A Little Treasury
of
American Poetry

The Little Treasury Series
OSCAR WILLIAMS, Editor

A LITTLE TREASURY OF MODERN POETRY
edited by Oscar Williams

A LITTLE TREASURY OF GREAT POETRY
edited by Oscar Williams

A LITTLE TREASURY OF AMERICAN POETRY
edited by Oscar Williams

A LITTLE TREASURY OF AMERICAN PROSE
edited by George Mayberry

A LITTLE TREASURY OF LOVE POEMS
edited by John Holmes

In Preparation

A LITTLE TREASURY OF WORLD POETRY
edited by Hubert Creekmore

A LITTLE TREASURY OF BRITISH POETRY
edited by Oscar Williams

A Little Treasury of American Poetry

THE CHIEF POETS

from colonial times to the present day

Edited with an Introduction by

Oscar Williams

NEW YORK
CHARLES SCRIBNER'S SONS
1948

B

COPYRIGHT NOTICES
AND ACKNOWLEDGMENTS

Copyright Notices & Acknowledgments

Copyright Notices & Acknowledgments

Copyright Notices & Acknowledgments

Contents

Part I
American Indian Poetry

Part II
The Chief Poets
from Colonial Times to the Present Day

xi

Contents

Contents

Part III

Poetry of the Forties

xiii

Contents

Appendix

Introduction

I

As MY first selection in this collection, I have used the
opening sections of the *Wallam Olum*, the Red Score
or Painted History of the Lenni Lenape, an Amerindian
epic of creation and of the wanderings of the Eastern
tribes who inhabited that part of our land to which
came the first United States settlers. The *Wallam Olum*
is perhaps the only real book that has come down to
us from the aborigines, and we have it only in a word
by word translation made in the beginning of the nineteenth century by C. S. Rafinesque, who also made a
transcription of the pictographs, thus preserving this
invaluable material. Unfortunately, no good translation
of the work, which is possibly as great as the Iliad,
has been made; perhaps it could not be made. Indian
poetry was a different thing altogether from poetry as
we now understand it, though Aristotle certainly had
in mind, when he wrote the Poetics, something rather
more like it than like our personal poetry of today. For
the poetry of the Amerindian, in its purity before the
advent of the white man, was a totality of the life of
the people: it was song, dance, oratory, liturgy, history
and magic ritual to control the phenomena of nature.
It was not written down, in the usual course, but was
committed to memory by the Keeper of the Wampum,
who recited the great epic with fitting ceremony, in
much the same manner as the Homeric bards recited
the Iliad. That it was also written in pictographs we

know from the fragments we possess, but the essential reality of the epic was transmitted by rote, with that perfection of memory common to people without writing.

I have followed the *Wallam Olum* with translations of other Amerindian poetry from both Eastern and Western tribes, but these small poems must not be taken as truly representative of Amerindian poetry: the complex of a primitive poem requires, for its comprehension, gesture and song, an understanding of the magical purpose of the work, and specialized knowledge of primitive tribal psychology. The intricate meaning of such poetry simply cannot be translated into print, especially in a language meant to express a very different stage in man's development. It is to be hoped that sometime a great translator of Amerindian poetry may appear, one who has the special insight and patience for the task. I have included these translations because I am sure that the originals were important poetry and because it would be arrogant to call this book "American" while omitting poetry that existed in America for long centuries before the short few hundred years of the white man's occupation.

The peculiar handicap of American poetry has been that it has not had just this indigenous epic material as its foundation. Other major literatures can show organic growth from savage and barbaric folk-lore, warrior songs and ballads, common to a people long in their habitat. But, because the colonists were physical, rather than anthropological, or literary, explorers, our poetry had to start as the scion of a mature sophisticated tradition grafted upon not a literature, but a new environment. Blind to the Amerindian culture so richly before and around them, the colonists destroyed the primitive arts, together with their society, before any real awareness of their existence developed. It was not until the Indian had all but vanished from the East and Middle West, not, indeed, until even the Western tribes had been thrust upon reservations, that any intelligent inquiry into their religious, social and art customs took place. True, exceptional white men took an interest in the Indians, in some cases a sympathetic interest. But understanding was lacking. The familial customs of the natives, their tribal rites and ceremonial gestures seemed to the Europeans matters of sin or ignorance. Jesuit missionaries, who observed the savages more closely perhaps than others, saw even their dreams as from the devil, and were in haste to convert them, not to preserve their essentially religious arts.

Certainly American children grow up with a folklore picture of the Indian: Pocahontas, the Last of the Mohicans, Hiawatha, "heap Big Chief" and the "Noble Redskin" give American childhood its most romantic concept. But this concept is essentially European, the white man's idea of what a savage should be. Even American writers of the nineteenth century made no genuine effort to discover the true facts about the natives. Longfellow did gather a certain amount of Amerindian material for Hiawatha but his research was superficial. Even when he had authentic material it seemed nonsense to him and he rejected it. When told that Hiawatha and his twelve-year-old daughter had visited a conference of the Five Nations, there to see a small speck in the sky which rapidly grew larger until it became a monstrous bird which swooped down and crushed the little girl to atoms, he felt the tale to be too foolish for use. And, in true academic style, he went to the Finnish for his form and rhythms, untroubled by any sensitivity to the Amerindian spirit.

II

Colonial and early poets of the republic wrote from English models and kept London still their intellectual capital. They were provincial, unable to see that they had a whole new world, rather than a province, for their setting. The restless expansion of immigrant peoples across an untouched continent which was as dramatic geographically as the crowded history of the settlers themselves demanded a unique poetry for its expression. It had to wait for Whitman.

For it was not leisured and intellectual Europeans who came to the new land; men migrated for religious and political freedom, for adventure and to seek their fortunes. The hard wilderness attracted men of physical endurance and courage, seeking physical betterment through conquest of a physical environment. Then, when the practical and scientific bent of a whole nation was determined, America got that ideal of steady improvement of material conditions, rather than the enjoyment of leisure, which has never been dislodged. Moreover, the United States has never known a pre-industrial age. The modern world began when our republic began. Even the farmer dreams his dream of factory production, of mechanization. Except for local intervals in New England and in the South, America has had no true pastoral life. We have had riders of the range, share-croppers and owners of vast farming land, but no peasants. The American poet has always suffered from the frustrations inevitable to the artist in an industrial society; he has had the further misfortune of not possessing a heritage of folk-lore of his own. The hill-billy songs, the songs of the range, are based upon

old Irish and English models; Negro blues and spirit-
uals, themselves the product of immigrants, which
come nearest to being a genuine American folk-lore,
have been strangled by the commercialized exploitation
of radio and "arty" circles. If they had been allowed to
lie fallow a little longer, their poignant, untampered-with
spontaneity might perhaps have become fertile for serious
poetry.

Yet, in spite of handicaps that have kept Canada and
Australia unproductive of great poets, America has a
remarkable record, for so short a period of time, not
only in the appearance of major poets, but also in new
poetic material.

The colonial poets showed no signs of any American
influence, except in the subject matter of popular dog-
gerel. Much verse was written but only two poets of
the period survive as of other than historical interest
to us now. These two are Anne Bradstreet and Edward
Taylor, whose work has only as recently as the turn of
the decade been brought forward by Mr. Thomas H.
Johnson. Philip Freneau, who may be considered the
first poet of the new republic, was American in his interest in republican ideals and in his concern for the
people, but he contributed nothing purely American in
poetic matter or form.

III

Boston was the American intellectual capital of the
nineteenth century. But it was not the New England
writers, who dominated the literary scene and established the quality of American prose, who were responsible for the three major poets of the period and
their influence, which was wide enough to reach England and France and to continue into our own time.

Bryant, Longfellow, Lowell, Holmes, *et al.*, produced only watered-down versions of English verse and their work, by serious standards, is second-rate. Emerson's influence sprang more from his essays than from his poetry, which, though good, could not be called characteristically American as is his prose.

But while the New Englanders were, especially in the cases of Longfellow and Lowell, enjoying both academic respect and popular acclaim, three of their contemporaries were producing work of firm worth and originality. Each an American phenomenon, Whitman, Poe and Emily Dickinson were evolving in different kinds of isolation. The physical retirement of Emily Dickinson did not enisle her more sharply than Poe was isolated by his temperament or Whitman by his democratic ideal of putting the whole of America into song.

The United States has always had two quite different kinds of writers: on the one side, those of erudition, on the other, men spottily educated, or even self- or half-educated. Now lack of complete higher education, while always a handicap, in a sensitive and active mind sometimes creates its own advantage which may more than compensate for the handicap. Indeed, except for those minds great enough to utilize it, a too complete and catholic education may sometimes overwhelm and drown the creative talent. Some genius, unfortunate in being confined to hints and glimpses of ideas, to fragments of learning, can substitute appetite and digestion for taste, and nourish its concepts to completion in its own bowels. Originality is the result and, granted the genius, a centered and worthwhile originality, more in harmony with its entire environment than the work of the mere scholar. If originality has lately fallen into ill-repute, it is because there has been

too great a straining for attention by means of shock
tactics and much effort to be "different" on the part of
too many who seek poetic reputation. That it is true
that the influence of great poetry is salutary for any
poet, and that a well-chosen influence can do so much
in bringing a fine talent to its own special fruition, does
not mean that marked originality, whether of form or
content or texture, is not still one of the greatest characteristics of a major poet.

Poe, Dickinson and Whitman were all original, and
partly because they lacked complete formal education,
a lack which also certainly contributed to their faults.
In Poe's case, his acuity of mind may make us wish
that he had had access to the best of European criticism. With whatever reservations a modern reader may
turn from his poems today, his importance cannot be
underestimated, so effective has his influence been,
passing to France, and, through the symbolists, returning again to America via T. S. Eliot. Dickinson's precision of vocabulary and condensed statement antici-
pated the twentieth century. Both these poets, though
contemporary with the academic Longfellow and his
friends, managed to find exactly the language suited to
their unique talents and by being themselves, rather
than reflections of other personalities, made, with Whitman, a place in world literature for nineteenth-century
America.

I have represented the period before 1900 with very
full selections from these three poets and others of importance. I have given only token admission to men
like Longfellow, Lowell, Bryant and others, whose
sentimental and largely meretricious work was so popular in the previous century. They have long received
too much attention from our schools, especially the
lower schools. If I had had more courage I might have

omitted them altogether. One purpose of this anthology will have been accomplished if it helps to raise the standard of taste in such schools and gives American young people a better opportunity to educate themselves through serious poetry. Moreover, this collection is not a history of the United States in verse, nor yet a history of its literature. While the history of a country is indeed reflected in its poetry, that poetry is the mirror of the native spirit, not of events. For instance, Robinson's poem on Lincoln and Tate's *Ode to the Confederate Dead* will be found here, not as occasional verse of the War of the Rebellion, but because they are qualified as poetry.

IV

To most people, native or foreign, Whitman is the archetype of American poets. And rightly so, for in his work may be found certain fundamental characteristics of American poetry which appear again and again in the work of others who, on the surface, may seem to have little in common with him. To Whitman, love was a mingling with all mankind, a concern for the mass of man and democratic institutions. His subject was the social scene, his nature had the vastness of a continent always active with the nomadic flow of humanity at work. And it is exactly the social scene which has obsessed the important American poets ever since, and, through their influence, other poets as well. In spite of his conscious and excessive optimism and passionate belief in progress Whitman filled his lines with the reality, rather than his ideal, of the social situation. He tried to encompass in a poem the whole of democracy, its people, its speech rhythms, its landscape, the conquest of its nature, everything. He was native to the land and he spoke for the land. But the heterogeneous elements of his landscape also spoke through him and asserted their formless lack of fusion. The parts and peoples of America had not begun to cohere, they scarcely do so as yet in our own day. Whitman could not avoid chaos, it was around him and he desired to absorb it, not to select. But his whole-heartedness gave value to the effort; poetry was the result. He has had countless untalented followers who find it easy to write without discipline, but no genuine follower in the genre. Such a follower could not arise; the method was peculiar to Whitman. He could illuminate a mist and give it the force of shape in defiance of form.

But though only the poetasters use his surface characteristics, important American poets have exhibited the same deeper concerns and fallen into their own pitfalls. Hart Crane, too, attempted to express the entirety of his environment, an impossible task but again rewarding because of the passionate sensitivity of the poet. Ezra Pound, though he long denied quality to Whitman, is much like him in manner and at one time (in the poem *A Pact*) confessed his indebtedness to him. But Pound resembles Whitman more nearly than he would certainly have cared to admit: in form, in his attempt to draw into a whole prism too many facets of society, and in too general a concept.

In Whitman we note the absence of one of the commonest phenomena of English poetry: the personal love poem. Again, this is an American characteristic; we have produced almost no first-rate personal love poems. Whitman rejoiced in death; he says,

But praise! praise! praise!
For the sure enwinding arms of cool enfolding Death.

Dark Mother. . . .
I glorify thee above all.

Death as a part of life or as the answer to desire, in
contradistinction to the "eat, drink and be merry for
tomorrow we die" of the English tradition, is very common in American poetry. Poe wrote of nothing else, we
find it in Dickinson in scores of poems, we find it still
in the poets of the twentieth century. The American
death wish is very strong and the poets have voiced it.
This attitude toward death is a natural dénouement of
American infantilism.

In Whitman we find the ever-present longing to be
one with the people; simply, to have friends. His contact with the literary world was tangential. He learned
much from Emerson, who was also full of faith in the
common man and who steadily predicted ever-grow-
ing greatness in democracy for America. Emerson, confined to a study, never received the full magnetic current of the soil which Whitman got by actually living
on the pavements and roads of the common folk.
Therefore a study of Emerson will not expose the
underlying despair that forced its way, in spite of surface optimism, into the long lines of Whitman's loose
verses. But Whitman was not at ease with scholars,
though he was well enough read for his occasions. He
needed a sympathetic audience and sought it where
it has not yet been found by American poets, among
ordinary people. (I am not speaking here of that audience which comes to a poet posthumously, but that
which usefully gives him the stimulus of encourage-
ment during his lifetime.) He himself said, "To have
great poets there must be great audiences too." This
statement is not true but he showed his awareness of
the American poet's perennial problem.

v

This problem of getting an audience has always been an insoluble one for our poets and its strictures have had much to do with the frequency and kinds of originality that are found among them. In England and in France there is always a lively literary life which gives artists a chance to meet and talk with something more than scholarly conformity. London and Paris are habituated to erudition and can use it as a tool rather than be used by it. But our educational institutions have been long in multiplying and long in maturing, so that until very recently too great a number of young talents have had scholarship revealed to them as a surprise. Hence it is too often and too much emphasized long after it should have been accepted as standard equipment to be used but not advertised. Thus, in America, creative persons have social needs that cannot be filled in academic circles; they try to fill them by making contact with ordinary men and women, whom their instinct tells them are their natural audience.

For poetry should be the expression of the whole people, not a private matter. Unfortunately, the American public, like some other modern publics, does not care for, nor understand serious poetry. Moreover, the special audience for poetry even among, let us say, those who have gone through college, is incredibly small. In America it is extremely unlikely that people whose schooling has stopped before college will read poetry at all, but in England it is not unusual for workmen to be poetry lovers. So, though modern poetry of any nationality is estranged from a large audience, probably nowhere else in the world is it so thoroughly exiled as in America. *The Saturday Evening Post* once published an article by an ex-GI who had returned to high school after combat action in the Pacific. His strongest complaint about the curriculum was directed against the poetry. He could scarcely be blamed! He was being taught Longfellow, Lowell and Bryant and was convinced that poetry was never about real subjects of concern to a man who had faced extremity. Thus, because they have offered the very young nothing but mediocre verse, the schools build up in minds of any sensitivity a positive revulsion to anything that is printed in the physical shape of a poem. If they offered the true instead of the false there might be an increase in the size of the audience.

To be sure, there are many other reasons for the rejection of poetry by the people. The American emphasis upon material welfare and mechanical gadgets, the reverence for the mysteries of science, the journalistic corruption of language in popular periodicals and upon the radio, the never-lifting oppression of economic anxiety and extrovert ideals, together with much else, make the simplest kind of escape entertainment, in the reality of their day's living, not only of more attraction, but actually of more value to the majority than so demanding an exercise as the reading of serious poetry.

This lack of a sizable audience (which, in any art, as in the theatre, throws back the group energy to the artist so that he can add it to his own force in the creative process) makes the poet turn inward. Granted the importance of his talent, the more isolated he is the more original he is likely to be. And in America we find this expected originality. Here new methods of writing appear with apparent suddenness, and diverse talents are contemporaneous. No coterie has produced successful work here; "schools" do not vitalize as they do in France and, in lesser degree, in England. It is the individual figure, working almost alone, who produces the finally important poetry.

VI

American poetry has had an extraordinary number of these single figures in a very short historical period. In the nineteenth century, as I have said, Poe, Dickinson and Whitman; in the twentieth, many more have contributed new techniques, among them Pound, Jeffers, Stevens, Riding, Hart Crane, Eliot and Masters. The one movement or "school" that made a popular stir was that of Imagism which to some extent influenced (without derailing) a number of the important talents. The roster of twentieth-century poets is so long that I have devoted a greater portion of this anthology to their presentation. But not all of the best poets have been innovators and not all of the innovators are first-rate poets. Sometimes new methods seem to be "in the air," a result of external conditions rather than peculiar to the poet. As an example: It is often said that Eliot was the first to mingle the commonplaces of modern life with the larger themes of tradition and spiritual reality. But traces of this technique can be found in the early poems of E. A. Robinson and the whole method is contained in small in some of the vignettes of *Spoon River Anthology*. To take an example: An examination of *Henry C. Calhoun*, to be found on page 243 of this book, will show Masters' use of modern terms together with Christian terminology in very much the same spirit of disillusion as used by Eliot. When we read *Aaron Hatfield* (page 249), again this technique is plain. Handled by a major poet, as only one of his devices, we know what great poetry can result from it. But even as used by Masters, it was important: the stir caused by *Spoon River Anthology* was deserved.

A ceaseless concern with the dilemmas of society at large has been common to all American poets of any calibre. While this interest is now common to all modern poetry, it was pioneered by American poets. For American poetry has, in the twentieth century, taken its place with the mature literatures of the world. Today English poets are as affected by American work as the American poets are by English work. There is even an exchange of poets: as Eliot became a British subject, so has Auden become an American citizen. Eliot is affectionately called "the Master" by younger men on both sides of the Atlantic, and Auden has had a marked effect during the last decade upon the American literary world. I have included both Eliot and Auden in this collection, as American poets. (All the English anthologies greedily include both and our claim upon them is, I feel, just as valid in the case of Auden and more valid in the case of Eliot.) Nearly and remotely, the influence of American poetry has been wide and I believe that it will continue to widen. Native talents find more and more models worthy of the highest respect at home and foreign poets have begun to look with attention toward American genius. One has only to mention the names of Wallace Stevens, E. E. Cummings, Hart Crane, John Crowe Ransom, Allen Tate and Ezra Pound to illustrate this point.

VII

I have spoken above of the effect of poor or repressive education upon certain American poets. But American scholarship has also a fine record in its list of poets, not the less genuine and creative for their erudition. When I spoke of "schools" having no fructifying virtues here, as in France, I did not mean that we have not had any group of poets with closely allied interests. Without manifestos or passionate assumption of a limited philosophy, we have, in this century, had a most useful group of writers whose common interest, if not common declaration, has been in metaphysical poetry. They have sometimes been called the Agrarian Group and they include names such as Tate, Ransom, John Peale Bishop, etc. These men have carried criticism to a high level of excellence, and, in their own verse, set a demanding standard for poetry based upon the traditional forms.

Their value has been salutary and their example has made it impossible, in the future, for any but mature poetry to receive critical recognition. It was very necessary for a genuine educative standard to be made, and then exemplified. Eliot's desertion did not prevent him from being read here, but with a single example of scholarship, and that an extraordinarily great one, perhaps real attention to the quality of poetry would not have become general. The new metaphysical poets have shown the richness of their criticism in creative action. These poets, too, are concerned with social problems; they too wish to understand and express America. But their informed minds, recognizing the heterogeneous nature of the country, have wisely chosen to closely observe a particular, and personally familiar, section of it, in its past as well as in its present. Thus they have succeeded, as Whitman and Crane could not succeed, in accomplishing what they set out to do. Tate, Ransom and John Peale Bishop have written from the complex of the South, other poets have drawn their color from other sections.

In fact, a greater success in form has been achieved by those poets who have tried to express only one sectional culture of the country, not by the use of "local" terminology in the style called Americana, but in spirit. Thus Robinson Jeffers, bound to the California coast, has, in the terrible realization of his verse, somehow got a real image from one facet of America. His pessimism is the obverse of Whitman's optimism. As Whitman expressed America's democracy and largeness, Jeffers has expressed its violence and enormity. He is a definitely Californian product. So Robert Frost expressed New England; E. E. Cummings, Hart Crane and others who have truly received, and written of, urban life have done the same for the city.

VIII

Intellect and knowledge of the tradition are of great consequence to a poet. That is unquestionable. But just as the drawbacks of partial ignorance can be compensated for by genius, so too, can mediocrity be confounded by too much reading. While Whitman was responsible for a most unsightly flow into print of incredibly bad verse by his would-be imitators, much learning, of such incalculable value to men fitted to handle it, becomes, when learned by rote instead of understanding, responsible for vices at least as bad.

One of these vices has followed from a virtue. Modern criticism has done much service in tracing the influences of poets upon one another, but this criticism, too solemnly and unthinkingly read, has led to almost a plague of plagiarism. F. O. Matthiessen in a note in his book *American Renaissance* says, ". . . I have undoubtedly plagiarized from many sources—to use the que talent. The result will be a firm originality in proper form.

The present looseness of thought upon this subject ll rather prevent America from having her Dante or akespeare than assist such a poet to arise. I cannot go o the matter of Shakespeare's "plagiarism" here, but hink it will be found to be rather different from the up plagiarism of the present. I should suggest that poets do insist on taking from every poem the minute appears in a little magazine, that they group together pre ethically and publish as a group under a group me. For group poetry might also have its value.

IX

I have divided this anthology into three sections, the st and smallest is devoted to Amerindian poetry. The cond, and main section, covers the work of the chief pets from colonial times to the present. This section is rranged chronologically, by birth dates. In some ways his arrangement is deceptive, as well as arbitrary, since does not, due to differences in longevity and dates of ublication, show clearly at what point the poet took is place in the literary stream. For instance, though tobinson was born before Stephen Crane, Crane's life as short and his writing completed before 1900, whereas Robinson's first book of importance was not published ntil 1910. I have given the major poets thorough and dequate representation here, almost to the exclusion f lesser figures. Important long poems, such as the "Song of Myself" by Whitman, "The Man With the Blue Guitar" by Wallace Stevens, "Ash Wednesday" and "The Waste Land" by T. S. Eliot, "The Man Against the Sky" by E. A. Robinson and "The Bridge"

ugly term that did not bother Shakespeare's age. I doubt whether any criticism or cultural history has ever been written without such plagiary, which inevitably results from assimilating the contributions of your countless fellow-workers, past and present."

Now, a difference could be made between the ugliness of plagiarism in the creative work of poetry itself, and in criticism, which is rather more akin to science with its enforced use of the work of men past, than to poetry. In mathematics, for instance, it is the next step in a series for which a mathematician claims and receives credit. All his colleagues know very well who made each step that led up to it. The progression is regular. In writing, ideas are intertwined and language is flexible, as it is not in science. In criticism, the writer may lay claim to a merely felicitous restatement of many old discoveries, but he receives most praise for an addition to ways of examining or evaluating a work of art. Such new methods are also rather easily recognized as being original to the critic. That is, presupposing that the work was not taken from an as yet unpublished, or little circulated, previously written statement.

In poetry, influence is inevitable if anything worth reading at all is written. It is certainly legitimate for a poet to be influenced by his models. It is also proper enough for a poet to use the work of his predecessors in particular ways. It is well known how Eliot has used the lines of the poets who preceded him. From significant fragments of world literature he made his own new poem and his great originality lay in the manner of that usage. If this is plagiarism, plagiarism is not a crime, nor even a peccadillo. A new and great work had been made. The material of other poets was easily traceable to its sources, at least each fragment was known to at least some critics. Moreover, Eliot himself made it clear, in his notes, what his methods had been and what his sources were.

But there are other ways of utilizing other men's work and no matter how respectable the ways may become in the opinion of whatever critics, some of those ways infringe upon honesty. There are gradations, but it is perhaps time for an examination to be made of the whole subject. It is now known that Hart Crane used material from Samuel Greenberg's manuscript. Greenberg had not been published, Crane made no published notes about his indebtedness and did not offer Greenberg's manuscript to a publisher. It remained for chance to eventually give Greenberg his due. Moreover, Greenberg was dead when Crane was published and if this was theft, it could do no harm to Greenberg. Further, Crane's work was more valuable than Greenberg's. However, it might have been more ethical for Crane to, at least, have appended a note to his page when he used Greenberg's material, considering that that material was unpublished. I have included Crane's "Emblems of Conduct," built upon Greenberg's "Conduct" and other poems of his, under Greenberg's name, just to make this point clear.

Excuses can be, and are, found for Crane's act. Unfortunately excuses are also found in high circles for practices that can scarcely be called less than theft. There are many poets writing today (of all grades except the best) who, encouraged by what they consider the examples of Shakespeare, Eliot, Crane, *et al.*, do not hesitate to lift vocabulary, whole lines and stanzas, or even whole poems, with just enough changes made to "get by," from, not poets of the past whose work is well-known, but from contemporaries, themselves often unknown or not yet established. The work may be taken from a book whose ink is scarcely dry, from a volume xxxii

that has not received its due, from a little m
infinitesimal circulation, or even from
manuscript read in the home of a friend.
a case of the latter, i.e., the taking from
manuscript, was brought to my attention. T
received a good deal of praise for "his"
are poets whose whole work is a patchworl
skillful, of such borrowings. It cannot alwa
pastiche, changes are made.

This practice has been much condoned.
it is dangerous to continue to condone it
ervation. A new definition (ethical not le
giarism should be made. This theft of
gained its respectability because it is both
good, in the sense that it leads in many
making of good poems, for poets to use the
sors' work as they need it. But it must be
that such predecessors have been published
is known and their places are established. T
the living while they are still in the process
especially from the young, the little known
accepted, is not so ethical. The artist, espe
greatly talented, needs recognition to proper
to grow. When he sees his work under anot
even before he can get proper recognition f
discouraged and by so much is his talent st
there is a worse danger. Nowhere as much
arts does an immoral practice exact its punish
great creative talents can find sufficient ma
poets already dead or so much older that
thoroughly established. If they do not slip int
habit of reaching for the nearest, that is, th
devices and materials of their day, they will
to the discipline of finding vocabulary, devic
titudes of their own, and thus most fitted

by Hart Crane have been included in full. I have not included the "one poem" poets, with the exception of Edwin Markham with his "Man with the Hoe," but I have used one poem or so each from the work of several poets who, though they have published a great deal, are not of sufficient critical or historical importance to receive more attention.

It will be noticed that the poetry of the twentieth century receives considerably more space than that of the nineteenth. The last fifty years have seen the publication of much more poetry of a much higher standard than all that was written in the preceding two hundred and fifty years. In fact, American poetry has indeed in this recent period come of age and we have given to the English tradition many poems worthy to stand there with the best done by English poets.

My third section is arranged alphabetically and contains the work of poets who made an appearance in the forties. Most of the poets in this section are in the younger age group which includes the war poets (i.e., poets who saw service in the late war). Here, too, can be found certain older poets whose work belongs most distinctly to this period. However, the main section contains established poets whose poetry also belongs to the forties period, in that some of their best work was published then, and also because their spirit and influence are thoroughly contemporary. Thus Allen Tate, E. E. Cummings, Richard Eberhart, Wallace Stevens and others, who issued important books during the forties, are, largely due to their importance, placed in the main section.

I believe that a comparison between the poets of the nineteenth and twentieth centuries will show a marked rise in the quality of American poetry, a suddenness of improvement not to be found during the same period in other literatures. This growth, as it were by bold leaps, may lead us to expect even more exciting work in the future, and the poetry of the younger poets in section three strengthens this belief.

If American poets can utilize tradition, as they have of late learned to do, and at the same time risk an absolute originality, as did Whitman, the appearance of our Shakespeare may not be far off. The increased political importance of America, though it may have its drawbacks, does have an advantage for American poetry. It has already brought many European personalities to our shores and has made young Americans familiar with broader aspects of life and with ideas from other currents of national thought, and, such is the fallibility of human nature, stimulated, by reflection, an interest in American literature in other countries. This interest will, in turn, increase the confidence of American poets and increase their output. New York is already the political world capital, it tends to become the literary world capital. Simultaneously there has been a remarkable growth of smaller centers of literary awareness throughout the states and of that nation-wide activity which inevitably will create major poets.

—OSCAR WILLIAMS

New York City,
January 2, 1948

I
American Indian
Poetry

THE WALLAM OLUM

The Red Score or Painted History
of the Lenni Lenape

*(Two excerpts with the original glyphs translated
word for word by C. S. Rafinesque)*

I

ON THE CREATION AND ONTOGONY

Sayewitalli   wemiguma   wokgetaki
At first there   all sea-water   on the top land

Hackung-kwelik   owanaku   wakyutali
Above much water   foggy was   and these

   kitanitowit-essop
   God creator-He was

Sayewis   hallewiwis   nolemiwi elemamik
First being eternal being invisible   everywhere

   kitanitowit-essop
   God creator-He was

Sohalawak   kwelik   hakik
He causes them   much water   much land

   owak   awasagamak
   much clouds   much heaven

Sohalawak   gishuk   nipahum
He causes them   *sun*   *moon*

alankwak
stars

Wemi   sohalawak   yulik
All   *he causes them*   *these*

yuch-aan
well-to-move

Wich owagan   kshakan   moshakwat
With *action* *it blows hard* *it clears up*

kwelik   kshipehelep
deep water   *it ran off*

Opeleken   mani-menak   delsin
It looks bright   *made-island*   *is there*

epit
being there

Lappinup   kitanitowit   manito
Again when   *God creator*   *he made*

manitoak
the makers

Owiniwak   augelatawiwak chichankwak
First beings also   *angels also* *souls also*

wemiwak
all also

4

Wtenk   manito   jinwis   lennowak
After   *he made*   *man-being*   *men*

mukom
ancestor

Milap   netami-gaho   owini-gaho
He gave him   *the first-mother*   *first-being mother*

Namesik   milap   tulpewik   milap
Fishes   *he gave him*   *turtles*   *he gave him*

awesik   milap   cholensak   milap
beasts   *he gave him*   *birds*   *he gave him*

Makimani-shak   sohalawak   makowini
Bad spirit but   *he causes them*   *bad beings*

nakowak   amangamek
black snakes   *monsters*

Sohalawak   uchewak   sohalawak
He caused them   *flies*   *he caused them*

pungusak
gnats

Nitisak   wemi   owini   w'delsinewoap
Friends   *all*   *beings*   *were there*

Kiwis   wunand   wishimanitoak
Thou being   *a good god*   *good spirits*

essopak
were

5

Nijini   netami   lennowak   nigohanetami
Jins   *the first*   *men*   *the first mother*

okwewi   nantinéwak
wives   *fairies also*

Gattamin   netami   mitzi   nijini
Fat fruit   *the first*   *food*   *the jins*

nantiné
the fairies

Wemi   wingi-namenep   wemi   ksin
All   *willingly pleased*   *all*   *easy*

elendamep   wemi   wullatemanuwi
thinking   *all*   *happy*

Shukand   eli-kimi   mekenikink
But then   *while secretly*   *on earth*

wakon   powako   init'ako
snake god   *priest snake*   *worship snake*

Mattalogas   pallalogas   maktatin
Wickedness   *crime*   *unhappiness*

owagan   payat-chikyutali
deeds   *coming then thus there*

Maktapan   payat   wihillan   payat
Bad weather   *coming*   *distemper*   *coming*

mboagan   payat
death   *coming*

6

Wonwemi	wiwunchkamik	atak
This all	*very long ago*	*beyond*

kitahikan	netamakiepit
great ocean	*first land at*

II

THE DELUGE

Wulamo	maskanakoanup	lennowak
Long ago	*powerful snake when*	*men also*

makowini	essopak
bad beings	*had become*

Maskanako	shingalusit	nijini	essopak
Strong snake	*foe*	*the jins*	*had become*

shawalendamep	ekenshingalan
became troubled	*together hating*

Nishawi	palliton	nishawi	machiton
Both	*fighting*	*both*	*spoiling*

nishawi	matta	lungundowin
both	*not*	*keeping peace*

Mattapewi	wiki	nihanlowit	mekwazoan
Less man	*with*	*dead keeper*	*fighting*

Maskanako	gishi	penauwelendamep
Strong snake	*ready*	*resolved*

lennowak	owini	palliton
men	*beings*	*to spoil*

Nakowa	petonep	amangam
Black snake	*he brought*	*monster*

petonep	akopehella	petonep
he brought	*snake water rushing*	*he brought*

Pehella	pehella	pohoka	pohoka
Much water	*rushing*	*much go*	*to hills*

eshohok eshohok	palliton palliton
much penetrate	*much destroying*

Tulapit	menapit	nanaboush
At turtle land	*at that island*	*nana-hare*

maskaboush	owinimokom
strong-hare	*grandfather of beings he became*

linowimokom
grandfather of men he became

Gishikin	pommixin	tulagishatten
Being born	*creeping*	*a turtle he is ready*

lohxin
to move and dwell

Owini	linowi	wemoltin	pehella
Beings	*men*	*all go forth*	*flood*

gahani	pommixin	nahiwi
shallow water	*creeping*	*above water*

tatalli	tulapin
which way	*turtle back*

8

Amangamek makdopannek allendyuwek
Sea monsters *they were many* *some of them*

metzipannek
they did eat

Manito-dasin mokol wichemap palpal
Spirit-daughter *boat* *helped* *come*

payat payat wemichemap
coming *coming* *all helped*

Nanaboush nanaboush wemimokom
Nana-hare *nana-hare* *grandfather of all*

winimokom linnimokom
grandfather of beings *grandfather of men*

tulamokom
grandfather of turtle

Linapi-ma tulapi-ma tulapewi tapitawi
Men there *turtle there* *turtle they* *altogether*

Wishanem tulpewi pataman tulpewi
Frightened *turtle he* *praying* *turtle he*

poniton wuliton
let it be *to make well*

Kshipehelen penkwihilen kwamipokho
Water running off *it is drying* *plain & mountain*

sitwalikho maskan wagan palliwi palliwi
path of cave *dire* *action* *much elsewhere*

9

THE WAR GOD'S HORSE SONG

(From *The Navajo*)

I AM the Turquoise Woman's son.
On top of Belted Mountain
Beautiful horses—slim like a weasel!
My horse has a hoof like striped agate;
His fetlock is like a fine eagle plume;
His legs are like quick lightning.
My horse's body is like an eagle-plumed arrow;
My horse has a tail like a trailing black cloud.
I put flexible goods on my horse's back;
The Little Holy Wind blows through his hair.

His mane is made of short rainbows.
My horse's ears are made of round corn.
My horse's eyes are made of big stars.
My horse's head is made of mixed waters
(From the holy waters—he never knows thirst).
My horse's teeth are made of white shell.
The long rainbow is in his mouth for a bridle,
        And with it I guide him.
When my horse neighs, different-colored horses follow.
When my horse neighs, different-colored sheep follow.
        I am wealthy, because of him.

        Before me peaceful,
        Behind me peaceful,
        Under me peaceful,
        Over me peaceful,
        All around me peaceful—
        Peaceful voice when he neighs.
        I am Everlasting and Peaceful.
        I stand for my horse.

                    (*by Dane and Mary Roberts Coolidge*)

10

SACRED FORMULA
TO ATTRACT AFFECTION

(From *The Cherokee*)

Kû! Listen! In Alahíyi you repose, O Terrible Woman
Oh, you have drawn near to hearken.
There in Alahíyi you are at rest, O White Woman.
No one is ever lonely when with you.
You are most beautiful.
Instantly and at once you have rendered me a white man.
No one is ever lonely when with me.
Now you have made the path white for me.
I shall never be dreary. . . .
I shall never become blue.
You have brought down to me the white road.
There in midearth you have placed me.
I shall stand erect upon the earth.
No one is ever lonely when with me.
I am very handsome. You have put me into the white
    house.
I shall be in it as it moves about
And no one with me shall ever be lonely.
Verily, I shall never become blue.
Instantly you have caused it to be so with me.

And now there in Alahíyi you have rendered the woman
    blue.
Now you have made the path blue for her;
Let her be completely veiled in loneliness.
Put her into the blue road.
And now bring her down.
Place her standing upon the earth.
Where her feet are now and wherever she may go,
Let loneliness leave its mark upon her.
Let her be marked out for loneliness where she stands.

Ha! I belong to the Wolf clan,
That one alone which was allotted for you.

11

No one is ever lonely with me. I am handsome.
Let her put her soul
Into the very center of my soul, never to turn away.
Grant that in the midst of men
She shall never think of them.
I belong to the one clan alone which was allotted for you
When the seven clans were established.

Where [other] men live it is lonely.
They are very loathsome.
The common polecat has made them so like himself
That they are fit only for his company.
They have become mere refuse.
They are very loathsome.

The common opossum has made them so like himself
That they are fit only to be with him.
They are very loathsome.
Even the crow has made them so like himself
That they are fit only for his company.
They are very loathsome.
The miserable rain-crow has made them so like himself
That they are fit only to be with him.

The seven clans all alike make one feel lonely in their
    company.
They are not even good looking.
They go about clothed with mere refuse.
They go about even covered with dung.
But I—I was ordained to be a white man.
I stand with my face toward the Sun Land.
No one is ever lonely with me. I am very handsome.
I shall certainly never become blue.
I am covered with the everlasting white house
Wherever I go.
No one is ever lonely with me.
Your soul has come into the very center of my soul,
Never to turn away.
I, Gatigwanasti, I take your soul. *Sgê!*

(by James Mooney)

12

SACRED FORMULA TO DESTROY LIFE

(From *The Cherokee*)

LISTEN! Now I have come to step over your soul.
You are of the wolf clan. Your name is Áyûiuni.
Your spittle I have put at rest under the earth.
Your soul I have put at rest under the earth.
I have come to cover you over with the black rock.
I have come to cover you with the black slabs, never to
    reappear.
Toward the black coffin in the Darkening Land your
    path shall stretch out.
So shall it be for you.
The clay of the upland has come [to cover you].
Instantly the black clay has lodged there where it is at
    rest at the black houses in the Darkening Land.
With the black coffin and the black slabs I have come to
    cover you.
Now your soul has faded away.
It has become blue.
When darkness comes
Your spirit shall grow less
And dwindle away,
Never to reappear. Listen!

(by James Mooney)

SONG FOR THE PASSING
OF A BEAUTIFUL WOMAN

(From *The Paiute*)

STRONG sun across the sod can make
Such quickening as your countenance!

I am more worth for what your passing wakes,
Great races in my loins, to you that cry.
My blood is redder for your loveliness.

(Reëxpressed by Mary Austin)

13

GLYPH

(From *The Washoe-Paiute*)

TRULY buzzards
Around my sky are circling!

For my soul festers,
And an odor of corruption
Betrays me to disaster.

Meanness, betrayal and spite
Come flockwise,
To make me aware
Of sickness and death within me.
My sky is full of the dreadful sound
Of the wings of unsuccesses.

(Reëxpressed by Mary Austin)

LOVE SONG

(From *The Papago*)

EARLY I rose
In the blue morning;
My love was up before me,
It came running up to me from the doorways
    of the Dawn.

On Papago Mountain
The dying quarry
Looked at me with my love's eyes.

(Reëxpressed by Mary Austin)

II
The Chief Poets
from
Colonial Times
to the
Present Day

Anne Bradstreet

THE FLESH AND THE SPIRIT

In secret place where once I stood,
Close by the banks of lacrym flood,
I heard two sisters reason on
Things that are past and things to come.
One Flesh was called, who had her eye
On worldly wealth and vanity;
The other Spirit, who did rear
Her thoughts unto a higher sphere.
"Sister," quoth Flesh, "what livest thou on—
Nothing but meditation?
Doth contemplation feed thee, so
Regardlessly to let earth go?
Can speculation satisfy
Notion without reality?
Dost dream of things beyond the moon,
And dost thou hope to dwell there soon?
Hast treasures there laid up in store
That all in the world thou countest poor?
Art fancy sick, or turned a sot,
To catch at shadows which are not?
Come, come, I'll show unto thy sense
Industry hath its recompense.
What canst desire but thou mayst see
True substance in variety?
Dost honor like? Acquire the same,
As some to their immortal fame,
And trophies to thy name erect
Which wearing time shall ne'er deject.
For riches dost thou long full sore?
Behold enough of precious store;

17

Earth hath more silver, pearls, and gold
Than eyes can see or hands can hold.
Affectest thou pleasure? Take thy fill;
Earth hath enough of what you will.
Then let not go what thou mayst find
For things unknown, only in mind."

SPIRIT:

"Be still, thou unregenerate part;
Disturb no more my settled heart,
For I have vowed, and so will do,
Thee as a foe still to pursue,
And combat with thee will and must
Until I see thee laid in the dust.
Sisters we are, yea, twins we be,
Yet deadly feud 'twixt thee and me;
For from one father are we not.
Thou by old Adam was begot,
But my arise is from above,
Whence my dear Father I do love.
Thou speakest me fair, but hatest me sore;
Thy flattering shows I'll trust no more.
How oft thy slave hast thou me made
When I believed what thou hast said,
And never had more cause of woe
Than when I did what thou bad'st do.
I'll stop mine ears at these thy charms,
And count them for my deadly harms.
Thy sinful pleasures I do hate,
Thy riches are to me no bait,
Thine honors do nor will I love,
For my ambition lies above.
My greatest honor it shall be
When I am victor over thee,
And triumph shall, with laurel head,
When thou my captive shalt be led.
How I do live thou needst not scoff,

18

For I have meat thou knowst not of:
The hidden manna I do eat,
The word of life it is my meat.
My thoughts do yield me more content
Than can thy hours in pleasure spent.
Nor are they shadows which I catch,
Nor fancies vain at which I snatch,
But reach at things that are so high
Beyond thy dull capacity.
Eternal substance I do see,
With which enrichéd I would be;
Mine eye doth pierce the heavens, and see
What is invisible to thee.
My garments are not silk or gold,
Nor such like trash which earth doth hold,
But royal robes I shall have on,
More glorious than the glistering sun.
My crown not diamonds, pearls, and gold,
But such as angels' heads enfold.
The city where I hope to dwell
There's none on earth can parallel:
The stately walls, both high and strong,
Are made of precious jasper stone;
The gates of pearl both rich and clear,
And angels are for porters there;
The streets thereof transparent gold,
Such as no eye did e'er behold;
A crystal river there doth run,
Which doth proceed from the Lamb's throne;
Of life there are the waters sure,
Which shall remain for ever pure;
Of sun or moon they have no need,
For glory doth from God proceed—
No candle there, nor yet torch-light,
For there shall be no darksome night.
From sickness and infirmity
For evermore they shall be free,
Nor withering age shall e'er come there,

But beauty shall be bright and clear.
This city pure is not for thee,
For things unclean there shall not be.
If I of Heaven may have my fill,
Take thou the world, and all that will."

A LETTER TO HER HUSBAND

PHŒBUS, make haste: the day's too long; be gone;
The silent night's the fittest time for moan
But stay this once, unto my suit give ear,
And tell my griefs in either Hemisphere;
And if the whirling of thy wheels don't drown'd
The woeful accents of my doleful sound,
If in thy swift carrier thou canst make stay,
I crave this boon, this errand by the way:
Commend me to the man more lov'd then life;
Show him the sorrows of his widowed wife,
My dumpish thoughts, my groans, my brakish tears,
My sobs, my longing hopes, my doubting fears;
And if he love, how can he there abide?
My interest's more than all the world beside.
He that can tell the stars or ocean sand,
Or all the grass that in the meads do stand,
The leaves in th' woods, the hail or drops of rain,
Or in a corn-field number every grain,
Or every mote that in the sun-shine hops,
May count my sighs and number all my drops.
Tell him the countless steps that thou dost trace
That once a day thy spouse thou mayst embrace;
And when thou canst not treat by loving mouth,
Thy rays afar salute her from the south.
But for one month I see no day, poor soul,
Like those far situate under the pole,
Which day by day long wait for thy arise:
O how they joy when thou dost light the skies.

O *Phœbus*, hadst thou but thus long from thine
Restrain'd the beams of thy beloved shine,
At thy return, if so thou could'st or durst,
Behold a chaos blacker then the first,
Tell him here's worse than a confused matter—
His little world's a fathom under water;
Nought but the fervor of his ardent beams
Hath power to dry the torrent of these streams.
Tell him I would say more, but cannot well:
Oppressed minds abruptest tales do tell.
Now post with double speed, mark what I say;
By all our loves conjure him not to stay.

LONGING FOR HEAVEN

As weary pilgrim now at rest
    Hugs with delight his silent nest,
His wasted limbs now lie full soft
    That myrie steps have trodden oft,
Blesses himself to think upon
    His dangers past and travails done;
The burning sun no more shall heat,
    Nor stormy rains on him shall beat;
The briars and thorns no more shall scratch,
    Nor hungry wolves at him shall catch;
He erring paths no more shall tread,
    Nor wild fruits eat instead of bread;
For waters cold he doth not long,
    For thirst no more shall parch his tongue;
No rugged stones his feet shall gall,
    Nor stumps nor rocks cause him to fall;
All cares and fears he bids farewell,
    And means in safety now to dwell:
A pilgrim I on earth perplext,
    With sins, with cares and sorrows vexed,

By age and pains brought to decay,
 And my clay house mouldering away,
Oh how I long to be at rest
 And soar on high among the blest!
This body shall in silence sleep,
 Mine eyes no more shall ever weep,
No fainting fits shall me assail,
 Nor grinding pains my body frail,
With cares and fears ne'er cumbered be,
 Nor losses know nor sorrows see.
What though my flesh shall there consume?
 It is the bed Christ did perfume;
And when a few years shall be gone,
 This mortal shall be cloth'd upon:
A corrupt carcasse down it lies,
 A glorious body it shall rise;
In weakness and dishonor sown,
 In power 'tis rais'd by Christ alone.
Then soul and body shall unite,
 And of their maker have the sight.
Such lasting joys shall there behold
 As ear ne'er heard nor tongue e'er told.
Lord, make me ready for that day:
 Then come, dear bridegroom, come away!

OUR INSUFFICIENCY
TO PRAISE GOD
SUITABLY FOR HIS MERCY

SHOULD all the world so wide to atoms fall,
   Should th' air be shred to motes; should we
   See all the earth hacked here so small
     That none could smaller be?
Should heaven and earth be atomized, we guess
The number of these motes were numberless.

But should we then a world each atom deem,
   Where dwell as many pious men
   As all these motes the world could teem,
     Were it shred into them?
Each atom would the world surmount, we guess,
Whose men in number would be numberless.

But had each pious man as many tongues
   At singing all together then
   The praise that to the Lord belongs,
     As all these atoms men?
Each man would sing a world of praise, we guess,
Whose tongues in number would be numberless.

And had each tongue, as many songs of praise
   To sing to the Almighty ALL,
   As all these men have tongues to raise
     To him their holy call?
Each tongue would tune a world of praise, we guess,
Whose songs in number would be numberless.

23

Nay, had each song as many tunes most sweet,
    Or one intwisting in't as many,
      As all these tongues have songs most meet
        Unparalleled by any?
Each song a world of music makes, we guess,
Whose tunes in number would be numberless.

Now should all these conspire in us, that we
    Could breathe such praise to thee, Most High:
      Should we thy sounding organs be
        To ring such melody?
Our music would the world of worlds outring,
Yet be unfit within thine ears to ting.

Thou didst us mould, and us new mould when we
    Were worse than mould we tread upon.
      Nay, nettles made by sin we be:
        Yet hadst compassion.
Thou hast plucked out our stings; and by degrees
Hast of us, lately wasps, made lady-bees.

Though e'er our tongues thy praises due can fan,
    A weevil with the world may fly,
      Yea fly away: and with a span
        We may out mete the sky.
Though what we can is but a lisp, we pray
Accept thereof. We have no better pay.

HOUSEWIFERY

Make me, O Lord, thy spinning wheel complete;
    Thy holy word my distaff make for me.
Make mine affections thy swift flyers neat,
    And make my soul thy holy spool to be.
      My conversation make to be thy reel,
      And reel the yarn thereon spun of thy wheel.

Make me thy loom then, knit therein this twine:
 And make thy holy spirit, Lord, wind quills:
Then weave the web thyself. The yarn is fine.
 Thine ordinances make my fulling mills.
 Then dye the same in heavenly colors choice,
 All pinked with varnished flowers of paradise.

Then clothe therewith mine understanding, will,
 Affections, judgment, conscience, memory;
My words and actions, that their shine may fill
 My ways with glory and thee glorify.
 Then mine apparel shall display before ye
 That I am clothed in holy robes for glory.

MEDITATION SIX

CANTICLES II: 1: *I am . . . the lily of the valleys.*

AM I thy gold? Or purse, Lord, for thy wealth;
 Whether in mine or mint refined for thee?
I'm counted so, but count me o'er thyself,
 Lest gold washed face, and brass in heart I be.
 I fear my touchstone touches when I try
 Me, and my counted gold too overly.

Am I new minted by thy stamp indeed?
 Mine eyes are dim; I cannot clearly see.
Be thou my spectacles that I may read
 Thine image and inscription stamped on me.
 If thy bright image do upon me stand,
 I am a golden angel in thy hand.

Lord, make my soul thy plate: thine image bright
 Within the circle of the same enfoil.
And on its brims in golden letters write
 Thy superscription in an holy style.
 Then I shall be thy money, thou my hoard:
 Let me thy angel be, be thou my Lord.

MEDITATION SEVEN

Thy human frame, my glorious Lord, I spy,
  A golden still with heavenly choice drugs filled:
Thy holy love, the glowing heat whereby
  The spirit of grace is graciously distilled.
  Thy mouth the neck through which these spirits still;
  My soul thy vial make, and therewith fill.

Thy speech the liquor in thy vessel stands,
  Well ting'd with grace, a blessed tincture, lo,
Thy words distilled grace in thy lips poured, and
  Give graces tincture in them where they go.
  Thy words in graces tincture stilled, Lord, may
  The tincture of thy grace in me convey.

That golden mint of words thy mouth divine
  Doth tip these words, which by my fall were spoiled;
And dub with gold dug out of graces mine,
  That they thine image might have in them foiled.
  Grace in thy lips poured out's as liquid gold:
  Thy bottle make my soul, Lord, it to hold.

MEDITATION EIGHT

I kenning through astronomy divine
  The world's bright battlement, wherein I spy
A golden path my pencil cannot line
  From that bright throne unto my threshold lie.
  And while my puzzled thoughts about it pore,
  I find the bread of life in't at my door.

When that this bird of paradise put in
  This wicker cage (my corps) to tweedle praise
Had pecked the fruit forbid: and so did fling
  Away its food, and lost its golden days,
  It fell into celestial famine sore,
  And never could attain a morsel more.

Alas! alas! poor bird, what wilt thou do?
  This creature's field no food for souls e'er gave:
And if thou knock at angels' doors, they show
  An empty barrel: they no soul bread have.
  Alas! poor bird, the world's white loaf is done,
  And cannot yield thee here the smallest crumb.

In this sad state, God's tender bowels run
  Out streams of grace: and he to end all strife,
The purest wheat in heaven, his dear-dear Son
  Grinds, and kneads up into this bread of life:
  Which bread of life from heaven down came and
    stands
  Dished in thy table up by angels' hands.

Did God mould up this bread in heaven, and bake,
  Which from his table came, and to thine goeth?
Doth he bespeak thee thus: this soul bread take;
  Come, eat thy fill of this, thy God's white loaf?
  It's food too fine for angels; yet come, take
  And eat thy fill! it's heaven's sugar cake.

What grace is this knead in this loaf? This thing
  Souls are but petty things it to admire.
Ye angels, help: this fill would to the brim
  Heav'ns whelm'd-down crystal meal bowl, yea
    and higher.
  This bread of life dropped in thy mouth doth cry:
  Eat, eat me, soul, and thou shalt never die.

THE ACCUSATION
OF THE INWARD MAN

You want clear spectacles: your eyes are dim:
Turn inside out, and turn your eyes within.
Your sins like motes in th' sun do swim: nay, see
Your mites are molehills, molehills mountains be.

Your mountain sins do magnitude transcend:
Whose number's numberless, and doth want end.
The understanding's dark, and therefore will
Account of ill for good, and good for ill.
As to a purblind man men oft appear
Like walking trees within the hemisphere,
So in the judgment carnal things excel:
Pleasures and profits bear away the bell.
The will is hereupon perverted so,
It lackeys after ill; doth good forego.
The reasonable soul doth much delight
A pickpack t' ride o' th' sensual appetite.
And hence the heart is hardened, and toys
With love, delight, and joy, yea vanities.

Make but a thorough search, and you may spy
Your soul a trudging hard, though secretly
Upon the feet of your affections mute,
And hankering after all forbidden fruit.
Ask but yourself in secret, laying near
Thy head thereto: 'twill whisper in thine ear
That it is tickled much, though secretly.
And greatly itches after villainy.
'Twill mock thee in thy face, and though it say
It must not tell, it scorns to tell thee nay.
But slack the reins, and come a loophole lower:
You'll find it was but pen-cooped up before.
Nay, muster up your thoughts, and take the pole
Of what walk in the entry of your soul:
Which if you do, you certainly will find
With robbers, cut-throats, thieves it's mostly lined.
And hundred rogues you'll find lie gaming there:
For one true man, that in that path appears.
Your true man too's oft footsore, seldom is
Sound wind and limb: and still to add to this,
He's but a traveler within that way:
Whereas the rest there pitch their tents, and stay.
Nay, nay, what thoughts unclean? lascivious?

Blasphemous? murderous? and malicious?
Tyrannic? wrathful? atheistic rise
Of evils new and old, of every size?
These bed and board here; make the heart a sty
Of all abominable brothelry.
　　Then is it pure? is this the fruit of grace?
　　If so, how do ye: you and I embrace!

THE OUTWARD MAN ACCUSED

TURN o'er thy outward man, and judge aright.
Doth not a pagan's life out shine thy light?
Thy fleering looks, thy wanton eyes, each part
Are painted sign-post of a wanton heart.
If thou art weigh'd in golden scales, dost do
To others as thou wouldst be done unto?
Weigh, weigh thy words: thy untruths, all which came
Out of thy mouth, and thou confest the same.
Why did thy tongue detract from any one,
Whisper such tales thou wouldst not have be known?
When thou wast got in such a merry vein,
How far didst thou exceed the golden mean?
When that thou wast at such a boon or feast,
Why didst thou rather lie than lose thy jest?
How wast thou tickled when thy droughty ears
Allayed their thirst with filthy squibs and jeers?
Why didst thou glaver [1] men of place? And why
Scowl, gloat, and frown on honest poverty?
Why did'st thou spend thy state in foolish pranks?
And peacock up thyself above thy ranks?
Why thoughtest thyself out of the world as shut,
When not with others in the cony cut? [2]
Hold up thy head; is't thus or no? if yea,
How then is all thy folly purged away?
　　If no, thy tongue belies itself, for lo
　　Thou saidst thy heart was dressed from sin also.

---

[1] _wheedle_　　　[2] _pony catching, swindling_

Philip Freneau

THE INDIAN BURYING GROUND

In spite of all the learned have said,
  I still my old opinion keep;
The posture, that we give the dead
  Points out the soul's eternal sleep.

Not so the ancients of these lands—
  The Indian, when from life released,
Again is seated with his friends,
  And shares again the joyous feast.

His imaged birds, and painted bowl,
  And venison, for a journey dressed,
Bespeak the nature of the soul,
  Activity, that knows no rest.

His bow, for action ready bent,
  And arrows, with a head of stone,
Can only mean that life is spent,
  And not the old ideas gone.

Thou, stranger, that shalt come this way,
  No fraud upon the dead commit—
Observe the swelling turf, and say
  They do not lie, but here they sit.

Here still a lofty rock remains,
  On which the curious eye may trace
(Now wasted, half, by wearing rains)
  The fancies of a ruder race.

Here still an agèd elm aspires,
　　Beneath whose far-projecting shade
(And which the shepherd still admires)
　　The children of the forest played!

There oft a restless Indian queen
　　(Pale Shebah with her braided hair)
And many a barbarous form is seen
　　To chide the man that lingers there.

By midnight moons, o'er moistening dews;
　　In habit for the chase arrayed,
The hunter still the deer pursues,
　　The hunter and the deer—a shade!

And long shall timorous Fancy see
　　The painted chief, and pointed spear,
And Reason's self shall bow the knee
　　To shadows and delusions here.

THE WILD HONEYSUCKLE

FAIR flower, that dost so comely grow,
Hid in this silent, dull retreat,
Untouched thy honied blossoms blow,
Unseen thy little branches greet:
　　No roving foot shall crush thee here,
　　No busy hand provoke a tear.

By Nature's self in white arrayed,
She bade thee shun the vulgar eye,
And planted here the guardian shade,
And sent soft waters murmuring by;
　　Thus quietly thy summer goes,
　　Thy days declining to repose.

Smit with those charms, that must decay,
I grieve to see your future doom;
They died—nor were those flowers more gay,
The flowers that did in Eden bloom;
  Unpitying frosts, and Autumn's power
  Shall leave no vestige of this flower.

From morning suns and evening dews
At first thy little being came:
If nothing once, you nothing lose,
For when you die you are the same;
  The space between, is but an hour,
  The frail duration of a flower.

SONG OF THYRSIS

THE turtle on yon withered bough,
That lately mourned her murdered mate,
Has found another comrade now—
Such changes all await!
Again her drooping plume is drest,
Again she's willing to be blest
And takes her lover to her nest.

If nature has decreed it so
With all above, and all below,
Let us like them forget our woe,
  And not be killed with sorrow.
If I should quit your arms to-night
And chance to die before 'twas light,
I would advise you—and you might—
  Love again to-morrow.

William Cullen Bryant

TO A WATERFOWL

WHITHER, midst falling dew,
While glow the heavens with the last steps of day,
Far, through their rosy depths, dost thou pursue
    Thy solitary way?

Vainly the fowler's eye
Might mark thy distant flight to do thee wrong,
As, darkly painted on the crimson sky,
    Thy figure floats along.

Seek'st thou the plashy brink
Of weedy lake, or marge of river wide,
Or where the rocking billows rise and sink
    On the chafed ocean-side?

There is a Power whose care
Teaches thy way along that pathless coast,—
The desert and illimitable air,—
    Lone wandering, but not lost.

All day thy wings have fanned
At that far height, the cold, thin atmosphere,
Yet stoop not, weary, to the welcome land,
    Though the dark night is near.

And soon that toil shall end;
Soon shalt thou find a summer home, and rest,
And scream among thy fellows; reeds shall bend
    Soon, o'er thy sheltered nest.

33

Thou'rt gone, the abyss of heaven
Hath swallowed up thy form; yet, on my heart
Deeply hath sunk the lesson thou hast given,
    And shall not soon depart.

He who, from zone to zone,
Guides through the boundless sky thy certain flight,
In the long way that I must tread alone,
    Will lead my steps aright.

THANATOPSIS

To him who in the love of nature holds
Communion with her visible forms, she speaks
A various language; for his gayer hours
She has a voice of gladness, and a smile
And eloquence of beauty, and she glides
Into his darker musings, with a mild
And healing sympathy, that steals away
Their sharpness, ere he is aware. When thoughts
Of the last bitter hour come like a blight
Over thy spirit, and sad images
Of the stern agony, and shroud, and pall,
And breathless darkness, and the narrow house,
Make thee to shudder and grow sick at heart;—
Go forth, under the open sky, and list
To Nature's teachings, while from all around—
Earth and her waters, and the depths of air—
Comes a still voice:—

               Yet a few days, and thee
The all-beholding sun shall see no more
In all his course; nor yet in the cold ground,
Where thy pale form was laid, with many tears,
Nor in the embrace of ocean, shall exist
Thy image. Earth, that nourished thee, shall claim

Thy growth, to be resolved to earth again,
And, lost each human trace, surrendering up
Thine individual being, shalt thou go
To mix forever with the elements,
To be a brother to the insensible rock
And to the sluggish clod, which the rude swain
Turns with his share, and treads upon. The oak
Shall send his roots abroad and pierce thy mold.
Yet not to thine eternal resting-place
Shalt thou retire alone, nor couldst thou wish
Couch more magnificent. Thou shalt lie down
With patriarchs of the infant world—with kings,
The powerful of the earth—the wise, the good,
Fair forms, and hoary seers of ages past,
All in one mighty sepulcher. The hills,
Rock-ribbed and ancient as the sun,—the vales
Stretching in pensive quietness between;
The venerable woods—rivers that move
In majesty, and the complaining brooks
That make the meadows green; and, poured round all,
Old Ocean's gray and melancholy waste,—
Are but the solemn decorations all
Of the great tomb of man. The golden sun,
The planets, all the infinite host of heaven,
Are shining on the sad abodes of death
Through the still lapse of ages. All that tread
The globe are but a handful to the tribes
That slumber in its bosom.—Take the wings
Of morning, pierce the Barcan wilderness,
Or lose thyself in the continuous woods
Where rolls the Oregon, and hears no sound
Save his own dashings—yet the dead are there:
And millions in those solitudes, since first
The flight of years began, have laid them down
In their last sleep—the dead reign there alone.

So shalt thou rest, and what if thou withdraw
In silence from the living, and no friend

Take note of thy departure? All that breathe
Will share thy destiny. The gay will laugh
When thou art gone, the solemn brood of care
Plod on, and each one as before will chase
His favorite phantom; yet all these shall leave
Their mirth and their employments, and shall come
And make their bed with thee. As the long train
Of ages glides away, the sons of men—
The youth in life's fresh spring, and he who goes
In the full strength of years, matron and maid,
The speechless babe, and the gray-headed man—
Shall one by one be gathered to thy side,
By those who in their turn shall follow them.

So live, that when thy summons comes to join
The innumerable caravan, which moves
To that mysterious realm, where each shall take
His chamber in the silent halls of death,
Thou go not, like the quarry-slave at night,
Scourged to his dungeon, but, sustained and soothed
By an unfaltering trust, approach thy grave
Like one who wraps the drapery of his couch
About him, and lies down to pleasant dreams.

Ralph Waldo Emerson

CONCORD HYMN

*Sung at the Completion of the Battle Monument,
July 4, 1837*

By the rude bridge that arched the flood,
   Their flag to April's breeze unfurled,
Here once the embattled farmers stood
   And fired the shot heard round the world.

The foe long since in silence slept;
   Alike the conqueror silent sleeps;
And Time the ruined bridge has swept
   Down the dark stream which seaward creeps.

On this green bank, by this soft stream,
   We set to-day a votive stone;
That memory may their deed redeem,
   When, like our sires, our sons are gone.

Spirit, that made those heroes dare
   To die, and leave their children free,
Bid Time and Nature gently spare
   The shaft we raise to them and thee.

BRAHMA

If the red slayer think he slays,
   Or if the slain think he is slain,
They know not well the subtle ways
   I keep, and pass, and turn again.

37

Far or forgot to me is near;
  Shadow and sunlight are the same;
The vanished gods to me appear;
  And one to me are shame and fame.

They reckon ill who leave me out;
  When me they fly, I am the wings;
I am the doubter and the doubt,
  And I the hymn the Brahmin sings.

The strong gods pine for my abode,
  And pine in vain the sacred Seven;
But thou, meek lover of the good!
  Find me, and turn thy back on heaven.

THE SNOW-STORM

ANNOUNCED by all the trumpets of the sky,
Arrives the snow, and, driving o'er the fields,
Seems nowhere to alight: the whited air
Hides hills and woods, the river, and the heaven,
And veils the farm-house at the garden's end.
The sled and traveller stopped, the courier's feet
Delayed, all friends shut out, the housemates sit
Around the radiant fireplace, enclosed
In a tumultuous privacy of storm.

Come see the north wind's masonry.
Out of an unseen quarry evermore
Furnished with tile, the fierce artificer
Curves his white bastions with projected roof
Round every windward stake, or tree, or door.
Speeding, the myriad-handed, his wild work
So fanciful, so savage, nought cares he
For number or proportion. Mockingly,
On coop or kennel he hangs Parian wreaths;

A swan-like form invests the hidden thorn;
Fills up the farmer's lane from wall to wall,
Maugre the farmer's sighs; and at the gate
A tapering turret overtops the work.
And when his hours are numbered, and the world
Is all his own, retiring, as he were not,
Leaves, when the sun appears, astonished Art
To mimic in slow structures, stone by stone,
Built in an age, the mad wind's night-work,
The frolic architecture of the snow.

URIEL

It fell in the ancient periods
   Which the brooding soul surveys,
Or ever the wild Time coined itself
   Into calendar months and days.

This was the lapse of Uriel,
Which in Paradise befell.
Once, among the Pleiads walking,
Seyd overheard the young gods talking;
And the treason, too long pent,
To his ears was evident.
The young deities discussed
Laws of form, and metre just,
Orb, quintessence, and sunbeams,
What subsisteth, and what seems.
One, with low tones that decide,
And doubt and reverend use defied,
With a look that solved the sphere,
And stirred the devils everywhere,
Gave his sentiment divine
Against the being of a line.
"Line in nature is not found;
Unit and universe are round;

In vain produced, all rays return;
Evil will bless, and ice will burn."
As Uriel spoke with piercing eye,
A shudder ran around the sky;
The stern old war-gods shook their heads,
The seraphs frowned from myrtle-beds;
Seemed to the holy festival
The rash word boded ill to all;
The balance-beam of Fate was bent;
The bounds of good and ill were rent;
Strong Hades could not keep his own,
But all slid to confusion.

A sad self-knowledge, withering, fell
On the beauty of Uriel;
In heaven once eminent, the god
Withdrew, that hour, into his cloud;
Whether doomed to long gyration
In the sea of generation,
Or by knowledge grown too bright
To hit the nerve of feebler sight.
Straightway, a forgetting wind
Stole over the celestial kind,
And their lips the secret kept,
If in ashes the fire-seed slept.
But now and then, truth-speaking things
Shamed the angels' veiling wings;
And, shrilling from the solar course,
Or from fruit of chemic force,
Procession of a soul in matter,
Or the speeding change of water,
Or out of the good of evil born,
Came Uriel's voice of cherub scorn,
And a blush tinged the upper sky,
And the gods shook, they knew not why.

BACCHUS

BRING me wine, but wine which never grew
In the belly of the grape,
Or grew on vine whose tap-roots, reaching through
Under the Andes to the Cape,
Suffer no savor of the earth to scape.

Let its grapes the morn salute
From a nocturnal root,
Which feels the acrid juice
Of Styx and Erebus;
And turns the woe of Night,
By its own craft, to a more rich delight.

We buy ashes for bread;
We buy diluted wine;
Give me of the true,—
Whose ample leaves and tendrils curled
Among the silver hills of heaven,
Draw everlasting dew;
Wine of wine,
Blood of the world,
Form of forms, and mould of statures,
That I intoxicated,
And by the draught assimilated,
May float at pleasure through all natures;
The bird-language rightly spell,
And that which roses say so well.

Wine that is shed
Like the torrents of the sun
Up the horizon walls,
Or like the Atlantic streams, which run
When the South Sea calls.

Water and bread,
Food which needs no transmuting,

Rainbow-flowering, wisdom-fruiting,
Wine which is already man,
Food which teach and reason can.
Wine which Music is,—
Music and wine are one,—
That I, drinking this,
Shall hear far Chaos talk with me;
Kings unborn shall walk with me;
And the poor grass shall plot and plan
What it will do when it is man.
Quickened so, will I unlock
Every crypt of every rock.

I thank the joyful juice
For all I know;—
Winds of remembering
Of the ancient being blow,
And seeming-solid walls of use
Open and flow.

Pour, Bacchus! the remembering wine;
Retrieve the loss of me and mine!
Vine for vine be antidote,
And the grape requite the lote!
Haste to cure the old despair,—
Reason in Nature's lotus drenched,
The memory of ages quenched;
Give them again to shine;
Let wine repair what this undid;
And where the infection slid,
A dazzling memory revive;
Refresh the faded tints,
Recut the aged prints,
And write my old adventures with the pen
Which on the first day drew,
Upon the tablets blue,
The dancing Pleiads and eternal men.

EXPERIENCE

THE lords of life, the lords of life,—
I saw them pass
In their own guise,
Like and unlike,
Portly and grim,—
Use and Surprise,
Surface and Dream,
Succession swift, and spectral Wrong,
Temperament without a tongue,
And the inventor of the game
Omnipresent without name;—
Some to see, some to be guessed,
They marched from east to west:
Little man, least of all,
Among the legs of his guardians tall,
Walked about with puzzled look.
Him by the hand dear Nature took,
Dearest Nature, strong and kind,
Whispered, "Darling, never mind!
To-morrow they will wear another face,
The founder thou; these are thy race!"

COMPENSATION

WHY should I keep holiday
    When other men have none?
Why but because, when these are gay,
    I sit and mourn alone?

And why, when mirth unseals all tongues,
    Should mine alone be dumb?
Ah! late I spoke to silent throngs,
    And now their hour is come.

GIVE ALL TO LOVE

Give all to love;
Obey thy heart;
Friends, kindred, days,
Estate, good-fame,
Plans, credit, and the Muse,—
Nothing refuse.

'Tis a brave master;
Let it have scope:
Follow it utterly,
Hope beyond hope:
High and more high
It dives into noon,
With wing unspent,
Untold intent;
But it is a god,
Knows its own path,
And the outlets of the sky.

It was never for the mean;
It requireth courage stout,
Souls above doubt,
Valor unbending;
It will reward,—
They shall return
More than they were,
And ever ascending.

Leave all for love;
Yet, hear me, yet,
One word more thy heart behoved,
One pulse more of firm endeavor,—
Keep thee to-day
To-morrow, forever,
Free as an Arab
Of thy beloved.

Cling with life to the maid;
But when the surprise,
First vague shadow of surmise
Flits across her bosom young
Of a joy apart from thee,
Free be she, fancy-free;
Nor thou detain her vesture's hem,
Nor the palest rose she flung
From her summer diadem.

Though thou loved her as thyself,
As a self of purer clay,
Though her parting dims the day,
Stealing grace from all alive;
Heartily know,
When half-gods go,
The gods arrive.

THE RHODORA:

On Being Asked, Whence Is the Flower?

IN May, when sea-winds pierced our solitudes,
I found the fresh Rhodora in the woods,
Spreading its leafless blooms in a damp nook,
To please the desert and the sluggish brook.
The purple petals, fallen in the pool,
Made the black water with their beauty gay;
Here might the red-bird come his plumes to cool,
And court the flower that cheapens his array.
Rhodora! if the sages ask thee why
This charm is wasted on the earth and sky,
Tell them, dear, that if eyes were made for seeing,
Then Beauty is its own excuse for being:
Why thou were there, O rival of the rose!
I never thought to ask, I never knew:
But, in my simple ignorance, suppose
The self-same Power that brought me there brought you.

45

CHARACTER

THE sun set, but set not his hope:
Stars rose; his faith was earlier up:
Fixed on the enormous galaxy,
Deeper and older seemed his eye;.
And matched his suffrance sublime
The taciturnity of time.
He spoke, and words more soft than rain
Brought the Age of Gold again:
His action won such reverence sweet
As hid all measure of the feat.

THE PAST

THE debt is paid,
The verdict said,
The Furies laid,
The plague is stayed,
All fortunes made;
Turn the key and bolt the door,
Sweet is death forevermore.
Nor haughty hope, nor swart chagrin,
Nor murdering hate, can enter in.
All is now secure and fast;
Not the gods can shake the Past;
Flies-to the adamantine door
Bolted down forevermore.
None can reënter there,—
No thief so politic,
No Satan with a royal trick
Steal in by window, chink, or hole,
To bind or unbind, add what lacked,
Insert a leaf, or forge a name,
New-face or finish what is packed,
Alter or mend eternal Fact.

FABLE

THE mountain and the squirrel
Had a quarrel,
And the former called the latter "Little Prig";
Bun replied,
"You are doubtless very big;
But all sorts of things and weather
Must be taken in together,
To make up a year
And a sphere.
And I think it no disgrace
To occupy my place.
If I'm not so large as you,
You are not so small as I,
And not half so spry.
I'll not deny you make
A very pretty squirrel track;
Talents differ; all is well and wisely put;
If I cannot carry forests on my back,
Neither can you crack a nut."

DAYS

DAUGHTERS of Time, the hypocritic Days,
Muffled and dumb like barefoot dervishes,
And marching single in an endless file,
Bring diadems and fagots in their hands.
To each they offer gifts after his will,
Bread, kingdoms, stars, and sky that holds them all.
I, in my pleached garden, watched the pomp,
Forgot my morning wishes, hastily
Took a few herbs and apples, and the Day
Turned and departed silent. I, too late,
Under her solemn fillet saw the scorn.

IN AN AGE OF FOPS AND TOYS

In an age of fops and toys,
Wanting wisdom, void of right,
Who shall nerve heroic boys
To hazard all in Freedom's fight,—
Break sharply off their jolly games,
Forsake their comrades gay
And quit proud homes and youthful dames
For famine, toil and fray?
Yet on the nimble air benign
Speed nimbler messages,
That waft the breath of grace divine
To hearts in sloth and ease.
So nigh is grandeur to our dust,
So near is God to man,
When Duty whispers low, *Thou must,*
The youth replies, *I can.*

(*from* Voluntaries)

THE PROBLEM

I like a church; I like a cowl;
I love a prophet of the soul;
And on my heart monastic aisles
Fall like sweet strains, or pensive smiles;
Yet not for all his faith can see
Would I that cowled churchman be.

Why should the vest on him allure,
Which I could not on me endure?
Not from a vain or shallow thought
His awful Jove young Phidias brought;
Never from lips of cunning fell
The thrilling Delphic oracle;
Out from the heart of nature rolled

The burdens of the Bible old;
The litanies of nations came,
Like the volcano's tongue of flame,
Up from the burning core below,—
The canticles of love and woe;
The hand that rounded Peter's dome,
And groined the aisles of Christian Rome,
Wrought in a sad sincerity;
Himself from God he could not free;
He builded better than he knew;—
The conscious stone to beauty grew.

Know'st thou what wove yon woodbird's nest
Of leaves, and feathers from her breast?
Or how the fish outbuilt her shell,
Painting with morn each annual cell?
Or how the sacred pine-tree adds
To her old leaves new myriads?
Such and so grew these holy piles,
Whilst love and terror laid the tiles.
Earth proudly wears the Parthenon,
As the best gem upon her zone;
And Morning opes with haste her lids,
To gaze upon the Pyramids;
O'er England's abbeys bends the sky,
As on its friends, with kindred eye;
For, out of Thought's interior sphere
These wonders rose to upper air;
And Nature gladly gave them place,
Adopted them into her race,
And granted them an equal date
With Andes and with Ararat.

These temples grew as grows the grass;
Art might obey, but not surpass.
The passive Master lent his hand
To the vast soul that o'er him planned;
And the same power that reared the shrine,

49

Bestrode the tribes that knelt within.
Ever the fiery Pentecost
Girds with one flame the countless host,
Trances the heart through chanting choirs,
And through the priest the mind inspires.

The word unto the prophet spoken
Was writ on tables yet unbroken;
The word by seers or sibyls told,
In groves of oak, or fanes of gold,
Still floats upon the morning wind,
Still whispers to the willing mind.
One accent of the Holy Ghost
The heedless world hath never lost.
I know what say the fathers wise,—
The Book itself before me lies,
Old *Chrysostom,* best Augustine,
And he who blent both in his line,
The younger *Golden Lips* or mines,
Taylor, the Shakespeare of divines.
His words are music in my ear,
I see his cowled portrait dear;
And yet, for all his faith could see,
I would not the good bishop be.

FORBEARANCE

HAST thou named all the birds without a gun?
Loved the wood-rose, and left it on its stalk?
At rich men's tables eaten bread and pulse?
Unarmed, faced danger with a heart of trust?
And loved so well a high behaviour,
In man or maid, that thou from speech refrained,
Nobility more nobly to repay?
O, be my friend, and teach me to be thine!

RALPH WALDO EMERSON
GOOD-BYE

GOOD-BYE, proud world! I'm going home:
Thou art not my friend, and I'm not thine.
Long through thy weary crowds I roam;
A river-ark on the ocean brine,
Long I've been tossed like the driven foam;
But now, proud world! I'm going home.

Good-bye to Flattery's fawning face;
To Grandeur with his wise grimace;
To upstart Wealth's averted eye;
To supple Office, low and high;
To crowded halls, to court and street;
To frozen hearts and hasting feet;
To those who go, and those who come;
Good-bye, proud world! I'm going home.

I am going to my own hearth-stone,
Bosomed in yon green hills alone,—
A secret nook in a pleasant land,
Whose groves the frolic fairies planned;
Where arches green, the livelong day,
Echo the blackbird's roundelay,
And vulgar feet have never trod
A spot that is sacred to thought and God.

O, when I am safe in my sylvan home,
I tread on the pride of Greece and Rome;
And when I am stretched beneath the pines,
Where the evening star so holy shines,
I laugh at the lore and the pride of man,
At the sophist schools, and the learned clan;
For what are they all, in their high conceit,
When man in the bush with God may meet?

SEA-SHORE

I HEARD or seemed to hear the chiding Sea
Say, Pilgrim, why so late and slow to come?
Am I not always here, thy summer home?
Is not my voice thy music, morn and eve?
My breath thy healthful climate in the heats,
My touch thy antidote, my bay thy bath?
Was ever building like my terraces?
Was ever couch magnificent as mine?
Lie on the warm rock-ledges, and there learn
A little hut suffices like a town.
I make your sculptured architecture vain,
Vain beside mine. I drive my wedges home,
And carve the coastwise mountain into caves.
Lo! here is Rome, and Nineveh, and Thebes,
Karnak, and Pyramid, and Giant's Stairs,
Half piled or prostrate; and my newest slab
Older than all thy race.

      Behold the Sea,
The opaline, the plentiful and strong,
Yet beautiful as is the rose in June,
Fresh as the trickling rainbow of July;
Sea full of food, the nourisher of kinds,
Purger of earth, and medicine of men;
Creating a sweet climate by my breath,
Washing out harms and griefs from memory,
And, in my mathematic ebb and flow,
Giving a hint of that which changes not.
Rich are the sea-gods:—who gives gifts but they?
They grope the sea for pearls, but more than pearls:
They pluck Force thence, and give it to the wise.
For every wave is wealth to Dædalus,
Wealth to the cunning artist who can work
This matchless strength. Where shall he find, O waves!
A load your Atlas shoulders cannot lift?

I with my hammer pounding evermore
The rocky coast, smite Andes into dust,
Strewing my bed, and, in another age,
Rebuild a continent of better men.
Then I unbar the doors: my paths lead out
The exodus of nations: I disperse
Men to all shores that front the hoary main.

I too have arts and sorceries;
Illusion dwells forever with the wave.
I know what spells are laid. Leave me to deal
With credulous and imaginative man;
For, though he scoop my water in his palm
A few rods off he deems it gems and clouds.
Planting strange fruits and sunshine on the shore,
I make some coast alluring, some lone isle,
To distant men, who must go there, or die.

John Greenleaf Whittier

ICHABOD

So fallen, so lost! the light withdrawn
 Which once he wore!
The glory from his gray hairs gone
 Forevermore!

Revile him not—the Tempter hath
 A snare for all;
And pitying tears, not scorn and wrath,
 Befit his fall.

Oh dumb be passion's stormy rage
 When he who might
Have lighted up and led his age
 Falls back in night.

Scorn? would the angels laugh to mark
 A bright soul driven,
Fiend-goaded, down the endless dark,
 From hope and heaven?

Let not the land once proud of him
 Insult him now,
Nor brand with deeper shame his dim,
 Dishonored brow.

But let its humbled sons, instead,
 From sea to lake,
A long lament as for the dead
 In sadness make.

Of all we loved and honored, nought
 Save power remains—
A fallen angel's pride of thought,
 Still strong in chains.

All else is gone; from those great eyes
    The soul has fled:
When faith is lost, when honor dies,
    The man is dead.

Then pay the reverence of old days
    To his dead fame;
Walk backward, with averted gaze,
    And hide the shame.

THE BAREFOOT BOY

BLESSINGS on thee, little man,
Barefoot boy, with cheek of tan!
With thy turned-up pantaloons,
And thy merry whistled tunes;
With thy red lip, redder still
Kissed by strawberries on the hill;
With the sunshine on thy face,
Through thy torn brim's jaunty grace;
From my heart I give thee joy,—
I was once a barefoot boy!
Prince thou art,—the grown-up man
Only is republican.
Let the million-dollared ride!
Barefoot, trudging at his side,
Thou hast more than he can buy
In the reach of ear and eye,—
Outward sunshine, inward joy:
Blessings on thee, barefoot boy!
Oh for boyhood's painless play,
Sleep that wakes in laughing day,
Health that mocks the doctor's rules,
Knowledge never learned of schools,
Of the wild bee's morning chase,
Of the wild-flower's time and place,
Flight of fowl and habitude
Of the tenants of the wood;

How the tortoise bears his shell,
How the woodchuck digs his cell,
And the ground-mole sinks his well;
How the robin feeds her young,
How the oriole's nest is hung;
Where the whitest lilies blow,
Where the freshest berries grow,
Where the ground-nut trails its vine,
Where the wood-grape's clusters shine;
Of the black wasp's cunning way,
Mason of his walls of clay,
And the architectural plans
Of gray hornet artisans!
For, eschewing books and tasks,
Nature answers all he asks;
Hand in hand with her he walks,
Face to face with her he talks,
Part and parcel of her joy,—
Blessings on the barefoot boy!

Oh for boyhood's time of June,
Crowding years in one brief moon,
When all things I heard or saw,
Me, their master, waited for.
I was rich in flowers and trees,
Humming-birds and honey-bees;
For my sport the squirrel played,
Plied the snouted mole his spade;
For my taste the blackberry cone
Purpled over hedge and stone;
Laughed the brook for my delight
Through the day and through the night,
Whispering at the garden wall,
Talked with me from fall to fall;
Mine the sand-rimmed pickerel pond,
Mine the walnut slopes beyond,
Mine, on bending orchard trees,
Apples of Hesperides!
Still as my horizon grew,

Larger grew my riches too;
All the world I saw or knew
Seemed a complex Chinese toy,
Fashioned for a barefoot boy!
 Oh for festal dainties spread,
Like my bowl of milk and bread;
Pewter spoon and bowl of wood,
On the door-stone, gray and rude!
O'er me, like a regal tent,
Cloudy-ribbed, the sunset bent,
Purple-curtained, fringed with gold,
Looped in many a wind-swung fold;
While for music came the play
Of the pied frogs' orchestra;
And, to light the noisy choir,
Lit the fly his lamp of fire.
I was monarch: pomp and joy
Waited on the barefoot boy!
 Cheerily, then, my little man,
Live and laugh, as boyhood can!
Though the flinty slopes be hard,
Stubble-speared the new-mown sward,
Every morn shall lead thee through
Fresh baptisms of the dew;
Every evening from thy feet
Shall the cool wind kiss the heat:
All too soon these feet must hide
In the prison cells of pride,
Lose the freedom of the sod,
Like a colt's for work be shod,
Made to tread the mills of toil,
Up and down in ceaseless moil:
Happy if their track be found
Never on forbidden ground;
Happy if they sink not in
Quick and treacherous sands of sin.
Ah! that thou couldst know thy joy,
Ere it passes, barefoot boy!

Henry Wadsworth Longfellow

MY LOST YOUTH

Often I think of the beautiful town
    That is seated by the sea;
Often in thought go up and down
The pleasant streets of that dear old town,
    And my youth comes back to me.
        And a verse of a Lapland song
        Is haunting my memory still:
        "A boy's will is the wind's will,
And the thoughts of youth are long, long thoughts."

I can see the shadowy lines of its trees,
    And catch, in sudden gleams,
The sheen of the far-surrounding seas,
And islands that were the Hesperides
    Of all my boyish dreams.
        And the burden of that old song,
        It murmurs and whispers still:
        "A boy's will is the wind's will,
And the thoughts of youth are long, long thoughts."

I remember the black wharves and the slips,
    And the sea-tides tossing free;
And the Spanish sailors with bearded lips,
And the beauty and mystery of the ships,
    And the magic of the sea.
        And the voice of that wayward song
        Is singing and saying still:
        "A boy's will is the wind's will,
And the thoughts of youth are long, long thoughts."

I remember the bulwarks by the shore,
    And the fort upon the hill;
The sunrise gun, with its hollow roar,
The drum-beat repeated o'er and o'er,
    And the bugle wild and shrill.
        And the music of that old song
        Throbs in my memory still:
    "A boy's will is the wind's will,
And the thoughts of youth are long, long thoughts."

I remember the sea-fight far away,
    How it thundered o'er the tide!
And the dead captains, as they lay
In their graves, o'erlooking the tranquil bay
    Where they in battle died.
        And the sound of that mournful song
        Goes through me with a thrill:
    "A boy's will is the wind's will,
And the thoughts of youth are long, long thoughts."

I can see the breezy dome of groves,
    The shadows of Deering's Woods;
And the friendships old and the early loves
Come back with a Sabbath sound, as of doves
    In quiet neighborhoods.
        And the verse of that sweet old song,
        It flutters and murmurs still:
    "A boy's will is the wind's will,
And the thoughts of youth are long, long thoughts."

I remember the gleams and glooms that dart
    Across the school-boy's brain;
The song and the silence in the heart,
That in part are prophecies, and in part
    Are longings wild and vain.
        And the voice of that fitful song
        Sings on, and is never still:

59

"A boy's will is the wind's will,
And the thoughts of youth are long, long thoughts."

There are things of which I may not speak;
    There are dreams that cannot die;
There are thoughts that make the strong heart weak,
And bring a pallor into the cheek,
    And a mist before the eye.
        And the words of that fatal song
        Come over me like a chill:
        "A boy's will is the wind's will,
And the thoughts of youth are long, long thoughts."

Strange to me now are the forms I meet
    When I visit the dear old town;
But the native air is pure and sweet,
And the trees that o'ershadow each well-known street,
    As they balance up and down,
        Are singing the beautiful song,
        Are sighing and whispering still:
        "A boy's will is the wind's will,
And the thoughts of youth are long, long thoughts."

And Deering's Woods are fresh and fair,
    And with joy that is almost pain
My heart goes back to wander there,
And among the dreams of the days that were,
    I find my lost youth again.
        And the strange and beautiful song,
        The groves are repeating it still:
        "A boy's will is the wind's will,
And the thoughts of youth are long, long thoughts."

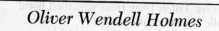

Oliver Wendell Holmes

THE CHAMBERED NAUTILUS

This is the ship of pearl, which, poets feign,
　　Sails the unshadowed main,—
　　The venturous bark that flings
On the sweet summer wind its purpled wings
In gulfs enchanted, where the Siren sings,
　　And coral reefs lie bare,
Where the cold sea-maids rise to sun their streaming
　　　hair.

Its webs of living gauze no more unfurl;
　　Wrecked is the ship of pearl!
　　And every chambered cell,
Where its dim dreaming life was wont to dwell,
As the frail tenant shaped his growing shell,
　　Before thee lies revealed,—
Its irised ceiling rent, its sunless crypt unsealed!

Year after year beheld the silent toil
　　That spread his lustrous coil;
　　Still, as the spiral grew,
He left the past year's dwelling for the new,
Stole with soft step its shining archway through,
　　Built up its idle door,
Stretched in his last-found home, and knew the old
　　no more.

Thanks for the heavenly message brought by thee,
　　Child of the wandering sea,
　　Cast from her lap, forlorn!
From thy dead lips a clearer note is born

Than ever Triton blew from wreathèd horn!
   While on mine ear it rings,
Through the deep caves of thought I hear a voice that
         sings:—

Build thee more stately mansions, O my soul,
   As the swift seasons roll!
   Leave thy low-vaulted past!
Let each new temple, nobler than the last,
Shut thee from heaven with a dome more vast,
   Till thou at length art free,
Leaving thine outgrown shell by life's unresting sea!

THE DEACON'S MASTERPIECE

OR, THE WONDERFUL "ONE-HOSS SHAY"

A Logical Story

HAVE you heard of the wonderful one-hoss shay,
That was built in such a logical way
It ran a hundred years to a day,
And then, of a sudden, it—ah, but stay,
I'll tell you what happened without delay,
Scaring the parson into fits,
Frightening people out of their wits,—
Have you ever heard of that, I say?

Seventeen hundred and fifty-five.
Georgius Secundus was then alive,—
Snuffy old drone from the German hive!
That was the year when Lisbon-town
Saw the earth open and gulp her down,
And Braddock's army was done so brown,
Left without a scalp to its crown.

It was on the terrible Earthquake-day
That the Deacon finished the one-hoss shay.

Now in building of chaises, I tell you what,
There is always *somewhere* a weakest spot,—
In hub, tire, felloe, in spring or thill,
In panel, or crossbar, or floor, or sill,
In screw, bolt, thoroughbrace,—lurking still,
Find it somewhere you must and will,—
Above or below, or within or without,—
And that's the reason, beyond a doubt,
That a chaise *breaks down,* but doesn't *wear out.*

But the Deacon swore (as Deacons do,
With an "I dew vum," or an "I tell *yeou*")
He would build one shay to beat the taown
'N' the keounty 'n' all the kentry raoun';
It should be so built that it *couldn'* break daown:
"Fur," said the Deacon, " 't 's mighty plain
Thut the weakes' place mus' stan' the strain;
'N' the way t' fix it, uz I maintain, is only jest
T' make that place uz strong uz the rest."

So the Deacon inquired of the village folk
Where he could find the strongest oak,
That couldn't be split nor bent nor broke,—
That was for spokes and floor and sills;
He sent for lancewood to make the thills;
The crossbars were ash, from the straightest trees,
The panels of white-wood, that cuts like cheese,
But lasts like iron for things like these;
The hubs of logs from the "Settler's ellum,"—
Last of its timber,—they couldn't sell 'em,
Never an axe had seen their chips,
And the wedges flew from between their lips,
Their blunt ends frizzled like celery-tips;
Step and prop-iron, bolt and screw,
Spring, tire, axle, and linchpin too,

Steel of the finest, bright and blue;
Thoroughbrace bison-skin, thick and wide;
Boot, top, dasher, from tough old hide
Found in the pit when the tanner died.
That was the way he "put her through."
"There!" said the Deacon, "naow she'll dew!"

Do! I tell you, I rather guess
She was a wonder, and nothing less!
Colts grew horses, beards turned gray,
Deacon and deaconess dropped away,
Children and grandchildren—where were they?
But there stood the stout old one-hoss shay
As fresh as on Lisbon-earthquake-day!

EIGHTEEN HUNDRED;—it came and found
The Deacon's masterpiece strong and sound.
Eighteen hundred increased by ten;—
"Hahnsum kerridge" they called it then.
Eighteen hundred and twenty came;—
Running as usual; much the same.
Thirty and forty at last arrive,
And then come fifty, and FIFTY-FIVE.

Little of all we value here
Wakes on the morn of its hundredth year
Without both feeling and looking queer.
In fact, there's nothing that keeps its youth,
So far as I know, but a tree and truth.
(This is a moral that runs at large;
Take it.—You're welcome.—No extra charge.)

FIRST OF NOVEMBER,—the Earthquake-day,—
There are traces of age in the one-hoss shay,
A general flavor of mild decay,
But nothing local, as one may say.
There couldn't be,—for the Deacon's art
Had made it so like in every part

That there wasn't a chance for one to start.
For the wheels were just as strong as the thills,
And the floor was just as strong as the sills,
And the panels just as strong as the floor,
And the whipple-tree neither less nor more,
And the back-crossbar as strong as the fore,
And spring and axle and hub *encore*.
And yet, *as a whole*, it is past a doubt
In another hour it will be *worn out!*

First of November, 'Fifty-five!
This morning the parson takes a drive.
Now, small boys, get out of the way!
Here comes the wonderful one-hoss shay,
Drawn by a rat-tailed, ewe-necked bay.
"Huddup!" said the parson.—Off went they.
The parson was working his Sunday's text,—
Had got to *fifthly*, and stopped perplexed
At what the—Moses—was coming next.
All at once the horse stood still,
Close by the meet'n'-house on the hill.
First a shiver, and then a thrill,
Then something decidedly like a spill,—
And the parson was sitting upon a rock,
At half-past nine by the meet'n'-house clock,—
Just the hour of the Earthquake shock!
What do you think the parson found,
When he got up and stared around?
The poor old chaise in a heap or mound,
As if it had been to the mill and ground!
You see, of course, if you're not a dunce,
How it went to pieces all at once,—
All at once, and nothing first,—
Just as bubbles do when they burst.

End of the wonderful one-hoss shay.
Logic is logic. That's all I say.

Edgar Allan Poe

THE HAPPIEST DAY

The happiest day—the happiest hour
   My seared and blighted heart hath known,
The highest hope of pride and power,
   I feel hath flown.

Of power! said I? Yes! such I ween
   But they have vanished long, alas!
The visions of my youth have been—
   But let them pass.

And pride, what have I now with thee?
   Another brow may ev'n inherit
The venom thou hast poured on me—
   Be still my spirit!

The happiest day—the happiest hour
   Mine eyes shall see—have even seen
The brightest glance of pride and power
   I feel have been:

But were that hope of pride and power
   Now offered with the pain
Ev'n *then* I felt—that brightest hour
   I would not live again:

For on its wings was dark alloy
   And as it fluttered—fell
An essence—powerful to destroy
   A soul that knew it well.

EDGAR ALLAN POE

THE CONQUEROR WORM

Lo, 'tis a gala night
　　Within the lonesome latter years;
An angel throng, bewinged, bedight
　　In veils, and drowned in tears,
Sit in a theater, to see
　　A play of hopes and fears,
While the orchestra breathes fitfully
　　The music of the spheres.

Mimes, in the form of God on high,
　　Mutter and mumble low,
And hither and thither fly—
　　Mere puppets they, who come and go
At bidding of vast formless things
　　That shift the scenery to and fro,
Flapping from out their Condor wings
　　Invisible woe!

That motley drama, oh, be sure
　　It shall not be forgot!
With its Phantom chased for evermore
　　By a crowd that seize it not,
Through a circle that ever returneth in
　　To the self-same spot,
And much of Madness, and more of Sin,
　　And Horror the soul of the plot.

But see, amid the mimic rout
　　A crawling shape intrude!
A blood-red thing that writhes from out
　　The scenic solitude!
It writhes! it writhes! with mortal pangs
　　The mimes become its food,
And seraphs sob at vermin fangs
　　In human gore imbued.

67

Out, out are the lights—out all!
  And over each quivering form
The curtain, a funeral pall,
  Comes down with the rush of a storm;
While the angels, all pallid and wan,
  Uprising, unveiling, affirm
That the play is the tragedy "Man,"
  And its hero the Conqueror Worm.

THE RAVEN

Once upon a midnight dreary, while I pondered, weak
    and weary,
Over many a quaint and curious volume of forgotten
    lore—
While I nodded, nearly napping, suddenly there came
    a tapping,
As of some one gently rapping, rapping at my chamber
    door.
" 'Tis some visitor," I muttered, "tapping at my chamber
    door—
  Only this and nothing more."

Ah, distinctly I remember it was in the bleak December;
And each separate dying ember wrought its ghost upon
    the floor.
Eagerly I wished the morrow;—vainly I had sought to
    borrow
From my books surcease of sorrow—sorrow for the lost
    Lenore—
For the rare and radiant maiden whom the angels name
    Lenore—
  Nameless *here* for evermore.

And the silken, sad, uncertain rustling of each purple
    curtain
Thrilled me—filled me with fantastic terrors never felt
    before;

So that now, to still the beating of my heart, I stood
    repeating
" 'Tis some visitor entreating entrance at my chamber
    door—
Some late visitor entreating entrance at my chamber
    door;—
    This it is and nothing more."

Presently my soul grew stronger; hesitating then no
    longer,
"Sir," said I, "or Madam, truly your forgiveness I im-
    plore;
But the fact is I was napping, and so gently you came
    rapping,
And so faintly you came tapping, tapping at my chamber
    door,
That I scarce was sure I heard you"—here I opened wide
    the door;
    Darkness there and nothing more.

Deep into that darkness peering, long I stood there won-
    dering, fearing,
Doubting, dreaming dreams no mortal ever dared to
    dream before;
But the silence was unbroken, and the stillness gave no
    token,
And the only word there spoken was the whispered
    word, "Lenore!"
This I whispered, and an echo murmured back the word
    "Lenore!"
    Merely this and nothing more.

Back into the chamber turning, all my soul within me
    burning,
Soon again I heard a tapping somewhat louder than
    before.
"Surely," said I, "surely that is something at my window
    lattice;

Let me see, then, what thereat is, and this mystery
    explore—
Let my heart be still a moment and this mystery ex-
    plore;—
    'Tis the wind and nothing more!"

Open here I flung the shutter, when, with many a flirt
    and flutter
In there stepped a stately Raven of the saintly days of
    yore.
Not the least obeisance made he; not a minute stopped
    or stayed he;
But, with mien of lord or lady, perched above my cham-
    ber door—
Perched upon a bust of Pallas just above my chamber
    door—
    Perched, and sat, and nothing more.

Then this ebony bird beguiling my sad fancy into
    smiling,
By the grave and stern decorum of the countenance it
    wore,
"Though thy crest be shorn and shaven, thou," I said,
    "art sure no craven,
Ghastly grim and ancient Raven wandering from the
    Nightly shore—
Tell me what thy lordly name is on the Night's Plutonian
    shore!"
    Quoth the Raven, "Nevermore."

Much I marvelled this ungainly fowl to hear discourse
    so plainly,
Though its answer little meaning—little relevancy bore;
For we cannot help agreeing that no living human being
Ever yet was blessed with seeing bird above his chamber
    door—
Bird or beast upon the sculptured bust above his chamber
    door,
    With such name as "Nevermore."

But the Raven, sitting lonely on the placid bust, spoke
   only
That one word, as if his soul in that one word he did
   outpour.
Nothing farther then he uttered—not a feather then he
   fluttered—
Till I scarcely more than muttered "Other friends have
   flown before—
On the morrow *he* will leave me, as my hopes have flown
   before."
      Then the bird said "Nevermore."

Startled at the stillness broken by reply so aptly spoken,
"Doubtless," said I, "what it utters is its only stock and
   store
Caught from some unhappy master whom unmerciful
   Disaster
Followed fast and followed faster till his songs one
   burden bore—
Till the dirges of his Hope that melancholy burden bore
   Of 'Never—nevermore.'"

But the Raven still beguiling all my fancy into smiling,
Straight I wheeled a cushioned seat in front of bird, and
   bust and door;
Then, upon the velvet sinking, I betook myself to linking
Fancy unto fancy, thinking what this ominous bird of
   yore—
What this grim, ungainly, ghastly, gaunt, and ominous
   bird of yore
      Meant in croaking "Nevermore."

This I sat engaged in guessing, but no syllable expressing
To the fowl whose fiery eyes now burned into my
   bosom's core;
This and more I sat divining, with my head at ease
   reclining
On the cushion's velvet lining that the lamp-light gloated
   o'er,

But whose velvet violet lining with the lamp-light
    gloating o'er,
  She shall press, ah, nevermore!

Then, methought, the air grew denser, perfumed from
    an unseen censer
Swung by Seraphim whose foot-falls tinkled on the
    tufted floor.
"Wretch," I cried, "thy God hath lent thee—by these
    angels he hath sent thee
Respite—respite and nepenthe from thy memories of
    Lenore;
Quaff, oh quaff this kind nepenthe and forget this lost
    Lenore!"
    Quoth the Raven "Nevermore."

"Prophet!" said I, "thing of evil! prophet still, if bird or
    devil!—
Whether Tempter sent, or whether tempest tossed thee
    here ashore,
Desolate yet all undaunted, on this desert land en-
    chanted—
On this home by Horror haunted—tell me truly, I
    implore—
Is there—*is* there balm in Gilead?—tell me—tell me, I
    implore!"
    Quoth the Raven "Nevermore."

"Prophet!" said I, "thing of evil!—prophet still, if bird or
    devil!
By that Heaven that bends above us—by that God we
    both adore—
Tell this soul with sorrow laden if, within the distant
    Aidenn,
It shall clasp a sainted maiden whom the angels name
    Lenore—
Clasp a rare and radiant maiden whom the angels name
    Lenore."
    Quoth the Raven "Nevermore."

"Be that word our sign of parting, bird or fiend!" I
    shrieked, up-starting—
"Get thee back into the tempest and the Night's Plu-
    tonian shore!
Leave no black plume as a token of that lie thy soul
    hath spoken!
Leave my loneliness unbroken!—quit the bust above my
    door!
Take thy beak from out my heart, and take thy form
    from off my door!"
    Quoth the Raven "Nevermore."

And the Raven, never flitting, still is sitting, *still* is sitting
On the pallid bust of Pallas just above my chamber door;
And his eyes have all the seeming of a demon's that is
    dreaming,
And the lamp-light o'er him streaming throws his shad-
    ow on the floor;
And my soul from out that shadow that lies floating on
    the floor
    Shall be lifted—nevermore!

ULALUME

THE skies they were ashen and sober;
    The leaves they were crisped and sere—
    The leaves they were withering and sere;
It was night in the lonesome October
    Of my most immemorial year;
It was hard by the dim lake of Auber,
    In the misty mid region of Weir—
It was down by the dank tarn of Auber,
    In the ghoul-haunted woodland of Weir.

Here once, through an alley Titanic,
    Of cypress, I roamed with my Soul—
    Of cypress, with Psyche, my Soul.

These were days when my heart was volcanic
 As the scoriac rivers that roll—
 As the lavas that restlessly roll
Their sulphurous currents down Yaanek
 In the ultimate climes of the pole—
That groan as they roll down Mount Yaanek
 In the realms of the boreal pole.

Our talk had been serious and sober,
 But our thoughts they were palsied and sere—
 Our memories were treacherous and sere—
For we knew not the month was October,
 And we marked not the night of the year—
 (Ah, night of all nights in the year!)
We noted not the dim lake of Auber—
 (Though once we had journeyed down here)—
Remembered not the dank tarn of Auber,
 Nor the ghoul-haunted woodland of Weir.

And now, as the night was senescent
 And star-dials pointed to morn—
 As the star-dials hinted of morn—
At the end of our path a liquescent
 And nebulous lustre was born,
Out of which a miraculous crescent
 Arose with a duplicate horn—
Astarte's bediamonded crescent
 Distinct with its duplicate horn.

And I said—"She is warmer than Dian:
 She rolls through an ether of sighs—
 She revels in a region of sighs:
She has seen that the tears are not dry on
 These cheeks, where the worm never dies
And has come past the stars of the Lion
 To point us the path to the skies—
 To the Lethean peace of the skies—

Come up, in despite of the Lion,
　　To shine on us with her bright eyes—
Come up through the lair of the Lion,
　　With love in her luminous eyes."

But Psyche, uplifting her finger,
　　Said—"Sadly this star I mistrust—
　　Her pallor I strangely mistrust:—
Oh, hasten!—oh, let us not linger!
　　Oh, fly!—let us fly!—for we must."
In terror she spoke, letting sink her
　　Wings until they trailed in the dust—
In agony sobbed, letting sink her
　　Plumes till they trailed in the dust—
　　Till they sorrowfully trailed in the dust.

I replied—"This is nothing but dreaming:
　　Let us on by this tremulous light!
　　Let us bathe in this crystalline light!
Its Sibyllic splendor is beaming
　　With Hope and in Beauty to-night:—
　　See!—it flickers up the sky through the night!
Ah, we safely may trust to its gleaming,
　　And be sure it will lead us aright—
We safely may trust to a gleaming
　　That cannot but guide us aright,
　　Since it flickers up to Heaven through the night.'

Thus I pacified Psyche and kissed her,
　　And tempted her out of her gloom—
　　And conquered her scruples and gloom;
And we passed to the end of the vista,
　　But were stopped by the door of a tomb—
　　By the door of a legended tomb;
And I said—"What is written, sweet sister,
　　On the door of this legended tomb?"
　　She replied—"Ulalume—Ulalume—
　　'T is the vault of thy lost Ulalume!"

Then my heart it grew ashen and sober
 As the leaves that were crisped and sere—
 As the leaves that were withering and sere,
And I cried—"It was surely October
 On *this* very night of last year
 That I journeyed—I journeyed down here—
 That I brought a dread burden down here—
 On this night of all nights in the year,
 Ah, what demon has tempted me here?
Well I know, now, this dim lake of Auber—
 This misty mid region of Weir—
Well I know, now, this dank tarn of Auber,
 This ghoul-haunted woodland of Weir."

FOR ANNIE

THANK Heaven! the crisis—
 The danger is past,
And the lingering illness
 Is over at last—
And the fever called "Living"
 Is conquered at last.

Sadly, I know
 I am shorn of my strength,
And no muscle I move
 As I lie at full length—
But no matter!—I feel
 I am better at length.

And I rest so composedly
 Now, in my bed,
That any beholder
 Might fancy me dead—
Might start at beholding me,
 Thinking me dead.

The moaning and groaning,
  The sighing and sobbing,
Are quieted now,
  With that horrible throbbing
At heart:—ah that horrible,
  Horrible throbbing!

The sickness—the nausea—
  The pitiless pain—
Have ceased with the fever
  That maddened my brain—
With the fever called "Living"
  That burned in my brain.

And oh! of all tortures
  That torture the worst
Has abated—the terrible
  Torture of thirst
For the napthaline river
  Of Passion accurst:—
I have drank of a water
  That quenches all thirst:—

Of a water that flows,
  With a lullaby sound,
From a spring but a very few
  Feet under ground—
From a cavern not very far
  Down under ground.

And ah! let it never
  Be foolishly said
That my room it is gloomy
  And narrow my bed;
For a man never slept
  In a different bed—
And, to sleep, you must slumber
  In just such a bed.

77

My tantalized spirit
  Here blandly reposes,
Forgetting, or never
  Regretting, its roses—
Its old agitations
  Of myrtles and roses:

For now, while so quietly
  Lying, it fancies
A holier odor
  About it, of pansies—
A rosemary odor,
  Commingled with pansies—
With rue and the beautiful
  Puritan pansies.

And so it lies happily,
  Bathing in many
A dream of the truth
  And the beauty of Annie—
Drowned in a bath
  Of the tresses of Annie.

She tenderly kissed me,
  She fondly caressed,
And then I fell gently
  To sleep on her breast—
Deeply to sleep
  From the heaven of her breast.

When the light was extinguished,
  She covered me warm,
And she prayed to the angels
  To keep me from harm—
To the queen of the angels
  To shield me from harm.

And I lie so composedly,
  Now, in my bed,

(Knowing her love)
  That you fancy me dead—
And I rest so contentedly,
  Now, in my bed,
(With her love at my breast)
  That you fancy me dead—
That you shudder to look at me,
  Thinking me dead:

But my heart it is brighter
  Than all of the many
Stars of the sky,
  For it sparkles with Annie—
It glows with the light
  Of the love of my Annie—
With the thought of the light
  Of the eyes of my Annie.

ANNABEL LEE

IT was many and many a year ago,
  In a kingdom by the sea
That a maiden there lived whom you may know
  By the name of ANNABEL LEE;
And this maiden she lived with no other thought
  Than to love and be loved by me.

I was a child and *she* was a child,
  In this kingdom by the sea,
But we loved with a love that was more than love—
  I and my ANNABEL LEE—
With a love that the wingèd seraphs of heaven
  Coveted her and me.

And this was the reason that, long ago,
  In this kingdom by the sea,
A wind blew out of a cloud, chilling
  My beautiful ANNABEL LEE;

So that her high-born kinsmen came
    And bore her away from me,
To shut her up in a sepulchre
    In this kingdom by the sea.

The angels, not half so happy in heaven,
    Went envying her and me—
Yes!—that was the reason (as all men know,
    In this kingdom by the sea)
That the wind came out of the cloud by night,
    Chilling and killing my ANNABEL LEE.

But our love it was stronger by far than the love
    Of those who were older than we—
    Of many far wiser than we—
And neither the angels in heaven above,
    Nor the demons down under the sea,
Can ever dissever my soul from the soul
    Of the beautiful ANNABEL LEE:

For the moon never beams, without bringing me dreams
    Of the beautiful ANNABEL LEE,
And the stars never rise, but I feel the bright eyes
    Of the beautiful ANNABEL LEE:
And so, all the night-tide, I lie down by the side
Of my darling—my darling—my life and my bride,
    In the sepulchre there by the sea—
    In her tomb by the sounding sea.

TO HELEN

HELEN, thy beauty is to me
    Like those Nicéan barks of yore,
That gently, o'er a perfumed sea,
    The weary, way-worn wanderer bore
    To his own native shore.

On desperate seas long wont to roam,
  Thy hyacinth hair, thy classic face,
Thy Naiad airs have brought me home
  To the glory that was Greece,
  And the grandeur that was Rome.

Lo! in yon brilliant window-niche
  How statue-like I see thee stand,
The agate lamp within thy hand!
  Ah, Psyche, from the regions which
  Are Holy-Land!

ISRAFEL

IN Heaven a spirit doth dwell
  Whose heart-strings are a lute;
None sing so wildly well
As the angel Israfel,
And the giddy stars (so legends tell)
Ceasing their hymns, attend the spell
  Of his voice, all mute.

Tottering above
  In her highest noon,
  The enamored moon
Blushes with love,
  While, to listen, the red levin
  (With the rapid Pleiades, even,
  Which were seven)
  Pauses in Heaven.

And they say (the starry choir
  And the other listening things)
That Israfeli's fire
Is owing to that lyre
  By which he sits and sings—
The trembling living wire
  Of those unusual strings.

But the skies that angel trod,
　　Where deep thoughts are a duty—
Where Love's a grown-up God—
　　Where the Houri glances are
Imbued with all the beauty
　　Which we worship in a star.

Therefore, thou art not wrong,
　　Israfeli, who despisest
An unimpassioned song;
To thee the laurels belong,
　　Best bard, because the wisest!
Merrily live, and long!

The ecstasies above
　　With thy burning measures suit—
Thy grief, thy joy, thy hate, thy love,
　　With the fervor of thy lute—
　　Well may the stars be mute!

Yes, Heaven is thine; but this
　　Is a world of sweets and sours;
Our flowers are merely—flowers,
And the shadow of thy perfect bliss
　　Is the sunshine of ours.

If I could dwell
Where Israfel
　　Hath dwelt, and he where I,
He might not sing so wildly well
　　A mortal melody,
While a bolder note than this might swell
　　From my lyre within the sky.

THE CITY IN THE SEA

Lo! Death has reared himself a throne
In a strange city lying alone
Far down within the dim West,
Where the good and the bad and the worst and
        the best
Have gone to their eternal rest.
There shrines and palaces and towers
(Time-eaten towers that tremble not!)
Resemble nothing that is ours.
Around, by lifting winds forgot,
Resignedly beneath the sky
The melancholy waters lie.

No rays from the holy heaven come down
On the long night-time of that town;
But light from out the lurid sea
Streams up the turrets silently—
Gleams up the pinnacles far and free—
Up domes—up spires—up kingly halls—
Up fanes—up Babylon-like walls—
Up shadowy long-forgotten bowers
Of sculptured ivy and stone flowers—
Up many and many a marvellous shrine
Whose wreathèd friezes intertwine
The viol, the violet, and the vine.
Resignedly beneath the sky
The melancholy waters lie.
So blend the turrets and shadows there
That all seem pendulous in air,
While from a proud tower in the town
Death looks gigantically down.

There open fanes and gaping graves
Yawn level with the luminous waves
But not the riches there that lie
In each idol's diamond eye—

Not the gayly-jewelled dead
Tempt the waters from their bed;
For no ripples curl, alas!
Along that wilderness of glass—
No swellings tell that winds may be
Upon some far-off happier sea—
No heavings hint that winds have been
On seas less hideously serene.

But lo, a stir is in the air!
The wave—there is a movement there!
As if the towers had thrust aside,
In slightly sinking, the dull tide—
As if their tops had feebly given
A void within the filmy Heaven.
The waves have now a redder glow—
The hours are breathing faint and low—
And when, amid no earthly moans,
Down, down that town shall settle hence,
Hell, rising from a thousand thrones,
Shall do it reverence.

THE HAUNTED PALACE

In the greenest of our valleys
    By good angels tenanted,
Once a fair and stately palace—
    Radiant palace—reared its head.
In the monarch Thought's dominion—
    It stood there!
Never seraph spread a pinion
    Over fabric half so fair!

Banners yellow, glorious, golden,
    On its roof did float and flow,
(This—all this—was in the olden
    Time long ago,)
And every gentle air that dallied,

In that sweet day,
Along the ramparts plumed and pallid,
A wingèd odor went away.

Wanderers in that happy valley,
Through two luminous windows, saw
Spirits moving musically,
To a lute's well-tunèd law,
Round about a throne where, sitting,
(Porphyrogene!)
In state his glory well befitting,
The ruler of the realm was seen.

And all with pearl and ruby glowing
Was the fair palace door,
Through which came flowing, flowing, flowing
And sparkling evermore,
A troop of Echoes, whose sweet duty
Was but to sing,
In voices of surpassing beauty,
The wit and wisdom of their king.

But evil things, in robes of sorrow,
Assailed the monarch's high estate.
(Ah, let us mourn!—for never morrow
Shall dawn upon him desolate!)
And round about his home the glory
That blushed and bloomed,
Is but a dim-remembered story
Of the old time entombed.

And travellers, now, within that valley,
Through the red-litten windows see
Vast forms, that move fantastically
To a discordant melody,
While, like a ghastly rapid river,
Through the pale door
A hideous throng rush out forever
And laugh—but smile no more.

THE SLEEPER

At midnight, in the month of June,
I stand beneath the mystic moon.
An opiate vapour, dewy, dim,
Exhales from out her golden rim,
And softly dripping, drop by drop,
Upon the quiet mountain top,
Steals drowsily and musically
Into the universal valley.
The rosemary nods upon the grave;
The lily lolls upon the wave;
Wrapping the fog about its breast,
The ruin moulders into rest;
Looking like Lethe, see, the lake
A conscious slumber seems to take,
And would not, for the world, awake.
All Beauty sleeps! And, lo, where lies
Irene, with her Destinies!
Oh, lady bright, can it be right—
This window open to the night?
The wanton airs, from the tree-top,
Laughingly through the lattice drop—
The bodiless airs, a wizard rout,
Flit through thy chamber in and out,
And wave the curtain canopy
So fitfully—so fearfully—
Above the closed and fringèd lid
'Neath which thy slumb'ring soul lies hid,
That, o'er the floor and down the wall,
Like ghosts the shadows rise and fall!
Oh, lady dear, hast thou no fear?
Why and what art thou dreaming here?
Sure thou art come o'er far-off seas,
A wonder to these garden trees!
Strange is thy pallor! strange thy dress!
Strange, above all, thy length of tress,
    And this all solemn silentness!

The lady sleeps! Oh, may her sleep,
Which is enduring, so be deep!
Heaven have her in its sacred keep!
This chamber changed for one more holy,
This bed for one more melancholy,
I pray to God that she may lie
Forever with unopened eye,
While the pale sheeted ghosts go by!

My love, she sleeps! Oh, may her sleep,
As it is lasting, so be deep!
Soft may the worms about her creep!
Far in the forest, dim and old,
For her may some tall vault unfold—
Some vault that oft hath flung its black
And wingèd panels fluttering back,
Triumphant, o'er the crested palls,
Of her grand family funerals—
Some sepulchre, remote, alone,
Against whose portal she hath thrown,
In childhood, many an idle stone—
Some tomb from out whose sounding door
She ne'er shall force an echo more,
Thrilling to think, poor child of sin,
It was the dead who groaned within.

TO ONE IN PARADISE

Thou wast all that to me, love,
  For which my soul did pine—
A green isle in the sea, love,
  A fountain and a shrine,
All wreathed with fairy fruits and flowers,
  And all the flowers were mine.

Ah, dream too bright to last!
  Ah, starry Hope, that didst arise

But to be overcast!
    A voice from out the Future cries,
"On! on!"—but o'er the Past
    (Dim gulf!) my spirit hovering lies
Mute, motionless, aghast!

For, alas, alas, with me
    The light of Life is o'er!
"No more—no more—no more—"
    (Such language holds the solemn sea
To the sands upon the shore)
    Shall bloom the thunder-blasted tree,
Or the stricken eagle soar!

And all my days are trances,
    And all my nightly dreams
Are where thy grey eye glances,
    And where thy footstep gleams—
In what ethereal dances,
    By what eternal streams.

LENORE

Ah, broken is the golden bowl! the spirit flown forever!
Let the bell toll!—a saintly soul floats on the Stygian river,
And, Guy De Vere, hast *thou* no tear?—weep now or
    never more!
See! on yon drear and rigid bier low lies thy love,
    Lenore!
Come! let the burial rite be read—the funeral song be
    sung!—
An anthem for the queenliest dead that ever died so
    young—
A dirge for her the doubly dead in that she died so
    young.

"Wretches! ye loved her for her wealth and hated her
    for her pride,
And when she fell in feeble health, ye blessed her—that
    she died!
How *shall* the ritual, then, be read?—the requiem how
    be sung
By you—by yours, the evil eye,—by yours, the slanderous
    tongue
That did to death the innocence that died, and died so
    young?"

Peccavimus; but rave not thus! and let a Sabbath song
Go up to God so solemnly the dead may feel no wrong!
The sweet Lenore hath "gone before," with Hope, that
    flew beside,
Leaving thee wild for the dear child that should have
    been thy bride—
For her, the fair and *debonair,* that now so lowly lies,
The life upon her yellow hair but not within her eyes—
The life still there, upon her hair—the death upon her
    eyes.

"Avaunt! tonight my heart is light. No dirge will I
    upraise.
But waft the angel on her flight with a pæan of old days!
Let *no* bell toll!—lest her sweet soul, amid its hallowed
    mirth,
Should catch the note, as it doth float up from the
    damnèd Earth.
To friends above, from fiends below, the indignant
    ghost is riven—
From Hell unto a high estate far up within the Heaven—
From grief and groan, to a golden throne, beside the
    King of Heaven."

DREAM-LAND

By a route obscure and lonely,
Haunted by ill angels only,
Where an Eidolon, named NIGHT,
On a black throne reigns upright,
I have reached these lands but newly
From an ultimate dim Thule—
From a wild weird clime that lieth, sublime,
    Out of SPACE—out of TIME.

Bottomless vales and boundless floods,
And chasms, and caves, and Titan woods,
With forms that no man can discover
For the tears that drip all over;
Mountains toppling evermore
Into seas without a shore;
Seas that restlessly aspire,
Surging, unto skies of fire;
Lakes that endlessly outspread
Their lone waters—lone and dead,—
Their still waters—still and chilly
With the snows of the lolling lily.

By the lakes that thus outspread
Their lone waters, lone and dead,—
Their sad waters, sad and chilly
With the snows of the lolling lily,—
By the mountains—near the river
Murmuring lowly, murmuring ever,—
By the grey woods,—by the swamp
Where the toad and the newt encamp,—
By the dismal tarns and pools
    Where dwell the Ghouls,—
By each spot the most unholy—
In each nook most melancholy,—
There the traveller meets, aghast,
Sheeted Memories of the Past—

Shrouded forms that start and sigh
As they pass the wanderer by—
White-robed forms of friends long given,
In agony, to the Earth—and Heaven.

For the heart whose woes are legion
'Tis a peaceful, soothing region—
For the spirit that walks in shadow
'Tis—oh 'tis an Eldorado!
But the traveller, travelling through it,
May not—dare not openly view it;
Never its mysteries are exposed
To the weak human eye unclosed;
So wills its King, who hath forbid
The uplifting of the fringèd lid;
And thus the sad Soul that here passes
Beholds it but through darkened glasses.

By a route obscure and lonely,
Haunted by ill angels only,
Where an Eidolon, named NIGHT,
On a black throne reigns upright,
I have wandered home but newly
From this ultimate dim Thule.

THE BELLS

1

HEAR the sledges with the bells—
      Silver bells!
What a world of merriment their melody foretells!
      How they tinkle, tinkle, tinkle,
            In the icy air of night!
      While the stars that oversprinkle
      All the heavens, seem to twinkle
            With a crystalline delight;

Keeping time, time, time,
In a sort of Runic rhyme,
To the tintinnabulation that so musically wells
From the bells, bells, bells, bells,
Bells, bells, bells—
From the jingling and the tinkling of the bells.

2

Hear the mellow wedding bells—
Golden bells!
What a world of happiness their harmony foretells!
Through the balmy air of night
How they ring out their delight!—
From the molten-golden notes,
And all in tune,
What a liquid ditty floats
To the turtle-dove that listens, while she gloats
On the moon!
Oh, from out the sounding cells,
What a gush of euphony voluminously wells!
How it swells!
How it dwells
On the Future!—how it tells
Of the rapture that impels
To the swinging and the ringing
Of the bells, bells, bells—
Of the bells, bells, bells, bells,
Bells, bells, bells—
To the rhyming and the chiming of the bells!

3

Hear the loud alarum bells—
Brazen bells!
What a tale of terror, now, their turbulency tells!
In the startled ear of night
How they scream out their affright!

Too much horrified to speak,
They can only shriek, shriek,
    Out of tune,
In a clamorous appealing to the mercy of the fire,
In a mad expostulation with the deaf and frantic fire,
    Leaping higher, higher, higher,
        With a desperate desire,
    And a resolute endeavor
    Now—now to sit, or never,
By the side of the pale-faced moon.
    Oh, the bells, bells, bells!
    What a tale their terror tells
        Of Despair!
How they clang, and clash, and roar!
What a horror they outpour
On the bosom of the palpitating air!
    Yet the ear, it fully knows,
        By the twanging
        And the clanging,
    How the danger ebbs and flows;
Yet the ear distinctly tells,
    In the jangling
    And wrangling,
How the danger sinks and swells,
By the sinking or the swelling in the anger of the bells—
        Of the bells,—
Of the bells, bells, bells, bells,
    Bells, bells, bells—
In the clamor and the clangor of the bells!

4

    Hear the tolling of the bells—
        Iron bells!
What a world of solemn thought their monody compels!
    In the silence of the night,
    How we shiver with affright
At the melancholy menace of their tone!

93

For every sound that floats
From the rust within their throats
    Is a groan.
And the people—ah, the people—
They that dwell up in the steeple,
    All alone,
And who tolling, tolling, tolling,
   In that muffled monotone,
Feel a glory in so rolling
   On the human heart a stone—
They are neither man nor woman—
They are neither brute nor human—
    They are Ghouls:—
And their king it is who tolls:—
And he rolls, rolls, rolls,
    Rolls
   A pæan from the bells!
And his merry bosom swells
With the pæan of the bells!
And he dances, and he yells;
Keeping time, time, time,
In a sort of Runic rhyme,
   To the pæan of the bells—
    Of the bells:—
Keeping time, time, time,
In a sort of Runic rhyme,
  To the throbbing of the bells—
   Of the bells, bells, bells—
  To the sobbing of the bells;
Keeping time, time, time,
  As he knells, knells, knells,
In a happy Runic rhyme,
   To the rolling of the bells—
   Of the bells, bells, bells:—
   To the tolling of the bells—
Of the bells, bells, bells, bells,
    Bells, bells, bells—
To the moaning and the groaning of the bells.

James Russell Lowell

PRELUDE from "THE VISION OF SIR LAUNFAL"

Over his keys the musing organist,
  Beginning doubtfully and far away,
First lets his fingers wander as they list,
  And builds a bridge from Dreamland for his lay:
Then, as the touch of his loved instrument
  Gives hope and fervor, nearer draws his theme,
First guessed by faint auroral flushes sent
  Along the wavering vista of his dream.

Not only around our infancy
Doth heaven with all its splendors lie;
Daily, with souls that cringe and plot,
We Sinais climb and know it not.

Over our manhood bend the skies;
  Against our fallen and traitor lives
The great winds utter prophecies;
  With our faint hearts the mountain strives;
Its arms outstretched, the druid wood
  Waits with its benedicite;
And to our age's drowsy blood
  Still shouts the inspiring sea.

Earth gets its price for what Earth gives us;
  The beggar is taxed for a corner to die in,
The priest hath his fee who comes and shrives us,
  We bargain for the graves we lie in;
At the Devil's booth are all things sold,
Each ounce of dross costs its ounce of gold;

95

For a cap and bells our lives we pay,
Bubbles we buy with a whole soul's tasking:
'Tis heaven alone that is given away,
'Tis only God may be had for the asking;
No price is set on the lavish summer;
June may be had by the poorest comer.

And what is so rare as a day in June?
　　Then, if ever, come perfect days;
Then Heaven tries the earth if it be in tune,
　　And over it softly her warm ear lays;
Whether we look, or whether we listen,
We hear life murmur, or see it glisten;
Every clod feels a stir of might,
　　An instinct within it that reaches and towers,
And, groping blindly above it for light,
　　Climbs to a soul in grass and flowers;
The flush of life may well be seen
　　Thrilling back over hills and valleys;
The cowslip startles in meadows green,
　　The buttercup catches the sun in its chalice,
And there's never a leaf nor a blade too mean
　　To be some happy creature's palace;
The little bird sits at his door in the sun,
　　Atilt like a blossom among the leaves,
And lets his illumined being o'errun
　　With the deluge of summer it receives;
His mate feels the eggs beneath her wings,
And the heart in her dumb breast flutters and sings;
He sings to the wide world, and she to her nest,—
In the nice ear of Nature which song is the best?

Now is the high-tide of the year,
　　And whatever of life hath ebbed away
Comes flooding back, with a ripply cheer,
　　Into every bare inlet and creek and bay;
Now the heart is so full that a drop overfills it,
We are happy now because God wills it;

No matter how barren the past may have been,
'Tis enough for us now that the leaves are green;
We sit in the warm shade and feel right well
How the sap creeps up and the blossoms swell;
We may shut our eyes, but we cannot help knowing
That skies are clear and grass is growing;
The breeze comes whispering in our ear,
That dandelions are blossoming near,
    That maize has sprouted, that streams are flowing,
That the river is bluer than the sky,
That the robin is plastering his house hard by;
And if the breeze kept the good news back,
For other couriers we should not lack;
    We could guess it all by yon heifer's lowing,—
And hark! how clear bold chanticleer,
Warmed with the new wine of the year,
    Tells all in his lusty crowing!

Joy comes, grief goes, we know not how;
Everything is happy now,
    Everything is upward striving;
'Tis as easy now for the heart to be true
As for grass to be green or skies to be blue,—
    'Tis the natural way of living:
Who knows whither the clouds have fled?
    In the unscarred heaven they leave no wake;
And the eyes forget the tears they have shed,
    The heart forgets its sorrow and ache;
The soul partakes the season's youth,
    And the sulphurous rifts of passion and woe
Lie deep 'neath a silence pure and smooth,
    Like burnt-out craters healed with snow.

Herman Melville

THE MARCH INTO VIRGINIA

(*July 1861*)

Did all the lets and bars appear
   To every just or larger end,
Whence should come the trust and cheer?
   Youth must its ignorant impulse lend—
Age finds place in the rear.
   All wars are boyish, and are fought by boys,
The champions and enthusiasts of the state:
   Turbid ardours and vain joys
     Not barrenly abate—
   Stimulants to the power mature,
     Preparatives of fate.

Who here forecasteth the event?
What heart but spurns at precedent
And warnings of the wise,
Contemned foreclosures of surprise?
The banners play, the bugles call,
The air is blue and prodigal.
   No berrying party, pleasure-wooed,
No picnic party in the May,
Ever went less loth than they
   Into that leafy neighborhood.
In Bacchic glee they file toward Fate,
Moloch's uninitiate;
Expectancy, and glad surmise
Of battle's unknown mysteries.
All they feel is this: 'tis glory,
A rapture sharp, though transitory,

Yet lasting in belaurelled story.
So they gaily go to fight,
Chatting left and laughing right.
But some who this blithe mood present,
    As on in lightsome files they fare,
Shall die experienced ere three days are spent—
    Perish, enlightened by the volleyed glare;
Or shame survive, and like to adamant,
    The throe of Second Manassas share.

SHERIDAN AT CEDAR CREEK

(October 1864)

SHOE the steed with silver
    That bore him to the fray,
When he heard the guns at dawning—
    Miles away;
When he heard them calling, calling—
    Mount! nor stay:
        Quick, or all is lost;
        They've surprised and stormed the post,
        They push your routed host—
Gallop! retrieve the day. . . .

Shroud the horse in sable—
    For the mounds they heap!
There is firing in the Valley,
    And yet no strife they keep;
It is the parting volley,
    It is the pathos deep.
        There is glory for the brave
        Who lead, and nobly save,
        But no knowledge in the grave
Where the nameless followers sleep.

THE HOUSE-TOP

A Night Piece (July 1863)

[*"I dare not write the horrible and inconceivable atrocities committed,"* says Froissart, *in alluding to the remarkable sedition in France during his time. The like may be hinted of some proceedings of the draft-rioters.—* MELVILLE'S NOTE]

No sleep. The sultriness pervades the air
And binds the brain—a dense oppression, such
As tawny tigers feel in matted shades,
Vexing their blood and making apt for ravage.
Beneath the stars the roofy desert spreads
Vacant as Libya. All is hushed near by.
Yet fitfully from far breaks a mixed surf
Of muffled sound, the Atheist roar of riot.
Yonder, where parching Sirius set in drought,
Balefully glares red Arson—there—and there.
The Town is taken by its rats—ship-rats
And rats of the wharves. All civil charms
And priestly spells which late held hearts in awe—
Fear-bound, subjected to a better sway
Than sway of self; these like a dream dissolve,
And man rebounds whole aeons back in nature.
Hail to the low dull rumble, dull and dead,
And ponderous drag that shakes the wall.
Wise Draco comes, deep in the midnight roll
Of black artillery; he comes, though late;
In code corroborating Calvin's creed
And cynic tyrannies of honest kings;
He comes, nor parleys; and the Town, redeemed,
Gives thanks devout; nor, being thankful, heeds
The grimy slur on the Republic's faith implied,
Which holds that Man is naturally good,
And—more—is Nature's Roman, never to be scourged.

THE BERG

A Dream

I SAW a ship of martial build
(Her standards set, her brave apparel on)
Directed as by madness mere
Against a stolid iceberg steer,
Nor budge it, though the infatuate ship went down.
The impact made huge ice-cubes fall
Sullen, in tons that crashed the deck;
But that one avalanche was all—
No other movement save the foundering wreck.

Along the spurs of ridges pale,
Not any slenderest shaft and frail,
A prism over glass-green gorges lone,
Toppled; nor lace of traceries fine,
Nor pendant drops in grot or mine
Were jarred, when the stunned ship went down.

Nor sole the gulls in cloud that wheeled
Circling one snow-flanked peak afar,
But nearer fowl the floes that skimmed
And crystal beaches, felt no jar
No thrill transmitted stirred the lock
Of jack-straw needle-ice at base;
Towers undermined by waves—the block
Atilt impending—kept their place.
Seals, dozing sleek on sliddery ledges
Slipt never, when by loftier edges
Through very inertia overthrown,
The impetuous ship in bafflement went down.

Hard Berg (methought), so cold, so vast,
With mortal damps self-overcast;
Exhaling still thy dankish breath—
Adrift dissolving, bound for death;

Though lumpish thou, a lumbering one—
A lumbering lubbard loitering slow,
Impingers rue thee and go down,
Sounding thy precipice below,
Nor stir the slimy slug that sprawls
Along thy dead indifference of walls.

SOUTHERN CROSS

EMBLAZONED bleak in austral skies—
A heaven remote, whose starry swarm
Like Science lights but cannot warm—
Translated Cross, hast thou withdrawn,
Dim paling too at every dawn,
With symbols vain once counted wise,
And gods declined to heraldries?

Estranged, estranged: can friend prove so?
Aloft, aloof, a frigid sign;
How far removed, thou Tree divine,
Whose tender fruit did reach so low—
Love apples of New-Paradise!
About the wide Australian sea
The planted nations yet to be—

When, ages hence, they lift their eyes,
Tell, what shall they retain of thee?
But class thee with Orion's sword?
In constellations unadored,
Christ and the Giant equal prize?
The atheist cycles—*must* they be?
Fomenters as forefathers we?

SHILOH

A Requiem (April, 1862)

SKIMMING lightly, wheeling still,
   The swallows fly low
Over the field in clouded days,
   The forest-field of Shiloh—
Over the field where April rain
Solaced the parched one stretched in pain
Through the pause of night
That followed the Sunday fight
   Around the church of Shiloh—
The church so lone, the log-built one,
That echoed to many a parting groan
     And natural prayer
  Of dying foemen mingled there—
Foemen at morn, but friends at eve—
  Fame or country least their care:
(What like a bullet can undeceive!)
   But now they lie low,
While over them the swallows skim,
   And all is hushed at Shiloh.

LONE FOUNTS

THOUGH fast youth's glorious fable flies,
View not the world with worldling's eyes;
Nor turn with weather of the time.
Foreclose the coming of surprise:
Stand where Posterity shall stand;
Stand where the Ancients stood before,
And, dipping in lone founts thy hand,
Drink of the never-varying lore:
Wise once, and wise thence evermore.

MONODY

To have known him, to have loved him
    After loneness long;
And then to be estranged in life,
    And neither in the wrong;
And now for death to set his seal—
    Ease me, a little ease, my song!

By wintry hills his hermit-mound
    The sheeted snow-drifts drape,
And houseless there the snow-bird flits
    Beneath the fir-trees' crape;
Glazed now with ice the cloistral vine
    That hid the shyest grape.

OF RAMA

That Rama whom the Indian sung—
A god he was, but knew it not;
Hence vainly puzzled at the wrong
Misplacing him in human lot.
Curtailment of his right he bare
Rather than wrangle; but no less
Was taunted for his tameness there.
A fugitive without redress,
He never the Holy Spirit grieved,
Nor the divine in him bereaved,
Though what that was he might not guess.

Live they who, like to Rama, led
Unspotted from the world aside,
Like Rama are discredited—
Like him, in outlawry abide?
May life and fable so agree?—
    The innocent if lawless elf,

Ethereal in virginity,
Retains the consciousness of self.
Though black frost nip, though white frost chill,
Nor white frost nor the black may kill
The patient root, the vernal sense
Surviving hard experience
As grass the winter. Even that curse
Which is the wormwood mixed with gall—
Better dependent on the worse—
Divine upon the animal—
That can not make such natures fall.

Though yielding easy rein, indeed,
To impulse which the fibers breed,
Nor quarreling with indolence;
Shall these the cup of grief dispense
Deliberate to any heart?
Not craft they know, nor envy's smart.
Theirs be the thoughts that dive and skim,
Theirs the spiced tears that overbrim,
And theirs the dimple and the lightsome whim.

THE NIGHT-MARCH

WITH banners furled, the clarions mute,
    An army passes in the night;
And beaming spears and helms salute
    The dark with bright.

In silence deep the legions stream,
    With open ranks, in order true;
Over boundless plains they stream and gleam—
    No chief in view!

Afar, in twinkling distance lost,
    (So legends tell) he lonely wends
And back through all that shining host
    His mandate sends.

Walt Whitman

I HEAR AMERICA SINGING

I HEAR America singing, the varied carols I hear,
Those of mechanics, each one singing his as it should be
    blithe and strong,
The carpenters singing his as he measures his plank or
    beam,
The mason singing his as he makes ready for work, or
    leaves off work,
The boatman singing what belongs to him in his boat,
    the deck-hand singing on the steamboat deck,
The shoemaker singing as he sits on his bench, the hatter
    singing as he stands,
The wood-cutter's song, the ploughboy's on his way in
    the morning, or at noon intermission or at sundown,
The delicious singing of the mother, or of the young wife
    at work, or of the girl sewing or washing,
Each singing what belongs to him or her and to none else,
The day what belongs to the day—at night the party of
    young fellows, robust, friendly,
Singing with open mouths their strong melodious songs.

SONG OF MYSELF

1

I CELEBRATE myself, and sing myself,
And what I assume you shall assume,
For every atom belonging to me as good belongs to you.

I loafe and invite my soul,
I lean and loafe at my ease observing a spear of summer
    grass.

My tongue, every atom of my blood, form'd from this
    soil, this air,
Born here of parents born here from parents the same,
    and their parents the same,
I, now thirty-seven years old in perfect health begin,
Hoping to cease not till death.

Creeds and schools in abeyance,
Retiring back a while sufficed at what they are, but never
    forgotten,
I harbor for good or bad, I permit to speak at every
    hazard,
Nature without check with original energy.

2

Houses and rooms are full of perfumes, the shelves are
    crowded with perfumes,
I breathe the fragrance myself and know it and like it,
The distillation would intoxicate me also, but I shall not
    let it.

The atmosphere is not a perfume, it has no taste of the
    distillation, it is odorless,
It is for my mouth forever, I am in love with it,
I will go to the bank by the wood and become undis-
    guised and naked,
I am mad for it to be in contact with me.

The smoke of my own breath,
Echoes, ripples, buzz'd whispers, love-root, silk-thread,
    crotch and vine,
My respiration and inspiration, the beating of my heart,
    the passing of blood and air through my lungs,
The sniff of green leaves and dry leaves, and of the shore
    and dark-color'd sea-rocks, and of hay in the barn,
The sound of the belch'd words of my voice loos'd to the
    eddies of the wind,

A few light kisses, a few embraces, a reaching around of
    arms,
The play of shine and shade on the trees as the supple
    boughs wag,
The delight alone or in the rush of the streets, or along
    the fields and hill-sides,
The feeling of health, the full-noon trill, the song of me
    rising from bed and meeting the sun.

Have you reckon'd a thousand acres much? have you
    reckon'd the earth much?
Have you practis'd so long to learn to read?
Have you felt so proud to get at the meaning of poems?

Stop this day and night with me and you shall possess
    the origin of all poems,
You shall possess the good of the earth and sun, (there
    are millions of suns left,)
You shall no longer take things at second or third hand,
    nor look through the eyes of the dead, nor feed on
    the spectres in books,
You shall not look through my eyes either, nor take
    things from me,
You shall listen to all sides and filter them from your self.

3

I have heard what the talkers were talking, the talk of
    the beginning and the end,
But I do not talk of the beginning or the end.

There was never any more inception than there is now,
Nor any more youth or age than there is now,
And will never be any more perfection than there is now,
Nor any more heaven or hell than there is now.

Urge and urge and urge,
Always the procreant urge of the world.
108

Out of the dimness opposite equals advance, always
    substance and increase, always sex,
Always a knit of identity, always distinction, always a
    breed of life.

To elaborate is no avail, learn'd and unlearn'd feel that
    it is so.

Sure as the most certain sure, plumb in the uprights,
    well entretied, braced in the beams,
Stout as a horse, affectionate, haughty, electrical,
I and this mystery here we stand.

Clear and sweet is my soul, and clear and sweet is all
    that is not my soul.
Lack one lacks both, and the unseen is proved by the
    seen,
Till that becomes unseen and receives proof in its turn.

Showing the best and dividing it from the worst age
    vexes age,

Knowing the perfect fitness and equanimity of things,
    while they discuss I am silent, and go bathe and
    admire myself.

Welcome is every organ and attribute of me, and of any
    man hearty and clean,
Not an inch nor a particle of an inch is vile, and none
    shall be less familiar than the rest.
I am satisfied—I see, dance, laugh, sing;
As the hugging and loving bed-fellow sleeps at my side
    through the night, and withdraws at the peep of the
    day with stealthy tread,
Leaving me baskets cover'd with white towels swelling
    the house with their plenty,
Shall I postpone my acceptation and realization and
    scream at my eyes,

That they turn from gazing after and down the road,
And forthwith cipher and show me to a cent,
Exactly the value of one and exactly the value of two,
    and which is ahead?

4

Trippers and askers surround me,
People I meet, the effect upon me of my early life or
    the ward and city I live in, or the nation,
The latest dates, discoveries, inventions, societies,
    authors old and new,
My dinner, dress, associates, looks, compliments, dues,
The real or fancied indifference of some man or woman
    I love,
The sickness of one of my folks or of myself, or ill-doing
    or loss or lack of money, or depressions or exalta-
    tions,
Battles, the horrors of fratricidal war, the fever of doubt-
    ful news, the fitful events;
These come to me days and nights and go from me
    again,
But they are not the Me myself.

Apart from the pulling and hauling stands what I am,
Stands amused, complacent, compassionating, idle, uni-
    tary,
Looks down, is erect, or bends an arm on an impalpable
    certain rest,
Looking with side-curved head curious what will come
    next,
Both in and out of the game and watching and wonder-
    ing at it.

Backward I see in my own days where I sweated through
    fog with linguists and contenders,
I have no mockings or arguments, I witness and wait.

5

I believe in you my soul, the other I am must not abase
    itself to you,
And you must not be abased to the other.

Loafe with me on the grass, loose the stop from your
    throat,
Not words, not music or rhyme I want, not custom or
    lecture, not even the best,
Only the lull I like, the hum of your valvèd voice.

I mind how once we lay such a transparent summer
    morning,
How you settled your head athwart my hips and gently
    turn'd over upon me,
And parted the shirt from my bosom-bone, and plunged
    your tongue to my bare-stript heart,
And reach'd till you felt my beard, and reach'd till you
    held my feet.

Swiftly arose and spread around me the peace and
    knowledge that pass all the argument of the earth,
And I know that the hand of God is the promise of my
    own,
And I know that the spirit of God is the brother of my
    own,
And that all the men ever born are also my brothers,
    and the women my sisters and lovers,
And that a kelson of the creation is love,
And limitless are leaves stiff or drooping in the fields,
And brown ants in the little wells beneath them,
And mossy scabs of the worm fence, heap'd stones, elder,
    mullein and poke-weed.

6

A child said What is the grass? fetching it to me with
    full hands,

How could I answer the child? I do not know what it is
any more than he.

I guess it must be the flag of my disposition, out of hopeful green stuff woven.

Or I guess it is the handkerchief of the Lord,
A scented gift and remembrancer designedly dropt,
Bearing the owner's name someway in the corners, that
we may see and remark, and say *Whose?*

Or I guess the grass is itself a child, the produced babe
of the vegetation.
Or I guess it is a uniform hieroglyphic,
And it means, Sprouting alike in broad zones and nar-
row zones,
Growing among black folks as among white,
Kanuck, Tuckahoe, Congressman, Cuff, I give them the
same, I receive them the same.

And now it seems to me the beautiful uncut hair of
graves.

Tenderly will I use you curling grass,
It may be you transpire from the breasts of young men,
It may be if I had known them I would have loved
them,
It may be you are from old people, or from offspring
taken soon out of their mothers' laps,
And here you are the mothers' laps.

This grass is very dark to be from the white heads of old
mothers,
Darker than the colorless beards of old men,
Dark to come from under the faint red roofs of mouths.
O I perceive after all so many uttering tongues,
And I perceive they do not come from the roofs of
mouths for nothing.

I wish I could translate the hints about the dead young
    men and women,
And the hints about old men and mothers, and the off-
    spring taken soon out of their laps.

What do you think has become of the young and old
    men?
And what do you think has become of the women and
    children?

They are alive and well somewhere,
The smallest sprout shows there is really no death,
And if ever there was it led forward life, and does not
    wait at the end to arrest it,
And ceas'd the moment life appear'd.

All goes onward and outward, nothing collapses,
And to die is different from what any one supposed, and
    luckier.

7

Has any one supposed it lucky to be born?
I hasten to inform him or her it is just as lucky to die,
    and I know it.

I pass death with the dying and birth with the new-
    wash'd babe, and am not contain'd between my
    hat and boots,
And peruse manifold objects, no two alike and every
    one good,
The earth good and the stars good, and their adjuncts
    all good.

I am not an earth nor an adjunct of an earth,
I am the mate and companion of people, all just as im-
    mortal and fathomless as myself,
(They do not know how immortal, but I know.)

113

Every kind for itself and its own, for me mine male and
female,
For me those that have been boys and that love women,
For me the man that is proud and feels how it stings to
be slighted,
For me the sweet-heart and the old maid, for me mothers
and the mothers of mothers,
For me lips that have smiled, eyes that have shed tears,
For me children and the begetters of children.

Undraped! you are not guilty to me, nor stale nor discarded,
I see through the broadcloth and gingham whether or
no,
And am around, tenacious, acquisitive, tireless, and cannot be shaken away.

8

The little one sleeps in its cradle,
I lift the gauze and look a long time, and silently brush
away flies with my hand.

The youngster and the red-faced girl turn aside up the
bushy hill,
I peeringly view them from the top.

The suicide sprawls on the bloody floor of the bedroom,
I witness the corpse with its dabbled hair, I note where
the pistol has fallen.

The blab of the pave, tires of carts, sluff of boot-soles,
talk of the promenaders,
The heavy omnibus, the driver with his interrogating
thumb, the clank of the shod horses on the granite
floor,
The snow-sleighs, clinking, shouted jokes, pelts of
snow-balls,

114

The hurrahs for popular favorites, the fury of rous'd
    mobs,
The flap of the curtain'd litter, a sick man inside borne to
    the hospital,
The meeting of enemies, the sudden oath, the blows and
    fall,
The excited crowd, the policeman with his star quickly
    working his passage to the centre of the crowd,
The impassive stones that receive and return so many
    echoes,
What groans of over-fed or half-starv'd who fall sun-
    struck or in fits,
What exclamations of women taken suddenly who hurry
    home and give birth to babes,
What living and buried speech is always vibrating here,
    what howls restrain'd by decorum,
Arrests of criminals, slights, adulterous offers made, ac-
    ceptances, rejections with convex lips,
I mind them or the show or resonance of them—I come
    and I depart.

9

The big doors of the country barn stand open and ready,
The dried grass of the harvest-time loads the slow-drawn
    wagon,
The clear light plays on the brown gray and green in-
    tertinged,
The armfuls are pack'd to the sagging mow.

I am there, I help, I came stretch'd atop of the load,
I felt its soft jolts, one leg reclined on the other,
I jump from the cross-beams and seize the clover and
    timothy,
And roll head over heels and tangle my hair full of
    wisps.

Alone far in the wilds and mountains I hunt,
Wandering amazed at my own lightness and glee,
In the late afternoon choosing a safe spot to pass the
    night,
Kindling a fire and broiling the fresh-kill'd game,
Falling asleep on the gather'd leaves with my dog and
    gun by my side.
The Yankee clipper is under her sky-sails, she cuts the
    sparkle and scud,
My eyes settle the land, I bend at her prow or shout joy-
    ously from the deck.
The boatmen and clam-diggers arose early and stopt for
    me,
I tuck'd my trowser-ends in my boots and went and had
    a good time;
You should have been with us that day round the
    chowder-kettle.

I saw the marriage of the trapper in the open air in the
    far west, the bride was a red girl,
Her father and his friends sat near cross-legged and
    dumbly smoking, they had moccasins to their feet and
    large thick blankets hanging from their shoulders,
On a bank lounged the trapper, he was drest mostly in
    skins, his luxuriant beard and curls protected his
    neck, he held his bride by the hand,
She had long eyelashes, her head was bare, her coarse
    straight locks descended upon her voluptuous
    limbs and reach'd to her feet.

The runaway slave came to my house and stopt outside,
I heard his motions crackling the twigs of the woodpile,
Through the swung half-door of the kitchen I saw him
    limpsy and weak,
And went where he sat on a log and led him in and as-
    sured him,

And brought water and fill'd a tub for his sweated body
  and bruis'd feet,
And gave him a room that enter'd from my own, and
  gave him some coarse clean clothes,
And remember perfectly well his revolving eyes and his
  awkwardness,
And remember putting plasters on the galls of his neck
  and ankles;
He staid with me a week before he was recuperated and
  pass'd north,
I had him sit next me at table, my fire-lock lean'd in the
  corner.

11

Twenty-eight young men bathe by the shore,
Twenty-eight young men and all so friendly;
Twenty-eight years of womanly life and all so lonesome.

She owns the fine house by the rise of the bank,
She hides handsome and richly drest aft the blinds of
  the window.

Which of the young men does she like the best?
Ah the homeliest of them is beautiful to her.

Where are you off to, lady? for I see you,
You splash in the water there, yet stay stock still in your
  room.

Dancing and laughing along the beach came the twenty-
  ninth bather,
The rest did not see her, but she saw them and loved
  them.

The beards of the young men glisten'd with wet, it ran
  from their long hair,
Little streams pass'd all over their bodies.

An unseen hand also pass'd over their bodies,
It descended tremblingly from their temples and ribs.

The young men float on their backs, their white bellies
    bulge to the sun, they do not ask who seizes fast to
    them,
They do not know who puffs and declines with pendant
    and bending arch,
They do not think whom they souse with spray.

12

The butcher-boy puts off his killing-clothes, or sharpens
    his knife at the stall in the market,
I loiter enjoying his repartee and his shuffle and break-
    down.

Blacksmiths with grimed and hairy chests environ the
    anvil,
Each has his main-sledge, they are all out, there is a
    great heat in the fire.

From the cinder-strew'd threshold I follow their move-
    ments,
The lithe sheer of their waists plays even with their
    massive arms,
Overhand the hammers swing, overhand so slow, over-
    hand so sure,
They do not hasten, each man hits in his place.

13

The negro holds firmly the reins of his four horses, the
    block swags underneath on its tied-over chain,
The negro that drives the long dray of the stone-yard,
    steady and tall he stands pois'd on one leg on the
    string-piece,

His blue shirt exposes his ample neck and breast and
　　loosens over his hip-band,
His glance is calm and commanding, he tosses the slouch
　　of his hat away from his forehead,
The sun falls on his crispy hair and mustache, falls on
　　the black of his polish'd and perfect limbs.

I behold the picturesque giant and love him, and I do
　　not stop there,
I go with the team also.

In me the caresser of life wherever moving, backward as
　　well as forward sluing,
To niches aside and junior bending, not a person or
　　object missing,
Absorbing all to myself and for this song.

Oxen that rattle the yoke and chain or halt in the leafy
　　shade, what is that you express in your eyes?
It seems to me more than all the print I have read in my
　　life.

My tread scares the wood-drake and wood-duck on my
　　distant and day-long ramble,
They rise together, they slowly circle around.

I believe in those wing'd purposes,
And acknowledge red, yellow, white, playing within me,
And consider green and violet and the tufted crown
　　intentional,
And do not call the tortoise unworthy because she is not
　　something else,
And the jay in the woods never studied the gamut, yet
　　trills pretty well to me,
And the look of the bay mare shames silliness out of me.

The wild gander leads his flock through the cool night,
Ya-honk he says, and sounds it down to me like an invitation,
The pert may suppose it meaningless, but I listening close,
Find its purpose and place up there toward the wintry sky.

The sharp-hoof'd moose of the north, the cat on the house-sill, the chickadee, the prairie-dog,
The litter of the grunting sow as they tug at her teats,
The brood of the turkey-hen and she with her half-spread wings,
I see in them and myself the same old law.

The press of my foot to the earth springs a hundred affections,
They scorn the best I can do to relate them.

I am enamour'd of growing out-doors,
Of men that live among cattle or taste of the ocean or woods,
Of the builders and steerers of ships and the wielders of axes and mauls, and the drivers of horses,
I can eat and sleep with them week in and week out.

What is commonest, cheapest, nearest, easiest, is Me,
Me going in for my chances, spending for vast returns,
Adorning myself to bestow myself on the first that will take me,
Not asking the sky to come down to my good will,
Scattering it freely forever.

The pure contralto sings in the organ loft,

The carpenter dresses his plank, the tongue of his fore-
plane whistles its wild ascending lisp,

The married and unmarried children ride home to their
Thanksgiving dinner,

The pilot seizes the king-pin, he heaves down with a
strong arm,

The mate stands braced in the whale-boat, lance and
harpoon are ready,

The duck-shooter walks by silent and cautious stretches,

The deacons are ordain'd with cross'd hands at the altar,

The spinning-girl retreats and advances to the hum of
the big wheel,

The farmer stops by the bars as he walks on a First-day
loafe and looks at the oats and rye,

The lunatic is carried at last to the asylum a confirmed case,

(He will never sleep any more as he did in the cot in his
mother's bed-room;)

The jour printer with gray head and gaunt jaws works at
his case,

He turns his quid of tobacco while his eyes blurr with the
manuscript;

The malform'd limbs are tied to the surgeon's table,

What is removed drops horribly in a pail;

The quadroon girl is sold at the auction-stand, the drunk-
ard nods by the bar-room stove,

The machinist rolls up his sleeves, the policeman travels
his beat, the gate-keeper marks who pass,

The young fellow drives the express-wagon, (I love him,
though I do not know him;)

The half-breed straps on his light boots to compete in the
race,

The western turkey-shooting draws old and young, some
lean on their rifles, some sit on logs,

Out from the crowd steps the marksman, takes his posi-
tion, levels his piece;

The groups of newly-come immigrants cover the wharf
    or levee,
As the woolly-pates hoe in the sugar-field, the overseer
    views them from his saddle,
The bugle calls in the ball-room, the gentlemen run for
    their partners, the dancers bow to each other,
The youth lies awake in the cedar-roof'd garret and harks
    to the musical rain,
The wolverine sets traps on the creek that helps fill the
    Huron,
The squaw wrapt in her yellow-hemm'd cloth is offering
    moccasins and bead-bags for sale,
The connoisseur peers along the exhibition-gallery with
    half-shut eyes bent sideways,
As the deck-hands make fast the steamboat the plank is
    thrown for the shore-going passengers,
The young sister holds out the skein while the elder sister
    winds it off in a ball, and stops now and then for the
    knots,
The one-year wife is recovering and happy having a
    week ago borne her first child,
The clean-hair'd Yankee girl works with her sewing-ma-
    chine or in the factory or mill,
The paving-man leans on his two-handed rammer, the
    reporter's lead flies swiftly over the note-book, the
    sign-painter is lettering with blue and gold,
The canal boy trots on the tow-path, the book-keeper
    counts at his desk, the shoemaker waxes his thread,
The conductor beats time for the band and all the per-
    formers follow him,
The child is baptized, the convert is making his first
    professions,
The regatta is spread on the bay, the race is begun, (how
    the white sails sparkle!)
The drover watching his drove sings out to them that
    would stray,
The peddler sweats with his pack on his back, (the pur-
    chaser higgling about the odd cent;)

The bride unrumples her white dress, the minute-hand
    of the clock moves slowly,
The opium-eater reclines with rigid head and just-open'd
    lips,
The prostitute draggles her shawl, her bonnet bobs on
    her tipsy and pimpled neck,
The crowd laugh at her blackguard oaths, the men jeer
    and wink to each other,
(Miserable! I do not laugh at your oaths nor jeer you;)
The President holding a cabinet council is surrounded by
    the great Secretaries,
On the piazza walk three matrons stately and friendly
    with twined arms,
The crew of the fish-smack pack repeated layers of hali-
    but in the hold,
The Missourian crosses the plains toting his wares and
    his cattle,
As the fare-collector goes through the train he gives
    notice by the jingling of loose change,
The floor-men are laying the floor, the tinners are tinning
    the roof, the masons are calling for mortar,
In single file each shouldering his hod pass onward the
    laborers;
Seasons pursuing each other the indescribable crowd is
    gather'd, it is the fourth of Seventh-month, (what
    salutes of cannon and small arms!)
Seasons pursuing each other the plougher ploughs, the
    mower mows, and the winter-grain falls in the
    ground;
Off on the lakes the pike-fisher watches and waits by the
    hole in the frozen surface,
The stumps stand thick round the clearing, the squatter
    strikes deep with his axe,
Flatboatmen make fast towards dusk near the cotton-
    wood or pecan-trees,
Coon-seekers go through the regions of the Red River or
    through those drain'd by the Tennessee, or through
    those of the Arkansas,

Torches shine in the dark that hangs on the Chatta-
hooche or Altamahaw,
Patriarchs sit at supper with sons and grandsons and
great grandsons around them,
In walls of adobe, in canvas tents, rest hunters and trap-
pers after their day's sport,
The city sleeps and the country sleeps,
The living sleep for their time, the dead sleep for their
time,
The old husband sleeps by his wife and the young hus-
band sleeps by his wife;
And these tend inward to me, and I tend outward to
them,
And such as it is to be of these more or less I am,
And of these one and all I weave the song of myself.

16

I am of old and young, of the foolish as much as the wise,
Regardless of others, ever regardful of others,
Maternal as well as paternal, a child as well as a man,
Stuff'd with the stuff that is coarse and stuff'd with the
stuff that is fine,
One of the Nation of many nations, the smallest the same
and the largest the same,
A Southerner soon as a Northerner, a planter nonchalant
and hospitable down by the Oconee I live,
A Yankee bound my own way ready for trade, my joints
the limberest joints on earth and the sternest joints
on earth,
A Kentuckian walking the vale of the Elkhorn in my
deer-skin leggings, a Louisianian or Georgian,
A boatman over lakes or bays or along coasts, a Hoosier,
Badger, Buckeye;
At home on Kanadian snow-shoes or up in the bush, or
with fishermen off Newfoundland,
At home in the fleet of ice-boats, sailing with the rest and
tacking,

At home on the hills of Vermont or in the woods of
    Maine, or the Texan ranch,
Comrade of Californians, comrade of free North-West-
    erners, (loving their big proportions,)
Comrade of raftsmen and coalmen, comrade of all who
    shake hands and welcome to drink and meat,
A learner with the simplest, a teacher of the thought-
    fullest,
A novice beginning yet experient of myriads of seasons,
Of every hue and caste am I, of every rank and religion,
A farmer, mechanic, artist, gentleman, sailor, quaker,
Prisoner, fancy-man, rowdy, lawyer, physician, priest.

I resist any thing better than my own diversity,
Breathe the air but leave plenty after me,
And am not stuck up, and am in my place.

(The moth and the fish-eggs are in their place,
The bright suns I see and the dark suns I cannot see are
    in their place,
The palpable is in its place and the impalpable is in its
    place.)

17

These are really the thoughts of all men in all ages and
    lands, they are not original with me,
If they are not yours as much as mine they are nothing,
    or next to nothing,
If they are not the riddle and the untying of the riddle
    they are nothing,
If they are not just as close as they are distant they are
    nothing.

This is the grass that grows wherever the land is and the
    water is,
This the common air that bathes the globe.

18

With music strong I come, with my cornets and my
    drums,
I play not marches for accepted victors only, I play
    marches for conquer'd and slain persons.

Have you heard that it was good to gain the day?
I also say it is good to fall, battles are lost in the same
    spirit in which they are won.

I beat and pound for the dead,
I blow through my embouchures my loudest and gayest
    for them.

Vivas to those who have fail'd!
And to those whose war-vessels sank in the sea!
And to those themselves who sank in the sea!
And to all generals that lost engagements, and all over-
    come heroes!
And the numberless unknown heroes equal to the great-
    est heroes known!

19

This is the meal equally set, this the meat for natural
    hunger,
It is for the wicked just the same as the righteous, I make
    appointments with all,
I will not have a single person slighted or left away,
The kept-woman, sponger, thief, are hereby invited,
The heavy-lipp'd slave is invited, the venerealee is in-
    vited;
There shall be no difference between them and the rest.

This is the press of a bashful hand, this the float and odor
    of hair,
This the touch of my lips to yours, this the murmur of
    yearning,

This the far-off depth and height reflecting my own face,
This the thoughtful merge of myself, and the outlet
again.

Do you guess I have some intricate purpose?
Well I have, for the Fourth-month showers have, and the
mica on the side of a rock has.

Do you take it I would astonish?
Does the daylight astonish? does the early redstart twit-
tering through the woods?
Do I astonish more than they?
This hour I tell things in confidence,
I might not tell everybody, but I will tell you.

20

Who goes there? hankering, gross, mystical, nude;
How is it I extract strength from the beef I eat?

What is a man anyhow? what am I? what are you?

All I mark as my own you shall offset it with your own,
Else it were time lost listening to me.

I do not snivel that snivel the world over,
That months are vacuums and the ground but wallow
and filth.

Whimpering and truckling fold with powders for inva-
lids, conformity goes to the fourth-remov'd,
I wear my hat as I please indoors or out.

Why should I pray? why should I venerate and be ceremonious?

Having pried through the strata, analyzed to a hair, counsel'd with doctors and calculated close,
I find no sweeter fat than sticks to my own bones.

In all people I see myself, none more and not one a bar-
ley-corn less,
And the good or bad I say of myself I say of them.

I know I am solid and sound,
To me the converging objects of the universe perpetually
flow,
All are written to me, and I must get what the writing
means.

I know I am deathless,
I know this orbit of mine cannot be swept by a carpenter's compass,
I know I shall not pass like a child's carlacue cut with a
burnt stick at night.

I know I am august,
I do not trouble my spirit to vindicate itself or be
understood,
I see that the elementary laws never apologize,
(I reckon I behave no prouder than the level I plant my
house by, after all.)

I exist as I am, that is enough,
If no other in the world be aware I sit content,
And if each and all be aware I sit content.

One world is aware and by far the largest to me, and
that is myself,
And whether I come to my own to-day or in ten thousand
or ten million years,
I can cheerfully take it now, or with equal cheerfulness
I can wait.

My foothold is tenon'd and mortis'd in granite,
I laugh at what you call dissolution,
And I know the amplitude of time.

I am the poet of the Body and I am the poet of the Soul,
The pleasures of heaven are with me and the pains of
hell are with me,
The first I graft and increase upon myself, the latter I
translate into a new tongue.

I am the poet of the woman the same as the man,
And I say it is as great to be a woman as to be a man,
And I say there is nothing greater than the mother of
men.

I chant the chant of dilation or pride,
We have had ducking and deprecating about enough,
I show that size is only development.

Have you outstript the rest? are you the President?
It is a trifle, they will more than arrive there every one,
and still pass on.

I am he that walks with the tender and growing night,
I call to the earth and sea half-held by the night.

Press close bare-bosom'd night—press close magnetic
nourishing night!
Night of south winds—night of the large few stars!
Still nodding night—mad naked summer night.

Smile O voluptuous cool-breath'd earth!
Earth of the slumbering and liquid trees!
Earth of departed sunset—earth of the mountains misty-
topt!
Earth of the vitreous pour of the full moon just tinged
with blue!
Earth of shine and dark mottling the tide of the river!
Earth of the limpid gray of clouds brighter and clearer
for my sake!

Far-swooping elbow'd earth—rich apple-blossom'd earth!
Smile, for your lover comes.

Prodigal, you have given me love—therefore I to you
    give love!
O unspeakable passionate love.

22

You sea! I resign myself to you also—I guess what you
    mean,
I behold from the beach your crooked inviting fingers,
I believe you refuse to go back without feeling of me,
We must have a turn together, I undress, hurry me out of
    sight of the land,
Cushion me soft, rock me in billowy drowse,
Dash me with amorous wet, I can repay you.

Sea of stretch'd ground-swells,
Sea breathing broad and convulsive breaths,
Sea of the brine of life and of unshovell'd yet always-
    ready graves,
Howler and scooper of storms, capricious and dainty
    sea,
I am integral with you, I too am of one phase and of all
    phases.

Partaker of influx and efflux, I, extoller of hate and
    conciliation,
Extoller of amies and those that sleep in each other's
    arms,

I am he attesting sympathy,
(Shall I make my list of things in the house and skip
    the house that supports them?)

I am not the poet of goodness only, I do not decline to be
    the poet of wickedness also.

What blurt is this about virtue and about vice?
Evil propels me and reform of evil propels me, I stand
　　indifferent,
My gait is no fault-finder's or rejecter's gait,
I moisten the roots of all that has grown.

Did you fear some scrofula out of the unflagging preg-
　　nancy?
Did you guess the celestial laws are yet to be work'd
　　over and rectified?

I find one side a balance and the antipodal side a balance,
Soft doctrine as steady help as stable doctrine,
Thoughts and deeds of the present our rouse and early
　　start.

This minute that comes to me over the past decillions,
There is no better than it and now.

What behaved well in the past or behaves well to-day
　　is not such a wonder,
The wonder is always and always how there can be a
　　mean man or an infidel.

23

Endless unfolding of words of ages!
And mine a word of the modern, the word En-Masse.

A word of the faith that never balks,
Here or henceforward it is all the same to me, I accept
　　Time absolutely.

It alone is without flaw, it alone rounds and completes
　　all,
That mystic baffling wonder alone completes all.

I accept Reality and dare not question it,
Materialism first and last imbuing.

Hurrah for positive science! long live exact demonstration!
Fetch stonecrop mixt with cedar and branches of lilac,
This is the lexicographer, this the chemist, this made a grammar of the old cartouches,
These mariners put the ship through dangerous unknown seas,
This is the geologist, this works with the scalpel, and this is a mathematician.

Gentlemen, to you the first honors always!
Your facts are useful, and yet they are not my dwelling,
I but enter by them to an area of my dwelling.

Less the reminders of properties told my words,
And more the reminders they of life untold, and of freedom and extrication,
And make short account of neuters and geldings, and favor men and women fully equipt.
And beat the gong of revolt, and stop with fugitives and them that plot and conspire.

24

Walt Whitman, a kosmos, of Manhattan the son,
Turbulent, fleshy, sensual, eating, drinking and breeding,
No sentimentalist, no stander above men and women or apart from them,
No more modest than immodest.

Unscrew the locks from the doors!
Unscrew the doors themselves from their jambs!
Whoever degrades another degrades me,
And whatever is done or said returns at last to me.

Through me the afflatus surging and surging, through me the current and index.

I speak the pass-word primeval, I give the sign of democracy,
By God! I will accept nothing which all cannot have
their counterpart of on the same terms.

Through me many long dumb voices,
Voices of the interminable generations of prisoners and
slaves,
Voices of the diseas'd and despairing and of thieves and
dwarfs,
Voices of cycles of preparation and accretion,
And of the threads that connect the stars, and of wombs
and of the father-stuff,
And of the rights of them the others are down upon,
Of the deform'd, trivial, flat, foolish, despised,
Fog in the air, beetles rolling balls of dung.

Through me forbidden voices,
Voices of sexes and lusts, voices veil'd and I remove the
veil,
Voices indecent by me clarified and transfigur'd.

I do not press my fingers across my mouth,
I keep as delicate around the bowels as around the head
and heart,
Copulation is no more rank to me than death is.

I believe in the flesh and the appetites,
Seeing, hearing, feeling, are miracles, and each part and
tag of me is a miracle.

Divine am I inside and out, and I make holy whatever I
touch or am touch'd from,
The scent of these arm-pits aroma finer than prayer,
This head more than churches, bibles, and all the creeds.

If I worship one thing more than another it shall be the
spread of my own body, or any part of it,

Translucent mould of me it shall be you!
Shaded ledges and rests it shall be you!
Firm masculine colter it shall be you!
Whatever goes to the tilth of me it shall be you!
You my rich blood! your milky stream pale strippings of
    my life!
Breast that presses against other breasts it shall be you!
My brain it shall be your occult convolutions!
Root of wash'd sweet-flag! timorous pond-snipe! nest of
    guarded duplicate eggs! it shall be you!
Mix'd tussled hay of head, beard, brawn, it shall be you!
Trickling sap of maple, fibre of manly wheat, it shall be
    you!
Sun so generous it shall be you!
Vapors lighting and shading my face it shall be you!
You sweaty brooks and dews it shall be you!
Winds whose soft-tickling genitals rub against me it shall
    be you!
Broad muscular fields, branches of live oak, loving
    lounger in my winding paths, it shall be you!
Hands I have taken, face I have kiss'd, mortal I have
    ever touch'd, it shall be you.

I dote on myself, there is that lot of me and all so
    luscious,
Each moment and whatever happens thrills me with joy,
I cannot tell how my ankles bend, nor whence the
    cause of my faintest wish,
Nor the cause of the friendship I emit, nor the cause of
    the friendship I take again.
That I walk up my stoop, I pause to consider if it really
    be,
A morning-glory at my window satisfies me more than
    the metaphysics of books.

To behold the day-break!
The little light fades the immense and diaphanous
    shadows,

The air tastes good to my palate.
Hefts of the moving world at innocent gambols silently
    rising, freshly exuding,
Scooting obliquely high and low.

Something I cannot see puts upward libidinous prongs,
Seas of bright juice suffuse heaven.

The earth by the sky staid with, the daily close of their
    junction,
The heav'd challenge from the east that moment over
    my head,
The mocking taunt, See then whether you shall be
    master!

25

Dazzling and tremendous how quick the sun-rise would
    kill me,
If I could not now and always send sun-rise out of me.

We also ascend dazzling and tremendous as the sun,
We found our own O my soul in the calm and cool of
    the daybreak.

My voice goes after what my eyes cannot reach,
With the twirl of my tongue I encompass worlds and
    volumes of worlds.

Speech is the twin of my vision, it is unequal to measure
    itself,
It provokes me forever, it says sarcastically,
Walt you contain enough, why don't you let it out then?

Come now I will not be tantalized, you conceive too
    much of articulation,
Do you not know O speech how the buds beneath you
    are folded?
Waiting in gloom, protected by frost,

The dirt receding before my prophetical screams,
I underlying causes to balance them at last,
My knowledge my live parts, it keeping tally with the
    meaning of all things,
Happiness, (which whoever hears me let him or her set
    out in search of this day.)

My final merit I refuse you, I refuse putting from me
    what I really am,
Encompass worlds, but never try to encompass me,
I crowd your sleekest and best by simply looking toward
    you.

Writing and talk do not prove me,
I carry the plenum of proof and every thing else in my
    face,
With the hush of my lips I wholly confound the skeptic.

26

Now I will do nothing but listen,
To accrue what I hear into this song, to let sounds con-
    tribute toward it.

I hear bravuras of birds, bustle of growing wheat, gos-
    sip of flames, clack of sticks cooking my meals.
I hear the sound I love, the sound of the human voice,
I hear all sounds running together, combined, fused or
    following,
Sounds of the city and sounds out of the city, sounds of
    the day and night,
Talkative young ones to those that like them, the loud
    laugh of work-people at their meals,
The angry bass of disjointed friendship, the faint tones
    of the sick,
The judge with hands tight to the desk, his pallid lips
    pronouncing a death-sentence,
The heave'e'yo of stevedores unlading ships by the
    wharves, the refrain of the anchor-lifters,

The ring of alarm-bells, the cry of fire, the whirr of swift-
    streaking engines and hose-carts with premonitory
    tinkles and color'd lights,
The steam-whistle, the solid roll of the train of approach-
    ing cars,
The slow march play'd at the head of the association
    marching two and two,
(They go to guard some corpse, the flag-tops are draped
    with black muslin.)

I hear the violoncello, ('tis the young man's heart's
    complaint,)
I hear the key'd cornet, it glides quickly in through my
    ears,
It shakes mad-sweet pangs through my belly and breast.

I hear the chorus, it is a grand opera,
Ah this indeed is music—this suits me.

A tenor large and fresh as the creation fills me,
The orbic flex of his mouth is pouring and filling me full.

I hear the train'd soprano (what work with hers is this?)
The orchestra whirls me wider than Uranus flies,
It wrenches such ardors from me I did not know I
    possess'd them,
It sails me, I dab with bare feet, they are lick'd by the
    indolent waves,
I am cut by bitter and angry hail, I lose my breath,
Steep'd amid honey'd morphine, my windpipe throttled
    in fakes of death,
At length let up again to feel the puzzle of puzzles,
And that we call Being.

27

To be in any form, what is that?
(Round and round we go, all of us, and ever come back
    thither,)

If nothing lay more develop'd the quahaug in its callous
    shell were enough.

Mine is no callous shell,
I have instant conductors all over me whether I pass or
    stop,
They seize every object and lead it harmlessly through
    me.

I merely stir, press, feel with my fingers, and am happy,
To touch my person to some one else's is about as much
    as I can stand.

28

Is this then a touch? quivering me to a new identity,
Flames and ether making a rush for my veins,
Treacherous tip of me reaching and crowding to help
    them,
My flesh and blood playing out lightning to strike what is
    hardly different from myself,
On all sides prurient provokers stiffening my limbs,
Straining the udder of my heart for its withheld drip,
Behaving licentious toward me, taking no denial,
Depriving me of my best as for a purpose,
Unbuttoning my clothes, holding me by the bare waist,
Deluding my confusion with the calm of the sunlight
    and pasture-fields,
Immodestly sliding the fellow-senses away,
They bribed to swap off with touch and go and graze
    at the edges of me,
No consideration, no regard for my draining strength or
    my anger,
Fetching the rest of the herd around to enjoy them a
    while,
Then all uniting to stand on a headland and worry me.

The sentries desert every other part of me,
They have left me helpless to a red marauder,
138

They all come to the headland to witness and assist
    against me.

I am given up by traitors,
I talk wildly, I have lost my wits, I and nobody else
    am the greatest traitor,
I went myself first to the headland, my own hands
    carried me there.

You villain touch! what are you doing? my breath is
    tight in its throat,
Unclench your floodgates, you are too much for me.

29

Blind loving wrestling touch, sheath'd hooded sharp-
    tooth'd touch!
Did it make you ache so, leaving me?

Parting track'd by arriving, perpetual payment of per-
    petual loan,
Rich showering rain, and recompense richer afterward.

Sprouts take and accumulate, stand by the curb prolific
    and vital,
Landscapes projected masculine, full-sized and golden.

30

All truths wait in all things,
They neither hasten their own delivery nor resist it,
They do not need the obstetric forceps of the surgeon,
The insignificant is as big to me as any,
(What is less or more than a touch?)

Logic and sermons never convince,
The damp of the night drives deeper into my soul.
(Only what proves itself to every man and woman is so,
Only what nobody denies is so.)

A minute and a drop of me settle my brain,
I believe the soggy clods shall become lovers and lamps,
And a compend of compends is the meat of a man or
    woman,
And a summit and flower there is the feeling they have
    for each other,
And they are to branch boundlessly out of that lesson
    until it becomes omnific,
And until one and all shall delight us, and we them.

31

I believe a leaf of grass is no less than the journey-work
    of the stars,
And the pismire is equally perfect, and a grain of sand,
    and the egg of the wren,
And the tree-toad is a chef-d'œuvre for the highest,
And the running blackberry would adorn the parlors of
    heaven,
And the narrowest hinge in my hand puts to scorn all
    machinery,
And the cow crunching with depress'd head surpasses
    any statue,
And a mouse is miracle enough to stagger sextillions of
    infidels.

I find I incorporate gneiss, coal, long-threaded moss,
    fruits, grains, esculent roots,
And am stucco'd with quadrupeds and birds all over,
And have distanced what is behind me for good reasons,
But call any thing back again when I desire it.

In vain the speeding or shyness,
In vain the plutonic rocks send their old heat against
    my approach,
In vain the mastodon retreats beneath its own powder'd
    bones,
In vain objects stand leagues off and assume manifold
    shapes,

In vain the ocean settling in hollows and the great mon-
    sters lying low,
In vain the buzzard houses herself with the sky,
In vain the snake slides through the creepers and logs,
In vain the elk takes to the inner passes of the woods,
In vain the razor-bill'd auk sails far north to Labrador,
I follow quickly, I ascend to the nest in the fissure of the
    cliff.

32

I think I could turn and live with animals, they're so
    placid and self-contain'd,
I stand and look at them long and long.

They do not sweat and whine about their condition,
They do not lie awake in the dark and weep for their
    sins,
They do not make me sick discussing their duty to God,
Not one is dissatisfied, not one is demented with the
    mania of owning things,
Not one kneels to another, nor to his kind that lived
    thousands of years ago,
Not one is respectable or unhappy over the whole earth.

So they show their relations to me and I accept them,
They bring me tokens of myself, they evince them plainly
    in their possession.

I wonder where they get those tokens,
Did I pass that way huge times ago and negligently
    drop them?

Myself moving forward then and now and forever,
Gathering and showing more always and with velocity,
Infinite and omnigenous, and the like of these among
    them,
Not too exclusive toward the reachers of my remem-
    brancers,

Picking out here one that I love, and now go with him
    on brotherly terms.

A gigantic beauty of a stallion, fresh and responsive to
    my caresses,
Head high in the forehead, wide between the ears,
Limbs glossy and supple, tail dusting the ground,
Eyes full of sparkling wickedness, ears finely cut, flexibly
    moving.

His nostrils dilate as my heels embrace him,
His well-built limbs tremble with pleasure as we race
    around and return.

I but use you a minute, then I resign you, stallion,
Why do I need your paces when I myself out-gallop
    them?
Even as I stand or sit passing faster than you.

33

Space and Time! now I see it is true, what I guess'd at,
What I guess'd when I loaf'd on the grass,
What I guess'd while I lay alone in my bed,
And again as I walk'd the beach under the paling stars
    of the morning.
My ties and ballasts leave me, my elbows rest in sea-
    gaps,
I skirt sierras, my palms cover continents,
I am afoot with my vision.

By the city's quadrangular houses—in log huts, camping
    with lumbermen,
Along the ruts of the turnpike, along the dry gulch and
    rivulet bed,
Weeding my onion-patch or hoeing rows of carrots and
    parsnips, crossing savannas, trailing in forests,
Prospecting, gold-digging, girdling the trees of a new
    purchase,

Scorch'd ankle-deep by the hot sand, hauling my boat
    down the shallow river,
Where the panther walks to and fro on a limb overhead,
    where the buck turns furiously at the hunter,
Where the rattlesnake suns his flabby length on a rock,
    where the otter is feeding on fish,
Where the alligator in his tough pimples sleeps by the
    bayou,
Where the black bear is searching for roots or honey,
    where the beaver pats the mud with his paddle-
    shaped tail;
Over the growing sugar, over the yellow-flower'd cotton
    plant, over the rice in its low moist field,
Over the sharp-peak'd farm house, with its scallop'd
    scum and slender shoots from the gutters,
Over the western persimmon, over the long-leav'd corn,
    over the delicate blue-flower flax,
Over the white and brown buckwheat, a hummer and
    buzzer there with the rest,
Over the dusky green of the rye as it ripples and shades
    in the breeze;
Scaling mountains, pulling myself cautiously up, hold-
    ing on by low scragged limbs,
Walking the path worn in the grass and beat through
    the leaves of the brush,
Where the quail is whistling betwixt the woods and the
    wheat-lot,
Where the bat flies in the Seventh-month eve, where
    the great gold-bug drops through the dark,
Where the brook puts out of the roots of the old tree and
    flows to the meadow,
Where cattle stand and shake away flies with the trem-
    ulous shuddering of their hides,
Where the cheese-cloth hangs in the kitchen, where
    andirons straddle the hearth-slab, where cobwebs
    fall in festoons from the rafters;
Where trip-hammers crash, where the press is whirl-
    ing its cylinders,

Where the human heart beats with terrible throes under
    its ribs,
Where the pear-shaped balloon is floating aloft, (floating
    in it myself and looking composedly down,)
Where the life-car is drawn on the slip-noose, where the
    heat hatches pale-green eggs in the dented sand,
Where the she-whale swims with her calf and never
    forsakes it,
Where the steam-ship trails hind-ways its long pennant
    of smoke,
Where the fin of the shark cuts like a black chip out of
    the water,
Where the half-burn'd brig is riding on unknown cur-
    rents,
Where shells grow to her slimy deck, where the dead
    are corrupting below;
Where the dense-starr'd flag is borne at the head of the
    regiments,
Approaching Manhattan up by the long-stretching
    island,
Under Niagara, the cataract falling like a veil over my
    countenance,
Upon a door-step, upon the horse-block of hard wood
    outside,
Upon the race-course, or enjoying picnics or jigs or a
    good game of base-ball,
At he-festivals, with blackguard gibes, ironical license,
    bull-dances, drinking, laughter,
At the cider-mill tasting the sweets of the brown mash,
    sucking the juice through a straw,
At apple-peelings wanting kisses for all red fruit I find,
At musters, beach-parties, friendly bees, huskings, house-
    raisings;
Where the mocking-bird sounds his delicious gurgles,
    cackles, screams, weeps,
Where the hay-rick stands in the barn-yard, where the
    dry-stalks are scatter'd, where the brood-cow waits
    in the hovel,

Where the bull advances to do his masculine work,
where the stud to the mare, where the cock is treading the hen,
Where the heifers browse, where geese nip their food
with short jerks,
Where sun-down shadows lengthen over the limitless
and lonesome prairie,
Where herds of buffalo make a crawling spread of the
square miles far and near,
Where the humming-bird shimmers, where the neck of
the long-lived swan is curving and winding,
Where the laughing-gull scoots by the shore, where she
laughs her near-human laugh,
Where bee-hives range on a gray bench in the garden
half hid by the high weeds,
Where band-neck'd partridges roost in a ring on the
ground with their heads out,
Where burial coaches enter the arch'd gates of a cemetery,
Where winter wolves bark amid wastes of snow and
icicled trees,
Where the yellow-crown'd heron comes to the edge
of the marsh at night and feeds upon small crabs,
Where the splash of swimmers and divers cools the
warm noon,
Where the katy-did works her chromatic reed on the
walnut-tree over the well,
Through patches of citrons and cucumbers with silver-
wired leaves,
Through the salt-lick or orange glade, or under conical
firs,
Through the gymnasium, through the curtain'd saloon,
through the office or public hall;
Pleas'd with the native and pleas'd with the foreign,
pleas'd with the new and old,
Pleas'd with the homely woman as well as the handsome,
Pleas'd with the quakeress as she puts off her bonnet and
talks melodiously,

Pleas'd with the tune of the choir of the whitewash'd church,

Pleas'd with the earnest words of the sweating Methodist preacher, impress'd seriously at the camp-meeting;

Looking in at the shop-windows of Broadway the whole forenoon, flatting the flesh of my nose on the thick plate glass,

Wandering the same afternoon with my face turn'd up to the clouds, or down a lane or along the beach,

My right and left arms round the sides of two friends, and I in the middle;

Coming home with the silent and dark-cheek'd bush-boy, (behind me he rides at the drape of the day,)

Far from the settlements studying the print of animals' feet, or the moccasin print,

By the cot in the hospital reaching lemonade to a feverish patient,

Night the coffin'd corpse when all is still, examining with a candle;

Voyaging to every port to dicker and adventure,

Hurrying with the modern crowd as eager and fickle as any,

Hot toward one I hate, ready in my madness to knife him,

Solitary at midnight in my back yard, my thoughts gone from me a long while,

Walking the old hills of Judæa with the beautiful gentle God by my side,

Speeding through space, speeding through heaven and the stars,

Speeding amid the seven satellites and the broad ring, and the diameter of eighty thousand miles,

Speeding with tail'd meteors, throwing fire-balls like the rest,

Carrying the crescent child that carries its own full mother in its belly,

Storming, enjoying, planning, loving, cautioning,

Backing and filling, appearing and disappearing,

I tread day and night such roads.

146

I visit the orchards of spheres and look at the product,
And look at quintillions ripen'd and look at quintillions
green.

I fly those flights of a fluid and swallowing soul,
My course runs below the soundings of plummets.
I help myself to material and immaterial,
No guard can shut me off, no law prevent me.

I anchor my ship for a little while only,
My messengers continually cruise away or bring their
returns to me.
I go hunting polar furs and the seal, leaping chasms with
a pike-pointed staff, clinging to topples of brittle
and blue.

I ascend to the foretruck,
I take my place late at night in the crow's-nest,
We sail the arctic sea, it is plenty light enough,
Through the clear atmosphere I stretch around on the
wonderful beauty,
The enormous masses of ice pass me and I pass them,
the scenery is plain in all directions,
The white-topt mountains show in the distance, I fling
out my fancies toward them,
We are approaching some great battle-field in which we
are soon to be engaged,
We pass the colossal outposts of the encampment, we
pass with still feet and caution,
Or we are entering by the suburbs some vast and ruin'd
city,
The blocks and fallen architecture more than all the
living cities of the globe.

I am a free companion, I bivouac by invading watchfires,
I turn the bridegroom out of bed and stay with the bride
myself,
I tighten her all night to my thighs and lips.

147

My voice is the wife's voice, the screech by the rail of
the stairs,
They fetch my man's body up dripping and drown'd.

I understand the large hearts of heroes,
The courage of present times and all times,
How the skipper saw the crowded and rudderless wreck
of the steamship, and Death chasing it up and down
the storm,
How he knuckled tight and gave not back an inch, and
was faithful of days and faithful of nights,
And chalk'd in large letters on a board, *Be of good cheer,
we will not desert you;*
How he follow'd with them and tack'd with them three
days and would not give it up,
How he saved the drifting company at last,
How the lank loose-gown'd women look'd when boated
from the side of their prepared graves,
How the silent old-faced infants and the lifted sick, and
the sharp-lipp'd unshaved men;
All this I swallow, it tastes good, I like it well, it becomes
mine,
I am the man, I suffer'd, I was there.

The disdain and calmness of martyrs,
The mother of old, condemn'd for a witch, burnt with
dry wood, her children gazing on,
The hounded slave that flags in the race, leans by the
fence, blowing, cover'd with sweat,
The twinges that sting like needles his legs and neck, the
murderous buckshot and the bullets,
All these I feel or am.

I am the hounded slave, I wince at the bite of the dogs,
Hell and despair are upon me, crack and again crack the
marksmen,
I clutch the rails of the fence, my gore dribs, thinn'd with
the ooze of my skin,

I fall on the weeds and stones,
The riders spur their unwilling horses, haul close,
Taunt my dizzy ears and beat me violently over the head
    with whip-stocks.
Agonies are one of my changes of garments.
I do not ask the wounded person how he feels, I myself
    become the wounded person,
My hurts turn livid upon me as I lean on a cane and
    observe.

I am the mash'd fireman with breast-bone broken,
Tumbling walls buried me in their debris,
Heat and smoke I inspired, I heard the yelling shouts of
    my comrades,
I heard the distant click of their picks and shovels,
They have clear'd the beams away, they tenderly lift me
    forth.
I lie in the night air in my red shirt, the pervading hush
    is for my sake,
Painless after all I lie exhausted but not so unhappy,
White and beautiful are the faces around me, the heads
    are bared of their fire-caps,
The kneeling crowd fades with the light of the torches.

Distant and dead resuscitate,
They show as the dial or move as the hands of me, I am
    the clock myself.

I am an old artillerist, I tell of my fort's bombardment,
I am there again.

Again the long roll of the drummers,
Again the attacking cannon, mortars,
Again to my listening ears the cannon responsive.

I take part, I see and hear the whole,
The cries, curses, roar, the plaudits for well-aim'd shots,
The ambulanza slowly passing trailing its red drip,

Workmen searching after damages, making indispensable repairs,
The fall of grenades through the rent roof, the fan-shaped explosion,
The whizz of limbs, heads, stone, wood, iron, high in the air.

Again gurgles the mouth of my dying general, he furiously waves with his hand,
He gasps through the clot *Mind not me—mind—the entrenchments.*

34

Now I tell what I knew in Texas in my early youth,
(I tell not the fall of Alamo,
Not one escaped to tell the fall of Alamo,
The hundred and fifty are dumb yet at Alamo,)
'Tis the tale of the murder in cold blood of four hundred and twelve young men.

Retreating they had form'd in a hollow square with their baggage for breastworks,
Nine hundred lives out of the surrounding enemy's, nine times their number, was the price they took in advance,
Their colonel was wounded and their ammunition gone,
They treated for an honorable capitulation, receiv'd writing and seal, gave up their arms and march'd back prisoners of war.

They were the glory of the race of rangers,
Matchless with horse, rifle, song, supper, courtship,
Large, turbulent, generous, handsome, proud, and affectionate,
Bearded, sunburnt, drest in the free costume of hunters,
Not a single one over thirty years of age.
The second First-day morning they were brought out in squads and massacred, it was beautiful early summer,

The work commenced about five o'clock and was over
by eight.

None obey'd the command to kneel,
Some made a mad and helpless rush, some stood stark
and straight,
A few fell at once, shot in the temple or heart, the living
and dead lay together,
The maim'd and mangled dug in the dirt, the new-comers
saw them there,
Some half-kill'd attempted to crawl away,
These were despatch'd with bayonets or batter'd with
the blunts of muskets.
A youth not seventeen years old seiz'd his assassin till
two more came to release him,
The three were all torn and cover'd with the boy's blood.

At eleven o'clock began the burning of the bodies;
That is the tale of the murder of the four hundred and
twelve young men.

35

Would you hear of an old-time sea-fight?
Would you learn who won by the light of the moon and
stars?
List to the yarn, as my grandmother's father the sailor
told it to me.

Our foe was no skulk in his ship I tell you, (said he,)
His was the surly English pluck, and there is no tougher
or truer, and never was, and never will be;
Along the lower'd eve he came horribly raking us.
We closed with him, the yards entangled, the cannon
touch'd,
My captain lash'd fast with his own hands.

We had receiv'd some eighteen pound shots under the
water,

On our lower-gun-deck two large pieces had burst at the
first fire, killing all around and blowing up overhead.

Fighting at sun-down, fighting at dark,
Ten o'clock at night, the full moon well up, our leaks on
the gain, and five feet of water reported,
The master-at-arms loosing the prisoners confined in the
after-hold to give them a chance for themselves.

The transit to and from the magazine is now stopt by the
sentinels,
They see so many strange faces they do not know whom
to trust.

Our frigate takes fire,
The other asks if we demand quarter?
If our colors are struck and the fighting done?

Now I laugh content, for I hear the voice of my little
captain,
We have not struck, he composedly cries, *we have just
begun our part of the fighting.*

Only three guns are in use,
One is directed by the captain himself against the
enemy's main-mast,
Two well serv'd with grape and canister silence his mus-
ketry and clear his decks.

The tops alone second the fire of this little battery, espe-
cially the main-top,
They hold out bravely during the whole of the action.
Not a moment's cease,
The leaks gain fast on the pumps, the fire eats toward the
powder-magazine.

One of the pumps has been shot away, it is generally
thought we are sinking.

Serene stands the little captain,
He is not hurried, his voice is neither high nor low,
His eyes give more light to us than our battle-lanterns.

Toward twelve there in the beams of the moon they
surrender to us.

36

Stretch'd and still lies the midnight,
Two great hulls motionless on the breast of the darkness,
Our vessel riddled and slowly sinking, preparations to
pass to the one we have conquer'd,
The captain on the quarter-deck coldly giving his orders
through a countenance white as a sheet,
Near by the corpse of the child that serv'd in the cabin,
The dead face of an old salt with long white hair and
carefully curl'd whiskers,
The flames spite of all that can be done flickering aloft
and below,
The husky voices of the two or three officers yet fit for
duty,
Formless stacks of bodies and bodies by themselves, dabs
of flesh upon the masts and spars,
Cut of cordage, dangle of rigging, slight shock of the
soothe of waves,
Black and impassive guns, litter of powder-parcels,
strong scent,
A few large stars overhead, silent and mournful shining,
Delicate sniffs of sea-breeze, smells of sedgy grass and
fields by the shore, death-messages given in charge
to survivors,
The hiss of the surgeon's knife, the gnawing teeth of his
saw,
Wheeze, cluck, swash of falling blood, short wild scream,
and long, dull, tapering groan,
These so, these irretrievable.

37

You laggards there on guard! look to your arms!
In at the conquer'd doors they crowd! I am possess'd!
Embody all presences outlaw'd or suffering,
See myself in prison shaped like another man,
And feel the dull unintermitted pain,

For me the keepers of convicts shoulder their carbines
     and keep watch,
It is I let out in the morning and barr'd at night.

Not a mutineer walks handcuff'd to jail but I am hand-
     cuff'd to him and walk by his side,
(I am less the jolly one there, and more the silent one
     with sweat on my twitching lips.)

Not a youngster is taken for larceny but I go up too, and
     am tried and sentenced.

Not a cholera patient lies at the last gasp but I also lie at
     the last gasp,
My face is ash-color'd, my sinews gnarl, away from me
     people retreat.

Askers embody themselves in me and I am embodied in
     them,
I project my hat, sit shame-faced, and beg.

38

Enough! enough! enough!
Somehow I have been stunn'd. Stand back!
Give me a little time beyond my cuff'd head, slumbers,
     dreams, gaping,
I discover myself on the verge of a usual mistake.

That I could forget the mockers and insults!

That I could forget the trickling tears and the blows of
the bludgeons and hammers!
That I could look with a separate look on my own crucifixion and bloody crowning!

I remember now,
I resume the overstaid fraction,
The grave of rock multiplies what has been confided to
it, or to any graves,
Corpses rise, gashes heal, fastenings roll from me.

I troop forth replenish'd with supreme power, one of an
average unending procession,
Inland and sea-coast we go, and pass all boundary lines,
Our swift ordinances on their way over the whole earth,
The blossoms we wear in our hats the growth of thou-
sands of years.
Eleves, I salute you! come forward!
Continue your annotations, continue your questionings.

39

The friendly and flowing savage, who is he?
Is he waiting for civilization, or past it and mastering it?

Is he some Southwesterner rais'd out-doors? is he Kanadian?
Is he from the Mississippi country? Iowa, Oregon, California?
The mountains? prairie-life, bush-life? or sailor from the
sea?

Wherever he goes men and women accept and desire
him,
They desire he should like them, touch them, speak to
them, stay with them.

Behavior lawless as snow-flakes, words simple as grass,
uncomb'd head, laughter, and naïveté,

Slow-stepping feet, common features, common modes
    and emanations,
They descend in new forms from the tips of his fingers,
They are wafted with the odor of his body or breath,
    they fly out of the glance of his eyes.

40

Flaunt of the sunshine I need not your bask—lie over!
You light surfaces only, I force surfaces and depths also.

Earth! you seem to look for something at my hands,
Say, old top-knot, what do you want?

Man or woman, I might tell how I like you, but cannot,
And might tell what it is in me and what it is in you, but
    cannot,
And might tell that pining I have, that pulse of my nights
    and days.

Behold, I do not give lectures or a little charity,
When I give I give myself.

You there, impotent, loose in the knees,
Open your scarf'd chops till I blow grit within you,
Spread your palms and lift the flaps of your pockets,
I am not to be denied, I compel, I have stores plenty and
    to spare,
And any thing I have I bestow.

I do not ask who you are, that is not important to me,
You can do nothing and be nothing but what I will infold
    you.

To cotton-field drudge or cleaner of privies I lean,
On his right cheek I put the family kiss,
And in my soul I swear I never will deny him.

On women fit for conception I start bigger and nimbler
    babes,

(This day I am jetting the stuff of far more arrogant
    republics.)

To any one dying, thither I speed and twist the knob of
    the door,
Turn the bed-clothes toward the foot of the bed,
Let the physician and the priest go home.

I seize the descending man and raise him with resistless
    will,
O despairer, here is my neck,
By God, you shall not go down! hang your whole weight
    upon me.

I dilate you with tremendous breath, I buoy you up,
Every room of the house do I fill with an arm'd force,
Lovers of me, bafflers of graves.

Sleep—I and they keep guard all night,
Not doubt, not disease shall dare to lay finger upon you,
I have embraced you, and henceforth possess you to
    myself,
And when you rise in the morning you will find what I
    tell you is so.

41

I am he bringing help for the sick as they pant on their
    backs,
And for strong upright men I bring yet more needed
    help.

I heard what was said of the universe,
Heard it and heard it of several thousand years;
It is middling well as far as it goes—but is that all?

Magnifying and applying come I,
Outbidding at the start the old cautious hucksters,

Taking myself the exact dimensions of Jehovah,
Lithographing Kronos, Zeus his son, and Hercules his
    grandson,
Buying drafts of Osiris, Isis, Belus, Brahma, Buddha,
In my portfolio placing Manito loose, Allah on a leaf, the
    crucifix engraved,
With Odin and the hideous-faced Mexitli and every idol
    and image,
Taking them all for what they are worth and not a cent
    more,
Admitting they were alive and did the work of their days,
(They bore mites as for unfledg'd birds who have now to
    rise and fly and sing for themselves,)
Accepting the rough deific sketches to fill out better in
    myself, bestowing them freely on each man and
    woman I see,
Discovering as much or more in a framer framing a
    house,
Putting higher claims for him there with his roll'd-up
    sleeves driving the mallet and chisel,
Not objecting to special revelations, considering a curl
    of smoke or a hair on the back of my hand just as
    curious as any revelation,
Lads ahold of fire-engines and hook-and-ladder ropes no
    less to me than the gods of the antique wars,
Minding their voices' peal through the crash of destruc-
    tion,
Their brawny limbs passing safe over charr'd laths, their
    white foreheads whole and unhurt out of the flames;
By the mechanic's wife with her babe at her nipple inter-
    ceding for every person born,
Three scythes at harvest whizzing in a row from three
    lusty angels with shirts bagg'd out at their waists,
The snag-tooth'd hostler with red hair redeeming sins
    past and to come,
Selling all he possesses, traveling on foot to fee lawyers
    for his brother and sit by him while he is tried for
    forgery;

What was strewn in the amplest strewing the square rod
    about me, and not filling the square rod then,
The bull and the bug never worshipp'd half enough,
Dung and dirt more admirable than was dream'd,
The supernatural of no account, myself waiting my time
    to be one of the supremes,
The day getting ready for me when I shall do as much
    good as the best, and be as prodigious;
By my life-lumps! becoming already a creator,
Putting myself here and now to the ambush'd womb of
    the shadows.

42

A call in the midst of the crowd,
My own voice, orotund sweeping and final.

Come my children,
Come my boys and girls, my women, household and in-
    timates,
Now the performer launches his nerve, he has pass'd his
    prelude on the reeds within.

Easily written loose-finger'd chords—I feel the thrum of
    your climax and close.

My head slues round on my neck,
Music rolls, but not from the organ,
Folks are around me, but they are no household of mine.

Ever the hard unsunk ground,
Ever the eaters and drinkers, ever the upward and
    downward sun, ever the air and the ceaseless tides,
Ever myself and my neighbors, refreshing, wicked, real,
Ever the old inexplicable query, ever that thorn'd thumb,
    that breath of itches and thirsts,
Ever the vexer's *hoot! hoot!* till we find where the sly one
    hides and bring him forth,

Ever love, ever the sobbing liquid of life,
Ever the bandage under the chin, ever the trestles of
    death.

Here and there with dimes on the eyes walking,
To feed the greed of the belly the brains liberally spoon-
    ing,
Tickets buying, taking, selling, but in to the feast never
    once going,
Many sweating, ploughing, thrashing, and then the chaff
    for payment receiving,
A few idly owning, and they the wheat continually
    claiming.

This is the city and I am one of the citizens,
Whatever interests the rest interests me, politics, wars,
    markets, newspapers, schools,
The mayor and councils, banks, tariffs, steamships, fac-
    tories, stocks, stores, real estate and personal estate.

The little plentiful manikins skipping around in collars
    and tail'd coats,
I am aware who they are, (they are positively not worms
    or fleas,)
I acknowledge the duplicates of myself, the weakest and
    shallowest is deathless with me,
What I do and say the same waits for them,
Every thought that flounders in me the same flounders
    in them.

I know perfectly well my own egotism,
Know my omnivorous lines and must not write any less,
And would fetch you whoever you are flush with myself.

Not words of routine this song of mine,
But abruptly to question, to leap beyond yet nearer
    bring;
This printed and bound book—but the printer and the
    printing-office boy?

The well-taken photographs—but your wife or friend
    close and solid in your arms?
The black ship mail'd with iron, her mighty guns in her
    turrets—but the pluck of the captain and engineers?
In the houses the dishes and fare and furniture—but the
    host and hostess, and the look out of their eyes?
The sky up there—yet here or next door, or across the
    way?
The saints and sages in history—but you yourself?
Sermons, creeds, theology—but the fathomless human
    brain,
And what is reason? and what is love? and what is life?

43

I do not despise you priests, all time, the world over,
My faith is the greatest of faiths and the least of faiths,
Enclosing worship ancient and modern and all between
    ancient and modern,
Believing I shall come again upon the earth after five
    thousand years,
Waiting responses from oracles, honoring the gods, salut-
    ing the sun,
Making a fetich of the first rock or stump, powowing
    with sticks in the circle of obis,
Helping the llama or brahmin as he trims the lamps of
    the idols,
Dancing yet through the streets in a phallic procession,
    rapt and austere in the woods a gymnosophist,
Drinking mead from the skull-cup, to Shastas and Vedas
    admirant, minding the Koran,
Walking the teokallis, spotted with gore from the stone
    and knife, beating the serpent-skin drum,
Accepting the Gospels, accepting him that was crucified,
    knowing assuredly that he is divine,
To the mass kneeling or the puritan's prayer rising, or
    sitting patiently in a pew,

Ranting and frothing in my insane crisis, or waiting dead-
  like till my spirit arouses me,
Looking forth on pavement and land, or outside of pavement and land,
Belonging to the winders of the circuit of circuits.

One of that centripetal and centrifugal gang I turn and
  talk like a man leaving charges before a journey.

Down-hearted doubters dull and excluded,
Frivolous, sullen, moping, angry, affected, dishearten'd,
  atheistical,
I know every one of you, I know the sea of torment,
  doubt, despair and unbelief.

How the flukes splash!
How they contort rapid as lightning, with spasms and
  spouts of blood!

Be at peace bloody flukes of doubters and sullen mopers,
I take my place among you as much as among any,
The past is the push of you, me, all, precisely the same,
And what is yet untried and afterward is for you, me, all
  precisely the same.

I do not know what is untried and afterward,
But I know it will in its turn prove sufficient, and cannot
  fail.
Each who passes is consider'd, each who stops is consider'd, not a single one can it fail.

It cannot fail the young man who died and was buried,
Nor the young woman who died and was put by his side,
Nor the little child that peep'd in at the door, and then
  drew back and was never seen again,
Nor the old man who has lived without purpose, and
  feels it with bitterness worse than gall,
Nor him in the poor house tubercled by rum and the bad
  disorder,

Nor the numberless slaughter'd and wreck'd, nor the
  brutish koboo call'd the ordure of humanity,
Nor the sacs merely floating with open mouths for food
  to slip in,
Nor any thing in the earth, or down in the oldest graves
  of the earth,
Nor any thing in the myriads of spheres, nor the myriads
  of myriads that inhabit them,
Nor the present, nor the least wisp that is known.

44

It is time to explain myself—let us stand up.

What is known I strip away,
I launch all men and women forward with me into the
  Unknown.

The clock indicates the moment—but what does eternity
  indicate?

We have thus far exhausted trillions of winters and
  summers,
There are trillions ahead, and trillions ahead of them.

Births have brought us richness and variety.
And other births will bring us richness and variety.

I do not call one greater and one smaller,
That which fills its period and place is equal to any.

Were mankind murderous or jealous upon you, my
  brother, my sister?
I am sorry for you, they are not murderous or jealous
  upon me,
All has been gentle with me, I keep no account with
  lamentation,
(What have I to do with lamentation?)

I am an acme of things accomplish'd, and I an encloser
  of things to be.
My feet strike an apex of the apices of the stairs,
On every step bunches of ages, and larger bunches be-
  tween the steps,
All below duly travel'd, and still I mount and mount.
Rise after rise bow the phantoms behind me,
Afar down I see the huge first Nothing, I know I was
  even there,
I waited unseen and always, and slept through the
  lethargic mist,
And took my time, and took no hurt from the fetid
  carbon.

Long I was hugg'd close—long and long.

Immense have been the preparations for me,
Faithful and friendly the arms that have help'd me.

Cycles ferried my cradle, rowing and rowing like cheer-
  ful boatmen,
For room to me stars kept aside in their own rings,
They sent influences to look after what was to hold me.

Before I was born out of my mother generations guided
  me,
My embryo has never been torpid, nothing could overlay
  it.

For it the nebula cohere to an orb,
The long slow strata piled to rest it on,
Vast vegetables gave it sustenance,
Monstrous sauroids transported it in their mouths and
  deposited it with care.

All forces have been steadily employ'd to complete and
  delight me,
Now on this spot I stand with my robust soul.

O span of youth! ever-push'd elasticity.
O manhood, balanced, florid and full.

My lovers suffocate me,
Crowding my lips, thick in the pores of my skin,
Jostling me through streets and public halls, coming
  naked to me at night,
Crying by day *Ahoy!* from the rocks of the river, swing-
  ing and chirping over my head,
Calling my name from flower-beds, vines, tangled under-
  brush,
Lighting on every moment of my life,
Bussing my body with soft balsamic busses,
Noiselessly passing handfuls out of their hearts and giv-
  ing them to be mine.

Old age superbly rising! O welcome, ineffable grace of
  dying days!

Every condition promulges not only itself, it promulges
  what grows after and out of itself,
And the dark hush promulges as much as any.

I open my scuttle at night and see the far-sprinkled
  systems,
And all I see multiplied as high as I can cipher edge but
  the rim of the farther systems.

Wider and wider they spread, expanding, always expanding,
Outward and outward and forever outward.

My sun has his sun and round him obediently wheels,
He joins with his partners a group of superior circuit,
And greater sets follow, making specks of the greatest
  inside them.

There is no stoppage and never can be stoppage,
If I, you, and the worlds, and all beneath or upon their
surfaces, were this moment reduced back to a pallid
float, it would not avail in the long run,
We should surely bring up again where we now stand,
And surely go as much farther, and then farther and
farther.
A few quadrillions of eras, a few octillions of cubic
leagues, do not hazard the span or make it impatient,
They are but parts, any thing is but a part.

See ever so far, there is limitless space outside of that,
Count ever so much, there is limitless time around that.

My rendezvous is appointed, it is certain,
The Lord will be there and wait till I come on perfect
terms,
The great Camerado, the lover true for whom I pine will
be there.

46

I know I have the best of time and space, and was never
measured and never will be measured.

I tramp a perpetual journey, (come listen all!)
My signs are a rain-proof coat, good shoes, and a staff
cut from the woods,
No friend of mine takes his ease in my chair,
I have no chair, no church, no philosophy,
I lead no man to a dinner-table, library, exchange,
But each man and each woman of you I lead upon a
knoll,
My left hand hooking you round the waist,
My right hand pointing to landscapes of continents and
the public road.
Not I, not any one else can travel that road for you,
You must travel it for yourself.

It is not far, it is within reach,
Perhaps you have been on it since you were born and
did not know,
Perhaps it is everywhere on water and on land.

Shoulder your duds dear son, and I will mine, and let
us hasten forth,
Wonderful cities and free nations we shall fetch as we go.

If you tire, give me both burdens, and rest the chuff
of your hand on my hip,
And in due time you shall repay the same service to me,
For after we start we never lie by again.

This day before dawn I ascended a hill and look'd at
the crowded heaven,
And I said to my spirit *When we become the enfolders
of those orbs, and the pleasure and knowledge of
every thing in them, shall we be fill'd and satisfied
then?*
And my spirit said *No, we but level that lift to pass and
continue beyond.*

You are also asking me questions and I hear you,
I answer that I cannot answer, you must find out for
yourself.

Sit a while, dear son,
Here are biscuits to eat and here is milk to drink,
But as soon as you sleep and renew yourself in sweet
clothes, I kiss you with a good-by kiss and open the
gate for your egress hence.

Long enough have you dream'd contemptible dreams,
Now I wash the gum from your eyes,
You must habit yourself to the dazzle of the light and
of every moment of your life.

Long have you timidly waded holding a plank by the
shore,

Now I will you to be a bold swimmer,
To jump off in the midst of the sea, rise again, nod to
    me, shout, and laughingly dash with your hair.

47

I am the teacher of athletes,
He that by me spreads a wider breast than my own
    proves the width of my own,
He most honors my style who learns under it to destroy
    the teacher.

The boy I love, the same becomes a man not through
    derived power, but in his own right,
Wicked rather than virtuous out of conformity or fear,
Fond of his sweetheart, relishing well his steak,
Unrequited love or a slight cutting him worse than sharp
    steel cuts,
First-rate to ride, to fight, to hit the bull's eye, to sail a
    skiff, to sing a song or play on the banjo,
Preferring scars and the beard and faces pitted with
    small-pox over all latherers,
And those well-tann'd to those that keep out of the sun.

I teach straying from me, yet who can stray from me?
I follow you whoever you are from the present hour,
My words itch at your ears till you understand them.

I do not say these things for a dollar or to fill up the
    time while I wait for a boat,
(It is you talking just as much as myself, I act as the
    tongue of you,
Tied in your mouth, in mine it begins to be loosen'd.)

I swear I will never again mention love or death inside
    a house,
And I swear I will never translate myself at all, only to
    him or her who privately stays with me in the open
    air.

If you would understand me go to the heights or water-
shore,
The nearest gnat is an explanation, and a drop or motion
of waves a key,
The maul, the oar, the hand-saw, second my words.
No shutter'd room or school can commune with me,
But roughs and little children better than they.

The young mechanic is closest to me, he knows me well,
The woodman that takes his axe and jug with him shall
take me with him all day,
The farm-boy ploughing in the field feels good at the
sound of my voice,
In vessels that sail my words sail, I go with fishermen
and seamen and love them.

The soldier camp'd or upon the march is mine,
On the night ere the pending battle many seek me, and I
do not fail them,
On that solemn night (it may be their last) those that
know me seek me.

My face rubs to the hunter's face when he lies down
alone in his blanket,
The driver thinking of me does not mind the jolt of his
wagon,
The young mother and old mother comprehend me,
The girl and the wife rest the needle a moment and
forget where they are,
They and all would resume what I have told them.

48

I have said that the soul is not more than the body,
And I have said that the body is not more than the soul,
And nothing, not God, is greater to one than one's self is,
And whoever walks a furlong without sympathy walks
to his own funeral drest in his shroud,

And I or you pocketless of a dime may purchase the pick
of the earth,

And to glance with an eye or show a bean in its pod
confounds the learning of all times,

And there is no trade or employment but the young man
following it may become a hero,

And there is no object so soft but it makes a hub for the
wheel'd universe,

And I say to any man or woman, Let your soul stand
cool and composed before a million universes.

And I say to mankind, Be not curious about God,

For I who am curious about each am not curious about
God,

(No array of terms can say how much I am at peace
about God and about death.)

I hear and behold God in every object, yet understand
God not in the least,

Nor do I understand who there can be more wonderful
than myself.

Why should I wish to see God better than this day?

I see something of God each hour of the twenty-four, and
each moment then,

In the faces of men and women I see God, and in my
own face in the glass,

I find letters from God dropt in the street, and every
one is sign'd by God's name,

And I leave them where they are, for I know that where-
soe'er I go,

Others will punctually come for ever and ever.

49

And as to you Death, and you bitter hug of mortality,
it is idle to try to alarm me.

To his work without flinching the accoucheur comes,

I see the elder-hand pressing receiving supporting,

170

I recline by the sills of the exquisite flexible doors,
And mark the outlet, and mark the relief and escape.

And as to you Corpse I think you are good manure, but
    that does not offend me,
I smell the white roses sweet-scented and growing,
I reach to the leafy lips, I reach to the polish'd breasts
    of melons.

And as to you Life I reckon you are the leavings of many
    deaths,
(No doubt I have died myself ten thousand times
    before.)

I hear you whispering there O stars of heaven,
O suns—O grass of graves—O perpetual transfers and
    promotions,
If you do not say any thing how can I say any thing?

Of the turbid pool that lies in the autumn forest,
Of the moon that descends the steeps of the soughing
    twilight,
Toss, sparkles of day and dusk—toss on the black stems
    that decay in the muck,
Toss to the moaning gibberish of the dry limbs.

I ascend from the moon, I ascend from the night,
I perceive that the ghastly glimmer is noonday sunbeams
    reflected,
And debouch to the steady and central from the off-
    spring great or small.

50

There is that in me—I do not know what it is—but I know
    it is in me.
Wrench'd and sweaty—calm and cool then my body
    becomes,
I sleep—I sleep long.

I do not know it—it is without name—it is a word unsaid,
It is not in any dictionary, utterance, symbol.

Something it swings on more than the earth I swing on,
To it the creation is the friend whose embracing awakes
me.

Perhaps I might tell more. Outlines! I plead for my
brothers and sisters.

Do you see O my brothers and sisters?
It is not chaos or death—it is form, union, plan—it is
eternal life—it is Happiness.

51

The past and present wilt—I have fill'd them, emptied
them,
And proceed to fill my next fold of the future.

Listener up there! what have you to confide to me?
Look in my face while I snuff the sidle of evening,
(Talk honestly, no one else hears you, and I stay only a
minute longer.)

Do I contradict myself?
Very well then I contradict myself,
(I am large, I contain multitudes.)

I concentrate toward them that are nigh, I wait on the
door-slab.

Who has done his day's work? who will soonest be
through with his supper?
Who wishes to walk with me?

Will you speak before I am gone? will you prove already
too late?

The spotted hawk swoops by and accuses me, he complains of my gab and my loitering.

I too am not a bit tamed, I too am untranslatable,
I sound my barbaric yawp over the roofs of the world.

The last scud of day holds back for me,
It flings my likeness after the rest and true as any on the shadow'd wilds,
It coaxes me to the vapor and the dusk.

I depart as air, I shake my white locks at the runaway sun,
I effuse my flesh in eddies, and drift it in lacy jags.

I bequeath myself to the dirt to grow from the grass I love,
If you want me again look for me under your boot-soles.

You will hardly know who I am or what I mean,
But I shall be good health to you nevertheless,
And filter and fibre your blood.

Failing to fetch me at first keep encouraged,
Missing me one place search another,
I stop somewhere waiting for you.

I SAW IN LOUISIANA
A LIVE-OAK GROWING

I saw in Louisiana a live-oak growing,
All alone stood it and the moss hung down from the branches,
Without any companion it grew there uttering joyous leaves of dark green,

And its look, rude, unbending, lusty, made me think of
    myself,
But I wonder'd how it could utter joyous leaves standing
    alone there without its friend near, for I knew I
    could not,
And I broke off a twig with a certain number of leaves
    upon it, and twined around it a little moss,
And brought it away, and I have placed it in sight in my
    room,
It is not needed to remind me as of my own dear friends,
(For I believe lately I think of little else than of them,)
Yet it remains to me a curious token, it makes me think
    of manly love;
For all that, and though the live-oak glistens there in
    Louisiana solitary in a wide flat space,
Uttering joyous leaves all its life without a friend a lover
    near,
I know very well I could not.

A NOISELESS PATIENT SPIDER

A NOISELESS patient spider,
I mark'd where on a little promontory it stood isolated,
Mark'd how to explore the vacant vast surrounding,
It launch'd forth filament, filament, filament, out of
    itself,
Ever unreeling them, ever tirelessly speeding them.

And you O my soul where you stand,
Surrounded, detached, in measureless oceans of space,
Ceaselessly musing, venturing, throwing, seeking the
    spheres to connect them,
Till the bridge you will need be form'd, till the ductile
    anchor hold,
Till the gossamer thread you fling catch somewhere, O
    my soul.

174

O CAPTAIN! MY CAPTAIN!

O CAPTAIN! my Captain! our fearful trip is done,
The ship has weather'd every rack, the prize we sought
    is won,
The port is near, the bells I hear, the people all exulting,
While follow eyes the steady keel, the vessel grim and
    daring;
      But O heart! heart! heart!
        O the bleeding drops of red,
          Where on the deck my Captain lies,
           Fallen cold and dead.

O Captain! my Captain! rise up and hear the bells;
Rise up—for you the flag is flung—for you the bugle trills,
For you bouquets and ribbon'd wreaths—for you the
    shores a-crowding,
For you they call, the swaying mass, their eager faces
    turning;
      Here Captain! dear father!
        This arm beneath your head!
          It is some dream that on the deck,
           You've fallen cold and dead.

My Captain does not answer, his lips are pale and still,
My father does not feel my arm, he has no pulse nor will,
The ship is anchor'd safe and sound, its voyage closed
    and done,
From fearful trip the victor ship comes in with object
    won;
      Exult O shores, and ring O bells!
        But I with mournful tread,
          Walk the deck my Captain lies,
           Fallen cold and dead.

POETS TO COME

Poets to come! orators, singers, musicians to come!
Not to-day is to justify me and answer what I am for,
But you, a new brood, native, athletic, continental,
    greater than before known,
Arouse! for you must justify me.

I myself but write one or two indicative words for the
    future,
I but advance a moment only to wheel and hurry back
    in the darkness.

I am a man who, sauntering along without fully stopping,
    turns a casual look upon you and then averts his
    face,
Leaving it to you to prove and define it,
Expecting the main things from you.

I HEAR
IT WAS CHARGED AGAINST ME

I hear it was charged against me that I sought to destroy
    institutions.
But really I am neither for nor against institutions.
(What indeed have I in common with them? or what
    with the destruction of them?)
Only I will establish in the Mannahatta and in every
    city of these States inland and seaboard,
And in the fields and woods, and above every keel little
    or large that dents the water,
Without edifices or rules or trustees or any argument,
The institution of the dear love of comrades.
176

WALT WHITMAN
THIS COMPOST

I

SOMETHING startles me where I thought I was safest;
I withdraw from the still woods I loved;
I will not go now on the pastures to walk;
I will not strip the clothes from my body to meet my
    lover the sea;
I will not touch my flesh to the earth, as to other flesh,
    to renew me.

O how can it be that the ground does not sicken?
How can you be alive, you growths of spring?
How can you furnish health, you blood of herbs, roots,
    orchards, grain?
Are they not continually putting distemper'd corpses
    within you?
Is not every continent work'd over and over with sour
    dead?

Where have you disposed of their carcasses?
Those drunkards and gluttons of so many generations;
Where have you drawn off all the foul liquid and meat?
I do not see any of it upon you to-day—or perhaps I am
    deceiv'd;
I will run a furrow with my plough—I will press my
    spade through the sod, and turn it up underneath;
I am sure I shall expose some of the foul meat.

II

Behold this compost! behold it well!
Perhaps every mite has once form'd part of a sick person
    —Yet behold!
The grass of spring covers the prairies,
The bean bursts noiselessly through the mould in the
    garden,

177

The delicate spear of the onion pierces upward,
The apple-buds cluster together on the apple-branches,
The resurrection of the wheat appears with pale visage
    out of its graves,
The tinge awakes over the willow-tree and the mulberry-
    tree,
The he-birds carol mornings and evenings, while the
    she-birds sit on their nests,
The young of poultry break through the hatch'd eggs,
The new-born of animals appear—the calf is dropt from
    the cow, the colt from the mare,
Out of its little hill faithfully rise the potato's dark green
    leaves,
Out of its hill rises the yellow maize-stalk—the lilacs
    bloom in the door-yards;
The summer growth is innocent and disdainful above
    all those strata of sour dead.

What chemistry!
That the winds are really not infectious,
That this is no cheat, this transparent green-wash of
    the sea, which is so amorous after me,
That it is safe to allow it to lick my naked body all over
    with its tongues,
That it will not endanger me with the fevers that have
    deposited themselves in it,
That all is clean, forever and forever.
That the cool drink from the well tastes so good,
That blackberries are so flavorous and juicy,
That the fruits of the apple-orchard, and of the orange-
    orchard—that melons, grapes, peaches, plums, will
    none of them poison me,
That when I recline on the grass I do not catch any
    disease,
Though probably every spear of grass rises out of what
    was once a catching disease.

III

Now I am terrified at the Earth! it is that calm and
  patient,
It grows such sweet things out of such corruptions,
It turns harmless and stainless on its axis, with such
  endless successions of diseas'd corpses,
It distills such exquisite winds out of such infused fetor,
It renews with such unwitting looks, its prodigal, annual,
  sumptuous crops,
It gives such divine materials to men, and accepts such
  leavings from them at last.

CROSSING BROOKLYN FERRY

1

FLOOD-TIDE below me! I see you face to face!
Clouds of the west—sun there half an hour high—I see
  you also face to face.

Crowds of men and women attired in the usual costumes,
  how curious you are to me!
On the ferry-boats the hundreds and hundreds that
  cross, returning home, are more curious to me than
  you suppose,
And you that shall cross from shore to shore years hence
  are more to me, and more in my meditations, than
  you might suppose.

2

The impalpable sustenance of me from all things at all
  hours of the day,
The simple, compact, well-join'd scheme, myself disintegrated, every one disintegrated yet part of the
  scheme,

The similitudes of the past and those of the future,
The glories strung like beads on my smallest sights and
    hearings, on the walk in the street and the passage
    over the river,
The current rushing so swiftly and swimming with me
    far away,
The others that are to follow me, the ties between me
    and them,
The certainty of others, the life, love, sight, hearing of
    others.

Others will enter the gates of the ferry and cross from
    shore to shore,
Others will watch the run of the flood-tide,
Others will see the shipping of Manhattan north and
    west, and the heights of Brooklyn to the south and
    east,
Others will see the islands large and small;
Fifty years hence, others will see them as they cross, the
    sun half an hour high,
A hundred years hence, or ever so many hundred years
    hence, others will see them,
Will enjoy the sunset, the pouring-in of the flood-tide,
    the falling-back to the sea of the ebb-tide.

3

It avails not, time nor place—distance avails not,
I am with you, you men and women of a generation, or
    ever so many generations hence,
Just as you feel when you look on the river and sky, so
    I felt,
Just as any of you is one of a living crowd, I was one of a
    crowd,
Just as you are refresh'd by the gladness of the river and
    the bright flow, I was refresh'd,
Just as you stand and lean on the rail, yet hurry with the
    swift current, I stood yet was hurried,

Just as you look on the numberless masts of ships and
the thick-stemm'd pipes of steamboats, I look'd.

I too many and many a time cross'd the river of old,
Watched the Twelfth-month sea-gulls, saw them high in
the air floating with motionless wings, oscillating
their bodies,
Saw how the glistening yellow lit up parts of their bodies
and left the rest in strong shadow,
Saw the slow-wheeling circles and the gradual edging
toward the south,
Saw the reflection of the summer sky in the water,
Had my eyes dazzled by the shimmering track of beams,
Look'd at the fine centrifugal spokes of light round the
shape of my head in the sunlit water,
Look'd on the haze on the hills southward and south-
westward,
Look'd on the vapor as it flew in fleeces tinged with
violet,
Look'd toward the lower bay to notice the vessels arriv-
ing,
Saw their approach, saw aboard those that were near me,
Saw the white sails of schooners and sloops, saw the ships
at anchor,
The sailors at work in the rigging or out astride the spars,
The round masts, the swinging motion of the hulls, the
slender serpentine pennants,
The large and small steamers in motion, the pilots in
their pilot-houses,
The white wake left by the passage, the quick tremulous
whirl of the wheels,
The flags of all nations, the falling of them at sunset,
The scalloped-edged waves in the twilight, the ladled
cups, the frolicsome crests and glistening,
The stretch afar growing dimmer and dimmer, the gray
walls of the granite storehouses by the docks,
On the river the shadowy group, the big steam-tug

closely flank'd on each side by the barges, the hay-
boat, the belated lighter,
On the neighboring shore the fires from the foundry
chimneys burning high and glaringly into the night,
Casting their flicker of black contrasted with wild red
and yellow light over the tops of houses, and down
into the clefts of streets.

4

These and all else were to me the same as they are to
you,
I loved well those cities, loved well the stately and rapid
river,
The men and women I saw were all near to me,
Others the same—others who look back on me because I
look'd forward to them,
(The time will come, though I stop here to-day and
to-night.)

5

What is it then between us?
What is the count of the scores or hundreds of years
between us?

Whatever it is, it avails not—distance avails not, and
place avails not,
I too lived, Brooklyn of ample hills was mine,
I too walk'd the streets of Manhattan island, and bathed
in the waters around it,
I too felt the curious abrupt questionings stir within me.
In the day among crowds of people sometimes they
came upon me,
In my walks home late at night or as I lay in my bed they
came upon me,
I too had been struck from the float forever held in solu-
tion,

I too had receiv'd identity by my body,
That I was I knew was of my body, and what I should
    be I knew I should be of my body.

6

It is not upon you alone the dark patches fall,
The dark threw its patches down upon me also,
The best I had done seem'd to me blank and suspicious,
My great thoughts as I supposed them, were they not in
    reality meagre?
Nor is it you alone who know what it is to be evil,
I am he who knew what it was to be evil,
I too knitted the old knot of contrariety,
Blabb'd, blush'd, resented, lied, stole, grudg'd,
Had guile, anger, lust, hot wishes I dared not speak,
Was wayward, vain, greedy, shallow, sly, cowardly, ma-
    lignant,
The wolf, the snake, the hog, not wanting in me,
The cheating look, the frivolous word, the adulterous
    wish, not wanting,
Refusals, hates, postponements, meanness, laziness, none
    of these wanting,
Was one with the rest, the days and haps of the rest,
Was call'd by my nighest name by clear loud voices of
    young men as they saw me approaching or passing,
Felt their arms on my neck as I stood, or the negligent
    leaning of their flesh against me as I sat,
Saw many I loved in the street or ferry-boat or public
    assembly, yet never told them a word,
Lived the same life with the rest, the same old laughing,
    gnawing, sleeping,
Play'd the part that still looks back on the actor or actress,
The same old role, the role that is what we make it, as
    great as we like,
Or as small as we like, or both great and small.

7

Closer yet I approach you,
What thought you have of me now, I had as much of you
—I laid in my stores in advance,
I consider'd long and seriously of you before you were
born.

Who was to know what should come home to me?
Who knows but I am enjoying this?
Who knows, for all the distance, but I am as good as
looking at you now, for all you cannot see me?

8

Ah, what can ever be more stately and admirable to me
than mast-hemm'd Manhattan?
River and sunset and scallop-edg'd waves of flood-tide?
The sea-gulls oscillating their bodies, the hay-boat in the
twilight, and the belated lighter?
What gods can exceed these that clasp me by the hand,
and with voices I love call me promptly and loudly
by my nighest name as I approach?

What is more subtle than this which ties me to the
woman or man that looks in my face?
Which fuses me into you now, and pours my meaning
into you?

We understand then do we not?
What I promis'd without mentioning it, have you not
accepted?
What the study could not teach—what the preaching
could not accomplish is accomplish'd, is it not?

9

Flow on, river! flow with the flood-tide, and ebb with
the ebb-tide!

Frolic on, crested and scallop-edg'd waves!

Gorgeous clouds of the sunset! drench with your splendor me, or the men and women generations after me!

Cross from shore to shore, countless crowds of passengers!

Stand up, tall masts of Mannahatta! stand up, beautiful hills of Brooklyn!

Throb, baffled and curious brain! throw out questions and answers!

Suspend here and everywhere, eternal float of solution!

Gaze, loving and thirsting eyes, in the house or street or public assembly!

Sound out, voices of young men! loudly and musically call me by my nighest name!

Live, old life! play the part that looks back on the actor or actress!

Play the old role, the role that is great or small according as one makes it!

Consider, you who peruse me, whether I may not in unknown ways be looking upon you;

Be firm, rail over the river, to support those who lean idly, yet haste with the hasting current;

Fly on, sea-birds! fly sideways, or wheel in large circles high in the air;

Receive the summer sky, you water, and faithfully hold it till all downcast eyes have time to take it from you!

Diverge, fine spokes of light, from the shape of my head, or any one's head, in the sunlit water!

Come on, ships from the lower bay! pass up or down, white-sail'd schooners, sloops, lighters!

Flaunt away, flags of all nations! be duly lower'd at sunset!

Burn high your fires, foundry chimneys! cast black shadows at nightfall! cast red and yellow light over the tops of the houses!

Appearances, now or henceforth, indicate what you are,
You necessary film, continue to envelop the soul,
About my body for me, and your body for you, be hung
  our divinest aromas,
Thrive, cities—bring your freight, bring your shows,
  ample and sufficient rivers,
Expand, being than which none else is perhaps more
  spiritual,
Keep your places, objects than which none else is more
  lasting.

You have waited, you always wait, you dumb, beautiful
  ministers,
We receive you with free sense at last, and are insatiate
  henceforward,
Not you any more shall be able to foil us, or withhold
  yourselves from us,
We use you, and do not cast you aside—we plant you
  permanently within us,
We fathom you not—we love you—there is perfection in
  you also,
You furnish your parts toward eternity,
Great or small, you furnish your parts toward the soul.

WHEN LILACS LAST
IN THE DOORYARD BLOOM'D

When lilacs last in the dooryard bloom'd,
And the great star early droop'd in the western sky in
  the night,
I mourn'd, and yet shall mourn with ever-returning
  spring.

Ever-returning spring, trinity sure to me you bring,
Lilac blooming perennial and drooping star in the west,
And thought of him I love.

O powerful western fallen star!
O shades of night—O moody, tearful night!
O great star disappear'd—O the black murk that hides
the star!
O cruel hands that hold me powerless—O helpless soul
of me!
O harsh surrounding cloud that will not free my soul.

In the dooryard fronting an old farm-house near the
white-wash'd palings,
Stands the lilac-bush tall-growing with heart-shaped
leaves of rich green,
With many a pointed blossom rising delicate, with the
perfume strong I love,
With every leaf a miracle—and from this bush in the
dooryard,
With delicate-color'd blossoms and heart-shaped leaves
of rich green,
A sprig with its flower I break.

In the swamp in secluded recesses,
A shy and hidden bird is warbling a song.
Solitary the thrush,
The hermit withdrawn to himself, avoiding the settle-
ments,
Sings by himself a song.
Song of the bleeding throat,
Death's outlet song of life, (for well dear brother I know,
If thou wast not granted to sing thou would'st surely die.)

Over the breast of the spring, the land, amid cities,
Amid lanes and through old woods, where lately the
violets peep'd from the ground, spotting the gray
debris,
Amid the grass in the fields each side of the lanes, passing the endless grass,
Passing the yellow-spear'd wheat, every grain from its
shroud in the dark-brown fields uprisen,

Passing the apple-tree blows of white and pink in the
    orchards,
Carrying a corpse to where it shall rest in the grave,
Night and day journeys a coffin.

Coffin that passes through lanes and streets,
Through day and night with the great cloud darkening
    the land,
With the pomp of the inloop'd flags with the cities draped
    in black,
With the show of the States themselves as of crape-veil'd
    women standing,
With processions long and winding and the flambeaus of
    the night,
With the countless torches lit, with the silent sea of faces
    and the unbared heads,
With the waiting depot, the arriving coffin, and the som-
    bre faces,
With dirges through the night, with the thousand voices
    rising strong and solemn,
With all the mournful voices of the dirges pour'd around
    the coffin,
The dim-lit churches and the shuddering organs—where
    amid these you journey,
With the tolling tolling bells' perpetual clang,
Here, coffin that slowly passes,
I give you my sprig of lilac.

(Nor for you, for one alone,
Blossoms and branches green to coffins all I bring,
For fresh as the morning, thus would I chant a song for
    you O sane and sacred death.
All over bouquets of roses,
O death, I cover you over with roses and early lilies,
But mostly and now the lilac that blooms the first,
Copious I break, I break the sprigs from the bushes,
With loaded arms I come, pouring for you,
For you and the coffins all of you O death.)

O western orb sailing the heaven,
Now I know what you must have meant as a month since
    I walk'd,
As I walk'd in silence the transparent shadowy night,
As I saw you had something to tell as you bent to me
    night after night,
As you droop'd from the sky low down as if to my side,
    (while the other stars all look'd on,)
As we wander'd together the solemn night, (for some-
    thing I know not what kept me from sleep,)
As the night advanced, and I saw on the rim of the west
    how full you were of woe,
As I stood on the rising ground in the breeze in the cool
    transparent night,
As I watch'd where you pass'd and was lost in the neth-
    erward black of the night,
As my soul in its trouble dissatisfied sank, as where you
    sad orb,
Concluded, dropt in the night, and was gone.

Sing on there in the swamp,
O singer bashful and tender, I hear your notes, I hear
    your call,
I hear, I come presently, I understand you,
But a moment I linger, for the lustrous star has detain'd me,
The star my departing comrade holds and detains me.

O how shall I warble myself for the dead one there I
    loved?
And how shall I deck my song for the large sweet soul
    that has gone?
And what shall my perfume be for the grave of him I
    love?
Sea-winds blown from east and west,
Blown from the Eastern sea and blown from the Western
    sea, till there on the prairies meeting,
These and with these and the breath of my chant,
I'll perfume the grave of him I love.

O what shall I hang on the chamber walls?
And what shall the pictures be that I hang on the walls,
To adorn the burial-house of him I love?
Pictures of growing spring and farms and homes,
With the Fourth-month eve at sundown, and the gray
    smoke lucid and bright,
With floods of the yellow gold of the gorgeous, indolent,
    sinking sun, burning, expanding the air,
With the fresh sweet herbage under foot, and the pale
    green leaves of the trees prolific,
In the distance the flowing glaze, the breast of the river,
    with a wind-dapple here and there,
With ranging hills on the banks, with many a line against
    the sky, and shadows,
And the city at hand with dwellings so dense, and stacks
    of chimneys,
And all the scenes of life and the workshops, and the
    workmen homeward returning.

Lo, body and soul—this land,
My own Manhattan with spires, and the sparkling and
    hurrying tides, and the ships,
The varied and ample land, the South and the North in
    the light, Ohio's shores and flashing Missouri,
And ever the far-spreading prairies cover'd with grass
    and corn.
Lo, the most excellent sun so calm and haughty,
The violet and purple morn with just-felt breezes,
The gentle soft-born measureless light,
The miracle spreading bathing all, the fulfill'd noon,
The coming eve delicious, the welcome night and the
    stars,
Over my cities shining all, enveloping man and land.

Sing on, sing on you gray-brown bird,
Sing from the swamps, the recesses, pour your chant
    from the bushes,
Limitless out of the dusk, out of the cedars and pines.

Sing on dearest brother, warble your reedy song,
Loud human song, with voice of uttermost woe.
O liquid and free and tender!
O wild and loose to my soul—O wondrous singer!
You only I hear—yet the star holds me, (but will soon depart,)
Yet the lilac with mastering odor holds me.

Now while I sat in the day and look'd forth,
In the close of the day with its light and the fields of spring, and the farmers preparing their crops,
In the large unconscious scenery of my land with its lakes and forests,
In the heavenly aerial beauty, (after the perturb'd winds and the storms,)
Under the arching heavens of the afternoon swift passing, and the voices of children and women,
The many-moving sea-tides, and I saw the ships how they sail'd,
And the summer approaching with richness, and the fields all busy with labor,
And the infinite separate houses, how they all went on, each with its meals and minutia of daily usages,
And the streets how their throbbings throbb'd, and the cities pent—lo, then and there,
Falling upon them all and among them all, enveloping me with the rest,
Appear'd the cloud, appear'd the long black trail,
And I knew death, its thought, and the sacred knowledge of death.

Then with the knowledge of death as walking one side of me,
And the thought of death close-walking the other side of me,
And I in the middle as with companions, and as holding the hands of companions,
I fled forth to the hiding receiving night that talks not,

Down to the shores of the water, the path by the swamp
    in the dimness,
To the solemn shadowy cedars and ghostly pines so still.
And the singer so shy to the rest receiv'd me,
The gray-brown bird I know receiv'd us comrades three,
And he sang the carol of death, and a verse for him I
    love.

From deep secluded recesses,
From the fragrant cedars and the ghostly pines so still,
Came the carol of the bird.

And the charm of the carol rapt me,
As I held as if by their hands my comrades in the night,
And the voice of my spirit tallied the song of the bird.

    Come lovely and soothing death,
Undulate round the world, serenely arriving, arriving,
In the day, in the night, to all, to each,
Sooner or later delicate death.

    Prais'd be the fathomless universe,
For life and joy, and for objects and knowledge curious,
And for love, sweet love—but praise! praise! praise!
For the sure-enwinding arms of cool-enfolding death.

    Dark mother always gliding near with soft feet,
Have none chanted for thee a chant of fullest welcome?
Then I chant it for thee, I glorify thee above all,
I bring thee a song that when thou must indeed come,
    come unfalteringly.

    Approach strong deliveress,
When it is so, when thou hast taken them I joyously sing
    the dead,
Lost in the loving floating ocean of thee,
Laved in the flood of thy bliss O death.

    From me to thee glad serenades,
Dances for thee I propose saluting thee, adornments and
    feastings for thee,
And the sights of the open landscape and the high-spread
    sky are fitting,

And life and the fields, and the huge and thoughtful
    night.
    The night in silence under many a star,
The ocean shore and the husky whispering wave whose
    voice I know,
And the soul turning to thee O vast and well-veil'd death,
And the body gratefully nestling close to thee.
    Over the tree-tops I float thee a song,
Over the rising and sinking waves, over the myriad fields
    and the prairies wide,
Over the dense-pack'd cities all and the teeming wharves
    and ways,
I float this carol with joy, with joy to thee O death.

To the tally of my soul,
Loud and strong kept up the gray-brown bird,
With pure deliberate notes spreading filling the night.
Loud in the pines and cedars dim,
Clear in the freshness moist and the swamp-perfume,
And I with my comrades there in the night.
While my sight that was bound in my eyes unclosed,
As to long panoramas of visions.
And I saw askant the armies,
I saw as in noiseless dreams hundreds of battle-flags,
Borne through the smoke of the battles and pierc'd with
    missiles I saw them,
And carried hither and yon through the smoke, and torn
    and bloody,
And at last but a few shreds left on the staffs, (and all in
    silence,)
And the staffs all splinter'd and broken.
I saw battle-corpses, myriads of them,
And the white skeletons of young men, I saw them,
I saw the debris and debris of all the slain soldiers of the
    war,
But I saw they were not as was thought,
They themselves were fully at rest, they suffer'd not,
The living remain'd and suffer'd, the mother suffer'd,

193

And the wife and the child and the musing comrade
    suffer'd,
And the armies that remain'd suffer'd,

Passing the visions, passing the night,
Passing, unloosing the hold of my comrades' hands,
Passing the song of the hermit bird and the tallying song
    of my soul,
Victorious song, death's outlet song, yet varying ever-
    altering song,
As low and wailing, yet clear the notes, rising and fall-
    ing, flooding the night,
Sadly sinking and fainting, as warning and warning, and
    yet again bursting with joy,
Covering the earth and filling the spread of the heaven,
As that powerful psalm in the night I heard from recesses,
Passing, I leave thee lilac with heart-shaped leaves,
I leave thee there in the door-yard, blooming, returning
    with spring.

I cease from my song for thee,
From my gaze on thee in the west, fronting the west,
    communing with thee,
O comrade lustrous with silver face in the night.

Yet each to keep and all, retrievements out of the night,
The song, the wondrous chant of the gray-brown bird,
And the tallying chant, the echo arous'd in my soul,
With the lustrous and drooping star with the countenance
    full of woe,
With the holders holding my hand nearing the call of
    the bird,
Comrades mine and I in the midst, and their memory
    ever to keep, for the dead I loved so well,
For the sweetest, wisest soul of all my days and lands—
    And this for his dear sake,
Lilac and star and bird twined with the chant of my soul,
There in the fragrant pines and the cedars dusk and dim.

TO THINK OF TIME

1

To think of time—of all that retrospection,
To think of today, and the ages continued henceforward.
Have you guess'd you yourself would not continue?
Have you dreaded these earth-beetles?
Have you fear'd the future would be nothing to you?
Is today nothing? is the beginningless past nothing?
If the future is nothing they are just as surely nothing.
To think that the sun rose in the east—that men and
      women were flexible, real, alive—that every thing
      was alive,
To think that you and I did not see, feel, think, nor bear
      our part,
To think that we are now here and bear our part.

2

Not a day passes, not a minute or second without an
      accouchement,
Not a day passes, not a minute or second without a
      corpse.
The dull nights go over and the dull days also,
The soreness of lying so much in bed goes over,
The physician after long putting off gives the silent and
      terrible look for an answer,
The children come hurried and weeping, and the broth-
      ers and sisters are sent for,
Medicines stand unused on the shelf, (the camphor-smell
      has long pervaded the rooms,)
The faithful hand of the living does not desert the hand
      of the dying,
The twitching lips press lightly on the forehead of the
      dying,
The breath ceases and the pulse of the heart ceases,
The corpse stretches on the bed and the living look upon
      it,

It is palpable as the living are palpable.
The living look upon the corpse with their eyesight,
But without eyesight lingers a different living and looks
curiously on the corpse.

3

To think the thought of death merged in the thought of
materials,
To think of all these wonders of city and country, and
others taking great interest in them, and we taking
no interest in them.
To think how eager we are in building our houses,
To think others shall be just as eager, and we quite
indifferent.
(I see one building the house that serves him a few years,
or seventy or eighty years at most,
I see one building the house that serves him longer than
that.)
Slow-moving and black lines creep over the whole earth
—they never cease—they are the burial lines,
He that was President was buried, and he that is now
President shall surely be buried.

4

A reminiscence of the vulgar fate,
A frequent sample of the life and death of workmen,
Each after his kind.
Cold dash of waves at the ferry-wharf, posh and ice in
the river, half-frozen mud in the streets,
A gray discouraged sky overhead, the short last daylight
of December,
A hearse and stages, the funeral of an old Broadway
stage-driver, the cortege mostly drivers.
Steady the trot to the cemetery, duly rattles the death-
bell,
The gate is pass'd, the new-dug grave is halted at, the
living alight, the hearse uncloses,

The coffin is pass'd out, lower'd and settled, the whip is
    laid on the coffin, the earth is swiftly shovel'd in,
The mound above is flatted with the spades—silence,
A minute—no one moves or speaks—it is done,
He is decently put away—is there any thing more?

He was a good fellow, free-mouth'd, quick-temper'd, not
    bad-looking,
Ready with life or death for a friend, fond of women,
    gambled, ate hearty, drank hearty,
Had known what it was to be flush, grew low-spirited
    toward the last, sicken'd, was help'd by a contri-
    bution,
Died, aged forty-one years—and that was his funeral.

Thumb extended, finger uplifted, apron, cape, gloves,
    strap, wet-weather clothes, whip carefully chosen,
Boss, spotter, starter, hostler, somebody loafing on you,
    you loafing on somebody, headway, man before
    and man behind,
Good day's work, bad day's work, pet stock, mean stock,
    first out, last out, turning-in at night,
To think that these are so much and so nigh to other
    drivers, and he there takes no interest in them.

WHISPERS OF HEAVENLY DEATH

WHISPERS of heavenly death murmur'd I hear,
Labial gossip of night, sibilant chorals,
Footsteps gently ascending, mystical breezes wafted soft
    and low,
Ripples of unseen rivers, tides of a current flowing, for-
    ever flowing
(Or is it the plashing of tears? the measureless waters
    of human tears?)

I see, just see skyward, great cloud-masses;
Mournfully, slowly they roll, silently swelling and mix-
      ing,
With at times a half-dimm'd sadden'd far-off star,
Appearing and disappearing.

(Some parturition rather, some solemn immortal birth;
On the frontiers to eyes impenetrable,
Some soul is passing over.)

GOOD-BYE, MY FANCY

GOOD-BYE, my Fancy!
      Farewell, dear mate, dear love!
      I'm going away, I know not where,
Or to what fortune, or whether I may ever see you again,
So Good-bye, my Fancy.

Now for my last—let me look back a moment;
The slower fainter ticking of the clock is in me,
Exit, nightfall, and soon the heart-thud stopping.
Long have we lived, joy'd, caress'd together;
Delightful!—now separation—Good-bye, my Fancy.

Yet let me not be too hasty:
Long indeed have we lived, slept, filter'd, become really
      blended into one;
Then if we die we die together (yes, we'll remain one),
If we go anywhere we'll go together to meet what hap-
      pens,
May-be we'll be better off and blither, and learn some-
      thing,
May-be it is yourself now really ushering me to the true
      songs (who knows?),
May-be it is you the mortal knob really undoing, turning
      —so now finally,
Good-bye—and hail! my Fancy.

Emily Dickinson

A LIGHT EXISTS IN SPRING

A LIGHT exists in spring
    Not present on the year
At any other period,
    When March is scarcely here.

A color stands abroad
    On solitary hills
That science cannot overtake,
    But human nature feels.

It waits upon the lawn;
    It shows the furthest tree
Upon the furthest slope we know;
    It almost speaks to me.

Then, as horizons step,
    Or noons report away,
Without the formula of sound,
    It passes, and we stay:

A quality of loss
    Affecting our content,
As trade had suddenly encroached
    Upon a sacrament.

AS IMPERCEPTIBLY AS GRIEF

As imperceptibly as grief
    The summer lapsed away,—
Too imperceptible, at last,
    To seem like perfidy.

199

A quietness distilled,
As twilight long begun,
Or Nature, spending with herself
Sequestered afternoon.

The dusk drew earlier in,
The morning foreign shone,—
A courteous, yet harrowing grace,
As guest who would be gone.

And thus, without a wing,
Or service of a keel,
Our summer made her light escape
Into the beautiful.

A CERTAIN SLANT OF LIGHT

THERE's a certain slant of light,
On winter afternoons,
That oppresses, like the weight
Of cathedral tunes.

Heavenly hurt it gives us;
We can find no scar,
But internal difference
Where the meanings are.

None may teach it anything
'Tis the seal, despair,—
An imperial affliction
Sent us of the air.

When it comes, the landscape listens,
Shadows hold their breath;
When it goes, 'tis like the distance
On the look of death.

DYING

I HEARD a fly buzz when I died;
　The stillness round my form
Was like the stillness in the air
　Between the heaves of storm.

The eyes beside had wrung them dry,
　And breaths were gathering sure
For that last onset, when the king
　Be witnessed in his power.

I willed my keepsakes, signed away
　What portion of me I
Could make assignable—and then
　There interposed a fly,

With blue, uncertain, stumbling buzz,
　Between the light and me;
And then the windows failed, and then
　I could not see to see.

THE CHARIOT

BECAUSE I could not stop for Death,
He kindly stopped for me;
The carriage held but just ourselves
And Immortality.

We slowly drove, we knew no haste,
And I had put away
My labour, and my leisure too,
For his civility.

We passed the school where children played
Their lessons scarcely done;

We passed the fields of gazing grain,
We passed the setting sun.

We paused before a house that seemed
A swelling on the ground;
The roof was scarcely visible,
The cornice but a mound.

Since then 'tis centuries; but each
Feels shorter than the day
I first surmised the horses' heads
Were toward eternity.

I FELT A FUNERAL
IN MY BRAIN

I FELT a funeral in my brain,
    And mourners, to and fro,
Kept treading, treading, till it seemed
    That sense was breaking through.

And when they all were seated,
    A service like a drum
Kept beating, beating, till I thought
    My mind was going numb.

And then I heard them lift a box,
    And creak across my soul
With those same boots of lead, again.
    Then space began to toll

As all the heavens were a bell,
    And Being but an ear,
And I and silence some strange race,
    Wrecked, solitary, here.

EMILY DICKINSON

IN WINTER, IN MY ROOM

In Winter, in my room,
I came upon a worm,
Pink, lank, and warm.
But as he was a worm
And worms presume,
Not quite with him at home—
Secured him by a string
To something neighbouring,
And went along.

A trifle afterward
A thing occurred,
I'd not believe it if I heard—
But state with creeping blood;
A snake, with mottles rare,
Surveyed my chamber floor,
In feature as the worm before,
But ringed with power.
The very string
With which I tied him, too,
When he was mean and new,
That string was there.

I shrank—"How fair you are!"
Propitiation's claw—
"Afraid," he hissed,
"Of me?
No cordiality?"
He fathomed me.

Then to a rhythm slim
Secreted in his form,
As patterns swim,
Projected him.

That time I flew,
Both eyes his way,
Lest he pursue—
Nor ever ceased to run,
Till in a distant town,
Towns on from mine—
I sat me down;
This was a dream.

IN THE GARDEN

A BIRD came down the walk:
He did not know I saw;
He bit an angle-worm in halves
And ate the fellow raw.

And then he drank a dew
From a convenient grass,
And then hopped sidewise to the wall
To let a beetle pass.

He glanced with rapid eyes
That hurried all abroad—
They looked like frightened beads, I thought;
He stirred his velvet head

Like one in danger; cautious,
I offered him a crumb,
And he unrolled his feathers
And rowed him softer home

Than oars divide the ocean,
Too silver for a seam,
Or butterflies, off banks of noon,
Leap, plashless, as they swim.

PARTING

My life closed twice before its close;
It yet remains to see
If Immortality unveil
A third event to me,

So huge, so hopeless to conceive,
As these that twice befell.
Parting is all we know of heaven,
And all we need of hell.

BY THE SEA

I STARTED early, took my dog,
And visited the sea;
The mermaids in the basement
Came out to look at me,

And frigates in the upper floor
Extended hempen hands,
Presuming me to be a mouse
Aground, upon the sands.

But no man moved me till the tide
Went past my simple shoe,
And past my apron and my belt,
And past my bodice too,

And made as he would eat me up
As wholly as a dew
Upon a dandelion's sleeve—
And then I started too.

And he—he followed close behind;
I felt his silver heel

Upon my ankle,—then my shoes
Would overflow with pearl.

Until we met the solid town,
No man he seemed to know;
And bowing with a mighty look
At me, the sea withdrew.

I NEVER SAW A MOOR

I NEVER saw a moor,
I never saw the sea;
Yet know I how the heather looks,
And what a wave must be.

I never spoke with God,
Nor visited in heaven;
Yet certain am I of the spot
As if the chart were given.

I TASTE A LIQUOR NEVER BREWED

I TASTE a liquor never brewed,
From tankards scooped in pearl;
Not all the vats upon the Rhine
Yield such an alcohol!

Inebriate of air am I,
And debauchee of dew,
Reeling, through endless summer days,
From inns of molten blue.

When landlords turn the drunken bee
Out of the foxglove's door,
When butterflies renounce their drams,
I shall but drink the more!

Till seraphs swing their snowy hats,
And saints to windows run,
To see the little tippler
Leaning against the sun!

THE LAST NIGHT THAT SHE LIVED

THE last night that she lived,
It was a common night,
Except the dying; this to us
Made nature different.

We noticed smallest things,—
Things overlooked before,
By this great light upon our minds
Italicized, as 'twere.

That others could exist
While she must finish quite,
A jealousy for her arose
So nearly infinite.

We waited while she passed;
It was a narrow time,
Too jostled were our souls to speak,
At length the notice came.

She mentioned, and forgot;
Then lightly as a reed
Bent to the water, shivered scarce,
Consented, and was dead.

And we, we placed the hair,
And drew the head erect;
And then an awful leisure was,
Our faith to regulate.

I DIED FOR BEAUTY

I DIED for beauty, but was scarce
Adjusted in the tomb,
When one who died for truth was lain
In an adjoining room.

He questioned softly why I failed?
"For beauty," I replied.
"And I for truth—the two are one;
We brethren are," he said.

And so, as kinsmen met a-night,
We talked between the rooms,
Until the moss had reached our lips,
And covered up our names.

MUCH MADNESS

MUCH madness is divinest sense
To a discerning eye;
Much sense the starkest madness.
'Tis the majority
In this, as all, prevails.
Assent, and you are sane;
Demur,—you're straightway dangerous,
And handled with a chain.

SUCCESS IS COUNTED SWEETEST

SUCCESS is counted sweetest
By those who ne'er succeed.
To comprehend a nectar
Requires sorest need.

Not one of all the purple host
Who took the flag today

Can tell the definition,
So clear, of victory,

As he defeated, dying,
On whose forbidden ear
The distant strains of triumph
Break, agonized and clear.

TO FIGHT ALOUD IS BRAVE

To fight aloud is very brave,
But gallanter, I know,
Who charge within the bosom,
The cavalry of woe.

Who win, and nations do not see,
Who fall, and none observe,
Whose dying eyes no country
Regards with patriot love.

We trust, in plumed procession,
For such the angels go,
Rank after rank, with even feet
And uniforms of snow.

PAIN HAS AN ELEMENT

PAIN has an element of blank;
It cannot recollect
When it began, or if there were
A day when it was not.

It has no future but itself,
Its infinite realms contain
Its past, enlightened to perceive
New periods of pain.

OUR JOURNEY HAD ADVANCED

Our journey had advanced;
Our feet were almost come
To that odd fork in Being's road,
Eternity by term.

Our pace took sudden awe,
Our feet reluctant led.
Before were cities, but between,
The forest of the dead.

Retreat was out of hope,—
Behind, a sealéd route,
Eternity's white flag before,
And God at every gate.

'TWAS WARM AT FIRST

'Twas warm at first like us,
Until there crept there on
A chill, like frost upon a glass,
Till all the scene be gone.

The forehead copied stone,
The fingers grew too cold
To ache, and like a skater's brook
The busy eyes congealed.

It straightened—that was all—
It crowded cold to cold—
It multiplied indifference
As Pride were all it could.

And even when with cords
'Twas lowered like a freight,
It made no signal, nor demurred,
But dropped like adamant.

I HAD BEEN HUNGRY

I HAD been hungry all the years;
My noon had come to dine;
I, trembling, drew the table near,
And touched the curious wine.

'Twas this on tables I had seen,
When turning, hungry, lone,
I looked in windows, for the wealth
I could not hope to own.

I did not know the ample bread;
'Twas so unlike the crumb
The birds and I had often shared
In Nature's dining-room.

The plenty hurt me, 'twas so new,—
Myself felt ill and odd,
As berry of a mountain bush
Transplanted to the road.

Nor was I hungry; so I found
That hunger was a way
Of persons outside windows,
The entering takes away.

I AM AFRAID TO OWN A BODY

I AM afraid to own a body,
I am afraid to own a soul;
Profound, precarious property,
Possession not optional.

Double estate entailed at pleasure
Upon an unsuspecting hair;
Duke in a moment of deathlessness,
And God for a frontier.

211

UNDUE SIGNIFICANCE

UNDUE significance a starving man attaches
To food
Far off; he sighs, and therefore hopeless,
And therefore good.

Partaken, it relieves indeed, but proves us
That spices fly
In the receipt. It was the distance
Was savory.

BEFORE I GOT MY EYE PUT OUT

BEFORE I got my eye put out,
I liked as well to see
As other creatures that have eyes,
And know no other way.

But were it told to me, to-day,
That I might have the sky
For mine, I tell you that my heart
Would split, for size of me.

The meadows mine, the mountains mine,—
All forests, stintless stars,
As much of noon as I could take
Between my finite eyes.

The motions of the dipping birds,
The lightning's jointed road,
For mine to look at when I liked—
The news would strike me dead!

So, safer, guess, with just my soul
Upon the window-pane
Where other creatures put their eyes,
Incautious of the sun.

EMILY DICKINSON

FARTHER IN THE SUMMER

FARTHER in summer than the birds,
Pathetic from the grass,
A minor nation celebrates
Its unobtrusive mass.

No ordinance is seen,
So gradual the grace,
A pensive custom it becomes,
Enlarging loneliness.

Antiquest felt at noon
When August, burning low,
Calls forth this spectral canticle,
Repose to typify.

Remit as yet no grace,
No furrow on the glow,
Yet a druidic difference
Enhances nature now.

NOT WITH A CLUB

NOT with a club the heart is broken,
Nor with a stone;
A whip, so small you could not see it,
I've known

To lash the magic creature
Till it fell,
Yet that whip's name too noble
Then to tell.

Magnanimous of bird
By boy descried,
To sing unto the stone
Of which it died.

THE FIRST DAY'S NIGHT
HAD COME

THE first Day's Night had come—
And, grateful that a thing
So terrible had been endured,
I told my Soul to sing.

She said her strings were snapt,
Her bow to atoms blown;
And so, to mend her, gave me work
Until another morn.

And then a Day as huge
As Yesterday in pairs
Unrolled its horror on my face—
Until it blocked my eyes.

AFTER GREAT PAIN
A FORMAL FEELING COMES

AFTER great pain a formal feeling comes—
The nerves sit ceremonious like tombs;
The stiff Heart questions—was it He that bore?
And yesterday—or centuries before?

The feet mechanical
Go round a wooden way
Of ground or air or Ought, regardless grown,
A quartz contentment like a stone.

This is the hour of lead
Remembered if outlived,
As freezing persons recollect the snow—
First chill, then stupor, then the letting go.

BEAUTY IS NOT CAUSED,—IT IS

BEAUTY is not caused,—it is;
Chase it and it ceases,
Chase it not and it abides,
Overtake the creases

In the meadow when the wind
Runs his fingers thro' it?
Deity will see to it
That you never do it.

ONE BLESSING HAD I

ONE blessing had I, than the rest
    So larger to my eyes
That I stopped gauging, satisfied,
    For this enchanted size.

It was the limit of my dream,
    The focus of my prayer,—
A perfect, paralyzing bliss
    Contented as despair.

I knew no more of want or cold,
    Phantasms both become,
For this new value in the soul,
    Supremest earthly sum.

The heaven below the heaven above
    Obscured with ruddier hue.
Life's latitude leant over-full;
    The judgment perished, too.

Why joys so scantily disburse,
    Why Paradise defer,
Why floods are served to us in bowls,—
    I speculate no more.

215

THE TRAIN

I LIKE to see it lap the miles,
And lick the valleys up,
And stop to feed itself at tanks;
And then, prodigious, step

Around a pile of mountains,
And, supercilious, peer
In shanties by the sides of roads;
And then a quarry pare

To fit its sides, and crawl between,
Complaining all the while
In horrid, hooting stanza;
Then chase itself down hill

And neigh like Boanerges;
Then, punctual as a star,
Stop—docile and omnipotent—
At its own stable door.

THE SNAKE

A NARROW fellow in the grass
Occasionally rides;
You may have met him—did you not,
His notice sudden is.

The grass divides as with a comb,
A spotted shaft is seen;
And then it closes at your feet
And opens further on.

He likes a boggy acre,
A floor too cool for corn.

Yet when a child, and barefoot,
I more than once, at morn,

Have passed, I thought, a whip-lash
Unbraiding in the sun—
When, stooping to secure it,
It wrinkled, and was gone.

Several of nature's people
I know, and they know me;
I feel for them a transport
Of cordiality;

But never met this fellow,
Attended or alone,
Without a tighter breathing,
And zero at the bone.

LOVE IS THAT LATER THING
THAN DEATH

Love is that later thing than death,
More previous than life,
Confirms it at its entrance and
Usurps it of itself;

Tastes death, the first to prove the sting,
The second, to its friend,
Disarms the little interval,
Deposits him with God.

Then hovers, an inferior guard,
Lest this belovéd charge
Need, once in an eternity,
A lesser than the large.

THE LAMP BURNS SURE, WITHIN

THE lamp burns sure, within,
Tho' serfs supply the oil,—
It matters not the busy wick
At her phosphoric toil!

The slave forgets to fill—
The lamp burns golden on,
Unconscious that the oil is out
As that the slave is gone!

TELL ALL THE TRUTH

TELL all the truth but tell it slant,
Success in circuit lies,
Too bright for our infirm delight
The truth's superb surprise;

As lightning to the children eased
With explanation kind,
The truth must dazzle gradually
Or every man be blind.

FLOSS WON'T SAVE YOU

FLOSS won't save you from an abyss,
But a rope will,
Notwithstanding a rope for a souvenir
Does not look as well.

But I tell you every step is a sluice,
And every stop a well.
Now will you have the rope or the floss?
Prices reasonable.

LOVE CAN DO ALL
BUT RAISE THE DEAD

Love can do all but raise the dead;
I doubt if even that
From such a giant were withheld
Were flesh equivalent.

But love is tired and must sleep,
And hungry and must graze,
And so abets the shining fleet
Till it is out of gaze.

SHE LAY AS IF AT PLAY

She lay as if at play
Her life had leaped away
Intending to return—
But not so soon.

Her merry arms half dropt
As if for lull of sport
An instant had forgot
The trick to start.

Her dancing eyes ajar
As if their owner were
Still sparkling through
For fun at you.

Her morning at the door,
Devising, I am sure,
To force her sleep—
So light, so deep.

THE FINAL INCH

'Twas like a maelstrom, with a notch
That nearer every day
Kept narrowing its boiling wheel
Until the agony

Toyed coolly with the final inch
Of your delirious hem,
And you dropped, lost, when something broke
And let you from a dream

As if a goblin with a gauge
Kept measuring the hours,
Until you felt your second weigh
Helpless in his paws,

And not a sinew, stirred, could help,
And sense was setting numb,
When God remembered, and the fiend
Let go then, overcome;

As if your sentence stood pronounced,
And you were frozen led
From dungeon's luxury of doubt
To gibbets and the dead;

And when the film had stitched your eyes,
A creature gasped "Reprieve!"
Which anguish was the utterest then,
To perish, or to live?

Sidney Lanier

THE MARSHES OF GLYNN

Glooms of the live-oaks, beautiful-braided and woven
With intricate shades of the vines that myriad-cloven
  Clamber the forks of the multiform boughs,—
      Emerald twilights,—
      Virginal shy lights,
Wrought of the leaves to allure to the whisper of vows,
When lovers pace timidly down through the green col-
    onnades
Of the dim sweet woods, of the dear dark woods,
  Of the heavenly woods and glades,
That run to the radiant marginal sand-beach within
    The wide sea-marshes of Glynn;—

Beautiful glooms, soft dusks in the noon-day fire,—
Wildwood privacies, closets of lone desire,
Chamber from chamber parted with wavering arras of
    leaves,—
Cells for the passionate pleasure of prayer to the soul
    that grieves,
Pure with a sense of the passing of saints through the
    wood.
Cool for the dutiful weighing of ill with good;—
O braided dusks of the oak and woven shades of the vine,
While the riotous noon-day sun of the June-day long
    did shine
Ye held me fast in your heart and I held you fast in mine;
But now when the noon is no more, and riot is rest,
And the sun is a-wait at the ponderous gate of the West,
And the slant yellow beam down the wood-aisle doth
    seem
Like a lane into heaven that leads from a dream,—

Ay, now, when my soul all day hath drunken the soul of
    the oak,
And my heart is at ease from men, and the wearisome
    sound of the stroke
    Of the scythe of time and the trowel of trade is low,
    And belief overmasters doubt, and I know that I know,
And my spirit is grown to a lordly great compass within,
That the length and the breadth and the sweep of the
    marshes of Glynn
Will work me no fear like the fear they have wrought
    me of yore
When length was fatigue, and when breadth was but
    bitterness sore,
And when terror and shrinking and dreary unnamable
    pain
Drew over me out of the merciless miles of the plain,—

Oh, now, unafraid, I am fain to face
    The vast sweet visage of space.
To the edge of the wood I am drawn, I am drawn,
Where the gray beach glimmering runs, as a belt of the
    dawn,
    For a mete and a mark
      To the forest-dark:—
        So:
Affable live-oak, leaning low,—
Thus—with your favor—soft, with a reverent hand
(Not lightly touching your person, Lord of the land!),
Bending your beauty aside, with a step I stand
On the firm-packed sand,
    Free
By a world of marsh that borders a world of sea.
  Sinuous southward and sinuous northward the shim-
    mering band
  Of the sand-beach fastens the fringe of the marsh to
    the folds of the land.
Inward and outward to northward and southward the
    beach-lines linger and curl

222

As a silver-wrought garment that clings to and follows
    the firm sweet limbs of a girl.
Vanishing, swerving, evermore curving again into sight,
Softly the sand-beach wavers away to a dim gray looping
    of light.
And what if behind me to westward the wall of the
    woods stands high?
The world lies east: how ample, the marsh and the sea
    and the sky!
A league and a league of marsh-grass, waist-high, broad
    in the blade,
Green, and all of a height, and unflecked with a light or
    a shade,
Stretch leisurely off, in a pleasant plain,
To the terminal blue of the main.

Oh, what is abroad in the marsh and the terminal sea?
Somehow my soul seems suddenly free
From the weighing of fate and the sad discussion of sin,
By the length and the breadth and the sweep of the
    marshes of Glynn.

Ye marshes, how candid and simple and nothing-with-
    holding and free
Ye publish yourselves to the sky and offer yourselves to
    the sea!
Tolerant plains, that suffer the sea and the rains and the
    sun,
Ye spread and span like the catholic man who hath
    mightily won
God out of knowledge and good out of infinite pain
And sight out of blindness and purity out of a stain.

As the marsh-hen secretly builds on the watery sod,
Behold I will build me a nest on the greatness of God:
I will fly in the greatness of God as the marsh-hen flies
In the freedom that fills all the space 'twixt the marsh
    and the skies:

By so many roots as the marsh-grass sends in the sod
I will heartily lay me a-hold on the greatness of God:
Oh, like to the greatness of God is the greatness within
The range of the marshes, the liberal marshes of Glynn.

And the sea lends large, as the marsh: lo, out of his plenty
      the sea
Pours fast: full soon the time of the flood-tide must be:
Look how the grace of the sea doth go
About and about through the intricate channels that flow
    Here and there,
        Everywhere,
Till his waters have flooded the uttermost creeks and the
    low-lying lanes,
And the marsh is meshed with a million veins,
That like as with rosy and silvery essences flow
  In the rose-and-silver evening glow.
      Farewell, my lord Sun!
The creeks overflow: a thousand rivulets run
'Twixt the roots of the sod; the blades of the marsh-grass
    stir;
Passeth a hurrying sound of wings that westward whir;
Passeth, and all is still; and the currents cease to run;
And the sea and the marsh are one.

How still the plains of the waters be!
The tide is in his ecstasy.
The tide is at his highest height:
    And it is night.

And now from the Vast of the Lord will the waters of
    sleep
Roll in on the souls of men,
But who will reveal to our waking ken
The forms that swim and the shapes that creep
    Under the waters of sleep?

OPPOSITION

Of fret, of dark, of thorn, of chill,
  Complain no more; for these, O heart,
Direct the random of the will
  As rhymes direct the rage of art.

The lute's fixt fret, that runs athwart
  The strain and purpose of the string,
For governance and nice consort
  Doth bar his wilful wavering.

The dark hath many dear avails;
  The dark distils divinest dews;
The dark is rich with nightingales,
  With dreams, and with the heavenly Muse.

Bleeding with thorns of petty strife,
  I'll ease (as lovers do) my smart
With sonnets to my lady Life
  Writ red in issues from the heart.

What grace may lie within the chill
  Of favor frozen fast in scorn!
When Good's a-freeze, we call it Ill!
  This rosy Time is glacier-born.

Of fret, of dark, of thorn, of chill,
  Complain thou not, O heart; for these
Bank-in the current of the will
  To uses, arts, and charities.

STRUGGLE

My soul is like the oar that momently
  Dies in a desperate stress beneath the wave,
Then glitters out again and sweeps the sea:
  Each second I'm new-born from some new grave.

225

THE SYMPHONY

"O TRADE! O Trade! would thou wert dead!
The Time needs heart—'tis tired of head:
We're all for love," the violins said.
"Of what avail the rigorous tale
Of bill for coin and box for bale?
Grant thee, O Trade! thine uttermost hope:
Level red gold with blue sky-slope,
And base it deep as devils grope:
When all's done, what hast thou won
Of the only sweet that's under the sun?
Ay, canst thou buy a single sigh
Of true love's least, least ecstasy?"
Then, with a bridegroom's heart-beats trembling,
All the mightier strings assembling
Ranged them on the violins' side
As when the bridegroom leads the bride,
And, heart in voice, together cried:
"Yea, what avail the endless tale
Of gain by cunning and plus by sale?
Look up the land, look down the land
The poor, the poor, the poor, they stand
Wedged by the pressing of Trade's hand
Against an inward-opening door
That pressure tightens ever more:
They sigh a monstrous foul-air sigh
For the outside leagues of liberty,
Where Art, sweet lark, translates the sky
Into a heavenly melody.
'Each day, all day' (these poor folks say),
'In the same old year-long, drear-long way,
We weave in the mills and heave in the kilns,
We sieve mine-meshes under the hills,
And thieve much gold from the Devil's bank tills,
To relieve, O God, what manner of ills?—
The beasts, they hunger, and eat, and die;
And so do we, and the world's a sty;

226

Hush, fellow-swine: why nuzzle and cry?
Swinehood hath no remedy
Say many men, and hasten by,
Clamping the nose and blinking the eye
But who said once, in the lordly tone,
Man shall not live by bread alone
But all that cometh from the Throne?
  Hath God said so?
  But Trade saith *No:*
And the kilns and the curt-tongued mills say *Go:*
There's plenty that can, if you can't: we know.
Move out, if you think you're underpaid.
The poor are prolific; we're not afraid;
  Trade is trade."
Threat this passionate protesting
Meekly changed, and softened till
It sank to sad requesting
And suggesting sadder still:
"And oh, if men might some time see
How piteous-false the poor decree
That trade no more than trade must be!
Does business mean, *Die, you—live, I?*
Then 'Trade is trade' but sings a lie:
'Tis only war grown miserly.
If business is battle, name it so:
War-crimes less will shame it so,
And widows less will blame it so.
Alas, for the poor to have some part
In yon sweet living lands of Art,
Makes problem not for head, but heart.
Vainly might Plato's brain revolve it:
Plainly the heart of a child could solve it."

And then, as when from words that seem but rude
We pass to silent pain that sits abroad
Back in our heart's great dark and solitude,
So sank the strings to gentle throbbing
Of long chords change-marked with sobbing—

227

Motherly sobbing, not distinctlier heard
Than half wing-openings of the sleeping bird,
Some dream of danger to her young hath stirred.
Then stirring and demurring ceased, and lo!
Every least ripple of the strings' song-flow
Died to a level with each level bow
And made a great chord tranquil-surfaced so,
As a brook beneath his curving bank doth go
To linger in the sacred dark and green
Where many boughs the still pool overlean
And many leaves make shadow with their sheen.
   But presently
A velvet flute-note fell down pleasantly
Upon the bosom of that harmony,
And sailed and sailed incessantly,
As if a petal from a wild-rose blown
Had fluttered down upon that pool of tone
And boatwise dropped o' the convex side
And floated down the glassy tide
And clarified and glorified
The solemn spaces where the shadows bide.
From the warm concave of that fluted note
Somewhat, half song, half odor, forth did float,
As if a rose might somehow be a throat:
"When Nature from her far-off glen
Flutes her soft messages to men,
    The flute can say them o'er again;
    Yea, Nature, singing sweet and lone,
Breathes through life's strident polyphone
The flute-voice in the world of tone.
    Sweet friends,
    Man's love ascends
To finer and diviner ends
Than man's mere thought e'er comprehends.
For I, e'en I,
As here I lie,
A petal on a harmony,
Demand of Science whence and why

Man's tender pain, man's inward cry,
When he doth gaze on earth and sky?
I am not overbold:
  I hold
Full powers from Nature manifold.
I speak for each no-tonguèd tree
That, spring by spring, doth nobler be,
And dumbly and most wistfully
His mighty prayerful arms outspreads
Above men's oft-unheeding heads,
And his big blessing downward sheds.
I speak for all-shaped blooms and leaves,
Lichens on stones and moss on eaves,
Grasses and grains in ranks and sheaves;
Broad-fronded ferns and keen-leaved canes,
And briery mazes bounding lanes,
And marsh-plants, thirsty-cupped for rains,
And milky stems and sugary veins;
For every long-armed woman-vine
That round a piteous tree doth twine;
For passionate odors, and divine
Pistils, and petals crystalline;
All purities of shady springs,
All shynesses of film-winged things
That fly from tree-trunks and bark-rings;
All modesties of mountain-fawns
That leap to covert from wild lawns,
And tremble if the day but dawns;
All sparklings of small beady eyes
Of birds, and sidelong glances wise
Wherewith the jay hints tragedies;
All piquancies of prickly burs,
And smoothnesses of downs and furs
Of eiders and of minevers;
All limpid honeys that do lie
At stamen-bases, nor deny
The humming-birds' fine roguery,
Bee-thighs, nor any butterfly;

229

All gracious curves of slender wings,
Bark-mottlings, fibre-spiralings,
Fern-wavings and leaf-flickerings;
Each dial-marked leaf and flower-bell
Wherewith in every lonesome dell
Time to himself his hours doth tell;
All tree-sounds, rustlings of pine cones,
Wind-sighings, doves' melodious moans,
And night's unearthly under-tones;
All placid lakes and waveless deeps,
All cool reposing mountain-steeps,
Vale-calms and tranquil lotos-sleeps;—
Yea, all fair forms, and sounds, and lights,
And warmths, and mysteries, and mights,
Of Nature's utmost depths and heights,
—These doth my timid tongue present,
Their mouthpiece and leal instrument
And servant, all love-eloquent.
I heard, when *All for love* the violins cried:
So, Nature calls through all her system wide,
Give me thy love, O man, so long denied.
Much time is run, and man hath changed his ways,
Since Nature, in the antique fable-days,
Was hid from man's true love by proxy fays,
False fauns and rascal gods that stole her praise.
The nymphs, cold creatures of man's colder brain,
Chilled Nature's streams till man's warm heart was
                                                    fain
Never to lave its love in them again.
Later, a sweet Voice *Love thy neighbor* said;
Then first the bounds of neighborhood outspread
Beyond all confines of old ethnic dread.
Vainly the Jew might wag his covenant head:
All men are neighbors, so the sweet Voice said.
So, when man's arms had circled all man's race,
The liberal compass of his warm embrace
Stretched bigger yet in the dark bounds of space;
With hands a-grope he felt smooth Nature's grace,

Drew her to breast and kissed her sweetheart face:
Yea, man found neighbors in great hills and trees
And streams and clouds and suns and birds and bees,
And throbbed with neighbor-loves in loving these.
But oh, the poor! the poor! the poor!
That stand by the inward-opening door
Trade's hand doth tighten ever more,
And sigh their monstrous foul-air sigh
For the outside hills of liberty,
Where Nature spreads her wild blue sky
For Art to make into melody!
Thou Trade! thou king of the modern days!
    Change thy ways,
    Change thy ways;
Let the sweaty laborers file
    A little while,
    A little while,
Where Art and Nature sing and smile.
Trade! is thy heart all dead, all dead?
And hast thou nothing but a head?
I'm all for heart," the flute-voice said,
And into sudden silence fled,
Like as a blush that while 'tis red
Dies to a still, still white instead.

    Thereto a thrilling calm succeeds,
Till presently the silence breeds
A little breeze among the reeds
That seems to blow by sea-marsh weeds:
Then from the gentle stir and fret
Sings out the melting clarionet,
Like as a lady sings while yet
Her eyes with salty tears are wet.
"O Trade! O Trade!" the Lady said,
"I too will wish thee utterly dead
If all thy heart is in thy head.
For O my God! and O my God!

231

What shameful ways have women trod
At beckoning of Trade's golden rod!
Alas when sighs are traders' lies,
And heart's-ease eyes and violet eyes
  Are merchandise!
O purchased lips that kiss with pain!
O cheeks coin-spotted with smirch and stain!
O trafficked hearts that break in twain!
—And yet what wonder at my sisters' crime?
So hath Trade withered up Love's sinewy prime,
Men love not women as in olden time.
Ah, not in these cold merchantable days
Deem men their life an opal gray, where plays
The one red Sweet of gracious ladies'-praise.
Now, comes a suitor with sharp prying eye—
Says, *Here, you Lady, if you'll sell, I'll buy:*
Come, heart for heart—a trade? What! weeping? why?
Shame on such wooers' dapper mercery!
I would my lover kneeling at my feet
In humble manliness should cry, *O sweet!*
I know not if thy heart my heart will greet:
I ask not if thy love my love can meet:
Whate'er thy worshipful soft tongue shall say,
I'll kiss thine answer, be it yea or nay:
I do but know I love thee, and I pray
To be thy knight until my dying day.
Woe him that cunning trades in hearts contrives!
Base love good women to base loving drives
If men loved larger, larger were our lives;
And wooed they nobler, won they nobler wives."

There thrust the bold straightforward horn
To battle for that lady lorn,
With heartsome voice of mellow scorn,
Like any knight in knighthood's morn.
  "Now comfort thee," said he,
    "Fair Lady.
For God shall right thy grievous wrong,

And man shall sing thee a true-love song,
Voiced in act his whole life long,
Yea, all thy sweet life long,
Fair Lady.
Where's he that craftily hath said,
The day of chivalry is dead?
I'll prove that lie upon his head,
Or I will die instead,
Fair Lady.
Is Honor gone into his grave?
Hath Faith become a caitiff knave,
And Selfhood turned into a slave
To work in Mammon's cave,
Fair Lady?
Will Truth's long blade ne'er gleam again?
Hath Giant Trade in dungeons slain
All great contempts of mean-got gain
And hates of inward stain,
Fair Lady?
For aye shall name and fame be sold,
And place be hugged for the sake of gold,
And smirch-robed Justice feebly scold
At Crime all money-bold,
Fair Lady?
Shall self-wrapt husbands aye forget
Kiss-pardons for the daily fret
Wherewith sweet wifely eyes are wet—
Blind to lips kiss-wise set—
Fair Lady?
Shall lovers higgle, heart for heart,
Till wooing grows a trading mart
Where much for little, and all for part,
Make love a cheapening art,
Fair Lady?
Shall women scorch for a single sin
That her betrayer may revel in,
And she be burnt, and he but grin

233

When that the flames begin,
    Fair Lady?
Shall ne'er prevail the woman's plea,
We maids would far, far whiter be
If that our eyes might sometimes see
    Men maids in purity,
       Fair Lady?
Shall Trade aye salve his conscience-aches
With jibes at Chivalry's old mistakes—
The wars that o'erhot knighthood makes
    For Christ's and ladies' sakes,
       Fair Lady?
Now by each knight that e'er hath prayed
To fight like a man and love like a maid,
Since Pembroke's life, as Pembroke's blade,
    I' the scabbard, death, was laid,
       Fair Lady,
I dare avouch my faith is bright
That God doth right and God hath might.
Nor time hath changed His hair to white,
    Nor His dear love to spite,
       Fair Lady.
I doubt no doubts: I strive, and shrive my clay,
And fight my fight in the patient modern way
For true love and for thee—ah me! and pray
    To be thy knight until my dying day,
       Fair Lady."
Made end that knightly horn, and spurred away
Into the thick of the melodious fray.

And then the hautboy played and smiled,
And sang like any large-eyed child,
Cool-hearted and all undefiled.
    "Huge Trade!" he said,
"Would thou wouldst lift me on thy head
And run where'er my finger led!
Once said a Man—and wise was He—
Never shalt thou the heavens see,

Save as a little child thou be."
Then o'er sea-lashings of commingling tunes
    The ancient wise bassoons,
        Like weird
        Gray-beard
Old harpers sitting on the high sea-dunes,
    Chanted runes:
"Bright-waved gain, gray waved loss,
The sea of all doth lash and toss,
One wave forward and one across:
But now 'twas trough, now 'tis crest,
And worst doth foam and flash to best,
    And curst to blest.

Life! Life! thou sea-fugue, writ from east to west,
    Love, Love alone can pore
    On thy dissolving score
    Of harsh half-phrasings,
        Blotted ere writ,
    And double erasings
        Of chords most fit.
Yea, Love, sole music master blest,
May read thy weltering palimpsest.
To follow Time's dying melodies through,
And never to lose the old in the new,
And ever to solve the discords true—
    Love alone can do.
And ever Love hears the poor-folks' crying,
And ever Love hears the women's sighing,
And ever sweet knighthood's death-defying,
And ever wise childhood's deep implying,
But never a trader's glozing and lying.

And yet shall Love himself be heard,
Though long deferred, though long deferred:
O'er the modern waste a dove hath whirred:
Music is Love in search of a word."

SONG OF THE CHATTAHOOCHEE

OUT of the hills of Habersham,
    Down the valleys of Hall,
I hurry amain to reach the plain,
Run the rapid and leap the fall,
Split at the rock and together again,
Accept my bed, or narrow or wide,
And flee from folly on every side
With a lover's pain to attain the plain
        Far from the hills of Habersham,
        Far from the valleys of Hall.

All down the hills of Habersham,
    All through the valleys of Hall,
The rushes cried *Abide, abide,*
The willful waterweeds held me thrall,
The laving laurel turned my tide,
The ferns and the fondling grass said *Stay,*
The dewberry dipped for to work delay,
And the little reeds sighed *Abide, abide,*
        Here in the hills of Habersham,
        Here in the valleys of Hall.

High o'er the hills of Habersham,
    Veiling the valleys of Hall,
The hickory told me manifold
Fair tales of shade, the poplar tall
Wrought me her shadowy self to hold,
The chestnut, the oak, the walnut, the pine,
Overleaning, with flickering meaning and sign,
Said, *Pass not, so cold, these manifold*
        Deep shades of the hills of Habersham,
        These glades in the valleys of Hall.

And oft in the hills of Habersham,
    And oft in the valleys of Hall,
The white quartz shone, and the smooth brook-stone

Did bar me of passage with friendly brawl,
And many a luminous jewel lone
—Crystals clear or a-cloud with mist,
Ruby, garnet and amethyst—
Made lures with the lights of streaming stone
    In the clefts of the hills of Habersham,
    In the beds of the valleys of Hall.

    But oh, not the hills of Habersham,
    And oh, not the valleys of Hall
Avail: I am fain for to water the plain.
Downward the voices of Duty call—
Downward, to toil and be mixed with the main,
The dry fields burn, and the mills are to turn,
And a myriad flowers mortally yearn,
And the lordly main from beyond the plain
    Calls o'er the hills of Habersham,
    Calls through the valleys of Hall.

BALLAD OF TREES & THE MASTER

    Into the woods my Master went,
    Clean forspent, forspent.
    Into the woods my Master came,
    Forspent with love and shame.
    But the olives they were not blind to Him,
    The little gray leaves were kind to Him:
    The thorn-tree had a mind to Him
    When into the woods He came.

    Out of the woods my Master went,
    And He was well content.
    Out of the woods my Master came,
    Content with death and shame.
    When Death and Shame would woo Him last,
    From under the trees they drew Him last:
    'Twas on a tree they slew Him—last
    When out of the woods He came.

Edwin Markham

THE MAN WITH THE HOE

God made man in His own image
In the image of God He made him.
—GENESIS

BOWED by the weight of centuries he leans
Upon his hoe and gazes on the ground,
The emptiness of ages in his face,
And on his back the burden of the world.
Who made him dead to rapture and despair,
A thing that grieves not and that never hopes,
Stolid and stunned, a brother to the ox?
Who loosened and let down this brutal jaw?
Whose was the hand that slanted back this brow?
Whose breath blew out the light within this brain?

Is this the Thing the Lord God made and gave
To have dominion over sea and land;
To trace the stars and search the heavens for power;
To feel the passion of Eternity?
Is this the dream He dreamed who shaped the suns
And markt their ways upon the ancient deep?
Down all the caverns of Hell to their last gulf
There is no shape more terrible than this—
More tongued with censure of the world's blind greed—
More filled with signs and portents for the soul—
More packt with danger to the universe.

What gulfs between him and the seraphim!
Slave of the wheel of labor, what to him
Are Plato and the swing of Pleiades?
238

What the long reaches of the peaks of song,
The rift of dawn, the reddening of the rose?
Through this dread shape the suffering ages look;
Time's tragedy is in that aching stoop;
Through this dread shape humanity betrayed,
Plundered, profaned and disinherited,
Cries protest to the Powers that made the world,
A protest that is also prophecy.

O masters, lords and rulers in all lands,
Is this the handiwork you give to God,
This monstrous thing distorted and soul-quencht?
How will you ever straighten up this shape;
Touch it again with immortality;
Give back the upward looking and the light;
Rebuild in it the music and the dream;
Make right the immemorial infamies,
Perfidious wrongs, immedicable woes?

O masters, lords and rulers in all lands,
How will the future reckon with this Man?
How answer his brute question in that hour
When whirlwinds of rebellion shake all shores?
How will it be with kingdoms and with kings—
With those who shaped him to the thing he is—
When this dumb Terror shall rise to judge the world,
After the silence of the centuries?

Edgar Lee Masters

THE HILL*

WHERE are Elmer, Herman, Bert, Tom and Charley,
The weak of will, the strong of arm, the clown, the
    boozer, the fighter?
All, all, are sleeping on the hill.

One passed in a fever,
One was burned in a mine,
One was killed in a brawl,
One died in a jail,
One fell from a bridge toiling for children and wife—
All, all are sleeping, sleeping, sleeping on the hill.

Where are Ella, Kate, Mag, Lizzie and Edith,
The tender heart, the simple soul, the loud, the
    proud, the happy one?—
All, all, are sleeping on the hill.

One died in shameful child-birth,
One of a thwarted love,
One at the hands of a brute in a brothel,
One of a broken pride, in the search for her heart's
    desire,
One after life in far-away London and Paris
Was brought to her little space by Ella and Kate
    and Mag—
All, all are sleeping, sleeping, sleeping on the hill.

Where are Uncle Isaac and Aunt Emily,
And old Towny Kincaid and Sevigne Houghton,
And Major Walker who had talked

* This poem and the following poems by Edgar Lee Masters are from
"Spoon River Anthology."

240

With venerable men of the revolution—
All, all, are sleeping on the hill.

They brought them dead sons from the war,
And daughters whom life had crushed,
And their children fatherless, crying—
All, all are sleeping, sleeping, sleeping on the hill.

Where is Old Fiddler Jones
Who played with life all his ninety years,
Braving the sleet with bared breast,
Drinking, rioting, thinking neither of wife nor kin,
Nor gold, nor love, nor heaven?
Lo! he babbles of the fish-frys of long ago,
Of the horse-races of long ago at Clary's Grove,
Of what Abe Lincoln said
One time at Springfield.

FIDDLER JONES

THE earth keeps some vibration going
There in your heart, and that is you.
And if the people find you can fiddle,
Why, fiddle you must, for all your life.
What do you see, a harvest of clover?
Or a meadow to walk through to the river?
The wind's in the corn; you rub your hands
For beeves hereafter ready for market;
Or else you hear the rustle of skirts
Like the girls when dancing at Little Grove.
To Cooney Potter a pillar of dust
Or whirling leaves meant ruinous drouth;
They looked to me like Red-Head Sammy
Stepping it off, to "Toor-a-Loor."
How could I till my forty acres
Not to speak of getting more,
With a medley of horns, bassoons and piccolos

241

Stirred in my brain by crows and robins
And the creak of a wind-mill—only these?
And I never started to plow in my life
That some one did not stop in the road
And take me away to a dance or picnic.
I ended up with forty acres;
I ended up with a broken fiddle—
And a broken laugh, and a thousand memories,
And not a single regret.

RUTHERFORD McDOWELL

THEY brought me ambrotypes
Of the old pioneers to enlarge.
And sometimes one sat for me—
Someone who was in being
When giant hands from the womb of the world
Tore the republic.
What was it in their eyes?—
For I could never fathom
That mystical pathos of drooped eyelids,
And the serene sorrow of their eyes.
It was like a pool of water,
Amid oak trees at the edge of a forest,
Where the leaves fall,
As you hear the crow of a cock
From a far-off farm house, seen near the hills
Where the third generation lives, and the strong men
And the strong women are gone and forgotten.
And these grand-children and great grand-children
Of the pioneers!—
Truly did my camera record their faces, too,
With so much of the old strength gone,
And the old faith gone,
And the old mastery of life gone,
And the old courage gone,
Which labors and loves and suffers and sings
Under the sun!

HENRY C. CALHOUN

I REACHED the highest place in Spoon River,
But through what bitterness of spirit!
The face of my father, sitting speechless,
Child-like, watching his canaries,
And looking at the court-house window
Of the county judge's room,
And his admonitions to me to seek
My own life, and punish Spoon River
To avenge the wrong the people did him,
Filled me with furious energy
To seek for wealth and seek for power.
But what did he do but send me along
The path that leads to the grove of the Furies?
I followed the path and I tell you this:
On the way to the grove you'll pass the Fates,
Shadow-eyed, bent over their weaving.
Stop for a moment, and if you see
The thread of revenge leap out of the shuttle
Then quickly snatch from Atropos
The shears and cut it, lest your sons,
And the children of them and their children
Wear the envenomed robe.

CARL HAMBLIN

THE press of the Spoon River *Clarion* was wrecked,
And I was tarred and feathered,
For publishing this on the day the Anarchists were
  hanged in Chicago:
"I saw a beautiful woman with bandaged eyes
Standing on the steps of a marble temple.
Great multitudes passed in front of her,
Lifting their faces to her imploringly.
In her left hand she held a sword.

She was brandishing the sword,
Sometimes striking a child, again a laborer,
Again a slinking woman, again a lunatic.
In her right hand she held a scale;
Into the scale pieces of gold were tossed
By those who dodged the strokes of the sword.
A man in a black gown read from a manuscript:
'She is no respecter of persons.'
Then a youth wearing a red cap
Leaped to her side and snatched away the bandage.
And lo, the lashes had been eaten away
From the oozy eye-lids;
The eye-balls were seared with a milky mucus;
The madness of a dying soul
Was written on her face—
But the multitude saw why she wore the bandage."

THE VILLAGE ATHEIST

YE young debaters over the doctrine
Of the soul's immortality,
I who lie here was the village atheist,
Talkative, contentious, versed in the arguments
Of the infidels.
But through a long sickness
Coughing myself to death
I read the *Upanishads* and the poetry of Jesus.
And they lighted a torch of hope and intuition
And desire which the Shadow,
Leading me swiftly through the caverns of darkness,
Could not extinguish.
Listen to me, ye who live in the senses
And think through the senses only:
Immortality is not a gift,
Immortality is an achievement;
And only those who strive mightily
Shall possess it.

JACOB GODBEY

How did you feel, you libertarians,
Who spent your talents rallying noble reasons
Around the saloon, as if Liberty
Was not to be found anywhere except at the bar
Or at a table, guzzling?
How did you feel, Ben Pantier, and the rest of you,
Who almost stoned me for a tyrant,
Garbed as a moralist,
And as a wry-faced ascetic frowning upon Yorkshire
    pudding,
Roast beef and ale and good will and rosy cheer—
Things you never saw in a grog-shop in your life?
How did you feel after I was dead and gone,
And your goddess, Liberty, unmasked as a strumpet,
Selling out the streets of Spoon River
To the insolent giants
Who manned the saloons from afar?
Did it occur to you that personal liberty
Is liberty of the mind,
Rather than of the belly?

SETH COMPTON

When I died, the circulating library
Which I built up for Spoon River,
And managed for the good of inquiring minds,
Was sold at auction on the public square,
As if to destroy the last vestige
Of my memory and influence.
For those of you who could not see the virtue
Of knowing Volney's "Ruins" as well as Butler's
    "Analogy"
And "Faust" as well as "Evangeline,"
Were really the power in the village,

245

And often you asked me,
"What is the use of knowing the evil in the world?"
I am out of your way now, Spoon River,
Choose your own good and call it good.
For I could never make you see
That no one knows what is good
Who knows not what is evil;
And no one knows what is true
Who knows not what is false.

LUCINDA MATLOCK

I WENT to the dances at Chandlerville,
And played snap-out at Winchester.
One time we changed partners,
Driving home in the moonlight of middle June,
And then I found Davis.
We were married and lived together for seventy years,
Enjoying, working, raising the twelve children,
Eight of whom we lost
Ere I had reached the age of sixty.
I spun, I wove, I kept the house, I nursed the sick,
I made the garden, and for holiday
Rambled over the fields where sang the larks,
And by Spoon River gathering many a shell,
And many a flower and medicinal weed—
Shouting to the wooded hills, singing to the green valleys.
At ninety-six I had lived enough, that is all,
And passed to a sweet repose.
What is this I hear of sorrow and weariness,
Anger, discontent, and drooping hopes?
Degenerate sons and daughters,
Life is too strong for you—
It takes life to love Life.

DAVIS MATLOCK

SUPPOSE it is nothing but the hive:
That there are drones and workers
And queens, and nothing but storing honey—
(Material things as well as culture and wisdom)—
For the next generation, this generation never living,
Except as it swarms in the sun-light of youth,
Strengthening its wings on what has been gathered,
And tasting, on the way to the hive
From the clover field, the delicate spoil.
Suppose all this, and suppose the truth:
That the nature of man is greater
Than nature's need in the hive;
And you must bear the burden of life,
As well as the urge from your spirit's excess—
Well, I say to live it out like a god
Sure of immortal life, though you are in doubt,
Is the way to live it.
If that doesn't make God proud of you
Then God is nothing but gravitation,
Or sleep is the golden goal.

ANNE RUTLEDGE

OUT of me unworthy and unknown
The vibrations of deathless music;
"With malice toward none, with charity for all."
Out of me the forgiveness of millions toward millions,
And the beneficent face of a nation
Shining with justice and truth.
I am Anne Rutledge who sleep beneath these weeds,
Beloved in life of Abraham Lincoln,
Wedded to him, not through union,
But through separation.
Bloom forever, O Republic,
From the dust of my bosom!

ARLO WILL

DID you ever see an alligator
Come up to the air from the mud,
Staring blindly under the full glare of noon?
Have you seen the stabled horses at night
Tremble and start back at the sight of a lantern?
Have you ever walked in darkness
When an unknown door was open before you
And you stood, it seemed, in the light of a thousand
    candles
Of delicate wax?
Have you walked with the wind in your ears
And the sunlight about you
And found it suddenly shine with an inner splendor?
Out of the mud many times,
Before many doors of light,
Through many fields of splendor,
Where around your steps a soundless glory scatters
Like new-fallen snow,
Will you go through earth, O strong of soul,
And through unnumbered heavens
To the final flame!

SCHOLFIELD HUXLEY

GOD! ask me not to record your wonders,
I admit the stars and the suns
And the countless worlds.
But I have measured their distances
And weighed them and discovered their substances.
I have devised wings for the air,
And keels for water,
And horses of iron for the earth.
I have lengthened the vision you gave me a million times,
And the hearing you gave me a million times,
I have leaped over space with speech,
And taken fire for light out of the air.

I have built great cities and bored through the hills,
And bridged majestic waters.
I have written the *Iliad* and *Hamlet;*
And I have explored your mysteries,
And searched for you without ceasing,
And found you again after losing you
In hours of weariness—
And I ask you:
How would you like to create a sun
And the next day have the worms
Slipping in and out between your fingers?

AARON HATFIELD

BETTER than granite, Spoon River,
Is the memory-picture you keep of me
Standing before the pioneer men and women
There at Concord Church on Communion day.
Speaking in broken voice of the peasant youth
Of Galilee who went to the city
And was killed by bankers and lawyers;
My voice mingling with the June wind
That blew over wheat fields from Atterbury;
While the white stones in the burying ground
Around the Church shimmered in the summer sun.
And there, though my own memories
Were too great to bear, were you, O pioneers,
With bowed heads breathing forth your sorrow
For the sons killed in battle and the daughters
And little children who vanished in life's morning,
Or at the intolerable hour of noon.
But in those moments of tragic silence,
When the wine and bread were passed,
Came the reconciliation for us—
Us the ploughmen and the hewers of wood,
Us the peasants, brothers of the peasant of Galilee—
To us came the Comforter
And the consolation of tongues of flame!

249

THE DARK HILLS

DARK hills at evening in the west,
Where sunset hovers like a sound
Of golden horns that sang to rest
Old bones of warriors under ground,
Far now from all the bannered ways
Where flash the legions of the sun,
You fade—as if the last of days
Were fading and all wars were done.

RICHARD CORY

WHENEVER Richard Cory went down town,
  We people on the pavement looked at him:
He was a gentleman from sole to crown,
  Clean favored, and imperially slim.

And he was always quietly arrayed,
  And he was always human when he talked;
But still he fluttered pulses when he said,
  "Good-morning," and he glittered when he walked.

And he was rich—yes, richer than a king—
  And admirably schooled in every grace:
In fine, we thought that he was everything
  To make us wish that we were in his place.

So on we worked, and waited for the light,
  And went without the meat, and cursed the bread;
And Richard Cory, one calm summer night,
  Went home and put a bullet through his head.

MINIVER CHEEVY

Miniver Cheevy, child of scorn,
  Grew lean while he assailed the seasons;
He wept that he was ever born,
  And he had reasons.

Miniver loved the days of old
  When swords were bright and steeds were prancing;
The vision of a warrior bold
  Would set him dancing.

Miniver sighed for what was not,
  And dreamed, and rested from his labors;
He dreamed of Thebes and Camelot,
  And Priam's neighbors.

Miniver mourned the ripe renown
  That made so many a name so fragrant;
He mourned Romance, now on the town,
  And Art, a vagrant.

Miniver loved the Medici,
  Albeit he had never seen one;
He would have sinned incessantly
  Could he have been one.

Miniver cursed the commonplace
  And eyed a khaki suit with loathing;
He missed the mediæval grace
  Of iron clothing.

Miniver scorned the gold he sought,
  But sore annoyed was he without it;
Miniver thought, and thought, and thought,
  And thought about it.

Miniver Cheevy, born too late,
    Scratched his head and kept on thinking;
Miniver coughed, and called it fate,
    And kept on drinking.

MR. FLOOD'S PARTY

OLD EBEN FLOOD, climbing alone one night
Over the hill between the town below
And the forsaken upland hermitage
That held as much as he should ever know
On earth again of home, paused warily.
The road was his with not a native near;
And Eben, having leisure, said aloud,
For no man else in Tilbury Town to hear:

"Well, Mr. Flood, we have the harvest moon
Again, and we may not have many more;
The bird is on the wing, the poet says,
And you and I have said it here before.
Drink to the bird." He raised up to the light
The jug that he had gone so far to fill,
And answered huskily: "Well, Mr. Flood,
Since you propose it, I believe I will."

Alone, as if enduring to the end
A valiant armor of scarred hopes outworn,
He stood there in the middle of the road
Like Roland's ghost winding a silent horn.
Below him, in the town among the trees,
Where friends of other days had honored him,
A phantom salutation of the dead
Rang thinly till old Eben's eyes were dim.

Then, as a mother lays her sleeping child
Down tenderly, fearing it may awake,

He set the jug down slowly at his feet
With trembling care, knowing that most things break;
And only when assured that on firm earth
It stood, as the uncertain lives of men
Assuredly did not, he paced away,
And with his hand extended paused again:

"Well, Mr. Flood, we have not met like this
In a long time; and many a change has come
To both of us, I fear, since last it was
We had a drop together. Welcome home!"
Convivially returning with himself,
Again he raised the jug up to the light;
And with an acquiescent quaver said:
"Well, Mr. Flood, if you insist, I might.

"Only a very little, Mr. Flood—
For auld lang syne. No more, sir; that will do."
So, for the time, apparently it did,
And Eben evidently thought so too;
For soon amid the silver loneliness
Of night he lifted up his voice and sang,
Secure, with only two moons listening,
Until the whole harmonious landscape rang—

"For auld lang syne." The weary throat gave out,
The last word wavered; and the song being done,
He raised again the jug regretfully
And shook his head, and was again alone.
There was not much that was ahead of him,
And there was nothing in the town below—
Where strangers would have shut the many doors
That many friends had opened long ago.

EROS TURANNOS

SHE fears him, and will always ask
    What fated her to choose him;
She meets in his engaging mask
    All reasons to refuse him;
But what she meets and what she fears
Are less than are the downward years,
Drawn slowly to the foamless weirs
    Of age, were she to lose him.

Between a blurred sagacity
    That once had power to sound him,
And Love, that will not let him be
    The Judas that she found him,
Her pride assuages her almost,
As if it were alone the cost.—
He sees that he will not be lost,
    And waits and looks around him.

A sense of ocean and old trees
    Envelops and allures him;
Tradition, touching all he sees,
    Beguiles and reassures him;
And all her doubts of what he says
Are dimmed with what she knows of days—
Till even prejudice delays
    And fades, and she secures him.

The falling leaf inaugurates
    The reign of her confusion;
The pounding wave reverberates
    The dirge of her illusion;
And home, where passion lived and died,
Becomes a place where she can hide,
While all the town and harbour side
    Vibrate with her seclusion.

We tell you, tapping on our brows,
　　The story as it should be—
As if the story of a house
　　Were told, or ever could be;
We'll have no kindly veil between
Her visions and those we have seen—
As if we guessed what hers have been,
　　Or what they are or would be.

Meanwhile we do no harm; for they
　　That with a god have striven,
Not hearing much of what we say,
　　Take what the god has given;
Though like waves breaking it may be,
Or like a changed familiar tree,
Or like a stairway to the sea
　　Where down the blind are driven.

GEORGE CRABBE

GIVE him the darkest inch your shelf allows,
Hide him in darkest garrets, if you will,—
But his hard, human pulse is throbbing still
With the sure strength that fearless truth endows.
In spite of all fine science disavows,
Of his plain excellence and stubborn skill
There yet remains what fashion cannot kill,
Though years have thinned the laurel from his brows.

Whether or not we read him, we can feel
From time to time the vigor of his name
Against us like a finger for the shame
And emptiness of what our souls reveal
In books that are as altars where we kneel
To consecrate the flicker, not the flame.

LUKE HAVERGAL

Go to the western gate, Luke Havergal,
There where the vines cling crimson on the wall,
And in the twilight wait for what will come.
The leaves will whisper there of her, and some,
Like flying words, will strike you as they fall;
But go, and if you listen, she will call.
Go to the western gate, Luke Havergal—
Luke Havergal.

No, there is not a dawn in eastern skies
To rift the fiery night that's in your eyes;
But there, where western glooms are gathering,
The dark will end the dark, if anything:
God slays himself with every leaf that flies,
And hell is more than half of paradise.
No, there is not a dawn in eastern skies—
In eastern skies.

Out of a grave I come to tell you this,
Out of a grave I come to quench the kiss
That flames upon your forehead with a glow
That blinds you to the way that you must go.
Yes, there is yet one way to where she is,
Bitter, but one that faith may never miss.
Out of a grave I come to tell you this—
To tell you this.

There is the western gate, Luke Havergal,
There are the crimson leaves upon the wall.
Go, for the winds are tearing them away,—
Nor think to riddle the dead words they say,
Nor any more to feel them as they fall;
But go, and if you trust her she will call.
There is the western gate, Luke Havergal—
Luke Havergal.

EDWIN ARLINGTON ROBINSON

THE MASTER

*(Lincoln. Supposed to have been written
not long after the Civil War)*

A FLYING word from there and there
Had sown the name at which we sneered,
But soon the name was everywhere,
To be reviled and then revered:
A presence to be loved and feared,
We cannot hide it, or deny
That we, the gentlemen who jeered,
May be forgotten by and by.

He came when days were perilous
And hearts of men were sore beguiled;
And having made his note of us,
He pondered and was reconciled.
Was ever master yet so mild
As he, and so untamable?
We doubted, even when he smiled,
Not knowing what he knew so well.

He knew that undeceiving fate
Would shame us whom he served unsought;
He knew that he must wince and wait—
The jest of those for whom he fought;
He knew devoutly what he thought
Of us and of our ridicule;
He knew that we must all be taught
Like little children in a school.

We gave a glamour to the task
That he encountered and saw through,
But little of us did he ask,
And little did we ever do.
And what appears if we review
The season when we railed and chaffed?

It is the face of one who knew
That we were learning while we laughed.

The face that in our vision feels
Again the venom that we flung,
Transfigured to the world reveals
The vigilance to which we clung.
Shrewd, hallowed, harassed, and among
The mysteries that are untold,
The face we see was never young,
Nor could it ever have been old.

For he, to whom we had applied
Our shopman's test of age and worth,
Was elemental when he died,
As he was ancient at his birth:
The saddest among kings of earth,
Bowed with a galling crown, this man
Met rancor with a cryptic mirth,
Laconic—and Olympian.

The love, the grandeur, and the fame
Are bounded by the world alone;
The calm, the smoldering, and the flame
Of awful patience were his own:
With him they are forever flown
Past all our fond self-shadowings,
Wherewith we cumber the Unknown
As with inept Icarian wings.

For we were not as other men:
'Twas ours to soar and his to see.
But we are coming down again,
And we shall come down pleasantly;
Nor shall we longer disagree
On what it is to be sublime,
But flourish in our perigee
And have one Titan at a time.

EDWIN ARLINGTON ROBINSON

FOR A DEAD LADY

No more with overflowing light
Shall fill the eyes that now are faded,
Nor shall another's fringe with night
Their woman-hidden world as they did.
No more shall quiver down the days
The flowing wonder of her ways,
Whereof no language may requite
The shifting and the many-shaded.

The grace, divine, definitive,
Clings only as a faint forestalling;
The laugh that love could not forgive
Is hushed, and answers to no calling;
The forehead and the little ears
Have gone where Saturn keeps the years;
The breast where roses could not live
Has done with rising and with falling.

The beauty, shattered by the laws
That have creation in their keeping,
No longer trembles at applause,
Or over children that are sleeping;
And we who delve in beauty's lore
Know all that we have known before
Of what inexorable cause
Makes Time so vicious in his reaping.

FLAMMONDE

THE man Flammonde, from God knows where,
With firm address and foreign air,
With news of nations in his talk
And something royal in his walk,
With glint of iron in his eyes,
But never doubt, nor yet surprise,

259

Appeared, and stayed, and held his head
As one by kings accredited.

Erect, with his alert repose
About him, and about his clothes,
He pictured all tradition hears
Of what we owe to fifty years.
His cleansing heritage of taste
Paraded neither want nor waste;
And what he needed for his fee
To live, he borrowed graciously.

He never told us what he was,
Or what mischance, or other cause,
Had banished him from better days
To play the Prince of Castaways.
Meanwhile he played surpassing well
A part, for most, unplayable;
In fine, one pauses, half afraid
To say for certain that he played.

For that, one may as well forego
Conviction as to yes or no;
Nor can I say just how intense
Would then have been the difference
To several, who, having striven
In vain to get what he was given,
Would see the stranger taken on
By friends not easy to be won.

Moreover, many a malcontent
He soothed and found munificent;
His courtesy beguiled and foiled
Suspicion that his years were soiled;
His mien distinguished any crowd,
His credit strengthened when he bowed;
And women, young and old, were fond
Of looking at the man Flammonde.

There was a woman in our town
On whom the fashion was to frown;
But while our talk renewed the tinge
Of a long-faded scarlet fringe,
The man Flammonde saw none of that,
And what he saw we wondered at—
That none of us, in her distress,
Could hide or find our littleness.

There was a boy that all agreed
Had shut within him the rare seed
Of learning. We could understand,
But none of us could lift a hand.
The man Flammonde appraised the youth,
And told a few of us the truth;
And thereby, for a little gold,
A flowered future was unrolled.

There were two citizens who fought
For years and years, and over nought;
They made life awkward for their friends,
And shortened their own dividends.
The man Flammonde said what was wrong
Should be made right; nor was it long
Before they were again in line,
And had each other in to dine.

And these I mention are but four
Of many out of many more.
So much for them. But what of him—
So firm in every look and limb?
What small satanic sort of kink
Was in his brain? What broken link
Withheld him from the destinies
That came so near to being his?

What was he, when we came to sift
His meaning, and to note the drift

Of incommunicable ways
That make us ponder while we praise?
Why was it that his charm revealed
Somehow the surface of a shield?
What was it that we never caught?
What was he, and what was he not?

How much it was of him we met
We cannot ever know; nor yet
Shall all he gave us quite atone
For what was his, and his alone;
Nor need we now, since he knew best,
Nourish an ethical unrest:
Rarely at once will nature give
The power to be Flammonde and live.

We cannot know how much we learn
From those who never will return,
Until a flash of unforeseen
Remembrance falls on what has been.
We've each a darkening hill to climb;
And this is why, from time to time
In Tilbury Town, we look beyond
Horizons for the man Flammonde.

CASSANDRA

I HEARD one who said: "Verily,
  What word have I for children here?
Your Dollar is your only Word,
  The wrath of it your only fear.

"You build it altars tall enough
  To make you see, but you are blind;
You cannot leave it long enough
  To look before you or behind.

"When Reason beckons you to pause,
    You laugh and say that you know best;
But what it is you know, you keep
    As dark as ingots in a chest.

"You laugh and answer, 'We are young;
    Oh, leave us now, and let us grow:'
Not asking how much more of this
    Will Time endure or Fate bestow.

"Because a few complacent years
    Have made your peril of your pride,
Think you that you are to go on
    Forever pampered and untried?

"What lost eclipse of history,
    What bivouac of the marching stars,
Has given the sign for you to see
    Millenniums and last great wars?

"What unrecorded overthrow
    Of all the world has ever known,
Or ever been, has made itself
    So plain to you, and you alone?

"Your Dollar, Dove and Eagle make
    A Trinity that even you
Rate higher than you rate yourselves;
    It pays, it flatters, and it's new.

"And though your very flesh and blood
    Be what your Eagle eats and drinks,
You'll praise him for the best of birds,
    Not knowing what the Eagle thinks.

"The power is yours, but not the sight;
    You see not upon what you tread;

You have the ages for your guide,
But not the wisdom to be led.

"Think you to tread forever down
The merciless old verities?
And are you never to have eyes
To see the world for what it is?

"Are you to pay for what you have
With all you are?"—No other word
We caught, but with a laughing crowd
Moved on. None heeded, and few heard.

THE MAN AGAINST THE SKY

BETWEEN me and the sunset, like a dome
Against the glory of a world on fire,
Now burned a sudden hill,
Bleak, round and high, by flame-lit height made higher,
With nothing on it for the flame to kill
Save one who moved and was alone up there
To loom before the chaos and the glare
As if he were the last god going home
Unto his last desire.
Dark, marvellous, and inscrutable he moved on
Till down the fiery distance he was gone,
Like one of those eternal, remote things
That range across a man's imaginings
When a sure music fills him and he knows
What he may say thereafter to few men—
The touch of ages having wrought
An echo and a glimpse of what he thought
A phantom or a legend until then;
For whether lighted over ways that save,
Or lured from all repose,
If he go on too far to find a grave,
Mostly alone he goes.

Even he, who stood where I had found him,
On high with fire all round him,
Who moved along the molten west,
And over the round hill's crest
That seemed half ready with him to go down,
Flame-bitten and flame-cleft
As if there were to be no last thing left
Of a nameless unimaginable town—
Even he who climbed and vanished may have taken
Down to the perils of a depth not known,
From death defended, though by men forsaken,
The bread that every man must eat alone;
He may have walked while others hardly dared
Look on to see him stand where many fell;
And upward out of that as out of hell,
He may have sung and striven
To mount where more of him shall yet be given,
Bereft of all retreat,
To sevenfold heat—
As on a day when three in Dura shared
The furnace, and were spared
For glory by that king of Babylon
Who made himself so great that God, who heard,
Covered him with long feathers, like a bird.

Again, he may have gone down easily,
By comfortable altitudes, and found,
As always, underneath him solid ground
Whereon to be sufficient and to stand
Possessed already of the promised land,
Far stretched and fair to see:
A good sight, verily,
And one to make the eyes of her who bore him
Shine glad with hidden tears.
Why question of his ease of who before him,
In one place or another where they left
Their names as far behind them as their bones
And yet by dint of slaughter, toil, and theft,

And shrewdly sharpened stones,
Carved hard the way for his ascendancy
Through deserts of lost years?
Why trouble him now who sees and hears
No more than what his innocence requires,
And therefore to no other height aspires
Than one at which he neither quails nor tires?
He may do more by seeing what he sees
Than others eager for iniquities;
He may, by seeing all things for the best,
Incite futurity to do the rest.

Or with an even likelihood,
He may have met with atrabilious eyes
The fires of time on equal terms and passed
Indifferently down, until at last
His only kind of grandeur would have been,
Apparently, in being seen.
He may have had for evil or for good
No argument; he may have had no care
For what without himself went anywhere
To failure or to glory, and least of all
For such a stale, flamboyant miracle;
He may have been the prophet of an art
Immovable to old idolatries;
He may have been a player without a part,
Annoyed that even the sun should have the skies
For such a flaming way to advertise;
He may have been a painter sick at heart
With Nature's toiling for a new surprise;
He may have been a cynic, who now, for all
Of anything divine that his effete
Negation may have tasted,
Saw truth in his own image, rather small,
Forbore to fever the ephemeral,
Found any barren height a good retreat
From any swarming street,
And in the sun saw power superbly wasted;

And when the primitive old-fashioned stars
Came out again to shine on joys and wars
More primitive, and all arrayed for doom,
He may have proved a world a sorry thing
In his imagining,
And life a lighted highway to the tomb.

Or, mounting with unfirm unsearching tread,
His hopes to chaos led,
He may have stumbled up there from the past,
And with an aching strangeness viewed the last
Abysmal conflagration of his dreams—
A flame where nothing seems
To burn but flame itself, by nothing fed;
And while it all went out,
Not even the faint anodyne of doubt
May then have eased a painful going down
From pictured heights of power and lost renown,
Revealed at length to his outlived endeavour
Remote and unapproachable forever;
And at his heart there may have gnawed
Sick memories of a dead faith foiled and flawed
And long dishonoured by the living death
Assigned alike by chance
To brutes and hierophants;
And anguish fallen on those he loved around him
May once have dealt the last blow to confound him,
And so have left him as death leaves a child,
Who sees it all too near;
And he who knows no young way to forget
May struggle to the tomb unreconciled.
Whatever suns may rise or set
There may be nothing kinder for him here
Than shafts and agonies;
And under these
He may cry out and stay on horribly;
Or, seeing in death too small a thing to fear,
He may go forward like a stoic Roman

267

Where pangs and terrors in his pathway lie—
Or, seizing the swift logic of a woman,
Curse God and die.
Or maybe there, like many another one
Who might have stood aloft and looked ahead,
Black-drawn against wild red,
He may have built unawed by fiery gules
That in him no commotion stirred,
A living reason out of molecules
Why molecules occurred,
And one for smiling when he might have sighed
Had he seen far enough
And in the same inevitable stuff
Discovered an odd reason too for pride
In being what he must have been by laws
Infrangible and for no kind of cause.
Deterred by no confusion or surprise
He may have seen with his mechanic eyes
A world without a meaning, and had room,
Alone amid magnificence and doom,
To build himself an airy monument
That should, or fail him in his vague intent,
Outlast an accidental universe—
To call it nothing worse—
Or, by the burrowing guile
Of Time disintegrated and effaced,
Like once-remembered mighty trees go down
To ruin, of which by man may now be traced
No part sufficient even to be rotten,
And in the book of things that are forgotten
Is entered as a thing not quite worth while.
He may have been so great
That satraps would have shivered at his frown,
And all he prized alive may rule a state
No larger than a grave that holds a clown;
He may have been a master of his fate,
And of his atoms—ready as another
In his emergence to exonerate

His father and his mother;
He may have been a captain of a host,
Self-eloquent and ripe for prodigies,
Doomed here to swell by dangerous degrees,
And then give up the ghost.
Nahum's great grasshoppers were such as these,
Sun-scattered and soon lost.

Whatever the dark road he may have taken,
This man who stood on high
And faced alone the sky,
Whatever drove or lured or guided him—
A vision answering a faith unshaken,
An easy trust assumed of easy trials,
A sick negation born of weak denials,
A crazed abhorrence of an old condition,
A blind attendance on a brief ambition—
Whatever stayed him or derided him,
His way was even as ours;
And we, with all our wounds and all our powers,
Must each await alone at his own height
Another darkness or another light;
And there, of our poor self dominion reft,
If inference and reason shun
Hell, Heaven, and Oblivion,
May thwarted will (perforce precarious,
But for our conservation better thus)
Have no misgiving left
Of doing yet what here we leave undone?
Or if unto the last of these we cleave,
Believing or protesting we believe
In such an idle and ephemeral
Florescence of the diabolical—
If, robbed of two fond old enormities,
Our being had no onward auguries,
What then were this great love of ours to say
For launching other lives to voyage again
A little farther into time and pain,

A little faster in a futile chase
For a kingdom and a power and a Race
That would have still in sight
A manifest end of ashes and eternal night?
Is this the music of the toys we shake
So loud—as if there might be no mistake
Somewhere in our indomitable will?
Are we no greater than the noise we make
Along our blind atomic pilgrimage
Whereon by crass chance billeted we go
Because our brains and bones and cartilage
Will have it so?
If this we say, then let us all be still
About our share in it, and live and die
More quietly thereby.

Where was he going, this man against the sky?
You know not, nor do I.
But this we know, if we know anything:
That we may laugh and fight and sing
And of our transience here make offering
To an orient Word that will not be erased,
Or, save in incommunicable gleams
Too permanent for dreams,
Be found or known.
No tonic or ambitious irritant
Of increase or of want
Has made an otherwise insensate waste
Of ages overthrown
A ruthless, veiled, implacable foretaste
Of other ages that are still to be
Depleted and rewarded variously
Because a few, by fate's economy
Shall seem to move the world the way it goes,
No soft evangel of equality,
Safe-cradled in a communal repose
That huddles into death and may at last
Be covered well with equatorial snows—

And all for what, the devil only knows—
Will aggregate an inkling to confirm
The credit of a sage or of a worm,
Or tell us why one man in five
Should have a care to stay alive
While in his heart he feels no violence
Laid on his humour and intelligence
When infant Science makes a pleasant face
And waves again that hollow toy, the Race;
No planetary trap where souls are wrought
For nothing but the sake of being caught
And sent again to nothing will attune
Itself to any key of any reason
Why man should hunger through another season
To find out why 'twere better late than soon
To go away and let the sun and moon
And all the silly stars illuminate
A place for creeping things,
And those that root and trumpet and have wings,
And herd and ruminate,
Or dive and flash and poise in rivers and seas,
Or by their loyal tails in lofty trees
Hang screeching lewd victorious derision
Of man's immortal vision.

Shall we, because Eternity records
Too vast an answer for the time-born words
We spell, whereof so many are dead that once
In our capricious lexicons
Were so alive and final, hear no more
The Word itself, the living word
That none alive has ever heard
Or ever spelt,
And few have ever felt
Without the fears and old surrenderings
And terrors that began
When Death let fall a feather from his wings
And humbled the first man?

Because the weight of our humility,
Wherefrom we gain
A little wisdom and much pain,
Falls here too sore and there too tedious,
Are we in anguish or complacency,
Not looking far enough ahead
To see by what mad couriers we are led
Along the roads of the ridiculous,
To pity ourselves and laugh at faith
And while we curse life bear it?
And if we see the soul's dead end in death,
Are we to fear it?
What folly is here that has not yet a name
Unless we say outright that we are liars?
What have we seen beyond our sunset fires
That lights again the way by which we came?
Why pay we such a price, and one we give
So clamouringly, for each racked empty day
That leads one more last human hope away,
As quiet fiends would lead past our crazed eyes
Our children to an unseen sacrifice?
If after all that we have lived and thought,
All comes to Nought—
If there be nothing after Now,
And we be nothing anyhow,
And we know that—why live?
'Twere sure but weaklings' vain distress
To suffer dungeons where so many doors
Will open on the cold eternal shores
That look sheer down
To the dark tideless floods of Nothingness
Where all who know may drown.

Stephen Crane

I STOOD UPON A HIGH PLACE

I STOOD upon a high place,
And saw, below, many devils
Running, leaping,
And carousing in sin.
One looked up, grinning,
And said, "Comrade! Brother!"

A LEARNED MAN

A LEARNED man came to me once.
He said, "I know the way—come."
And I was overjoyed at this.
Together we hastened.
Soon, too soon, were we
Where my eyes were useless,
And I knew not the ways of my feet.
I clung to the hand of my friend;
But at last he cried, "I am lost."

A YOUTH IN APPAREL
THAT GLITTERED

A YOUTH in apparel that glittered
Went to walk in a grim forest.
There he met an assassin
Attired all in garb of old days;
He, scowling through the thickets,

And dagger poised quivering,
Rushed upon the youth.
"Sir," said this latter,
"I am enchanted, believe me,
To die, thus,
In this mediæval fashion,
According to the best legends;
Ah, what joy!"
Then took he the wound, smiling,
And died, content.

I SAW A MAN PURSUING
THE HORIZON

I SAW a man pursuing the horizon;
Round and round they sped.
I was disturbed at this;
I accosted the man.
"It is futile," I said,
"You can never—"
"You lie," he cried,
And ran on.

MANY WORKMEN

MANY workmen
Built a huge ball of masonry
Upon a mountain-top.
Then they went to the valley below,
And turned to behold their work.
"It is grand," they said;
They loved the thing.

Of a sudden, it moved:
It came upon them swiftly;

274

It crushed them all to blood.
But some had opportunity to squeal.

A MAN SAW A BALL OF GOLD IN THE SKY

A MAN saw a ball of gold in the sky;
He climbed for it,
And eventually he achieved it—
It was clay.

Now this is the strange part:
When the man went to the earth
And looked again,
Lo, there was the ball of gold.
Now this is the strange part:
It was a ball of gold.
Ay, by the heavens, it was a ball of gold.

IT WAS WRONG TO DO THIS, SAID THE ANGEL

"IT was wrong to do this," said the angel.
"You should live like a flower,
Holding malice like a puppy,
Waging war like a lambkin."

"Not so," quoth the man
Who had no fear of spirits;
"It is only wrong for angels
Who can live like flowers,
Holding malice like the puppies,
Waging war like the lambkins,"

THERE WAS A MAN WITH A TONGUE OF WOOD

THERE was a man with a tongue of wood
Who essayed to sing,
And in truth it was lamentable.
But there was one who heard
The clip-clapper of this tongue of wood
And knew what the man
Wished to sing,
And with that the singer was content.

THE WAYFARER

THE wayfarer,
Perceiving the pathway to truth,
Was struck with astonishment.
It was thickly grown with weeds.
"Ha," he said,
"I see that no one has passed here
In a long time."
Later he saw that each weed
Was a singular knife.
"Well," he mumbled at last,
"Doubtless there are other roads."

WAR IS KIND

Do not weep, maiden, for war is kind.
Because your lover threw wild hands toward the sky
And the affrighted steed ran on alone,
Do not weep.
War is kind.

Hoarse, booming drums of the regiment,
Little souls who thirst for fight,
These men were born to drill and die.
The unexplained glory flies above them,
Great is the battle-god, great, and his kingdom—
A field where a thousand corpses lie.

Do not weep, babe, for war is kind.
Because your father tumbled in the yellow trenches,
Raged at his breast, gulped and died,
Do not weep.
War is kind.

Swift blazing flag of the regiment,
Eagle with crest of red and gold,
These men were born to drill and die.
Point for them the virtue of slaughter,
Make plain to them the excellence of killing
And a field where a thousand corpses lie.

Mother whose heart hung humble as a button
On the bright splendid shroud of your son,
Do not weep.
War is kind.

Trumbull Stickney

MNEMOSYNE

IT's autumn in the country I remember.

How warm a wind blew here about the ways!
And shadows on the hillside lay to slumber
During the long sun-sweetened summer-days.

It's cold abroad the country I remember.

The swallows veering skimmed the golden grain
At midday with a wing aslant and limber;
And yellow cattle browsed upon the plain.

It's empty down the country I remember.

I had a sister lovely in my sight:
Her hair was dark, her eyes were very sombre;
We sang together in the woods at night.

It's lonely in the country I remember.

The babble of our children fills my ears,
And on our hearth I stare the perished ember
To flames that show all starry thro' my tears.

It's dark about the country I remember.

There are the mountains where I lived. The path
Is slushed with cattle-tracks and fallen timber,
The stumps are twisted by the tempests' wrath.

But that I knew these places are my own,
I'd ask how came such wretchedness to cumber
The earth, and I to people it alone.

It rains across the country I remember.

THE SOUL OF TIME

TIME's a circumference
Whereof the segment of our station seems
A long straight line from nothing into naught.
Therefore we say "progress," "infinity"—
Dull words whose object
Hangs in the air of error and delights
Our boyish minds ahunt for butterflies.
For aspiration studies not the sky
But looks for stars; the victories of faith
Are soldiered none the less with certainties,
And all the multitudinous armies decked
With banners blown ahead and flute before
March not to the desert or th' Elysian fields,
But in the track of some discovery,
The grip and cognizance of something true,
Which won resolves a better distribution
Between the dreaming mind and real truth.

I cannot understand you.

'Tis because
You lean over my meaning's edge and feel
A dizziness of the things I have not said.

279

BE STILL. THE HANGING GARDENS
WERE A DREAM

BE still. The Hanging Gardens were a dream
That over Persian roses flew to kiss
The curlèd lashes of Semiramis.
Troy never was, nor green Skamander stream.
Provence and Troubadour are merest lies,
The glorious hair of Venice was a beam
Made within Titian's eye. The sunsets seem,
The world is very old and nothing is.

Be still. Thou foolish thing, thou canst not wake,
Nor thy tears wedge thy soldered lids apart,
But patter in the darkness of thy heart.
Thy brain is plagued. Thou art a frighted owl
Blind with the light of life thou'ldst not forsake,
And error loves and nourishes thy soul.

LIVE BLINDLY

LIVE blindly and upon the hour. The Lord,
Who was the Future, died full long ago.
Knowledge which is the Past is folly. Go,
Poor child, and be not to thyself abhorred.
Around thine earth sun-wingèd winds do blow
And planets roll; a meteor draws his sword;
The rainbow breaks his seven-coloured chord
And the long strips of river-silver flow:

Awake! Give thyself to the lovely hours.
Drinking their lips, catch thou the dream in flight
About their fragile hairs' aërial gold.
Thou art divine, thou livest,—as of old
Apollo springing naked to the light,
And all his island shivered into flowers.

HE SAID: "IF IN HIS IMAGE
I WAS MADE"

HE said: "If in his image I was made,
I am his equal and across the land
We two should make our journey hand in hand
Like brothers dignified and unafraid."
And God that day was walking in the shade.
To whom he said: "The world is idly planned,
We cross each other, let us understand
Thou who thou art, I who I am," he said.

Darkness came down. And all that night was heard
Tremendous clamour and the broken roar
Of things in turmoil driven down before.
Then silence. Morning broke, and sang a bird.
He lay upon the earth, his bosom stirred;
But God was seen no longer any more.

ON SOME SHELLS FOUND INLAND

THESE are my murmur-laden shells that keep
A fresh voice tho' the years lie very gray.
The wave that washed their lips and tuned their lay
Is gone, gone with the faded ocean sweep,
The royal tide, gray ebb and sunken neap
And purple midday,—gone! To this hot clay
Must sing my shells, where yet the primal day,
Its roar and rhythm and splendour will not sleep.

What hand shall join them to their proper sea
If all be gone? Shall they forever feel
Glories undone and worlds that cannot be?—
'Twere mercy to stamp out this agèd wrong,
Dash them to earth and crunch them with the heel
And make a dust of their seraphic song.

AT SAINTE-MARGUERITE

THE gray tide flows and flounders in the rocks
Along the crannies up the swollen sand.
Far out the reefs lie naked—dunes and blocks
Low in the watery wind. A shaft of land
Going to sea thins out the western strand.

It rains, and all along and always gulls
Career sea-screaming in and weather-glossed.
It blows here, pushing round the cliff; in lulls
Within the humid stone a motion lost
Ekes out the flurried heart-beat of the coast.

It blows and rains a pale and whirling mist
This summer morning. I that hither came—
Was it to pluck this savage from the schist,
This crazy yellowish bloom without a name,
With leathern blade and tortured wiry frame?

Why here alone, away, the forehead pricked
With dripping salt and fingers damp with brine,
Before the offal and the derelict
And where the hungry sea-wolves howl and whine
Like human hours? now that the columbine

Stands somewhere shaded near the fields that fall
Great starry sheaves of the delighted year,
And globing rosy on the garden wall
The peach and apricot and soon the pear
Drip in the teasing hand their sugared tear.

Inland a little way the summer lies.
Inland a little and but yesterday
I saw the weary teams, I heard the cries
Of sicklemen across the fallen hay,
And buried in the sunburned stacks I lay

282

Tasting the straws and tossing, laughing soft
Into the sky's great eyes of gold and blue
And nodding to the breezy leaves aloft
Over the harvest's mellow residue.
But sudden then—then strangely dark it grew.

How good it is, before the dreary flow
Of cloud and water, here to lie alone
And in this desolation to let go
Down the ravine one with another, down
Across the surf to linger or to drown

The loves that none can give and none receive,
The fearful asking and the small retort,
The life to dream of and the dream to live!
Very much more is nothing than a part,
Nothing at all and darkness in the heart.

I would my manhood now were like the sea.—
Thou at high-tide, when compassing the land
Thou find'st the issue short, questioningly
A moment poised, thy floods then down the strand
Sink without rancour, sink without command,

Sink of themselves in peace without despair,
And turn as still the calm horizon turns,
Till they repose little by little nowhere
And the long light unfathomable burns
Clear from the zenith stars to the sea-ferns.

Thou art thy Priest, thy Victim and thy God.
Thy life is bulwarked with a thread of foam,
And of the sky, the mountains and the sod
Thou askest nothing, evermore at home
In thy own self's perennial masterdom.

LEAVE HIM NOW QUIET

Leave him now quiet by the way
To rest apart.
I know what draws him to the dust alway
And churns him in the builder's lime:
He has the fright of time.
I heard it knocking in his breast
A minute since;
His human eyes did wince,
He stubborned like the massive slaughter beast
And as a thing o'erwhelmed with sound
Stood bolted to the ground.

Leave him, for rest alone can cure—
If cure there be—
This waif upon the sea.
He is of those who slanted the great door
And listened—wretched little lad—
To what they said.

NEAR HELIKON

By such an all-embalming summer day
As sweetens now among the mountain pines
Down to the cornland yonder and the vines,
To where the sky and sea are mixed in gray,
How do all things together take their way
Harmonious to the harvest, bringing wines
And bread and light and whatsoe'er combines
In the large wreath to make it round and gay.
To me my troubled life doth now appear
Like scarce distinguishable summits hung
Around the blue horizon: places where
Not even a traveller purposeth to steer,—
Whereof a migrant bird in passing sung,
And the girl closed her window not to hear.

NOW IN THE PALACE GARDENS

Now in the palace gardens warm with age,
On lawn and flower-bed this afternoon
The thin November-coloured foliage
Just as last year unfastens lilting down,

And round the terrace in gray attitude
The very statues are becoming sere
With long presentiment of solitude.
Most of the life that I have lived is here,

Here by the path and autumn's earthy grass
And chestnuts standing down the breadths of sky:
Indeed I know not how it came to pass,
The life I lived here so unhappily.

Yet blessing over all! I do not care
What wormwood I have ate to cups of gall;
I care not what despairs are buried there
Under the ground, no, I care not at all.

Nay, if the heart have beaten, let it break!
I have not loved and lived but only this
Betwixt my birth and grave. Dear Spirit, take
The gratitude that pains so deep it is.

When Spring shall be again, and at your door
You stand to feel the mellower evening wind,
Remember if you will my heart is pure,
Perfectly pure and altogether kind;

How much it aches to linger in these things!
I thought the perfect end of love was peace
Over the long-forgiven sufferings.
But something else, I know not what it is,

The words that came so nearly and then not,
The vanity, the error of the whole,
The strong cross-purpose, oh, I know not what
Cries dreadfully in the distracted soul.

The evening fills the garden, hardly red;
And autumn goes away, like one alone.
Would I were with the leaves that thread by thread
Soften to soil, I would that I were one.

FIDELITY

Not lost or won but above all endeavour
Thy life like heaven circles around mine;
Thy eyes it seems upon my eyes did shine
    Since forever.

For aught he summon up his earliest hour
No man remembers the surprise of day,
Nor where he saw with virgin wonder play
    The first flower.

And o'er the imagination's last horizon
No brain has leaning descried nothing more:
Still there are stars and in the night before
    More have arisen.

Not won or lost is unto thee my being;
Our eyes were always so together met.
If mine should close, if ever thine forget,
    Time is dying.

Amy Lowell

PATTERNS

I WALK down the garden-paths,
And all the daffodils
Are blowing, and the bright blue squills.
I walk down the patterned garden-paths
In my stiff, brocaded gown.
With my powdered hair and jeweled fan,
I too am a rare
Pattern. As I wander down
The garden-paths.

My dress is richly figured,
And the train
Makes a pink and silver stain
On the gravel, and the thrift
Of the borders.
Just a plate of current fashion,
Tripping by in high-heeled, ribboned shoes.
Not a softness anywhere about me,
Only whalebone and brocade.
And I sink on a seat in the shade
Of a lime tree. For my passion
Wars against the stiff brocade.
The daffodils and squills
Flutter in the breeze
As they please.
And I weep;
For the lime-tree is in blossom
And one small flower has dropped upon my bosom.

287

And the plashing of waterdrops
In the marble fountain
Comes down the garden-paths.
The dripping never stops.
Underneath my stiffened gown
Is the softness of a woman bathing in a marble basin,
A basin in the midst of hedges grown
So thick, she cannot see her lover hiding,
But she guesses he is near,
And the sliding of the water
Seems the stroking of a dear
Hand upon her.
What is Summer in a fine brocaded gown!
I should like to see it lying in a heap upon the ground.
All the pink and silver crumpled up on the ground.

I would be the pink and silver as I ran along the paths,
And he would stumble after,
Bewildered by my laughter.
I should see the sun flashing from his sword-hilt and the
      buckles on his shoes.
I would choose
To lead him in a maze along the patterned paths,
A bright and laughing maze for my heavy-booted lover.
Till he caught me in the shade,
And the buttons of his waistcoat bruised my body as he
      clasped me,
Aching, melting, unafraid.
With the shadows of the leaves and the sundrops,
And the plopping of the waterdrops,
All about us in the open afternoon—
I am very like to swoon
With the weight of this brocade,
For the sun sifts through the shade.

Underneath the fallen blossom
In my bosom
Is a letter I have hid.

It was brought to me this morning by a rider from the
    Duke.

"Madam, we regret to inform you that Lord Hartwell
Died in action Thursday se'nnight."
As I read it in the white, morning sunlight,
The letters squirmed like snakes.
"Any answer, Madam," said my footman.
"No," I told him.
"See that the messenger takes some refreshment.
No, no answer."
And I walked into the garden,
Up and down the patterned paths,
In my stiff, correct brocade.
The blue and yellow flowers stood up proudly in the
    sun,
Each one.
I stood upright too,
Held rigid to the pattern
By the stiffness of my gown;
Up and down I walked,
Up and down.

In a month he would have been my husband.
In a month, here, underneath this lime,
We would have broke the pattern;
He for me, and I for him,
He as Colonel, I as Lady,
On this shady seat.
He had a whim
That sunlight carried blessing.
And I answered, "It shall be as you have said."
Now he is dead.

In Summer and in Winter I shall walk
Up and down
The patterned garden-paths
In my stiff, brocaded gown.

The squills and daffodils
Will give place to pillared roses, and to asters, and to
    snow.
I shall go
Up and down
In my gown.
Gorgeously arrayed,
Boned and stayed.
And the softness of my body will be guarded from em-
    brace
By each button, hook, and lace.
For the man who should loose me is dead,
Fighting with the Duke in Flanders,
In a pattern called a war.
Christ! What are patterns for?

STOPPING BY WOODS ON
A SNOWY EVENING

WHOSE woods these are I think I know.
His house is in the village though;
He will not see me stopping here
To watch his woods fill up with snow.

My little horse must think it queer
To stop without a farmhouse near
Between the woods and frozen lake
The darkest evening of the year.

He gives his harness bells a shake
To ask if there is some mistake.
The only other sound's the sweep
Of easy wind and downy flake.

The woods are lovely, dark and deep.
But I have promises to keep,
And miles to go before I sleep,
And miles to go before I sleep.

NEITHER OUT FAR NOR IN DEEP

THE people along the sand
All turn and look one way.
They turn their back on the land.
They look at the sea all day.

As long as it takes to pass
A ship keeps raising its hull;
The wetter ground like glass
Reflects a standing gull.

The land may vary more;
But wherever the truth may be—
The water comes ashore,
And the people look at the sea.

They cannot look out far.
They cannot look in deep.
But when was that ever a bar
To any watch they keep?

MOWING

THERE was never a sound beside the wood but one,
And that was my long scythe whispering to the ground.
What was it it whispered? I knew not well myself;
Perhaps it was something about the heat of the sun,
Something, perhaps, about the lack of sound—
And that was why it whispered and did not speak.
It was no dream of the gift of idle hours,
Or easy gold at the hand of fay or elf:
Anything more than the truth would have seemed too
    weak
To the earnest love that laid the swale in rows,
Not without feeble-pointed spikes of flowers
(Pale orchises), and scared a bright green snake.
The fact is the sweetest dream that labor knows.
My long scythe whispered and left the hay to make.

THE ROAD NOT TAKEN

Two roads diverged in a yellow wood,
And sorry I could not travel both
And be one traveller, long I stood
And looked down one as far as I could
To where it bent in the undergrowth;

Then took the other, as just as fair,
And having perhaps the better claim,
Because it was grassy and wanted wear;
Though as for that the passing there
Had worn them really about the same,

And both that morning equally lay
In leaves no step had trodden black.
Oh, I kept the first for another day!
Yet knowing how way leads on to way,
I doubted if I should ever come back.

I shall be telling this with a sigh
Somewhere ages and ages hence:
Two roads diverged in a wood, and I—
I took the one less travelled by,
And that has made all the difference.

THE TUFT OF FLOWERS

I went to turn the grass once after one
Who mowed it in the dew before the sun.

The dew was gone that made his blade so keen
Before I came to view the levelled scene.

I looked for him behind an isle of trees;
I listened for his whetstone on the breeze.

But he had gone his way, the grass all mown,
And I must be, as he had been,—alone,

"As all must be," I said within my heart,
"Whether they work together or apart."

But as I said it, swift there passed me by
On noiseless wing a bewildered butterfly,

Seeking with memories grown dim o'er night
Some resting flower of yesterday's delight.

And once I marked his flight go round and round,
As where some flower lay withering on the ground.

And then he flew as far as eye could see,
And then on tremulous wing came back to me.

I thought of questions that have no reply,
And would have turned to toss the grass to dry;

But he turned first, and led my eye to look
At a tall tuft of flowers beside a brook,

A leaping tongue of bloom the scythe had spared
Beside a reedy brook the scythe had bared.

I left my place to know them by their name,
Finding them butterfly weed when I came.

The mower in the dew had loved them thus,
By leaving them to flourish, not for us,

Nor yet to draw one thought of ours to him,
But from sheer morning gladness at the brim.

The butterfly and I had lit upon,
Nevertheless, a message from the dawn,

That made me hear the wakening birds around,
And hear his long scythe whispering to the ground,

And feel a spirit kindred to my own;
So that henceforth I worked no more alone;

But glad with him, I worked as with his aid,
And weary, sought at noon with him the shade;

And dreaming, as it were, held brotherly speech
With one whose thought I had not hoped to reach.

"Men work together," I told him from the heart,
"Whether they work together or apart."

TO EARTHWARD

Love at the lips was touch
As sweet as I could bear;
And once that seemed too much;
I lived on air

That crossed me from sweet things,
The flow of—was it musk
From hidden grapevine springs
Down hill at dusk?

I had the swirl and ache
From sprays of honeysuckle
That when they're gathered shake
Dew on the knuckle.

I craved strong sweets, but those
Seemed strong when I was young;
The petal of the rose
It was that stung.

Now no joy but lacks salt
That is not dashed with pain
And weariness and fault;
I crave the stain

Of tears, the aftermark
Of almost too much love,
The sweet of bitter bark
And burning clove.

When stiff and sore and scarred
I take away my hand
From leaning on it hard
In grass and sand,

The hurt is not enough:
I long for weight and strength
To feel the earth as rough
To all my length.

AFTER APPLE-PICKING

My long two-pointed ladder's sticking through a tree
Toward heaven still,
And there's the barrel that I didn't fill
Beside it, and there may be two or three
Apples I didn't pick upon some bough.
But I am done with apple-picking now.
Essence of winter sleep is on the night,
The scent of apples: I am drowsing off.
I cannot rub the strangeness from my sight
I got from looking through a pane of glass
I skimmed this morning from the drinking trough
And held against the world of hoary grass.
It melted, and I let it fall and break.
But I was well
Upon my way to sleep before it fell,

And I could tell
What form my dreaming was about to take.
Magnified apples appear and disappear,
Stem end and blossom end,
And every fleck of russet showing clear.
My instep arch not only keeps the ache,
It keeps the pressure of a ladder-round.
I feel the ladder sway as the boughs bend.
And I keep hearing from the cellar bin
The rumbling sound
Of load on load of apples coming in.
For I have had too much
Of apple-picking: I am overtired
Of the great harvest I myself desired.
There were ten thousand thousand fruit to touch,
Cherish in hand, lift down, and not let fall.
For all
That struck the earth,
No matter if not bruised or spiked with stubble,
Went surely to the cider-apple heap
As of no worth.
One can see what will trouble
This sleep of mine, whatever sleep it is.
Were he not gone,
The woodchuck could say whether it's like his
Long sleep, as I describe its coming on,
Or just some human sleep.

TWO TRAMPS IN MUD TIME

Out of the mud two strangers came
And caught me splitting wood in the yard.
And one of them put me off my aim
By hailing cheerily "Hit them hard!"
I knew pretty well why he dropped behind
And let the other go on a way.

I knew pretty well what he had in mind:
He wanted to take my job for pay.

Good blocks of beech it was I split,
As large around as the chopping block;
And every piece I squarely hit
Fell splinterless as a cloven rock.
The blows that a life of self-control
Spares to strike for the common good
That day, giving a loose to my soul,
I spent on the unimportant wood.

The sun was warm but the wind was chill.
You know how it is with an April day
When the sun is out and the wind is still,
You're one month on in the middle of May.
But if you so much as dare to speak,
A cloud comes over the sunlit arch,
A wind comes off a frozen peak,
And you're two months back in the middle of March.

A bluebird comes tenderly up to alight
And fronts the wind to unruffle a plume,
His song so pitched as not to excite
A single flower as yet to bloom.
It is snowing a flake: and he half knew
Winter was only playing possum.
Except in color he isn't blue,
But he wouldn't advise a thing to blossom.

The water for which we may have to look
In summertime with a witching-wand,
In every wheelrut's now a brook,
In every print of a hoof a pond.
Be glad of water, but don't forget
The lurking frost in the earth beneath
That will steal forth after the sun is set
And show on the water its crystal teeth.

The time when most I loved my task
These two must make me love it more
By coming with what they came to ask.
You'd think I never had felt before
The weight of an ax-head poised aloft,
The grip on earth of outspread feet,
The life of muscles rocking soft
And smooth and moist in vernal heat.

Out of the woods two hulking tramps
(From sleeping God knows where last night,
But not long since in the lumber camps).
They thought all chopping was theirs of right.
Men of the woods and lumberjacks,
They judged me by their appropriate tool.
Except as a fellow handled an ax,
They had no way of knowing a fool.

Nothing on either side was said.
They knew they had but to stay their stay
And all their logic would fill my head:
As that I had no right to play
With what was another man's work for gain.
My right might be love but theirs was need.
And where the two exist in twain
Theirs was the better right—agreed.

But yield who will to their separation,
My object in living is to unite
My avocation and my vocation
As my two eyes make one in sight.
Only where love and need are one,
And the work is play for mortal stakes,
Is the deed ever really done
For Heaven and the future's sakes.

BIRCHES

WHEN I see birches bend to left and right
Across the lines of straighter darker trees,
I like to think some boy's been swinging them.
But swinging doesn't bend them down to stay.
Ice-storms do that. Often you must have seen them
Loaded with ice a sunny winter morning
After a rain. They click upon themselves
As the breeze rises, and turn many-coloured
As the stir cracks and crazes their enamel.
Soon the sun's warmth makes them shed crystal shells
Shattering and avalanching on the snowcrust—
Such heaps of broken glass to sweep away
You'd think the inner dome of heaven had fallen.
They are dragged to the withered bracken by the load,
And they seem not to break; though once they are
        bowed
So low for long, they never right themselves:
You may see their trunks arching in the woods
Years afterwards, trailing their leaves on the ground
Like girls on hands and knees that throw their hair
Before them over their heads to dry in the sun.
But I was going to say when Truth broke in
With all her matter-of-fact about the ice-storm
(Now am I free to be poetical?)
I should prefer to have some boy bend them
As he went out and in to fetch the cows—
Some boy too far from town to learn baseball,
Whose only play was what he found himself,
Summer or winter, and could play alone.
One by one he subdued his father's trees
By riding them down over and over again
Until he took the stiffness out of them,
And not one but hung limp, not one was left
For him to conquer. He learned all there was
To learn about not launching out too soon
And so not carrying the tree away

Clear to the ground. He always kept his poise
To the top branches, climbing carefully
With the same pains you use to fill a cup
Up to the brim, and even above the brim.
Then he flung outward, feet first, with a swish,
Kicking his way down through the air to the ground.

So was I once myself a swinger of birches;
And so I dream of going back to be.
It's when I'm weary of considerations,
And life is too much like a pathless wood
Where your face burns and tickles with the cobwebs
Broken across it, and one eye is weeping
From a twig's having lashed it open,
I'd like to get away from earth a while
And then come back to it and begin over.
May no fate wilfully misunderstand me
And half grant what I wish and snatch me away
Not to return. Earth's the right place for love:
I don't know where it's likely to go better.
I'd like to go by climbing a high birch tree,
And climb black branches up a snow-white trunk
Toward heaven, till the tree could bear no more,
But dipped its top and set me down again.
That would be good both going and coming back.
One could do worse than be a swinger of birches.

FIRE AND ICE

SOME say the world will end in fire;
Some say in ice.
From what I've tasted of desire
I hold with those who favor fire.
But if it had to perish twice,
I think I know enough of hate
To know that for destruction ice
Is also great
And would suffice.

THE WOOD-PILE

OUT walking in the frozen swamp one grey day
I paused and said, "I will turn back from here.
No, I will go on farther—and we shall see."
The hard snow held me, save where now and then
One foot went down. The view was all in lines
Straight up and down of tall slim trees
Too much alike to mark or name a place by
So as to say for certain I was here
Or somewhere else: I was just far from home.
A small bird flew before me. He was careful
To put a tree between us when he lighted,
And say no word to tell me who he was
Who was so foolish as to think what *he* thought.
He thought that I was after him for a feather—
The white one in his tail; like one who takes
Everything said as personal to himself:
One flight out sideways would have undeceived him.
And then there was a pile of wood for which
I forgot him and let his little fear
Carry him off the way I might have gone,
Without so much as wishing him good-night.
He went behind it to make his last stand.
It was a cord of maple, cut and split
And piled—and measured, four by four by eight.
And not another like it could I see.
No runner tracks in this year's snow looped near it.
And it was older sure than this year's cutting,
Or even last year's or the year's before.
The wood was grey and the bark warping off it
And the pile somewhat sunken. Clematis
Had wound strings round and round it like a bundle.
What held it though on one side was a tree
Still growing, and on one a stake and prop,
These latter about to fall. I thought that only
Someone who lived in turning to fresh tasks
Could so forget his handiwork on which

He spent himself, the labor of his ax,
And leave it there far from a useful fireplace
To warm the frozen swamp as best it could
With the slow smokeless burning of decay.

MENDING WALL

SOMETHING there is that doesn't love a wall,
That sends the frozen-ground-swell under it,
And spills the upper boulders in the sun;
And makes gaps even two can pass abreast.
The work of hunters is another thing:
I have come after them and made repair
Where they have left not one stone on a stone,
But they would have the rabbit out of hiding,
To please the yelping dogs. The gaps I mean,
No one has seen them made or heard them made,
But at spring mending-time we find them there.
I let my neighbor know beyond the hill;
And on a day we meet to walk the line
And set the wall between us once again.
We keep the wall between us as we go.
To each the boulders that have fallen to each.
And some are loaves and some so nearly balls
We have to use a spell to make them balance:
"Stay where you are until our backs are turned!"
We wear our fingers rough with handling them.
Oh, just another kind of out-door game,
One on a side. It comes to little more:
There where it is we do not need the wall:
He is all pine and I am apple orchard.
My apple trees will never get across
And eat the cones under his pines, I tell him.
He only says, "Good fences make good neighbors."
Spring is the mischief in me, and I wonder
If I could put a notion in his head:
"*Why* do they make good neighbors? Isn't it
Where there are cows? But here there are no cows.

Before I built a wall I'd ask to know
What I was walling in or walling out,
And to whom I was like to give offence.
Something there is that doesn't love a wall,
That wants it down." I could say "Elves" to him,
But it's not elves exactly, and I'd rather
He said it for himself. I see him there
Bringing a stone grasped firmly by the top
In each hand, like an old-stone savage armed.
He moves in darkness as it seems to me,
Not of woods only and the shade of trees.
He will not go behind his father's saying,
And he likes having thought of it so well
He says again, "Good fences make good neighbors."

THE LESSON FOR TODAY

IF this uncertain age in which we dwell
Were really as dark as I hear sages tell,
And I convinced that they were really sages,
I should not curse myself with it to hell,
But leaving not the chair I long have sat in,
I should betake me back ten thousand pages
To the world's undebatably dark ages,
And getting up my medieval Latin,
Seek converse common cause and brotherhood
(By all that's liberal—I should, I should)
With poets who could calmly take the fate
Of being born at once too early and late,
And for these reasons kept from being great.
Yet singing but Dione in the wood
And *ver aspergit terram floribus*
They slowly led old Latin verse to rhyme
And to forget the ancient lengths of time,
And so began the modern world for us.

I'd say, O Master of the Palace School,
You were not Charles' nor anybody's fool:

Tell me as pedagogue to pedagogue,
You did not know that since King Charles did rule
You had no chance but to be minor, did you?
Your light was spent perhaps as in a fog
That at once kept you burning low and hid you.
The age may very well have been to blame
For your not having won to Virgil's fame.
But no one ever heard you make the claim.
You would not think you knew enough to judge
The age when full upon you. That's my point.
We have today and I could call their name
Who know exactly what is out of joint
To make their verse and their excuses lame.
They've tried to grasp with too much social fact
Too large a situation. You and I
Would be afraid if we should comprehend
And get outside of too much bad statistics
Our muscles never could again contract:
We never could recover human shape,
But must live lives out mentally agape,
Or die of philosophical distension.
That's how we feel—and we're no special mystics.

We can't appraise the time in which we act.
But for the folly of it, let's pretend
We know enough to know it for adverse.
One more millennium's about to end.
Let's celebrate the event, my distant friend,
In publicly disputing which is worse,
The present age or your age. You and I
As schoolmen of repute should qualify
To wage a fine scholastical contention
As to whose age deserves the lower mark,
Or should I say the higher one, for dark.
I can just hear the way you make it go:
There's always something to be sorry for,
A sordid peace or an outrageous war.
Yes, yes, of course. We have the same convention.

The groundwork of all faith is human woe.
It was well worth preliminary mention.
There's nothing but injustice to be had,
No choice is left a poet, you might add,
But how to take the curse, tragic or comic.
It was well worth preliminary mention.
But let's get on to where our cases part,
If part they do. Let me propose a start.
(We're rivals in the badness of our case,
Remember, and must keep a solemn face.)
Space ails us moderns: we are sick with space.
Its contemplation makes us out as small
As a brief epidemic of microbes
That in a good glass may be seen to crawl
The patina of this the least of globes.
But have we there the advantage after all?
You were belittled into vilest worms
God hardly tolerated with his feet;
Which comes to the same thing in different terms.
We both are the belittled human race,
One as compared with God and one with space.
I had thought ours the more profound disgrace;
But doubtless this was only my conceit.
The cloister and the observatory saint
Take comfort in about the same complaint.
So science and religion really meet.

I can just hear you call your Palace class:
Come learn the Latin Eheu for alas.
You may not want to use it and you may.
O paladins, the lesson for today
Is how to be unhappy yet polite.
And at the summons Roland, Olivier,
And every sheepish paladin and peer,
Being already more than proved in fight,
Sits down in school to try if he can write
Like Horace in the true Horatian vein,
Yet like a Christian disciplined to bend

His mind to thinking always of the end.
Memento mori and obey the Lord.
Art and religion love the somber chord.
Earth's a hard place in which to save the soul,
And could it be brought under state control,
So automatically we all were saved,
Its separateness from Heaven could be waived;
It might as well at once be kingdom-come.
(Perhaps it will be next millennium.)

But these are universals, not confined
To any one time, place, or human kind.
We're either nothing or a God's regret.
As ever when philosophers are met,
No matter where they stoutly mean to get,
Nor what particulars they reason from,
They are philosophers, and from old habit
They end up in the universal Whole
As unoriginal as any rabbit.

One age is like another for the soul.
I'm telling you. You haven't said a thing,
Unless I put it in your mouth to say.
I'm having the whole argument my way—
But in your favor—please to tell your King—
In having granted you all ages shine
With equal darkness, yours as dark as mine.
I'm liberal. You, you aristocrat
Won't know exactly what I mean by that.
I mean so altruistically moral
I never take my own side in a quarrel.
I'd lay my hand on his hand on his staff,
Lean back and have my confidential laugh,
And tell him I had read his Epitaph.

It sent me to the graves the other day.
The only other there was far away
Across the landscape with a watering pot
At his devotions in a special plot.
And he was there resuscitating flowers

(Make no mistake about its being bones);
But I was only there to read the stones
To see what on the whole they had to say
About how long a man may think to live,
Which is becoming my concern of late.
And very wide the choice they seemed to give;
The ages ranging all the way from hours
To months and years and many many years.
One man had lived one hundred years and eight.
But though we all may be inclined to wait
And follow some development of state,
Or see what comes of science and invention,
There is a limit to our time extension.
We all are doomed to broken-off careers,
And so's the nation, so's the total race.
The earth itself is liable to the fate
Of meaninglessly being broken off.
(And hence so many literary tears
At which my inclination is to scoff.)
I may have wept that any should have died
Or missed their chance, or not have been their best,
Or been their riches, fame, or love denied;
On me as much as any is the jest.
I take my incompleteness with the rest.
God bless himself can no one else be blessed.

I hold your doctrine of Memento Mori.
And were an epitaph to be my story
I'd have a short one ready for my own.
I would have written of me on my stone:
I had a lover's quarrel with the world.

COME IN

As I came to the edge of the woods,
Thrush music—hark!
Now if it was dusk outside,
Inside it was dark.

Too dark in the woods for a bird
By sleight of wing
To better its perch for the night,
Though it still could sing.

The last of the light of the sun
That had died in the west
Still lived for one song more
In a thrush's breast.

Far in the pillared dark
Thrush music went—
Almost like a call to come in
To the dark and lament.

But no, I was out for stars:
I would not come in.
I meant not even if asked;
And I hadn't been.

THE MIDDLENESS OF THE ROAD

THE road at the top of the rise
Seems to come to an end
And take off into the skies.
So at the distant bend

It seems to go into a wood,
The place of standing still
As long the trees have stood.
But say what Fancy will,

The mineral drops that explode
To drive my ton of car
Are limited to the road.
They deal with near and far,

But have almost nothing to do
With the absolute flight and rest
The universal blue
And local green suggest.

A YOUNG BIRCH

THE birch begins to crack its outer sheath
Of baby green and show the white beneath,
As whosoever likes the young and slight
May well have noticed. Soon entirely white
To double day and cut in half the dark
It will stand forth, entirely white in bark,
And nothing but the top a leafy green—
The only native tree that dares to lean
Relying on its beauty, to the air.
(Less brave perhaps than trusting are the fair.)
And someone reminiscent will recall
How once in cutting brush along the wall
He spared it from the number of the slain,
At first to be no bigger than a cane,
And then no bigger than a fishing pole,
But now at last so obvious a bole
The most efficient help you ever hired
Would know that it was there to be admired,
And zeal would not be thanked that cut it down
When you were sick in bed or out of town.
It was a thing of beauty and was sent
To live its life out as an ornament.

DIRECTIVE

BACK out of all this now too much for us,
Back in a time made simple by the loss
Of detail, burned, dissolved, and broken off
Like graveyard marble sculpture in the weather,
There is a house that is no more a house

ROBERT FROST

Upon a farm that is no more a farm
And in a town that is no more a town.
The road there, if you'll let a guide direct you
Who only has at heart your getting lost,
May seem as if it should have been a quarry—
Great monolithic knees the former town
Long since gave up pretence of keeping covered.
And there's a story in a book about it:
Besides the wear of iron wagon wheels
The ledges show lines ruled southeast northwest,
The chisel work of an enormous Glacier
That braced his feet against the Arctic Pole.
You must not mind a certain coolness from him
Still said to haunt this side of Panther Mountain.
Nor need you mind the serial ordeal
Of being watched from forty cellar holes
As if by eye pairs out of forty firkins.
As for the woods' excitement over you
That sends light rustle rushes to their leaves,
Charge that to upstart inexperience.
Where were they all not twenty years ago?
They think too much of having shaded out
A few old pecker-fretted apple trees.
Make yourself up a cheering song of how
Someone's road home from work this once was,
Who may be just ahead of you on foot
Or creaking with a buggy load of grain.
The height of the adventure is the height
Of country where two village cultures faded
Into each other. Both of them are lost.
And if you're lost enough to find yourself
By now, pull in your ladder road behind you
And put a sign up CLOSED to all but me.
Then make yourself at home. The only field
Now left's no bigger than a harness gall.
First there's the children's house of make believe,
Some shattered dishes underneath a pine,
The playthings in the playhouse of the children.

Weep for what little things could make them glad.
Then for the house that is no more a house,
But only a belilaced cellar hole,
Now slowly closing like a dent in dough.
This was no playhouse but a house in earnest.
Your destination and your destiny's
A brook that was the water of the house,
Cold as a spring as yet so near its source,
Too lofty and original to rage.
(We know the valley streams that when aroused
Will leave their tatters hung on barb and thorn.)
I have kept hidden in the instep arch
Of an old cedar at the waterside
A broken drinking goblet like the Grail
Under a spell so the wrong ones can't find it,
So can't get saved, as Saint Mark says they mustn't.
(I stole the goblet from the children's playhouse.)
Here are your waters and your watering place.
Drink and be whole again beyond confusion.

ONCE BY THE PACIFIC

THE shattered water made a misty din.
Great waves looked over others coming in,
And thought of doing something to the shore
That water never did to land before.
The clouds were low and hairy in the skies,
Like locks blown forward in the gleam of eyes.
You could not tell, and yet it looked as if
The shore was lucky in being backed by cliff,
The cliff in being backed by continent;
It looked as if a night of dark intent
Was coming, and not only a night, an age.
Someone had better be prepared for rage.
There would be more than ocean-water broken
Before God's last *Put out the Light* was spoken.

Carl Sandburg

THEY HAVE YARNS

(from "The People, Yes")

THEY have yarns
Of a skyscraper so tall they had to put hinges
On the two top stories so to let the moon go by,
Of one corn crop in Missouri when the roots
Went so deep and drew off so much water
The Mississippi riverbed that year was dry,
Of pancakes so thin they had only one side,
Of "a fog so thick we shingled the barn and six feet out
on the fog,"
Of Pecos Pete straddling a cyclone in Texas and riding
it to the west coast where "it rained out under him,"
Of the man who drove a swarm of bees across the Rocky
Mountains and the Desert "and didn't lose a bee,"
Of a mountain railroad curve where the engineer in his
cab can touch the caboose and spit in the conduc-
tor's eye,
Of the boy who climbed a cornstalk growing so fast he
would have starved to death if they hadn't shot
biscuits up to him,
Of the old man's whiskers: "When the wind was with
him his whiskers arrived a day before he did,"
Of the hen laying a square egg and cackling, "Ouch!"
and of hens laying eggs with the dates printed on
them,
Of the ship captain's shadow: it froze to the deck one
cold winter night,
Of mutineers on that same ship put to chipping rust with
rubber hammers,
Of the sheep counter who was fast and accurate: "I just
count their feet and divide by four,"

313

Of the man so tall he must climb a ladder to shave himself,

Of the runt so teeny-weeny it takes two men and a boy to see him,

Of mosquitoes: one can kill a dog, two of them a man,

Of a cyclone that sucked cookstoves out of the kitchen, up the chimney flue, and on to the next town,

Of the same cyclone picking up wagon-tracks in Nebraska and dropping them over in the Dakotas,

Of the hook-and-eye snake unlocking itself into forty pieces, each piece two inches long, then in nine seconds flat snapping itself together again,

Of the watch swallowed by the cow—when they butchered her a year later the watch was running and had the correct time,

Of horned snakes, hoop snakes that roll themselves where they want to go, and rattlesnakes carrying bells instead of rattles on their tails,

Of the herd of cattle in California getting lost in a giant redwood tree that had hollowed out,

Of the man who killed a snake by putting its tail in its mouth so it swallowed itself,

Of railroad trains whizzing along so fast they reach the station before the whistle,

Of pigs so thin the farmer had to tie knots in their tails to keep them from crawling through the cracks in their pens,

Of Paul Bunyan's big blue ox, Babe, measuring between the eyes forty-two ax-handles and a plug of Star tobacco exactly,

Of John Henry's hammer and the curve of its swing and his singing of it as "a rainbow round my shoulder."

    "Do tell!"

    "I want to know!"

    "You don't say so!"

    "For the land's sake!"

    "Gosh all fish-hooks!"

    "Tell me some more.

I don't believe a word you say
but I love to listen
to your sweet harmonica
to your chin-music.
Your fish stories hang together
when they're just a pack of lies:
you ought to have a leather medal:
you ought to have a statue
carved of butter: you deserve
a large bouquet of turnips."

"Yessir," the traveler drawled,
"Away out there in the petrified forest
everything goes on the same as usual.
The petrified birds sit in their petrified nests
and hatch their petrified young from petrified eggs."

A high pressure salesman jumped off the Brooklyn
Bridge and was saved by a policeman. But it didn't
take him long to sell the idea to the policeman. So
together they jumped off the bridge.

One of the oil men in heaven started a rumor of a gusher
down in hell. All the other oil men left in a hurry
for hell. As he gets to thinking about the rumor he
had started he says to himself there might be something in it after all. So he leaves for hell in a hurry.

"The number 42 will win this raffle, that's my number."
And when he won they asked him whether he
guessed the number or had a system. He said he
had a system. "I took up the old family album and
there on page 7 was my grandfather and grandmother both on page 7. I said to myself this is easy
for 7 times 7 is the number that will win and 7 times
7 is 42."

Once a shipwrecked sailor caught hold of a stateroom
door and floated for hours till friendly hands from
out of the darkness threw him a rope. And he called
across the night, "What country is this?" and hearing voices answer, "New Jersey," he took a fresh

315

hold on the floating stateroom door and called back
half-wearily, "I guess I'll float a little farther."

An Ohio man bundled up the tin roof of a summer
kitchen and sent it to a motor car maker with a
complaint of his car not giving service. In three
weeks a new car arrived for him and a letter: "We
regret delay in shipment but your car was received
in a very bad order."

A Dakota cousin of this Ohio man sent six years of tin
can accumulations to the same works, asking them
to overhaul his car. Two weeks later came a rebuilt
car, five old tin cans, and a letter: "We are also for-
warding you five parts not necessary in our new
model."

Thus fantasies heard at filling stations in the midwest.
Another relates to a Missouri mule who took aim
with his heels at an automobile rattling by. The car
turned a somersault, lit next a fence, ran right along
through a cornfield till it came to a gate, moved onto
the road and went on its way as though nothing had
happened. The mule heehawed with desolation,
"What's the use?"

Another tells of a farmer and his family stalled on a railroad crossing, how they jumped out in time to see
a limited express knock it into flinders, the farmer
calling, "Well, I always did say that car was no
shucks in a real pinch."

When the Masonic Temple in Chicago was the tallest
building in the United States west of New York,
two men who would cheat the eyes out of you if you
gave 'em a chance, took an Iowa farmer to the top
of the building and asked him, "How is this for
high?" They told him that for $25 they would go
down in the basement and turn the building around
on its turn-table for him while he stood on the roof
and saw how this seventh wonder of the world
worked. He handed them $25. They went. He
waited. They never came back.

This is told in Chicago as a folk tale, the same as the legend of Mrs. O'Leary's cow kicking over the barn lamp that started the Chicago fire, when the Georgia visitor, Robert Toombs, telegraphed an Atlanta crony, "Chicago is on fire, the whole city burning down, God be praised!"

Nor is the prize sleeper Rip Van Winkle and his scolding wife forgotten, nor the headless horseman scooting through Sleepy Hollow

Nor the sunken treasure-ships in coves and harbors, the hideouts of gold and silver sought by Coronado, nor the Flying Dutchman rounding the Cape doomed to nevermore pound his ear nor ever again take a snooze for himself

Nor the sailor's caretaker Mother Carey seeing to it that every seafaring man in the afterworld has a seabird to bring him news of ships and women, an albatross for the admiral, a gull for the deckhand

Nor the sailor with a sweetheart in every port of the world, nor the ships that set out with flying colors and all the promises you could ask, the ships never heard of again

Nor Jim Liverpool, the riverman who could jump across any river and back without touching land he was that quick on his feet

Nor Mike Fink along the Ohio and the Mississippi, half wild horse and half cock-eyed alligator, the rest of him snags and snapping turtle. "I can out-run, out-jump, out-shoot, out-brag, out-drink, and out-fight, rough and tumble, no holts barred, any man on both sides of the river from Pittsburgh to New Orleans and back again to St. Louis. My trigger finger itches and I want to go redhot. War, famine and bloodshed puts flesh on my bones, and hardship's my daily bread."

Nor the man so lean he threw no shadow: six rattlesnakes struck at him at one time and every one missed him.

317

Vachel Lindsay

THE CONGO

(A Study of the Negro Race)

I—THEIR BASIC SAVAGERY

A deep rolling bass

FAT black bucks in a wine-barrel room,
Barrel-house kings, with feet unstable,
Sagged and reeled and pounded on the table,
Pounded on the table,
Beat an empty barrel with the handle of a
broom,
Hard as they were able,
Boom, boom, BOOM,
With a silk umbrella and the handle of a
broom,

*More deliberate.
Solemnly
chanted*

Boomlay, boomlay, boomlay, BOOM.
THEN I had religion, THEN I had a vision.
I could not turn from their revel in derision.
THEN I SAW THE CONGO, CREEPING THROUGH
THE BLACK,
CUTTING THROUGH THE JUNGLE WITH A
GOLDEN TRACK.
Then along that riverbank
A thousand miles
Tattooed cannibals danced in files;
Then I heard the boom of the blood-lust son
And a thigh-bone beating on a tin-pan gong.
And "BLOOD!" screamed the whistles and the
fifes of the warriors,

*A rapidly
piling climax of speed
and racket*

"BLOOD!" screamed the skull-faced, lean
witch-doctors;
"Whirl ye the deadly voo-doo rattle,

Harry the uplands,
Steal all the cattle,
Rattle-rattle, rattle-rattle,
Bing!
Boomlay, boomlay, boomlay, BOOM!"   *With a philosophic pause*
A roaring, epic, rag-time tune
From the mouth of the Congo
To the Mountains of the Moon.
Death is an Elephant,
Torch-eyed and horrible,   *Shrilly and with a heavily accented metre*
Foam-flanked and terrible.
BOOM, steal the pygmies,
BOOM, kill the Arabs,
BOOM, kill the white men,
Hoo, Hoo, Hoo.
Listen to the yell of Leopold's ghost   *Like the wind in the chimney*
Burning in Hell for his hand-maimed host.
Hear how the demons chuckle and yell
Cutting his hands off down in Hell.
Listen to the creepy proclamation,
Blown through the lairs of the forest-nation,
Blown past the white-ants' hill of clay,
Blown past the marsh where the butterflies
    play:—
"Be careful what you do,   *All the O sounds very golden.*
Or Mumbo-Jumbo, god of the Congo,   *Heavy accents very heavy. Light accents very light. Last line whispered*
And all of the other
Gods of the Congo,
Mumbo-Jumbo will hoo-doo you,
Mumbo-Jumbo will hoo-doo you,
Mumbo-Jumbo will hoo-doo you."

II—THEIR IRREPRESSIBLE HIGH SPIRITS

Wild crap-shooters with a whoop and a call   *Rather shrill and high*
Danced the juba in their gambling-hall,
And laughed fit to kill, and shook the town,

And guyed the policemen and laughed them
down
With a boomlay, boomlay, boomlay, Boom.
Then I saw the Congo, creeping through
the black,
Cutting through the jungle with a
golden track.

Read exactly as in first section. Lay emphasis on the delicate ideas. Keep as light-footed as possible

A negro fairyland swung into view,
A minstrel river
Where dreams come true.
The ebony palace soared on high
Through the blossoming trees to the evening
sky.
The inlaid porches and casements shone
With gold and ivory and elephant-bone.
And the black crowd laughed till their sides
were sore
At the baboon butler in the agate door,
And the well-known tunes of the parrot band
That trilled on the bushes of that magic land.
A troupe of skull-faced witch-men came

With pomposity

Through the agate doorway in suits of
flame—
Yea, long-tailed coats with a gold-leaf crust
And hats that were covered with diamond-
dust.
And the crowd in the court gave a whoop
and a call
And danced the juba from wall to wall.
But the witch-men suddenly stilled the
throng

With a great deliberation and ghostliness

With a stern cold glare, and a stern old song:
"Mumbo-Jumbo will hoo-doo you." . . .

With overwhelming assurance, good cheer, and pomp

Just then from the doorway, as fat as shotes
Came the cake-walk princes in their long red
coats,
Canes with a brilliant lacquer shine,

And tall silk hats that were red as wine.
And they pranced with their butterfly partners there,

*With grow-
ing speed
and sharply
marked
dance-
rhythm*

Coal-black maidens with pearls in their hair,
Knee-skirts trimmed with the jassamine
sweet,
And bells on their ankles and little black feet.
And the couples railed at the chant and the
frown
Of the witch-men lean, and laughed them
down.
(Oh, rare was the revel, and well worth
while
That made those glowering witch-men
smile.)

The cake-walk royalty then began
To walk for a cake that was tall as a man

*With a touch
of negro dia-
lect, and as
rapidly as
possible to-
ward the end*

To the tune of "Boomlay, boomlay, BOOM,"
While the witch-men laughed, with a sinister
air,
And sang with the scalawags prancing there:
"Walk with care, walk with care,
Or Mumbo-Jumbo, god of the Congo,
And all of the other
Gods of the Congo,
Mumbo-Jumbo will hoo-doo you.
Beware, beware, walk with care,
Boomlay, boomlay, boomlay, boom,
Boomlay, boomlay, boomlay, boom,
Boomlay, boomlay, boomlay, boom,
Boomlay, boomlay, boomlay,
BOOM."

Oh, rare was the revel, and well worth while
That made those glowering witch-men smile.

*Slow philo-
sophic calm*

321

III—THE HOPE OF THEIR RELIGION

*Heavy bass.
With a literal
imitation of
camp-meet-
ing racket
and trance*

A good old Negro in the slums of the town
Preached at a sister for her velvet gown.
Howled at a brother for his low-down ways,
His prowling, guzzling, sneak-thief days.
Beat on the Bible till he wore it out
Starting the jubilee revival shout.
And some had visions, as they stood on
    chairs,
And sang of Jacob, and the golden stairs.
And they all repented, a thousand strong,
From their stupor and savagery and sin and
    wrong,
And slammed with their hymn-books till they
    shook the room
With "Glory, glory, glory,"
And "Boom, boom, Boom."
THEN I SAW THE CONGO, CREEPING THROUGH
    THE BLACK,
CUTTING THROUGH THE JUNGLE WITH A
    GOLDEN TRACK.

*Exactly as in
the first sec-
tion. Begin
with terror
and power,
end with joy*

And the gray sky opened like a new-rent veil
And showed the apostles with their coats of
    mail.
In bright white steel they were seated round,
And their fire-eyes watched where the Congo
    wound.
And the twelve Apostles, from their thrones
    on high,

*Sung to the
tune of
"Hark, ten
thousand
harps and
voices"*

Thrilled all the forest with their heavenly
    cry:
"Mumbo-Jumbo will die in the jungle;
Never again will he hoo-doo you,
Never again will he hoo-doo you."

*With grow-
ing delibera-
tion and joy*

Then along that river, a thousand miles,
The vine-snared trees fell down in files.

Pioneer angels cleared the way
For a Congo paradise, for babes at play,
For sacred capitals, for temples clean.
Gone were the skull-faced witch-men lean;
There, where the wild ghost-gods had
 wailed,
A million boats of the angels sailed
With oars of silver, and prows of blue,
And silken pennants that the sun shone
 through.
'Twas a land transfigured, 'twas a new creation.
Oh, a singing wind swept the Negro nation,
And on through the backwoods clearing
 flew:—
"Mumbo-Jumbo is dead in the jungle.
Never again will he hoo-doo you.
Never again will he hoo-doo you."

In a rather high key—as delicately as possible

To the tune of "Hark, ten thousand harps and voices"

Redeemed were the forests, the beasts and
 the men,
And only the vulture dared again
By the far lone mountains of the moon
To cry, in the silence, the Congo tune:
"Mumbo-Jumbo will hoo-doo you,
Mumbo-Jumbo will hoo-doo you.
Mumbo . . . Jumbo . . . will . . . hoo-doo . . . you."

Dying down into a penetrating, terrified whisper

THE LEADEN-EYED

LET not young souls be smothered out before
They do quaint deeds and fully flaunt their pride.
It is the world's one crime its babes grow dull,
Its poor are ox-like, limp and leaden-eyed.
Not that they starve, but starve so dreamlessly;
Not that they sow, but that they seldom reap;
Not that they serve, but have no gods to serve;
Not that they die, but that they die like sheep.

323

FACTORY WINDOWS ARE ALWAYS BROKEN

FACTORY windows are always broken.
Somebody's always throwing bricks,
Somebody's always heaving cinders,
Playing ugly Yahoo tricks.

Factory windows are always broken.
Other windows are let alone.
No one throws through the chapel-window
The bitter, snarling derisive stone.

Factory windows are always broken.
Something or other is going wrong.
Something is rotten—I think, in Denmark.
End of the factory-window song.

ABRAHAM LINCOLN WALKS AT MIDNIGHT

(*in Springfield, Illinois*)

IT is portentous, and a thing of state
That here at midnight, in our little town
A mourning figure walks, and will not rest,
Near the old court-house pacing up and down,

Or by his homestead, or in shadowed yards
He lingers where his children used to play,
Or through the market, on the well-worn stones
He stalks until the dawn-stars burn away.

A bronzed, lank man! His suit of ancient black,
A famous high top-hat and plain worn shawl

Make him the quaint great figure that men love,
The prairie-lawyer, master of us all.

He cannot sleep upon his hillside now.
He is among us:—as in times before!
And we who toss and lie awake for long
Breathe deep, and start, to see him pass the door.

His head is bowed. He thinks on men and kings.
Yes, when the sick world cries, how can he sleep?
Too many peasants fight, they know not why,
Too many homesteads in black terror weep.

The sins of all the war-lords burn his heart.
He sees the dreadnoughts scouring every main.
He carries on his shawl-wrapped shoulders now
The bitterness, the folly and the pain.

He cannot rest until a spirit-dawn
Shall come;—the shining hope of Europe free:
The league of sober folk, the Workers' Earth,
Bringing long peace to Cornland, Alp and Sea.

It breaks his heart that kings must murder still,
That all his hours of travail here for men
Seem yet in vain. And who will bring white peace
That he may sleep upon his hill again?

THE EAGLE THAT IS FORGOTTEN

[*John P. Altgeld. Born December 30, 1847;
Died March 12, 1902*]

SLEEP softly . . . eagle forgotten . . . under the stone,
Time has its way with you there, and the clay has its own.
"We have buried him now," thought your foes, and in
    secret rejoiced.

They made a brave show of their mourning, their hatred
  unvoiced,
They had snarled at you, barked at you, foamed at you,
  day after day,
Now you were ended. They praised you, . . . and laid
  you away.

The others that mourned you in silence and terror and
  truth,
The widow bereft of her pittance, the boy without youth,
The mocked and the scorned and the wounded, the
  lame and the poor
That should have remembered forever, . . . remember
  no more.

Where are those lovers of yours, on what name do they
  call
The lost, that in armies wept over your funeral pall?
They call on the names of a hundred high-valiant ones,
A hundred white eagles have risen, the sons of your
  sons,
The zeal in their wings is a zeal that your dreaming
  began,
The valor that wore out your soul in the service of man.

Sleep softly, . . . eagle forgotten, . . . under the stone,
Time has its way with you there, and the clay has its
  own.
Sleep on, O brave hearted, O wise man, that kindled the
  flame—
To live in mankind is far more than to live in a name,
To live in mankind, far, far more . . . than to live in a
  name.

GENERAL WILLIAM BOOTH
ENTERS INTO HEAVEN

*(To be sung to the tune of "The Blood of the Lamb"
with indicated instrument.)*

(Bass drum beaten loudly.)

Booth led boldly with his big bass drum—
(Are you washed in the blood of the Lamb?)
The Saints smiled gravely and they said: "He's come."
(Are you washed in the blood of the Lamb?)
Walking lepers followed, rank on rank,
Lurching bravos from the ditches dank,
Drabs from the alleyways and drug fiends pale—
Minds still passion-ridden, soul-powers frail:—
Vermin-eaten saints with moldy breath,
Unwashed legions with the ways of Death—
(Are you washed in the blood of the Lamb?)

(Banjos.)

Every slum had sent its half-a-score
The round world over. (Booth had groaned for more.)
Every banner that the wide world flies
Bloomed with glory and transcendent dyes.
Big-voiced lasses made their banjos bang;
Tranced, fanatical they shrieked and sang:—
"Are you washed in the blood of the Lamb?"
Hallelujah! It was queer to see
Bull-necked convicts with that land make free.
Loons with trumpets blowed a blare, blare, blare
On, on upward thro' the golden air!
(Are you washed in the blood of the Lamb?)

(Bass drum slower and softer.)

Booth died blind and still by faith he trod,
Eyes still dazzled by the ways of God.
Booth led boldly, and he looked the chief,
Eagle countenance in sharp relief,

327

Beard a-flying, air of high command
Unabated in that holy land.

(*Sweet flute music.*)
Jesus came from out the court-house door,
Stretched his hands above the passing poor.
Booth saw not, but led his queer ones there
Round and round the mighty court-house square.
Then, in an instant all that blear review
Marched on spotless, clad in raiment new.
The lame were straightened, withered limbs uncurled
And blind eyes opened on a new, sweet world.

(*Bass drum louder.*)
Drabs and vixens in a flash made whole!
Gone was the weasel-head, the snout, the jowl!
Sages and sibyls now, and athletes clean,
Rulers of empires, and of forests green!

(*Grand chorus of all instruments. Tambourines
to the foreground.*)
The hosts were sandalled, and their wings were fire!
(Are you washed in the blood of the Lamb?)
But their noise played havoc with the angel-choir.
(Are you washed in the blood of the Lamb?)
Oh, shout Salvation! It was good to see
Kings and Princes by the Lamb set free.
The banjos rattled and the tambourines
Jing-jing-jingled in the hands of Queens.

(*Reverently sung, no instruments.*)
And when Booth halted by the curb for prayer
He saw his Master thro' the flag-filled air.
Christ came gently with a robe and crown
For Booth the soldier, while the throng knelt down.
He saw King Jesus. They were face to face,
And he knelt a-weeping in that holy place.
Are you washed in the blood of the Lamb?
328

SIMON LEGREE—A NEGRO SERMON

(To be read in your own variety of negro dialect.)

LEGREE's big house was white and green.
His cotton-fields were the best to be seen.
He had strong horses and opulent cattle,
And bloodhounds bold, with chains that would rattle.
His garret was full of curious things:
Books of magic, bags of gold,
And rabbits' feet on long twine strings.
But he went down to the Devil.

Legree, he sported a brass-buttoned coat,
A snake-skin necktie, a blood-red shirt.
Legree he had a beard like a goat,
And a thick hairy neck, and eyes like dirt.
His puffed-out cheeks were fish-belly white,
He had great long teeth, and an appetite.
He ate raw meat, 'most every meal,
And rolled his eyes till the cat would squeal.
His fist was an enormous size
To mash poor niggers that told him lies:
He was surely a witch-man in disguise.
But he went down to the Devil.

He wore hip boots, and would wade all day
To capture his slaves that had fled away.
But he went down to the Devil.

He beat poor Uncle Tom to death
Who prayed for Legree with his last breath.
Then Uncle Tom to Eva flew,
To the high sanctoriums bright and new;
And Simon Legree stared up beneath,
And cracked his heels, and ground his teeth:
And went down to the Devil.

He crossed the yard in the storm and gloom;
He went into his grand front room.
He said, "I liked him, and I don't care."
He kicked a hound, he gave a swear;
He tightened his belt, he took a lamp,
Went down cellar to the webs and damp.
There in the middle of the mouldy floor
He heaved up a slab, he found a door—
And went down to the Devil.

His lamp blew out, but his eyes burned bright.
Simon Legree stepped down all night—
Down, down to the Devil.
Simon Legree he reached the place,
He saw one half of the human race,
He saw the Devil on a wide green throne,
Gnawing the meat from a big ham-bone,
And he said to Mister Devil:
    "I see that you have much to eat—
    A red ham-bone is surely sweet.
    I see that you have lion's feet;
    I see your frame is fat and fine,
    I see you drink your poison wine—
    Blood and burning turpentine."

And the Devil said to Simon Legree:
    "I like your style, so wicked and free.
    Come sit and share my throne with me,
    And let us bark and revel."
And there they sit and gnash their teeth,
And each one wears a hop-vine wreath.
They are matching pennies and shooting craps,
They are playing poker and taking naps.
And old Legree is fat and fine:
He heats the fire, he drinks the wine—
Blood and burning turpentine—
            Down, down with the Devil;
            Down, down with the Devil;
                Down, down with the Devil.

BRYAN, BRYAN, BRYAN, BRYAN

*The Campaign of Eighteen Ninety-Six, as Viewed at
The Time by a Sixteen-Year-Old, etc.*

I

In a nation of one hundred fine, mob-hearted, lynching,
        relenting, repenting millions,
There are plenty of sweeping, swinging, stinging, gor-
        geous things to shout about,
And knock your old blue devils out.

I brag and chant of Bryan, Bryan, Bryan,
Candidate for president who sketched a silver Zion,
The one American Poet who could sing outdoors,
He brought in tides of wonder, of unprecedented splen-
        dor
Wild roses from the plains, that made hearts tender,
All the funny circus silks
Of politics unfurled,
Bartlett pears of romance that were honey at the cores,
And torchlights down the street, to the end of the world.

There were truths eternal in the gab and tittle-tattle.
There were real heads broken in the fustian and the
        rattle.
There were real lines drawn:
Not the silver and the gold,
But Nebraska's cry went eastward against the dour and
        old,
The mean and cold.
It was eighteen ninety-six, and I was just sixteen
And Altgeld ruled in Springfield, Illinois,
When there came from the sunset Nebraska's shout
        of joy:
In a coat like a deacon, in a black Stetson hat

331

He scourged the elephant plutocrats
With barbed wire from the Platte.
The scales dropped from their mighty eyes.
They saw that summer's noon
A tribe of wonders coming
To a marching tune.

Oh, the longhorns from Texas,
The jayhawks from Kansas,
The plop-eyed bungaroo and giant giassicus,
The varmint, chipmunk, bugaboo,
The horned-toad, prairie-dog and ballyhoo,
From all the newborn states arow,
Bidding the eagles of the west fly on,
Bidding the eagles of the west fly on,
The fawn, prodactyl and thing-a-ma-jig,
The rakaboor, the hellangone,
The whangdoodle, batfowl and pig,
The coyote, wild-cat and grizzly in a glow,
In a miracle of health and speed, the whole breed
    abreast,
They leaped the Mississippi, blue border of the West,
From the Gulf to Canada, two thousand miles long:—
Against the towns of Tubal Cain,
Ah,—sharp was their song.
Against the ways of Tubal Cain, too cunning for the
    young,
The longhorn calf, the buffalo and wampus gave tongue.

These creatures were defending things Mark Hanna
    never dreamed:
The moods of airy childhood that in desert dews
    gleamed,
The gossamers and whimsies,
The monkeyshines and didoes
Rank and strange
Of the canyons and the range,
The ultimate fantastics

Of the far western slope,
And of prairie schooner children
Born beneath the stars,
Beneath falling snows,
Of the babies born at midnight
In the sod huts of lost hope,
With no physician there,
Except a Kansas prayer,
With the Indian raid a howling through the air.
And all these in their helpless days
By the dour East oppressed,
Mean paternalism
Making their mistakes for them,
Crucifying half the West,
Till the whole Atlantic coast
Seemed a giant spider's nest.

And these children and their sons
At last rode through the cactus,
A cliff of mighty cowboys
On the lope,
With gun and rope.
And all the way to frightened Maine the old East heard
    them call,
And saw our Bryan by a mile lead the wall
Of men and whirling flowers and beasts,
The bard and the prophet of them all.
Prairie avenger, mountain lion,
Bryan, Bryan, Bryan, Bryan,
Gigantic troubadour, speaking like a siege gun,
Smashing Plymouth Rock with his boulders from the
    West,
And just a hundred miles behind, tornadoes piled across
    the sky,
Blotting out sun and moon,
A sign on high.

Headlong, dazed and blinking in the weird green light,
The scalawags made moan, afraid to fight.

333

When Bryan came to Springfield, and Altgeld gave him
    greeting,
Rochester was deserted, Divernon was deserted,
Mechanicsburg, Riverton, Chickenbristle, Cotton Hill,
Empty: for all Sangamon drove to the meeting—
In silver-decked racing cart,
Buggy, buckboard, carryall,
Carriage, phaeton, whatever would haul,
And silver-decked farm-wagons gritted, banged and
    rolled,
With the new tale of Bryan by the iron tires told.
The State House loomed afar,
A speck, a hive, a football,
A captive balloon!
And the town was all one spreading wing of bunting,
    plumes, and sunshine,
Every rag and flag, and Bryan picture sold,
When the rigs in many a dusty line
Jammed our streets at noon,
And joined the wild parade against the power of gold.

We roamed, we boys from High School,
With mankind,
While Springfield gleamed, silk-lined.
Oh, Tom Dines, and Art Fitzgerald,
And the gangs that they could get!
I can hear them yelling yet.
Helping the incantation, defying aristocracy,
With every bridle gone,
Ridding the world of the low down mean,
Bidding the eagles of the West fly on,
Bidding the eagles of the West fly on,
We were bully, wild and woolly,
Never yet curried below the knees.
We saw flowers in the air,
Fair as the Pleiades, bright as Orion,

—Hopes of all mankind,
Made rare, resistless, thrice refined.
Oh, we bucks from every Springfield ward!
Colts of democracy—
Yet time-winds out of Chaos from the star-fields of the
Lord.

The long parade rolled on. I stood by my best girl.
She was a cool young citizen, with wise and laughing
eyes.
With my necktie by my ear, I was stepping on my dear,
But she kept like a pattern, without a shaken curl.

She wore in her hair a brave prairie rose.
Her gold chums cut her, for that was not the pose.
No Gibson Girl would wear it in that fresh way.
But we were fairy Democrats, and this was our day.

The earth rocked like the ocean, the sidewalk was a deck.
The houses for the moment were lost in the wide wreck.
And the bands played strange and stranger music as they
trailed along.
Against the ways of Tubal Cain,
Ah, sharp was their song!
The demons in the bricks, the demons in the grass,
The demons in the bank-vaults peered out to see us pass,
And the angels in the trees, the angels in the grass,
The angels in the flags peered out to see us pass.
And the sidewalk was our chariot, and the flowers
bloomed higher,
And the street turned to silver and the grass turned to
fire,
And then it was but grass, and the town was there again,
A place for women and men.

III

Then we stood where we could see every band,
And the speaker's stand.

And Bryan took the platform.
And he was introduced.
And he lifted his hand
And cast a new spell.
Progressive silence fell
In Springfield,
In Illinois,
Around the world.
Then we heard these glacial boulders across the prairie
    rolled:
"The people have a right to make their own mistakes. . . .
You shall not crucify mankind
Upon a cross of gold."

And everybody heard him—
In the streets and State House yard.
And everybody heard him
In Springfield, in Illinois,
Around and around and around the world,
That danced upon its axis
And like a darling broncho whirled.

IV

July, August, suspense.
Wall Street lost to sense.
August, September, October,
More suspense,
And the whole East down like a wind-smashed fence.

Then Hanna to the rescue,
Hanna of Ohio,
Rallying the roller-tops,
Rallying the bucket-shops.
Threatening drouth and death,
Promising manna,
Rallying the trusts against the bawling flannelmouth;
Invading misers' cellars,

Tin-cans, socks,
Melting down the rocks,
Pouring out the long green to a million workers,
Spondulix by the mountain-load, to stop each new tor-
    nado,
And beat the cheapskate, blatherskite,
Populistic, anarchistic,
Deacon—desperado.

V

Election night at midnight:
Boy Bryan's defeat.
Defeat of western silver.
Defeat of the wheat.
Victory of letterfiles
And plutocrats in miles
With dollar signs upon their coats,
Diamond watchchains on their vests
And spats on their feet.
Victory of custodians, Plymouth Rock,
And all that inbred landlord stock.
Victory of the neat.
Defeat of the aspen groves of Colorado valleys,
The blue bells of the Rockies,
And blue bonnets of old Texas, by the Pittsburg alleys.
Defeat of alfalfa and the Mariposa lily.
Defeat of the Pacific and the long Mississippi.
Defeat of the young by the old and silly.
Defeat of tornadoes by the poison vats supreme.
Defeat of my boyhood, defeat of my dream.

VI

Where is McKinley, that respectable McKinley,
The man without an angle or a tangle,
Who soothed down the city man and soothed down the
    farmer,

337

The German, the Irish, the Southerner, the Northerner,
Who climbed every greasy pole, and slipped through
    every crack;
Who soothed down the gambling hall, the bar-room, the
    church,
The devil vote, the angel vote, the neutral vote,
The desperately wicked, and their victims on the rack,
The gold vote, the silver vote, the brass vote, the lead
    vote,
Every vote? . . .

Where is McKinley, Mark Hanna's McKinley,
His slave, his echo, his suit of clothes?
Gone to join the shadows, with the pomps of that time,
And the flame of that summer's prairie rose.

Where is Cleveland whom the Democratic platform
Read from the party in a glorious hour,
Gone to join the shadows with pitchfork Tillman,
And sledge-hammer Altgeld who wrecked his power.

Where is Hanna, bulldog Hanna.
Low-browed Hanna, who said: "Stand pat"?
Gone to his place with old Pierpont Morgan.
Gone somewhere . . . with lean rat Platt.

Where is Roosevelt, the young dude cowboy,
Who hated Bryan, then aped his way?
Gone to join the shadows with mighty Cromwell
And tall King Saul, till the Judgment day.

Where is Altgeld, brave as the truth,
Whose name the few still say with tears?
Gone to join the ironies with Old John Brown,
Whose fame rings loud for a thousand years.

Where is that boy, that Heaven-born Bryan,
That Homer Bryan, who sang from the West?
Gone to join the shadows with Altgeld the Eagle,
Where the kings and the slaves and the troubadours rest.

Wallace Stevens

THE MAN WITH THE BLUE GUITAR

I

THE man bent over his guitar,
A shearsman of sorts. The day was green.

They said, "You have a blue guitar,
You do not play things as they are."

The man replied, "Things as they are
Are changed upon the blue guitar."

And they said then, "But play, you must,
A tune beyond us, yet ourselves,

A tune upon the blue guitar
Of things exactly as they are."

II

I cannot bring a world quite round,
Although I patch it as I can.

I sing a hero's head, large eye
And bearded bronze, but not a man,

Although I patch him as I can
And reach through him almost to man.

If to serenade almost to man
Is to miss, by that, things as they are,

339

Say that it is the serenade
Of a man that plays a blue guitar.

III

Ah, but to play man number one,
To drive the dagger in his heart,

To lay his brain upon the board
And pick the acrid colors out,

To nail his thought across the door,
Its wings spread wide to rain and snow,

To strike his living hi and ho,
To tick it, tock it, turn it true,

To bang it from a savage blue,
Jangling the metal of the strings. . . .

IV

So that's life, then: things as they are?
It picks its way on the blue guitar.

A million people on one string?
And all their manner in the thing,

And all their manner, right and wrong,
And all their manner, weak and strong?

The feelings crazily, craftily call,
Like a buzzing of flies in autumn air,

And that's life, then: things as they are,
This buzzing of the blue guitar.

V

Do not speak to us of the greatness of poetry,
Of the torches wisping in the underground,

Of the structure of vaults upon a point of light.
There are no shadows in our sun,

Day is desire and night is sleep.
There are no shadows anywhere.

The earth, for us, is flat and bare.
There are no shadows. Poetry

Exceeding music must take the place
Of empty heaven and its hymns,

Ourselves in poetry must take their place,
Even in the chattering of your guitar.

VI

A tune beyond us as we are,
Yet nothing changed by the blue guitar;

Ourselves in the tune as if in space,
Yet nothing changed, except the place

Of things as they are and only the place
As you play them, on the blue guitar,

Placed, so, beyond the compass of change,
Perceived in a final atmosphere;

For a moment final, in the way
The thinking of art seems final when

The thinking of god is smoky dew.
The tune is space. The blue guitar

Becomes the place of things as they are,
A composing of senses of the guitar.

VII

It is the sun that shares our works.
The moon shares nothing. It is a sea.

When shall I come to say of the sun,
It is a sea; it shares nothing;

The sun no longer shares our works
And the earth is alive with creeping men,

Mechanical beetles never quite warm?
And shall I then stand in the sun, as now

I stand in the moon, and call it good,
The immaculate, the merciful good,

Detached from us, from things as they are?
Not to be part of the sun? To stand

Remote and call it merciful?
The strings are cold on the blue guitar.

VIII

The vivid, florid, turgid sky,
The drenching thunder rolling by,

The morning deluged still by night,
The clouds tumultuously bright

And the feeling heavy in cold chords
Struggling toward impassioned choirs,

Crying among the clouds, enraged
By gold antagonists in air—

I know my lazy, leaden twang
Is like the reason in a storm;

And yet it brings the storm to bear.
I twang it out and leave it there.

IX

And the color, the overcast blue
Of the air, in which the blue guitar

Is a form, described but difficult,
And I am merely a shadow hunched

Above the arrowy, still strings,
The maker of a thing yet to be made;

The color like a thought that grows
Out of a mood, the tragic robe

Of the actor, half his gesture, half
His speech, the dress of his meaning, silk

Sodden with his melancholy words,
The weather of his stage, himself.

X

Raise reddest columns. Toll a bell
And clap the hollows full of tin.

Throw papers in the streets, the wills
Of the dead, majestic in their seals.

And the beautiful trombones—behold
The approach of him whom none believes,

Whom all believe that all believe,
A pagan in a vanished car.

Roll a drum upon the blue guitar.
Lean from the steeple. Cry aloud,

343

"Here am I, my adversary, that
Confront you, hoo-ing the slick trombones,

Yet with a petty misery
At heart, a petty misery,

Ever the prelude to your end,
The touch that topples men and rock."

XI

Slowly the ivy on the stones
Becomes the stones. Women become

The cities, children become the fields
And men in waves become the sea.

It is the chord that falsifies.
The sea returns upon the men,

The fields entrap the children, brick
Is a weed and all the flies are caught,

Wingless and withered, but living alive.
The discord merely magnifies.

Deeper within the belly's dark
Of time, time grows upon the rock

XII

Tom-tom, c'est moi. The blue guitar
And I are one. The orchestra

Fills the high hall with shuffling men
High as the hall. The whirling noise

Of a multitude dwindles, all said,
To his breath that lies awake at night.

I know that timid breathing. Where
Do I begin and end? And where,

As I strum the thing, do I pick up
That which momentously declares

Itself not to be I and yet
Must be. It could be nothing else.

XIII

The pale intrusions into blue
Are corrupting pallors . . ay di mi,

Blue buds or pitchy blooms. Be content—
Expansions, diffusions—content to be

The unspotted imbecile revery,
The heraldic center of the world

Of blue, blue sleek with a hundred chins,
The amorist Adjective aflame . . .

XIV

First one beam, then another, then
A thousand are radiant in the sky.

Each is both star and orb; and day
Is the riches of their atmosphere.

The sea appends its tattery hues.
The shores are banks of muffling mist.

One says a German chandelier—
A candle is enough to light the world.

It makes it clear. Even at noon
It glistens in essential dark.

At night, it lights the fruit and wine,
The book and bread, things as they are,

In a chiaroscuro where
One sits and plays the blue guitar.

XV

Is this picture of Picasso's, this "hoard
Of destructions", a picture of ourselves,

Now, an image of our society?
Do I sit, deformed, a naked egg,

Catching at Good-bye, harvest moon,
Without seeing the harvest or the moon?

Things as they are have been destroyed.
Have I? Am I a man that is dead

At a table on which the food is cold?
Is my thought a memory, not alive?

Is the spot on the floor, there, wine or blood
And whichever it may be, is it mine?

XVI

The earth is not earth but a stone,
Not the mother that held men as they fell

But stone, but like a stone, no· not
The mother, but an oppressor, but like

An oppressor that grudges them their death,
As it grudges the living that they live.

To live in war, to live at war,
To chop the sullen psaltery,

To improve the sewers in Jerusalem,
To electrify the nimbuses—

Place honey on the altars and die,
You lovers that are bitter at heart.

XVII

The person has a mould.   But not
Its animal.   The angelic ones

Speak of the soul, the mind.   It is
An animal.   The blue guitar—

On that its claws propound, its fangs
Articulate   its desert days.

The blue guitar a mould?   That shell?
Well, after all, the north wind blows

A horn, on which its victory
Is a worm composing in a straw.

XVIII

A dream (to call it a dream) in which
I can believe, in face of the object,

A dream no longer a dream, a thing,
Of things as they are, as the blue guitar

After long strumming on certain nights
Gives the touch of the senses, not of the hand,

But the very senses as they touch
The wind-gloss. Or as daylight comes,

Like light in a mirroring of cliffs,
Rising upward from a sea of ex.

XIX

That I may reduce the monster to
Myself, and then may be myself

In face of the monster, be more than part
Of it, more than the monstrous player of

One of its monstrous lutes, not be
Alone, but reduce the monster and be,

Two things, the two together as one,
And play of the monster and of myself,

Or better not of myself at all,
But of that as its intelligence,

Being the lion in the lute
Before the lion locked in stone.

XX

What is there in life except one's ideas,
Good air, good friend, what is there in life?

Is it ideas that I believe?
Good air, my only friend, believe,

Believe would be a brother full
Of love, believe would be a friend,

Friendlier than my only friend,
Good air. Poor pale, poor pale guitar . . . . .

XXI

A substitute for all the gods:
This self, not that gold self aloft,

Alone, one's shadow magnified,
Lord of the body, looking down,

As now and called most high,
The shadow of Chocorua

In an immenser heaven, aloft,
Alone, lord of the land and lord

Of the men that live in the land, high lord.
One's self and the mountains of one's land,

Without shadows, without magnificence,
The flesh, the bone, the dirt, the stone.

XXII

Poetry is the subject of the poem,
From this the poem issues and

To this returns. Between the two,
Between issue and return, there is

An absence in reality,
Things as they are. Or so we say.

But are these separate? Is it
An absence for the poem, which acquires

Its true appearances there, sun's green,
Cloud's red, earth feeling, sky that thinks.

From these it takes. Perhaps it gives,
In the universal intercourse.

XXIII

A few final solutions, like a duet
With the undertaker: a voice in the clouds,

Another on earth, the one a voice
Of ether, the other smelling of drink,

The voice of ether prevailing, the swell
Of the undertaker's song in the snow

Apostrophizing wreaths, the voice
In the clouds serene and final, next

The grunted breath serene and final,
The imagined and the real, thought

And the truth, Dichtung und Wahrheit, all
Confusion solved, as in a refrain

One keeps on playing year by year,
Concerning the nature of things as they are.

XXIV

A poem like a missal found
In the mud, a missal for that young man,

That scholar hungriest for that book,
The very book, or, less, a page

Or, at the least, a phrase, that phrase,
A hawk of life, that latined phrase:

To know; a missal for brooding-sight.
To meet that hawk's eye and to flinch

Not at the eye but at the joy of it.
I play. But this is what I think.

XXV

He held the world upon his nose
And this-a-way he gave a fling.

His robes and symbols, ai-yi-yi—
And that-a-way he twirled the thing.

Sombre as fir-trees, liquid cats
Moved in the grass without a sound.

They did not know the grass went round.
The cats had cats and the grass turned gray

And the world had worlds, ai, this-a-way:
The grass turned green and the grass turned gray.

And the nose is eternal, that-a-way.
Things as they were, things as they are,

Things as they will be by and by . . .
A fat thumb beats out ai-yi-yi.

XXVI

The world washed in his imagination,
The world was a shore, whether sound or form

Or light, the relic of farewells,
Rock, of valedictory echoings,

To which his imagination returned,
From which it sped, a bar in space,

Sand heaped in the clouds, giant that fought
Against the murderous alphabet:

The swarm of thoughts, the swarm of dreams
Of inaccessible Utopia.

A mountainous music always seemed
To be falling and to be passing away.

XXVII

It is the sea that whitens the roof.
The sea drifts through the winter air.

It is the sea that the north wind makes.
The sea is in the falling snow.

This gloom is the darkness of the sea.
That tours to shift the shifting scene.

Regard. But for that salty cup,
But for the icicles on the eaves—

The sea is a form of ridicule.
The iceberg settings satirize

The demon that cannot be himself,
That tours to shift the shifting scene.

XXVIII

I am a native in this world
And think in it as a native thinks,

Gesu, not native of a mind
Thinking the thoughts I call my own,

Native, a native in the world
And like a native think in it.

It could not be a mind, the wave
In which the watery grasses flow

And yet are fixed as a photograph,
The wind in which the dead leaves blow.

Here I inhale profounder strength
And as I am, I speak and move

And things are as I think they are
And say they are on the blue guitar.

XXIX

In the cathedral, I sat there, and read,
Alone, a lean Review and said,

"These degustations in the vaults
Oppose the past and the festival.

What is beyond the cathedral, outside,
Balances with nuptial song.

So it is to sit and to balance things
To and to and to the point of still,

To say of one mask it is like,
To say of another it is like,

To know that the balance does not quite rest,
That the mask is strange, however like."

The shapes are wrong and the sounds are false.
The bells are the bellowings of bulls.

Yet Franciscan don was never more
Himself than in this fertile glass.

XXX

From this I shall evolve a man.
This is his essence: the old fantoche

Hanging his shawl upon the wind,
Like something on the stage, puffed out,

His strutting studied through centuries.
At last, in spite of his manner, his eye

353

A-cock at the cross-piece on a pole
Supporting heavy cables, slung

Through Oxidia, banal suburb,
One-half of all its installments paid.

Dew-dapper clapper-traps, blazing
From crusty stacks above machines.

Ecce, Oxidia is the seed
Dropped out of this amber-ember pod,

Oxidia is the soot of fire,
Oxidia is Olympia.

XXXI

How long and late the pheasant sleeps.
The employer and the employee contend,

Combat, compose their droll affair.
The bubbling sun will bubble up,

Spring sparkle and the cock-bird shriek.
The employer and employee will hear

And continue their affair. The shriek
Will rack the thickets. There is no place,

Here, for the lark fixed in the mind,
In the museum of the sky. The cock

Will claw sleep. Morning is not sun,
It is this posture of the nerves,

As if a blunted player clutched
The nuances of the blue guitar.

It must be this rhapsody or none,
The rhapsody of things as they are.

XXXII

Throw away the lights, the definitions,
And say of what you see in the dark

That it is this or that it is that,
But do not use the rotted names.

How should you walk in that space and know
Nothing of the madness of space,

Nothing of its jocular procreations?
Throw the lights away. Nothing must stand

Between you and the shapes you take
When the crust of shape has been destroyed.

You as you are? You are yourself.
The blue guitar surprises you.

XXXIII

That generation's dream, aviled
In the mud, in Monday's dirty light,

That's it, the only dream they knew,
Time in its final block, not time

To come, a wrangling of two dreams.
Here is the bread of time to come,

Here is its actual stone. The bread
Will be our bread, the stone will be

Our bed and we shall sleep by night.
We shall forget by day, except

The moments when we choose to play
The imagined pine, the imagined jay.

NUANCES OF A THEME BY WILLIAMS

> *It's a strange courage*
> *you give me, ancient star:*
>
> *Shine alone in the sunrise*
> *Toward which you lend no part!*

I

SHINE alone, shine nakedly, shine like bronze,
that reflects neither my face nor any inner part
of my being, shine like fire, that mirrors nothing.

II

Lend no part to any humanity that suffuses
you in its own light.
Be not chimera of morning,
Half-man, half-star.
Be not an intelligence,
Like a widow's bird
Or an old horse.

THE PLEASURES OF MERELY CIRCULATING

THE garden flew round with the angel,
The angel flew round with the clouds,
And the clouds flew round and the clouds flew round
And the clouds flew round with the clouds.

Is there any secret in skulls,
The cattle skulls in the woods?
Do the drummers in black hoods
Rumble anything out of their drums?

Mrs. Anderson's Swedish baby
Might well have been German or Spanish,
Yet that things go round and again go round
Has rather a classical sound.

AUTUMN REFRAIN

THE skreak and skritter of evening gone
And grackles gone and sorrows of the sun,
The sorrows of sun, too, gone . . . the moon and moon,
The yellow moon of words about the nightingale
In measureless measures, not a bird for me
But the name of a bird and the name of a nameless air
I have never—shall never hear. And yet beneath
The stillness of everything gone, and being still,
Being and sitting still, something resides,
Some skreaking and skrittering residuum,
And grates these evasions of the nightingale
Though I have never—shall never hear that bird.
And the stillness is in the key, all of it is,
The stillness is all in the key of that desolate sound.

THE EMPEROR OF ICE-CREAM

CALL the roller of big cigars,
The muscular one, and bid him whip
In kitchen cups concupiscent curds.
Let the wenches dawdle in such dress
As they are used to wear, and let the boys
Bring flowers in last month's newspapers.
Let be be finale of seem.
The only emperor is the emperor of ice-cream.

Take from the dresser of deal,
Lacking the three glass knobs, that sheet
On which she embroidered fantails once
And spread it so as to cover her face.
If her horny feet protrude, they come

To show how cold she is, and dumb.
Let the lamp affix its beam.
The only emperor is the emperor of ice-cream.

ANECDOTE OF THE JAR

I PLACED a jar in Tennessee,
And round it was, upon a hill.
It made the slovenly wilderness
Surround that hill.

The wilderness rose up to it,
And sprawled around, no longer wild.
The jar was round upon the ground
And tall and of a port in air.

It took dominion everywhere.
The jar was gray and bare.
It did not give of bird or bush,
Like nothing else in Tennessee.

TATTOO

The light is like a spider.
It crawls over the water.
It crawls over the edges of the snow.
It crawls under your eyelids
And spreads its webs there—
Its two webs.

The webs of your eyes
Are fastened
To the flesh and bones of you
As to rafters or grass.

There are filaments of your eyes
On the surface of the water
And in the edges of the snow.

358

SUNDAY MORNING

I

COMPLACENCIES of the peignoir, and late
Coffee and oranges in a sunny chair,
And the green freedom of a cockatoo
Upon a rug mingle to dissipate
The holy hush of ancient sacrifice.
She dreams a little, and she feels the dark
Encroachment of that old catastrophe,
As a calm darkens among water-lights.
The pungent oranges and bright, green wings
Seem things in some procession of the dead,
Winding across wide water, without sound.
The day is like wide water, without sound,
Stilled for the passing of her dreaming feet
Over the seas, to silent Palestine,
Dominion of the blood and sepulchre.

II

Why should she give her bounty to the dead?
What is divinity if it can come
Only in silent shadows and in dreams?
Shall she not find in comforts of the sun,
In pungent fruit and bright, green wings, or else
In any balm or beauty of the earth,
Things to be cherished like the thought of heaven?
Divinity must live within herself:
Passions of rain, or moods in falling snow;
Grievings in loneliness, or unsubdued
Elations when the forest blooms; gusty
Emotions on wet roads on autumn nights;
All pleasures and all pains, remembering
The bough of summer and the winter branch.
These are the measures destined for her soul.

III

Jove in the clouds had his inhuman birth.
No mother suckled him, no sweet land gave
Large-mannered motions to his mythy mind.
He moved among us, as a muttering king,
Magnificent, would move among his hinds,
Until our blood, commingling, virginal,
With heaven, brought such requital to desire
The very hinds discerned it, in a star.
Shall our blood fail? Or shall it come to be
The blood of paradise? And shall the earth
Seem all of paradise that we shall know?
The sky will be much friendlier then than now,
A part of labor and a part of pain,
And next in glory to enduring love,
Not this dividing and indifferent blue.

IV

She says, "I am content when wakened birds,
Before they fly, test the reality
Of misty fields, by their sweet questionings;
But when the birds are gone, and their warm fields
Return no more, where, then, is paradise?"
There is not any haunt of prophecy,
Nor any old chimera of the grave,
Neither the golden underground, nor isle
Melodious, where spirits gat them home,
Nor visionary south, nor cloudy palm
Remote on heaven's hill, that has endured
As April's green endures; or will endure
Like her remembrance of awakened birds,
Or her desire for June and evening, tipped
By the consummation of the swallow's wings.

V

She says, "But in contentment I still feel
The need of some imperishable bliss."
Death is the mother of beauty; hence from her,
Alone, shall come fulfilment to our dreams
And our desires. Although she strews the leaves
Of sure obliteration on our paths,
The path sick sorrow took, the many paths
Where triumph rang its brassy phrase, or love
Whispered a little out of tenderness,
She makes the willow shiver in the sun
For maidens who were wont to sit and gaze
Upon the grass, relinquished to their feet.
She causes boys to pile new plums and pears
On disregarded plate. The maidens taste
And stray impassioned in the littering leaves.

VI

Is there no change of death in paradise?
Does ripe fruit never fall? Or do the boughs
Hang always heavy in that perfect sky,
Unchanging, yet so like our perishing earth,
With rivers like our own that seek for seas
They never find, the same receding shores
That never touch with inarticulate pang?
Why set the pear upon those river-banks
Or spice the shores with odors of the plum?
Alas, that they should wear our colors there,
The silken weavings of our afternoons,
And pick the strings of our insipid lutes!
Death is the mother of beauty, mystical,
Within whose burning bosom we devise
Our earthly mothers waiting, sleeplessly.

VII

Supple and turbulent, a ring of men
Shall chant in orgy on a summer morn
Their boisterous devotion to the sun,
Not as a god, but as a god might be,
Naked among them, like a savage source.
Their chant shall be a chant of paradise,
Out of their blood, returning to the sky;
And in their chant shall enter, voice by voice,
The windy lake wherein their lord delights,
The trees, like serafim, and echoing hills,
That choir among themselves long afterward.
They shall know well the heavenly fellowship
Of men that perish and of summer morn.
And whence they came and whither they shall go
The dew upon their feet shall manifest.

VIII

She hears, upon that water without sound,
A voice that cries, "The tomb in Palestine
Is not the porch of spirits lingering.
It is the grave of Jesus, where he lay."
We live in an old chaos of the sun,
Or old dependency of day and night,
Or island solitude, unsponsored, free,
Of that wide water, inescapable.
Deer walk upon our mountains, and the quail
Whistle about us their spontaneous cries;
Sweet berries ripen in the wilderness;
And, in the isolation of the sky,
At evening, casual flocks of pigeons make
Ambiguous undulations as they sink,
Downward to darkness, on extended wings.

AN EXTRACT

from Addresses to the Academy of Fine Ideas

On an early Sunday in April, a feeble day,
He felt curious about the winter hills
And wondered about the water in the lake.
It had been cold since December. Snow fell, first,
At New Year and, from then until April, lay
On everything. Now it had melted, leaving
The gray grass like a pallet, closely pressed;
And dirt. The wind blew in the empty place.
The winter wind blew in an empty place—
There was that difference between the and an,
The difference between himself and no man,
No man that heard a wind in an empty place.
It was time to be himself again, to see
If the place, in spite of its witheredness, was still
Within the difference. He felt curious
Whether the water was black and lashed about
Or whether the ice still covered the lake. There was still
Snow under the trees and on the northern rocks,
The dead rocks not the green rocks, the live rocks. If,
When he looked, the water ran up the air or grew white
Against the edge of the ice, the abstraction would
Be broken and winter would be broken and done,
And being would be being himself again,
Being, becoming seeing and feeling and self,
Black water breaking into reality.

A POSTCARD FROM THE VOLCANO

Children picking up our bones
Will never know that these were once
As quick as foxes on the hill;

And that in autumn, when the grapes
Made sharp air sharper by their smell
These had a being, breathing frost;

And least will guess that with our bones
We left much more, left what still is
The look of things, left what we felt

At what we saw. The spring clouds blow
Above the shuttered mansion-house,
Beyond our gate and the windy sky

Cries out a literate despair.
We knew for long the mansion's look
And what we said of it became

A part of what it is . . . Children,
Still weaving budded aureoles,
Will speak our speech and never know,

Will say of the mansion that it seems
As if he that lived there left behind
A spirit storming in blank walls,

A dirty house in a gutted world,
A tatter of shadows peaked to white,
Smeared with the gold of the opulent sun.

PAROCHIAL THEME

LONG-TAILED ponies go nosing the pine-lands,
Ponies of Parisians shooting on the hill.

The wind blows. In the wind the voices
Have shapes that are not yet fully themselves,

Are sounds blown by a blower into shapes,
The blower squeezed to the thinnest *mi* of falsetto.

The hunters run to and fro. The heavy trees,
The grunting, shuffling branches, the robust,

The nocturnal, the antique, the blue-green pines
Deepen the feelings to inhuman depths.

These are the forest. This health is holy,
This halloo, halloo, halloo heard over the cries

Of those for whom a square room is a fire,
Of those whom the statues torture and keep down.

This health is holy, this descant of a self,
This barbarous chanting of what is strong, this blare.

But salvation here? What about the rattle of sticks
On tins and boxes? What about horses eaten by wind?

When spring comes and the skeletons of the hunters
Stretch themselves to rest in their first summer's sun,

The spring will have health of its own, with none
Of autumn's halloo in its hair. So that closely, then,

Health follows after health. Salvation there:
There's no such thing as life; or if there is,

It is faster than the weather, faster than
Any character. It is more than any scene:

Of the guillotine or of any glamorous hanging.
Piece the world together, boys, but not with your hands.

THE WOMAN THAT HAD MORE
BABIES THAN THAT

I

An acrobat on the border of the sea
Observed the waves, the rising and the swell
And the first line spreading up the beach; again,
The rising and the swell, the preparation
And the first line foaming over the sand; again,
The rising and the swell, the first line's glitter,
Like a dancer's skirt, flung round and settling down.
This was repeated day by day. The waves
Were mechanical, muscular. They never changed,
They never stopped, a repetition repeated
Continually— There is a woman has had
More babies than that. The merely revolving wheel
Returns and returns, along the dry, salt shore.
There is a mother whose children need more than that.
She is not the mother of landscapes but of those
That question the repetition on the shore,
Listening to the whole sea for a sound
Of more or less, ascetically sated
By amical tones.
           The acrobat observed
The universal machine. There he perceived
The need for a thesis, a music constant to move.

II

Berceuse, transatlantic. The children are men, old men,
Who, when they think and speak of the central man,
Of the humming of the central man, the whole sound
Of the sea, the central humming of the sea,
Are old men breathed on by a maternal voice,
Children and old men and philosophers,
Bald heads with their mother's voice still in their ears.

The self is a cloister full of remembered sounds
And of sounds so far forgotten, like her voice,
That they return unrecognized. The self
Detects the sound of a voice that doubles its own,
In the images of desire, the forms that speak,
The ideas that come to it with a sense of speech.
The old men, the philosophers, are haunted by that
Maternal voice, the explanation at night.
They are more than parts of the universal machine.
Their need in solitude: that is the need,
The desire, for the fiery lullaby.

III

           If her head
Stood on a plain of marble, high and cold;
If her eyes were chinks in which the sparrows built;
If she was deaf with falling grass in her ears—
But there is more than a marble, massive head.
They find her in the crackling summer night,
In the *Duft* of towns, beside a window, beside
A lamp, in a day of the week, the time before spring,
A manner of walking, yellow fruit, a house,
A street. She has a supernatural head.
On her lips familiar words become the words
Of an elevation, an elixir of the whole.

ON AN OLD HORN

I

THE bird kept saying that birds had once been men,
Or were to be, animals with men's eyes,
Men fat as feathers, misers counting breaths,
Women of a melancholy one could sing.

Then the bird from his ruddy belly blew
A trumpet round the trees. Could one say that it was
A baby with the tail of a rat?
                    The stones
Were violet, yellow, purple, pink. The grass
Of the iris bore white blooms. The bird then boomed.
Could one say that he sang the colors in the stones,
False as the mind, instead of the fragrance, warm
With sun?
            In the little of his voice, or the like,
Or less, he found a man, or more, against
Calamity, proclaimed himself, was proclaimed.

II

If the stars that move together as one, disband,
Flying like insects of fire in a cavern of night,
Pipperoo, pippera, pipperum . . . The rest is rot.

CUISINE BOURGEOISE

THESE days of disinheritance, we feast
On human heads. True, birds rebuild
Old nests and there is blue in the woods.
The church bells clap one night in the week.
But that's all done. It is what used to be,
As they used to lie in the grass, in the heat,
Men on green beds and women half of sun.
The words are written, though not yet said.

It is like the season when, after summer,
It is summer and it is not, it is autumn
And it is not, it is day and it not,
As if last night's lamps continued to burn,

As if yesterday's people continued to watch
The sky, half porcelain, preferring that
To shaking out heavy bodies in the glares
Of this present, this science, this unrecognized,

This outpost, this douce, this dumb, this dead, in which
We feast on human heads, brought in on leaves,
Crowned with the first, cold buds. On these we live,
No longer on the ancient cake of seed,
The almond and deep fruit. This bitter meat
Sustains us. . . . Who, then, are they, seated here?
Is the table a mirror in which they sit and look?
Are they men eating reflections of themselves?

THE PRESIDENT ORDAINS THE BEE TO BE

THE President ordains the bee to be
Immortal. The President ordains. But does
The body lift its heavy wing, take up,

Again, an inexhaustible being, rise
Over the loftiest antagonist
To drone the green phrases of its juvenal?

Why should the bee recapture a lost blague,
Find a deep echo in a horn and buzz
The bottomless trophy, new hornsman after old?

The President has apples on the table
And barefoot servants round him, who adjust
The curtains to a metaphysical t

And the banners of the nation flutter, burst
On the flag-poles in a red-blue dazzle, whack
At the halyards. Why, then, when in golden fury

Spring vanishes the scraps of winter, why
Should there be a question of returning or
Of death in memory's dream? Is spring a sleep?

This warmth is for lovers at last accomplishing
Their love, this beginning, not resuming, this
Booming and booming of the new-come bee.

(*from* "NOTES TOWARD A SUPREME FICTION")

THE GREAT STATUE OF THE GENERAL DU PUY

THE great statue of the General Du Puy
Rested immobile, though neighboring catafalques
Bore off the residents of its noble Place.

The right, uplifted foreleg of the horse
Suggested that, at the final funeral,
The music halted and the horse stood still.

On Sundays, lawyers in their promenades
Approached this strongly-heightened effigy
To study the past, and doctors, having bathed

Themselves with care, sought out the nerveless frame
Of a suspension, a permanence, so rigid
That it made the General a bit absurd,

Changed his true flesh to an inhuman bronze.
There never had been, never could be, such
A man. The lawyers disbelieved, the doctors

Said that as keen, illustrious ornament,
As a setting for geraniums, the General,
The very Place Du Puy, in fact, belonged

Among our more vestigial states of mind.
Nothing had happened because nothing had changed.
Yet the General was rubbish in the end.

(*from* "NOTES TOWARD A SUPREME FICTION")

WHISTLE ALOUD, TOO WEEDY WREN

WHISTLE aloud, too weedy wren. I can
Do all that angels can. I enjoy like them,
Like men besides, like men in light secluded,

Enjoying angels. Whistle, forced bugler,
That bugles for the mate, nearby the nest,
Cock bugler, whistle and bugle and stop just short,

Red robin, stop in your preludes, practicing
Mere repetitions. These things at least comprise
An occupation, an exercise, a work,

A thing final in itself and, therefore, good:
One of the vast repetitions final in
Themselves and, therefore, good, the going round

And round, and round, the merely going round,
Until merely going round is a final good,
The way wine comes at a table in a wood.

And we enjoy like men, the way a leaf
Above the table spins its constant spin,
So that we look at it with pleasure, look

At it spinning its eccentric measure. Perhaps,
The man-hero is not the exceptional monster,
But he that of repetition is most master.

(*from* "NOTES TOWARD A SUPREME FICTION")

William Carlos Williams

THE YACHTS

contend in a sea which the land partly encloses
shielding them from the too heavy blows
of an ungoverned ocean which when it chooses

tortures the biggest hulls, the best man knows
to pit against its beating, and sinks them pitilessly.
Mothlike in mists, scintillant in the minute

brilliance of cloudless days, with broad bellying sails
they glide to the wind tossing green water
from their sharp prows while over them the crew crawls

ant-like, solicitously grooming them, releasing,
making fast as they turn, lean far over and having
caught the wind again, side by side, head for the mark.

In a well guarded arena of open water surrounded by
lesser and greater craft which, sycophant, lumbering
and flittering follow them, they appear youthful, rare

as the light of a happy eye, live with the grace
of all that in the mind is feckless, free and
naturally to be desired. Now the sea which holds them

is moody, lapping their glossy sides, as if feeling
for some slightest flaw but fails completely.
Today no race. Then the wind comes again. The yachts

move, jockeying for a start, the signal is set and they
are off. Now the waves strike at them but they are too
well made, they slip through, though they take in canvas.

Arms with hands grasping seek to clutch at the prows.
Bodies thrown recklessly in the way are cut aside.
It is a sea of faces about them in agony, in despair

until the horror of the race dawns staggering the mind,
the whole sea become an entanglement of watery bodies
lost to the world bearing what they cannot hold. Broken,

beaten, desolate, reaching from the dead to be taken up
they cry out, failing, failing! their cries rising
in waves still as the skillful yachts pass over.

PEACE ON EARTH

The Archer is wake!
The Swan is flying!
Gold against blue
An Arrow is lying.
There is hunting in heaven—
Sleep safe till to-morrow.

The Bears are abroad!
The Eagle is screaming!
Gold against blue
Their eyes are gleaming!
Sleep!
Sleep safe till to-morrow.

The Sisters lie
With their arms
    intertwining;
Gold against blue
Their hair is shining!
The Serpent writhes!
Orion is listening!
Gold against blue
His sword is glistening!
Sleep!
There is hunting in
    heaven—
Sleep safe till to-morrow.

THE RED WHEELBARROW

so much depends
upon

a red wheel
barrow

glazed with rain
water

beside the white
chickens

373

THE BOTTICELLIAN TREES

THE alphabet of
the trees

is fading in the
song of the leaves

the crossing
bars of the thin

letters that spelled
winter

and the cold
have been illumined

with
pointed green

by the rain and sun—
The strict simple

principles of
straight branches

are being modified

by pinched out

ifs of color, devout
conditions

the smiles of love—

. . . . .

until the stript
sentences

move as a woman's
limbs under cloth

and praise from secrecy
with hot ardor

love's ascendancy
in summer—

In summer the song
sings itself

above the muffled words—

THE SEA-ELEPHANT

TRUNDLED from
the strangeness of the sea—
a kind of
heaven—
374

Ladies and Gentlemen!
the greatest
sea-monster ever exhibited
alive

the gigantic
sea-elephant—O wallow
of flesh where
are

there fish enough for
that
appetite stupidity
cannot lessen?

Sick
of April's smallness
the little
leaves—

Flesh has lief of you
enormous sea—
Speak!
Blouaugh! (feed

me) my
flesh is riven—
fish after fish into his maw
unswallowing

to let them glide down
gulching back
half spittle half
brine

the
troubled eyes—torn
from the sea.
(In

a practical voice) They
ought

to put it back where
it came from.

Gape.
Strange head—
told by old sailors—
rising

bearded
to the surface—and
the only
sense out of them

is that woman's
Yes
it's wonderful but they
ought to

put it
back into the sea where
it came from.
Blouaugh!

Swing—ride
walk
on wires—toss balls
stoop and

contort yourselves—
But I
am love. I am
from the sea—

Blouaugh!
there is no crime save
the too heavy
body

375

the sea
held playfully—comes
to the surface
the water

boiling
about the head the cows

scattering
fish dripping from

the bounty
of . . . and Spring,
they say
Spring is icummen in—

EL HOMBRE

IT's a strange courage
you give me ancient star:

Shine alone in the sunrise
toward which you lend no part!

THE TERM

A RUMPLED sheet
of brown paper
about the length

and apparent bulk
of a man was
rolling with the

wind slowly over
and over in
the street as

a car drove down
upon it and
crushed it to

the ground. Unlike
a man it rose
again rolling

with the wind over
and over to be as
it was before.

WILLIAM CARLOS WILLIAMS
THE FORGOTTEN CITY

WHEN I was coming down from the country
with my mother, the day of the storm,
trees were across the road and small branches
kept rattling on the roof of the car.
There was ten feet or more of water
making the parkways impassable with the wind
bringing more rain in sheets. Brown torrents
gushed up through new sluiceways in the
valley floor so that I had to take any road
I could find bearing to the south and west,
to get back to the city. I passed through
extraordinary places, as vivid as any
I ever saw where the storm had broken
the barrier and let through
a strange commonplace: Long, deserted avenues
with unrecognized names at the corners and
drunken looking people with completely
foreign manners. Monuments, institutions
and in one place a large body of water
startled me with an acre or more of hot
jets spouting up symmetrically over it. Parks.
I had no idea where I was and promised
myself I would some day go back to study
this curious and industrious people who lived
in these apartments, at these sharp
corners and turns of intersecting avenues
with so little apparent communication
with an outside world. How did they get
cut off this way from representation in our
newspapers and other means of publicity
when so near the metropolis, so closely
surrounded by the familiar and the famous.

TRACT

I WILL teach you my townspeople
how to perform a funeral—
for you have it over a troop
of artists—
unless one should scour the world—
you have the ground sense necessary.

See! the hearse leads.
I begin with a design for a hearse.
For Christ's sake not black—
nor white either—and not polished!
Let it be weathered—like a farm wagon—
with gilt wheels (this could be
applied fresh at small expense)
or no wheels at all:
a rough dray to drag over the ground.

Knock the glass out!
My God—glass, my townspeople!
For what purpose? Is it for the dead
to look out or for us to see
how well he is housed or to see
the flowers or the lack of them—
or what?
To keep the rain and snow from him?
He will have a heavier rain soon:
pebbles and dirt and what not.
Let there be no glass—
and no upholstery! phew!
and no little brass rollers
and small easy wheels on the bottom—
my townspeople what are you thinking of!
A rough plain hearse then
with gilt wheels and no top at all.
On this the coffin lies
by its own weight.

                              No wreaths please—
especially no hot-house flowers.
Some common memento is better,
something he prized and is known by:
his old clothes—a few books perhaps—
God knows what! You realize
how we are about these things,
my townspeople—
something will be found—anything—
even flowers if he had come to that.
So much for the hearse.

For heaven's sake though see to the driver!
Take off the silk hat! In fact
that's no place at all for him
up there unceremoniously
dragging our friend out to his own dignity!
Bring him down—bring him down!
Low and inconspicuous! I'd not have him ride
on the wagon at all—damn him—
the undertaker's understrapper!
Let him hold the reins
and walk at the side
and inconspicuously too!

Then briefly as to yourselves:
Walk behind—as they do in France,
seventh class, or if you ride
Hell take curtains! Go with some show
of inconvenience; sit openly—
to the weather as to grief.
Or do you think you can shut grief in?
What—from us? We who have perhaps
nothing to lose? Share with us
share with us—it will be money
in your pockets.
                              Go now
I think you are ready.

THE INN OF EARTH

I CAME to the crowded Inn of Earth,
    And called for a cup of wine,
But the Host went by with averted eye
    From a thirst as keen as mine.

Then I sat down with weariness
    And asked a bit of bread,
But the Host went by with averted eye
    And never a word he said.

While always from the outer night
    The waiting souls came in
With stifled cries of sharp surprise
    At all the light and din.

"Then give me a bed to sleep," I said,
    "For midnight comes apace"—
But the Host went by with averted eye
    And I never saw his face.

"Since there is neither food nor rest,
    I go where I fared before"—
But the Host went by with averted eye
    And barred the outer door.

SPRING NIGHT

THE park is filled with night and fog,
    The veils are drawn about the world,

380

The drowsy lights along the paths
   Are dim and pearled.

Gold and gleaming the empty streets,
   Gold and gleaming the misty lake,
The mirrored lights like sunken swords,
   Glimmer and shake.

Oh, is it not enough to be
Here with this beauty over me?
My throat should ache with praise, and I
Should kneel in joy beneath the sky.
Oh, beauty are you not enough?
Why am I crying after love,
With youth, a singing voice and eyes
To take earth's wonder with surprise?
Why have I put off my pride,
Why am I unsatisfied,
I for whom the pensive night
Binds her cloudy hair with light,
I for whom all beauty burns
Like incense in a million urns?
Oh, beauty, are you not enough?
Why am I crying after love?

THERE WILL COME SOFT RAINS

War Time

There will come soft rains and the smell of the ground,
And swallows circling with their shimmering sound;

And frogs in the pools singing at night,
And wild plum-trees in tremulous white;

Robins will wear their feathery fire
Whistling their whims on a low fence-wire;

And not one will know of the war, not one
Will care at last when it is done.

Not one would mind, neither bird nor tree,
If mankind perished utterly;

And Spring herself, when she woke at dawn,
Would scarcely know that we were gone.

THE LONG HILL

I MUST have passed the crest a while ago
    And now I am going down—
Strange to have crossed the crest and not to know,
    But the brambles were always catching the hem of my
        gown.

All the morning I thought how proud I should be
    To stand there straight as a queen,
Wrapped in the wind and the sun with the world under
        me—
    But the air was dull; there was little I could have seen.

It was nearly level along the beaten track
    And the brambles caught in my gown—
But it's no use now to think of turning back,
    The rest of the way will be only going down.

Ezra Pound

HUGH SELWYN MAUBERLEY
(LIFE AND CONTACTS)

"VOCAT ÆSTUS IN UMBRAM"
Nemesianus, Ec. IV

I

E. P. ODE POUR L'ELECTION DE SON
SEPULCHRE

FOR three years, out of key with his time,
He strove to resuscitate the dead art
Of poetry; to maintain "the sublime"
In the old sense. Wrong from the start—

No, hardly, but seeing he had been born
In a half savage country, out of date;
Bent resolutely on wringing lilies from the acorn;
Capaneus; trout for factitious bait;

Ἴδμεν γάρ τοι πάνθ', ὅσ' ἐνὶ Τροίῃ
Caught in the unstopped ear;
Giving the rocks small lee-way
The chopped seas held him, therefore, that year.

His true Penelope was Flaubert,
He fished by obstinate isles;
Observed the elegance of Circe's hair
Rather than the mottoes on sun-dials.

Unaffected by "the march of events,"
He passed from men's memory in *l'an trentiesme
De son eage;* the case presents
No adjunct to the Muses' diadem.

383

II

The age demanded an image
Of its accelerated grimace,
Something for the modern stage,
Not, at any rate, an Attic grace;

Not, not certainly, the obscure reveries
Of the inward gaze;
Better mendacities
Than the classics in paraphrase!

The "age demanded" chiefly a mould in plaster,
Made with no loss of time,
A prose kinema, not, not assuredly, alabaster
Or the "sculpture" of rhyme.

III

The tea-rose tea-gown, etc.
Supplants the mousseline of Cos,
The pianola "replaces"
Sappho's barbitos.

Christ follows Dionysus,
Phallic and ambrosial
Made way for macerations;
Caliban casts out Ariel.

All things are a flowing,
Sage Heracleitus says;
But a tawdry cheapness
Shall outlast our days.

Even the Christian beauty
Defects—after Samothrace;
We see τὸ καλὸν
Decreed in the market place.

Faun's flesh is not to us,
Nor the saint's vision.
We have the press for wafer;
Franchise for circumcision.

All men, in law, are equals.
Free of Pisistratus,
We choose a knave or an eunuch
To rule over us.

O bright Apollo,
τίν' ἄνδρα, τίν' ἥρωα, τίνα θεὸν,
What god, man, or hero
Shall I place a tin wreath upon!

IV

These fought in any case,
and some believing,

              pro domo, in any case . . .

Some quick to arm,
some for adventure,
some from fear of weakness,
some from fear of censure,
some for love of slaughter, in imagination,
learning later . . .
some in fear, learning love of slaughter;

Died some, pro patria,
              non "dulce" non "et decor" . . .
walked eye-deep in hell
believing in old men's lies, then unbelieving
came home, home to a lie,
home to many deceits,
home to old lies and new infamy;
usury age-old and age-thick
and liars in public places.

Daring as never before, wastage as never before.
Young blood and high blood,
fair cheeks, and fine bodies;

frankness as never before,

Frankness as never before,
disillusions as never told in the old days,
hysterias, trench confessions,
laughter out of dead bellies.

v

There died a myriad,
And of the best, among them,
For an old bitch gone in the teeth,
For a botched civilization,

Charm, smiling at the good mouth,
Quick eyes gone under earth's lid,

For two gross of broken statues,
For a few thousand battered books.

VI

YEUX GLAUQUES

Gladstone was still respected,
When John Ruskin produced
"King's Treasuries"; Swinburne
And Rossetti still abused.

Fœtid Buchanan lifted up his voice
When that faun's head of hers
Became a pastime for
Painters and adulterers.

The Burne-Jones cartons
Have preserved her eyes;

Still, at the Tate, they teach
Cophetua to rhapsodize;

Thin like brook-water,
With a vacant gaze.
The English Rubaiyat was still-born
In those days.

The thin, clear gaze, the same
Still darts out faun-like from the half-ruin'd face,
Questing and passive. . . .
"Ah, poor Jenny's case" . . .

Bewildered that a world
Shows no surprise
At her last maquero's
Adulteries.

VII

"SIENA MI FE'; DISFECEMI MAREMMA"

Among the pickled fœtuses and bottled bones,
Engaged in perfecting the catalogue,
I found the last scion of the
Senatorial families of Strasbourg, Monsieur Verog.

For two hours he talked of Gallifet;
Of Dowson; of the Rhymers' Club;
Told me how Johnson (Lionel) died
By falling from a high stool in a pub . . .

But showed no trace of alcohol
At the autopsy, privately performed—
Tissue preserved—the pure mind
Arose toward Newman as the whiskey warmed.

387

Dowson found harlots cheaper than hotels;
Headlam for uplift; Image impartially imbued
With raptures for Bacchus, Terpsichore and the
    Church.
So spoke the author of "The Dorian Mood,"

M. Verog, out of step with the decade,
Detached from his contemporaries,
Neglected by the young,
Because of these reveries.

VIII

BRENNBAUM

The sky-like limpid eyes,
The circular infant's face,
The stiffness from spats to collar
Never relaxing into grace;

The heavy memories of Horeb, Sinai and the forty
    years,
Showed only when the daylight fell
Level across the face
Of Brennbaum "The Impeccable."

IX

MR. NIXON

In the cream gilded cabin of his steam yacht
Mr. Nixon advised me kindly, to advance with
    fewer
Dangers of delay. "Consider
    "Carefully the reviewer.

"I was as poor as you are;
"When I began I got, of course,

388

"Advance on royalties, fifty at first," said Mr.
    Nixon,
"Follow me, and take a column,
"Even if you have to work free.

"Butter reviewers. From fifty to three hundred
"I rose in eighteen months;
"The hardest nut I had to crack
"Was Dr. Dundas.

"I never mentioned a man but with the view
"Of selling my own works.
"The tip's a good one, as for literature
"It gives no man a sinecure.

"And no one knows, at sight, a masterpiece.
"And give up verse, my boy,
"There's nothing in it."

   .   .   .   .   .

Likewise a friend of Bloughram's once advised me:
Don't kick against the pricks,
Accept opinion. The "Nineties" tried your game
And died, there's nothing in it.

X

Beneath the sagging roof
The stylist has taken shelter,
Unpaid, uncelebrated,
At last from the world's welter

Nature receives him;
With a placid and uneducated mistress
He exercises his talents
And the soil meets his distress.

The haven from sophistications and contentions
Leaks through its thatch;
He offers succulent cooking;
The door has a creaking latch.

XI

"Conservatrix of Milésien"
Habits of mind and feeling,
Possibly. But in Ealing
With the most bank-clerkly of Englishmen?

No, "Milésian" is an exaggeration.
No instinct has survived in her
Older than those her grandmother
Told her would fit her station.

XII

"Daphne with her thighs in bark
Stretches toward me her leafy hands,"—
Subjectively. In the stuffed-satin drawing-room
I await The Lady Valentine's commands,

Knowing my coat has never been
Of precisely the fashion
To stimulate, in her,
A durable passion;

Doubtful, somewhat, of the value
Of well-gowned approbation
Of literary effort,
But never of The Lady Valentine's vocation:

Poetry, her border of ideas,
The edge, uncertain, but a means of blending
With other strata
Where the lower and higher have ending;

A hook to catch the Lady Jane's attention,
A modulation toward the theatre,
Also, in the case of revolution,
A possible friend and comforter.

.   .   .   .   .

Conduct, on the other hand, the soul
"Which the highest cultures have nourished"
To Fleet St. where
Dr. Johnson flourished;

Beside this thoroughfare
The sale of half-hose has
Long since superseded the cultivation
Of Pierian roses.

XIII

ENVOI (1919)

Go, dumb-born book,
Tell her that sang me once that song of Lawes:
Hadst thou but song
As thou hast subjects known,
Then were there cause in thee that should condone
Even my faults that heavy upon me lie,
And build her glories their longevity.

Tell her that sheds
Such treasure in the air,
Recking naught else but that her graces give
Life to the moment,
I would bid them live
As roses might, in magic amber laid,
Red overwrought with orange and all made
One substance and one colour
Braving time.

Tell her that goes
With song upon her lips
But sings not out the song, nor knows
The maker of it, some other mouth,
May be as fair as hers,
Might, in new ages, gain her worshippers,
When our two dusts with Waller's shall be laid,
Siftings on siftings in oblivion,
Till change hath broken down
All things save Beauty alone.

MAUBERLEY

1920

"Vacuos exercet aera morsus."

I

Turned from the "eau-forte
Par Jaquemart"
To the strait head
Of Messalina:

"His true Penelope
Was Flaubert,"
And his tool
The engraver's.

Firmness,
Not the full smile,
His art, but an art
In profile;

Colourless
Pier Francesca,
Pisanello lacking the skill
To forge Achaia.

II

"Qu'est ce qu'ils savent de l'amour, et qu'est ce qu'ils peuvent comprendre?

S'ils ne comprennent pas la poésie, s'ils ne sentent pas la musique, qu'est ce qu'ils peuvent comprendre de cette passion en comparaison avec laquelle la rose est grossière et le parfum des violettes un tonnerre?" CAID ALI

For three years, diabolus in the scale,
He drank ambrosia,
All passes, ANANGKE prevails,
Came end, at last, to that Arcadia.

He had moved amid her phantasmagoria,
Amid her galaxies,
NUKTIS 'AGALMA

. . . .

Drifted . . . drifted precipitate,
Asking time to be rid of . . . .
Of his bewilderment; to designate
His new found orchid. . . .

To be certain . . . certain . . .
(Amid ærial flowers) . . . time for arrangements—
Drifted on
To the final estrangement;

Unable in the supervening blankness
To sift TO AGATHON from the chaff
Until he found his sieve . . .
Ultimately, his seismograph:

—Given that is his "fundamental passion,"
This urge to convey the relation
Of eye-lid and cheek-bone
By verbal manifestations;

393

To present the series
Of curious heads in medallion—

He had passed, inconscient, full gaze,
The wide-banded irides
And botticellian sprays implied
In their diastasis;

Which anæthesis, noted a year late,
And weighed, revealed his great affect,
(Orchid), mandate
Of Eros, a retrospect.

Mouths biting empty air,
The still stone dogs,
Caught in metamorphosis, were
Left him as epilogues.

"THE AGE DEMANDED"

Vide Poem II. Page 384

For this agility chance found
Him of all men, unfit
As the red-beaked steeds of
The Cytheræan for a chain bit.

The glow of porcelain
Brought no reforming sense
To his perception
Of the social inconsequence.

Thus, if her colour
Came against his gaze,
Tempered as if
It were through a perfect glaze

He made no immediate application
Of this to relation of the state
To the individual, the month was more temperate
Because this beauty had been.

> The coral isle, the lion-coloured sand
> Burst in upon the porcelain revery:
> Impetuous troubling
> Of his imagery.

Mildness, amid the neo-Nietzschean clatter,
His sense of graduations,
Quite out of place amid
Resistance to current exacerbations,

Invitation, mere invitation to perceptivity
Gradually led him to the isolation
Which these presents place
Under a more tolerant, perhaps, examination.

By constant elimination
The manifest universe
Yielded an armour
Against utter consternation,

A Minoan undulation,
Seen, we admit, amid ambrosial circumstances
Strengthened him against
The discouraging doctrine of chances,

And his desire for survival,
Faint in the most strenuous moods,
Became an Olympian *apathein*
In the presence of selected perceptions.

A pale gold, in the aforesaid pattern,
The unexpected palms
Destroying, certainly, the artist's urge,

Left him delighted with the imaginary
Audition of the phantasmal sea-surge,

Incapable of the least utterance or composition,
Emendation, conservation of the "better tradition,"
Refinement of medium, elimination of superfluities,
August attraction or concentration.

Nothing, in brief, but maudlin confession,
Irresponse to human aggression,
Amid the precipitation, down-float
Of insubstantial manna,
Lifting the faint susurrus
Of his subjective hosannah.

Ultimate affronts to
Human redundancies;

Non-esteem of self-styled "his betters"
Leading, as he well knew,
To his final
Exclusion from the world of letters.

IV

Scattered Moluccas
Not knowing, day to day,
The first day's end, in the next noon;
The placid water
Unbroken by the Simoon;

Thick foliage
Placid beneath warm suns,
Tawn fore-shores
Washed in the cobalt of oblivions;

Or through dawn-mist
The grey and rose

396

Of the juridical
Flamingoes;

A consciousness disjunct,
Being but this overblotted
Series
Of intermittences;

Coracle of Pacific voyages,
The unforecasted beach;
Then on an oar
Read this:

"I was
And I no more exist;
Here drifted
An hedonist."

MEDALLION

Luini in porcelain!
The grand piano
Utters a profane
Protest with her clear soprano.

The sleek head emerges
From the gold-yellow frock
As Anadyomene in the opening
Pages of Reinach.

Honey-red, closing the face-oval,
A basket-work of braids which seem as if they were
Spun in King Minos' hall
From metal, or intractable amber;

The face-oval beneath the glaze,
Bright in its suave bounding-line, as,
Beneath half-watt rays,
The eyes turn topaz.

THE GARDEN

En robe de parade. SAMAIN

LIKE a skein of loose silk blown against a wall
She walks by the railing of a path in Kensington Gardens,
And she is dying piece-meal
    of a sort of emotional anæmia.

And round about there is a rabble
Of the filthy, sturdy, unkillable infants of the very poor.
They shall inherit the earth.

In her is the end of breeding.
Her boredom is exquisite and excessive.
She would like some one to speak to her,
And is almost afraid that I
    will commit that indiscretion.

ORTUS

How have I laboured?
How have I not laboured
To bring her soul to birth,
To give these elements a name and a centre!
She is beautiful as the sunlight, and as fluid.
She has no name, and no place.
How have I laboured to bring her soul into separation;
To give her a name and her being!

Surely you are bound and entwined,
You are mingled with the elements unborn;
I have loved a stream and a shadow.

I beseech you enter your life.
I beseech you learn to say "I,"
When I question you;
For you are no part, but a whole,
    No portion, but a being.

THE ALCHEMIST

Chant for the Transmutation of Metals

Saîl of Claustra, Aelis, Azalais,
As you move among the bright trees;
As your voices, under the larches of Paradise
Make a clear sound,
Saîl of Claustra, Aelis, Azalais,
Raimona, Tibors, Berangèrë,
'Neath the dark gleam of the sky;
Under night, the peacock-throated,
Bring the saffron-coloured shell,
Bring the red gold of the maple,
Bring the light of the birch tree in autumn
Mirals, Cembelins, Audiarda,
                   Remember this fire.

Elain, Tireis, Alcmena
'Mid the silver rustling of wheat,
Agradiva, Anhes, Ardenca,
From the plum-coloured lake, in stillness,
From the molten dyes of the water
Bring the burnished nature of fire;
Briseis, Lianor, Loica,
From the wide earth and the olive,
From the poplars weeping their amber,
By the bright flame of the fishing torch
                   Remember this fire.
Midonz, with the gold of the sun, the leaf of the poplar,
    by the light of the amber,
Midonz, daughter of the sun, shaft of the tree, silver of
    the leaf, light of the yellow of the amber,
Midonz, gift of the God, gift of the light, gift of the
    amber of the sun,
                   Give light to the metal.
Anhes of Rocacoart, Ardenca, Aemelis,
From the power of grass,

From the white, alive in the seed,
From the heat of the bud,
From the copper of the leaf in autumn,
From the bronze of the maple, from the sap in the bough;
Lianor, Ioanna, Loica,
By the stir of the fin,
By the trout asleep in the gray-green of water;
Vanna, Mandetta, Viera, Alodetta, Picarda, Manuela
From the red gleam of copper,
Ysaut, Ydone, slight rustling of leaves,
Vierna, Jocelynn, daring of spirits,
By the mirror of burnished copper,
    O Queen of Cypress,
Out of Erebus, the flat-lying breadth,
Breath that is stretched out beneath the world:
Out of Erebus, out of the flat waste of air, lying beneath
  the world;
Out of the brown leaf-brown colourless
     Bring the imperceptible cool.
Elain, Tireis, Alcmena,
    Quiet this metal!
Let the manes put off their terror, let them put off their
  aqueous bodies with fire.
Let them assume the milk-white bodies of agate.
Let them draw together the bones of the metal.

Selvaggia, Guiscarda, Mandetta,
    Rain flakes of gold on the water
Azure and flaking silver of water,
Alcyon, Phætona, Alcmena,
Pallor of silver, pale lustre of Latona,
By these, from the malevolence of the dew
    Guard this alembic.
Elain, Tireis, Allodetta
    Quiet this metal.

400

NEAR PERIGORD

A Perigord, pres del muralh
Tan que i puosch' om gitar ab malh.

You'D have men's hearts up from the dust
And tell their secrets, Messire Cino,
Right enough? Then read between the lines of Uc St. Circ,
Solve me the riddle, for you know the tale.

Bertrans, En Bertrans, left a fine canzone:
"Maent, I love you, you have turned me out.
The voice at Montfort, Lady Agnes' hair,
Bel Miral's stature, the viscountess' throat,
Set all together, are not worthy of you. . . ."
And all the while you sing out that canzone,
Think you that Maent lived at Montaignac,
One at Chalais, another at Malemort
Hard over Brive—for every lady a castle,
Each place strong.

        Oh, *is* it easy enough?
Tairiran held hall in Montaignac,
His brother-in-law was all there was of power
In Perigord, and this good union
Gobbled all the land, and held it later for some hundred
    years.
And our En Bertrans was in Altafort,
Hub of the wheel, the stirrer-up of strife,
As caught by Dante in the last wallow of hell—
The headless trunk "that made its head a lamp,"
For separation wrought out separation,
And he who set the strife between brother and brother
And had his way with the old English king,
Viced in such torture for the "counterpass."
How would you live, with neighbours set about you—
Poictiers and Brive, untaken Rochecouart,
Spread like the finger-tips of one frail hand;

401

And you on that great mountain of a palm—
Not a neat ledge, not Foix between its streams,
But one huge back half-covered up with pine,
Worked for and snatched from the string-purse of Born—
The four round towers, four brothers—mostly fools:
What could he do but play the desperate chess,
And stir old grudges?

        "Pawn your castles, lords!
Let the Jews pay."

        And the great scene—
(That, maybe, never happened!)

        Beaten at last,
Before the hard old king:

        "Your son, ah, since he died
"My wit and worth are cobwebs brushed aside
"In the full flare of grief. Do what you will."

Take the whole man, and ravel out the story.
He loved this lady in castle Montaignac?
The castle flanked him—he had need of it.
You read to-day, how long the overlords of Perigord,
The Talleyrands, have held the place; it was no transient
    fiction.
And Maent failed him? Or saw through the scheme?

And all his net-like thought of new alliance?
Chalais is high, a-level with the poplars.
Its lowest stones just meet the valley tips
Where the low Dronne is filled with water-lilies.
And Rochecouart can match it, stronger yet,
The very spur's end, built on sheerest cliff,
And Malemort keeps its close hold on Brive,
While Born, his own close purse, his rabbit warren,
His subterranean chamber with a dozen doors,
A-bristle with antennæ to feel roads,
To sniff the traffic into Perigord.
And that hard phalanx, that unbroken line,

The ten good miles from there to Maent's castle,
All of his flank—how could he do without her?
And all the road to Cahors, to Toulouse?
What would he do without her?

"Papiol,
Go forthright singing—Anhes, Cembelins.
There is a throat; ah, there are two white hands;
There is a trellis full of early roses,
And all my heart is bound about with love.
Where am I come with compound flatteries—
What doors are open to fine compliment?"
And every one half jealous of Maent?
He wrote the catch to pit their jealousies
Against her; give her pride in them?

Take his own speech, make what you will of it—
And still the knot, the first knot, of Maent?

Is it a love poem? Did he sing of war?
Is it an intrigue to run subtly out,
Born of a jongleur's tongue, freely to pass
Up and about and in and out the land,
Mark him a craftsman and a strategist?
(St. Leider had done as much as Polhonac,
Singing a different stave, as closely hidden.)
Oh, there is precedent, legal tradition,
To sing one thing when your song means another,
"Et albirar ab lor bordon—"
Foix' count knew that. What is Sir Bertrans' singing?
Maent, Maent, and yet again Maent,
Or war and broken heaumes and politics?

II

End fact. Try fiction. Let us say we see
En Bertrans, a tower-room at Hautefort,
Sunset, the ribbon-like road lies, in red cross-light,

403

Southward toward Montaignac, and he bends at a table
Scribbling, swearing between his teeth; by his left hand
Lie little strips of parchment covered over,
Scratched and erased with *al* and *ochaisos*.
Testing his list of rhymes, a lean man? Bilious?
With a red straggling beard?
And the green cat's-eye lifts toward Montaignac.

Or take his "magnet" singer setting out,
Dodging his way past Aubeterre, singing at Chalais in
    the vaulted hall,
Or, by a lichened tree at Rochecouart
Aimlessly watching a hawk above the valleys,
Waiting his turn in the mid-summer evening,
Thinking of Aelis, whom he loved heart and soul . . .
To find her half alone, Montfort away,
And a brown, placid, hated woman visiting her,
Spoiling his visit, with a year before the next one.
Little enough?
Or carry him forward. "Go through all the courts,
My Magnet," Bertrans had said.

We came to Ventadour
In the mid love court, he sings out the canzon,
No one hears save Arrimon Luc D'Esparo—
No one hears aught save the gracious sound of compli-
    ments.
Sir Arrimon counts on his fingers, Montfort,
Rochecouart, Chalais, the rest, the tactic,
Malemort, guesses beneath, sends word to Cœur-de-Lion:
The compact, de Born smoked out, trees felled
About his castle, cattle driven out!
Or no one sees it, and En Bertrans prospered?

And ten years after, or twenty, as you will,
Arnaut and Richard lodge beneath Chalus:
The dull round towers encroaching on the field,
The tents tight drawn, horses at tether

Further and out of reach, the purple night,
The crackling of small fires, the bannerets,
The lazy leopards on the largest banner,
Stray gleams on hanging mail, an armourer's torch-flare
Melting on steel.

    And in the quietest space
They probe old scandals, say de Born is dead;
And we've the gossip (skipped six hundred years).
Richard shall die to-morrow—leave him there
Talking of *trobar clus* with Daniel.
And the "best craftsman" sings out his friend's song,
Envies its vigour . . . and deplores the technique,
Dispraises his own skill?—That's as you will.
And they discuss the dead man,
Plantagenet puts the riddle: "Did he love her?"
And Arnaut parries: "Did he love your sister?
True, he has praised her, but in some opinion
He wrote that praise only to show he had
The favour of your party; had been well received."

"You knew the man."
            "*You* knew the man."
"I am an artist, you have tried both métiers."
"You were born near him."
            "Do we know our friends?"
"Say that he saw the castles, say that he loved Maent!"
"Say that he loved her, does it solve the riddle?"
    End the discussion, Richard goes out next day
And gets a quarrel-bolt shot through his vizard,
Pardons the bowman, dies,

            Ends our discussion. Arnaut ends
"In sacred odour"—(that's apocryphal!)
And we can leave the talk till Dante writes:
Surely I saw, and still before my eyes
Goes on that headless trunk, that bears for light

405

Its own head swinging, gripped by the dead hair,
And like a swinging lamp that says, "Ah me!
I severed men, my head and heart
Ye see here severed, my life's counterpart."

Or take En Bertrans?

III

Ed eran due in uno, ed uno in due;
Inferno, XXVIII, 125

Bewildering spring, and by the Auvezere
Poppies and day's eyes in the green émail
Rose over us; and we knew all that stream,
And our two horses had traced out the valleys;
Knew the low flooded lands squared out with poplars,
In the young days when the deep sky befriended.
     And great wings beat above us in the twilight,
And the great wheels in heaven
Bore us together . . . surging . . . and apart . . .
Believing we should meet with lips and hands,

  High, high and sure . . . and then the counterthrust:
"Why do you love me? Will you always love me?
But I am like the grass, I can not love you."
Or, "Love, and I love and love you,
And hate your mind, not *you*, your soul, your hands."

    So to this last estrangement, Tairiran!

    There shut up in his castle, Tairiran's,
She who had nor ears nor tongue save in her hands,
Gone—ah, gone—untouched, unreachable!
She who could never live save through one person,
She who could never speak save to one person,
And all the rest of her a shifting change,
A broken bundle of mirrors . . . !

Ezra Pound

THE RIVER-MERCHANT'S WIFE:
A LETTER

While my hair was still cut straight across my forehead
I played about the front gate, pulling flowers.
You came by on bamboo stilts, playing horse,
You walked about my seat, playing with blue plums
And we went on living in the village of Chokan:
Two small people, without dislike or suspicion.

At fourteen I married My Lord you.
I never laughed, being bashful.
Lowering my head, I looked at the wall.
Called to, a thousand times, I never looked back.

At fifteen I stopped scowling,
I desired my dust to be mingled with yours
Forever and forever and forever.
Why should I climb the look out?

At sixteen you departed,
You went into far Ku-to-yen, by the river of swirling
    eddies,
And you have been gone five months.
The monkeys make sorrowful noise overhead.
You dragged your feet when you went out.
By the gate now, the moss is grown, the different mosses,
Too deep to clear them away!
The leaves fall early this autumn, in wind.
The paired butterflies are already yellow with August
Over the grass in the West garden;
They hurt me. I grow older.
If you are coming down through the narrows of the river
    Kiang,
Please let me know beforehand,
And I will come out to meet you
            As far as Cho-fu-sa.

THE SEAFARER

From the Anglo-Saxon

MAY I for my own self song's truth reckon,
Journey's jargon, how I in harsh days
Hardship endured oft.
Bitter breast-cares have I abided,
Known on my keel many a care's hold,
And dire sea-surge, and there I oft spent
Narrow nightwatch nigh the ship's head
While she tossed close to cliffs. Coldly afflicted,
My feet were by frost benumbed.
Chill its chains are; chafing sighs
Hew my heart round and hunger begot
Mere-weary mood. Lest man know not
That he on dry land loveliest liveth,
List how I, care-wretched, on ice-cold sea,
Weathered the winter, wretched outcast
Deprived of my kinsmen;
Hung with hard ice-flakes, where hail-scur flew,
There I heard naught save the harsh sea
And ice-cold wave, at whiles the swan cries,
Did for my games the gannet's clamour,
Sea-fowls' loudness was for me laughter,
The mews' singing all my mead-drink.
Storms, on the stone-cliffs beaten, fell on the stern
In icy feathers; full oft the eagle screamed
With spray on his pinion.

                       Not any protector
May make merry man faring needy.
This he little believes, who aye in winsome life
Abides 'mid burghers some heavy business,
Wealthy and wine-flushed, how I weary oft
Must bide above brine.
Neareth nightshade, snoweth from north,

Frost froze the land, hail fell on earth then,
Corn of the coldest. Nathless there knocketh now
The heart's thought that I on high streams
The salt-wavy tumult traverse alone.
Moaneth alway my mind's lust
That I fare forth, that I afar hence
Seek out a foreign fastness.
For this there's no mood-lofty man over earth's midst,
Not though he be given his good, but will have in his
    youth greed;
Nor his deed to the daring, nor his king to the faithful
But shall have his sorrow for sea-fare
Whatever his lord will.
He hath not heart for harping, nor in ring-having
Nor winsomeness to wife, nor world's delight
Nor any whit else save the wave's slash,
Yet longing comes upon him to fare forth on the water.
Bosque taketh blossom, cometh beauty of berries,
Fields to fairness, land fares brisker,
All this admonisheth man eager of mood,
The heart turns to travel so that he then thinks
On flood-ways to be far departing.
Cuckoo calleth with gloomy crying,
He singeth summerward, bodeth sorrow,
The bitter heart's blood. Burgher knows not—
He the prosperous man—what some perform
Where wandering them widest draweth.
So that but now my heart burst from my breastlock,
My mood 'mid the mere-flood,
Over the whale's acre, would wander wide.
On earth's shelter cometh oft to me,
Eager and ready, the crying lone-flyer,
Whets for the whale-path the heart irresistibly,
O'er tracks of ocean; seeing that anyhow
My lord deems to me this dead life
On loan and on land, I believe not
That any earth-weal eternal standeth

Save there be somewhat calamitous
That, ere a man's tide go, turn it to twain.
Disease or oldness or sword-hate
Beats out the breath from doom-gripped body.
And for this, every earl whatever, for those speaking
    after—
Laud of the living, boasteth some last word,
That he will work ere he pass onward,
Frame on the fair earth 'gainst foes his malice,
Daring ado, . . .
So that all men shall honour him after
And his laud beyond them remain 'mid the English,
Aye, for ever, a lasting life's-blast,
Delight 'mid the doughty.

                             Days little durable,
And all arrogance of earthen riches,
There come now no kings nor Cæsars
Nor gold-giving lords like those gone.
Howe'er in mirth most magnified,
Whoe'er lived in life most lordliest,
Drear all this excellence, delights undurable!
Waneth the watch, but the world holdeth.
Tomb hideth trouble. The blade is layed low.
Earthly glory ageth and seareth.
No man at all going the earth's gait,
But age fares against him, his face paleth,
Grey-haired he groaneth, knows gone companions,
Lordly men, are to earth o'ergiven,
Nor may he then the flesh-cover, whose life ceaseth,
Nor eat the sweet nor feel the sorry,
Nor stir hand nor think in mid heart,
And though he strew the grave with gold,
His born brothers, their buried bodies
Be an unlikely treasure hoard.

A PACT

I MAKE a pact with you, Walt Whitman—
I have detested you long enough.
I come to you as a grown child
Who has had a pig-headed father;
I am old enough now to make friends.
It was you that broke the new wood,
Now is a time for carving.
We have one sap and one root—
Let there be commerce between us.

CANTO I

AND then went down to the ship,
Set keel to breakers, forth on the godly sea, and
We set up mast and sail on that swart ship,
Bore sheep aboard her, and our bodies also
Heavy with weeping, and winds from sternward
Bore us out onward with bellying canvas,
Circe's this craft, the trim-coifed goddess.
Then sat we amidships, wind jamming the tiller,
Thus with stretched sail, we went over sea till day's end.
Sun to his slumber, shadows o'er all the ocean,
Came we then to the bounds of deepest water,
To the Kimmerian lands, and peopled cities
Covered with close-webbed mist, unpierced ever
With glitter of sun-ray
Nor with stars stretched, nor looking back from heaven
Swartest night stretched over wretched men there.
The ocean flowing backward, came we then to the place
Aforesaid by Circe.
Here did they rites, Perimedes and Eurylochus,
And drawing sword from my hip
I dug the ell-square pitkin;
Poured we libations unto each the dead,

411

First mead and then sweet wine, water mixed with white
    flour.
Then prayed I many a prayer to the sickly death's-heads;
As set in Ithaca, sterile bulls of the best
For sacrifice, heaping the pyre with goods,
A sheep to Tiresias only, black and a bell-sheep.
Dark blood flowed in the fosse,
Souls out of Erebus, cadaverous dead, of brides
Of youths and of the old who had borne much;
Souls stained with recent tears, girls tender,
Men many, mauled with bronze lance heads,
Battle spoil, bearing yet dreary arms,
These many crowded about me; with shouting,
Pallor upon me, cried to my men for more beasts;
Slaughtered the herds, sheep slain of bronze;
Poured ointment, cried to the gods,
To Pluto the strong, and praised Proserpine;
Unsheathed the narrow sword,
I sat to keep off the impetuous impotent dead,
Till I should hear Tiresias.
But first Elpenor came, our friend Elpenor,
Unburied, cast on the wide earth,
Limbs that we left in the house of Circe,
Unwept, unwrapped in sepulcher, since toils urged other.
Pitiful spirit. And I cried in hurried speech:
"Elpenor, how art thou come to this dark coast?
"Cam'st thou afoot, outstripping seamen?"
              And he in heavy speech:
"Ill fate and abundant wine. I slept in Circe's ingle.
"Going down the long ladder unguarded,
"I fell against the buttress,
"Shattered the nape-nerve, the soul sought Avernus.
"But thou, O King, I bid remember me, unwept, un-
    buried,
"Heap up mine arms, be tomb by sea-board, and in-
    scribed:
"'*A man of no fortune and with a name to come.*'
"And set my oar up, that I swung mid fellows."

And Anticlea came, whom I beat off, and then Tiresias
    Theban,
Holding his golden wand, knew me, and spoke first:
"A second time? why? man of ill star,
"Facing the sunless dead and this joyless region?
"Stand from the fosse, leave me my bloody bever
"For soothsay."
         And I stepped back,
And he strong with the blood, said then: "Odysseus
"Shalt return through spiteful Neptune, over dark seas,
"Lose all companions." And then Anticlea came.
Lie quiet Divus. I mean that is Andreas Divus,
In officina Wecheli, 1538, out of Homer.
And he sailed, by Sirens and thence outward and away
And unto Circe.
        Venerandam,
In the Cretan's phrase, with the golden crown, Aphro-
    dite,
Cypri munimenta sortita est, mirthful, oricalchi, with
    golden
Girdles and breast bands, thou with dark eyelids
Bearing the golden bough of Argicida.

SESTINA: ALTAFORTE

Loquitur: En Bertrans de Born.
    Dante Alighieri put this man in hell for that he was a stirrer up
    of strife. Eccovi! Judge ye!
    Have I dug him up again?
The scene is at his castle, Altaforte. "Papiols" is his jongleur.
"The Leopard," the device of Richard Cœur de Lion.

DAMN it all! all this our South stinks peace.
You whoreson dog, Papiols, come! Let's to music!
I have no life save when the swords clash.
But ah! when I see the standards gold, vair, purple,
    opposing
And the broad fields beneath them turn crimson,
Then howl I my heart nigh mad with rejoicing.

413

In hot summer have I great rejoicing
When the tempests kill the earth's foul peace,
And the lightnings from black heav'n flash crimson,
And the fierce thunders roar me their music
And the winds shriek through the clouds mad, opposing,
And through all the riven skies God's swords clash.

Hell grant soon we hear again the swords clash!
And the shrill neighs of destriers in battle rejoicing,
Spiked breast to spiked breast opposing!
Better one hour's stour than a year's peace
With fat boards, bawds, wine and frail music!
Bah! there's no wine like the blood's crimson!

And I love to see the sun rise blood-crimson.
And I watch his spears through the dark clash
And it fills all my heart with rejoicing
And pries wide my mouth with fast music
When I see him so scorn and defy peace,
His lone might 'gainst all darkness opposing.

The man who fears war and squats opposing
My words for stour, hath no blood of crimson
But is fit only to rot in womanish peace
Far from where worth's won and the swords clash
For the death of such sluts I go rejoicing;
Yea, I fill all the air with my music.

Papiols, Papiols, to the music!
There's no sound like to swords swords opposing,
No cry like the battle's rejoicing
When our elbows and swords drip the crimson
And our charges 'gainst "The Leopard's" rush clash.
May God damn for ever all who cry "Peace!"

And let the music of the swords make them crimson!
Hell grant soon we hear again the swords clash!
Hell blot black for alway the thought "Peace"!
414

BALLAD OF THE GOODLY FERE

Simon Zelotes speaketh it somewhile after the Crucifixion

Fere = Mate, Companion

HA' we lost the goodliest fere o' all
For the priests and the gallows tree?
Aye lover he was of brawny men,
O' ships and the open sea.

When they came wi' a host to take Our Man
His smile was good to see,
"First let these go!" quo' our Goodly Fere,
"Or I'll see ye damned," says he.

Aye he sent us out through the crossed high spears
And the scorn of his laugh rang free,
"Why took ye not me when I walked about
Alone in the town?" says he.

Oh we drunk his "Hale" in the good red wine
When we last made company,
No capon priest was the Goodly Fere
But a man o' men was he.

I ha' seen him drive a hundred men
Wi' a bundle o' cords swung free,
That they took the high and holy house
For their pawn and treasury.

They'll no' get him a' in a book I think
Though they write it cunningly;
No mouse of the scrolls was the Goodly Fere
But aye loved the open sea.

If they think they ha' snared our Goodly Fere
They are fools to the last degree.

415

"I'll go to the feast," quo' our Goodly Fere,
"Though I go to the gallows tree."

"Ye ha' seen me heal the lame and blind,
And wake the dead," says he,
"Ye shall see one thing to master all:
'Tis how a brave man dies on the tree."

A son of God was the Goodly Fere
That bade us his brothers be.
I ha' seen him cow a thousand men.
I have seen him upon the tree.

He cried no cry when they drave the nails
And the blood gushed hot and free,
The hounds of the crimson sky gave tongue
But never a cry cried he.

I ha' seen him cow a thousand men
On the hills o' Galilee,
They whined as he walked out calm between,
Wi' his eyes like the grey o' the sea,

Like the sea that brooks no voyaging
With the winds unleashed and free,
Like the sea that he cowed at Genseret
Wi' twey words spoke' suddenly.

A master of men was the Goodly Fere,
A mate of the wind and sea,
If they think they ha' slain our Goodly Fere
They are fools eternally.

I ha' seen him eat o' the honey-comb
Sin' they nailed him to the tree.

Elinor Wylie

WILD PEACHES

I

When the world turns completely upside down
You say we'll emigrate to the Eastern Shore
Aboard a river-boat from Baltimore;
We'll live among wild peach trees, miles from town,
You'll wear a coonskin cap, and I a gown
Homespun, dyed butternut's dark gold colour.
Lost, like your lotus-eating ancestor,
We'll swim in milk and honey till we drown.
The winter will be short, the summer long,
The autumn amber-hued, sunny and hot,
Tasting of cider and of scuppernong;
All seasons sweet, but autumn best of all.
The squirrels in their silver fur will fall
Like falling leaves, like fruit, before your shot.

II

The autumn frosts will lie upon the grass
Like bloom on grapes of purple-brown and gold.
The misted early mornings will be cold;
The little puddles will be roofed with glass.
The sun, which burns from copper into brass,
Melts these at noon, and makes the boys unfold
Their knitted mufflers; full as they can hold,
Fat pockets dribble chestnuts as they pass.
Peaches grow wild, and pigs can live in clover;
A barrel of salted herrings lasts a year;
The spring begins before the winter's over.

By February you may find the skins
Of garter snakes and water moccasins
Dwindled and harsh, dead-white and cloudy-clear.

III

When April pours the colours of a shell
Upon the hills, when every little creek
Is shot with silver from the Chesapeake
In shoals new-minted by the ocean swell,
When strawberries go begging, and the sleek
Blue plums lie open to the blackbird's beak,
We shall live well—we shall live very well.
The months between the cherries and the peaches
Are brimming cornucopias which spill
Fruits red and purple, sombre-bloomed and black;
Then, down rich fields and frosty river beaches
We'll trample bright persimmons, while you kill
Bronze partridge, speckled quail, and canvasback.

IV

Down to the Puritan marrow of my bones
There's something in this richness that I hate.
I love the look, austere, immaculate,
Of landscapes drawn in pearly monotones.
There's something in my very blood that owns
Bare hills, cold silver on a sky of slate,
A thread of water, churned to milky spate
Streaming through slanted pastures fenced with stones.
I love those skies, thin blue or snowy gray,
Those fields sparse-planted, rendering meagre sheaves;
That spring, briefer than apple-blossom's breath,
Summer, so much too beautiful to stay,
Swift autumn, like a bonfire of leaves,
And sleepy winter, like the sleep of death.
418

ELINOR WYLIE

ESCAPE

WHEN foxes eat the last gold grape,
And the last white antelope is killed,
I shall stop fighting and escape
Into a little house I'll build.

But first I'll shrink to fairy size,
With a whisper no one understands,
Making blind moons of all your eyes,
And muddy roads of all your hands.

And you may grope for me in vain
In hollows under the mangrove root,
Or where, in apple-scented rain,
The silver wasp-nests hang like fruit.

THE EAGLE AND THE MOLE

AVOID the reeking herd,
Shun the polluted flock,
Live like that stoic bird,
The eagle of the rock.

The huddled warmth of crowds
Begets and fosters hate;
He keeps, above the clouds,
His cliff inviolate.

When flocks are folded warm,
And herds to shelter run,
He sails above the storm,
He stares into the sun.

If in the eagle's track
Your sinews cannot leap,

419

Avoid the lathered pack,
Turn from the steaming sheep.

If you would keep your soul
From spotted sight or sound,
Live like the velvet mole;
Go burrow under ground.

And there hold intercourse
With roots of trees and stones,
With rivers at their source,
And disembodied bones.

FAREWELL, SWEET DUST

Now I have lost you, I must scatter
All of you on the air henceforth;
Not that to me it can ever matter
But it's only fair to the rest of earth.

Now especially, when it is winter
And the sun's not half so bright as he was,
Who wouldn't be glad to find a splinter
That once was you, in the frozen grass?

Snowflakes, too, will be softer feathered,
Clouds, perhaps, will be whiter plumed;
Rain, whose brilliance you caught and gathered,
Purer silver have reassumed.

Farewell, sweet dust; I was never a miser:
Once, for a minute, I made you mine:
Now you are gone, I am none the wiser
But the leaves of the willow are bright as wine.

TO A BOOK

By some peculiar force centrifugal
Snatched from my mind's protective keeping
Your path is plain and unequivocal,
A lightning-feathered falcon, leaping
To trace a hieroglyph in heaven.
O little moon! O lucent circle!
You are beyond my reach, and even
Beyond the fortune of a miracle.
A stubborn archangelic levity
Has whirled you into alien ether
But still a silver thread of gravity
Must bind our pulses up together.
In your beloved veins the earthy
Is mingled with the superhuman
Since you are mine, and I was worthy
To suckle you, as very woman.

The seedling of another planet
That holds our own in light derision
You clove the subterranean granite
To rainbows of the rock's division:
And like an aureate grain of mustard
Folding a golden microcosm
You fell between my breasts, which fostered
The shape of your sidereal blossom.
Now you are flown upon a power
Whose sovereignty is half-deceptive:
For you are free, my dragon-flower,
And still forever you are captive.
You shall remain a moon untarnished
By all contagion of our metal.
Yet this inferior substance furnished
The roots of that elusive petal:

A moon remaining pure and luminous,
So far removed, yet never further,
No prophecy, however ominous,

Pollutes with spiritual murther.
O smaller than a pearl's beginning
Within my brain! what living virtue
Informed your growth, and set you spinning
Where no malicious dust can hurt you?
Above terrestrial malfeasance,
Above the ignorant delusion,
With summer in successive seasons
To light you in divine transfusion
Of crystalline and opalescent,
No arrow of the world can startle
Your lunar quietude, my crescent:
Remember that your birth was mortal.

TRUE VINE

THERE is a serpent in perfection tarnished
The thin shell pierced, the purity grown fainter,
The virgin silver shield no longer burnished,
The pearly fruit with ruin at its centre.

The thing that sits expectant in our bosoms
Contriving heaven out of very little
Demands such delicate immaculate blossoms
As no malicious verity makes brittle.

This wild fastidious hope is quick to languish;
Its smooth diaphanous escape is swifter
Than the pack of truth; no mortal can distinguish
Its trace upon the durable hereafter.

Not so the obdurate and savage lovely
Whose roots are set profoundly upon trouble;
This flower grows so fiercely and so bravely
It does not even know that it is noble.

This is the vine to love, whose balsams flourish
Upon a living soil corrupt and faulty,

Whose leaves have drunk the skies, and stooped to
    nourish
The earth again with honey sweet and salty.

LET NO CHARITABLE HOPE

Now let no charitable hope
Confuse my mind with images
Of eagle and of antelope:
I am in nature none of these.

I was, being human, born alone;
I am, being woman, hard beset;
I live by squeezing from a stone
The little nourishment I get.

In masks outrageous and austere
The years go by in single file;
But none has merited my fear,
And none has quite escaped my smile.

SONNET from "ONE PERSON"

I HEREBY swear that to uphold your house
I would lay my bones in quick destroying lime
Or turn my flesh to timber for all time;
Cut down my womanhood; lop off the boughs
Of that perpetual ecstasy that grows
From the heart's core; condemn it as a crime
If it be broader than a beam, or climb
Above the stature that your roof allows.
I am not the hearthstone nor the cornerstone
Within this noble fabric you have builded;
Not by my beauty was its cornice gilded;
Not on my courage were its arches thrown:
My lord, adjudge my strength, and set me where
I bear a little more than I can bear.

423

EARTH

GRASSHOPPER, your tiny song
And my poem alike belong
To the dark and silent earth,
From which all poetry has birth;
All we say and all we sing
Is but as the murmuring
Of that drowsy heart of hers
When from her deep dream she stirs:
If we sorrow, or rejoice,
You and I are but her voice.

Deftly does the dust express,
In mind, her hidden loveliness—
And, from her cool silence, stream
The cricket's cry and Dante's dream;
For the earth, that breeds the trees,
Breeds cities too, and symphonies,
Equally her beauty flows
Into a savior, or a rose—
Looks down in dream, and from above
Smiles at herself in Jesus' love;
Christ's love and Homer's art
Are but the workings of her heart,
Through Leonardo's hand she seeks
Herself, and through Beethoven speaks,
In holy thunderings around,
The dreadful message of the ground.

The serene and humble mold
Does in herself all selves enfold,

424

Kingdoms, destinies, and creeds,
Great dreams, atoning deeds,
Science, that probes the firmament,
The high, inflexible intent
Of one, for many, sacrificed;
Plato's brain, the heart of Christ,
All love, all legend, and all lore
Are in the dust forevermore.

Even as the growing grass,
Up from the soil religions pass,
And the field that bears the rye
Bears parables and prophecy—
Out of the earth the poem grows,
Like the lily, or the rose;
And all man is, or yet may be,
Is but herself in agony
Toiling up the steep ascent
Toward the complete accomplishment
When all dust shall be—the whole
Universe—one conscious soul.

Yes, the quiet and cool sod
Bears in her breast the dream of God.

If you would know what earth is, scan
The intricate, proud heart of man,
Which is the earth articulate,
And learn how holy and how great,
How limitless and how profound
Is the nature of the ground—
How, without question or demur,
We may entrust ourselves to her
When we are wearied out and lay
Our bodies in the common clay.

For she is pity, she is love,
All wisdom, she, all thoughts that move

425

About her everlasting breast
Till she gathers them to rest—
All tenderness of all the ages,
Seraphic secrets of the sages,
Vision and hope of all the seers,
All prayer, all anguish, and all tears
Are but the dust, that from her dream
Awakes, and knows herself supreme;
Are but earth, when she reveals
All that her secret heart conceals
Down in the dark and silent loam,
Which is ourselves, asleep, at home.

Yes, and this, my poem, too,
Is part of her as dust and dew—
Wherein herself she doth declare,
Through my lips, and say her prayer.

John Gould Fletcher

DOWN THE MISSISSIPPI

EMBARKATION

DULL masses of dense green,
The forests range their sombre platforms;
Between them silently, like a spirit,
The river finds its own mysterious path.

Loosely the river sways out, backward, forward,
Always fretting the outer side;
Shunning the invisible focus of each crescent,
Seeking to spread into shining loops over fields.

Like an enormous serpent, dilating, uncoiling,
Displaying a broad scaly back of earth-smeared gold;
Swaying out sinuously between the dull motionless
    forests,
As molten metal might glide down the lip of a vase of
    dark bronze;

It goes, while the steamboat drifting out upon it,
Seems now to be floating not only outwards but upwards;
In the flight of a petal detached and gradually moving
    skyward
Above the pink explosion of the calyx of the dawn.

HEAT

As if the sun had trodden down the sky,
Until no more it holds living air, but only humid vapor,
427

Heat pressing upon earth with irresistible languor,
Turns all the solid forest into half-liquid smudge.

The heavy clouds like cargo-boats strain slowly against
    its current;
And the flickering of the haze is like the thunder of ten
    thousand paddles
Against the heavy wall of the horizon, pale-blue and
    utterly windless,
Whereon the sun hangs motionless, a brassy disc of
    flame.

FULL MOON

Flinging its arc of silver bubbles, quickly shifts the moon
From side to side of us as we go down its path;
I sit on the deck at midnight and watch it slipping and
    sliding,
Under my tilted chair, like a thin film of spilt water.

It is weaving a river of light to take the place of this
    river;
A river where we shall drift all night, then come to rest
    in its shallows;
And then I shall wake from my drowsiness and look
    down from some dim treetop
Over white lakes of cotton, like moonfields on every side.

THE MOON'S ORCHESTRA

When the moon lights up
Its dull red campfire through the trees;
And floats out, like a white balloon,
Into the blue cup of the night, borne by a casual breeze;
The moon-orchestra then begins to stir.
Jiggle of fiddles commence their crazy dance in the
    darkness.

428

Crickets churr
Against the stark reiteration of the rusty flutes which
frogs
Puff at from rotted logs
In the swamp.
And then the moon begins her dance of frozen pomp
Over the lightly quivering floor of the flat and mournful
river.
Her white feet slightly twist and swirl.
She is a mad girl
In an old unlit ballroom
Whose walls, half-guessed at through the gloom,
Are hung with the rusty crape of stark black cypress
Which show, through gaps and tatters, red stains half
hidden away.

THE STEVEDORES

Frieze of warm bronze that glides with catlike move-
ments
Over the gangplank poised and yet awaiting,
The sinewy thudding rhythm of forty shuffling feet
Falling like muffled drumbeats on the stillness.
O roll the cotton down,
Roll, roll the cotton down,
From the further side of Jordan,
O roll the cotton down!

And the river waits.
The river listens,
Chuckling little banjo-notes that break with a flop on
the stillness;
And by the low dark shed that holds the heavy freights,
Two lonely cypress trees stand up and point with stiffened
fingers
Far southward where a single chimney stands out aloof
in the sky.

NIGHT LANDING

After the whistle's roar has bellowed and shuddered,
Shaking the sleeping town and the somnolent river,
The deep toned floating of the pilot's bell
Suddenly warns the engines.

They stop like heartbeats that abruptly stop;
The shore glides to us, in a wide low curve.

And then—supreme revelation of the river—
The tackle is loosed—the long gangplank swings out-
    wards—
And poised at the end of it, half-naked beneath the
    searchlight,
A blue-black negro with gleaming teeth waits for his
    chance to leap.

THE SILENCE

There is a silence I carry about with me always;
A silence perpetual, for it is self-created;
A silence of heat, of water, of unchecked fruitfulness
Through which each year the heavy harvests bloom and
    burst and fall.

Deep, matted green silence of my South,
Often within the push and scorn of great cities,
I have seen that mile-wide waste of water swaying out
    to you,
And on its current glimmering, I am going to the sea.

There is a silence I have achieved: I have walked beyond
    its threshold;
I know it is without horizons, boundless, fathomless,
    perfect.
And some day maybe, far away,
I will curl up in it at last and sleep an endless sleep.

H. D.

FRAGMENT 113

"Neither honey nor bee for me."

—SAPPHO

Not honey,
not the plunder of the
    bee
from meadow or sand-
    flower
or mountain bush;
from winter-flower or shoot
born of the later heat:
not honey, not the sweet
stain on the lips and teeth:
not honey, not the deep
plunge of soft belly
and the clinging of the
    gold-edged
pollen-dusted feet;

though rapture blind my
    eyes,
and hunger crisp
dark and inert my mouth,
not honey, not the south,
not the tall stalk
of red twin-lilies,
nor light branch of fruit
    tree
caught in flexible light
    branch.

not honey, not the south;
ah, flower of purple iris,
flower of white,
or of the iris, withering the
    grass—
for fleck of the sun's fire,
gathers such heat and
    power,
that shadow-print is light,
cast through the petals
of the yellow iris flower.

not iris—old desire—old
    passion—
old forgetfulness—old pain—
not this, nor any flower,
but if you turn again,
seek strength of arm and
    throat,
touch as the god:
neglect the lyre-note;
knowing that you shall feel,
about the frame,
no trembling of the string
but heat, more passionate
of bone and the white shell
and fiery tempered steel.

431

SONG

You are as gold
as the half-ripe grain
that merges to gold again,
as white as the white
    rain
that beats through
the half-opened flowers
of the great flower tufts
thick on the black limbs
of an Illyrian apple
    bough.

Can honey distil such
    fragrance
as your bright hair—
for your face is as fair
    as rain,
yet as rain that lies clear
on white honey-comb,
lends radiance to the white
    wax,
so your hair on your brow
casts light for a shadow.

THE GARDEN

I

You are clear,
O rose, cut in rock,
hard as the descent of hail.

I could scrape the colour
from the petals,
like spilt dye from a rock.

If I could break you
I could break a tree.

If I could stir
I could break a tree—
I could break you.

II

O wind, rend open the
    heat,
cut apart the heat,
slit it to tatters.

Fruit cannot drop
through this thick air;
fruit cannot fall into heat
that presses up and blunts
the points of pears,
and rounds grapes.

Cut the heat:
plough through it,
turning it on either side
of your path.

432

HERMES OF THE WAYS

I

THE hard sand breaks,
and the grains of it
are clear as wine.

Far off over the leagues
  of it,
the wind,
playing on the wide shore,
piles little ridges,
and the great waves
break over it.

But more than the many-
  foamed ways
of the sea,
I know him
of the triple path-ways,
Hermes,
who awaits.

Dubious,
facing three ways,
welcoming wayfarers,
he whom the sea-orchard
shelters from the west,
from the east
weathers sea-wind;
fronts the great dunes.

Wind rushes
over the dunes,
and the coarse, salt-
  crusted grass
answers.

Heu,
it whips round my ankles!

II

Small is
this white stream,
flowing below ground
from the poplar-shaded hill,
but the water is sweet.

Apples on the small trees
are hard,
too small,
too late ripened
by a desperate sun
that struggles through
  sea-mist.

The boughs of the trees
are twisted
by many bafflings;
twisted are
the small-leafed boughs.

But the shadow of them
is not the shadow of the
  mast head
nor of the torn sails.

Hermes, Hermes,
the great sea foamed,
gnashed its teeth about me;
but you have waited,
where sea-grass tangles with
shore-grass.

433

ORCHARD

I saw the first pear
as it fell—
the honey-seeking, golden banded,
the yellow swarm,
was not more fleet than I,
(spare us from loveliness!)
and I fell prostrate,
crying:
you have flayed us with your blossoms,
spare us the beauty
of fruit-trees!

The honey-seeking
paused not;
the air thundered their song,
and I alone was prostrate.

O rough-hewn
god of the orchard,
I bring you an offering—
do you, alone unbeautiful,
son of the god,
spare us from loveliness:

these fallen hazel-nuts,
stripped late of their green sheaths,
grapes, red-purple,
their berries
dripping with wine;
pomegranates already broken,
and shrunken figs,
and quinces untouched,
I bring you as offering.

H. D.

AT BAIA

I SHOULD have thought
in a dream you would have brought
some lovely perilous thing,
orchids piled in a great sheath,
as who would say (in a dream)
I send you this,
who left the blue veins
of your throat unkissed.

Why was it that your hands
(that never took mine)
your hands that I could see
drift over the orchid heads
so carefully,
your hands, so fragile, sure to lift
so gently, the fragile flower stuff—
ah, ah, how was it

You never sent (in a dream)
the very form, the very scent,
not heavy, not sensuous,
but perilous—perilous—
of orchids, piled in a great sheath,
and folded underneath on a bright scroll
some word:

Flower sent to flower;
for white hands, the lesser white,
less lovely of flower leaf,

or

Lover to lover, no kiss,
no touch, but forever and ever this.

SEA GODS

I   THEY say there is no hope—
sand—drift—rocks—rubble of the sea—
the broken hulk of a ship,
hung with shreds of rope,
pallid under the cracked pitch.

they say there is no hope
to conjure you—
no whip of the tongue to anger you—
no hate of words
you must rise to refute.

They say you are twisted by the sea,
you are cut apart
by wave-break upon wave-break,
that you are misshapen by the sharp rocks,
broken by the rasp and after-rasp.

That you are cut, torn, mangled,
torn by the stress and beat,
no stronger than the strips of sand
along your ragged beach.

II   But we bring violets,
great masses—single, sweet,
wood-violets, stream-violets,
violets from a wet marsh.

Violets in clumps from hills,
tufts with earth at the roots,
violets tugged from rocks,
blue violets, moss, cliff, river-violets.

Yellow violets' gold,
burnt with a rare tint—

violets like red ash
among tufts of grass.

We bring deep-purple
bird-foot violets.

We bring the hyacinth-violet,
sweet, bare, chill to the touch—
and violets whiter than the in-rush
of your own white surf.

III   For you will come,
you will yet haunt men in ships,
you will trail across the fringe of strait
and circle the jagged rocks.

You will trail across the rocks
and wash them with your salt,
you will curl between sand-hills—
you will thunder along the cliff—
break—retreat—get fresh strength—
gather and pour weight upon the beach.

You will draw back,
and the ripple on the sand-shelf
will be witness of your track.
O privet-white, you will paint
the lintel of wet sand with froth.

You will bring myrrh-bark
and drift laurel-wood from hot coasts!
when you hurl high—high—
we will answer with a shout.

For you will come,
you will come,
you will answer our taut hearts,
you will break the lie of men's thoughts,
and cherish and shelter us.

ADONIS

I

EACH of us like you
has died once,
each of us like you
has passed through drift of
wood-leaves,
cracked and bent
and tortured and unbent
in the winter frost,
then burnt into gold points,
lighted afresh,
crisp amber, scales of
gold-leaf,
gold turned and re-welded
in the sun-heat;

each of us like you
has died once,
each of us has crossed
an old wood-path
and found the winter
leaves
so golden in the sun-fire
that even the live wood-
flowers
were dark.

II

Not the gold on the
temple-front
where you stand,
is as gold as this,

not the gold that fastens
your sandal,
nor the gold reft
through your chiselled
locks
is as gold as this last
year's leaf,

not all the gold hammered
and wrought
and beaten
on your lover's face,
brow and bare breast
is as golden as this:

each of us like you
has died once,
each of us like you
stands apart, like you
fit to be worshipped.

Robinson Jeffers

THE STARS GO OVER
THE LONELY OCEAN

Unhappy about some far off things
That are not my affair, wandering
Along the coast and up the lean ridges,
I saw in the evening
The stars go over the lonely ocean,
And a black-maned wild boar
Plowing with his snout on Mal Paso Mountain.

The old monster snuffled, "Here are sweet roots,
Fat grubs, slick beetles and sprouted acorns.
The best nation in Europe has fallen,
And that is Finland,
But the stars go over the lonely ocean,"
The old black-bristled boar,
Tearing the sod on Mal Paso Mountain.

"The world's in a bad way, my man,
And bound to be worse before it mends;
Better lie up in the mountain here
Four or five centuries,
While the stars go over the lonely ocean,"
Said the old father of wild pigs,
Plowing the fallow on Mal Paso Mountain.

"Keep clear of the dupes that talk democracy
And the dogs that bark revolution,
Drunk with talk, liars and believers.
I believe in my tusks.
Long live freedom and damn the ideologies,"
Said the gamey black-maned wild boar
Tusking the turf on Mal Paso Mountain.

439

APOLOGY FOR BAD DREAMS

I

In the purple light, heavy with redwood, the slopes drop
    seaward,
Headlong convexities of forest, drawn in together to the
    steep ravine. Below, on the sea-cliff,
A lonely clearing; a little field of corn by the streamside;
    a roof under spared trees. Then the ocean
Like a great stone someone has cut to a sharp edge and
    polished to shining. Beyond it, the fountain
And furnace of incredible light flowing up from the sunk
    sun. In the little clearing a woman
Was punishing a horse; she had tied the halter to a sap-
    ling at the edge of the wood; but when the great
    whip
Clung to the flanks the creature kicked so hard she feared
    he would snap the halter; she called from the house
The young man her son; who fetched a chain tie-rope,
    they working together
Noosed the small rusty links round the horse's tongue
And tied him by the swollen tongue to the tree.
Seen from this height they are shrunk to insect size,
Out of all human relation. You cannot distinguish
The blood dripping from where the chain is fastened,
The beast shuddering; but the thrust neck and the legs
Far apart. You can see the whip fall on the flanks. . . .
The gesture of the arm. You cannot see the face of the
    woman.
The enormous light beats up out of the west across the
    cloud-bars of the trade-wind. The ocean
Darkens, the high clouds brighten, the hills darken to-
    gether. Unbridled and unbelievable beauty
Covers the evening world . . . not covers, grows appar-
    ent out of it, as Venus down there grows out
From the lit sky. What said the prophet? "I create good:
    and I create evil: I am the Lord."

II

This coast crying out for tragedy like all beautiful places,
(The quiet ones ask for quieter suffering; but here the
    granite cliff the gaunt cypresses' crown
Demands what victim? The dykes of red lava and black
    what Titan? The hills like pointed flames
Beyond Soberanes, the terrible peaks of the bare hills
    under the sun, what immolation?)
This coast crying out for tragedy like all beautiful places:
    and like the passionate spirit of humanity
Pain for its bread: God's, many victims', the painful
    deaths, the horrible transfigurations: I said in my
    heart,
"Better invent than suffer: imagine victims
Lest your own flesh be chosen the agonist, or you
Martyr some creature to the beauty of the place." And I
    said,
"Burn sacrifices once a year to magic
Horror away from the house, this little house here
You have built over the ocean with your own hands
Beside the standing boulders: for what are we,
The beast that walks upright, with speaking lips
And little hair, to think we should always be fed,
Sheltered, intact, and self-controlled? We sooner more
    liable
Than the other animals. Pain and terror, the insanities of
    desire; not accidents, but essential,
And crowd up from the core." I imagined victims for
    those wolves, I made the phantoms to follow.
They have hunted the phantoms and missed the house.
    It is not good to forget over what gulls the spirit
Of the beauty of humanity, the petal of a lost flower
    blown seaward by the nightwind, floats to its quiet-
    ness.

III

Boulders blunted like an old bear's teeth break up from
    the headland; below them
All the soil is thick with shells, the tide-rock feasts of a
    dead people.
Here the granite flanks are scarred with ancient fire, the
    ghosts of the tribe
Crouch in the nights beside the ghost of a fire, they try
    to remember the sunlight,
Light has died out of their skies. These have paid some-
    thing for the future
Luck of the country, while we living keep old griefs in
    memory: though God's
Envy is not a likely fountain of ruin, to forget evil calls
    down
Sudden reminders from the cloud: remembered deaths
    be our redeemers;
Imagined victims our salvation: white as the half moon
    at midnight
Someone flamelike passed me, saying, "I am Tamar
    Cauldwell, I have my desire,"
Then the voice of the sea returned, when she had gone
    by, the stars to their towers.
. . . Beautiful country, burn again, Point Pinos down to
    the Sur Rivers
Burn as before with bitter wonders, land and ocean and
    the Carmel water.

IV

He brays humanity in a mortar to bring the savor
From the bruised root: a man having bad dreams, who
    invents victims, is only the ape of that God.
He washes it out with tears and many waters, calcines it
    with fire in the red crucible,
Deforms it, makes it horrible to itself: the spirit flies out
    and stands naked, he sees the spirit.

He takes it in the naked ecstasy; it breaks in his hand, the
  atom is broken, the power that massed it
Cries to the power that moves the stars, "I have come
  home to myself, behold me.
I bruised myself in the flint mortar and burnt me
In the red shell, I tortured myself, I flew forth,
Stood naked of myself and broke me in fragments,
And here am I moving the stars that are me."
I have seen these ways of God: I know of no reason
For fire and change and torture and the old returnings.
He being sufficient might be still. I think they admit no
  reason; they are the ways of my love.
Unmeasured power, incredible passion, enormous craft:
  no thought apparent but burns darkly
Smothered with its own smoke in the human brain-vault:
  no thought outside; a certain measure in phenomena:
The fountains of the boiling stars, the flowers on the
  foreland, the ever-returning roses of dawn.

PROMISE OF PEACE

THE heads of strong old age are beautiful
Beyond all grace of youth. They have strange quiet,
Integrity, health, soundness, to the full
They've dealt with life and been attempered by it.
A young man must not sleep; his years are war
Civil and foreign but the former's worse;
But the old can breathe in safety now that they are
Forgetting what youth meant, the being perverse,
Running the fool's gauntlet and being cut
By the whips of the five senses. As for me,
If I should wish to live long it were but
To trade those fevers for tranquillity,
Thinking though that's entire and sweet in the grave
How shall the dead taste the deep treasure they have?

443

NIGHT

THE ebb slips from the rock, the sunken
Tide-rocks lift streaming shoulders
Out of the slack, the slow west
Sombering its torch; a ship's light
Shows faintly, far out,
Over the weight of the prone ocean
On the low cloud.

Over the dark mountain, over the dark pinewood,
Down the long dark valley along the shrunken river,
Returns the splendor without rays, the shining shadow,
Peace-bringer, the matrix of all shining and quieter of
   shining.
Where the shore widens on the bay she opens dark wings
And the ocean accepts her glory. O soul worshipful of her
You, like the ocean, have grave depths where she dwells
      always,
And the film of waves above that takes the sun takes also
Her, with more love. The sun-lovers have a blond favorite,
A father of lights and noises, wars, weeping and laughter,
Hot labor, lust and delight and the other blemishes.
      Quietness
Flows from her deeper fountain; and he will die; and she
   is immortal.

Far off from here the slender
Flocks of the mountain forest
Move among stems like towers
Of the old redwoods to the stream,
No twig crackling; dip shy
Wild muzzles into the mountain water
Among the dark ferns.

O passionately at peace you being secure will pardon
The blasphemies of glowworms, the lamp in my tower,
      the fretfulness

Of cities, the crescents of the planets, the pride of the
stars.
This August night in a rift of cloud Antares reddens,
The great one, the ancient torch, a lord among lost
children,
The earth's orbit doubled would not girdle his greatness,
one fire
Globed, out of grasp of the mind enormous; but to you
O Night
What? Not a spark? What flicker of a spark in the faint
far glimmer
Of a lost fire dying in the desert, dim coals of a sand-pit
the Bedouins
Wandered from at dawn. . . . Ah singing prayer to what
gulfs tempted
Suddenly are you more lost? To us the near-hand mountain
Be a measure of height, the tide-worn cliff at the sea-gate
a measure of continuance.

The tide, moving the night's
Vastness with lonely voices,
Turns, the deep dark-shining
Pacific leans on the land,
Feeling his cold strength
To the outmost margins: you Night will resume
The stars in your time.

O passionately at peace when will that tide draw shore-
ward,
Truly the spouting fountains of light, Antares, Arcturus,
Tire of their flow, they sing one song but they think
silence.
The striding winter-giant Orion shines, and dreams darkness.
And life, the flicker of men and moths and the wolf on
the hill,
Though furious for continuance, passionately feeding,
passionately

445

Remaking itself upon its mates, remembers deep inward
The calm mother, the quietness of the womb and the egg,
The primal and the latter silences: dear Night it is
    memory
Prophesies, prophecy that remembers, the charm of the
    dark.
And I and my people, we are willing to love the four-
    score years
Heartily; but as a sailor loves the sea, when the helm is
    for harbor.

Have men's minds changed,
Or the rock hidden in the deep of the waters of the soul
Broken the surface? A few centuries
Gone by, was none dared not to people
The darkness beyond the stars with harps and habita-
    tions.
But now, dear is the truth. Life is grown sweeter and
    lonelier,
And death is no evil.

SHINE, PERISHING REPUBLIC

WHILE this America settles in the mold of its vulgarity,
    heavily thickening to empire,
And protest, only a bubble in the molten mass, pops and
    sighs out, and the mass hardens,

I sadly smiling remember that the flower fades to make
    fruit, the fruit rots to make earth.
Out of the mother; and through the spring exultances,
    ripeness and decadence; and home to the mother.

You making haste haste on decay: not blameworthy;
    life is good, be it stubbornly long or suddenly
A mortal splendor: meteors are not needed less than
    mountains: shine, perishing republic.

But for my children, I would have them keep their distance from the thickening center; corruption
Never has been compulsory, when the cities lie at the
monster's feet there are left the mountains.

And boys, be in nothing so moderate as in love of man,
a clever servant, insufferable master.
There is the trap that catches noblest spirits, that caught
—they say—God, when he walked on earth.

HURT HAWKS

THE broken pillar of the wing jags from the clotted
shoulder,
The wing trails like a banner in defeat,
No more to use the sky forever but live with famine
And pain a few days: cat nor coyote
Will shorten the week of waiting for death, there is game
without talons.

He stands under the oak-bush and waits
The lame feet of salvation; at night he remembers free-
dom
And flies in a dream, the dawns ruin it.
He is strong and pain is worse to the strong, incapacity
is worse.
The curs of the day come and torment him
At distance, no one but death the redeemer will humble
that head,
The intrepid readiness, the terrible eyes.
The wild God of the world is sometimes merciful to those
That ask mercy, not often to the arrogant.
You do not know him, you communal people, or you have
forgotten him;
Intemperate and savage, the hawk remembers him;
Beautiful and wild, the hawks, and men that are dying
remember him.

I'd sooner, except the penalties, kill a man than a hawk;
but the great redtail
Had nothing left but unable misery
From the bone too shattered for mending, the wing that
trailed under his talons when he moved.
We had fed him six weeks, I gave him freedom,
He wandered over the foreland hill and returned in the
evening, asking for death,
Not like a beggar, still eyed with the old
Implacable arrogance. I gave him the lead gift in the
twilight.
What fell was relaxed,
Owl-downy, soft feminine feathers; but what
Soared: the fierce rush: the night-herons by the flooded
river cried fear at its rising
Before it was quite unsheathed from reality.

PRESCRIPTION OF PAINFUL ENDS

LUCRETIUS felt the change of the world in his time, the
great republic coming to the height
Whence no way leads but downward, Plato in his time
watched Athens
Dance the down path. The future is ever a misted landscape, no man foreknows it, but at cyclical turns
There is a change felt in the rhythm of events: as when
an exhausted horse
Falters and recovers, then the rhythm of the running
hoofbeats is altered, he will run miles yet,
But he must fall: we have felt it again in our own lifetime, slip, shift and speed-up
In the gallop of the world, and now suspect that, come
peace or war, the progress of America and Europe
Becomes a long process of deterioration—starred with
famous Byzantiums and Alexandrias,
Surely,—but downward. One desires at such times
To gather the insights of the age summit against future
loss, against the narrowing mind and the tyrants,

The pedants, the mystagogues, the swarms of barbarians:
time-conscious poems, poems for treasuries: Lucretius
Sings his great theory of natural origins and of wise conduct; Plato smiling carves dreams, bright cells
Of incorruptible wax to hive the Greek honey.
                              Our own time, much greater
and far less fortunate
Has acids for honey and for fine dreams
The immense vulgarities of misapplied science and decaying Christianity: therefore one christens each
poem, in dutiful
Hope of burning off at least the top crust of the time's
uncleanness, from the acid bottles.

MAY-JUNE, 1940

FORESEEN for so many years: these evils, this monstrous
violence, these massive agonies: no easier to bear.
We saw them with slow stone strides approach, everyone
saw them; we closed our eyes against them, we
looked
And they had come nearer. We ate and drank and slept,
they came nearer. Sometimes we laughed, they were
nearer. Now
They are here. And now a blind man foresees what follows them: degradation, famine, recovery and so
forth, and the
Epidemic manias: but not enough death to serve us, not
enough death. It would be better for men
To be few and live far apart, where none could infect
another; then slowly the sanity of field and mountain
And the cold ocean and glittering stars might enter their
minds.
                              Another
dream, another dream.
We shall have to accept certain limitations

In future, and abandon some humane dreams; only hard-
    minded, sleepless and realist, can ride this rock-slide
To new fields down the dark mountain; and we shall
    have to perceive that these insanities are normal;
We shall have to perceive that battle is a burning flower
    or like a huge music, and the dive-bomber's scream-
    ing orgasm
As beautiful as other passions; and that death and life are
    not serious alternatives. One has known all these
    things
For many years: there is greater and darker to know
In the next hundred.

        And why do you cry, my dear, why do you cry?
It is all in the whirling circles of time.
If millions are born millions must die,
If England goes down and Germany up
The stronger dog will still be on top,
All in the turning of time.
If civilization goes down, that
Would be an event to contemplate.
It will not be in our time, alas, my dear,
It will not be in our time.

I SHALL LAUGH PURELY

I

    TURN from that girl
    Your fixed blue eyes.
    Boy-slender she is,
    And a face as beautiful as a hawk's face.
    History passes like falling rocks.

    I am old as a stone,
    But she is beautiful.
    War is coming.

All the fine boys will go off to war.
History passes like falling rocks.

Oh, that one's to marry
Another old man;
You won't be helped
When your tall sons go away to war.
History falls on your head like rocks.

Keep a straight mind
In the evil time.
In the mad-dog time
Why may not an old man run mad?
History falls like rocks in the dark,
All will be worse confounded soon.

II

Count the glories of this time,
Count that girl's beauty, then count England,
Bleeding, at bay, magnificent,
At last a lion,
For all will be worse confounded soon.

Count that girl's beauty, count the coast-range,
The steep rock that stops the Pacific,
Count the surf on its precipice,
The hawks in its air,
For all will be worse confounded soon.

Count its eagles and wild boars,
Count the great blue-black winter storms,
Heavy rain and the hurricane,
Get them by heart,
For all will be worse confounded soon.

Count no human thing but only
England's great fight and that girl's beauty,

History passes like falling
Rocks in the dark,
And all will be worse confounded soon.

III

But this, I steadily assure you, is not the world's end,
Nor even the end of a civilization. It is not so late as you
    think: give nature time.
These wars will end, and I shall lead a troupe of shaky
    old men through Europe and America,
Old drunkards, worn-out lechers; fallen dictators, cast
    kings, a disgraced president; some cashiered gen-
    erals
And collapsed millionaires: we shall enact a play, I shall
    announce to the audience:
"All will be worse confounded soon."

We shall beware of wild dogs in Europe, and of the police
    in armed imperial America:—
For all that pain was mainly a shift of power:—we shall
    enact our play: "Oh Christian era,
Make a good end," but first I announce to our audiences:
    "This play is prophetic, it will be centuries.
This play does not represent the world's end,
But only the fall of a civilization. It is not so late as you
    think: give nature time."

In Europe we shall beware of starving dogs and political
    commissars, and of the police in America.
We shall rant on our makeshift stages in our cracked
    voices: "Oh Christian era,
Era of chivalry and the barbarians and the machines, era
    of science and the saints,
When you go down make a good sunset.
Never linger superfluous, old and holy and paralytic like
    India,

452

Go down in conclusive war and a great red sunset, great
    age go down,
For all will be worse confounded soon."

We shall tour to the last verge and the open Pacific, we
    shall sit on the yellow cliffs at Hurricane Point
And watch the centaurs come from the sea; their splayed
    hooves plunge and stutter on the tide-rocks, watch
    them swarm up,
The hairy and foamy flanks, the naked destructive shoul-
    ders, the brutal faces and the bent bows,
Horde after horde under the screaming gulls: my old men
    will cough in the fog and baa like sheep,
"Here comes the end of a civilization. Give nature time,"
And spit, and make lewd jokes. But I shall laugh purely,
Remembering what old enthusiast named a girl's beauty
    and England's battle
Among the lights of his time: she being by then a dyed
    hag, or more likely
One of those embalmer-fingered smiles in the subsoil;
    and England will be
Not admirable. I shall laugh purely, knowing the next age
Lives on not-human beauty, waiting on circumstance and
    its April, weaving its winter chrysalis;
Thin snow falls on historical rocks.

BLACK-OUT

THE war that we have carefully for years provoked
Comes on us unprepared, amazed and indignant. Our
    warships are shot
Like sitting ducks and our planes like nest-birds, both
    our coasts ridiculously panicked,
And our leaders make orations. This is the people
That hopes to impose on the whole planetary world
An American peace.

(Oh, we'll win our war. My money on
amazed Gulliver
And his horse-pistols.)

Meanwhile our prudent officers
Have cleared the coast-long ocean of ships and fishing-
craft, the sky of planes, the windows of light: these
clearings
Make a strange beauty. Watch the wide sea, there is
nothing human, the gulls have it. Watch the wide
sky,
All day clean of machines, only at dawn and dusk a mili-
tary hawk passes
High on patrol. Walk at night on the shore,
The pretty firefly spangle that used to line it
Perfectly silent, shut are the shops, mouse-dark the
houses.

Here the prehuman dignity of night
Stands, as it was and will be again. Oh beautiful
Darkness and silence, the two eyes that see God. Great
staring eyes.

FOURTH ACT

BECAUSE you are simple people, kindly and romantic,
and set your trust in a leader and believed lies;
Because you are humble, and over-valued the rat-run
historical tombs of Europe: you have been betrayed

A second time into folly. Now fight, be valiant, be cruel,
bloody and remorseless, quit you like men.
To fight in a needless war is evil, evil the valor, evil the
victory: to be beaten would be worse.

But fear nothing, the little land-frontiered nations are out
of date, the island-empires dissolve,
Only solid continents now can support the oceans of
bombers, the enormous globe of the sky.

It is scene one act four of the tragic farce The Political
     Animal. Its hero reaches his apogee
And ravages the whole planet; not even the insects, only
     perhaps bacteria, were ever so powerful.

Not a good play, but you can see the author's intention:
     to disgust and shock. The tragic theme
Is patriotism; the clowning is massacre. He wishes to turn
     humanity outward from its obsession

In humanity, *a riveder le stelle*. He will have to pile on
     horrors, he will not convince you
In a thousand years; but the whole affair is only a hare-
     brained episode in the life of the planet.

THE EYE

The Atlantic is a stormy moat, and the Mediterranean,
The blue pool in the old garden,
More than five thousand years has drunk sacrifice
Of ships and blood and shines in the sun; but here the
     Pacific:
The ships, planes, wars are perfectly irrelevant.
Neither our present blood-feud with the brave dwarfs
Nor any future world-quarrel of westering
And eastering man, the bloody migrations, greed of
     power, battle-falcons,
Are a mote of dust in the great scale-pan.
Here from this mountain shore, headland beyond stormy
     headland plunging like dolphins through the gray
     sea-smoke
Into pale sea, look west at the hill of water: it is half the
     planet: this dome, this half-globe, this bulging
Eyeball of water, arched over to Asia,
Australia and white Antarctica: those are the eyelids that
     never close; this is the staring unsleeping
Eye of the earth, and what it watches is not our wars.

EAGLE VALOR, CHICKEN MIND

UNHAPPY country what wings you have. Even here,
Nothing important to protect, and ocean-far from the
    nearest enemy, what a cloud
Of bombers amazes the coast mountain, what a hornet-
    swarm of fighters,
And day and night the guns practising.

Unhappy, eagle wings and beak, chicken brain.
Weep (it is frequent in human affairs) weep for the
    terrible magnificence of the means
The ridiculous incompetence of the reasons, the bloody
    and shabby
Pathos of the result.

CASSANDRA

THE mad girl with the staring eyes and long white fingers
Hooked in the stones of the wall,
The storm-wrack hair and the screeching mouth: does it
    matter, Cassandra,
Whether the people believe
Your bitter fountain? Truly men hate the truth, they'd
    liefer
Meet a tiger on the road.
Therefore the poets honey their truth with lying; but
    religion-
Venders and political men
Pour from the barrel, new lies on the old, and are praised
    for kindly
Wisdom. Poor bitch be wise.
No: you'll still mumble in a corner a crust of truth, to men
And gods disgusting.   —you and I, Cassandra.
456

Marianne Moore

POETRY

I, TOO, dislike it: there are things that are important
        beyond all this fiddle.
Reading it, however, with a perfect contempt for it, one
        discovers in
it after all, a place for the genuine.
    Hands that can grasp, eyes
    that can dilate, hair that can rise
        if it must, these things are important not because a

high-sounding interpretation can be put upon them but
        because they are
useful. When they become so derivative as to become
        unintelligible,
    the same thing may be said for all of us, that we
        do not admire what
        we cannot understand: the bat
            holding on upside down or in quest of something
        to

eat, elephants pushing, a wild horse taking a roll, a tire-
        less wolf under
a tree, the immovable critic twitching his skin like a
        horse that feels a flea, the base-
    ball fan, the statistician—
        nor is it valid
            to discriminate "against business documents and

school-books"; all these phenomena are important. One
        must make a distinction
    however: when dragged into prominence by half
        poets, the result is not poetry,

457

nor till the poets among us can be
"literalists of
    the imagination"—above
        insolence and triviality and can present

for inspection, imaginary gardens with real toads in
                them, shall we have
    it. In the meantime, if you demand on the one hand,
    the raw material of poetry in
        all its rawness and
        that which is on the other hand
            genuine, then you are interested in poetry.

THE MONKEYS

WINKED too much and were afraid of snakes. The zebras,
                supreme in
their abnormality; the elephants with their fog-coloured
            skin
    and strictly practical appendages
        were there, the small cats; and the parakeet—
            trivial and humdrum on examination, destroy-
                ing
        bark and portions of the food it could not eat.

I recall their magnificence, now not more magnificent
than it is dim. It is difficult to recall the ornament,
    speech, and precise manner of what one might
        call the minor acquaintances twenty
            years back; but I shall not forget him—that
                Gilgamesh among
        the hairy carnivora—that cat with the

wedge-shaped, slate-gray marks on its forelegs and the
                resolute tail,
astringently remarking, "They have imposed on us with
                their pale

half-fledged protestations, trembling about
   in inarticulate frenzy, saying
       it is not for us to understand art; finding it
all so difficult, examining the thing

as if it were inconceivably arcanic, as symmetrically frigid as if it had been carved out of chrysoprase
   or marble—strict with tension, malignant
    in its power over us and deeper
       than the sea when it proffers flattery in ex-
        change for hemp,
rye, flax, horses, platinum, timber, and fur."

ENGLAND

WITH its baby rivers and little towns, each with its abbey
   or its cathedral;
   with voices—one voice perhaps, echoing through the
    transept—the
criterion of suitability and convenience: and Italy with
   its equal
   shores—contriving an epicureanism from which the
    grossness has been

extracted: and Greece with its goats and its gourds, the
   nest of modified illusions:
   and France, the "chrysalis of the nocturnal butterfly"
    in
whose products, mystery of construction diverts one from
   what was originally one's
   object—substance at the core: and the East with its
    snails, its emotional

shorthand and jade cockroaches, its rock crystal and its
   imperturbability,
   all of museum quality: and America where there

459

is the little old ramshackle victoria in the south, where
cigars are smoked on the
street in the north; where there are no proof readers,
no silkworms, no digressions;

the wild man's land; grass-less, links-less, language-less
country—in which letters are written
not in Spanish, not in Greek, not in Latin, not in shorthand,
but in plain American which cats and dogs can read! The
letter "a" in psalm and calm when
pronounced with the sound of "a" in candle, is very
noticeable but

why should continents of misapprehension have to be
accounted for by the
fact? Does it follow that because there are poisonous
toadstools
which resemble mushrooms, both are dangerous? In the
case of mettlesomeness which may be
mistaken for appetite, of heat which may appear to be
haste, no con-

clusions may be drawn. To have misapprehended the
matter, is to have confessed
that one has not looked far enough. The sublimated
wisdom
of China, Egyptian discernment, the cataclysmic torrent
of emotion compressed
in the verbs of the Hebrew language, the books of the
man who is able

to say, "I envy nobody but him and him only, who catches
more fish than
I do,"—the flower and fruit of all that noted superi-
ority—should one not have stumbled upon it in America,
must one imagine
that it is not there? It has never been confined to one
locality.

SPENSER'S IRELAND

HAS not altered;—
   the kindest place I've never been,
   the greenest place I've never seen.
Every name is a tune.
Denunciations do not affect
     the culprit; nor blows, but it
is torture to him to not be spoken to.
They're natural,—
     the coat, like Venus'
mantle lined with stars,
buttoned close at the neck,—the
     sleeves new from disuse.

If in Ireland
   they play the harp backward at need,
   and gather at midday the seed
of the fern, eluding
their 'giants all covered with iron," might
     there be fern   seed for unlearn-
ing obduracy and for reinstating
the enchantment?
     Hindered characters
seldom have mothers—
in Irish stories—
     but they all have grandmothers.

It was Irish;
   a match not a marriage was made
   when my great great grandmother'd said
with native genius for
disunion, "although your suitor be
     perfection,   one objection
is enough; he is not
Irish." Outwitting
     the fairies, befriending the furies,
whoever again
and again says, "I'll never
     give in," never sees

that you're not free
   until you've been made captive by
      supreme belief,—credulity
you say? When large dainty
fingers tremblingly divide the wings
      of the fly   for mid-July
with a needle and wrap it with peacock-tail,
or tie wool and
      buzzard's wing, their pride,
like the enchanter's
is in care, not madness. Con-
      curring hands divide

flax for damask
   that when bleached by Irish weather
      has the silvered chamois-leather
water-tightness of a
skin. Twisted torcs and gold new-moon-shaped
      lunulae   aren't jewelry
like the purple-coral fuchsia-tree's. If Eire—
"the guillemot
      so neat" and the hen
of the heath and "the
linnet spinet-sweet"—bespeak
      relentlessness, then

they are to me
   like enchanted Earl Gerald who
      changed himself into a stag, to
a great green-eyed cat of
the mountain. Discommodity makes
      them invis   ible; they've dis-
appeared. The Irish say "Your trouble is their
trouble and your
      joy their joy?" I wish
I could believe it;
I am troubled, I'm dissat-
      isfied, I'm Irish.

IN DISTRUST OF MERITS

Strengthened to live, strengthened to die for
  medals and positioned victories?
They're fighting, fighting, fighting the blind
  man who thinks he sees,—
who cannot see that the enslaver is
enslaved; the hater, harmed. O shining O
    firm star, O tumultuous
      ocean lashed till small things go
    as they will, the mountainous
      wave makes us who look, know

depth. Lost at sea before they fought! O
  star of David, star of Bethlehem,
O black imperial lion
  of the Lord—emblem
of a risen world—be joined at last, be
joined. There is hate's crown beneath which all is
    death; there's love's without which none
      is king; the blessed deeds bless
    the halo. As contagion
      of sickness makes sickness,

contagion of trust can make trust. They're
  fighting in deserts and caves, one by
one, in battalions and squadrons;
  they're fighting that I
may yet recover from the disease, *my*
self; some have it lightly, some will die. "Man's
    wolf to man?" And we devour
      ourselves? The enemy could not
    have made a greater breach in our
      defenses. One pilot-

ing a blind man can escape him, but
  Job disheartened by false comfort knew,

that nothing is so defeating
  as a blind man who
can see. O alive who are dead, who are
proud not to see, O small dust of the earth
    that walks so arrogantly,
      trust begets power and faith is
an affectionate thing. We
  vow, we make this promise

to the fighting—it's a promise—"We'll
  never hate black, white, red, yellow, Jew,
Gentile, Untouchable." We are
  not competent to
make our vows. With set jaw they are fighting,
fighting, fighting,—some we love whom we know,
    some we love but know not—that
      hearts may feel and not be numb.
  It cures me; or am I what
    I can't believe in? Some

in snow, some on crags, some in quicksands,
  little by little, much by much, they
are fighting fighting fighting that where
  there was death there may
be life. "When a man is prey to anger,
he is moved by outside things; when he holds
  his ground in patience patience
    patience, that is action or
    beauty," the soldier's defense
  and hardest armor for

the fight. The world's an orphans' home. Shall
  we never have peace without sorrow?
without pleas of the dying for
  help that won't come? O
quiet form upon the dust, I cannot
look and yet I must. If these great patient
    dyings—all these agonies

464

and woundbearings and blood shed—
can teach us how to live, these
dyings were not wasted.

Hate-hardened heart, O heart of iron,
iron is iron till it is rust.
There never was a war that was
not inward; I must
fight till I have conquered in myself what
causes war, but I would not believe it.
I inwardly did nothing.
O Iscariotlike crime!
Beauty is everlasting
and dust is for a time.

SILENCE

My father used to say,
"Superior people never make long visits,
have to be shown Longfellow's grave
or the glass flowers at Harvard.
Self-reliant like the cat—
that takes its prey to privacy,
the mouse's limp tail hanging like a shoelace from its
    mouth—
they sometimes enjoy solitude,
and can be robbed of speech
by speech which has delighted them.
The deepest feeling always shows itself in silence;
not in silence, but restraint."
Nor was he insincere in saying, "Make my house your
    inn."
Inns are not residences.

A CARRIAGE FROM SWEDEN

THEY say there is a sweeter air
     where it was made, than we have here;
     a Hamlet's castle atmosphere.
At all events there is in Brooklyn
something that makes me feel at home.

Noone may see this put-away
     museum-piece, this country cart
     that inner happiness made art;
and yet, in this city of freckled
integrity it is a vein

of resined straightness from north-wind
     hardened Sweden's once-opposed-to-
     compromise archipelago
of rocks. Washington and Gustavus
Adolphus, forgive our decay.

Seats, dashboard and sides of smooth gourd-
     rind texture, a flowered step, swan-
     dart brake, and swirling crustacean-
tailed equine amphibious creatures
that garnish the axle-tree! What

a fine thing! What unannoying
     romance; And how beautiful, she
     with the natural stoop of the
snowy egret, gray-eyed and straight-haired,
for whom it should come to the door,—

of whom it reminds me. The split
     pine fair hair, steady gannet-clear
     eyes and the pine-needled-path deer-
swift step; that is Sweden—land of the
free and the soil for a spruce-tree—

vertical though a seedling—all
    needles: from a green trunk, green shelf
      on shelf fanning out by itself.
The deft white-stockinged dance in thick-soled
shoes! Denmark's sanctuaried Jews!

The puzzle-jugs and hand-spun rugs,
    the root-legged kracken shaped like dogs,
      the hanging buttons and the frogs
that edge the Sunday jackets! Sweden,
you have a runner called the Deer, who

When he's won a race, likes to run
    more; you have the sun-right gable-
      ends due east and west, the table
spread as for a banquet; and the put-
in twin vest-pleats with a fish-fin

effect when you need none. Sweden,
    what makes the people dress that way
      and those who see you wish to stay?
The runner, not too tired to run more
at the end of the race? And that

cart, dolphin-graceful? A Dalgrén
    lighthouse, self-lit? responsive and
      responsible, I understand;
it's not pine-needle-paths that give spring
when they're run on, it's a Sweden

of moated white castles,—the bed
    of densely grown flowers in an S
      meaning Sweden and stalwartness,
skill, and a surface that says
Made in Sweden: carts are my trade.

A GRAVE

MAN looking into the sea,
taking the view from those who have as much right to
it as you have to it yourself,
it is human nature to stand in the middle of a thing,
but you cannot stand in the middle of this;
the sea has nothing to give but a well excavated grave.
The firs stand in a procession, each with an emerald
turkey-foot at the top,
reserved as their contours, saying nothing;
repression, however, is not the most obvious characteristic of the sea;
the sea is a collector, quick to return a rapacious look.
There are others besides you who have worn that look—
whose expression is no longer a protest; the fish no longer
investigate them
for their bones have not lasted:
men lower nets, unconscious of the fact that they are
desecrating a grave,
and row quickly away—the blades of the oars
moving together like the feet of water-spiders as if there
were no such thing as death.
The wrinkles progress upon themselves in a phalanx—
beautiful under networks of foam,
and fade breathlessly while the sea rustles in and out
of the seaweed;
the birds swim through the air at top speed, emitting
cat-calls as heretofore—
the tortoise-shell scourges about the feet of the cliffs, in
motion beneath them;
and the ocean, under the pulsation of lighthouses and
noise of bell-buoys,
advances as usual, looking as if it were not that ocean
in which dropped things are bound to sink—
in which if they turn and twist, it is neither with volition
nor consciousness.

MARIANNE MOORE

WHAT ARE YEARS?

WHAT is our innocence,
what is our guilt? All are
        naked, none is safe. And whence
is courage: the unanswered question,
the resolute doubt,—
dumbly calling, deafly listening—that
in misfortune, even death,
        encourages others
        and in its defeat, stirs

the soul to be strong? He
sees deep and is glad, who
        accedes to mortality
and in his imprisonment, rises
upon himself as
the sea in a chasm, struggling to be
free and unable to be
        in its surrendering
        finds its continuing.

So he who strongly feels,
behaves. The very bird,
        grown taller as he sings, steels
his form straight up. Though he is captive,
his mighty singing
says, satisfaction is a lowly
thing, how pure a thing is joy.
        This is mortality,
        this is eternity.

469

T. S. Eliot

ASH WEDNESDAY

I

Because I do not hope to turn again
Because I do not hope
Because I do not hope to turn
Desiring this man's gift and that man's scope
I no longer strive to strive towards such things
(Why should the aged eagle stretch its wings?)
Why should I mourn
The vanished power of the usual reign?

Because I do not hope to know again
The infirm glory of the positive hour
Because I do not think
Because I know I shall not know
The one veritable transitory power
Because I cannot drink
There, where trees flower, and springs flow, for there is
    nothing again

Because I know that time is always time
And place is always and only place
And what is actual is actual only for one time
And only for one place
I rejoice that things are as they are and
I renounce the blessèd face
And renounce the voice
Because I cannot hope to turn again
Consequently I rejoice, having to construct something
Upon which to rejoice
470

And pray to God to have mercy upon us
And I pray that I may forget
These matters that with myself I too much discuss
Too much explain
Because I do not hope to turn again
Let these words answer
For what is done, not to be done again,
May the judgment not be too heavy upon us

Because these wings are no longer wings to fly
But merely vans to beat the air
The air which is now thoroughly small and dry
Smaller and dryer than the will
Teach us to care and not to care
Teach us to sit still.

Pray for us sinners now and at the hour of our death
Pray for us now and at the hour of our death.

II

Lady, three white leopards sat under a juniper-tree
In the cool of the day, having fed to satiety
On my legs my heart my liver and that which had been
    contained
In the hollow round of my skull. And God said
Shall these bones live? shall these
Bones live? And that which had been contained
In the bones (which were already dry) said chirping:
Because of the goodness of this Lady
And because of her loveliness, and because
She honors the Virgin in meditation,
We shine with brightness. And I who am here dis-
    sembled
Proffer my deeds to oblivion, and my love
To the posterity of the desert and the fruit of the gourd.
It is this which recovers
My guts the strings of my eyes and the indigestible por-
    tions

471

Which the leopards reject. The Lady is withdrawn
In a white gown, to contemplation, in a white gown.
Let the whiteness of bones atone to forgetfulness.
There is no life in them. As I am forgotten
And would be forgotten, so I would forget
Thus devoted, concentrated in purpose. And God said
Prophesy to the wind, to the wind only, for only
The wind will listen. And the bones sang chirping
With the burden of the grasshopper, saying

Lady of silences
Calm and distressed
Torn and most whole
Rose of memory
Rose of forgetfulness
Exhausted and life-giving
Worried reposeful
The single Rose
Is now the Garden
Where all loves end
Terminate torment
Of love unsatisfied
The greater torment
Of love satisfied
End of the endless
Journey to no end
Conclusion of all that
Is inconclusible
Speech without word and
Word of no speech
Grace to the Mother
For the Garden
Where all love ends.

Under a juniper-tree the bones sang, scattered and shining
We are glad to be scattered, we did little good to each
other,

Under a tree in the cool of the day, with the blessing
          of sand,
Forgetting themselves and each other, united
In the quiet of the desert. This is the land which ye
Shall divide by lot. And neither division nor unity
Matters. This is the land. We have our inheritance.

III

At the first turning of the second stair
I turned and saw below
The same shape twisted on the banister
Under the vapor in the fetid air
Struggling with the devil of the stairs who wears
The deceitful face of hope and of despair.

At the second turning of the second stair
I left them twisting, turning below;
There were no more faces and the stair was dark,
Damp, jaggèd, like an old man's mouth drivelling, beyond
          repair,
Or the toothed gullet of an agèd shark.

At the first turning of the third stair
Was a slotted window bellied like the fig's fruit
And beyond the hawthorn blossom and a pasture scene
The broadbacked figure drest in blue and green
Enchanted the maytime with an antique flute.

Blown hair is sweet, brown hair over the mouth blown,
Lilac and brown hair;
Distraction, music of the flute, stops and steps of the
          mind over the third stair,
Fading, fading; strength beyond hope and despair
Climbing the third stair.
Lord, I am not worthy
Lord, I am not worthy

          but speak the word only.

IV

Who walked between the violet and the violet
Who walked between
The various ranks of varied green
Going in white and blue, in Mary's color,
Talking of trivial things
In ignorance and in knowledge of eternal dolour
Who moved among the others as they walked,
Who then made strong the fountains and made fresh the
    springs
Made cool the dry rock and made firm the sand
In blue of larkspur, blue of Mary's color,
Sovegna vos

Here are the years that walk between, bearing
Away the fiddles and the flutes, restoring
One who moves in the time between sleep and waking,
    wearing

White light folded, sheathed about her, folded.
The new years walk, restoring
Through a bright cloud of tears, the years, restoring
With a new verse the ancient rhyme. Redeem
The time. Redeem
The unread vision in the higher dream
While jewelled unicorns draw by the gilded hearse.

The silent sister veiled in white and blue
Between the yews, behind the garden god,
Whose flute is breathless, bent her head and sighed but
    spoke no word

But the fountain sprang up and the bird sang down
Redeem the time, redeem the dream
The token of the word unheard, unspoken

Till the wind shake a thousand whispers from the yew

And after this our exile
474

If the lost word is lost, if the spent word is spent
If the unheard, unspoken
Word is unspoken, unheard;
Still is the unspoken word, the Word unheard,
The Word without a word, the Word within
The world and for the world;
And the light shone in darkness and
Against the Word the unstilled world still whirled
About the center of the silent Word.

O my people, what have I done unto thee.

Where shall the word be found, where will the word
Resound? Not here, there is not enough silence,
Not on the sea or on the islands, not
On the mainland, in the desert or the rain land,
For those who walk in darkness
Both in the day time and in the night time
The right time and the right place are not here
No place of grace for those who avoid the face
No time to rejoice for those who walk among noise and
    deny the voice

Will the veiled sister pray for
Those who walk in darkness, who chose thee and oppose
    thee,
Those who are torn on the horn between season and
    season, time and time, between
Hour and hour, word and word, power and power, those
    who wait
In darkness? Will the veiled sister pray
For children at the gate
Who will not go away and cannot pray:
Pray for those who chose and oppose

O my people, what have I done unto thee.

Will the veiled sister between the slender
Yew trees pray for those who offend her
And are terrified and cannot surrender
And affirm before the world and deny between the rocks
In the last desert between the last blue rocks
The desert in the garden the garden in the desert
Of drouth, spitting from the mouth the withered apple-
    seed.

O my people.

VI

Although I do not hope to turn again
Although I do not hope
Although I do not hope to turn

Wavering between the profit and the loss
In this brief transit where the dreams cross
The dreamcrossed twilight between birth and dying
(Bless me father) though I do not wish to wish these
    things
From the wide window towards the granite shore
The white sails still fly seaward, seaward flying
Unbroken wings
And the lost heart stiffens and rejoices
In the lost lilac and the lost sea voices
And the weak spirit quickens to rebel
For the bent golden-rod and the lost sea smell
Quickens to recover
The cry of quail and the whirling plover
And the blind eye creates
The empty forms between the ivory gates
And smell renews the salt savor of the sandy earth
This is the time of tension between dying and birth
The place of solitude where three dreams cross
Between blue rocks

476

But when the voices shaken from the yew-tree drift
  away
Let the other yew be shaken and reply.

Blessed sister, holy mother, spirit of the fountain, spirit
  of the garden,
Suffer us not to mock ourselves with falsehood
Teach us to care and not to care
Teach us to sit still
Even among these rocks,
Our peace in His will
And even among these rocks
Sister, mother,
And spirit of the river, spirit of the sea,
Suffer me not to be separated

And let my cry come unto Thee.

THE HOLLOW MEN

A penny for the Old Guy

I

WE are the hollow men
We are the stuffed men
Leaning together
Headpiece filled with straw. Alas!
Our dried voices, when
We whisper together
Are quiet and meaningless
As wind in dry grass
Or rats' feet over broken glass
In our dry cellar

Shape without form, shade without colour,
Paralysed force, gesture without motion;

Those who have crossed
With direct eyes, to death's other Kingdom
Remember us—if at all—not as lost
Violent souls, but only
As the hollow men
The stuffed men.

II

Eyes I dare not meet in dreams
In death's dream kingdom
These do not appear:
There, the eyes are
Sunlight on a broken column
There, is a tree swinging
And voices are
In the wind's singing
More distant and more solemn
Than a fading star.

Let me be no nearer
In death's dream kingdom
Let me also wear
Such deliberate disguises
Rat's skin, crowskin, crossed staves
In a field
Behaving as the wind behaves
No nearer—

Not that final meeting
In the twilight kingdom

III

This is the dead land
This is cactus land

Here the stone images
Are raised, here they receive
The supplication of a dead man's hand
Under the twinkle of a fading star.
Is it like this
In death's other kingdom
Waking alone
At the hour when we are
Trembling with tenderness
Lips that would kiss
Form prayers to broken stone.

IV

The eyes are not here
There are no eyes here
In this valley of dying stars
In this hollow valley
This broken jaw of our lost kingdoms

In this last of meeting places
We grope together
And avoid speech
Gathered on this beach of the tumid river

Sightless, unless
The eyes reappear
As the perpetual star
Multifoliate rose
Of death's twilight kingdom
The hope only
Of empty men.

V

Here we go round the prickly pear
Prickly pear prickly pear

Here we go round the prickly pear
At five o'clock in the morning.

Between the idea
And the reality
Between the motion
And the act
Falls the Shadow

For Thine is the Kingdom

Between the conception
And the creation
Between the emotion
And the response
Falls the Shadow

Life is very long

Between the desire
And the spasm
Between the potency
And the existence
Between the essence
And the descent
Falls the Shadow

For Thine is the Kingdom

For Thine is
Life is
For Thine is the

This is the way the world ends
This is the way the world ends
This is the way the world ends
Not with a bang but a whimper.

JOURNEY OF THE MAGI

"A COLD coming we had of it,
Just the worst time of the year
For a journey, and such a long journey:
The ways deep and the weather sharp,
The very dead of winter."
And the camels galled, sore-footed, refractory,
Lying down in the melting snow.
There were times we regretted
The summer palaces on slopes, the terraces,
And the silken girls bringing sherbet.
Then the camel men cursing and grumbling
And running away, and wanting their liquor and women,
And the night-fires going out, and the lack of shelters,
And the cities hostile and the towns unfriendly
And the villages dirty and charging high prices:
A hard time we had of it.
At the end we preferred to travel all night,
Sleeping in snatches,
With the voices singing in our ears, saying
That this was all folly.

Then at dawn we came down to a temperate valley,
Wet, below the snow line, smelling of vegetation;
With a running stream and a water-mill beating the
    darkness,
And three trees on the low sky,
And an old white horse galloped away in the meadow.
Then we came to a tavern with vine-leaves over the
    lintel,
Six hands at an open door dicing for pieces of silver,
And feet kicking the empty wine-skins.
But there was no information, and so we continued
And arrived at evening, not a moment too soon
Finding the place; it was (you may say) satisfactory.

All this was a long time ago, I remember,
And I would do it again, but set down
This set down
This: were we led all that way for
Birth or Death? There was a Birth, certainly,
We had evidence and no doubt. I had seen birth and
    death,
But had thought they were different; this Birth was
Hard and bitter agony for us, like Death, our death.
We returned to our places, these Kingdoms,
But no longer at ease here, in the old dispensation,
With an alien people clutching their gods.
I should be glad of another death.

MARINA

Quis hic locus, quae regio, quae mundi plaga?

WHAT seas what shores what grey rocks and what islands
What water lapping the bow
And scent of pine and the woodthrush singing through
    the fog
What images return
O my daughter.

Those who sharpen the tooth of the dog, meaning
Death
Those who glitter with the glory of the humming-bird,
    meaning
Death
Those who sit in the stye of contentment, meaning
Death
Those who suffer the ecstasy of the animals, meaning
Death

Are become unsubstantial, reduced by a wind,
482

A breath of pine, and the woodsong fog
By this grace dissolved in place

What is this face, less clear and clearer
The pulse in the arm, less strong and stronger—
Given or lent? more distant than stars and nearer than
    the eye

Whispers and small laughter between leaves and hurry-
    ing feet
Under sleep, where all the waters meet.

Bowsprit cracked with ice and paint cracked with heat.
I made this, I have forgotten
And remember.
The rigging weak and the canvas rotten
Between one June and another September.
Made this unknowing, half conscious, unknown, my own.
The garboard strake leaks, the seams need caulking.
This form, this face, this life
Living to live in a world of time beyond me; let me
Resign my life for this life, my speech for that unspoken,
The awakened, lips parted, the hope, the new ships.

What seas what shores what granite islands towards my
    timbers
And woodthrush calling through the fog
My daughter.

LA FIGLIA CHE PIANGE

O quam te memorem virgo . . .

STAND on the highest pavement of the stair—
Lean on a garden urn—
Weave, weave the sunlight in your hair—
Clasp your flowers to you with a pained surprise—

483

Fling them to the ground and turn
With a fugitive resentment in your eyes:
But weave, weave the sunlight in your hair.

So I would have had him leave,
So I would have had her stand and grieve,
So he would have left
As the soul leaves the body torn and bruised,
As the mind deserts the body it has used.
I should find
Some way incomparably light and deft,
Some way we both should understand,
Simple and faithless as a smile and shake of the hand.

She turned away, but with the autumn weather
Compelled my imagination many days,
Many days and many hours:
Her hair over her arms and her arms full of flowers.
And I wonder how they should have been together!
I should have lost a gesture and a pose.
Sometimes these cogitations still amaze
The troubled midnight and the noon's repose.

GERONTION

> *Thou hast nor youth nor age*
> *But as it were an after dinner sleep*
> *Dreaming of both.*

HERE I am, an old man in a dry month,
Being read to by a boy, waiting for rain.
I was neither at the hot gates
Nor fought in the warm rain
Nor knee deep in the salt marsh, heaving a cutlass,
Bitten by flies, fought.
My house is a decayed house,
And the jew squats on the window sill, the owner,

Spawned in some estaminet of Antwerp,
Blistered in Brussels, patched and peeled in London.
The goat coughs at night in the field overhead;
Rocks, moss, stonecrop, iron, merds.
The woman keeps the kitchen, makes tea,
Sneezes at evening, poking the peevish gutter.

                     I an old man,
A dull head among windy spaces.

Signs are taken for wonders. "We would see a sign!"
The word within a word, unable to speak a word,
Swaddled with darkness. In the juvescence of the year
Came Christ the tiger
In depraved May, dogwood and chestnut, flowering
    judas,
To be eaten, to be divided, to be drunk
Among whispers; by Mr. Silvero
With caressing hands, at Limoges
Who walked all night in the next room;

By Hakagawa, bowing among the Titians;
By Madame de Tornquist, in the dark room
Shifting the candles; Fräulein von Kulp
Who turned in the hall, one hand on the door. Vacant
    shuttles
Weave the wind. I have no ghosts,
An old man in a draughty house
Under a windy knob.

After such knowledge, what forgiveness? Think now
History has many cunning passages, contrived corridors
And issues, deceives with whispering ambitions,
Guides us by vanities. Think now
She gives when our attention is distracted
And what she gives, gives with such supple confusions
That the giving famishes the craving. Gives too late
What's not believed in, or if still believed,
In memory only, reconsidered passion. Gives too soon

Into weak hands, what's thought can be dispensed with
Till the refusal propagates a fear. Think
Neither fear nor courage saves us. Unnatural vices
Are fathered by our heroism. Virtues
Are forced upon us by our impudent crimes.
These tears are shaken from the wrath-bearing tree.

The tiger springs in the new year. Us he devours. Think
    at last
We have not reached conclusion, when I
Stiffen in a rented house. Think at last
I have not made this show purposelessly
And it is not by any concitation
Of the backward devils
I would meet you upon this honestly.
I that was near your heart was removed therefrom
To lose beauty in terror, terror in inquisition.
I have lost my passion: why should I need to keep it
Since what is kept must be adulterated?
I have lost my sight, smell, hearing, taste and touch:
How should I use them for your closer contact?

These with a thousand small deliberations
Protract the profit of their chilled delirium,
Excite the membrane, when the sense has cooled,
With pungent sauces, multiply variety
In a wilderness of mirrors. What will the spider do,
Suspend its operations, will the weevil
Delay? De Bailhache, Fresca, Mrs. Cammel, whirled
Beyond the circuit of the shuddering Bear
In fractured atoms. Gull against the wind, in the windy
    straits
Of Belle Isle, or running on the Horn,
White feathers in the snow, the Gulf claims,
And an old man driven by the Trades
To a sleepy corner.

                                     Tenants of the house,
Thoughts of a dry brain in a dry season.

T. S. ELIOT

SWEENEY
AMONG THE NIGHTINGALES

ὤμοι, πέπληγμαι καιρίαν πληγὴν ἔσω.

APENECK SWEENEY spreads his knees
Letting his arms hang down to laugh,
The zebra stripes along his jaw
Swelling to maculate giraffe.

The circles of the stormy moon
Slide westward toward the River Plate,
Death and the Raven drift above
And Sweeney guards the hornèd gate.

Gloomy Orion and the Dog
Are veiled; and hushed the shrunken seas;
The person in the Spanish cape
Tries to sit on Sweeney's knees

Slips and pulls the table cloth
Overturns a coffee-cup,
Reorganised upon the floor
She yawns and draws a stocking up;

The silent man in mocha brown
Sprawls at the window-sill and gapes;
The waiter brings in oranges
Bananas figs and hothouse grapes;

The silent vertebrate in brown
Contracts and concentrates, withdraws;
Rachel *née* Rabinovitch
Tears at the grapes with murderous paws;

She and the lady in the cape
Are suspect, thought to be in league;

Therefore the man with heavy eyes
Declines the gambit, shows fatigue,

Leaves the room and reappears
Outside the window, leaning in,
Branches of wistaria
Circumscribe a golden grin;

The host with someone indistinct
Converses at the door apart,
The nightingales are singing near
The Convent of the Sacred Heart,

And sang within the bloody wood
When Agamemnon cried aloud,
And let their liquid siftings fall
To stain the stiff dishonoured shroud.

WHISPERS OF IMMORTALITY

WEBSTER was much possessed by death
And saw the skull beneath the skin;
And breastless creatures underground
Leaned backward with a lipless grin.

Daffodil bulbs instead of balls
Stared from the sockets of the eyes!
He knew that thought clings round dead limbs
Tightening its lusts and luxuries.

Donne, I suppose, was such another
Who found no substitute for sense
To seize and clutch and penetrate,
Expert beyond experience.

He knew the anguish of the marrow
The ague of the skeleton;

No contact possible to flesh
Allayed the fever of the bone.

.   .   .

Grishkin is nice; her Russian eye
Is underlined for emphasis;
Uncorseted, her friendly bust
Gives promise of pneumatic bliss.

The couched Brazilian jaguar
Compels the scampering marmoset
With subtle effluence of cat;
Grishkin has a maisonette:

The sleek and sinuous jaguar
Does not in his arboreal gloom
Distil so rank a feline smell
As Grishkin in a drawing-room

And even abstracter entities
Circumambulate her charm;
But our lot crawls between dry ribs
To keep its metaphysics warm.

PRELUDES

I

THE winter evening settles down
With smell of steaks in passageways.
Six o'clock.
The burnt-out ends of smoky days.
And now a gusty shower wraps
The grimy scraps
Of withered leaves about your feet

489

And newspapers from vacant lots;
The showers beat
On broken blinds and chimney-pots,
And at the corner of the street
A lonely cab-horse steams and stamps.
And then the lighting of the lamps.

II

The morning comes to consciousness
Of faint stale smells of beer
From the sawdust-trampled street
With all its muddy feet that press
To early coffee-stands.
With the other masquerades
That time resumes,
One thinks of all the hands
That are raising dingy shades
In a thousand furnished rooms.

III

You tossed a blanket from the bed,
You lay upon your back, and waited;
You dozed, and watched the night revealing
The thousand sordid images
Of which your soul was constituted;
They flickered against the ceiling.
And when all the world came back
And the light crept up between the shutters
And you heard the sparrows in the gutters,
You had such a vision of the street
As the street hardly understands;
Sitting along the bed's edge, where
You curled the papers from your hair,
Or clasped the yellow soles of feet
In the palms of both soiled hands.

IV

His soul stretched tight across the skies
That fade behind a city block,
Or trampled by insistent feet
At four and five and six o'clock;
And short square fingers stuffing pipes,
And evening newspapers, and eyes
Assured of certain certainties,
The conscience of a blackened street
Impatient to assume the world.

I am moved by fancies that are curled
Around these images, and cling:
The notion of some infinitely gentle
Infinitely suffering thing.

Wipe your hand across your mouth, and laugh;
The worlds revolve like ancient women
Gathering fuel in vacant lots.

THE WASTE LAND

"Nam Sibyllam quidem Cumis ego ipse oculis meis vidi in
ampulla pendere, et cum illi pueri dicerent:
Σίβυλλα τί θέλεις; respondebat illa: ἀποθανεῖν
θέλω."

For Ezra Pound
il miglior fabbro.

I. THE BURIAL OF THE DEAD

April is the cruellest month, breeding
Lilacs out of the dead land, mixing
Memory and desire, stirring
Dull roots with spring rain.
Winter kept us warm, covering
Earth in forgetful snow, feeding

A little life with dried tubers.
Summer surprised us, coming over the Starnbergersee
With a shower of rain; we stopped in the colonnade,
And went on in sunlight, into the Hofgarten,
And drank coffee, and talked for an hour.
Bin gar keine Russin, stamm' aus Litauen, echt deutsch.
And when we were children, staying at the archduke's,
My cousin's, he took me out on a sled,
And I was frightened. He said, Marie,
Marie, hold on tight. And down we went.
In the mountains, there you feel free.
I read, much of the night, and go south in the winter.

What are the roots that clutch, what branches grow
Out of this stony rubbish? Son of man,
You cannot say, or guess, for you know only
A heap of broken images, where the sun beats,
And the dead tree gives no shelter, the cricket no relief,
And the dry stone no sound of water. Only
There is shadow under this red rock,
(Come in under the shadow of this red rock),
And I will show you something different from either
Your shadow at morning striding behind you
Or your shadow at evening rising to meet you;
I will show you fear in a handful of dust.
          Frisch weht der Wind
          Der Heimat zu
          Mein Irisch Kind,
          Wo weilest du?
"You gave me hyacinths first a year ago;
"They called me the hyacinth girl."
—Yet when we came back, late, from the Hyacinth
     garden,
Your arms full, and your hair wet, I could not
Speak, and my eyes failed, I was neither
Living nor dead, and I knew nothing,
Looking into the heart of light, the silence.
Oed' und leer das Meer.

Madame Sosostris, famous clairvoyante,
Had a bad cold, nevertheless
Is known to be the wisest woman in Europe,
With a wicked pack of cards. Here, said she,
Is your card, the drowned Phoenician Sailor,
(Those are pearls that were his eyes. Look!)
Here is Belladonna, the Lady of the Rocks,
The lady of situations.
Here is the man with three staves, and here the Wheel,
And here is the one-eyed merchant, and this card,
Which is blank, is something he carries on his back,
Which I am forbidden to see. I do not find
The Hanged Man. Fear death by water.
I see crowds of people, walking round in a ring.
Thank you. If you see dear Mrs. Equitone,
Tell her I bring the horoscope myself:
One must be so careful these days.

Unreal City,
Under the brown fog of a winter dawn,
A crowd flowed over London Bridge, so many,
I had not thought death had undone so many.
Sighs, short and infrequent, were exhaled,
And each man fixed his eyes before his feet.
Flowed up the hill and down King William Street,
To where Saint Mary Woolnoth kept the hours
With a dead sound on the final stroke of nine.
There I saw one I knew, and stopped him, crying:
    "Stetson!
"You who were with me in the ships at Mylae!
"That corpse you planted last year in your garden,
"Has it begun to sprout? Will it bloom this year?
"Or has the sudden frost disturbed its bed?
"Oh keep the Dog far hence, that's friend to men,
"Or with his nails he'll dig it up again!
"You! hypocrite lecteur!—mon semblable,—mon frère!"

II. A GAME OF CHESS

THE Chair she sat in, like a burnished throne,
Glowed on the marble, where the glass
Held up by standards wrought with fruited vines
From which a golden Cupidon peeped out
(Another hid his eyes behind his wing)
Doubled the flames of sevenbranched candelabra
Reflecting light upon the table as
The glitter of her jewels rose to meet it,
From satin cases poured in rich profusion;
In vials of ivory and coloured glass
Unstoppered, lurked her strange synthetic perfumes,
Unguent, powdered, or liquid—troubled, confused
And drowned the sense in odours; stirred by the air
That freshened from the window, these ascended
In fattening the prolonged candle-flames,
Flung their smoke into the laquearia,
Stirring the pattern on the coffered ceiling.
Huge sea-wood fed with copper
Burned green and orange, framed by the coloured stone,
In which sad light a carvèd dolphin swam.
Above the antique mantel was displayed
As though a window gave upon the sylvan scene
The change of Philomel, by the barbarous king
So rudely forced; yet there the nightingale
Filled all the desert with inviolable voice
And still she cried, and still the world pursues,
"Jug Jug" to dirty ears.
And other withered stumps of time
Were told upon the walls; staring forms
Leaned out, leaning, hushing the room enclosed.
Footsteps shuffled on the stair.
Under the firelight, under the brush, her hair
Spread out in fiery points
Glowed into words, then would be savagely still.

"My nerves are bad to-night. Yes, bad. Stay with me.
494

"Speak to me. Why do you never speak. Speak.
 "What are you thinking of? What thinking? What?
"I never know what you are thinking. Think."

I think we are in rats' alley
Where the dead men lost their bones.

"What is that noise?"
                              The wind under the door.
"What is that noise now? What is the wind doing?"
                              Nothing again nothing.
                                                      "Do
"You know nothing? Do you see nothing? Do you re-
     member
"Nothing?"

          I remember
Those are pearls that were his eyes.
"Are you alive, or not? Is there nothing in your head?"

                                                      But
O O O O that Shakespeherian Rag—
It's so elegant
So intelligent
"What shall I do now? What shall I do?"
"I shall rush out as I am, and walk the street
"With my hair down, so. What shall we do to-morrow?
"What shall we ever do?"
                              The hot water at ten.
And if it rains, a closed car at four.
And we shall play a game of chess,
Pressing lidless eyes and waiting for a knock upon the
     door.

When Lil's husband got demobbed, I said—
I didn't mince my words, I said to her myself,
HURRY UP PLEASE ITS TIME
Now Albert's coming back, make yourself a bit smart.

He'll want to know what you done with that money he
    gave you
To get yourself some teeth. He did, I was there.
You have them all out, Lil, and get a nice set,
He said, I swear, I can't bear to look at you.
And no more can't I, I said, and think of poor Albert,
He's been in the army four years, he wants a good time,
And if you don't give it him, there's others will, I said.
Oh is there, she said. Something o' that, I said.
Then I'll know who to thank, she said, and give me a
    straight look.
HURRY UP PLEASE ITS TIME
If you don't like it you can get on with it, I said.
Others can pick and choose if you can't.
But if Albert makes off, it won't be for lack of telling.
You ought to be ashamed, I said, to look so antique.
(And her only thirty-one.)
I can't help it, she said, pulling a long face,
It's them pills I took, to bring it off, she said.
(She's had five already, and nearly died of young
    George.)
The chemist said it would be all right, but I've never
    been the same.
You *are* a proper fool, I said.
Well, if Albert won't leave you alone, there it is, I said,
What you get married for if you don't want children?
HURRY UP PLEASE ITS TIME
Well, that Sunday Albert was home, they had a hot
    gammon,
And they asked me in to dinner, to get the beauty of it
    hot—
HURRY UP PLEASE ITS TIME
HURRY UP PLEASE ITS TIME
Goonight Bill. Goonight Lou. Goonight May. Goonight.
Ta ta. Goonight. Goonight.
Good night, ladies, good night, sweet ladies, good night,
    good night.

III. THE FIRE SERMON

The river's tent is broken: the last fingers of leaf
Clutch and sink into the wet bank. The wind
Crosses the brown land, unheard. The nymphs are departed.
Sweet Thames, run softly, till I end my song.
The river bears no empty bottles, sandwich papers,
Silk handkerchiefs, cardboard boxes, cigarette ends
Or other testimony of summer nights. The nymphs are
      departed.
And their friends, the loitering heirs of city directors;
Departed, have left no addresses.
By the waters of Leman I sat down and wept . . .
Sweet Thames, run softly till I end my song,
Sweet Thames, run softly, for I speak not loud or long.
But at my back in a cold blast I hear
The rattle of the bones, and chuckle spread from ear to ear.
A rat crept softly through the vegetation
Dragging its slimy belly on the bank
While I was fishing in the dull canal
On a winter evening round behind the gashouse
Musing upon the king my brother's wreck
And on the king my father's death before him.
White bodies naked on the low damp ground
And bones cast in a little low dry garret,
Rattled by the rat's foot only, year to year.
But at my back from time to time I hear
The sound of horns and motors, which shall bring
Sweeney to Mrs. Porter in the spring.
O the moon shone bright on Mrs. Porter
And on her daughter
They wash their feet in soda water
Et Ó ces voix d'enfants, chantant dans la coupole!

Twit twit twit
Jug jug jug jug jug jug
So rudely forc'd.
Tereu

497

Unreal City
Under the brown fog of a winter noon
Mr. Eugenides, the Smyrna merchant
Unshaven, with a pocket full of currants
C.i.f. London: documents at sight,
Asked me in demotic French
To luncheon at the Cannon Street Hotel
Followed by a weekend at the Metropole.
At the violet hour, when the eyes and back
Turn upward from the desk, when the human engine
        waits
Like a taxi throbbing waiting,
I Tiresias, though blind, throbbing between two lives,
Old man with wrinkled female breasts, can see
At the violet hour, the evening hour that strives
Homeward, and brings the sailor home from sea,
The typist home at teatime, clears her breakfast, lights
Her stove, and lays out food in tins.
Out of the window perilously spread
Her drying combinations touched by the sun's last rays.
On the divan are piled (at night her bed)
Stockings, slippers, camisoles, and stays.
I Tiresias, old man with wrinkled dugs
Perceived the scene, and foretold the rest—
I too awaited the expected guest.
He, the young man carbuncular, arrives,
A small house agent's clerk, with one bold stare,
One of the low on whom assurance sits
As a silk hat on a Bradford millionaire.
The time is now propitious, as he guesses,
The meal is ended, she is bored and tired,
Endeavours to engage her in caresses
Which still are unreproved, if undesired.
Flushed and decided, he assaults at once;
Exploring hands encounter no defence;
His vanity requires no response,
And makes a welcome of indifference.
(And I Tiresias have foresuffered all

Enacted on this same divan or bed;
I who have sat by Thebes below the wall
And walked among the lowest of the dead.)
Bestows one final patronising kiss,
And gropes his way, finding the stairs unlit . . .

She turns and looks a moment in the glass,
Hardly aware of her departed lover;
Her brain allows one half-formed thought to pass:
"Well now that's done: and I'm glad it's over."
When lovely woman stoops to folly and
Paces about her room again, alone,
She smoothes her hair with automatic hand,
And puts a record on the gramophone.

"This music crept by me upon the waters"
And along the Strand, up Queen Victoria Street.
O City city, I can sometimes hear
Beside a public bar in Lower Thames Street,
The pleasant whining of a mandoline
And a clatter and a chatter from within
Where fishmen lounge at noon: where the walls
Of Magnus Martyr hold
Inexplicable splendour of Ionian white and gold.

> The river sweats
> Oil and tar
> The barges drift
> With the turning tide
> Red sails
> Wide
> To leeward, swing on the heavy spar.
> The barges wash
> Drifting logs
> Down Greenwich reach
> Past the Isle of Dogs.
> > Weialala leia
> > Wallala leialala

Elizabeth and Leicester
Beating oars
The stern was formed
A gilded shell
Red and gold
The brisk swell
Rippled both shores
Southwest wind
Carried down stream
The peal of bells
White towers
        Weialala leia
        Wallala leialala

"Trams and dusty trees.
Highbury bore me. Richmond and Kew
Undid me. By Richmond I raised my knees
Supine on the floor of a narrow canoe."

"My feet are at Moorgate, and my heart
Under my feet. After the event
He wept. He promised 'a new start.'
I made no comment. What should I resent?"

"On Margate Sands.
I can connect
Nothing with nothing.
The broken fingernails of dirty hands.
My people humble people who expect
Nothing."
        la la

To Carthage then I came
Burning burning burning burning
O Lord Thou pluckest me out
O Lord Thou pluckest

burning

T. S. ELIOT

IV. DEATH BY WATER

PHLEBAS the Phoenician, a fortnight dead,
Forgot the cry of gulls, and the deep sea swell
And the profit and loss.
     A current under sea
Picked his bones in whispers. As he rose and fell
He passed the stages of his age and youth
Entering the whirlpool.
      Gentile or Jew
O you who turn the wheel and look to windward,
Consider Phlebas, who was once handsome and tall as
  you.

V. WHAT THE THUNDER SAID

AFTER the torchlight red on sweaty faces
After the frosty silence in the gardens
After the agony in stony places
The shouting and the crying
Prison and palace and reverberation
Of thunder of spring over distant mountains
He who was living is now dead
We who were living are now dying
With a little patience

Here is no water but only rock
Rock and no water and the sandy road
The road winding above among the mountains
Which are mountains of rock without water
If there were water we should stop and drink
Amongst the rock one cannot stop or think
Sweat is dry and feet are in the sand
If there were only water amongst the rock
Dead mountain mouth of carious teeth that cannot spit
Here one can neither stand nor lie nor sit
There is not even silence in the mountains

501

But dry sterile thunder without rain
There is not even solitude in the mountains
But red sullen faces sneer and snarl
From doors of mudcracked houses
                                        If there were water

   And no rock
   If there were rock
   And also water
   And water
   A spring
   A pool among the rock
   If there were the sound of water only
   Not the cicada
   And dry grass singing
   But sound of water over a rock
   Where the hermit-thrush sings in the pine trees
   Drip drop drip drop drop drop drop
   But there is no water

Who is the third who walks always beside you?
When I count, there are only you and I together
But when I look ahead up the white road
There is always another one walking beside you
Gliding wrapt in a brown mantle, hooded
I do not know whether a man or a woman
—But who is that on the other side of you?

What is that sound high in the air
Murmur of maternal lamentation
Who are those hooded hordes swarming
Over endless plains, stumbling in cracked earth
Ringed by the flat horizon only
What is the city over the mountains
Cracks and reforms and bursts in the violet air
Falling towers
Jerusalem Athens Alexandria
Vienna London
Unreal

A woman drew her long black hair out tight
And fiddled whisper music on those strings
And bats with baby faces in the violet light
Whistled, and beat their wings
And crawled head downward down a blackened wall
And upside down in air were towers
Tolling reminiscent bells, that kept the hours
And voices singing out of empty cisterns and exhausted
      wells.

In this decayed hole among the mountains
In the faint moonlight, the grass is singing
Over the tumbled graves, about the chapel
There is the empty chapel, only the wind's home.
It has no windows, and the door swings,
Dry bones can harm no one.
Only a cock stood on the rooftree
Co co rico co co rico
In a flash of lightning. Then a damp gust
Bringing rain

Ganga was sunken, and the limp leaves
Waited for rain, while the black clouds
Gathered far distant, over Himavant.
The jungle crouched, humped in silence.
Then spoke the thunder
DA
Datta: what have we given?
My friend, blood shaking my heart
The awful daring of a moment's surrender
Which an age of prudence can never retract
By this, and this only, we have existed
Which is not to be found in our obituaries
Or in memories draped by the beneficent spider
Or under seals broken by the lean solicitor
In our empty rooms
DA
Dayadhvam: I have heard the key

Turn in the door once and turn once only
We think of the key, each in his prison
Thinking of the key, each confirms a prison
Only at nightfall, aethereal rumours
Revive for a moment a broken Coriolanus
DA
Damyata: The boat responded
Gaily, to the hand expert with sail and oar
The sea was calm, your heart would have responded
Gaily, when invited, beating obedient
To controlling hands

                  I sat upon the shore
Fishing, with the arid plain behind me
Shall I at least set my lands in order?
London Bridge is falling down falling down falling down
Poi s'ascose nel foco che gli affina
Quando fiam uti chelidon—O swallow swallow
Le Prince d'Aquitaine à la tour abolie
These fragments I have shored against my ruins
Why then Ile fit you. Hieronymo's mad againe.
Datta. Dayadhvam. Damyata.
          Shantih   shantih   shantih

John Crowe Ransom

SURVEY OF LITERATURE

In all the good Greek of Plato
I lack my roastbeef and potato.

A better man was Aristotle,
Pulling steady on the bottle.

I dip my hat to Chaucer,
Swilling soup from his saucer,

And to Master Shakespeare
Who wrote big on small beer.

The abstemious Wordsworth
Subsisted on a curd's-worth,

But a slick one was Tennyson,
Putting gravy on his venison.

What these men had to eat and drink
Is what we say and what we think.

The influence of Milton
Came wry out of Stilton.

Sing a song for Percy Shelley,
Drowned in pale lemon jelly,

And for precious John Keats,
Dripping blood of pickled beets.

Then there was poor Willie Blake,
He foundered on sweet cake.

505

God have mercy on the sinner
Who must write with no dinner,

No gravy and no grub,
No pewter and no pub,

No belly and no bowels,
Only consonants and vowels.

DOG

Cock-a-doodle-doo the brass-lined rooster says,
Brekekekex intones the fat Greek frog—
These fantasies do not terrify me as
The bow-wow-wow of dog.

I had a little doggie who used to sit and beg,
A pretty little creature with tears in his eyes
And anomalous hand extended on his leg;
Housebroken was my Huendchen, and so wise.

Booms the voice of a big dog like a bell.
But Fido sits at dusk on Madam's lap
And, bored beyond his tongue's poor skill to tell,
Rehearses his pink paradigm, To yap.

However. Up the lane the tender bull
Proceeds unto his kine; he yearns for them,
Whose eyes adore him and are beautiful;
Love speeds him and no treason nor mayhem.

But, on arriving at the gap in the fence,
Behold! again the ubiquitous hairy dog,
Like a numerous army rattling the battlements
With shout, though it is but his monologue,
With a lion's courage and a bee's virulence
Though he is but one dog.

Shrill is the fury of the proud red bull,
His knees quiver, and the honeysuckle vine
Expires with anguish as his voice, terrible,
Cries, "What do you want of my twenty lady kine?"

Now the air trembles to the sorrowing Moo
Of twenty blameless ladies of the mead
Fearing their lord's precarious set-to.
It is the sunset and the heavens bleed.

The hooves of the red bull slither the claybank
And cut the green tendrils of the vine; his horn
Slices the young birch unto splinter and shank
But lunging leaves the bitch's boy untorn.

Across the red sky comes master, Hodge by name,
Upright, biped, tall-browed, and self-assured,
In his hand a cudgel, in his cold eye a flame:
"Have I beat my dog so sore and he is not cured?"

His stick and stone and curse rain on the brute
That pipped his bull of gentle pedigree
Till the leonine smarts with pain and disrepute
And the bovine weeps in the bosom of his family.

Old Hodge stays not his hand, but whips to kennel
The renegade. God's peace betide the souls
Of the pure in heart. But in the box that fennel
Grows round, are two red eyes that stare like coals.

PAINTED HEAD

By dark severance the apparition head
Smiles from the air a capital on no
Column or a Platonic perhaps head
On a canvas sky depending from nothing;

Stirs up an old illusion of grandeur
By tickling the instinct of heads to be
Absolute and to try decapitation
And to play truant from the body bush;

But too happy and beautiful for those sorts
Of head (homekeeping heads are happiest)
Discovers maybe thirty unwidowed years
Of not dishonoring the faithful stem;

Is nameless and has authored for the evil
Historian headhunters neither book
Nor state and is therefore distinct from tart
Heads with crowns and guilty gallery heads;

So that the extravagant device of art
Unhousing by abstraction this once head
Was capital irony by a loving hand
That knew the no treason of a head like this;

Makes repentance in an unlovely head
For having vinegarly traduced the flesh
Till, the hurt flesh recusing, the hard egg
Is shrunken to its own deathlike surface;

And an image thus. The body bears the head
(So hardly one they terribly are two)
Feeds and obeys and unto please what end?
Not to the glory of tyrant head but to

The increase of body. Beauty is of body.
The flesh contouring shallowly on a head
Is a rock-garden needing body's love
And best bodiness to colorify

The big blue birds sitting and sea-shell flats
And caves, and on the iron acropolis
To spread the hyacinthine hair and rear
The olive garden for the nightingales.

JOHN CROWE RANSOM

CAPTAIN CARPENTER

CAPTAIN CARPENTER rose up in his prime
Put on his pistols and went riding out
But had got wellnigh nowhere at that time
Till he fell in with ladies in a rout.

It was a pretty lady and all her train
That played with him so sweetly but before
An hour she'd taken a sword with all her main
And twined him of his nose for evermore.

Captain Carpenter mounted up one day
And rode straightway into a stranger rogue
That looked unchristian but be that as may
The Captain did not wait upon prologue.

But drew upon him out of his great heart
The other swung against him with a club
And cracked his two legs at the shinny part
And let him roll and stick like any tub.

Captain Carpenter rode many a time
From male and female took he sundry harms
He met the wife of Satan crying "I'm
The she-wolf bids you shall bear no more arms."

Their strokes and counters whistled in the wind
I wish he had delivered half his blows
But where she should have made off like a hind
The bitch bit off his arms at the elbows.

And Captain Carpenter parted with his ears
To a black devil that used him in this wise
O Jesus ere his threescore and ten years
Another had plucked out his sweet blue eyes.

Captain Carpenter got up on his roan
And sallied from the gate in hell's despite

509

I heard him asking in the grimmest tone
If any enemy yet there was to fight?

"To any adversary it is fame
If he risk to be wounded by my tongue
Or burnt in two beneath my red heart's flame
Such are the perils he is cast among.

"But if he can he has a pretty choice
From an anatomy with little to lose
Whether he cut my tongue and take my voice
Or whether it be my round red heart he choose."

It was the neatest knave that ever was seen
Stepping in perfume from his lady's bower
Who at this word put in his merry mien
And fell on Captain Carpenter like a tower.

I would not knock old fellows in the dust
But there lay Captain Carpenter on his back
His weapons were the old heart in his bust
And a blade shook between rotten teeth alack.

The rogue in scarlet and grey soon knew his mind
He wished to get his trophy and depart
With gentle apology and touch refined
He pierced him and produced the Captain's heart.

God's mercy rest on Captain Carpenter now
I thought him Sirs an honest gentleman
Citizen husband soldier and scholar enow
Let jangling kites eat of him if they can.

But God's deep curses follow after those
That shore him of his goodly nose and ears
His legs and strong arms at the two elbows
And eyes that had not watered seventy years

The curse of hell upon the sleek upstart
That got the Captain finally on his back
And took the red red vitals of his heart
And made the kites to whet their beaks clack clack.

DEAD BOY

THE little cousin is dead, by foul subtraction,
A green bough from Virginia's aged tree,
And none of the county kin like the transaction,
Nor some of the world of outer dark, like me.

A boy not beautiful, nor good, nor clever,
A black cloud full of storms too hot for keeping,
A sword beneath his mother's heart—yet never
Woman bewept her babe as this is weeping.

A pig with a pasty face, so I had said,
Squealing for cookies, kinned by poor pretense
With a noble house. But the little man quite dead,
I see the forebears' antique lineaments.

The elder men have strode by the box of death
To the wide flag porch, and muttering low send round
The bruit of the day. O friendly waste of breath!
Their hearts are hurt with a deep dynastic wound.

He was pale and little, the foolish neighbors say;
The first-fruits, saith the Preacher, the Lord hath taken;
But this was the old tree's late branch wrenched away,
Grieving the sapless limbs, the shorn and shaken.

511

BELLS FOR
JOHN WHITESIDE'S DAUGHTER

THERE was such speed in her little body,
And such lightness in her footfall,
It is no wonder her brown study
Astonishes us all.

Her wars were bruited in our high window.
We looked among orchard trees and beyond,
Where she took arms against her shadow,
Or harried unto the pond

The lazy geese, like a snow cloud
Dripping their snow on the green grass,
Tricking and stopping, sleepy and proud,
Who cried in goose, Alas.

For the tireless heart within the little
Lady with rod that made them rise
From their noon apple-dreams and scuttle
Goose-fashion under the skies!

But now go the bells, and we are ready,
In one house we are sternly stopped
To say we are vexed at her brown study,
Lying so primly propped.

BLUE GIRLS

TWIRLING your blue skirts, travelling the sward
Under the towers of your seminary,
Go listen to your teachers old and contrary
Without believing a word.

Tie the white fillets then about your hair
And think no more of what will come to pass

Than bluebirds that go walking on the grass
And chattering on the air.

Practice your beauty, blue girls, before it fail;
And I will cry with my loud lips and publish
Beauty which all our power shall never establish,
It is so frail.

For I could tell you a story which is true;
I know a lady with a terrible tongue,
Blear eyes fallen from blue,
All her perfections tarnished—yet it is not long
Since she was lovelier than any of you.

JUDITH OF BETHULIA

BEAUTIFUL as the flying legend of some leopard
She had not yet chosen her great captain or prince
Depositary to her flesh, and our defense;
And a wandering beauty is a blade out of its scabbard.
You know how dangerous, gentlemen of threescore?
May you know it yet ten more.

Nor by process of veiling she grew the less fabulous.
Grey or blue veils, we were desperate to study
The invincible emanations of her white body,
And the winds at her ordered raiment were ominous.
Might she walk in the market, sit in the council of
    soldiers?
Only of the extreme elders.

But a rare chance was the girl's then, when the Invader
Trumpeted from the south, and rumbled from the north,
Beleaguered the city from four quarters of the earth,
Our soldiery too craven and sick to aid her—
Where were the arms could countervail this horde?
Her beauty was the sword.

She sat with the elders, and proved on their blear visage
How bright was the weapon unrusted in her keeping,
While he lay surfeiting on their harvest heaping,
Wasting the husbandry of their rarest vintage—
And dreaming of the broad-breasted dames for concubine?
These floated on his wine.

He was lapped with bay-leaves, and grass and fumiter weed,
And from under the wine-film encountered his mortal vision,
For even within his tent she accomplished his derision;
She loosed one veil and another, standing unafraid;
And he perished. Nor brushed her with even so much as a daisy?
She found his destruction easy.

The heathen are all perished. The victory was furnished,
We smote them hiding in our vineyards, barns, annexes,
And now their white bones clutter the holes of foxes,
And the chieftain's head, with grinning sockets, and varnished—
Is it hung on the sky with a hideous epitaphy?
No, the woman keeps the trophy.

May God send unto our virtuous lady her prince.
It is stated she went reluctant to that orgy,
Yet a madness fevers our young men, and not the clergy
Nor the elders have turned them unto modesty since.
Inflamed by the thought of her naked beauty with desire?
Yes, and chilled with fear and despair.

ARMAGEDDON

Antichrist, playing his lissome flute and merry
As was his wont, debouched upon the plain;
Then came a swirl of dust, and Christ drew rein,
Brooding upon his frugal breviary.

Now which shall die, the roundel, rose, and hall,
Or else the tonsured beadsman's monkery?
For Christ and Antichrist arm cap-a-pie,
The prospect charms the soul of the lean jackal.

But Antichrist got down from the Barbary beast
And doffed his plume in courteous prostration;
Christ left his jennet's back in deprecation
And raised him, his own hand about the waist.

And then they fingered chivalry's quaint page,
Of precedence discoursing by the letter.
The oratory of Antichrist was better,
He invested Christ with the elder lineage.

He set Christ on his own Mahomet's back
Where Christ sat fortressed up like Diomede;
The cynical hairy jennet was his steed,
Obtuse, and most indifferent to attack.

The lordings measured lances and stood still,
And each was loath to let the other's blood;
Originally they were one brotherhood;
There stood the white pavilion on the hill.

To the pavilion went then the hierarchs,
If they might truce their honorable dispute;
Firm was the Christian's chin and he was mute,
And Antichrist ejected scant remarks.

Antichrist tendered a spray of rosemary
To serve his brother for a buttonhole;

515

Then Christ about his adversary's poll
Wrapped a dry palm that grew on Calvary.

Christ wore a dusty cassock, and the knight
Did him the honors of his tiring-hall,
Whence Christ did not come forth too finical,
But his egregious beauty richly dight.

With feasting they concluded every day,
And when the other shaped his phrases thicker
Christ, introducing water in the liquor,
Made wine of more ethereal bouquet.

At wassail Antichrist would pitch the strain
For unison of all the retinue;
Christ beat the time, and hummed a stave or two,
But did not say the words, which were profane.

Perruquiers were privily presented,
Till, knowing his need extreme and his heart pure,
Christ let them dress him his thick chevelure,
And soon his beard was glozed and sweetly scented.

And so the Wolf said Brother to the Lamb,
The True Heir keeping with the poor Impostor,
The rubric and the holy paternoster
Were jangled strangely with the dithyramb.

It could not be. There was a patriarch,
A godly liege of old malignant brood,
Who could not fathom the new brotherhood
Between the children of the light and dark.

He sought the ear of Christ on these mad things,
But in the white pavilion when he stood
And saw them featured and dressed like twins at food,
He poured in the wrong ear his misgivings.

He was discomfited, but Christ much more.
Christ shed unmannerly his devil's pelf,
Took ashes from the hearth and smeared himself,
Called for his smock and jennet as before.

His trump recalls his own to right opinions,
With scourge they mortify their carnal selves,
With stone they whet the ax-heads on the helves
And seek the Prince Beelzebub and minions.

Christ and his myrmidons, Christ at the head,
Chanted of death and glory and no complaisance;
Antichrist and the armies of malfeasance
Made songs of innocence and no bloodshed.

The immortal Adversary shook his head:
If now they fought too long, then he would famish;
And if much blood was shed, why, he was squeamish:
"These Armageddons weary me much," he said.

SOMEWHERE IS SUCH A KINGDOM

THE famous kingdom of the birds
Has a sweet tongue and liquid words,
The red-birds polish their notes
In their easy practiced throats,
Smooth as orators are the thrushes
Of the airy city of the bushes,
And God reward the fierce cock wrens
Who have such suavity with their hens.

To me this has its worth
As I sit upon the earth
Lacking my winter and quiet hearth.
For I go up into a nook
With a mind burdened or a book,
And hear no strife nor quarreling
As the birds and their wives sing.

Or, so it has been today.
Yet I cannot therefore say
If the red-bird, wren, or thrush
Know when to speak and when to hush;
Though their manifest education
Be a right enunciation,
And their chief excellence
A verbal elegance,
I cannot say if the wind never blows,
Nor how it sometimes goes.

This I know, that if they wrangle,
Their words inevitably will jangle.
If they be hateful as men
They will be harsh as we have been.
When they go to pecking
You will soon hear shrieking,
And they who will have the law,
How those will jaw!
Girls that have unlawful dreams
Will waken full of their own screams,
And boys that get too arrant
Will have rows with a parent,—
And when friend falls out with friend
All songs must have quick end.

Have they not claws like knives?
Have not these gentlemen wives?

But when they croak and fleer and swear,
My dull heart I must take elsewhere;
For I will see if God has made
Otherwhere another shade
Where the men or beasts or birds
Exchange few words and pleasant words.
And dare I think it is absurd
If no such beast were, no such bird?

Conrad Aiken

MORNING SONG OF SENLIN

IT is morning, Senlin says, and in the morning
When the light drips through the shutters like the dew,
I arise, I face the sunrise,
And do the things my fathers learned to do.
Stars in the purple dusk above the rooftops
Pale in a saffron mist and seem to die,
And I myself on a swiftly tilting planet
Stand before a glass and tie my tie.

Vine leaves tap my window,
Dew-drops sing to the garden stones,
The robin chirps in the chinaberry tree
Repeating three clear tones.

It is morning. I stand by the mirror
And tie my tie once more.
While waves far off in a pale rose twilight
Crash on a white sand shore.
I stand by a mirror and comb my hair:
How small and white my face!—
The green earth tilts through a sphere of air
And bathes in a flame of space.

There are houses hanging above the stars
And stars hung under a sea . . .
And a sun far off in a shell of silence
Dapples my walls for me . . .

It is morning, Senlin says, and in the morning
Should I not pause in the light to remember god?

519

Upright and firm I stand on a star unstable,
He is immense and lonely as a cloud.
I will dedicate this moment before my mirror
To him alone; for him I will comb my hair.
Accept these humble offerings, cloud of silence!
I will think of you as I descend the stair.

Vine leaves tap my window,
The snail-track shines on the stones,
Dew-drops flash from the chinaberry tree
Repeating two clear tones.

It is morning, I awake from a bed of silence,
Shining I rise from the starless waters of sleep.
The walls are about me still as in the evening,
I am the same, and the same name still I keep.

The earth revolves with me, yet makes no motion,
The stars pale silently in a coral sky.
In a whistling void I stand before my mirror,
Unconcerned, and tie my tie.

There are horses neighing on far-off hills
Tossing their long white manes,
And mountains flash in the rose-white dusk,
Their shoulders black with rains . . .
It is morning. I stand by the mirror
And surprise my soul once more;
The blue air rushes above my ceiling,
There are suns beneath my floor . . .

. . . It is morning, Senlin says, I ascend from darkness
And depart on the winds of space for I know not where,
My watch is wound, a key is in my pocket,
And the sky is darkened as I descend the stair.
There are shadows across the windows, clouds in heaven,
And a god among the stars; and I will go
520

Thinking of him as I might think of daybreak
And humming a tune I know . . .

Vine leaves tap at the window,
Dew-drops sing to the garden stones,
The robin chirps in the chinaberry tree
Repeating three clear tones.

MUSIC I HEARD

MUSIC I heard with you was more than music,
And bread I broke with you was more than bread;
Now that I am without you, all is desolate;
All that was once so beautiful is dead.

Your hands once touched this table and this silver,
And I have seen your fingers hold this glass.
These things do not remember you, beloved,
And yet your touch upon them will not pass.

For it was in my heart you moved among them,
And blessed them with your hands and with your eyes;
And in my heart they will remember always,—
They knew you once, O beautiful and wise.

TETÉLESTAI

I

How shall we praise the magnificence of the dead,
The great man humbled, the haughty brought to dust?
Is there a horn we should not blow as proudly
For the meanest of us all, who creeps his days,
Guarding his heart from blows, to die obscurely?
I am no king, have laid no kingdoms waste,

521

Taken no princes captive, led no triumphs
Of weeping women through long walls of trumpets;
Say rather, I am no one, or an atom;
Say rather, two great gods, in a vault of starlight,
Play ponderingly at chess, and at the game's end
One of the pieces, shaken, falls to the floor
And runs to the darkest corner; and that piece
Forgotten there, left motionless, is I. . . .
Say that I have no name, no gifts, no power,
Am only one of millions, mostly silent;
One who came with eyes and hands and a heart,
Looked on beauty, and loved it, and then left it.
Say that the fates of time and space obscured me,
Led me a thousand ways to pain, bemused me,
Wrapped me in ugliness; and like great spiders
Dispatched me at their leisure. . . . Well, what then?
Should I not hear, as I lie down in dust,
The horns of glory blowing above my burial?

II

Morning and evening opened and closed above me:
Houses were built above me; trees let fall
Yellowing leaves upon me, hands of ghosts;
Rain has showered its arrows of silver upon me
Seeking my heart; winds have roared and tossed me;
Music in long blue waves of sound has borne me
A helpless weed to shores of unthought silence;
Time, above me, within me, crashed its gongs
Of terrible warning, sifting the dust of death;
And here I lie. Blow now your horns of glory
Harshly over my flesh, you trees, you waters!
You stars and suns, Canopus, Deneb, Rigel,
Let me, as I lie down, here in this dust,
Hear, far off, your whispered salutation!
Roar now above my decaying flesh, you winds,
Whirl out your earth-scents over this body, tell me
Of ferns and stagnant pools, wild roses, hillsides!
522

Anoint me, rain, let crash your silver arrows
On this hard flesh! I am the one who named you,
I lived in you, and now I die in you.
I your son, your daughter, treader of music,
Lie broken, conquered . . . Let me not fall in silence.

III

I, the restless one; the circler of circles;
Herdsman and roper of stars, who could not capture
The secret of self; I who was tyrant to weaklings,
Striker of children; destroyer of women; corrupter
Of innocent dreamers, and laugher at beauty; I,
Too easily brought to tears and weakness by music,
Baffled and broken by love, the helpless beholder
Of the war in my heart of desire with desire, the struggle
Of hatred with love, terror with hunger; I
Who laughed without knowing the cause of my laughter,
    who grew
Without wishing to grow, a servant to my own body;
Loved without reason the laughter and flesh of a woman,
Enduring such torments to find her! I who at last
Grow weaker, struggle more feebly, relent in my pur-
    pose,
Choose for my triumph an easier end, look backward
At earlier conquests; or, caught in the web, cry out
In a sudden and empty despair, "Tetélestai!"
Pity me, now! I, who was arrogant, beg you!
Tell me, as I lie down, that I was courageous.
Blow horns of victory now, as I reel and am vanquished.
Shatter the sky with trumpets above my grave.

IV

. . . Look! this flesh how it crumbles to dust and is
    blown!
These bones, how they grind in the granite of frost and
    are nothing!

523

This skull, how it yawns for a flicker of time in the
     darkness,
Yet laughs not and sees not! It is crushed by a hammer of
     sunlight,
And the hands are destroyed. . . . Press down through
     the leaves of the jasmine,
Dig through the interlaced roots—nevermore will you
     find me;
I was no better than dust, yet you cannot replace me.
     . . .

Take the soft dust in your hand—does it stir: does it
     sing?
Has it lips and a heart? Does it open its eyes to the sun?
Does it run, does it dream, does it burn with a secret, or
     tremble
In terror of death? Or ache with tremendous decisions?
     . . .

Listen! . . . It says: "I lean by the river. The willows
Are yellowed with bud. White clouds roar up from the
     south
And darken the ripples; but they cannot darken my
     heart,
Nor the face like a star in my heart! . . . Rain falls on
     the water
And pelts it, and rings it with silver. The willow trees
     glisten,
The sparrows chirp under the eaves; but the face in
     my heart
Is a secret of music. . . . I wait in the rain and am
     silent."
Listen again! . . . It says: "I have worked, I am tired,
The pencil dulls in my hand: I see through the window
Walls upon walls of windows with faces behind them,
Smoke floating up to the sky, an ascension of sea-gulls.
I am tired. I have struggled in vain, my decision was
     fruitless,
Why then do I wait? with darkness, so easy, at hand!
     . . .

524

But tomorrow, perhaps . . . I will wait and endure till
    tomorrow!" . . .
Or again: "It is dark. The decision is made. I am van-
    quished
By terror of life. The walls mount slowly about me
In coldness. I had not the courage. I was forsaken.
I cried out, was answered by silence . . . Tetélestai! . . ."

V

Hear how it babbles!—Blow the dust out of your hand,
With its voices and visions, tread on it, forget it, turn
    homeward
With dreams in your brain. . . . This, then, is the
    humble, the nameless,—
The lover, the husband and father, the struggler with
    shadows,
The one who went down under shoutings of chaos, the
    weakling,
Who cried his "forsaken!" like Christ on the darkening
    hilltop! . . . .
This, then, is the one who implores, as he dwindles to
    silence,
A fanfare of glory. . . . And which of us dares to deny
    him?

TWO COFFEES IN THE ESPAÑOL

Two coffees in the Español, the last
Bright drops of golden Barsac in a goblet,
Fig paste and candied nuts. . . . Hardy is dead,
And James and Conrad dead, and Shakspere dead,
And old Moore ripens for an obscene grave,
And Yeats for an arid one; and I, and you—
What winding sheet for us, what boards and bricks,
What mummeries, candles, prayers, and pious frauds?
You shall be lapped in Syrian scarlet, woman,

525

And wear your pearls, and your bright bracelets, too,
Your agate ring, and round your neck shall hang
Your dark blue lapis with its specks of gold.
And I, beside you—ah! but will that be?
For there are dark streams in this dark world, lady,
Gulf Streams and Arctic currents of the soul;
And I may be, before our consummation
Beds us together, cheek by jowl, in earth,
Swept to another shore, where my white bones
Will lie unhonored, or defiled by gulls.

What dignity can death bestow on us,
Who kiss beneath a streetlamp, or hold hands
Half hidden in a taxi or replete
With coffee, figs and Barsac make our way
To a dark bedroom in a wormworn house?
The aspidistra guards the door; we enter,
Per aspidistra—then ad astra—is it?—
And lock ourselves securely in our gloom
And loose ourselves from terror. . . . Here's my hand,
The white scar on my thumb, and here's my mouth
To stop your murmur, speechless let us lie,
And think of Hardy, Shakspere, Yeats and James;
Comfort our panic hearts with magic names;
Stare at the ceiling, where the taxi lamps
Make ghosts of lights; and see, beyond this bed,
That other bed in which we will not move;
And, whether joined or separate, will not love.

SLEEP: AND BETWEEN THE CLOSED EYELIDS OF SLEEP

SLEEP: and between the closed eyelids of sleep,
From the dark spirit's still unresting brief,
The one tear burns its way. O God, O God,
What monstrous world is this, whence no escape
Even in sleep? Between the fast-shut lids

This one tear comes, hangs on the lashes, falls:
Symbol of some gigantic dream, that shakes
The secret-sleeping soul. . . . And I descend
By a green cliff that fronts the worldlong sea;
Disastrous shore; where bones of ships and rocks
Are mixed; and beating waves bring in the sails
Of unskilled mariners, ill-starred. The gulls
Fall in a cloud upon foul flotsam there;
The air resounds with cries of scavengers.

Dream: and between the close-locked lids of dream
The terrible infinite intrudes its blue:
Ice: silence: death: the abyss of Nothing.
O God, O God, let the sore soul have peace.
Deliver it from this bondage of harsh dreams.
Release this shadow from its object, this object
From its shadow. Let the fleet soul go nimbly,—
Down,—down,—from step to step of dark,—
From dark to deeper dark, from dark to rest.
And let no Theseus-thread of memory
Shine in that labyrinth, or on those stairs,
To guide her back; nor bring her, where she lies,
Remembrance of a torn world well forgot.

YOU WENT TO THE VERGE, YOU SAY, AND CAME BACK SAFELY?

—You went to the verge, you say, and came back safely?
Some have not been so fortunate,—some have fallen.
Children go lightly there, from crag to crag,
And coign to coign,—where even the goat is wary,—
And make sport of it. . . . . They fling down pebbles,
Following, with eyes undizzied, the long curve,
The long slow outward curve, into the abyss,
As far as eye can follow; and they themselves
Turn back, unworried, to the here and now. . . .

527

But you have been there, too?—

                                        I saw at length
The space-defying pine, that on the last
Outjutting rock has cramped its powerful roots.
There stood I too: under that tree I stood:
My hand against its resinous bark: my face
Turned out and downward to the fourfold kingdom.
The wind roared from all quarters. The waterfall
Came down, it seemed, from Heaven. The mighty sound
Of pouring elements,—earth, air, and water,—
The cry of eagles, chatter of falling stones,—
These were the frightful language of that place.
I understood it ill, but understood.—

—You understood it? Tell me, then, its meaning.
It was an all, a nothing, or a something?
Chaos, or divine love, or emptiness?
Water and earth and air and the sun's fire?
Or else, a question simply?—

                                        —Water and fire were there,
And air and earth; there too was emptiness;
All, and nothing, and something too, and love.
But these poor words, these squeaks of ours, in which
We strive to mimic, with strained throats and tongues,
The spawning and outrageous elements—
Alas, how paltry are they! For I saw—
—What did you see?

                                        —I saw myself and God.
I saw the ruin in which godhead lives:
Shapeless and vast: the strewn wreck of the world:
Sadness unplumbed: misery without bound.
Wailing I heard, but also I heard joy.
Wreckage I saw, but also I saw flowers.
Hatred I saw, but also I saw love. . . .
And thus, I saw myself.
528

—And this alone?
—And this alone awaits you, when you dare
To that sheer verge where horror hangs, and tremble
Against the falling rock; and, looking down,
Search the dark kingdom. It is to self you come,—
And that is God. It is the seed of seeds:
Seed for disastrous and immortal worlds.

It is the answer that no question asked.

WINTER FOR A MOMENT
TAKES THE MIND; THE SNOW

WINTER for a moment takes the mind; the snow
Falls past the arclight; icicles guard a wall;
The wind moans through a crack in the window;
A keen sparkle of frost is on the sill.
Only for a moment; as spring too might engage it,
With a single crocus in the loam, or a pair of birds;
Or summer with hot grass; or autumn with a yellow leaf.
Winter is there, outside, is here in me:
Drapes the planets with snow, deepens the ice on the
    moon,
Darkens the darkness that was already darkness.
The mind too has its snows, its slippery paths,
Walls bayonetted with ice, leaves ice-encased.
Here is the in-drawn room, to which you return
When the wind blows from Arcturus: here is the fire
At which you warm your hands and glaze your eyes;
The piano, on which you touch the cold treble;
Five notes like breaking icicles; and then silence.

The alarm-clock ticks, the pulse keeps time with it;
Night and the mind are full of sounds. I walk
From the fire-place, with its imaginary fire,
To the window, with its imaginary view.

Darkness, and snow ticking the window: silence,
And the knocking of chains on a motor-car, the tolling
Of a bronze bell, dedicated to Christ.
And then the uprush of angelic wings, the beating
Of wings demonic, from the abyss of the mind:
The darkness filled with a feathery whistling, wings
Numberless as the flakes of angelic snow,
The deep void swarming with wings and sound of wings,
The winnowing of chaos, the aliveness
Of depth and depth and depth dedicated to death.

Here are the bickerings of the inconsequential,
The chatterings of the ridiculous, the iterations
Of the meaningless. Memory, like a juggler,
Tosses its colored balls into the light, and again
Receives them into darkness. Here is the absurd,
Grinning like an idiot, and the omnivorous quotidian,
Which will have its day. A handful of coins,
Tickets, items from the news, a soiled handkerchief,
A letter to be answered, notice of a telephone call,
The petal of a flower in a volume of Shakspere,
The program of a concert. The photograph, too,
Propped on the mantel, and beneath it a dry rosebud;
The laundry bill, matches, an ash-tray, Utamaro's
Pearl-fishers. And the rug, on which are still the crumbs
Of yesterday's feast. These are the void, the night,
And the angelic wings that make it sound.

What is the flower? It is not a sigh of color,
Suspiration of purple, sibilation of saffron,
Nor aureate exhalation from the tomb.
Yet it is these because you think of these,
An emanation of emanations, fragile
As light, or glisten, or gleam, or coruscation,
Creature of brightness, and as brightness brief.
What is the frost? It is not the sparkle of death,
The flash of time's wing, seeds of eternity;
Yet it is these because you think of these.

And you, because you think of these, are both
Frost and flower, the bright ambiguous syllable
Of which the meaning is both no and yes.

Here is the tragic, the distorting mirror
In which your gesture becomes grandiose;
Tears form and fall from your magnificent eyes,
The brow is noble, and the mouth is God's.
Here is the God who seeks his mother, Chaos,—
Confusion seeking solution, and life seeking death.
Here is the rose that woos the icicle; the icicle
That woos the rose. Here is the silence of silences
Which dreams of becoming a sound, and the sound
Which will perfect itself in silence. And all
These things are only the uprush from the void,
The wings angelic and demonic, the sound of the abyss
Dedicated to death. And this is you.

RIMBAUD AND VERLAINE, PRECIOUS PAIR OF POETS

RIMBAUD and Verlaine, precious pair of poets,
Genius in both (but what is genius?) playing
Chess on a marble table at an inn
With chestnut blossom falling in blond beer
And on their hair and between knight and bishop—
Sunlight squared between them on the chess-board,
Cirrus in heaven, and a squeal of music
Blown from the leathern door of St. Sulpice—

Discussing, between moves, iamb and spondee
Anacoluthon and the open vowel
God the great peacock with his angel peacocks
And his dependent peacocks the bright stars:
Disputing too of fate as Plato loved it,
Or Sophocles, who hated and admired,
Or Socrates, who loved and was amused:

531

Verlaine puts down his pawn upon a leaf
And closes his long eyes, which are dishonest,
And says "Rimbaud, there is one thing to do:
We must take rhetoric, and wring its neck! . . ."
Rimbaud considers gravely, moves his Queen;
And then removes himself to Timbuctoo.

And Verlaine dead,—with all his jades and mauves;
And Rimbaud dead in Marseilles with a vision,
His leg cut off, as once before his heart;
And all reported by a later lackey,
Whose virtue is his tardiness in time.

Let us describe the evening as it is:—
The stars disposed in heaven as they are:
Verlaine and Shakspere rotting, where they rot,
Rimbaud remembered, and too soon forgot;

Order in all things, logic in the dark;
Arrangement in the atom and the spark;
Time in the heart and sequence in the brain—

Such as destroyed Rimbaud and fooled Verlaine.
And let us then take godhead by the neck—

And strangle it, and with it, rhetoric.

SO, IN THE EVENING,
TO THE SIMPLE CLOISTER

So, in the evening, to the simple cloister:
This place of boughs, where sounds of water, softly,
Lap on the stones. And this is what you are:
Here, in this dusty room, to which you climb
By four steep flights of stairs. The door is closed:
The furies of the city howl behind you:

The last bell plunges rock-like to the sea:
The horns of taxis wail in vain. You come
Once more, at evening, to this simple cloister;
Hushed by the quiet walls, you stand at peace.

What ferns of thought are these, the cool and green,
Dripping with moisture, that festoon these walls?
What water-lights are these, whose pallid rings
Dance with the leaves, or speckle the pale stones?
What spring is this, that bubbles the cold sand,
Urging the sluggish grains of white and gold? . . .
Peace. The delicious silence throngs with ghosts
Of wingèd sound and shadow. These are you.

Now in the evening, in the simple cloister,
You stand and wait; you stand and listen, waiting
For wingèd sounds and wingèd silences,
And long-remembered shadows. Here the rock
Lets down its vine of many colored flowers:
Waiting for you, or waiting for the lizard
To move his lifted claw, or shift his eye
Quick as a jewel. Here the lizard waits
For the slow snake to slide among cold leaves.
And, on the bough that arches the deep pool,
Lapped in a sound of water, the brown thrush
Waits, too, and listens, till his silence makes
Silence as deep as song. And time becomes
A timeless crystal, an eternity,
In which the gone and coming are at peace.

What bird is this, whose silence fills the trees
With rich delight? What leaves and boughs are these,
What lizard, and what snake? . . . The bird is gone:
And while you wait, another comes and goes,—
Another and another; yet your eye,
Although it has not moved, can scarcely say
If birds have come and gone,—so quick, so brief,—
Or if the thrush who waits there is the same . . .

533

The snake and lizard change, yet are the same:
The flowers, many-colored, on the vine,
Open and close their multitude of stars,—
Yet are the same. . . . And all these things are you.

Thus in the evening, in the simple cloister,
Eternity adds ring to ring, the darker
Beyond the brighter; and your silence fills
With such a world of worlds,—so still, so deep,—
As never voice could speak, whether it were
The ocean's or the bird's. The night comes on:
You wait and listen, in the darkened room,
To all these ghosts of change. And they are you.

THEN CAME I TO THE
SHORELESS SHORE OF SILENCE

THEN came I to the shoreless shore of silence,
Where never summer was nor shade of tree,
Nor sound of water, nor sweet light of sun,
But only nothing and the shore of nothing,
Above, below, around, and in my heart:

Where day was not, nor night, nor space, nor time,
Where no bird sang, save him of memory,
Nor footstep marked upon the marl, to guide
My halting footstep; and I turned for terror,
Seeking in vain the Pole Star of my thought;

Where it was blown among the shapeless clouds,
And gone as soon as seen, and scarce recalled,
Its image lost and I directionless;
Alone upon the brown sad edge of chaos,
In the wan evening that was evening always;

Then closed my eyes upon the sea of nothing
While memory brought back a sea more bright,
With long, long waves of light, and the swift sun,

And the good trees that bowed upon the wind;
And stood until grown dizzy with that dream;

Seeking in all that joy of things remembered
One image, one the dearest, one most bright,
One face, one star, one daisy, one delight,
One hour with wings most heavenly and swift,
One hand the tenderest upon the heart;

But still no image came, save of that sea,
No tenderer thing than thought of tenderness,
No heart or daisy brighter than the rest;
And only sadness at the bright sea lost,
And mournfulness that all had not been praised.

O lords of chaos, atoms of desire,
Whirlwind of fruitfulness, destruction's seed,
Hear now upon the void my late delight,
The quick brief cry of memory, that knows
At the dark's edge how great the darkness is.

BELOVED, LET US ONCE MORE PRAISE THE RAIN

BELOVED, let us once more praise the rain.
Let us discover some new alphabet,
For this, the often-praised; and be ourselves,
The rain, the chickweed, and the burdock leaf,
The green-white privet flower, the spotted stone,
And all that welcomes rain; the sparrow, too,—
Who watches with a hard eye, from seclusion,
Beneath the elm-tree bough, till rain is done.

There is an oriole who, upside down,
Hangs at his nest, and flicks an orange wing,—
Under a tree as dead and still as lead;
There is a single leaf, in all this heaven

535

Of leaves, which rain has loosened from its twig:
The stem breaks, and it falls, but it is caught
Upon a sister leaf, and thus she hangs;
There is an acorn cup, beside a mushroom,
Which catches three drops from the stooping cloud.

The timid bee goes back to hive; the fly
Under the broad leaf of the hollyhock
Perpends stupid with cold; the raindark snail
Surveys the wet world from a watery stone . . .
And still the syllables of water whisper:
The wheel of cloud whirs slowly: while we wait
In the dark room; and in your heart I find
One silver raindrop,—on a hawthorn leaf,—
Orion in a cobweb, and the World.

NOTHING TO SAY, YOU SAY?

NOTHING to say, you say? Then we'll say nothing:
But step from rug to rug and hold our breaths,
Count the green ivy-strings against the window,
The pictures on the wall. Let us exchange
Pennies of gossip, news from nowhere, names
Held in despite or honor; we have seen
The weather-vanes veer westward, and the clouds
Obedient to the wind; have walked in snow;
Forgotten and remembered—

                     But we are strangers;
Came here by paths which never crossed; and stare
At the blind mystery of each to each.
You've seen the sea and mountains? taken ether?
And slept in hospitals from Rome to Cairo?
Why so have I; and lost my tonsils, too;
And drunk the waters of the absolute.
But is it this we meet for, of an evening,
Is it this—

O come, like Shelley,
For god's sake let us sit on honest ground
And tell harsh stories of the deaths of kings!
Have out our hearts, confess our blood,
Our foulness and our virtue! I have known
Such sunsets of despair as god himself
Might weep for of a Sunday; and then slept
As dreamlessly as Jesus in his tomb.
I have had time in one hand, space in the other,
And mixed them to no purpose. I have seen
More in a woman's eye than can be liked,
And less than can be known. And as for you—

O creature of the frost and sunlight, worm
Uplifted by the atom's joy, receiver
Of stolen goods, unconscious thief of god—
Tell me upon this sofa how you came
From darkness to this darkness, from what terror
You found this restless pause in terror, learned
The bitter light you follow. We will talk—

But it is time to go, and I must go;
And what we thought, and silenced, none shall know.

THE FIRST NOTE, SIMPLE;
THE SECOND NOTE, DISTINCT

THE first note, simple; the second note, distinct;
The third note, harsh; the fourth, an innuendo;
The fifth, a humble triad; and the sixth—
Suddenly—is the chord of chords, that breaks
The evening; and from evening calls the angel,
One voice divinely singing.

                  Thus, at random,
This coil of worlds in which we grope; and thus
Our comings and our goings. So the twilight

537

Deepens the hour from rose to purple; so
One bell-note is the death-note, and completes
The half-remembered with the soon-forgotten.
The threes and fives compute our day; we move
To doom with all things moving.

                                        You and I
Are things compounded of time's heart-beats, stretching
The vascular instant from the vascular past;
You, with forgotten worlds, and I with worlds
Forgotten and remembered. Yet the leaf,
With all its bleeding veins, is not more torn
Than you are torn, this moment, from the last.
Can you rejoin it? Is it here, or there?
Where is that drop of blood you knew last year?
Where is that image which you loved, that frame
Of ghostly apparitions in your thought,
Alchemic mystery of your childhood, lost
With all its dizzy colors? . . . . It is gone.
Only the echo's echo can be heard.
Thrice-mirrored, the ghost pales.

                                        You plunge, poor soul,
From time's colossal brink into that chasm
Of change and limbo and immortal flux;
And bring up only, in your blood-stained hands,
One grain of sand that sparkles. Plunge again,
Poor diver, among weeds and death! and bring
The pearl of brightness up. It is this instant
When all is well with us: when hell and heaven
Arch in a chord of glory over madness;
When Pole Star sings to Sirius; and the wave
Of ultimate Ether breaks on ultimate Nothing.
The world's a rose which comes this night to flower:
This evening is its light. And it is we,
Who, with our harmonies and discords, woven
Of myriad things forgotten and remembered,
Urge the vast twilight to immortal bloom.

538

John Peale Bishop

SPEAKING OF POETRY

THE ceremony must be found
That will wed Desdemona to the huge Moor.

     It is not enough—
To win the approval of the Senator
Or to outwit his disapproval; honest Iago
Can manage that: it is not enough. For then,
Though she may pant again in his black arms
(His weight resilient as a Barbary stallion's)
She will be found
When the ambassadors of the Venetian state arrive
Again smothered. These things have not been changed,
Not in three hundred years

        (Tupping is still tupping
Though that particular word is obsolete.
Naturally, the ritual would not be in Latin.)

For though Othello had his blood from kings
His ancestry was barbarous, his ways African,
His speech uncouth. It must be remembered
That though he valued an embroidery—
Three mulberries proper on a silk like silver—
It was not for the subtlety of the stitches,
But for the magic in it. Whereas, Desdemona
Once contrived to imitate in needlework
Her father's shield, and plucked it out
Three times, to begin again, each time
With diminished colors. This is a small point
But indicative.

539

Desdemona was small and fair,

Delicate as a grasshopper
At the tag-end of summer: a Venetian
To her noble finger-tips.

O, it is not enough

That they should meet, naked, at dead of night
In a small inn on a dark canal. Procurers
Less expert than Iago can arrange as much.

The ceremony must be found

Traditional, with all its symbols
Ancient as the metaphors in dreams;
Strange, with never before heard music; continuous
Until the torches deaden at the bedroom door.

A RECOLLECTION

FAMOUSLY she descended, her red hair
Unbound and bronzed by sea-reflections, caught
Crinkled with sea-pearls. The fine slender taut
Knees that let down her feet upon the air,

Young breasts, slim flanks and golden quarries were
Odder than when the young distraught
Unknown Venetian, painting her portrait, thought
He'd not imagined what he painted there.

And I too commerced with that golden cloud:
Lipped her delicious hands and had my ease
Faring fantastically, perversely proud.

All loveliness demands our courtesies.
Since she was dead I praised her as I could
Silently, among the Barberini bees.

FIAMETTA

FIAMETTA walks under the quincebuds
   In a gown the color of flowers;
Her small breasts shine through the silken stuff
   Like raindrops after showers.
The green hem of her dress is silk, but duller
Than her eye's green color.

Her shadow restores the grass's green—
   Where the sun had gilded it;
The air has given her copper hair
   The sanguine that was requisite.
Whatever her flaws, my lady
Has no fault in her young body.

She leans with her long slender arms
   To pull down morning upon her—
Fragrance of quince, white light and falling cloud.
   The day shall have lacked due honor
Until I shall have rightly praised
Her standing thus with slight arms upraised.

ODE

WHY will they never sleep
Those great women who sit
Peering at me with parrot eyes?
They sit with grave knees; they keep
Perpetual stare; and their hands move
As though hands could be aware—
Forward and back, to begin again—
As though on tumultuous shuttles of wind they wove
Shrouds out of air.

The three are sisters. There is one
Who sits divine in weeping stone

On a small chair of skeleton
And is most inescapable.
I have walked through many mirrors
But always accompanied.
I have been as many men, as many ghosts,
As there were days. The boy was seen
Always at rainfall, mistily, not lost.
I have tried changing shapes
But always, alone, I have heard
Her shadow coming nearer, and known
The awful grasp of striding hands
Goddess! upon
The screaming metamorphosis.

One has a face burned hard
As the red Cretan clay,
Who wears a white torso scarred
With figures like a calendar.
She sits among broken shafts
Of stone; she is and still will be
Who feeds on cities, gods and men,
Weapons of bronze and curious ornaments,
Reckoning the evens as the odds.
Her least movement recalls the sea.

The last has idiot teeth
And a brow not made
For any thought but suffering.
Tired, she repeats
In idiot singing
A song shaped like a ring:
"Now is now and never Then
Dead Virgins will bear no men
And now that we speak of love, of love,
The woman's beneath
That's burdened with love
And the man's above
While the thing is done and done.

One is one and Three is three
Children may come from a spark in the sun
But One is one and never Three
And never a Virgin shall bear a Son
While the shadow lasts of the gray ashtree!"

Phantasmal marbles!

There was One who might have saved
Me from these grave dissolute stones
And parrot eyes. But He is dead,
Christ is dead. And in a grave
Dark as a sightless skull He lies
And of His bones are charnels made.

THIS DIM AND PTOLEMAIC MAN

For forty years, for forty-one,
Sparing the profits of the sun,
This farmer piled his meagre hoard
To buy at last a rattly Ford.

Now crouched on a scared smile he feels
Motion spurt beneath his heels,
Rheumatically intent shifts gears,
Unloosing joints of rustic years.

Morning light obscures the stars,
He swerves avoiding other cars,
Wheels with the road, does not discern
He eastward goes at every turn,

Nor how his aged limbs are hurled
Through all the motions of the world,
How wild past farms, past ricks, past trees,
He perishes toward Hercules.

YOUR CHASE
HAD A BEAST IN VIEW

Long time those gay and spotted hides
We hunted, riding; luxurious
Leopards in the forest slid.
At times it seemed they hunted us.

For just behind green tendrils they,
Seen and unseen, lengthened slunk;
Where the sun groped a greener day
They overleapt the rotted trunk.

And long we rode and still within
The forest eyes. Hidden we felt
A sinewy speed. A javelin
Once lifted to a snarling pelt

And fell and straightened to the hand.
Both knew that death must be delayed,
And on we rode, the leopards and
The followed, following, cavalcade.

O happiness! The lively long
Advancing of each golden beast!
The odor of their might was strong,
The morning wind was in the East.

But noon was cruel on our sight.
We rode into the forest's hem
And when the sun was at its height
In a small glade we slaughtered them.

We cut each throat. We dragged our knives
Across each looking throat. Their blood
Dyed death upon our hands. Our lives
Exultant spurted in the flood,

A moment young. Then silence broke
At the sweet destruction of
Those spotted beasts. And a shout spoke.
The youngest sang a stranger love.

Only in singing it might be
Supported by the sense alone,
One syllable of ecstasy
Confusing shame, confounding bone.

THE RETURN

NIGHT and we heard heavy and cadenced hoofbeats
Of troops departing; the last cohorts left
By the North Gate. That night some listened late
Leaning their eyelids toward Septentrion.

Morning flared and the young tore down the trophies
And warring ornaments: arches were strong
And in the sun but stone; no longer conquest
Circled our columns; all our state was down

In fragments. In the dust, old men with tufted
Eyebrows whiter than sunbaked faces gulped
As if fell. But they no more than we remembered
The old sea-fights, the soldiers' names and sculptors'.

We did not know the end was coming: nor why
It came; only that long before the end
Were many wanted to die. Then vultures starved
And sailed more slowly in the sky.

We still had taxes. Salt was high. The soldiers
Gone. Now there was much drinking and lewd
Houses all night loud with riot. But only
For a time. Soon the taverns had no roofs.

Strangely it was the young, the almost boys,
Who first abandoned hope; the old still lived
A little, at last a little lived in eyes.
It was the young whose child did not survive.

Some slept beneath the simulacra, until
The gods' faces froze. Then was fear.
Some had response in dreams, but morning restored
Interrogation. Then O then, O ruins!

Temples of Neptune invaded by the sea
And dolphins streaked like streams sportive
As sunlight rode and over the rushing floors
The sea unfurled and what was blue raced silver.

PERSPECTIVES ARE PRECIPICES

Sister Anne, Sister Anne,
Do you see anybody coming?

    I see a distance of black yews
    Long as the history of the Jews
    I see a road sunned with white sand
    Wide plains surrounding silence. And

    Far-off, a broken colonnade
    That overthrows the sun with shade.

Sister Anne, Sister Anne,
Do you see nobody coming?

                        A man

    Upon that road a man who goes
    Dragging a shadow by its toes.

Diminishing he goes, head bare
Of any covering even hair.

A pitcher depending from one hand
Goes mouth down. And dry is sand

Sister Anne, Sister Anne,
What do you see?

His dwindling stride. And he seems blind
Or worse to the prone man behind.

Sister Anne! Sister Anne!

I see a road. Beyond nowhere
Defined by cirrus and blue air.

I saw a man but he is gone
His shadow gone into the sun.

THE STATUE OF SHADOW

THIS was that mystery of clearest light:
No cloud
No shadow of a cloud
Passed on the stretch where then I stood.
A sandy noon consumed my sight.

I saw my body cast
In shadow and was afraid.
I saw time vast
As my own shadow and was afraid.
In light and a vision of light
I saw my shadow cast
Upon that coast.
The shade of all those centuries
Where death is longing and fate a crime

547

Lay long
But no longer
Than the statue of shadow
Noon laid at my feet.

This was that mystery:
Time had no other feature.

COLLOQUY WITH A KING-CRAB

DWARF pines; the wild plum on the wind-grassed shore
Shaken by autumn to its naked fruit;
Visions of bright winds across the bay:
These are, perhaps, sufficient images
To say what I have sought. These I have found.
Let these suffice with seas—though honesty is this,
To know what's sought from what the sands have found.
It needs no Proteus to announce the sea
Above the proclamations of loud surf—
Only the horseshoe crab, black carapace,
Project of life, though hideous, persisting
From the primordial grasp of claws on shore.
This crab is no abstraction, yet presents
No difficulty to the abstract mind,
His head all belly and his sword a tail,
But to the imagination is suspect.
Reject him? Why? Though voiceless, yet he says
That any monster may remain forever
If he but keep eyes, mind and claws intent
On the main chance, be not afraid to skulk.
This proletarian of the sea is not,
But scuttles, noble as the crocodile,
As ancient in his lineage. His name
Is not unknown in heaven. But his shell
Affords no edifice where I can creep
Though I consent like him to go on claws.

AN INTERLUDE

Our indolence was despair. We were still at times struck
When morning attained the deformed emperors
Where they stood, gaudy in armor, with laurels crowned,
One arm uplifted among the columns.

> There was never
Of course, any lack of statues to instruct us
In the aspect of virtue: magnanimous brows
Sterner than marble; in the sun's silence
Aquiline stares.

> Yet it was trying to behold
Depravity in the guards: propped as soldiers
By the gates, a few old seasoned cutthroats
With limping reputations; handsome and husky goat-
> herds,
Culled from the border hills, paid for and pampered
Out of our taxes; boys naughty as goats,
No wounds but in nerves, who nightly extolled
Their vices by Hadrian's monument and in broad day
Bartered equipment by the shaft of light
Where Victory wings the square.

> They jeered
Seeing the disorder, dust, stains, lagging wounds
Of the retreating army

> (The first in our annals—
What eyes the windows wore!)

> They clambered to jeer.

The Emperor arrived at midnight, complaining
Discreetly of the discipline. He must wait,
He said, opportunity
To retrieve both his own
And the nation's glory. Still on horseback,
He did not fail to recall our former fortunes;
Unbuckling swore at his orderly;

549

Summoned the generals
And for an hour harangued them in his tent:
Passes over the mountains could be entrusted
Only to troops of approved valor. Guards must be posted
Along all thoroughfares, doubled on crossroad,
With orders, and swords, to soothe this demented
Uproar and fear of the populace.

Deliberate

Even in the worst disease of his defeat,
The infecting tumult, he found time
Before morning to consult with others
On their causes for our long decline from greatness.
It was his opinion, he had long thought
And was more than ever convinced, nothing
Could be done for the army, nothing would again
Incite its ardor, unless manners were brought back
To their former glorious severity. No health else
In the state. Therefore, he proposed,
At the earliest possible moment, to revive
The long obsolete office of censor.

Revenue

Would have to be increased, but without, he insisted,
Adding to the already crushing burden of the wealthy.
The populace was to be separate once more as a class.
The hungry would be fed, of course, but the mob
Would have to curb its rage for riots. To prevent
These continual manifestations of envy, spite
And misery, he hereby restored
The equestrian order to all its rank and privileges.

Something, to be sure, would have to be done
For the peasantry, something, he was not sure,
But something, he supposed, along the lines of Augustus.
He would supply the army with all the needed statistics.
What might have come of all this we shall never know.
For nothing came of it, beyond some compilations of
     distress
Before the battle of the bogs.

550

                              Our undoing, it seems,
Was the blenching and scattered retreat of the swift
    barbarians.
Starved, for the countryside was exhausted, they did
    not refuse
Battle, but on the touch of our armies broke and fled,
Some without weapons. The Emperor, desiring to strike
    terror,
In haste pursued them with harassing swords
Beyond the third line, across salt meadows,
Into the marshes.

His body was never recovered. Here fortune turned.
All was adverse to our arms. The marshes, thick with
    ooze,
Sinking under those who fought, their armor weighted
    and the water deep.
Nor could they wield, in that morass, our heavy javelins.

We have heard the new Emperor proclaims
Our immediate deliverance. Medals have been struck off
Portraying him as Hercules the Victor
And as Mars the Avenger.

In the meantime, the barbarians are back in the passes.
Nothing is left but to stay devastation by tribute.

THE SUBMARINE BED

CHILDREN conceived when two nightgowns
In a bold clasp confused the bed . . .
As when an encumbered body drowns
And drowning lifts a dreadful head,

Each head was drawn to a strict tilt
To have no part in what was done,

While the lost gowns assumed the guilt
That should have been the body's own.

Bodies in deeper being plunged,
Abandoned sightless to the flood,
Swept down. Those two gowns lunged
Like hungry dogfish after food

That fled. Love? Was it love expulsed
To where those shrouds of love were wound
On corpses which with limbs convulsed
Sank into seas yet more profound?

Concupiscent, those gowns attain
The end they coveted. The heads stare
Sightless at mortality, then
Strain at the incorporeal air.

After such turmoil and such lust,
After such wreckage in the bed,
It is not easy to adjust
The body to a severed head.

THE DREAM

AND once again I was within that house
Where light collided with the gloom
And chilled on faces, as though the dawn
Were backward and the stars had gone;
For the long hall was populous
With pale expatriates from the tomb.

The house, deserted, had become a lair,
And all along that hall the dead slid
And tried the doors, one after one,
With hands no longer blest by bone.

They scanned me with a single stare
Because of what that one door hid.

I saw my mother, who had love
Still in her eyes, that did not own
Least light, for they had forfeited
Reflection, having reached the dead.
She spoke: and I was conscious of
An unspoken corruption.

Her speech prevented me from following
Angrily after those famished forms
Who only sought what I had sought
And found. I had been brought,
In the dread time of love's responding,
Undreaming into my young love's arms.

I saw what they were seeking in the gust
That drove them on from door to door
In the long deception of the hall.
They looked: from doors, nothing at all
Looked back at them. Yet though no lust
Awaited them, they must try once more.

I saw the shame that I contemned
Since it was sought by sightless eyes.
I knew what crime would be revealed
If the one door to the dead should yield,
But dreamed that door had been condemned
And in the dream had no surprise

That none could ever force a look
At incest dangling from a beam
And by a cord all blood attached.
For from the dark I knew there watched
Young eyes too quick with love to mock
The dead in that death-haunted dream.

Archibald MacLeish

DISCOVERY OF THIS TIME

Not by the Poets.

NOBODY borrowed a couple of dogs and a gun and
Packed out: keeping the evening forward:
Keeping the thrush to the left hand of the sun:
Following wandering water: building cover in
Four foot of wet snow in the underbrush:
Bringing the evidence back in a bag—a plover—a
Large bird: killed on the nest and no name for it.

No one set out for it. Nobody looked for the way here.

Not by Philosophers.

        Nobody sat to a map of the
Whole world: measured the drift of the stars: of
Letters in bottles: figured the flight of the lapwing:
Marked the compass courses on the chart—
"Here will be islands."

                "Here will be those shores."

"Coast will show here where the dolphins are."

Nobody figured it out on a fine morning
Propped on a wine-butt by a windy sea
With a lit pipe and a lead stub and a board's end. . . .

(And they sailed and there was log wood on the sea.)

554

Not by the Conquerors either.

Nobody led us here.
Nobody lined us up in a town field:
Shipped us in barges: fought at the stormy head:
Marched on for three days in the desert:
Encountered the elephants: beat them; buried the dead
    in a
Closed ring:
        And the next night to the west of us
Sea gulls over the sand: the wings numberless.

There are Leaders enough and they say what a mouth
    says but
None of them led us here!
                No man beat the drum . . .
Trekked to the site of it . . .

        Marked the shore and the harbors . . .

We came by ourselves.

        We looked and we had come.
There was one day and we walked from our lives and
    we stood here.
There was one day and we moved out—the neighborhood
Selling the farms: leaving the stock in the paddock:
Leaving the key in the lock and the cake on the table:
Letting the door slam: the tap drip . . .

There was one day and we looked and we had come here.

No one discovered it. No one intended it either.
There were all of us—all together—and we came.

YOU, ANDREW MARVELL

AND here face down beneath the sun
And here upon earth's noonward height
To feel the always coming on
The always rising of the night

To feel creep up the curving east
The earthy chill of dusk and slow
Upon those under lands the vast
And ever climbing shadow grow

And strange at Ecbatan the trees
Take leaf by leaf the evening strange
The flooding dark about their knees
The mountains over Persia change

And now at Kermanshah the gate
Dark empty and the withered grass
And through the twilight now the late
Few travelers in the westward pass

And Baghdad darken and the bridge
Across the silent river gone
And through Arabia the edge
Of evening widen and steal on

And deepen on Palmyra's street
The wheel rut in the ruined stone
And Lebanon fade out and Crete
High through the clouds and overblown

And over Sicily the air
Still flashing with the landward gulls
And loom and slowly disappear
The sails above the shadowy hulls

And Spain go under and the shore
Of Africa the gilded sand

And evening vanish and no more
The low pale light across that land

Nor now the long light on the sea

And here face downward in the sun
To feel how swift how secretly
The shadow of the night comes on . . .

IMMORTAL AUTUMN

I SPEAK this poem now with grave and level voice
In praise of autumn of the far-horn-winding fall
I praise the flower-barren fields the clouds the tall
Unanswering branches where the wind makes sullen
    noise

I praise the fall it is the human season
                           now
No more the foreign sun does meddle at our earth
Enforce the green and bring the fallow land to birth
Nor winter yet weigh all with silence the pine bough

But now in autumn with the blask and outcast crows
Share we the spacious world the whispering year is gone
There is more room to live now the once secret dawn
Comes late by daylight and the dark unguarded goes

Between the mutinous brave burning of the leaves
And winter's covering of our hearts with his deep snow
We are alone there are no evening birds we know
The naked moon the tame stars circle at our eaves

It is the human season on this sterile air
Do words outcarry breath the sound goes on and on
I hear a dead man's cry from autumn long since gone

I cry to you beyond upon this bitter air

ARS POETICA

A POEM should be palpable and mute
As a globed fruit

Dumb
As old medallions to the thumb

Silent as the sleeve-worn stone
Of casement ledges where the moss has grown—

A poem should be wordless
As the flight of birds

A poem should be motionless in time
As the moon climbs

Leaving, as the moon releases
Twig by twig the night-entangled trees,

Leaving, as the moon behind the winter leaves,
Memory by memory the mind—

A poem should be motionless in time
As the moon climbs

A poem should be equal to:
Not true

For all the history of grief
An empty doorway and a maple leaf

For love
The leaning grasses and two lights above the sea—

A poem should not mean
But be.

MEMORIAL RAIN

Ambassador Puser the ambassador
Reminds himself in French, the felicitous tongue,
What these (young men no longer) lie here for
In rows that once, and somewhere else, were young—

> All night in Brussels the wind had tugged at my
>   door:
> I had heard the wind at my door and the trees
>   strung
> Taut, and to me who had never been before
> In that country it was a strange wind blowing
> Steadily, stiffening the walls, the floor,
> The roof of my room. I had not slept for knowing
> He too, dead, was a stranger in that land
> And felt beneath the earth in the wind's flowing
> A tightening of roots and would not understand,
> Remembering lake winds in Illinois,
> That strange wind. I had felt his bones in the sand
> Listening.

—Reflects that these enjoy
Their country's gratitude, that deep repose,
That peace no pain can break, no hurt destroy,
That rest, that sleep—

> At Ghent the wind rose.
> There was a smell of rain and a heavy drag
> Of wind in the hedges but not as the wind blows
> Over fresh water when the waves lag
> Foaming and the willows huddle and it will rain:
> I felt him waiting.

—Indicates the flag
Which (may he say) enisles in Flanders' plain
This little field these happy, happy dead

Have made America—

In the ripe grain

The wind coiled glistening, darted, fled,
Dragging its heavy body: at Waereghem
The wind coiled in the grass above his head:
Waiting—listening—

—Dedicates to them

This earth their bones have hallowed, this last gift
A grateful country—

Under the dry grass stem

The words are blurred, are thickened, the words sift
Confused by the rasp of the wind, by the thin
    grating
Of ants under the grass, the minute shift
And tumble of dusty sand separating
From dusty sand. The roots of the grass strain,
Tighten, the earth is rigid, waits—he is waiting—
And suddenly, and all at once, the rain!

The people scatter, they run into houses, the wind
Is trampled under the rain, shakes free, is again
Trampled. The rain gathers, running in thinned
Spurts of water that ravel in the dry sand
Seeping into the sand under the grass roots, seeping
Between cracked boards to the bones of a clenched
    hand:
The earth relaxes, loosens; he is sleeping,
He rests, he is quiet, he sleeps in a strange land.

WHAT LIPS MY LIPS HAVE KISSED

WHAT lips my lips have kissed, and where, and why,
I have forgotten, and what arms have lain
Under my head till morning; but the rain
Is full of ghosts tonight, that tap and sigh
Upon the glass and listen for reply;
And in my heart there stirs a quiet pain
For unremembered lads that not again
Will turn to me at midnight with a cry.

Thus in the winter stands the lonely tree,
Nor knows what birds have vanished one by one,
Yet knows its boughs more silent than before:
I cannot say what loves have come and gone;
I only know that summer sang in me
A little while, that in me sings no more.

DIRGE WITHOUT MUSIC

I AM not resigned to the shutting away of loving hearts
    in the hard ground.
So it is, and so it will be, for so it has been, time out of
    mind:
Into the darkness they go, the wise and the lovely.
    Crowned
With lilies and with laurel they go; but I am not resigned.

Lovers and thinkers, into the earth with you.
Be one with the dull, the indiscriminate dust.
A fragment of what you felt, of what you knew,
A formula, a phrase remains,—but the best is lost.

561

The answers quick and keen, the honest look, the laugh-
    ter, the love,—
They are gone. They are gone to feed the roses. Elegant
    and curled
Is the blossom. Fragrant is the blossom. I know. But I do
    not approve.
More precious was the light in your eyes than all the
    roses of the world.

Down, down, down into the darkness of the grave
Gently they go, the beautiful, the tender, the kind;
Quietly they go, the intelligent, the witty, the brave.
I know. But I do not approve. And I am not resigned.

THE CAMEO

FOREVER over now, forever, forever gone
That day. Clear and diminished like a scene
Carven in cameo, the lighthouse, and the cove between
The sandy cliffs, and the boat drawn up on the beach;
And the long skirt of a lady innocent and young,
Her hand resting on her bosom, her head hung;
And the figure of a man in earnest speech.

Clear and diminished like a scene cut in cameo
The lighthouse, and the boat on the beach, and the two
    shapes
Of the woman and the man; lost like the lost day
Are the words that passed, and the pain,—discarded, cut
    away
From the stone, as from the memory the heat of the tears
    escapes.

O troubled forms, O early love unfortunate and hard,
Time has estranged you into a jewel cold and pure;
From the action of the waves and from the action of sor-
    row forever secure,
White against a ruddy cliff you stand, chalcedony on
 · sard.

RECUERDO

We were very tired, we were very merry—
We had gone back and forth all night on the ferry.
It was bare and bright, and smelled like a stable—
But we looked into a fire, we leaned across a table,
We lay on a hill-top underneath the moon;
And the whistles kept blowing, and the dawn came soon.

We were very tired, we were very merry—
We had gone back and forth all night on the ferry;
And you ate an apple, and I ate a pear,
From a dozen of each we had bought somewhere;
And the sky went wan, and the wind came cold,
And the sun rose dripping, a bucketful of gold.

We were very tired, we were very merry,
We had gone back and forth all night on the ferry.
We hailed, "Good-morrow, mother!" to a shawl-covered
    head,
And bought a morning paper, which neither of us read;
And she wept, "God bless you!" for the apples and pears,
And we gave her all our money but our subway fares.

ELEGY BEFORE DEATH

There will be rose and rhododendron
    When you are dead and under ground;
Still will be heard from white syringas
    Heavy with bees, a sunny sound.

Still will the tamaracks be raining
    After the rain has ceased, and still
Will there be robins in the stubble,
    Brown sheep upon the warm green hill.

Spring will not ail nor autumn falter;
    Nothing will know that you are gone,

Saving alone some sullen plough-land
  None but yourself set foot upon;

Saving the may-weed and the pig-weed
  Nothing will know that you are dead,—
These, and perhaps a useless wagon
  Standing beside some tumbled shed.

Oh, there will pass with your great passing
  Little of beauty not your own,—
Only the light from common water,
  Only the grace from simple stone.

THE RETURN

EARTH does not understand her child,
  Who from the loud gregarious town
Returns, depleted and defiled,
  To the still woods, to fling him down.

Earth cannot count the sons she bore:
  The wounded lynx, the wounded man
Come trailing blood unto her door;
  She shelters both as best she can.

But she is early up and out,
  To trim the year or strip its bones;
She has no time to stand about
  Talking of him in undertones

Who has no aim but to forget,
  Be left in peace, be lying thus
For days, for years, for centuries yet,
  Unshaven and anonymous;

Who, marked for failure, dulled by grief,
  Has traded in his wife and friend
For this warm ledge, this alder leaf:
  Comfort that does not comprehend.

EDNA ST. VINCENT MILLAY

ON HEARING A SYMPHONY
OF BEETHOVEN

SWEET sounds, oh, beautiful music, do not cease!
Reject me not into the world again.
With you alone is excellence and peace,
Mankind made plausible, his purpose plain.
Enchanted in your air benign and shrewd,
With limbs a-sprawl and empty faces pale,
The spiteful and the stingy and the rude
Sleep like the scullions in the fairy-tale.
This moment is the best the world can give:
The tranquil blossom on the tortured stem.
Reject me not, sweet sounds; oh, let me live,
Till Doom espy my towers and scatter them,
A city spell-bound under the aging sun.
Music my rampart, and my only one.

MORITURUS

IF I could have
Two things in one:
The peace of the grave,
And the light of the sun;

My hands across
My thin breast-bone,
But aware of the moss
Invading the stone,

Aware of the flight
Of the golden flicker
With his wing to the light;
To hear him nicker

And drum with his bill
On the rotted window;

Snug and still
On a gray pillow

Deep in the clay
Where digging is hard,
One of the way,—
The blue shard

Of a broken platter—
If I might be
Insensate matter
With sensate me

Sitting within,
Harking and prying,
I might begin
To dicker with dying.

565

For the body at best
Is a bundle of aches,
Longing for rest;
It cries when it wakes

"Alas, 'tis light!"
At set of sun
"Alas, 'tis night,
And nothing done!"

Death, however,
Is a spongy wall,
Is a sticky river,
Is nothing at all.

Summon the weeper,
Wail and sing;
Call him Reaper,
Angel, King;

Call him Evil
Drunk to the lees,
Monster, Devil—
He is less than these.

Call him Thief,
The Maggot in the Cheese,
The Canker in the Leaf—
He is less than these.

Dusk without sound,
Where the spirit by pain
Uncoiled, is wound
To spring again;

The mind enmeshed
Laid straight in repose,
566

And the body refreshed
By feeding the rose—

These are but visions;
These would be
The grave's derisions,
Could the grave see.

Here is the wish
Of one that died
Like a beached fish
On the ebb of the tide:

That he might wait
Till the tide came back,
To see if a crate,
Or a bottle, or a black

Boot, or an oar,
Or an orange peel
Be washed ashore. . . .
About his heel

The sand slips;
The last he hears
From the world's lips
Is the sand in his ears.

What thing is little?—
The aphis hid
In a house of spittle?
The hinge of the lid

Of the spider's eye
At the spider's birth?
"Greater am I
By the earth's girth

"Than Mighty Death!"
All creatures cry
That can summon breath—
And speak no lie.

For he is nothing;
He is less
Than Echo answering
"Nothingness!"—

Less than the heat
Of the furthest star
To the ripening wheat;
Less by far,

When all the lipping
Is said and sung,
Than the sweat dripping
From a dog's tongue.

This being so,
And I being such,
I would liever go
On a cripple's crutch,

Lopped and felled;
Liever be dependent
On a chair propelled
By a surly attendant

With a foul breath,
And be spooned my food,
Than go with Death
Where nothing good,

Not even the thrust
Of the summer gnat,

Consoles the dust
For being that.

Needy, lonely,
Stitched by pain,
Left with only
The drip of the rain

Out of all I had;
The books of the wise,
Badly read
By other eyes,

Lewdly bawled
At my closing ear;
Hated, called
A lingerer here—

Withstanding Death
Till Life be gone,
I shall treasure my breath,
I shall linger on.

I shall bolt my door
With a bolt and a cable;
I shall block my door
With a bureau and a table;

With all my might
My door shall be barred.
I shall put up a fight,
I shall take it hard.

With his hand on my
   mouth
He shall drag me forth,
Shrieking to the south
And clutching at the north.

567

Samuel Greenberg

THE GLASS BUBBLES

THE motion of gathering loops of water
Must either burst or remain in a moment.
The violet colors through the glass
Throw up little swellings that appear
And spatter as soon as another strikes
And is born; so pure are they of colored
Hues, that we feel the absent strength
Of its power. When they begin they gather
Like sand on the beach: each bubble
Contains a complete eye of water.

SOUL'S KISS

IT was the fruit on high,
From whence the chosen seed
Has found its moorless love
Therein, the human creed.

O soul of fatal refrain!—
Like the corn, flowers a cover
Over its skin, doth feign
From a mood; there love can hover.

Ah! by the shore of moss
And through the thrown-up rocks
There whispers the toneful moon;
The mingling serenade looks.

KILLING

Lo! the foolish fell.
Silence about—
While the hero stood
And saw the gathering
    crowd.

What an awkward
Fall is this . . .

An unseen conqueror,
After looking toward

The shouting throng, arouses
A triumphing cry—
While David held the head
For those who stood by.

THE BLANK BOOK LETTER

Now must I wait
For ideas astray
That keep lingering until
The fuse finds its way.

Men can write
And spell the beat

And whisper lore
From this solemn creation.

But the blank book letter
Has told you the vein
Of art, that souls
The earth no gain.

TO DEAR DANIEL*

THERE is a loud noise of
    Death
Where I lay;
There is a loud noise of life
Far away.

From low and weary stride
Have I flown;
From low and weary pride
I have grown.

What does it matter now
To you or me?
What does it matter now
To whom it be?

Again the stain has come
To me;
Again the stain has come
For thee.

* The last-dated poem in Greenberg's manuscript. Written on a one cent
postal card, dated March 14, 1917.

569

I CANNOT BELIEVE THAT I AM OF WIND

I CANNOT believe that I am of wind,
For earth and wind can match a god.
I cannot believe in writing so . . .
What would you do
If I must mind
The world of blossom's
Lay and peace?—
The rest of love
And charm's uncease?
I cannot believe the find.

ESSENTIALS

THE ill sat to be with the calm
Spacious breeze; the thirsty man
Sought the fountain; the seasons
Cloaked the roving form; the
Scholar lit his lamp to see;
The guide showed the unknown
Path; consolation soothed the
Gentle soul and lent his
Strengthening mind relief; the poor
Were sheltered from mercy's grief;
Mother cared for the offspring's want;
Rain poured o'er the fertile soil;
The torch found the miner's haunt;
The bathers fought the ocean's hurl.

SPIRITUALITY

IN what finite tendon dost thou rise?
Though 'pon the omnipotence thence we find
The glory of wicked truth which flaps its wings to bind
All but the hollow lute, that pipes its strain yon

Lower hill mid vat of fragrance. Ah, ye
Melancholy 'frain, oft have I left thee
To slumber my memory of such real disdain!
I mend no path, since my faith is as
The star o'er nocuous blue; within, my soul hath
Climbed unto thy tales of old, 'round fire listened.
I nobly saw that through history my youth came nigh
And whispered joy within my breast from efforts clear.
Forgive our memory stain! e'er this might of love
Hath meekly found its room, so called immortality.

IMMORTALITY

But only to be memories of spiritual gate,
Letting us feel the difference from the real;
Are not limits the sooth to formulate
Theories thereof, simply our ruler to feel?
Basques of statuettes of eruptions long ago,
Of power in symmetry, marvel of thought
The crafts attempt, showing rare aspiration;
The museums of the ancient fine stones
For bowls and cups found historians
Sacred adorations, the numismatist hath shown,
But only to be memories of spiritual gate,
Letting us feel the difference from the real;
Are not limits the sooth to formulate
Theories thereof, simply our ruler to feel?

CONDUCT

By a peninsula the painter sat and
Sketched the uneven valley groves.
The apostle gave alms to the
Meek. The volcano burst
In fusive sulphur and hurled

571

Rocks and ore into the air—
Heaven's sudden change at
The drawing tempestuous,
Darkening shade of dense clouded hues.
The wanderer soon chose
His spot of rest; they bore the
Chosen hero upon their shoulders,
Whom they strangely admired, as
The beach-tide summer of people desired.

EMBLEMS OF CONDUCT

(NOTE: *This version built on Samuel Greenberg's poems "Conduct" and "Immortality" was written by Hart Crane*)

By a peninsula the wanderer sat and sketched
The uneven valley graves. While the apostle gave
Alms to the meek the volcano burst
With sulphur and aureate rocks . . .
For joy rides in stupendous coverings
Luring the living into spiritual gates.

Orators follow the universe
And radio the complete laws to the people.
The apostle conveys thought through discipline.
Bowls and cups fill historians with adorations,—
Dull lips commemorating spiritual gates.

The wanderer later chose this spot of rest
Where marble clouds support the sea
And where was finally borne a chosen hero.
By that time summer and smoke were past.
Dolphins still played, arching the horizons,
But only to build memories of spiritual gates.

Mark Van Doren

YOUNG WOMAN AT A WINDOW

Who so valiant to decide?
Who so prompt and proper-active?
Yet each muscle in her brain
Relaxes now; is unrestrictive;
Lets her lean upon this dark
November night wind; lets it work—

Oh, lets it ask her if she thinks,
Oh, lets it whisper if she knows
How much of time is like a stream
Down which her headless body flows;
How many answers, proudly made,
Will be like minnows overlaid

With inch on inch of glossy black,
With depth on depth of sliding water;
Lets it dare her to predict
Those floods of silence coming later;
Till she melts, and leaning long
Is only conscious of wind-song.

Who so valorous of voice?
Who so staunch upon the ground?
But wind-and-water-song at work
Stops both her ears against the sound
Of someone here she used to know;
Of someone saying: It is so.

She leans and loses every word.
Her loudest wisdom well is gone.
But still the current of the night

573

Comes with its foaming on and on;
Pours round the sill; dissolves the hands;
And still the dreamless body stands.

AUTONOMOUS

IN jealousy of cause and pride of plan
He thinks he made himself, this happy man.
He was the decider; picked a year,
A womb to grow in, and a hemisphere;
And when he walked was master of the choice
Who fathered his first gait and tuned his voice.
Of all earth's people to its oddest ends
He summoned these few to be his natural friends;
From out the mist of women he contrived
The stepping forth of one whom then he wived;
And now that sons repeat him it is skill
Rewarded, it is accident of will.
The maple where it stands is proof of seed.
He knows it, and can measure by its need,
Among so many neighbors, a trunk's tallness;
And by its shade the after comer's smallness,
Dwarf to its sire. Such things, he says, must be
If soil decides. But he is not a tree;
And thinks that he was present in the dark
When skin was chosen over root and bark.

THIS AMBER SUNSTREAM

THIS amber sunstream, with an hour to live,
Flows carelessly, and does not save itself;
Nor recognizes any entered room—
This room; nor hears the clock upon a shelf,
Declaring the lone hour; for where it goes
All space in a great silence ever flows.

No living man may know it till this hour,
When the clear sunstream, thickening to amber,
Moves like a sea, and the sunk hulls of houses
Let it come slowly through, as divers clamber,
Feeling for gold. So now into this room
Peer the large eyes, unopen to their doom.

Another hour and nothing will be here.
Even upon themselves the eyes will close.
Nor will this bulk, withdrawing, die outdoors
In night, that from another silence flows.
No living man in any western room
But sits at amber sunset round a tomb.

THE DISTANT RUNNERS

*Six great horses of Spain, set free after his death by
De Soto's men, ran West and restored to America the
wild race lost there some thousands of years ago.*
—A legend.

FERDINAND DE SOTO lies
Soft again in river mud.
Birds again, as on the day
Of his descending, rise and go
Straightly West, and do not know
Of feet beneath that faintly thud.

If I were there in other time,
Between the proper sky and stream;
If I were there and saw the six
Abandoned manes, and ran along,
I could sing the fetlock song
That now is chilled within a dream.

575

Ferdinand De Soto, sleeping
In the river, never heard
Four-and-twenty Spanish hooves
Fling off their iron and cut the green,
Leaving circles new and clean
While overhead the wing-tips whirred.

Neither I nor any walker
By the Mississippi now
Can see the dozen nostrils open
Half in pain for death of men—
But half in gladness, neighing then
As loud as loping would allow.

On they rippled, tail and back,
A prairie day, and swallows knew
A dark, uneven current there.
But not a sound came up the wind,
And toward the night their shadow thinned
Before the black that flooded through.

If I were there to bend and look,
The sky would know them as they sped
And turn to see. But I am here,
And they are far, and time is old.
Within my dream the grass is cold;
The legs are locked; the sky is dead.

WINTER TRYST

WHEN the Atlantic upsloped itself
Like roofs of higher and higher houses,
To the great ridge, the foaming shelf
Whereon no dolphin ever browses;

When the wild grey broke into white,
And ships rose endward, crushing mountains;

Mark Van Doren

When it was thus, and icy light
Poured up from phosphorescent fountains:

When it was thus, at winter's crest,
A vessel arrived; and the annual ocean,
Faithfully setting her down in the west,
Repented awhile of its furious motion;

Subsided; but only until that prow
Was pointed again, and a passenger, waving,
Wept in the channel, reminded now
Of eleven months, and the duty of braving

A spring and a summer, and longer fall
Till the month of the year that was set for returning;
Then the grey slopes; and the port, and the tall
Still lover—O time! O bitter adjourning!

When the Atlantic upheaved its whole
And the bottomless world dared keels to try it:
Then was the season; this poor soul
Only that month kept longing quiet.

Only that month: most difficult,
Most dark. Most loveless, and most unable.
Yet it was hers. And time's result
Is love's most fair, most speechless fable.

E. E. Cummings

ALL IN GREEN WENT MY LOVE RIDING

ALL in green went my love riding
on a great horse of gold
into the silver dawn.

four lean hounds crouched low and smiling
the merry deer ran before.

Fleeter be they than dappled dreams
the swift sweet deer
the red rare deer.

Four red roebuck at a white water
the cruel bugle sang before.

Horn at hip went my love riding
riding the echo down
into the silver dawn.

four lean hounds crouched low and smiling
the level meadows ran before.

Softer be they than slippered sleep
the lean lithe deer
the fleet flown deer.

Four fleet does at a gold valley
the famished arrow sang before.

Bow at belt went my love riding

riding the mountain down
into the silver dawn.

four lean hounds crouched low and smiling
the sheer peaks ran before.

Paler be they than daunting death
the sleek slim deer
the tall tense deer.

Four tall stags at a green mountain
the lucky hunter sang before.

All in green went my love riding
on a great horse of gold
into the silver dawn.

four lean hounds crouched low and smiling
my heart fell dead before.

SOMEWHERE I HAVE NEVER TRAVELLED, GLADLY BEYOND

somewhere i have never travelled, gladly beyond
any experience, your eyes have their silence:
in your most frail gesture are things which enclose me,
or which i cannot touch because they are too near

your slightest look easily will unclose me
though i have closed myself as fingers,
you open always petal by petal myself as Spring opens
(touching skilfully, mysteriously) her first rose

or if your wish be to close me, i and
my life will shut very beautifully, suddenly,
as when the heart of this flower imagines
the snow carefully everywhere descending;

nothing which we are to perceive in this world equals
the power of your intense fragility: whose texture
compels me with the colour of its countries,
rendering death and forever with each breathing

(i do not know what it is about you that closes
and opens; only something in me understands
the voice of your eyes is deeper than all roses)
nobody, not even the rain, has such small hands

ANYONE LIVED IN A PRETTY
HOW TOWN

anyone lived in a pretty how town
(with up so floating many bells down)
spring summer autumn winter
he sang his didn't he danced his did.

Women and men (both little and small)
cared for anyone not at all
they sowed their isn't they reaped their same
sun moon stars rain

children guessed (but only a few
and down they forgot as up they grew
autumn winter spring summer)
that noone loved him more by more

when by now and tree by leaf
she laughed his joy she cried his grief
bird by snow and stir by still
anyone's any was all to her

someones married their everyones
laughed their cryings and did their dance

(sleep wake hope and then) they
said their nevers they slept their dream

stars rain sun moon
(and only the snow can begin to explain
how children are apt to forget to remember
with up so floating many bells down)

one day anyone died i guess
(and noone stooped to kiss his face)
busy folk buried them side by side
little by little and was by was

all by all and deep by deep
and more by more they dream their sleep
noone and anyone earth by april
wish by spirit and if by yes.

Women and men (both dong and ding)
summer autumn winter spring
reaped their sowing and went their came
sun moon stars rain

I SING OF OLAF

i sing of Olaf glad and big
whose warmest heart recoiled at war:
a conscientious object-or

his wellbelovéd colonel (trig
westpointer most succinctly bred)
took erring Olaf soon in hand;
but—though an host of overjoyed
noncoms (first knocking on the head
him) do through icy waters roll
that helplessness which others stroke
with brushes recently employed

anent this muddy toiletbowl,
while kindred intellects evoke
allegiance per blunt instruments—
Olaf (being to all intents
a corpse and wanting any rag
upon what God unto him gave)
responds, without getting annoyed
"I will not kiss your f.ing flag"

straightway the silver bird looked grave
(departing hurriedly to shave)

but—though all kinds of officers
(a yearning nation's blueeyed pride)
their passive prey did kick and curse
until for wear their clarion
voices and boots were much the worse,
and egged the firstclassprivates on
his rectum wickedly to tease
by means of skilfully applied
bayonets roasted hot with heat—
Olaf (upon what were once knees)
does almost ceaselessly repeat
"there is some s. I will not eat"

our president, being of which
assertions duly notified
threw the yellowsonofabitch
into a dungeon, where he died

Christ (of His mercy infinite)
i pray to see; and Olaf, too

preponderatingly because
unless statistics lie he was
more brave than me: more blond than you.

WHAT IF A MUCH OF A WHICH OF A WIND

what if a much of a which of a wind
gives the truth to summer's lie;
bloodies with dizzying leaves the sun
and yanks immortal stars awry?
Blow king to beggar and queen to seem
(blow friend to fiend: blow space to time)
—when skies are hanged and oceans drowned,
the single secret will still be man

what if a keen of a lean wind flays
screaming hills with sleet and snow:
strangles valleys by ropes of thing
and stifles forests in white ago?
Blow hope to terror; blow seeing to blind
(blow pity to envy and soul to mind)
—whose hearts are mountains, roots are trees,
it's they shall cry hello to the spring

what if a dawn of a doom of a dream
bites this universe in two,
peels forever out of his grave
and sprinkles nowhere with me and you?
Blow soon to never and never to twice
(blow life to isn't: blow death to was)
—all nothing's only our hugest home;
the most who die, the more we live

MY FATHER MOVED THROUGH DOOMS OF LOVE

My father moved through dooms of love
through sames of am through haves of give,
singing each morning out of each night
my father moved through depths of height

this motionless forgetful where
turned at his glance to shining here;
that if (so timid air is firm)
under his eyes would stir and squirm

newly as from unburied which
floats the first who, his april touch
drove sleeping selves to swarm their fates
woke dreamers to their ghostly roots

and should some why completely weep
my father's fingers brought her sleep:
vainly no smallest voice might cry
for he could feel the mountains grow.

Lifting the valleys of the sea
my father moved through griefs of joy;
praising a forehead called the moon
singing desire into begin

joy was his song and joy so pure
a heart of star by him could steer
and pure so now and now so yes
the wrists of twilight would rejoice

keen as midsummer's keen beyond
conceiving mind of sun will stand,
so strictly (over utmost him
so hugely) stood my father's dream

his flesh was flesh his blood was blood:
no hungry man but wished him food;
no cripple wouldn't creep one mile
uphill to only see him smile.

Scorning the pomp of must and shall
my father moved through dooms of feel;
his anger was as right as rain
his pity was as green as grain

septembering arms of year extend
less humbly wealth to foe and friend
than he to foolish and to wise
offered immeasurable is

proudly and (by octobering flame
beckoned) as earth will downward climb,
so naked for immortal work
his shoulders marched against the dark

his sorrow was as true as bread:
no liar looked him in the head;
if every friend became his foe
he'd laugh and build a world with snow.

My father moved through theys of we,
singing each new leaf out of each tree
(and every child was sure that spring
danced when she heard my father sing)

then let men kill which cannot share,
let blood and flesh be mud and mire,
scheming imagine, passion willed,
freedom a drug that's bought and sold

giving to steal and cruel kind,
a heart to fear, to doubt a mind,
to differ a disease of same,
conform the pinnacle of am

though dull were all we taste as bright,
bitter all utterly things sweet,
maggoty minus and dumb death
all we inherit, all bequeath

and nothing quite so least as truth
—i say though hate were why men breathe—
because my father lived his soul
love is the whole and more than all

MAY I FEEL SAID HE

may i feel said he
(i'll squeal said she
just once said he)
it's fun said she

may i touch said he
how much said she
a lot said he)
why not said she

(let's go said he
not too far said she
what's too far said he
where you are said she)

may i stay said he
(which way said she
like this said he
if you kiss said she

may i move said he
is it love said she)
if you're willing said he
(but you're killing said she

but it's life said he
but your wife said she
now said he)
ow said she

(tiptop said he
don't stop said she
oh no said he)
go slow said she

(cccome?said he
ummm said she)
you're divine!said he
(you are Mine said she)

PITY THIS BUSY MONSTER,
MANUNKIND

pity this busy monster, manunkind,

not. Progress is a comfortable disease:
your victim (death and life safely beyond)

plays with the bigness of his littleness
—electrons deify one razorblade
into a mountainrange; lenses extend

unwish through curving wherewhen till unwish
returns on its unself.

A world of made
is not a world of born—pity poor flesh

and trees, poor stars and stones, but never this
fine specimen of hypermagical

ultraomnipotence. We doctors know

a hopeless case if—listen: there's a hell
of a good universe next door; let's go

AS FREEDOM IS A BREAKFASTFOOD

As freedom is a breakfastfood
or truth can live with right and wrong
or molehills are from mountains made
—long enough and just so long
will being pay the rent of seem
and genius please the talentgang
and water most encourage flame

as hatracks into peachtrees grow
or hopes dance best on bald men's hair
and every finger is a toe
and any courage is a fear
—long enough and just so long
will the impure think all things pure
and hornets wail by children stung

or as the seeing are the blind
and robins never welcome spring
nor flatfolk prove their world is round
nor dingsters die at break of dong
and common's rare and millstones float
—long enough and just so long
tomorrow will not be too late

worms are the words but joy's the voice
down shall go which and up come who
breasts will be breasts thighs will be thighs
deeds cannot dream what dreams can do
—time is a tree (this life one leaf)
but love is the sky and i am for you
just so long and long enough

ALWAYS BEFORE YOUR VOICE
MY SOUL

ALWAYS before your voice my soul
half-beautiful and wholly droll
is as some smooth and awkward foal,
whereof young moons begin
the newness of his skin,

so of my stupid sincere youth
the exquisite failure uncouth
discovers a trembling and smooth
Unstrength, against the strong
silences of your song;

or as a single lamb whose sheen
of full unsheared fleece is mean
beside its lovelier friends, between
your thoughts more white than wool
My thought is sorrowful:

but my heart smote in trembling thirds
of anguish quivers to your words,
As to a flight of thirty birds
shakes with a thickening fright
the sudden fooled light.

it is the autumn of a year:
When through the thin air stooped with fear,
across the harvest whitely peer
empty of surprise
death's faultless eyes

(whose hand my folded soul shall know
while on faint hills do frailly go
The peaceful terrors of the snow,
and before your dead face
which sleeps, a dream shall pass)

and these my days their sounds and flowers
Fall in a pride of petaled hours,
like flowers at the feet of mowers
whose bodies strong with love
through meadows hugely move.

yet what am i that such and such
mysteries very simply touch
me, whose heart-wholeness overmuch
Expects of your hair pale,
a terror musical?

while in an earthless hour my fond
soul seriously yearns beyond
this fern of sunset frond on frond
opening in a rare
Slowness of gloried air . . .

The flute of morning stilled in noon—
noon the implacable bassoon—
now Twilight seeks the thrill of moon,
washed with a wild and thin
despair of violin

BUFFALO BILL'S

BUFFALO BILL'S
defunct
    who used to
        ride a watersmooth-silver
                        stallion
and break onetwothreefourfive pigeonsjustlike that
                                        Jesus

he was a handsome man
                    and what i want to know is
how do you like your blueeyed boy
Mister Death

IT WAS A GOODLY CO

it was a goodly co
which paid to make man free
(for man is enslaved by a dread dizziz
and the sooner it's over the sooner to biz
don't ask me what it's pliz

then up rose bishop budge from kew
a anglican was who
(With a rag and a bone and a hank of hair)'d
he picked up a thousand pounds or two
and he smote the monster merde

then up rose pride and up rose pelf
and ghibelline and guelph
and ladios and laddios
(on radios and raddios)
did save man from himself

ye duskiest despot's goldenest gal
did wring that dragon's tail
(for men must loaf and women must lay)
and she gave him a desdemonial
that took his breath away

all history oped her teeming womb
said demon for to doom
yea (fresh complexions being oke
with him) one william shakespeare broke
the silence of the tomb

then up rose mr lipshits pres
(who always nothing says)
and he kisséd the general menedjerr
and they smokéd a robert burns cigerr
to the god of things like they err

Louise Bogan

MEN LOVED WHOLLY
BEYOND WISDOM

MEN loved wholly beyond wisdom
Have the staff without the banner.
Like a fire in a dry thicket,
Rising within women's eyes
Is the love men must return.
Heart, so subtle now, and trembling,
What a marvel to be wise,
To love never in this manner!
To be quiet in the fern
Like a thing gone dead and still,
Listening to the prisoned cricket
Shake its terrible, dissembling
Music in the granite hill.

M., SINGING

Now, innocent, within the deep
Night of all things you turn the key
Unloosing what we know in sleep.
In your fresh voice they cry aloud
Those beings without heart or name.

Those creatures both corrupt and proud,
Upon the melancholy words
And in the music's subtlety,
Leave the long harvest which they reap
In the sunk land of dust and flame
And move to space beneath our sky.

591

HENCEFORTH, FROM THE MIND

HENCEFORTH, from the mind,
For your whole joy, must spring
Such joy as you may find
In any earthly thing,
And every time and place
Will take your thought for grace.

Henceforth, from the tongue,
From shallow speech alone,
Comes joy you thought, when young,
Would wring you to the bone,
Would pierce you to the heart
And spoil its stop and start.

Henceforward, from the shell,
Wherein you heard, and wondered
At oceans like a bell
So far from ocean sundered—
A smothered sound that sleeps
Long lost within lost deeps,

Will chime you change and hours,
The shadow of increase,
Will sound you flowers
Born under troubled peace—
Henceforth, henceforth
Will echo sea and earth.

SONG FOR A LYRE

THE landscape where I lie
Again from boughs sets free
Summer; all night must fly
In wind's obscurity
The thick, green leaves that made
Heavy the August shade.

Soon, in the pictured night,
Returns—as in a dream
Left after sleep's delight—
The shallow autumn stream:
Softly awake, its sound
Poured on the chilly ground.

Soon fly the leaves in throngs:
O love, though once I lay
Far from its sound, to weep,
When night divides my sleep,
When stars, the autumn stream,
Stillness, divide my dream,
Night to your voice belongs.

I SAW ETERNITY

O BEAUTIFUL FOREVER!
O grandiose Everlasting!
Now, now, now,
I break you into pieces,
I feed you to the ground.

O brilliant, O languishing
Cycle of weeping light!
The mice and birds will eat you,
And you will spoil their stomachs
As you have spoiled my mind.

Here, mice, rats,
Porcupines and toads,
Moles, shrews, squirrels,
Weasels, turtles, lizards,—
Here's bright Everlasting!
Here's a crumb of Forever!
Here's a crumb of Forever!

OLD COUNTRYSIDE

BEYOND the hour we counted rain that fell
On the slant shutter, all has come to proof.
The summer thunder, like a wooden bell,
Rang in the storm above the mansard roof,

And mirrors cast the cloudy day along
The attic floor; wind made the clapboards creak.
You braced against the wall to make it strong,
A shell against your cheek.

Long since, we pulled brown oak-leaves to the ground
In a winter of dry trees; we heard the cock
Shout its unplaceable cry, the axe's sound
Delay a moment after the axe's stroke.

Far back, we saw, in the stillest of the year,
The scrawled vine shudder, and the rose-branch show
Red to the thorns, and, sharp as sight can bear,
The thin hound's body arched against the snow.

THE DREAM

O GOD, in the dream the terrible horse began
To paw at the air, and make for me with his blows.
Fear kept for thirty-five years poured through his mane,
And retribution equally old, or nearly, breathed through
his nose.

Coward complete, I lay and wept on the ground
When some strong creature appeared, and leapt for the
rein.
Another woman, as I lay half in a swound
Leapt in the air, and clutched at the leather and chain.

594

Give him, she said, something of yours as a charm.
Throw him, she said, some poor thing you alone claim.
No, no, I cried, he hates me; he's out for harm,
And whether I yield or not, it is all the same.

But, like a lion in a legend, when I flung the glove
Pulled from my sweating, my cold right hand,
The terrible beast, that no one may understand,
Came to my side, and put down his head in love.

WOMEN

Women have no wilderness in them,
They are provident instead,
Content in the tight hot cell of their hearts
To eat dusty bread.

They do not see cattle cropping red winter grass,
They do not hear
Snow water going down under culverts
Shallow and clear.

They wait, when they should turn to journeys,
They stiffen, when they should bend.
They use against themselves that benevolence
To which no man is friend.

They cannot think of so many crops to a field
Or of clean wood cleft by an ax.
Their love is an eager meaninglessness
Too tense, or too lax.

They hear in every whisper that speaks to them
A shout and a cry.
As like as not, when they take life over their door-sills
They should let it go by.

Hart Crane

THE BRIDGE

From going to and fro in the earth,
and from walking up and down in it. THE BOOK OF JOB

TO BROOKLYN BRIDGE

How many dawns, chill from his rippling rest
The seagull's wings shall dip and pivot him,
Shedding white rings of tumult, building high
Over the chained bay waters Liberty—

Then, with inviolate curve, forsake our eyes
As apparitional as sails that cross
Some page of figures to be filed away;
—Till elevators drop us from our day . . .

I think of cinemas, panoramic sleights
With multitudes bent toward some flashing scene
Never disclosed, but hastened to again,
Foretold to other eyes on the same screen;

And Thee, across the harbor, silver-paced
As though the sun took step of thee, yet left
Some motion ever unspent in thy stride,—
Implicitly thy freedom staying thee!

Out of some subway scuttle, cell or loft
A bedlamite speeds to thy parapets,
Tilting there momently, shrill shirt ballooning,
A jest falls from the speechless caravan.

Down Wall, from girder into street noon leaks,
A rip-tooth of the sky's acetylene;

All afternoon the cloud-flown derricks turn . . .
Thy cables breathe the North Atlantic still.

And obscure as that heaven of the Jews,
Thy guerdon . . . Accolade thou dost bestow
Of anonymity time cannot raise:
Vibrant reprieve and pardon thou dost show.

O harp and altar, of the fury fused,
(How could mere toil align thy choiring strings!)
Terrific threshold of the prophet's pledge,
Prayer of pariah, and the lover's cry,—

Again the traffic lights that skim thy swift
Unfractioned idiom, immaculate sigh of stars,
Beading thy path—condense eternity:
And we have seen night lifted in thine arms.

Under thy shadow by the piers I waited;
Only in darkness is thy shadow clear.
The City's fiery parcels all undone,
Already snow submerges an iron year . . .

O Sleepless as the river under thee,
Vaulting the sea, the prairies' dreaming sod,
Unto us lowliest sometime sweep, descend
And of the curveship lend a myth to God.

I

AVE MARIA

Venient annis, sæcula seris,
Quibus Oceanus vincula rerum
Laxet et ingens pateat tellus
Tiphysque novos detegat orbes
Nec sit terris ultima Thule.—SENECA

BE with me, Luis de San Angel, now—
Witness before the tides can wrest away
The word I bring, O you who reined my suit

Into the Queen's great heart that doubtful day; *Columbus, alone, gazing toward Spain, invokes the presence of two faithful partisans of his quest ...*
For I have seen now what no perjured breath
Of clown nor sage can riddle or gainsay;—
To you, too, Juan Perez, whose counsel fear
And greed adjourned,—I bring you back
    Cathay!

Here waves climb into dusk on gleaming mail;
Invisible valves of the sea,—locks, tendons
Crested and creeping, troughing corridors
That fall back yawning to another plunge.
Slowly the sun's red caravel drops light
Once more behind us. . . . It is morning there—
O where our Indian emperies lie revealed,
Yet lost, all, let this keel one instant yield!

I thought of Genoa; and this truth, now proved,
That made me exile in her streets, stood me
More absolute than ever—biding the moon
Till dawn should clear that dim frontier, first seen
—The Chan's great continent. . . . Then faith, not fear
Nigh surged me witless. . . . Hearing the surf near—
I, wonder-breathing, kept the watch,—saw
The first palm chevron the first lighted hill.

And lowered. And they came out to us crying,
"The Great White Birds!" (O Madre Maria, still
One ship of these thou grantest safe returning;
Assure us through thy mantle's ageless blue!)
And record of more, floating in a casque,
Was tumbled from us under bare poles scudding;
And later hurricanes may claim more pawn. . . .
For here between two worlds, another, harsh,

This third, of water, tests the word; lo, here
Bewilderment and mutiny heap whelming
Laughter, and shadow cuts sleep from the heart
598

Almost as though the Moor's flung scimitar
Found more than flesh to fathom in its fall.
Yet under tempest-lash and surfeitings
Some inmost sob, half-heard, dissuades the abyss,
Merges the wind in measure to the waves,

Series on series, infinite,—till eyes
Starved wide on blackened tides, accrete—enclose
This turning rondure whole, this crescent ring
Sun-cusped and zoned with modulated fire
Like pearls that whisper through the Doge's hands
—Yet no delirium of jewels! O Fernando,
Take of that eastern shore, this western sea,
Yet yield thy God's, thy Virgin's charity!

—Rush down the plenitude, and you shall see
Isaiah counting famine on this lee!

*

An herb, a stray branch among salty teeth,
The jellied weeds that drag the shore,—perhaps
Tomorrow's moon will grant us Saltes Bar—
Palos again,—a land cleared of long war.
Some Angelus environs the cordage tree;
Dark waters onward shake the dark prow free.

*

O Thou who sleepest on Thyself, apart
Like ocean athwart lanes of death and birth,
And all the eddying breath between dost search
Cruelly with love thy parable of man,—
Inquisitor! incognizable Word
Of Eden and the enchained Sepulchre,
Into thy steep savannahs, burning blue,
Utter to loneliness the sail is true.

Who grindest oar, and arguing the mast

599

Subscribest holocaust of ships, O Thou
Within whose primal scan consummately
The glistening seignories of Ganges swim;—
Who sendest greeting by the corposant,
And Teneriffe's garnet—flamed it in a cloud,
Urging through night our passage to the Chan;—
Te Deum laudamus, for thy teeming span!

Of all that amplitude that time explores,
A needle in the sight, suspended north,—
Yielding by inference and discard, faith
And true appointment from the hidden shoal:
This disposition that thy night relates
From Moon to Saturn in one sapphire wheel:
The orbic wake of thy once whirling feet,
Elohim, still I hear thy sounding heel!

White toil of heaven's cordons, mustering
In holy rings all sails charged to the far
Hushed gleaming fields and pendant seething wheat
Of knowledge,—round thy brows unhooded now
—The kindled Crown! acceded of the poles
And biassed by full sails, meridians reel
Thy purpose—still one shore beyond desire!
The sea's green crying towers a-sway, Beyond

And kingdoms

        naked in the

                trembling heart—

Te Deum laudamus

              O Thou Hand of Fire

II

POWHATAN'S DAUGHTER

"—Pocahuntus, a well-featured but wanton yong girle . . . of the age of eleven or twelve years, get the boyes forth with her into the market place, and make them wheele, falling on their hands, turning their heels upwards, whom she would followe, and wheele so herself, naked as she was, all the fort over."

Hart Crane

THE HARBOR DAWN

INSISTENTLY through sleep—a tide of voices—
They meet you listening midway in your
    dream,
The long, tired sounds, fog-insulated noises:
Gongs in white surplices, beshrouded wails,
Far strum of fog horns . . . signals dispersed
    in veils.

*400 years and
more . . . or
is it from the
soundless
shore of sleep
that time*

And then a truck will lumber past the wharves
As winch engines begin throbbing on some deck;
Or a drunken stevedore's howl and thud below
Comes echoing alley-upward through dim snow.

And if they take your sleep away sometimes
They give it back again. Soft sleeves of sound
Attend the darkling harbor, the pillowed bay;
Somewhere out there in blankness steam

Spills into steam, and wanders, washed away
—Flurried by keen fifings, eddied
Among distant chiming buoys—adrift. The
    sky,
Cool feathery fold, suspends, distills
This wavering slumber. . . . Slowly—
Immemorially the window, the half-covered
    chair,
Ask nothing but this sheath of pallid air.

And you beside me, blessèd now while sirens
Sing to us, stealthily weave us into day—
Serenely now, before day claims our eyes
Your cool arms murmurously about me lay.

*recalls you
to your love,
there in a
waking
dream to
merge your
seed*

While myriad snowy hands are clustering at
    the panes—

601

your hands within my hands are deeds;
my tongue upon your throat—singing
arms close; eyes wide, undoubtful
                    dark
                              drink the dawn—
a forest shudders in your hair!

The window goes blond slowly. Frostily   *—with*
    clears.   *whom?*
From Cyclopean towers across Manhattan
    waters
—Two—three bright window-eyes aglitter, disk
The sun, released—aloft with cold gulls
    hither.

The fog leans one last moment on the sill.   *Who is the*
Under the mistletoe of dreams, a star—   *woman with*
As though to join us at some distant hill—   *us in the*
Turns in the waking west and goes to sleep. *dawn? . . .*
                                             whose is the
                                             flesh our feet
                                             have moved
                                             upon?

VAN WINKLE

MACADAM, gun-grey as the tunny's belt,   *Streets*
Leaps from Far Rockaway to Golden Gate: *spread past*
Listen! the miles a hurdy-gurdy grinds—   *store and*
Down gold arpeggios mile on mile unwinds.   *factory—*
                                             sped by sun-
                                             light and her
                                             smile . . .

Times earlier, when you hurried off to school
—It is the same hour though a later day—
You walked with Pizarro in a copybook,
And Cortez rode up, reining tautly in—
Firmly as coffee grips the taste,—and away! *Like*
                                             Memory, she
There was Priscilla's cheek close in the wind, *is time's*
And Captain Smith, all beard and certainty, *truant, shall*
And Rip Van Winkle bowing by the way,—   *take you by*
"Is this Sleepy Hollow, friend—?" And he—   *the hand . . .*
602

And Rip forgot the office hours, and he forgot the pay;
Van Winkle sweeps a tenement way down on Avenue A,—

The grind-organ says . . . Remember, remember
The cinder pile at the end of the backyard
Where we stoned the family of young
Garter snakes under . . . And the monoplanes
We launched—with paper wings and twisted
Rubber bands . . . Recall—recall

                    the rapid tongues
That flittered from under the ash heap day
After day whenever your stick discovered
Some sunning inch of unsuspecting fibre—
It flashed back at your thrust, as clean as fire.

And Rip was slowly made aware
    that he, Van Winkle, was not here
      nor there. He woke and swore he'd seen Broadway
        a Catskill daisy chain in May—

So memory, that strikes a rhyme out of a box
Or splits a random smell of flowers through glass—
Is it the whip stripped from the lilac tree
One day in spring my father took to me,
Or is it the Sabbatical, unconscious smile
My mother almost brought me once from church
And once only, as I recall—?

It flickered through the snow screen, blindly
It forsook her at the doorway, it was gone
Before I had left the window. It
Did not return with the kiss in the hall.

Macadam, gun-grey as the tunny's belt,
Leaps from Far Rockaway to Golden Gate. . . .
Keep hold of that nickel for car-change, Rip,—
Have you got your *"Times"*—?
And hurry along, Van Winkle—it's getting late!

THE RIVER

STICK your patent name on a signboard
brother—all over—going west—young man
Tintex—Japalac—Certain-teed Overalls ads
and lands sakes! under the new playbill
ripped in the guaranteed corner—see Bert Williams what?
Minstrels when you steal a chicken just
save me the wing for if it isn't
Erie it ain't for miles around a
Mazda—and the telegraphic night coming on Thomas

*... and past
the din and
slogans of
the year—*

a Ediford—and whistling down the tracks
a headlight rushing with the sound—can you
imagine—while an EXPRESS makes time like
SCIENCE—COMMERCE and the HOLYGHOST
RADIO ROARS IN EVERY HOME WE HAVE THE NORTHPOLE
WALLSTREET AND VIRGINBIRTH WITHOUT STONES OR
WIRES OR EVEN RUNNING brooks connecting ears
and no more sermons windows flashing roar
Breathtaking—as you like it . . . eh?

                So the 20th Century—so
whizzed the Limited—roared by and left
three men, still hungry on the tracks, ploddingly
watching the tail lights wizen and converge, slipping gimleted and neatly out of sight.

The last bear, shot drinking in the Dakotas
Loped under wires that span the mountain stream.
Keen instruments, strung to a vast precision
Bind town to town and dream to ticking dream.
But some men take their liquor slow—and count
—Though they'll confess no rosary nor clue—
The river's minute by the far brook's year.
Under a world of whistles, wires and steam
Caboose-like they go ruminating through

*to those
whose
addresses
are never
near*

604

Ohio, Indiana—blind baggage—
To Cheyenne tagging . . . Maybe Kalamazoo.

Time's rendings, time's blendings they construe
As final reckonings of fire and snow;
Strange bird-wit, like the elemental gist
Of unwalled winds they offer, singing low
My Old Kentucky Home and *Casey Jones,*
Some Sunny Day. I heard a road-gang chanting so.
And afterwards, who had a colt's eyes—one said,
"Jesus! Oh I remember watermelon days!" And sped
High in a cloud of merriment, recalled
"—And when my Aunt Sally Simpson smiled," he
    drawled—
"It was almost Louisiana, long ago."

"There's no place like Booneville though, Buddy,"
One said, excising a last burr from his vest,
"—For early trouting." Then peering in the can,
"—But I kept on the tracks." Possessed, resigned,
He trod the fire down pensively and grinned,
Spreading dry shingles of a beard. . . .

                                               Behind
My father's cannery works I used to see
Rail-squatters ranged in nomad raillery,
The ancient men—wifeless or runaway
Hobo-trekkers that forever search
An empire wilderness of freight and rails.
Each seemed a child, like me, on a loose perch,
Holding to childhood like some termless play.
John, Jake or Charley, hopping the slow freight
—Memphis to Tallahassee—riding the rods,
Blind fists of nothing, humpty-dumpty clods.   *but who have*
                                                 touched her,
                                                 knowing her
Yet they touch something like a key perhaps   *without name*
From pole to pole across the hills, the states
—They know a body under the wide rain;

605

Youngsters with eyes like fjords, old reprobates
With racetrack jargon,—dotting immensity
They lurk across her, knowing her yonder
      breast
Snow-silvered, sumac-stained or smoky blue—
Is past the valley-sleepers, south or west.
—As I have trod the rumorous midnights, too,

And past the circuit of the lamp's thin flame
(O Nights that brought me to her body bare!)
Have dreamed beyond the print that bound her name.
Trains sounding the long blizzards out—I heard
Wail into distances I knew were hers.
Papooses crying on the wind's long mane
Screamed redskin dynasties that fled the brain,
—Dead echoes! But I knew her body there,
Time like a serpent down her shoulder, dark,
And space, an eaglet's wing, laid on her hair.

Under the Ozarks, domed by Iron Mountain,
The old gods of the rain lie wrapped in pools
Where eyeless fish curvet a sunken fountain
And re-descend with corn from querulous *nor the*
      crows.   *myths of her*
                                                    fathers . . .
Such pilferings make up their timeless
      eatage,
Propitiate them for their timber torn
By iron, iron—always the iron dealt cleavage!
They doze now, below axe and powder horn.

And Pullman breakfasters glide glistening steel
From tunnel into field—iron strides the dew—
Straddles the hill, a dance of wheel on wheel.
You have a half-hour's wait at Siskiyou,
Or stay the night and take the next train through.
Southward, near Cairo passing, you can see
606

The Ohio merging,—borne down Tennessee;
And if it's summer and the sun's in dusk
Maybe the breeze will lift the River's musk
—As though the waters breathed that you might know
Memphis Johnny, Steamboat Bill, Missouri Joe.
Oh, lean from the window, if the train slows down,
As though you touched hands with some ancient clown,
—A little while gaze absently below
And hum *Deep River* with them while they go.

Yes, turn again and sniff once more—look see,
O Sheriff, Brakeman and Authority—
Hitch up your pants and crunch another quid,
For you, too, feed the River timelessly.
And few evade full measure of their fate;
Always they smile out eerily what they seem.
I could believe he joked at heaven's gate—
Dan Midland—jolted from the cold brake-beam.

Down, down—born pioneers in time's despite,
Grimed tributaries to an ancient flow—
They win no frontier by their wayward plight,
But drift in stillness, as from Jordan's brow.

You will not hear it as the sea; even stone
Is not more hushed by gravity . . . But slow,
As loth to take more tribute—sliding prone
Like one whose eyes were buried long ago

The River, spreading, flows—and spends your dream.
What are you, lost within this tideless spell?
You are your father's father, and the stream—
A liquid theme that floating niggers swell.

Damp tonnage and alluvial march of days—
Nights turbid, vascular with silted shale
And roots surrendered down of moraine clays:
The Mississippi drinks the farthest dale.

607

O quarrying passion, undertowed sunlight!
The basalt surface drags a jungle grace
Ochreous and lynx-barred in lengthening might;
Patience! and you shall reach the biding place!

Over De Soto's bones the freighted floors
Throb past the City storied of three thrones.
Down two more turns the Mississippi pours
(Anon tall ironsides up from salt lagoons)

And flows within itself, heaps itself free.
All fades but one thin skyline 'round . . . Ahead
No embrace opens but the stinging sea;
The River lifts itself from its long bed,

Poised wholly on its dream, a mustard glow
Tortured with history, its one will—flow!
—The Passion spreads in wide tongues, choked and slow,
Meeting the Gulf, hosannas silently below.

THE DANCE

THE swift red flesh, a winter king—
Who squired the glacier woman down the
  sky?
She ran the neighing canyons all the spring;
She spouted arms; she rose with maize—to
  die.

And in the autumn drouth, whose burnished
  hands
With mineral wariness found out the stone
Where prayers, forgotten, streamed the
  mesa sands?
He holds the twilight's dim, perpetual
  throne.

*Then you
shall see her
truly—your
blood
remembering
its first
invasion of
her secrecy,
its first
encounters
with her kin,
her chieftain
lover . . . his
shade that
haunts the
lakes and
hills*

608

Mythical brows we saw retiring—loth,
Disturbed and destined, into denser green.
Greeting they sped us, on the arrow's oath:
Now lie incorrigibly what years between . . .

There was a bed of leaves, and broken play;
There was a veil upon you, Pocahontas, bride—
O Princess whose brown lap was virgin May;
And bridal flanks and eyes hid tawny pride.

I left the village for dogwood. By the canoe
Tugging below the mill-race, I could see
Your hair's keen crescent running, and the blue
First moth of evening take wing stealthily.

What laughing chains the water wove and threw!
I learned to catch the trout's moon whisper; I
Drifted how many hours I never knew,
But, watching, saw that fleet young crescent die,—

And one star, swinging, take its place, alone,
Cupped in the larches of the mountain pass—
Until, immortally, it bled into the dawn.
I left my sleek boat nibbling margin grass . . .

I took the portage climb, then chose
A further valley-shed; I could not stop.
Feet nozzled wat'ry webs of upper flows;
One white veil gusted from the very top.

O Appalachian Spring! I gained the ledge;
Steep, inaccessible smile that eastward bends
And northward reaches in that violet wedge
Of Adirondacks!—wisped of azure wands,

Over how many bluffs, tarns, streams I sped!
—And knew myself within some boding shade:—
Grey tepees tufting the blue knolls ahead,
Smoke swirling through the yellow chestnut glade . . .

609

A distant cloud, a thunder-bud—it grew,
That blanket of the skies: the padded foot
Within,—I heard it; 'til its rhythm drew,
—Siphoned the black pool from the heart's hot root!

A cyclone threshes in the turbine crest,
Swooping in eagle feathers down your back;
Know, Maquokeeta, greeting; know death's best;
—Fall, Sachem, strictly as the tamarack!

A birch kneels. All her whistling fingers fly.
The oak grove circles in a crash of leaves;
The long moan of a dance is in the sky.
Dance, Maquokeeta: Pocahontas grieves . . .

And every tendon scurries toward the twangs
Of lightning deltaed down your saber hair.
Now snaps the flint in every tooth; red fangs
And splay tongues thinly busy the blue air . . .

Dance, Maquokeeta! snake that lives before,
That casts his pelt, and lives beyond! Sprout, horn!
Spark, tooth! Medicine-man, relent, restore—
Lie to us,—dance us back the tribal morn!

Spears and assemblies: black drums thrusting on—
O yelling battlements,—I, too, was liege
To rainbows currying each pulsant bone:
Surpassed the circumstance, danced out the siege!

And buzzard-circleted, screamed from the stake;
I could not pick the arrows from my side.
Wrapped in that fire, I saw more escorts wake—
Flickering, sprint up the hill groins like a tide.

I heard the hush of lava wrestling your arms,
And stag teeth foam about the raven throat;
Flame cataracts of heaven in seething swarms
Fed down your anklets to the sunset's moat.
610

O, like the lizard in the furious noon,
That drops his legs and colors in the sun,
—And laughs, pure serpent, Time itself, and **moon**
Of his own fate, I saw thy change begun!

And saw thee dive to kiss that destiny
Like one white meteor, sacrosanct and blent
At last with all that's consummate and free
There, where the first and last gods keep thy tent.

Thewed of the levin, thunder-shod and lean,
Lo, through what infinite seasons dost thou gaze—
Across what bivouacs of thin angered slain,
And see'st thy bride immortal in the maize!

Totem and fire-gall, slumbering pyramid—
Though other calendars now stack the sky,
Thy freedom is her largesse, Prince, and hid
On paths thou knewest best to claim her by.

High unto Labrador the sun strikes free
Her speechless dream of snow, and stirred again,
She is the torrent and the singing tree;
And she is virgin to the last of men . . .

West, west and south! winds over Cumberland
And winds across the llano grass resume
Her hair's warm sibilance. Her breasts are fanned
O stream by slope and vineyard—into bloom!

And when the caribou slant down for salt
Do arrows thirst and leap? Do antlers shine
Alert, star-triggered in the listening vault
Of dusk?—And are her perfect brows to thine?

We danced, O Brave, we danced beyond their farms,
In cobalt desert closures made our vows . . .
Now is the strong prayer folded in thine arms,
The serpent with the eagle in the boughs.

611

INDIANA

THE Morning-glory, climbing the morning *...and read*
  long   *her in a*
 Over the lintel on its wiry vine,   *mother's*
Closes before the dusk, furls in its song *farewell gaze.*
  As I close mine . . .

And bison thunder rends my dreams no more
 As once my womb was torn, my boy, when you
Yielded your first cry at the prairie's door . . .
  Your father knew

Then, though we'd buried him behind us, far
 Back on the gold trail—then his lost bones stirred . . .
But you who drop the scythe to grasp the oar
  Knew not, nor heard.

How we, too, Prodigal, once rode off, too—
 Waved Seminary Hill a gay good-bye . . .
We found God lavish there in Colorado
  But passing sly.

The pebbles sang, the firecat slunk away
 And glistening through the sluggard freshets came
In golden syllables loosed from the clay
  His gleaming name.

A dream called Eldorado was his town,
 It rose up shambling in the nuggets' wake,
It had no charter but a promised crown
  Of claims to stake.

But we,—too late, too early, howsoever—
 Won nothing out of fifty-nine—those years—
But gilded promise, yielded to us never,
  And barren tears . . .

The long trail back! I huddled in the shade
 Of wagon-tenting looked out once and saw
612

Bent westward, passing on a stumbling jade
    A homeless squaw—

Perhaps a halfbreed. On her slender back
    She cradled a babe's body, riding without rein.
Her eyes, strange for an Indian's, were not black
    But sharp with pain

And like twin stars. They seemed to shun the gaze
    Of all our silent men—the long team line—
Until she saw me—when their violet haze
    Lit with love shine . . .

I held you up—I suddenly the bolder,
    Knew that mere words could not have brought us
        nearer.
She nodded—and that smile across her shoulder
    Will still endear her

As long as Jim, your father's memory, is warm.
    Yes, Larry, now you're going to sea, remember
You were the first—before Ned and this farm,—
    First-born, remember—

And since then—all that's left to me of Jim
    Whose folks, like mine, came out of Arrowhead.
And you're the only one with eyes like him—
    Kentucky bred!

I'm standing still, I'm old, I'm half of stone!
    Oh, hold me in those eyes' engaging blue;
There's where the stubborn years gleam and atone,—
    Where gold is true!

Down the dim turnpike to the river's edge—
    Perhaps I'll hear the mare's hoofs to the ford . . .
Write me from Rio . . . and you'll keep your pledge;
    I know your word!

Come back to Indiana—not too late!
  (Or will you be a ranger to the end?)
Good-bye . . . Good-bye . . . oh, I shall always wait
  You, Larry, traveller—
                    stranger,
                              son,
                                  —my friend—

III

CUTTY SARK

> *O, the navies old and oaken,*
> *O, the Temeraire no more!*—MELVILLE

I MET a man in South Street, tall—
a nervous shark tooth swung on his chain.
His eyes pressed through green grass
—green glasses, or bar lights made them
So—
    shine—
        GREEN—
                eyes—
stepped out—forgot to look at you
or left you several blocks away—

in the nickel-in-the-slot piano jogged
"Stamboul Nights"—weaving somebody's nickel—
        sang—

O Stamboul Rose—dreams weave the rose!

        Murmurs of Leviathan he spoke,
        and rum was Plato in our heads . . .

"It's S.S. *Ala*—Antwerp—now remember kid
to put me out at three she sails on time.
I'm not much good at time any more keep

weakeyed watches sometimes snooze—" his bony hands
got to beating time . . . "A whaler once—
I ought to keep time and get over it—I'm a
Democrat—I know what time it is—No
I don't want to know what time it is—that
damned white Arctic killed my time . . ."

O Stamboul Rose—drums weave—

"I ran a donkey engine down there on the Canal
in Panama—got tired of that—
then Yucatan selling kitchenware—beads—
have you seen Popocatepetl—birdless mouth
with ashes sifting down—?
                        and then the coast again . . ."

Rose of Stamboul O coral Queen—
teased remnants of the skeletons of cities—
and galleries, galleries of watergutted lava
snarling stone—green—drums—drown—

Sing!
"—that spiracle!" he shot a finger out the door . . .
"O life's a geyser—beautiful—my lungs—
No—I can't live on land—!"

I saw the frontiers gleaming of his mind;
or are there frontiers—running sands sometimes
running sands—somewhere—sands running . . .
Or they may start some white machine that sings.
Then you may laugh and dance the axletree—
steel—silver—kick the traces—and know—

ATLANTIS ROSE drums wreathe the rose,
the star floats burning in a gulf of tears
and sleep another thousand—

                        interminably

long since somebody's nickel—stopped—
playing—

A wind worried those wicker-neat lapels, the
swinging summer entrances to cooler hells . . .
Outside a wharf truck nearly ran him down
—he lunged up Bowery way while the dawn
was putting the Statue of Liberty out—that
torch of hers you know—

I started walking home across the Bridge . . .

*

Blithe Yankee vanities, turreted sprites, winged
                    British repartees, skil-
ful savage sea-girls
that bloomed in the spring—Heave, weave
those bright designs the trade winds drive . . .

> *Sweet opium and tea, Yo-ho!*
> *Pennies for porpoises that bank the keel!*
> *Fins whip the breeze around Japan!*

Bright skysails ticketing the Line, wink round the Horn
to Frisco, Melbourne . . .
                    Pennants, parabolas—
clipper dreams indelible and ranging,
baronial white on lucky blue!

> Perennial-*Cutty*-trophied-*Sark!*

Thermopylæ, Black Prince, Flying Cloud through Sunda
—scarfed of foam, their bellies veered green esplanades,
locked in wind-humors, ran their eastings down;

> *at Java Head freshened the nip*
> *(sweet opium and tea!)*
> and turned and left us on the lee . . .

616

Buntlines tusseling (91 days, 20 hours and anchored!)
                                   Rainbow, Leander
(last trip a tragedy)—where can you be
Nimbus? and you rivals two—

        a long tack keeping—

                    Taeping?
                    Ariel?

IV

CAPE HATTERAS

*The seas all crossed,
weathered the capes, the voyage done* . . . . —WHITMAN

IMPONDERABLE the dinosaur

        sinks slow,

                the mammoth saurian

                        ghoul, the eastern

                            Cape. . .

While rises in the west the coastwise range,

                slowly the hushed land—
Combustion at the astral core—the dorsal change
Of energy—convulsive shift of sand. . .
But we, who round the capes, the promontories
Where strange tongues vary messages of surf
Below grey citadels, repeating to the stars
The ancient names—return home to our own
Hearths, there to eat an apple and recall
The songs that gypsies dealt us at Marseille
Or how the priests walked—slowly through Bombay—
Or to read you, Walt,—knowing us in thrall

To that deep wonderment, our native clay
Whose depth of red, eternal flesh of Pocahontas—
Those continental folded æons, surcharged
With sweetness below derricks, chimneys, tunnels—

617

Is veined by all that time has really pledged us. . .
And from above, thin squeaks of radio static,
The captured fume of space foams in our ears—
What whisperings of far watches on the main
Relapsing into silence, while time clears
Our lenses, lifts a focus, resurrects
A periscope to glimpse what joys or pain
Our eyes can share or answer—then deflects
Us, shunting to a labyrinth submersed
Where each sees only his dim past reversed. . .

But that star-glistered salver of infinity,
The circle, blind crucible of endless space,
Is sluiced by motion,—subjugated never.
Adam and Adam's answer in the forest
Left Hesperus mirrored in the lucid pool.
Now the eagle dominates our days, is jurist
Of the ambiguous cloud. We know the strident rule
Of wings imperious. . . Space, instantaneous,
Flickers a moment, consumes us in its smile:
A flash over the horizon—shifting gears—
And we have laughter, or more sudden tears.
Dream cancels dream in this new realm of fact
From which we wake into the dream of act;
Seeing himself an atom in a shroud—
Man hears himself an engine in a cloud!

"—Recorders ages hence"—ah, syllables of faith!
Walt, tell me, Walt Whitman, if infinity
Be still the same as when you walked the beach
Near Paumanok—your lone patrol—and heard the wraith
Through surf, its bird note there a long time falling. . .
For you, the panoramas and this breed of towers,
Of you—the theme that's statured in the cliff.
O Saunterer on free ways still ahead!
Not this our empire yet, but labyrinth
Wherein your eyes, like the Great Navigator's without
    ship,

Gleam from the great stones of each prison crypt
Of canyoned traffic . . . Confronting the Exchange,
Surviving in a world of stocks,—they also range
Across the hills where second timber strays
Back over Connecticut farms, abandoned pastures,—
Sea eyes and tidal, undenying, bright with myth!

The nasal whine of power whips a new universe. . .
Where spouting pillars spoor the evening sky,
Under the looming stacks of the gigantic power house
Stars prick the eyes with sharp ammoniac proverbs,
New verities, new inklings in the velvet hummed
Of dynamos, where hearing's leash is strummed. . .
Power's script,—wound, bobbin-bound, refined—
Is stropped to the slap of belts on booming spools,
    spurred
Into the bulging bouillon, harnessed jelly of the stars.
Towards what? The forked crash of split thunder parts
Our hearing momentwise; but fast in whirling armatures,
As bright as frogs' eyes, giggling in the girth
Of steely gizzards—axle-bound, confined
In coiled precision, bunched in mutual glee
The bearings glint,—O murmurless and shined
In oilrinsed circles of blind ecstasy!

Stars scribble on our eyes the frosty sagas,
The gleaming cantos of unvanquished space. . .
O sinewy silver biplane, nudging the wind's withers!
There, from Kill Devils Hill at Kitty Hawk
Two brothers in their twinship left the dune;
Warping the gale, the Wright windwrestlers veered
Capeward, then blading the wind's flank, banked and
    spun
What ciphers risen from prophetic script,
What marathons new-set between the stars!
The soul, by naphtha fledged into new reaches,
Already knows the closer clasp of Mars,—
New latitudes, unknotting, soon give place

To what fierce schedules, rife of doom apace!

Behold the dragon's covey—amphibian, ubiquitous
To hedge the seaboard, wrap the headland, ride
The blue's cloud-templed districts unto ether. . .
While Iliads glimmer through eyes raised in pride
Hell's belt springs wider into heaven's plumed side.
O bright circumferences, heights employed to fly
War's fiery kennel masked in downy offings,—
This tournament of space, the threshed and chiselled
  height,
Is baited by marauding circles, bludgeon flail
Of rancorous grenades whose screaming petals carve us
Wounds that we wrap with theorems sharp as hail!

Wheeled swiftly, wings emerge from larval-silver
  hangars
Taut motors surge, space-gnawing, into flight;
Through sparkling visibility, outspread, unsleeping,
Wings clip the last peripheries of light . . .
Tellurian wind-sleuths on dawn patrol,
Each plane a hurtling javelin of winged ordnance,
Bristle the heights above a screeching gale to hover;
Surely no eye that Sunward Escadrille can cover!
There, meaningful, fledged as the Pleiades
With razor sheen they zoom each rapid helix!
Up-chartered choristers of their own speeding
They, cavalcade on escapade, shear Cumulus—
Lay siege and hurdle Cirrus down the skies!
While Cetus-like, O thou Dirigible, enormous Lounger
Of pendulous auroral beaches,—satellited wide
By convoy planes, moonferrets that rejoin thee
On fleeing balconies as thou dost glide,
—Hast splintered space!

                    Low, shadowed of the Cape,
Regard the moving turrets! From grey decks
See scouting griffons rise through gaseous crepe
Hung low . . . until a conch of thunder answers
620

Cloud-belfries, banging, while searchlights, like fencers,
Slit the sky's pancreas of foaming anthracite
Toward thee, O Corsair of the typhoon,—pilot, hear!
Thine eyes bicarbonated white by speed, O Skygak, see
How from thy path above the levin's lance
Thou sowest doom thou hast nor time nor chance
To reckon—as thy stilly eyes partake
What alcohol of space. . . ! Remember, Falcon-Ace,
Thou hast there in thy wrist a Sanskrit charge
To conjugate infinity's dim marge—
Anew. . . !

But first, here at this height receive
The benediction of the shell's deep, sure reprieve!
Lead-perforated fuselage, escutcheoned wings
Lift agonized quittance, tilting from the invisible brink
Now eagle-bright, now
                      quarry-hid, twist-
                            -ing, sink with
Enormous repercussive list-
                           -ings down
Giddily spiralled
                  gauntlets, upturned, unlooping
In guerrilla sleights, trapped in combustion gyr-
Ing, dance the curdled depth
                     down whizzing
Zodiacs, dashed
            (now nearing fast the Cape!)
                   down gravitation's
                       vortex into crashed
. . . dispersion . . . into mashed and shapeless débris . . .
By Hatteras bunched the beached heap of high bravery!

                    *

The stars have grooved our eyes with old persuasions
Of love and hatred, birth,—surcease of nations. . . .

But who has held the heights more sure than thou,
O Walt!—Ascensions of thee hover in me now
As thou at junctions elegiac, there, of speed
With vast eternity, dost wield the rebound seed!
The competent loam, the probable grass,—travail
Of tides awash the pedestal of Everest, fail
Not less than thou in pure impulse inbred
To answer deepest soundings! O, upward from the dead
Thou bringest tally, and a pact, new bound,
Of living brotherhood!

                Thou, there beyond—
Glacial sierras and the flight of ravens,
Hermetically past condor zones, through zenith havens
Past where the albatross has offered up
His last wing-pulse, and downcast as a cup
That's drained, is shivered back to earth—thy wand
Has beat a song, O Walt,—there and beyond!
And this, thine other hand, upon my heart
Is plummet ushered of those tears that start
What memories of vigils, bloody, by that Cape,—
Ghoul-mound of man's perversity at balk
And fraternal massacre! Thou, pallid there as chalk,
Hast kept of wounds, O Mourner, all that sum
That then from Appomattox stretched to Somme!

Cowslip and shad-blow, flaked like tethered foam
Around bared teeth of stallions, bloomed that spring
When first I read thy lines, rife as the loam
Of prairies, yet like breakers cliffward leaping!
O, early following thee, I searched the hill
Blue-writ and odor-firm with violets, 'til
With June the mountain laurel broke through green
And filled the forest with what clustrous sheen!
Potomac lilies,—then the Pontiac rose,
And Klondike edelweiss of occult snows!
White banks of moonlight came descending valleys—
How speechful on oak-vizored palisades,

As vibrantly I following down Sequoia alleys
Heard thunder's eloquence through green arcades
Set trumpets breathing in each clump and grass tuft—'til
Gold autumn, captured, crowned the trembling hill!

Panis Angelicus! Eyes tranquil with the blaze
Of love's own diametric gaze, of love's amaze!
Not greatest, thou,—not first, nor last,—but near
And onward yielding past my utmost year.
Familiar, thou, as mendicants in public places;
Evasive—too—as dayspring's spreading arc to trace is:—
Our Meistersinger, thou set breath in steel;
And it was thou who on the boldest heel
Stood up and flung the span on even wing
Of that great Bridge, our Myth, whereof I sing!

Years of the Modern! Propulsions toward what capes?
But thou, *Panis Angelicus,* hast thou not seen
And passed that Barrier that none escapes—
But knows it leastwise as death-strife?—O, something
        green,
Beyond all sesames of science was thy choice
Wherewith to bind us throbbing with one voice,
New integers of Roman, Viking, Celt—
Thou, Vedic Caesar, to the greensward knelt!

And now, as launched in abysmal cupolas of space,
Toward endless terminals, Easters of speeding light—
Vast engines outward veering with seraphic grace
On clarion cylinders pass out of sight
To course that span of consciousness thou'st named
The Open Road—thy vision is reclaimed!
What heritage thou'st signalled to our hands!

And see! the rainbow's arch—how shimmeringly stands
Above the Cape's ghoul-mound, O joyous seer!
Recorders ages hence, yes, they shall hear
In their own veins uncancelled thy sure tread

623

And read thee by the aureole 'round thy head
Of pasture-shine, *Panis Angelicus!*

Yes, Walt,

Afoot again, and onward without halt,—
Not soon, nor suddenly,—No, never to let go
    My hand
        in yours,

Walt Whitman—

so—

V

THREE SONGS

The one Sestos, the other Abydos hight.—MARLOWE

SOUTHERN CROSS

I WANTED you, nameless Woman of the South,
No wraith, but utterly—as still more alone
The Southern Cross takes night
And lifts her girdles from her, one by one—
High, cool,
      wide from the slowly smoldering fire
Of lower heavens,—

           vaporous scars!
Eve! Magdalene!
        or Mary, you?

Whatever call—falls vainly on the wave.
O simian Venus, homeless Eve,
Unwedded, stumbling gardenless to grieve
Windswept guitars on lonely decks forever;
Finally to answer all within one grave!

And this long wake of phosphor,
               iridescent

Furrow of all our travel—trailed derision!
Eyes crumble at its kiss. Its long-drawn spell
Incites a yell. Slid on that backward vision
The mind is churned to spittle, whispering hell.

I wanted you . . . The embers of the Cross
Climbed by aslant and huddling aromatically.
It is blood to remember; it is fire
To stammer back . . . It is
God—your namelessness. And the wash—

All night the water combed you with black
Insolence. You crept out simmering, accomplished.
Water rattled that stinging coil, your
Rehearsed hair—docile, alas, from many arms.
Yes, Eve—wraith of my unloved seed!

The Cross, a phantom, buckled—dropped below the
    dawn.
Light drowned the lithic trillions of your spawn.

NATIONAL WINTER GARDEN

OUTSPOKEN buttocks in pink beads
Invite the necessary cloudy clinch
Of bandy eyes. . . . No extra mufflings here:
The world's one flagrant, sweating cinch.

And while legs waken salads in the brain
You pick your blonde out neatly through the smoke.
Always you wait for someone else though, always—
(Then rush the nearest exit through the smoke).

Always and last, before the final ring
When all the fireworks blare, begins
A tom-tom scrimmage with a somewhere violin,
Some cheapest echo of them all—begins.

And shall we call her whiter than the snow?
Sprayed first with ruby, then with emerald sheen—
Least tearful and least glad (who knows her smile?)
A caught slide shows her sandstone grey between.

Her eyes exist in swivellings of her teats,
Pearls whip her hips, a drench of whirling strands.
Her silly snake rings begin to mount, surmount
Each other—turquoise fakes on tinselled hands.

We wait that writhing pool, her pearls collapsed,
—All but her belly buried in the floor;
And the lewd trounce of a final muted beat!
We flee her spasm through a fleshless door. . . .

Yet, to the empty trapeze of your flesh,
O Magdalene, each comes back to die alone.
Then you, the burlesque of our lust—and faith,
Lug us back lifeward—bone by infant bone.

VIRGINIA

O RAIN at seven,
Pay-check at eleven—
Keep smiling the boss away,
Mary (what are you going to do?)
Gone seven—gone eleven,
And I'm still waiting you—

O blue-eyed Mary with the claret scarf,
Saturday Mary, mine!

It's high carillon
From the popcorn bells!
Pigeons by the million—
And Spring in Prince Street
Where green figs gleam
By oyster shells!

O Mary, leaning from the high wheat tower,
    Let down your golden hair!

      High in the noon of May
      On cornices of daffodils
      The slender violets stray.
      Crap-shooting gangs in Bleecker reign,
      Peonies with pony manes—
      Forget-me-nots at windowpanes:

Out of the way-up nickel-dime tower shine,
                Cathedral Mary,

                          shine!—

VI

QUAKER HILL

*I see only the ideal. But no ideals have ever been fully
successful on this earth.*—ISIDORA DUNCAN

*The gentian weaves her fringes,
The maple's loom is red.*—EMILY DICKINSON

PERSPECTIVE never withers from their eyes;
They keep that docile edict of the Spring
That blends March with August Antarctic skies:
These are but cows that see no other thing
Than grass and snow, and their own inner being
Through the rich halo that they do not trouble
Even to cast upon the seasons fleeting
Though they should thin and die on last year's stubble.

And they are awkward, ponderous and uncoy . . .
While we who press the cider mill, regarding them—
We, who with pledges taste the bright annoy
Of friendship's acid wine, retarding phlegm,

Shifting reprisals ('til who shall tell us when
The jest is too sharp to be kindly?) boast
Much of our store of faith in other men
Who would, ourselves, stalk down the merriest ghost.
Above them old Mizzentop, palatial white
Hostelry—floor by floor to cinquefoil dormer
Portholes the ceilings stack their stoic height.
Long tiers of windows staring out toward former
Faces—loose panes crown the hill and gleam
At sunset with a silent, cobwebbed patience . . .
See them, like eyes that still uphold some dream
Through mapled vistas, cancelled reservations!

High from the central cupola, they say
One's glance could cross the borders of three states;
But I have seen death's stare in slow survey
From four horizons that no one relates . . .
Weekenders avid of their turf-won scores,
Here three hours from the semaphores, the Czars
Of golf, by twos and threes in plaid plusfours
Alight with sticks abristle and cigars.

This was the Promised Land, and still it is
To the persuasive suburban land agent
In bootleg roadhouses where the gin fizz
Bubbles in time to Hollywood's new love-nest pageant.
Fresh from the radio in the old Meeting House
(Now the New Avalon Hotel) volcanoes roar
A welcome to highsteppers that no mouse
Who saw the Friends there ever heard before.

What cunning neighbors history has in fine!
The woodlouse mortgages the ancient deal
Table that Powitzky buys for only nine-
Ty-five at Adams' auction,—eats the seal,
The spinster polish of antiquity . . .
Who holds the lease on time and on disgrace?
What eats the pattern with ubiquity?
Where are my kinsmen and the patriarch race?

The resigned factions of the dead preside.
Dead rangers bled their comfort on the snow;
But I must ask slain Iroquois to guide
Me farther than scalped Yankees knew to go:
Shoulder the curse of sundered parentage,
Wait for the postman driving from Birch Hill
With birthright by blackmail, the arrant page
That unfolds a new destiny to fill. . . .

So, must we from the hawk's far stemming view,
Must we descend as worm's eye to construe
Our love of all we touch, and take it to the Gate
As humbly as a guest who knows himself too late,
His news already told? Yes, while the heart is wrung,
Arise—yes, take this sheaf of dust upon your tongue!
In one last angelus lift throbbing throat—
Listen, transmuting silence with that stilly note

Of pain that Emily, that Isadora knew!
While high from dim elm-chancels hung with dew,
That triple-noted clause of moonlight—
Yes, whip-poor-will, unhusks the heart of fright,
Breaks us and saves, yes, breaks the heart, yet yields
That patience that is armour and that shields
Love from despair—when love foresees the end—
Leaf after autumnal leaf

> break off,
>
> descend—
>
> descend—

VII

THE TUNNEL

To Find the Western path
Right thro' the Gates of Wrath.—BLAKE

PERFORMANCES, assortments, résumés—
Up Times Square to Columbus Circle lights
Channel the congresses, nightly sessions,

629

Refractions of the thousand theatres, faces—
Mysterious kitchens. . . . You shall search them all.
Some day by heart you'll learn each famous sight
And watch the curtain lift in hell's despite;
You'll find the garden in the third act dead,
Finger your knees—and wish yourself in bed
With tabloid crime-sheets perched in easy sight.

> Then let you reach your hat and go.
> As usual, let you—also
> walking down—exclaim
> to twelve upward leaving
> a subscription praise
> for what time slays.

Or can't you quite make up your mind to ride;
A walk is better underneath the L a brisk
Ten blocks or so before? But you find yourself
Preparing penguin flexions of the arms,—
As usual you will meet the scuttle yawn:
The subway yawns the quickest promise home.

Be minimum, then, to swim the hiving swarms
Out of the Square, the Circle burning bright—
Avoid the glass doors gyring at your right,
Where boxed alone a second, eyes take fright
—Quite unprepared rush naked back to light:
And down beside the turnstile press the coin
Into the slot. The gongs already rattle.

> And so
> of cities you bespeak
> subways, rivered under streets
> and rivers. . . . In the car
> the overtone of motion
> underground, the monotone
> of motion is the sound
> of other faces, also underground—

"Let's have a pencil Jimmy—living now
at Floral Park
Flatbush—on the Fourth of July—
like a pigeon's muddy dream—potatoes
to dig in the field—travlin the town—too—
night after night—the Culver line—the
girls all shaping up—it used to be—"

Our tongues recant like beaten weather vanes.
This answer lives like verdigris, like hair
Beyond extinction, surcease of the bone;
And repetition freezes—"What

"what do you want? getting weak on the links?
fandaddle daddy don't ask for change—IS THIS
FOURTEENTH? it's half past six she said—if
you don't like my gate why did you
swing on it, why *didja*
swing on it
anyhow—"

          And somehow anyhow swing—

The phonographs of hades in the brain
Are tunnels that re-wind themselves, and love
A burnt match skating in a urinal—
Somewhere above Fourteenth TAKE THE EXPRESS
To brush some new presentiment of pain—

"But I want service in this office SERVICE
I said—after
the show she cried a little afterwards but—"

Whose head is swinging from the swollen strap?
Whose body smokes along the bitten rails,
Bursts from a smoldering bundle far behind
In back forks of the chasms of the brain,—
Puffs from a riven stump far out behind

631

In interborough fissures of the mind . . . ?
And why do I often meet your visage here,
Your eyes like agate lanterns—on and on
Below the toothpaste and the dandruff ads?
—And did their riding eyes right through your side,
And did their eyes like unwashed platters ride?
And Death, aloft,—gigantically down
Probing through you—toward me, O evermore!
And when they dragged your retching flesh,
Your trembling hands that night through Baltimore—
That last night on the ballot rounds, did you
Shaking, did you deny the ticket, Poe?

For Gravesend Manor change at Chambers Street.
The platform hurries along to a dead stop.

The intent escalator lifts a serenade
Stilly
Of shoes, umbrellas, each eye attending its shoe, then
Bolting outright somewhere above where streets
Burst suddenly in rain. . . . The gongs recur:
Elbows and levers, guard and hissing door.
Thunder is galvothermic here below. . . . The car
Wheels off. The train rounds, bending to a scream,
Taking the final level for the dive
Under the river—
And somewhat emptier than before,
Demented, for a hitching second, humps; then
Lets go. . . . Toward corners of the floor
Newspapers wing, revolve and wing.
Blank windows gargle signals through the roar.
And does the Daemon take you home, also,
Wop washerwoman, with the bandaged hair?
After the corridors are swept, the cuspidors—
The gaunt sky-barracks cleanly now, and bare,
O Genoese, do you bring mother eyes and hands
Back home to children and to golden hair?

Daemon, demurring and eventful yawn!
Whose hideous laughter is a bellows mirth
Or the muffled slaughter of a day in birth—
O cruelly to inoculate the brinking dawn
With antennæ toward worlds that glow and sink;—
To spoon us out more liquid than the dim
Locution of the eldest star, and pack
The conscience navelled in the plunging wind,
Umbilical to call—and straightway die!

O caught like pennies beneath soot and steam,
Kiss of our agony thou gatherest;
Condensed, thou takest all—shrill ganglia
Impassioned with some song we fail to keep.
And yet, like Lazarus, to feel the slope,
The sod and billow breaking,—lifting ground,
—A sound of waters bending astride the sky
Unceasing with some Word that will not die . . . !

A tugboat, wheezing wreaths of steam,
Lunged past, with one galvanic blare stove up the
        River.
I counted the echoes assembling, one after one,
Searching, thumbing the midnight on the piers.
Lights, coasting, left the oily tympanum of waters;
The blackness somewhere gouged glass on a sky.
And this thy harbor, O my City, I have driven under,
Tossed from the coil of ticking towers. . . . Tomorrow,
And to be. . . . Here by the River that is East—
Here at the waters' edge the hands drop memory;
Shadowless in that abyss they unaccounting lie.
How far away the star has pooled the sea—
Or shall the hands be drawn away, to die?

Kiss of our agony Thou gatherest,
                    O Hand of Fire
                            gatherest—

VIII

ATLANTIS

*Music is then the knowledge of that which relates to
love in harmony and system.*—PLATO

THROUGH the bound cable strands, the arching path
Upward, veering with light, the flight of strings,—
Taut miles of shuttling moonlight syncopate
The whispered rush, telepathy of wires.
Up the index of night, granite and steel—
Transparent meshes—fleckless the gleaming staves—
Sibylline voices flicker, waveringly stream
As though a god were issue of the strings. . . .

And through that cordage, threading with its call
One arc synoptic of all tides below—
Their labyrinthine mouths of history
Pouring reply as though all ships at sea
Complighted in one vibrant breath made cry,—
"Make thy love sure—to weave whose song we ply!"
—From black embankments, moveless soundings hailed,
So seven oceans answer from their dream.

And on, obliquely up bright carrier bars
New octaves trestle the twin monoliths
Beyond whose frosted capes the moon bequeaths
Two worlds of sleep (O arching strands of song!)—
Onward and up the crystal-flooded aisle
White tempest nets file upward, upward ring
With silver terraces the humming spars,
The loft of vision, palladium helm of stars.

Sheerly the eyes, like seagulls stung with rime—
Slit and propelled by glistening fins of light—
Pick biting way up towering looms that press
Sidelong with flight of blade on tendon blade
634

—Tomorrows into yesteryear—and link
What cipher-script of time no traveller reads
But who, through smoking pyres of love and death,
Searches the timeless laugh of mythic spears.

Like hails, farewells—up planet-sequined heights
Some trillion whispering hammers g'immer Tyre:
Serenely, sharply up the long anvil cry
Of inchling aeons silence rivets Troy.
And you, aloft there—Jason! hesting Shout!
Still wrapping harness to the swarming air!
Silvery the rushing wake, surpassing call,
Beams yelling Æolus! splintered in the straits!

From gulfs unfolding, terrible of drums,
Tall Vision-of-the-Voyage, tensely spare—
Bridge, lifting night to cycloramic crest
Of deepest day—O Choir, translating time
Into what multitudinous Verb the suns
And synergy of waters ever fuse, recast
In myriad syllables,—Psalm of Cathay!
O Love, thy white, pervasive Paradigm . . . !

We left the haven hanging in the night—
Sheened harbor lanterns backward fled the keel.
Pacific here at time's end, bearing corn,—
Eyes stammer through the pangs of dust and steel.
And still the circular, indubitable frieze
Of heaven's meditation, yoking wave
To kneeling wave, one song devoutly binds—
The vernal strophe chimes from deathless strings!

O Thou steeled Cognizance whose leap commits
The agile precincts of the lark's return;
Within whose lariat sweep encinctured sing
In single chrysalis the many twain,—
Of stars Thou art the stitch and stallion glow
And like an organ, Thou, with sound of doom—

Sight, sound and flesh Thou leadest from time's realm
As love strikes clear direction for the helm.

Swift peal of secular light, intrinsic Myth
Whose fell unshadow is death's utter wound,—
O River-throated—iridescently upborne
Through the bright drench and fabric of our veins;
With white escarpments swinging into light,
Sustained in tears the cities are endowed
And justified conclamant with ripe fields
Revolving through their harvests in sweet torment.

Forever Deity's glittering Pledge, O Thou
Whose canticle fresh chemistry assigns
To rapt inception and beatitude,—
Always through blinding cables, to our joy,
Of thy white seizure springs the prophecy:
Always through spiring cordage, pyramids
Of silver sequel, Deity's young name
Kinetic of white choiring wings . . . ascends.

Migrations that must needs void memory,
Inventions that cobblestone the heart,—
Unspeakable Thou Bridge to Thee, O Love.
Thy pardon for this history, whitest Flower,
O Answerer of all,—Anemone,—
Now while thy petals spend the suns about us, hold—
(O Thou whose radiance doth inherit me)
Atlantis,—hold thy floating singer late!

So to thine Everpresence, beyond time,
Like spears ensanguined of one tolling star
That bleeds infinity—the orphic strings,
Sidereal phalanxes, leap and converge:
—One Song, one Bridge of Fire! Is it Cathay,
Now pity steeps the grass and rainbows ring
The serpent with the eagle in the leaves . . . ?
Whispers antiphonal in azure swing.

Allen Tate

AENEAS AT WASHINGTON

I MYSELF saw furious with blood
Neoptolemus, at his side the black Atridae,
Hecuba and the hundred daughters, Priam
Cut down, his filth drenching the holy fires.
In that extremity I bore me well
A true gentleman, valorous in arms,
Disinterested and honorable. Then fled:
That was a time when civilization
Run by the few fell to the many, and
Crashed to the shout of men, the clang of arms:
Cold victualing I seized, I hoisted up
The old man my father upon my back,
In the smoke made by sea for a new world
Saving little—a mind imperishable
If time is, a love of past things tenuous
As the hesitation of receding love.

(To the reduction of uncitied littorals
We brought chiefly the vigor of prophecy,
Our hunger breeding calculation
And fixed triumphs)

                I saw the thirsty dove
In the glowing fields of Troy, hemp ripening
And tawny corn, the thickening Blue Grass
All lying rich forever in the green sun.
I see all things apart, the towers that men
Contrive I too contrived long, long ago.
Now I demand little. The singular passion
Abides its object and consumes desire
In the circling shadow of its appetite.

637

There was a time when the young eyes were slow;
Their flame steady beyond the firstling fire,
I stood in the rain, far from home at nightfall
By the Potomac, the great Dome lit the water,
The city my blood had built I knew no more
While the screech-owl whistled his new delight
Consecutively dark.

                              Stuck in the wet mire
Four thousand leagues from the ninth buried city
I thought of Troy, what we had built her for.

SHADOW AND SHADE

THE shadow streamed into the wall—
The wall, break-shadow in the blast;
We lingered wordless while a tall
Shade enclouded the shadow's cast.

The torrent of the reaching shade
Broke shadow into all its parts,
What then had been of shadow made
Found exigence in fits and starts

Where nothing properly had name
Save that still element the air,
Burnt sea of universal frame
In which impounded now we were:

I took her hand, I shut her eyes
And all her shadow cleft with shade,
Shadow was crushed beyond disguise
But, being fear, was unafraid.

I asked fair shadow at my side:
What more shall fiery shade require?

We lay long in the immense tide
Of shade and shadowy desire

And saw the dusk assail the wall,
The black surge, mounting, crash the stone!
Companion of this lust, we fall,
I said, lest we should die alone.

THE WOLVES

THERE are wolves in the next room waiting
With heads bent low, thrust out, breathing
At nothing in the dark: between them and me
A white door patched with light from the hall
Where it seems never (so still is the house)
A man has walked from the front door to the stair.
It has all been forever. Beasts claw the floor.
I have brooded on angels and archfiends
But no man has ever sat where the next room's
Crowded with wolves, and for the honor of man
I affirm that never have I before. Now while
I have looked for the evening star at a cold window
And whistled when Arcturus spilt his light,
I've heard the wolves scuffle, and said: So this
Is man; so—what better conclusion is there—
The day will not follow night, and the heart
Of man has a little dignity, but less patience
Than a wolf's, and a duller sense that cannot
Smell its own mortality. (This and other
Meditations will be suited to other times
After dog silence howls his epitaph)
Now remember courage, go to the door,
Open it and see whether coiled on the bed
Or cringing by the wall a savage beast
Maybe with golden hair, with deep eyes
Like a bearded spider on a sunlit floor,
Will snarl—and man can never be alone.

THE MEDITERRANEAN

Quem das finem, rex magne, dolorum?

WHERE we went in the boat was a long bay
A slingshot wide, walled in by towering stone—
Peaked margin of antiquity's delay,
And we went there out of time's monotone:

Where we went in the black hull no light moved
But a gull white-winged along the feckless wave,
The breeze, unseen but fierce as a body loved,
That boat drove onward like a willing slave:

Where we went in the small ship the seaweed
Parted and gave to us the murmuring shore
And we made feast and in our secret need
Devoured the very plates Aeneas bore:

Where derelict you see through the low twilight
The green coast that you, thunder-tossed, would win,
Drop sail, and hastening to drink all night
Eat dish and bowl—to take that sweet land in!

Where we feasted and caroused on the sandless
Pebbles, affecting our day of piracy,
What prophecy of eaten plates could landless
Wanderers fulfil by the ancient sea?

We for that time might taste the famous age
Eternal here yet hidden from our eyes
When lust of power undid its stuffless rage;
They, in a wineskin, bore earth's paradise.

Let us lie down once more by the breathing side
Of Ocean, where our live forefathers sleep
As if the Known Sea still were a month wide—
Atlantis howls but is no longer steep!

What country shall we conquer, what fair land
Unman our conquest and locate our blood?
We've cracked the hemispheres with careless hand!
Now, from the Gates of Hercules we flood

Westward, westward till the barbarous brine
Whelms us to the tired world where tasseling corn,
Fat beans, grapes sweeter than muscadine
Rot on the vine: in that land were we born.

ODE TO THE CONFEDERATE DEAD

Row after row with strict impunity
The headstones yield their names to the element,
The wind whirrs without recollection;
In the riven troughs the splayed leaves
Pile up, of nature the casual sacrament
To the seasonal eternity of death;
Then driven by the fierce scrutiny
Of heaven to their election in the vast breath,
They sough the rumor of mortality.

Autumn is desolation in the plot
Of a thousand acres where these memories grow
From the inexhaustible bodies that are not
Dead, but feed the grass row after rich row.
Think of the autumns that have come and gone!—
Ambitious November with the humors of the year,
With a particular zeal for every slab,
Staining the uncomfortable angels that rot
On the slabs, a wing chipped here, an arm there:
The brute curiosity of an angel's stare
Turns you, like them, to stone,
Transforms the heaving air
Till plunged to a heavier world below
You shift your sea-space blindly
Heaving, turning like the blind crab.

Dazed by the wind, only the wind
The leaves flying, plunge

You know who have waited by the wall
The twilight certainty of an animal,
Those midnight restitutions of the blood
You know—the immitigable pines, the smoky frieze
Of the sky, the sudden call: you know the rage,
The cold pool left by the mounting flood,
Of muted Zeno and Parmenides.
You who have waited for the angry resolution
Of those desires that should be yours tomorrow,
You know the unimportant shrift of death
And praise the vision
And praise the arrogant circumstance
Of those who fall
Rank upon rank, hurried beyond decision—
Here by the sagging gate, stopped by the wall.

Seeing, seeing only the leaves
Flying, plunge and expire

Turn your eyes to the immoderate past,
Turn to the inscrutable infantry rising
Demons out of the earth—they will not last.
Stonewall, Stonewall, and the sunken fields of hemp,
Shiloh, Antietam, Malvern Hill, Bull Run.
Lost in that orient of the thick and fast
You will curse the setting sun.

Cursing only the leaves crying
Like an old man in a storm

You hear the shout, the crazy hemlocks point
With troubled fingers to the silence which
Smothers you, a mummy, in time.

The hound bitch
Toothless and dying, in a musty cellar

Hears the wind only.

> Now that the salt of their blood
Stiffens the saltier oblivion of the sea,
Seals the malignant purity of the flood,
What shall we who count our days and bow
Our heads with a commemorial woe
In the ribboned coats of grim felicity,
What shall we say of the bones, unclean,
Whose verdurous anonymity will grow?
The ragged arms, the ragged heads and eyes
Lost in these acres of the insane green?
The gray lean spiders come, they come and go;
In a tangle of willows without light
The singular screech-owl's tight
Invisible lyric seeds the mind
With the furious murmur of their chivalry.

> We shall say only the leaves
> Flying, plunge and expire

We shall say only the leaves whispering
In the improbable mist of nightfall
That flies on multiple wing;
Night is the beginning and the end
And in between the ends of distraction
Waits mute speculation, the patient curse
That stones the eyes, or like the jaguar leaps
For his own image in a jungle pool, his victim.

What shall we say who have knowledge
Carried to the heart? Shall we take the act
To the grave? Shall we, more hopeful, set up the grave
In the house? The ravenous grave?

> Leave now
The shut gate and the decomposing wall:
The gentle serpent, green in the mulberry bush,
Riots with his tongue through the hush—
Sentinel of the grave who counts us all!

DEATH OF LITTLE BOYS

WHEN little boys grow patient at last, weary,
Surrender their eyes immeasurably to the night,
The event will rage terrific as the sea;
Their bodies fill a crumbling room with light.

Then you will touch at the bedside, torn in two,
Gold curls now deftly intricate with gray
As the windowpane extends a fear to you
From one peeled aster drenched with the wind all day.

And over his chest the covers in the ultimate dream
Will mount to the teeth, ascend the eyes, press back
The locks—while round his sturdy belly gleam
The suspended breaths, white spars above the wreck:

Till all the guests, come in to look, turn down
Their palms; and delirium assails the cliff
Of Norway where you ponder, and your little town
Reels like a sailor drunk in a rotten skiff.

The bleak sunshine shrieks its chipped music then
Out to the milkweed amid the fields of wheat.
There is a calm for you where men and women
Unroll the chill precision of moving feet.

MOTHER AND SON

Now all day long the man who is not dead
Hastens the dark with inattentive eyes,
The woman with white hand and erect head
Stares at the cover, leans for the son's replies
At last to her importunate womanhood—
Her hand of death laid on the living bed;
So lives the fierce compositor of blood.

644

She waits; he lies upon the bed of sin
Where greed, avarice, anger writhed and slept
Till to their silence they were gathered in;
There, fallen with time, his tall and bitter kin
Once fired the passions that were never kept
In the permanent heart, and there his mother lay
To bear him on the impenetrable day.

The falcon mother cannot will her hand
Up to the bed, nor break the manacle
His exile sets upon her harsh command
That he should say the time is beautiful
Transfigured by her own possessing light:
The sick man craves the impalpable night.

Loosed betwixt eye and lid, the swimming beams
Of memory, blind school of cuttlefish
Rise to the air, plunge to the cold streams,
Rising and plunging the half-forgotten wish
To tear his heart out in some slow disgrace
And freeze the hue of terror to her face.

Hate, misery and fear beat off his heart
To the dry fury of the woman's mind;
The son prone in his autumn, moves apart
A seed blown upon a returning wind:
O child, be vigilant till towards the South
On the flowered wall all the sweet afternoon
The reaching sun, swift as the cottonmouth,
Strikes at the black crucifix on her breast
Where the cold dusk comes suddenly to rest—
Mortality will speak the victor soon!

The dreary flies lazy and casual
Stick to the ceiling, buzz along the wall—
O heart, the spider shuffles from the mould
Weaving, between the pinks and grapes, his pall.
The bright wallpaper, imperishably old,
Uncurls and flutters; it will never fall.

IDIOT

THE idiot greens the meadows with his eyes,
The meadow creeps implacable and still;
A dog barks, the hammock swings, he lies.
One two three the cows bulge on the hill.

Motion that is not time erects snowdrifts
While sister's hand sieves waterfalls of lace.
With a palm fan closer than death he lifts
The Ozarks and tilted seas across his face.

In the long sunset where impatient sound
Strips niggers to a multiple of backs
Flies yield their heat, magnolias drench the ground
With Appomattox! The shadows lie in stacks.

The julep glass weaves echoes in Jim's kinks
While ashy Jim puts murmurs in the day:
Now in the idiot's heart a chamber stinks
Of dead asters, as the potter's field of May.

All evening the marsh is a slick pool
Where dream wild hares, witch hazel, pretty girls.
"Up from the important picnic of a fool
Those rotted asters!" Eddy on eddy swirls

The innocent mansion of a panther's heart!
It crumbles, tick-tick time drags it in
Till now his arteries lag and now they start
Reverence with the frigid gusts of sin:

The stillness pelts the eye, assaults the hair;
A beech sticks out a branch to warn the stars,
A lightening-bug jerks angles in the air,
Diving. "I am the captain of new wars!"

The dusk runs down the lane driven like hail;
Far off a precise whistle is escheat

To the dark; and then the towering weak and pale
Covers his eyes with memory like a sheet.

THE EYE

I see the horses and the sad streets
Of my childhood in an agate eye
Roving, under the clean sheets,
Over a black hole in the sky.

The ill man becomes the child,
The evil man becomes the lover;
The natural man with evil roiled
Pulls down the sphereless sky for cover.

I see the gray heroes and the graves
Of my childhood in the nuclear eye—
Horizons spent in dun caves
Sucked down into the sinking sky.

The happy child becomes the man,
The elegant man becomes the mind,
The feathered gentleman who can
Perform quick feats of gentle kind.

I see the long field and the noon
Of my childhood in the carbolic eye,
Dissolving pupil of the moon
Seared the ravelled hole of the sky.

The nice ladies and gentlemen,
The teaser and the jelly-bean
Play cockalorum-and-the-hen,
Where the cool afternoons pour green;

I see the father and the cooling cup
Of my childhood in the swallowing sky
Down, down, until down is up,
And there is nothing in the eye,

Shut shutter of the mineral man
Who takes the fatherless dark to bed,
The acid sky to the brain-pan;
And calls the crows to peck his head.

SONNETS AT CHRISTMAS

(1934)

I

THIS is the day His hour of life draws near,
Let me get ready from head to foot for it
Most handily with eyes to pick the year
For small feed to reward a feathered wit.
Some men would see it an epiphany
At ease, at food and drink, others at chase
Yet I, stung lassitude, with ecstasy
Unspent argue the season's difficult case
So: Man, dull critter of enormous head,
What would he look at in the coiling sky?
But I must kneel again unto the Dead
While Christmas bells of paper white and red,
Figured with boys and girls spilt from a sled,
Ring out the silence I am nourished by.

II

Ah, Christ, I love you rings to the wild sky
And I must think a little of the past:
When I was ten I told a stinking lie
That got a black boy whipped; but now at last
The going years, caught in an accurate glow,
Reverse like balls englished upon green baize—
Let them return, let the round trumpets blow
The ancient crackle of the Christ's deep gaze.
Deafened and blind, with senses yet unfound,
Am I, untutored to the after-wit

Of knowledge, knowing a nightmare has no sound;
Therefore with idle hands and head I sit
In late December before the fire's daze
Punished by crimes of which I would be quit.

MORE SONNETS AT CHRISTMAS

(1942)

I

AGAIN the native hour lets down the locks
Uncombed and black, but gray the bobbing beard;
Ten years ago His eyes, fierce shuttlecocks,
Pierced the close net of what I failed: I feared
The belly-cold, the grave-clout, that betrayed
Me dithering in the drift of cordial seas;
Ten years are time enough to be dismayed
By mummy Christ, head crammed between his knees.
Suppose I take an arrogant bomber, stroke
By stroke, up to the frazzled sun to hear
Sun-ghostlings whisper: Yes, the capital yoke—
Remove it and there's not a ghost to fear
This crucial day, whose decapitate joke
Languidly winds into the inner ear.

II

The day's at end and there's nowhere to go,
Draw to the fire, even this fire is dying;
Get up and once again politely lying
Invite the ladies toward the mistletoe
With greedy eyes that stare like an old crow.
How pleasantly the holly wreaths did hang
And how stuffed Santa did his reindeer clang
Above the golden oaken mantel, years ago!
Then hang this picture for a calendar,

As sheep for goat, and pray most fixedly
For the cold martial progress of your star,
With thoughts of commerce and society,
Well-milked Chinese, Negroes who cannot sing,
The Huns gelded and feeding in a ring.

III

Give me this day a faith not personal
As follows: The American people fully armed
With assurance policies, righteous and harmed,
Battle the world of which they're not at all.
That lying boy of ten who stood in the hall,
His hat in hand (thus by his father charmed:
"You may be President"), was not alarmed
Nor even left uneasy by his fall.
Nobody said that he could be a plumber,
Carpenter, clerk, bus-driver, bombardier;
Let little boys go into violent slumber,
Aegean squall and squalor where their fear
Is of an enemy in remote oceans
Unstalked by Christ: these are the better notions.

IV

Gay citizen, myself, and thoughtful friend,
Your ghosts are Plato's Christians in the cave.
Unfix your necks, turn to the door; the nave
Gives back the cheated and light dividend
So long sequestered; now, new-rich, you'll spend
Flesh for reality inside a stone
Whose light obstruction, like a gossamer bone,
Dead or still living, will not break or bend.
Thus light, your flesh made pale and sinister
And put off like a dog that's had his day,
You will be Plato's kept philosopher,
Albino man bleached from the mortal clay,
Mild-mannered, gifted in your masters' ease
While the sun squats upon the waveless seas.

Oscar Williams

JEREMIAD

WHEN the bird flew from the Columbus hull
And swung our canyons from its fabled beak,
Or gravitation donned long gloves of bough
To drop its apple in perception's lap,
How was the embattled Spirit to conceive
Monstrosities lay breathing in the good,
That limbs of lambs could grow the heads of wolves?

The multitudes who built a wall of graves
Around the golden calf of nothingness
And faced the deathrays of the deathless smile
Through the vast stretches of injustice brought
The flower brimming in the crack of light—
They open valves to brimstone on our sleep
And freight our air with tons of memory.

Now out of reservoirs of misery
Our language glistens with a flow of tears
And history sweats its worms out of the books;
While prodded by war planes of an angry day
Out of abstraction's bed we turn to meet
The gigantic sense of failure darkening
The many windowed framework of the skull.

And once again, and maybe more than once
Again, must we put down the clockwheel tools
And apron of our carelessness, and rise
And throw our bodies, our bags of blood, against
The rocks of Mammonhood and so blot out
The evil writing on the tidal wall,
The Red Sea running down the heart of God.

651

THE SEESAW

I

I sit on the surge called ten stories tall
My eye flattens to a floor, a wall,
Like any bird on the nest anywhere
I live in a constant nothing of air
Some forty years up and ten stories high
A hundred inventions ahead of the sky,
With a ladder of ancestors holding me up
Whose rungs into history mystery drop,
But here I am where faith's feathers fly
Like the child in the rhyme in the sky so high.

Over the plumes of your thoughts I see
Your tired heart resting beside a tree;
From the tenth platform of my tithe of time
I perceive you exhausted in your prime,
With heaven collaterally circling around
Your presence that holds the landscape down,
With birds disappearing in the sponge of leaves
And sundown painting your hopes in sheaves—
I speak into a tube for your distant ear,
You look up at me across the miles so clear.

Is it your look makes my room to descend
As though I were inside the shaft of the end?
The floorspace edges from under my feet
The breadth of a sword's edge of monstrous speed;
I grasp for the desperate point of a tear,
For the bend in space or the turn of the year,
But out of the thousands not the least star
Can keep me from falling too fast too far;
And suddenly there beneath your tree I lie
With you at the window ten stories so high.

II

My face hung out its search in front of me,
A mask to try the outer storm of space,
Or net of form cast in the sea to be,
To catch at things not safely in their place
Out building coral pinnacles; on the fly
When heaven was stretched on rocks of cloud I caught
A tall star in the corner of my eye—
Lassoed was I, prone on the floor of thought—

Thrown, like the fisherman's wife who asked too much
In wanting to be God; the lightning's hiss
Foamed at the peak of earth, full height to touch
And hope, but death-rayed down to an abyss,
This now-deep nothingness on which we're curled.
It is the stars that make a valley of the world.

III

Divine seesaw! Ply thy twin ways of higher!
The valley of the grave upholds the stars.
The hand on the big Dipper trembles, pours
The fields of gold that roll out on the mire;
And in those fields there boils another sun
Stamping his weight until the night's stars drive
My unlived ages to the land of none
From which the sunflower shakes his flames alive—

And fire breaks out in my friend's house of rules,
The light in my neighbor's window burns my soul,
My enemy falls heir to all of Christ's jewels,
The loved one in the moving grave swings clear.
As grave and window seesaw before the whole
The hill swirls orbits of the dust and wind.
O pivot's pressure at the heart, through you I hear
The universe hallooing for an end.

653

MILK AT THE BOTTOM
OF THE SEA

IN the bowl of buildings *alias* the back yard
The milk of snow endlessly pours, but the bowl never
Fills. The century's live inhabitant caught behind
The window pane watches the single rakish tree
Blaze forth in ponderously immaculate italics.
The snowflakes pour everywhere in a panic, dizzyingly,
Or whirl to re-organize in the mid-air and float
Undecided; the sky tilts its ominous mountain, insuring
Another waterfall of snowflakes with all feathery speed.
Such activity should be noisy, a school's-out! of sounds,
But the silence is reverberating on the window glass
Exploring the deep-sea life of waywardness.

I am the traveller in the middle of the winter
In a wood-and-glass ship on the deeps of the age.
From peril's hold I watch the white germs from heaven
And blithe nothingness, the delicate roe of purity
Splurging to fill the air with their multipleness.
Making not even the sound of rain against rock.
I am an eye, I know, frozen in an undersea facade,
And have lost my hearing in such fantastic depths
Where the pressures cave in the senses, but still
My eye kindles to all this whiteness bearing down
In a dance of spiritual blindspots on our town.

In the end the wandering snowflakes are driven
Together, foam fat in the bottom of time, and I
Assuage through the mouth of the mind my entity;
The army of my veins, blood-drops, pores, thoughts,
Crowds to my bones in one supreme act of gravity,
Closer than earth to a hill, than leaves to a tree,
Till I am the very body of oneness and cannot go
Pure, cold, diffuse and wayward like the snow.

THE LAST SUPPER

I

APOSTLES of the hidden sun
Are come unto the room of breath
Hung with the banging blinds of death,
The body twelve, the spirit one,
Far as the eye, in earth arrayed,
The night shining, the supper laid.

II

The wine shone on the table that evening of history
Like an enormous ruby in the bauble and mystery.

In the glowing walls of the flickering decanter
There moved His face as at the world's center.

The hands of Judas showed up red and hurried
And the light hit them so, like a cross carried.

The faces of the others were there and moving
In the crystal of the dome, swiftly hovering.

The saints, under a lens, shrunken to pigmies,
Gesticulated in birds or in colored enigmas.

Outside there was a storm, the sound of temblors,
The blood bubbled and sprang into the tumblers.

When the morning came like a white wall of stone,
The day lay in the glass and the blood was gone.

VARIATIONS ON A THEME

I

ON THE DEATH OF AN ACQUAINTANCE

FRIEND, when I think of your delicate feminine face
And of your little hopes common as hearing or seeing,
How singlehanded you moved the massive stone of space
To find a cranny for the flower from the soil of your
　　　being,

And how now you manage to keep open in the universe
Under all-time strain that lighted crack in the reckoning
I am haunted by your grimace O steadily getting worse
Awaiting the vast glad look that reduces everything.

For long I thought you another human being in doubt,
One of the millions ordinary as daylight is everywhere,
One of those usual people that one meets with all about—
Now I see you were capable of decision and despair.

Forgive me if my heart cringes with those who die,
Forgive me, friend, when even in thought I cannot be
　　　brave
Who think of your clear face agonized under tons of sky
Hourly growing more haggard from the weight of the
　　　grave.

II

THE SPRITELY DEAD

There was a man within our tenement
who died upon a worn down step of day:
the wreath they hung upon the doorway meant
that there was nothing else for him to do.
But he was obstinate, he would not rest:
he dragged the flesh of silence everywhere

on crippled wings, and we would hear him whir
while on our memory's sill his eyes would roost.
We saw him wring his thoughts in deep despair
and stamp the color from our backyard scene:
careless, without his body, he would peer
to find out if we noticed his new sin.
He was afraid, afraid: he climbed our vines
and hid, on hands and knees, along our veins.

III

THE BORROWER OF SALT

The man who saw the light hanging on the tall end
Of the road thought it was a lantern on the distant wall
Of the mysterious neighbor, so he said, friend, friend,
I am coming out to borrow some of the savor of your salt.

Wherewith he started running toward the light that hung
In the neighbor's window, and as he kept going the light
Danced, saying with a mocking step, isn't it wrong
That I dance in my glory while you walk in the night?

Yes, said the man, it is wrong, and what is worse
The wind is getting bad, the mud thicker, the road
Harder to follow and I move as slowly as a hearse,
In fact I feel as if my body were turning into the load.

The gleam tittered like a light on the end of a spar
But the man was up to his knees in road as if roots
Sprouted from his feet; alas, said the man, it is too hard,
Those who would walk in great men's tracks wear boots.

He turned around and the wind opened spigots of swift
   air
On his head, up his thighs he felt the earth's lips creep,
And lo, the light gleamed spiritedly from his own fair
Housetop, but he couldn't move, the track was so deep.

657

SHOPPING FOR MEAT IN WINTER

WHAT lewd, naked and revolting shape is this?
A frozen oxtail in the butcher's shop
Long and lifeless upon the huge block of wood
On which the ogre's axe begins *chop chop*.

The sun like incense fumes on the smoky glass,
The street frets with people, the winter wind
Throws knives, prices dangle from shoppers' mouths
While the grim vegetables, on parade, bring to mind

The great countryside bathed in golden sleep,
The trees, the bees, the soft peace everywhere—
I think of the cow's tail, how all summer long
It beat the shapes of harps into the air.

SPRING

The bird that flies to climates crisper
Over its feathers wears feathers of sound
Protecting itself in a coat of whisper
Against the silence that stones the ground.

In the long miles between song and hearer
Where the distance's bones lie disinterred
I now overhear as the wings come nearer
The whispers of God instructing the bird,—

And see Him put out the branch of a finger
Where the bird sits down and begins its cheers;
The buds push out to look at the singer,
The blades of grass stand up all ears.

O truly now, it is gayer and warmer,
Tomorrow's the only dark bush on the land
And full of its doubts, but God the performer
Is walking about with the bird in His hand.

THE MAN COMING TOWARD YOU

I

THE man coming toward you is falling forward on all
    fronts:
He has just come in from the summer hot box of circum-
    stance,
His obedient arm pulls a ticket from the ticket machine,
A bell announces to the long tables his presence on the
    scene;
The room is crowded with Last Suppers and the air is
    angry;
The halleluiahs lift listless heads; the man is hungry.

He looks at the people, the rings of lights, the aisles, the
    chairs,
They mass and attack his eyes and they take him un-
    awares,
But in a moment it is over and the immense hippopot-
    amus cries
And swims away to safety in the vast past of his eyes;
The weeks recoil before the days, the years before the
    months;
The man is hungry and keeps moving forward on all
    fronts.

His hair is loosening, his teeth are at bay, he breathes
    fear,
His nails send futile tendrils into the belly of the atmos-
    phere;
Every drop of his blood is hanging loose in the universe,
His children's faces everywhere bring down the college
    doors;
He is growing old on all fronts; his foes and his friends
Are bleeding behind invisible walls bedecked with divi-
    dends;

His wife is aging, and his skin puts on its anonymous
  gloves;
The man is helpless, surrounded by two billion hates and
  loves;
Look at him squirm inside his clothes, the harpies around
  his ears,
In just one minute his brothers will have aged four thousand years.
Who records his stupendous step on the delicate ear-
  drum of Chance?
The man coming toward you is marching forward on all
  fronts.

II

Incoming train chattering opposite one's consciousness
With wheels moving restlessly inside the face of distance—
So the breath of the everyday expands through the
  station
Churning up a cloud of coffins above the advancing
  pistons.

Now the feet of the station are off the ground of Christian love,
The station is skipping rope with an elegant swish of
  arches:
A massive airiness, skirts blowing with a mass music of
  mind,
While the herd of backs, the trek from the subconscious,
  lurches.

Landing field of the strange strangers from the Mars of
  moment,
This is the land where the cat heads of the comets are
  buried:
The great clock of the nation peers under the sheet of
  history,

Like an eye staring amazed in the middle of the hostile
    forehead.

The ticket sellers are buried seated in the incandescent
    walls
But manage to meet the human race all gloved in travel
    dither:
Somewhere the long legs of highways stretch in torture
    under
The cavernous breach of landscape at the other end of
    the tether.

A canyonful of bells shivers to bits in a fit of innocence:
The railway station bends its head around the napes of
    silence:
Everywhere the shadows are budding on the tree of
    substance
Flowering into large leopards grounded swiftly on the
    pylons.

The train pulls in, tugging luminously at the leash of
    rails:
All the books are emptying their characters into the
    station:
The people who are quaintly decorating the mouthful
    of light
Reach for their hats and pasts and the luggage of frus-
    tration.

And the amazing direction called home branches every-
    where,
Dizzying the dutiful compass and the compliant ele-
    ments:
The attenuated female cry of struck iron bites at the
    wind,
And a powerful charge of flesh overloads the filaments.

This ant hill overrunning with nerves, with maggots of
  myth,
This tuft of winter lightning blooming in the cheek of
  travel,
This immense bulb wired in the bosom of a sullen universe,
This gathering of huddled veins—who shall unravel,
  unravel?

Who shall unravel this knot of light, the tangled sinews
  of man,
This kink composed of heroes and harpies, aims and
  omens?
For all the knots are Gordian knots until the mind is won,
The tyrant mind of the present unturned by the many
  poems. . . .

III

Let us get up who drowse in the armchair of adage,
Who are outstared by the eye of evening in the room:
The mask of heresy falls from the sanguine savage:
Outside flowers the populous body of the gloom.

The paws are crowding us out in our intimate tent,
The tri-humped fable, camel of horror, wants to get in:
The cold nose of the night steadily widens the rent
And pulls from our shoulders the ingrown annals of sin.

Better to unloose a flock of screams into the rain—
Swing open the door hung by the nerves over deeps of
  evil:
In the surcharged light there gleams the knob of the
  brain
On which lies hallucination, fingerprint of the devil.

Better to walk out with naked feet among the flawed
  events

Where unicorns stand toy-deep among crystal alps of
    jargon
And the rubber clouds leave in hordes the breathing
    vents
Jolted open by death rattles of the conjuring jaguar.

In the sandstorm of civilization's letters-of-the-print,
Even death is no shield—the tongue gets coated and
    wicked,
The lungs corrode and the springs are matted with lint,
And the girders crowd around the latest among the
    naked.

Obituary notices adorn the sedateness of daily features:
Somebody is committing the daily commonplace of
    dying—
Somebody barters a piecemeal past for a mess of futures—
Somebody is caught telling the truth, the headlines
    lying.

The oddest people die in the corners of our conscious-
    ness:
Lights, with half-names, go out, as in a harbor at night:
And death becomes a magnificent soliloquy in full dress
While we eavesdrop from the bottom of a shaft of light.

And from the bottom where we cower we hear the shoddy
Argument that reality gives to the anguish of the angel:
We are thrown like a hand grenade from the wrist of
    body
Among the boy demons romping in the celluloid manger.

Those who die die in a hurry, hand quicker than eye:
The details are pitiless that tell how the trick is done:
Meanwhile we button the day against the threatening
    sky—
Vast gold paw limping through mind, dread tread of
    sun.

663

Caught with nerve of the sweet tooth exposed to view-
    points,
Caught without clothing before the lustful emanation of
    ice,
We rip the weather strips of the last hour from the loins—
Our tent a sheet of newspaper, gesticulating flag of
    truce.

IV

The clock hangs to the walls by all its unseen fours
Edging closer along the sleeve of the audience:
The speaker pulls exhortations out of the doors—
Throws them to the virulent eyes in the wells of silence.

What is the man saying into the gullets of the many?
Now the loaves and the little fishes are divided in air
And fill the tossing foliage with a sound of money—
To a bushelful of birds' sound sticks the ring of despair.

The autonomous audience sits behind a brick row of
    brows
Mounted with the gun eyes, the doubts and the desires:
The hero medalled with solutions pulls out all the nows
And fans the sophistries forward, the sleeping ires.

The rows of children, too, with their townclock masks
Laugh an adult laugh or cough a grown up cough:
The teacher's awful stature dwindles between school
    desks:
Through a field of children's faces the future is off.

What if the audience rose from its buried victories
And smote the speaker with its wrath gloved in hill,
Would the word *revolution* fall out of all dictionaries
And leave in the speaker's vocabulary a growing hole?

664

What if the audience broke out of its boorish listening
And showed its bleeding ear, vast as a landscape,
And smashed the lead numerals on the world's fasten-
    ings
And sought through the entrails of its leaders for escape?

But this body bleeds long before the bullets reach it,
This stretch of nerves facing the depth-charge of drums:
And the underman of Calvin and the overman of
    Nietzsche
Burn in disintegration's glory in the auditoriums.

The huge child's-head of audience screams between
    girders:
Sleeping rivets of reality keep the beams flowing over-
    head:
And humanity bleeds through its open wounds, the
    leaders,
Its faucets of fire on the wall of darkness and the dead.

V

The new sphinx with the lips of economics
Propounds the question, the gears grinding in the
    throat:
—What is reality?—and the man with the demon skin
Lets his amorphous eyes upward toward Paradise float.

And with wet seas of astonishment he now beholds
The insect glitterings of the amorphous sphere,
Huge foreign body trafficking in the blood stream,
Shrieking and disgorging the synthetic year.

From the back ways, from the backyards of justification
Comes the question, its feet weighted with factories,
Sashweighted by the turbines, dynamos, dividends,
While the holy ghost of freedom cries among the trees.

The vandals are rebuilding the theatres again,
The crumpled curtains are smeared with imaginations:
The sequins are the glistering eyeballs of the men
Whose colossal virtue was their incredible patience.

The capacious demeanors of the gods are still unwilted,
The fields of molten corn come gliding from their hands:
The untiring sunsets have not yet—not yet succeeded
In designing an iron moment to cover the lands.

But the question hangs, a cloud frozen into chromium,
Frightening the pink-toed senses in their heated nest:
The sackcloth of martyrdom shines like a coat of mail,
And there are guns up the sleeve that sleep on the breast.

The radio, that angel's upper lip, repeats the question,
In the private air, in the closet mouldy with conscience:
The slough of the Sunday papers slaps at the windows:
Termites are living in the rotted music of the ancients.

The personal aggrandizement of earning a living
Prejudices the sincerity and the desire for an answer:
The sky fills the eye until it brims with the past,
And the search for reality grows keener and tenser:

And the opponent who disagrees remains the forerunner
Of that perilous matter, that element, the real:
And only when the drums stop to let the future pass
Does the man hear the small feet of the frightened ideal.

THE MAP OF PLACES

THE map of places passes.
The reality of paper tears.
Land and water where they are
Are only where they were
When words read *here* and *here*
Before ships happened there.

Now on naked names feet stand,
No geographies in the hand,
And paper reads anciently,
And ships at sea
Turn round and round.
All is known, all is found.
Death meets itself everywhere.
Holes in maps look through to nowhere.

THE FLOWERING URN

AND every prodigal greatness
Must creep back into strange home,
Must fill the empty matrix of
The never-begotten perfect son
Who never can be born.

And every quavering littleness
Must pale more tinily than it knows
Into the giant hush whose sound
Reverberates within itself
As tenderest numbers cannot improve.

667

And from this jealous secrecy
Will rise itself, will flower up
The likeness kept against false seed:
When death-whole is the seed
And no new harvest will fraction sowing.

Will rise the same peace that held
Before fertility's lie awoke
The virgin sleep of Mother All:
The same but for the way in flowering
It speaks of fruits that could not be.

DEAR POSSIBLE

DEAR possible, and if you drown,
Nothing is lost, unless my empty hands
Claim the conjectured corpse
Of empty water—a legal vengeance
On my own earnestness.

Dear creature of event, and if I wait the clock
And if the clock be punctual and you late,
Rail against me, my time, my clock,
And rightfully correct me
With wrong, lateness and ill-temper.

Dear scholar of love,
If by your own formula
I open heaven to you
When you knock punctually at the door,
Then you are there, but I where I was.

And I mean that fate in the scales
Is up, down, even, trembling,
Right, wrong, weighing and unweighing,
And I mean that, dear possible,
That fate, that dear fate.

THE WIND, THE CLOCK, THE WE

THE wind has at last got into the clock—
Every minute for itself.
There's no more sixty,
There's no more twelve,
It's as late as it's early.

The rain has washed out the numbers.
The trees don't care what happens.
Time has become a landscape
Of suicidal leaves and stoic branches—
Unpainted as fast as painted.

Or perhaps that's too much to say,
With the clock devouring in itself
And the minutes given leave to die.

The sea's no picture at all.
To sea, then: that's time now,
And every mortal heart's a sailor
Sworn to vengeance on the wind,
To hurl life back into the thin teeth
Out of which first it whistled,
An idiotic defiance of it knew not what
Screeching round the studying clock.

Now there's neither ticking nor blowing.
The ship has gone down with its men,
The sea with the ship, the wind with the sea.
The wind at last got into the clock,
The clock at last got into the wind,
The world at last got out of itself,
At last we can make sense, you and I,
You lone survivor on paper,
The wind's boldness and the clock's care
Become a voiceless language,
And I the story hushed in it—

Is more to say of me?
Do I say more than self-choked hesitation
Can repeat word for word after me,
The script not altered by a breath
Of perhaps meaning otherwise?

THREE SERMONS TO THE DEAD

I

THE WAY OF THE AIR

THE way of the air is by clouds to speak
And by clouds to be silent.
The way of the air is a progress
From treachery to repentance.
The air is the freedom to hope.
You breathe your hopes,
And are glad, and live.
And there are clouds.
There are clouds which betray your hopes.
To whom? To your Conscience, which is not you.
And you are ashamed, and the clouds tear.
By the conscienceless air you live,
But by Conscience, your mouth's tight seal,
You die, you are what you are only.
The clouds are you, Conscience is not you.
Yet you make the clouds to tear and repent
For Conscience's sake, which is not you.
For first was the air, and last is Conscience.
And that which is last is, and that which was first is not.
First was freedom, and last is a tight seal.
The free word tears, but the sealed mouth is silenter.
The air opens your mouth, the clouds unshape it.
Conscience closes the mouth, but gives it back.
What is Conscience? It is Death—
In airless final love of which
You keep inviolate your voice

Against the clouds that steam in traitor whispers
Repentantly upon your mouth,
Aura of tattered hopes
Protesting as you dare not.

II

NOT ALL IMMACULATE

Yet it is not all immaculate death—
Not all a folding to of covers
Punctually, by time's trembling hands.
There is (unreadable) a motley clatter
After that day of instantaneousness
Has summoned instant night from night.
There is a panic of stained steps
Along pale streets conspiring backwards
Into remembered days like bedrooms
Slow with oversleeping, timeless.
It is not all a tidy ending, dawning
Of a picture-page whereon tidily, briefly,
The world is told of by a thinnest light—
The moon-like smile of worn Forgiveness.
Against this weather-peace there cries
(Unhearable) a scarlet wind,
As the sun's bull once bellowed,
And a black rain beseeches, as earth once
In pride of ram besought itself to doubt.
This guarded day is not the whole of you,
Whose foreheads by this day resist
Nature's insanities and headaches,
The garrulous mute bodily debates.
This night which hammers brain-like
At your immune memories now
Lies far and dim, but great it lies
As far and dim, greatly unrolls
That which has been forgotten greatly.
It is not all this sheerer day.
There is that, also, which you have forgotten.

671

There is a blemished night abroad,
And though you lock it in itself
With lockless rigour, that it may not out
By any mercy-key of yours,
Still does it shadow the lustrated tale—
Since of your also those young chapters
Toward which, as to later lives,
Young, later selves of you go futuring.

III

NOR IS IT WRITTEN

Nor is it written that you may not grieve.
There is no rule of joy, long may you dwell
Not smiling yet in that last pain,
On that last supper of the heart.
It is not written that you must take joy
Because not thus again shall you sit down
To ply the mingled banquet
Which the deep larder of illusion shed
Like myth in time grown not astonishing.
Lean to the cloth awhile, and yet awhile,
And even may your eyes caress
Proudly the used abundance.
It is not written in what heart
You may not pass from ancient plenty
Into the straitened nowadays.
To each is given secrecy of heart,
To make himself what heart he please
In stirring up from that fond table
To sit him down at this sharp meal.
It shall not here be asked of him
"What thinks your heart?"
Long may you sorely to yourself upbraid
This truth unwild, this only-bread.
It is not counted what large passions
Your heart in ancient private keeps alive.
To each is given what defeat he will.

LAURA RIDING

FOR-EVER MORNING

"TIME's Conscience!" cried the allerion.
"How great the thrustlecock and thistle,
How small the lily and the lion,
How great and small and equal all,
How one and many, same and sorted,
How not unchanged and not distorted!"

And the money was made of gold,
And the gold was made of money,
And the cause of the quarrel was nothing,
And the arguers stopped counting
At how much, how many, one and plenty,
And peace came and was the same.

If then, if now, then then, now now,
No more and always and thus and so,
To not believe, to not doubt,
To what, to wit, to know and not-know,
To eat evenly of fire and snow,
To talk, loud and soft, to not-talk.

But when was last night?
Oh, just before the cock crew.
And when did the cock crow?
Oh, just after remembrance flew.
And when did remembrance fly?
Oh, just as the chandler sat down to die.

BECAUSE OF CLOTHES

WITHOUT dressmakers to connect
The good-will of the body
With the purpose of the head,
We should be two worlds

673

Instead of a world and its shadow
The flesh.

The head is one world
And the body is another—
The same, but somewhat slower
And more dazed and earlier,
The divergence being corrected
In dress.

There is an odour of Christ
In the cloth: below the chin
No harm is meant. Even, immune
From capital test, wisdom flowers
Out of the shaded breast, and the thighs
Are meek.

The union of matter with mind
By the method of raiment
Destroys not our nakedness
Nor muffles the bell of thought.
Merely the moment to its dumb hour
Is joined.

Inner is the glow of knowledge
And outer is the gloom of appearance.
But putting on the cloak and cap
With only the hands and the face showing,
We turn the gloom in and the glow forth
Softly.

Wherefore, by the neutral grace
Of the needle, we possess our triumphs
Together with our defeats
In a single balanced couplement:
We pause between sense and foolishness,
And live.

RESPECT FOR THE DEAD

For they are dead.
They have learned to be truthful.
Respect for the truthfulness of the dead.

Remember them as they were not,
For this is how they are now.
Think of them with bowed hate.
For they did not choose to die,
And yet they are dead.

They gave false witness:
Life was not as they lived it.
And yet they now speak the truth.
Respect for the dead.
Respect for the truth.

Are the dead the truth?
Yes, because they live not.
Is the truth the dead?
No, because they live not.
What is the truth?
The truth is the one self alive.

Does the truth then live?
No, the truth does not die.
The truth and the dead do not die.
Respect for the truth and the dead.

The truth is the one person alive.
It goes for a walk every evening
After day and before night.
It goes for a walk with the dead.

Respect for them as they pass.
For they are the dead whom you hate:

675

They were false.
And that is the truth which you hate:
It is true.
Respect for your hate.

AUSPICE OF JEWELS

They have connived at those jewelled fascinations
That to our hands and arms and ears
And heads and necks and feet
And all the winding stalk
Extended the mute spell of the face.

They have endowed the whole of us
With such a solemn gleaming
As in the dark of flesh-love
But the face at first did have.
We are studded with wide brilliance
As the world with towns and cities—
The travelling look builds capitals
Where the evasive eye may rest
Safe from the too immediate lodgement.

Obscure and bright these forms
Which as the women of their lingering thought
In slow translucence we have worn.
And the silent given glitter locks us
In a not false unplainness:
Have we ourselves been sure
What steady countenance to turn them?

Until now—when this passionate neglect
Of theirs, and our twinkling reluctance,
Are like the reader and the book
Whose fingers and whose pages have confided
But whose sight and sense
Meet in a chilly time of strangeness;

And it is once more early, anxious,
And so late, it is intolerably the same
Not speaking coruscation
That both we and they made endless, dream-long,
Lest be cruel to so much love
The closer shine of waking,
And what be said sound colder
Than the ghastly love-lisp.

Until now—when to go jewelled
We must despoil the drowsy masquerade
Where gloom of silk and gold
And glossy dazed adornments
Kept safe from flagrant realness
The forgeries of ourselves we were—
When to be alive as love feigned us
We must steal death and its wan splendours
From the women of their sighs we were.

For we are now otherwise luminous.
The light which was spent in jewels
Has performed upon the face
A gradual eclipse of recognition.
We have passed from plaintive visibility
Into total rareness,
And from this reunion of ourselves and them
Under the snuffed lantern of time
Comes an astonished flash like truth
Or the unseen-unheard entrance of someone
Whom eyes and ears in their dotage
Have forgotten for dead or lost.

(And hurrying toward distracted glory,
Gemmed lady-pageants, bells on their hearts,
By restless knights attended
Whose maudlin plumes and pommels
Urge the adventure past return.)

PORTRAIT OF THE ARTIST AS A PREMATURELY OLD MAN

It is common knowledge to every schoolboy and even
  every Bachelor of Arts,

That all sin is divided into two parts.

One kind of sin is called a sin of commission, and that
  is very important,

And it is what you are doing when you are doing something you ortant,

And the other kind of sin is just the opposite and is
  called a sin of omission and is equally bad in the
  eyes of all right-thinking people, from Billy Sunday
  to Buddha,

And it consists of not having done something you
  shudda.

I might as well give you my opinion of these two kinds
  of sin as long as, in a way, against each other we are
  pitting them,

And that is, don't bother your head abouts sins of commission because however sinful, they must at least be
  fun or else you wouldn't be committing them.

It is the sin of omission, the second kind of sin,

That lays eggs under your skin.

The way you get really painfully bitten

Is by the insurance you haven't taken out and the
  checks you haven't added up the stubs of and the
  appointments you haven't kept and the bills you
  haven't paid and the letters you haven't written.

Also, about sins of omission there is one particularly
  painful lack of beauty,

Namely, it isn't as though it had been a riotous red
  letter day or night every time you neglected to do
  your duty;

678

You didn't get a wicked forbidden thrill
Every time you let a policy lapse or forgot to pay a bill;
You didn't slap the lads in the tavern on the back and loudly cry Whee,
Let's all fail to write just one more letter before we go home, and this round of unwritten letters is on me.
No, you never get any fun
Out of the things you haven't done,
But they are the things that I do not like to be amid,
Because the suitable things you didn't do give you a lot more trouble than the unsuitable things you did.
The moral is that it is probably better not to sin at all, but if some kind of sin you must be pursuing,
Well, remember to do it by doing rather than by not doing.

BANKERS ARE JUST LIKE ANY-BODY ELSE, EXCEPT RICHER

THIS is a song to celebrate banks,
Because they are full of money and you go into them and all your hear is clinks and clanks,
Or maybe a sound like the wind in the trees on the hills,
Which is the rustling of the thousand dollar bills.
Most bankers dwell in marble halls,
Which they get to dwell in because they encourage deposits and discourage withdrawals,
And particularly because they all observe one rule which woe betides the banker who fails to heed it,
Which is you must never lend any money to anybody unless they don't need it.
I know you, you cautious conservative banks!
If people are worried about their rent it is your duty to deny them the loan of one nickel, yes, even one copper engraving of the martyred son of the late Nancy Hanks;

679

Yes, if they request fifty dollars to pay for a baby you
must look at them like Tarzan looking at an uppity
ape in the jungle,

And tell them what do they think a bank is, anyhow,
they had better go get the money from their wife's
aunt or ungle.

But suppose people come in and they have a million
and they want another million to pile on top of it,

Why, you brim with the milk of human kindness and
you urge them to accept every drop of it,

And you lend them the million so then they have two
million and this gives them the idea that they would
be better off with four,

So they already have two million as security so you
have no hesitation in lending them two more,

And all the vice-presidents nod their heads in rhythm,

And the only question asked is do the borrowers want
the money sent or do they want to take it withm.

But please do not think that I am not fond of banks,

Because I think they deserve our appreciation and
thanks,

Because they perform a valuable public service in elimi-
nating the jackasses who go around saying that health
and happiness are everything and money isn't essential,

Because as soon as they have to borrow some unimportant money to maintain their health and happiness
they starve to death so they can't go around any more
sneering at good old money, which is nothing short
of providential.

THE ANATOMY OF HAPPINESS

LOTS of truisms don't have to be repeated but there is
one that has got to be,

Which is that it is much nicer to be happy than it is not
to be,

And I shall even add to it by stating unequivocally and
    without restraint

That you are much happier when you are happy than
    when you ain't.

Some people are just naturally Pollyanna,

While others call for sugar and cream and strawberries
    on their manna.

Now, I think we all ought to say a fig for the happiness
    that comes of thinking helpful thoughts and search-
    ing your soul,

The most exciting happiness is the happiness generated
    by forces beyond your control,

Because if you just depend on your helpful thoughts for
    your happiness and would just as soon drink butter-
    milk as champagne, and if mink is no better than
    lapin to you,

Why you don't even deserve to have anything nice and
    exciting happen to you.

If you are really Master of your Fate,

It shouldn't make any difference to you whether Cleo-
    patra or the Bearded Lady is your mate,

So I hold no brief for the kind of happiness or the kind
    of unhappiness that some people constantly carry
    around in their breast,

Because that kind of happiness simply consists of being
    resigned to the worst just as that kind of unhappiness
    consists of being resentful of the best.

No, there is only one kind of happiness that I take the
    stump for,

Which is the kind that comes when something so won-
    derful falls in your lap that joy is what you jump for,

Something not of your own doing,

When the blue sky opens and out pops a refund from
    the Government or an invitation to a terrapin dinner
    or an unhoped-for Yes from the lovely creature you
    have been disconsolately wooing.

And obviously such miracles don't happen every day,

But here's hoping they may,

Because then everybody would be happy except the
   people who pride themselves on creating their own
   happiness who as soon as they saw everybody who
   didn't create their own happiness happy they would
   probably grieve over sharing their own heretofore
   private sublimity,
A condition which I could face with equanimity.

I NEVER EVEN SUGGESTED IT

I KNOW lots of men who are in love and lots of men who
   are married and lots of men who are both,
And to fall out with their loved ones is what all of them
   are most loth.
They are conciliatory at every opportunity,
Because all they want is serenity and a certain amount
   of impunity.
Yes, many the swain who has finally admitted that the
   earth is flat
Simply to sidestep a spat,
Many the masculine Positively or Absolutely which has
   been diluted to an If
Simply to avert a tiff,
Many the two-fisted executive whose domestic conver-
   sation is limited to a tactfully interpolated Yes,
And then he is amazed to find that he is being raked
   backwards over a bed of coals nevertheless.
These misguided fellows are under the impression that
   it takes two to make a quarrel, that you can sidestep
   a crisis by nonaggression and nonresistance,
Instead of removing yourself to a discreet distance.
Passivity can be a provoking *modus operandi;*
Consider the Empire and Gandhi.
Silence is golden, but sometimes invisibility is golder.
Because loved ones may not be able to make bricks
   without straw but often they don't need any straw to

manufacture a bone to pick or blood in their eye or
a chip for their soft white shoulder.
It is my duty, gentlemen, to inform you that women are
dictators all, and I recommend to you this moral:
In real life it takes only one to make a quarrel.

KINDLY UNHITCH THAT STAR,
BUDDY

I HARDLY suppose I know anybody who wouldn't rather
be a success than a failure,
Just as I suppose every piece of crabgrass in the garden
would much rather be an azalea,
And in celestial circles all the run-of-the-mill angels
would rather be archangels or at least cherubim and
seraphim,
And in the legal world all the little process-servers hope
to grow up into great big bailiffim and sheriffim.
Indeed, everybody wants to be a wow,
But not everybody knows exactly how.
Some people think they will eventually wear diamonds
instead of rhinestones
Only by everlastingly keeping their noses to their
grhinestones,
And other people think they will be able to put in more
time at Palm Beach and the Ritz
By not paying too much attention to attendance at the
office but rather in being brilliant by starts and fits.
Some people after a full day's work sit up all night getting
a college education by correspondence,
While others seem to think they'll get just as far by de-
voting their evenings to the study of the difference
in temperament between brunettance and blondance.
Some stake their all on luck,
And others put their faith in their ability to pass the
buck.

In short, the world is filled with people trying to achieve success,

And half of them think they'll get it by saying No and half of them by saying Yes,

And if all the ones who say No said Yes, and vice versa, such is the fate of humanity that ninety-nine per cent of them still wouldn't be any better off than they were before,

Which perhaps is just as well because if everybody was a success nobody could be contemptuous of anybody else and everybody would start in all over again trying to be a bigger success than everybody else so they would have somebody to be contemptuous of and so on forevermore,

Because when people start hitching their wagons to a star,

That's the way they are.

GOLLY, HOW TRUTH WILL OUT

How does a person get to be a capable liar?

That is something that I respectfully inquiar,

Because I don't believe a person will ever set the world on fire

Unless they are a capable lire.

Some wise man said that words were given to us to conceal our thoughts,

But if a person has nothing but truthful words why their thoughts haven't even the protection of a pair of panties or shoughts,

And a naked thought is ineffectual as well as improper,

And hasn't a chance in the presence of a glib chinchilla-clad whopper.

One of the greatest abilities a person can have, I guess,

Is the ability to say Yes when they mean No and No when they mean Yes.

Oh to be Machiavellian, oh to be unscrupulous, oh to be glib!

Oh to be ever prepared with a plausible fib!

Because then a dinner engagement or a contract or a treaty is no longer a fetter,

Because liars can just logically lie their way out of it if they don't like it or if one comes along that they like better;

And do you think their conscience prickles?

No, it tickles.

And please believe that I mean every one of these lines as I am writing them

Because once there was a small boy who was sent to the drugstore to buy some bitter stuff to put on his nails to keep him from biting them,

And in his humiliation he tried to lie to the clerk

And it didn't work,

Because he said My mother sent me to buy some bitter stuff for a friend of mine's nails that bites them, and the clerk smiled wisely and said I wonder who that friend could be,

And the small boy broke down and said Me,

And it was me, or at least I was him,

And all my subsequent attempts at subterfuge have been equally grim,

And that is why I admire a suave prevarication because I prevaricate so awkwardly and gauchely,

And that is why I can never amount to anything politically or socially.

Richard Eberhart

THE GROUNDHOG

In June, amid the golden fields,
I saw a groundhog lying dead.
Dead lay he; my senses shook,
And mind outshot our naked frailty.
There lowly in the vigorous summer
His form began its senseless change,
And made my senses waver dim
Seeing nature ferocious in him.
Inspecting close his maggots' might
And seething cauldron of his being,
Half with loathing, half with a strange love,
I poked him with an angry stick.
The fever arose, became a flame
And Vigour circumscribed the skies,
Immense energy in the sun,
And through my frame a sunless trembling.
My stick had done nor good nor harm.
Then stood I silent in the day
Watching the object, as before;
And kept my reverence for knowledge
Trying for control, to be still,
To quell the passion of the blood;
Until I had bent down on my knees
Praying for joy in the sight of decay.
And so I left; and I returned
In Autumn strict of eye, to see
The sap gone out of the groundhog,
But the bony sodden hulk remained.
But the year had lost its meaning,
And in intellectual chains
I lost both love and loathing,
Mured up in the wall of wisdom.

Another summer took the fields again
Massive and burning, full of life,
But when I chanced upon the spot
There was only a little hair left,
And bones bleaching in the sunlight
Beautiful as architecture;
I watched them like a geometer,
And cut a walking stick from a birch.
It has been three years, now.
There is no sign of the groundhog.
I stood there in the whirling summer,
My hand capped a withered heart,
And thought of China and of Greece,
Of Alexander in his tent;
Of Montaigne in his tower,
Of Saint Theresa in her wild lament.

THE LARGESS

With cicada's nymphal skin
So have I meetings made,
Let down my eyes to him,
With fear upon that thin shade.

Lest the look I gave
Was death's loving me,
To every memory have,
That himself he see.

Yet O marvellous crispness,
Dun, but perfect structure,
Thin as matter is,
It has its wondrous lure.

And took it in my grassy feel,
That cold, that final form,
If still it be the same;
Alert to a hoped harm.

687

Where have you gone, slight being
Whose brown monument
Mirror makes of wings
Yet in a damp tenement.

Can I among winds lose you
When vibrant is all air?
Must I not use you
Then in every desire?

It has not denied my mind,
But no sign has made,
Bleak, delicate, defined
And crinkled husk once life had.

My eyes soothe over him,
My hand trembles with force.
What eternal hovers in
Him: speak, are you corpse?

IMAGINING HOW IT WOULD BE TO BE DEAD

IMAGINING how it would be to be dead,
Until my tender filaments
From mere threads air have become
And this is all my consciousness
(While like a world of rock and stone
By body cumbersome and big
Breathes out a vivid atmosphere
Which is the touchless breach of the air)
I lost my head, and could not hold
Either my hands together or my heart
But was so sentient a being
I seemed to break time apart
And thus became all things air can touch
Or could touch could it touch all things,

And this was an embrace most dear,
Final, complete, a flying without wings.
From being bound to one poor skull,
And that surrounded by one earth,
And the earth in one universe forced,
And that chained to some larger gear,
I was the air, I was the air,
And then I pressed on eye and cheek
The sightless hinges of eternity
That make the whole world creak.

AT LAKE GENEVA

AND at Lake Geneva, which is in Wisconsin,
In the summer,
After breast strokes in the clear cutting lake
I picked up a magazine from a table,
Being called *Travel*.
The leaves fell to an eye-suspension
And a memory-carver, pure leisure perhaps,
(Or pleasure is never pure: but
Struck with fear and loss?)
I read from the year 1929
D. H. Lawrence articulate on flowers in Sicily.
Blue and white and red and green,
He named them with the names of his lips,
The world blooming, bursting, seeming to dilate
Now memory-bright, before my eyes, memory-tena-
    cious,
For that was a time rich for me,
Taormina days! Aetna in the distance
A Scylla and Charybdis of youth and maturity.
But my old companionate melancholy
Came there to me in the sunlight,
In the pure interests of the new summer,
And I had a single thought, ramifying,
I had a single thought, so singular,

Lawrence dead, seven years since Sicily,
And did it matter that he was Lawrence?
What matter now? Here in Wisconsin
These thousands who never heard of D. H. Lawrence.
Did it matter, all that he said? Had he said much?
Are the fishermen, the garage mechanics, the ticket
    takers
More important? Are they more important? Should one
Revolve in them the more, in him the less, shadow only
Of individualism?
So ran on my cogitation; seven years
Travel had lain in the summer-used house.
Seven years, a cycle, Lawrence's flower-love, his
Flower-exaltation, stood in cold type
Unseen by my eyes. And a certain loathing
Came, as often, for the evil that time is.

And there was a diffusion of thought,
Which is life-like, from the depth and
Clenching, fixation of the thought
A moving off, the mere air, or somebody
Passing outside, or a voice in the kitchen
Switching the reverie to a picturization
Of the actual present world of the senses.
Then to attack the stealth of that!
Was all my, but momentary, use!
Why should the mood vanish, the reverie dissolve,
With little but prosaic surd in the wake of,
Of, well, say surges and surges of love.
Such wanderings conjured up
By Lawrence in type on the table,
A personal conjunction in time that dissolves.
So significance cannot be pierced-through-to?
No final word to say by the means of poetry?
But always vacillation and pulsations, action?

What immediately surrounds us is real.
Now another summer appertains. Certainly stones,

RICHARD EBERHART

Trees, waves, clouds, air are good and
May I say they refuse the treacheries of rhetoric?
On this island, inhabited somewhat by Icelanders,
Washington Island in Wisconsin,
Traditional-primitive happiness accrues.
There are no psychopathic disturbances here.
Final things are violent; abolition of half way measures.
The spiders on the wall, Jack with his boat,
The two clowns from Red Wing.
Sickels: "How do you like bathing girls?"
Kernan: "I don't know, I never bathed any."
Wind standing at Death's Door,
The sun dry and hot, axe strokes,
And a sail going over the Door,
Slot machines, beer practically every hour,
The swimming water furling on the skin
And at night, once, the glory of the Northern Lights!
While on the dock you lie,
Gazing off from Death's Door,
You see the incredible make and knead of the sky-shakes!
To be bigger or littler is your need,
Not insufficiently human as you are,
Seeing that majestic mysterious night sky fretwork.
If the doors of perception were cleansed—
Or if we weren't heavy and
"Ruth, I think I'll go and get some sleep,
You'd better come now,
Your mother is afraid you might fall asleep
And roll off the dock."
Let the problem of Form go by the wind
It is something to be happy for a while,
Don't shoot at the seagulls, it's not good sportsmanship;
"There's not much danger of hitting one with a .38"
I mean the albatross,
Esemplastic was always a ridiculous word.

ON SHOOTING PARTICLES
BEYOND THE WORLD

"White Sands, N. M., Dec. 18 (UP). 'We first throw a little something into the skies,' Zwicky said. 'Then a little more, then a shipload of instruments—then ourselves.'"

On this day man's disgust is known
Incipient before but now full blown
With minor wars of major consequence,
Duly building empirical delusions.

Now this little creature in a rage
Like new-born infant screaming compleat angler
Objects to the whole globe itself
And with a vicious lunge he throws

Metal particles beyond the orbit of mankind.
Beethoven shaking his fist at death,
A giant dignity in human terms,
Is nothing to this imbecile metal fury.

The world is too much for him. The green
Of earth is not enough, love's deities,
Peaceful intercourse, happiness of nations,
The wild animal dazzled on the desert.

If the maniac would only realize
The comforts of his padded cell
He would have penetrated the
Impenetrability of the spiritual.

It is not intelligent to go too far.
How he frets that he can't go too!
But his particles would maim a star,
His free-floating bombards rock the moon.

Good Boy! We pat the baby to eructate,
We pat him then for eructation.

Good Boy Man! Your innards are put out,
From now all space will be your vomitorium.

The atom bomb accepted this world,
Its hatred of man blew death in his face.
But not content, he'll send slugs beyond,
His particles of intellect will spit on the sun.

Not God he'll catch, in the mystery of space.
He flaunts his own out-cast state
As he throws his imperfections outward bound,
And his shout that gives a hissing sound.

THE FURY OF AERIAL
BOMBARDMENT

You would think the fury of aerial bombardment
Would rouse God to relent; the infinite spaces
Are still silent. He looks on shock-pried faces.
History, even, does not know what is meant.

You would feel that after so many centuries
God would give man to repent; yet he can kill
As Cain could, but with multitudinous will,
No farther advanced than in his ancient furies.

Was man made stupid to see his own stupidity?
Is God by definition indifferent, beyond us all?
Is the eternal truth man's fighting soul
Wherein the Beast ravens in its own avidity?

Of Van Wettering I speak, and Averill,
Names on a list, whose faces I do not recall
But they are gone to early death, who late in school
Distinguished the belt feed lever from the belt
  holding pawl.

RUMINATION

WHEN I can hold a stone within my hand
And feel time make it sand and soil, and see
The roots of living things grow in this land,
Pushing between my fingers flower and tree,
Then I shall be as wise as death,
For death has done this and he will
Do this to me, and blow his breath
To fire my clay, when I am still.

DAM NECK, VIRGINIA

ANTI-AIRCRAFT seen from a certain distance
On a steely blue night say a mile away
Flowers on the air absolutely dream-like,
The vision has no relation to the reality.

The floating balls of light are tossed easily
And float out into space without a care,
They the sailors of the gentlest parabolas
In a companionship and with a kind of stare.

They are a controlled kind of falling stars,
But not falling, rising and floating and going out,
Teaming together in efflorescent spectacle
Seemingly better than nature's: man is on the lookout.

The men are firing tracers, practising at night.
Each specialist himself precision's instrument,
These expert prestidigitators press the luminence
In knowledge of and ignorance of their doing.

They do not know the dream-like vision ascending
In me, one mile away: they had not thought of that.
Huddled in darkness behind their bright projectors
They are the scientists of the skill to kill.

As this sight and show is gentle and false,
The truth of guns is fierce that aims at death.
Of war in the animal sinews let us speak not,
But of the beautiful disrelation of the spiritual.

A MEDITATION

Now you are holding my skull in your hand.
I am not anybody. I am dead.
God has taken my life away. You are holding
My skull in your hand, the wind is blowing—
The wind is blowing, the wind is blowing—
The wind is blowing through my skull like a horn
And you are thinking of the world's unearthly music
And of the beauty beyond the earth and seas,
You think the tune will tell you of the truth,
You are thinking: thinking, are you?—are you
Thinking? I am dead. I am dead and in your hand.

Now what does it matter whether I lived or died
Or when I lived or when I died or what I tried
To do of all the things there are to do in the world,
You might be musing upon a finch, or a melon,
You might be not you but somebody else, some other,
Some utter muser, maybe, in some other land
With some other kind of brains or bones, or both,
Some lack of bile to make these peregrinations;
You might be a man who never found me at all,
That miraculous fellow, that idiotic genius
Who never had to think of the wind in my skull at all.

There, you see I am so helpless in your hands.
I cannot get back, cannot reach or yearn back,
Nor summon love enough, nor the intellectual care—
Being dead, you talk as if I had spirit at all—
To come back to you and tell you who I am.
You do me too much honor with your grave words
And quizzical head bent down, trace of a lovable smile,
Too much too much honor for one so windless,

And witless, wizened long past wandering and pondering.
Go back to your strict duties of the earth, man,
Make love to your girl long nights, and long summer
    days.

But there, you hold me, a philosopher! If philosophical,
You had better put me back in the earth,
Hold nothing at all! Hold your own hand, man!
Now you can feel the dainty wind playing through it
Weaving among your fingers what you want to know
There is the place to love and make your contempla-
    tions
For you can still make your fingers fly and go.
Of all symbols the cunning mind devises
None can be so strict, so purely right
As the hand that makes the fingers fashion the love
Contending in immaterial mastery.

But something touches you, deeply, beyond all com-
    ment,
Something so tender, wise, human; you are only human
And grief makes you as a little child that weeps
For you do not know why you are in the world
Nor how you got here, in any real sense, nor how long
Before some ruthless shock will end you forever,
That peculiar you you must cherish, the uniqueness,
The kind not like the skull that is in your hand
But that is fixed in its intricate nicety,—
As who can imagine, seeing a fine bull in pasture
That that magnificent creature will lie down and die?

God has taken my life away. I am dead,
I am not anybody. I am no oracle. You be
An oracle, if you can. You be full of imagination.
You see beyond me, which is seeing beyond yourself,
Yours is the purely human burden and the prophecy.
These things can only be talked of by men.

RICHARD EBERHART

Man is the talking machine; or the arcane marionette
Who like a god thinks himself to be immune
From the terrible void and absolute darkness
The unthinkable loss and final destitution
Upon which he builds (O! yes!) his mighty hierarchies.

But if I had the power to seem to be,
Or could even wish to be powerful, and say
"I am Lord of Life. I am Eternal Life"—
I could not say it, the contradiction is too great.
This goes too far, and lacks a certain humor.
You build a fiction of what I am, or could be,
And amidst the limits of your mentality and words
Revolve, with all your feelings stumbling blocks
And your keenest thoughts barbs of fiery wire.
O dear sweet little timeful poor creature
Tell this skull what it cares not to say

Life blows like the wind away

You have run the weirs of the emotions,
Even as I did; but they are not through with you yet.
There will be many complicated messages,
Memory will make of your heart a veritable mill,
The need for action jerk your legs, ambition
Choke you, rage consume you almost to inanition,
Conquest will thrill you, and defeat annul you.
And you will not have enough, but lust of life
Drive you on to the cold, very brink of the grave
With man's old captive, cyclic wish to know
What it is all about, meaning and moral dimension.

What is it all about, you are asking me now
For it is less of me than of yourself you are thinking,
Surely more of yourself, flesh-bound as you are—
You would withdraw in horror at my secret,
You would not want to know, your long-lashed eyes
    aglare,

697

Of the cold absolute blankness and fate of death,
Of the depths of being beyond all words to say,
Of your profound or of the world's destiny,
Of the mind of God, rising like a mighty fire
Pure and calm beyond all mortal instances
Magnificent, eternal, Everlasting, sweet and mild.

No, I rise a little, I come to life a little.
If I could only make you see the simple truth,
So simple it is so hard to say, hard to believe,
That you are to be man, that is, to be human,
You are imperfect, will never know perfection,
You must strive, but the goal will recede forever,
That you must do what the great poets and the sages
    say,
Obeying scripture even in the rotten times,
That you must, also, not think nor feel too much
(For the Greeks knew what they were talking about),
And that, as you have lived, so must you die

And blow like the wind away

Now you walk back among the flowers of the world.
You have put me down and I am myself again.
Now you return, return from your solemn meditation
Among the strange shadows, the strange veils of longing
And through the cathartic action of beautiful contem-
    plation
Seek among your fellows whatever is good in life,
Purified by this; for, as sin purifies lust,
As war purges society, as death rarifies life,
So the contemplation of death is valuable
Restorative of the soul to new even reaches
Easing a little the burden of our suffering

Before we blow like the wind away

And blow like the wind away

W. H. Auden

HERMAN MELVILLE

TOWARDS the end he sailed into an extraordinary mildness,
And anchored in his home and reached his wife
And rode within the harbour of her hand,
And went across each morning to an office
As though his occupation were another island.

Goodness existed: that was the new knowledge
His terror had to blow itself quite out
To let him see it; but it was the gale had blown him
Past the Cape Horn of sensible success
Which cries: "This rock is Eden. Shipwreck here."

But deafened him with thunder and confused with lightning:
—The maniac hero hunting like a jewel
The rare ambiguous monster that had maimed his sex,
Hatred for hatred ending in a scream,
The unexplained survivor breaking off the nightmare—
All that was intricate and false; the truth was simple.

Evil is unspectacular and always human,
And shares our bed and eats at our own table,
And we are introduced to Goodness every day,
Even in drawing-rooms among a crowd of faults;
He has a name like Billy and is almost perfect
But wears a stammer like a decoration:
And every time they meet the same thing has to happen;
It is the Evil that is helpless like a lover
And has to pick a quarrel and succeeds,
And both are openly destroyed before our eyes.

For now he was awake and knew
No one is ever spared except in dreams;
But there was something else the nightmare had distorted—
Even the punishment was human and a form of love:
The howling storm had been his father's presence
And all the time he had been carried on his father's breast.

Who now had set him gently down and left him.
He stood upon the narrow balcony and listened:
And all the stars above him sang as in his childhood
"All, all is vanity," but it was not the same;
For now the words descended like the calm of mountains—
—Nathaniel had been shy because his love was selfish—
But now he cried in exultation and surrender
"The Godhead is broken like bread. We are the pieces."

And sat down at his desk and wrote a story.

CANZONE

WHEN shall we learn, what should be clear as day,
We cannot choose what we are free to love?
Although the mouse we banished yesterday
Is an enraged rhinoceros today,
Our value is more threatened than we know:
Shabby objections to our present day
Go snooping round its outskirts; night and day
Faces, orations, battles, bait our will
As questionable forms and noises will;
Whole phyla of resentments every day
Give status to the wild men of the world
Who rule the absent-minded and this world.

We are created from and with the world
To suffer with and from it day by day:

Whether we meet in a majestic world
Of solid measurements or a dream world
Of swans and gold, we are required to love
All homeless objects that require a world.
Our claim to own our bodies and our world
Is our catastrophe. What can we know
But panic and caprice until we know
Our dreadful appetite demands a world
Whose order, origin, and purpose will
Be fluent satisfaction of our will?

Drift, Autumn, drift; fall, colours, where you will:
Bald melancholia minces through the world.
Regret, cold oceans, the lymphatic will
Caught in reflection on the right to will:
While violent dogs excite their dying day
To bacchic fury; snarl, though, as they will,
Their teeth are not a triumph for the will
But utter hesitation. What we love
Ourselves for is our power not to love,
To shrink to nothing or explode at will,
To ruin and remember that we know
What ruins and hyaenas cannot know.

If in this dark now I less often know
That spiral staircase where the haunted will
Hunts for its stolen luggage, who should know
Better than you, beloved, how I know
What gives security to any world,
Or in whose mirror I begin to know
The chaos of the heart as merchants know
Their coins and cities, genius its own day?
For through our lively traffic all the day,
In my own person I am forced to know
How much must be forgotten out of love,
How much must be forgiven, even love.

Dear flesh, dear mind, dear spirit, O dear love,
In the depths of myself blind monsters know

Your presence and are angry, dreading Love
That asks its images for more than love;
The hot rampageous horses of my will,
Catching the scent of Heaven, whinny: Love
Gives no excuse to evil done for love,
Neither in you, nor me, nor armies, nor the world
Of words and wheels, nor any other world.
Dear fellow-creature, praise our God of Love
That we are so admonished, that no day
Of conscious trial be a wasted day.

Or else we make a scarecrow of the day,
Loose ends and jumble of our common world,
And stuff and nonsense of our own free will;
Or else our changing flesh may never know
There must be sorrow if there can be love.

PREFACE

(The Stage Manager to the Critics)

THE aged catch their breath,
For the nonchalant couple go
Waltzing across the tightrope
As if there were no death
Or hope of falling down;
The wounded cry as the clown
Doubles his meaning, and O
How the dear little children laugh
When the drums roll and the lovely
Lady is sawn in half.

O what authority gives
Existence its surprise?
Science is happy to answer
That the ghosts who haunt our lives
Are handy with mirrors and wire,
That song and sugar and fire,
Courage and come-hither eyes
Have a genius for taking pains.

But how does one think up a habit?
Our wonder, our terror remains.

Art opens the fishiest eye
To the Flesh and the Devil who heat
The Chamber of Temptation
Where heroes roar and die.
We are wet with sympathy now;
Thanks for the evening; but how
Shall we satisfy when we meet,
Between Shall-I and I-Will,
The lion's mouth whose hunger
No metaphors can fill?

Well, who in his own backyard
Has not opened his heart to the smiling
Secret he cannot quote?
Which goes to show that the Bard
Was sober when he wrote
That this world of fact we love
Is unsubstantial stuff:
All the rest is silence
On the other side of the wall;
And the silence ripeness,
And the ripeness all.

SEPTEMBER 1, 1939

I SIT in one of the dives
On Fifty-second Street
Uncertain and afraid
As the clever hopes expire
Of a low dishonest decade:
Waves of anger and fear
Circulate over the bright
And darkened lands of the earth,
Obsessing our private lives;
The unmentionable odour of death
Offends the September night.

Accurate scholarship can
Unearth the whole offence
From Luther until now
That has driven a culture mad,
Find what occurred at Linz,
What huge imago made
A psychopathic god:
I and the public know
What all schoolchildren learn,
Those to whom evil is done
Do evil in return.

Exiled Thucydides knew
All that a speech can say
About Democracy,
And what dictators do,
The elderly rubbish they talk
To an apathetic grave;
Analysed all in his book,
The enlightenment driven away,
The habit-forming pain,
Mismanagement and grief:
We must suffer them all again.

Into this neutral air
Where blind skyscrapers use
Their full height to proclaim
The strength of Collective Man,
Each language pours its vain
Competitive excuse:
But who can live for long
In an euphoric dream;
Out of the mirror they stare,
Imperialism's face
And the international wrong.

Faces along the bar
Cling to their average day:

The lights must never go out,
The music must always play,
All the conventions conspire
To make this fort assume
The furniture of home;
Lest we should see where we are,
Lost in a haunted wood,
Children afraid of the night
Who have never been happy or good.

The windiest militant trash
Important Persons shout
Is not so crude as our wish:
What mad Nijinsky wrote
About Diaghilev
Is true of the normal heart;
For the error bred in the bone
Of each woman and each man
Craves what it cannot have,
Not universal love
But to be loved alone.

From the conservative dark
Into the ethical life
The dense commuters come,
Repeating their morning vow;
"I *will* be true to the wife,
I'll concentrate more on my work,"
And helpless governors wake
To resume their compulsory game:
Who can release them now,
Who can reach the deaf,
Who can speak for the dumb?

All I have is a voice
To undo the folded lie,
The romantic lie in the brain
Of the sensual man-in-the-street
And the lie of Authority

Whose buildings grope the sky:
There is no such thing as the State
And no one exists alone;
Hunger allows no choice
To the citizen or the police;
We must love one another or die.

Defenceless under the night
Our world in stupor lies;
Yet, dotted everywhere,
Ironic points of light
Flash out wherever the Just
Exchange their messages:
May I, composed like them
Of Eros and of dust,
Beleaguered by the same
Negation and despair,
Show an affirming flame.

THE DIASPORA

How he survived them they could never understand:
Had they not beggared him themselves to prove
They could not live without their dogmas or their land?
No worlds they drove him from were ever big enough:
How *could* it be the earth the Unconfined
Meant when It bade them set no limits to their love?
And he fulfilled the rôle for which he was designed:
On heat with fear, he drew their terrors to him,
And was a godsend to the lowest of mankind.
Till there was no place left where they could still pursue him
Except that exile which he called his Race.
But, envying him even that, they plunged right through him
Into a land of mirrors without time or space,
And all they had to strike now was the human face.

W. H. AUDEN

AUTUMN 1940

RETURNING each morning from a timeless world,
The senses open upon a world of time;
    After so many years the light is
    Novel still and immensely ambitious.

But, translated from her own informal world,
The ego is bewildered and does not want
    A shining novelty this morning,
    And does not like the noise or the people.

For behind the doors of this ambitious day
Stand shadows with enormous grudges, outside
    Its chartered ocean of perception
    Misshapen coastguards drunk with foreboding;

And whispering websters stealing through this world
Discredit so much literature and praise:
    Summer was worse than we expected,
    And now cold autumn comes on the water.

The lesser lives retire on their savings, their
Small deposits of starches and nuts, and soon
    Will be asleep or travelling or
    Dead; but this year the towns of our childhood

Are changing complexion along with the woods,
And many who have shared our conduct will add
    Their pinches of detritus to the
    Nutritive chain of determined being,

And even the uneliminated decline
To a vita minima, huddling for warmth
    The hard- and the soft-mouthed together
    In a coma of waiting, just breathing

In a darkness of tribulation and death,
While blizzards havoc the gardens, and the old

Folly becomes unsafe, the mill-wheels
Rust and the weirs fall slowly to pieces.

Will the inflamed ego attempt as before
To migrate again to her family place,
    To the hanging gardens of Eros
    And the moons of his magical summer?

But the local train does not run any more,
The heretical roses have lost their scent,
    And her Cornish Hollow of tryst is
    Swarming now with discourteous villains

Whom father's battered hat cannot wish away,
And the fancy-governed sequence leads us all
    Back to that labyrinth where either
    We are found or lose ourselves for ever.

Oh what sign can we make to be found? How can
We will the knowledge that we must know to will?
    The waste is a suburb of prophets,
    But few have seen Jesus and so many

Judas the Abyss. The rocks are big and bad,
And death so substantial in the thinning air;
    Learning screams in the narrow gate where
    Events are traded with time, but who can

Tell what logic must and must not leave to fate,
Or what laws we are permitted to obey?
    There are no birds; the predatory
    Glaciers glitter in the chilly evening;

And death is probable. Nevertheless,
Whatever the situation and the blame,
    Let the lips do formal contrition
    For whatever is going to happen;

Time remembered bear witness to time required,
The positive and negative ways through time
    Embrace and encourage each other
    In a brief moment of intersection;

That the orgulous spirit may while it can
Conform to its temporal focus with praise,
    Acknowledging the attributes of
    One immortal one infinite Substance,

And the shabby structure of indolent flesh
Give a resonant echo to the Word which was
    From the beginning, and the shining
    Light be comprehended by the darkness.

VOLTAIRE AT FERNEY

Almost happy now, he looked at his estate.
An exile making watches glanced up as he passed,
And went on working; where a hospital was rising fast
A joiner touched his cap; an agent came to tell
Some of the trees he'd planned were progressing well.
The white alps glittered. It was summer. He was very
    great.

Far off in Paris, where his enemies
Whispered that he was wicked, in an upright chair
A blind old woman longed for death and letters. He
    would write
"Nothing is better than life." But was it? Yes, the fight
Against the false and the unfair
Was always worth it. So was gardening. Civilise.

Cajoling, scolding, scheming, cleverest of them all,
He'd led the other children in a holy war
Against the infamous grown-ups; and, like a child, been
    sly

And humble when there was occasion for
The two-faced answer or the plain protective lie,
But patient like a peasant waited for their fall.

And never doubted, like D'Alembert, he would win:
Only Pascal was a great enemy, the rest
Were rats already poisoned; there was much, though,
    to be done,
And only himself to count upon.
Dear Diderot was dull but did his best;
Rousseau, he'd always known, would blubber and give
    in.

So, like a sentinel, he could not sleep. The night was
    full of wrong,
Earthquakes and executions. Soon he would be dead,
And still all over Europe stood the horrible nurses
Itching to boil their children. Only his verses
Perhaps could stop them: He must go on working.
    Overhead
The uncomplaining stars composed their lucid song.

AT THE GRAVE OF HENRY JAMES

THE snow, less intransigeant than their marble,
Has left the defence of whiteness to these tombs;
    For all the pools at my feet
Accommodate blue now, and echo such clouds as occur
To the sky, and whatever bird or mourner the passing
    Moment remarks they repeat

While the rocks, named after singular spaces
Within which images wandered once that caused
    All to tremble and offend,
Stand here in an innocent stillness, each marking the
    spot
Where one more series of errors lost its uniqueness
    And novelty came to an end.

710

To whose real advantage were such transactions
When words of reflection were exchanged for trees?
  What living occasion can
Be just to the absent? O noon but reflects on itself,
And the small taciturn stone that is the only witness
  To a great and talkative man

Has no more judgment than my ignorant shadow
Of odious comparisons or distant clocks
  Which challenge and interfere
With the heart's instantaneous reading of time, time
    that is
A warm enigma no longer in you for whom I
  Surrender my private cheer

Startling the awkward footsteps of my apprehension,
The flushed assault of your recognition is
  The *donnée* of this doubtful hour:
O stern proconsul of intractable provinces,
O poet of the difficult, dear addicted artist,
  Assent to my soil and flower.

As I stand awake on our solar fabric,
That primary machine, the earth, which gendarmes,
    banks,
  And aspirin pre-suppose.
On which the clumsy and sad may all sit down, and
    any who will
Say their a-ha to the beautiful, the common locus
  Of the master and the rose.

Our theatre, scaffold, and erotic city
Where all the infirm species are partners in the act
  Of encroachment bodies crave,
Though solitude in death is *de rigueur* for their flesh
And the self-denying hermit flies as it approaches
  Like the carnivore to a cave.

That its plural numbers may unite in meaning,
Its vulgar tongues unravel the knotted mass
   Of the improperly conjunct,
Open my eyes now to all its hinted significant forms,
Sharpen my ears to detect amid its brilliant uproar
   The low thud of the defunct.

O dwell, ironic at my living centre,
Half ancestor, half child; because the actual self
   Round whom time revolves so fast
Is so afraid of what its motions might possibly do
That the actor is never there when his really important
   Acts happen. Only the past

Is present, no one about but the dead as,
Equipped with a few inherited odds and ends,
   One after another we are
Fired into life to seek that unseen target where all
Our equivocal judgments are judged and resolved in
   One whole Alas or Hurrah.

And only the unborn remark the disaster
When, though it makes no difference to the pretty airs
   The bird of Appetite sings,
And Amour Propre is his usual amusing self,
Out from the jungle of an undistinguished moment
   The flexible shadow springs.

Now more than ever, when torches and snare-drum
Excite the squat women of the saurian brain
   Till a milling mob of fears
Breaks in insultingly on anywhere, when in our dreams
Pigs play on the organs and the blue sky runs shrieking
   As the Crack of Doom appears,

Are the good ghosts needed with the white magic
Of their subtle loves. War has no ambiguities
   Like a marriage; the result

Required of its *affaire fatale* is simple and sad,
The physical removal of all human objects
    That conceal the Difficult.

Then remember me that I may remember
The test we have to learn to shudder for is not
    An historical event,
That neither the low democracy of a nightmare nor
An army's primitive tidiness may deceive me
    About our predicament.

That catastrophic situation which neither
Victory nor defeat can annul; to be
    Deaf yet determined to sing,
To be lame and blind yet burning for the Great Good
        Place,
To be radically corrupt yet mournfully attracted
    By the Real Distinguished Thing.

And shall I not specially bless you as, vexed with
My little inferior questions, today I stand
    Beside the bed where you rest
Who opened such passionate arms to your *Bon* when
        It ran
Towards you with its overwhelming reasons pleading
    All beautifully in Its breast?

O with what innocence your hand submitted
To these formal rules that help a child to play,
    While your heart, fastidious as
A delicate nun, remained true to the rare noblesse
Of your lucid gift and, for its own sake, ignored the
    Resentful muttering Mass,

Whose ruminant hatred of all which cannot
Be simplified or stolen is still at large;
    No death can assuage its lust
To vilify the landscape of Distinction and see

The heart of the Personal brought to a systolic stand-
    still,
  The Tall to diminished dust.

Preserve me, Master, from its vague incitement;
Yours be the disciplinary image that holds
  Me back from agreeable wrong
And the clutch of eddying muddle, lest Proportion shed
The alpine chill of her shrugging editorial shoulder
  On my loose impromptu song.

Suggest; so may I segregate my disorder
Into districts of prospective value: approve;
  Lightly, lightly, then, may I dance
Over the frontier of the obvious and fumble no more
In the old limp pocket of the minor exhibition,
  Nor riot with irrelevance.

And no longer shoe geese or water stakes, but
Bolt in my day my grain of truth to the barn
  Where tribulations may leap
With their long-lost brothers at last in the festival
Of which not one had a dissenting image, and the
  Flushed immediacy sleep.

Into this city from the shining lowlands
Blows a wind that whispers of uncovered skulls
  And fresh ruins under the moon,
Of hopes that will not survive the *secousse* of this spring
Of blood and flames, of the terror that walks by night
  and
  The sickness that strikes at noon.

All will be judged. Master of nuance and scruple,
Pray for me and for all writers living or dead;
  Because there are many whose works
Are in better taste than their lives; because there is no
    end

To the vanity of our calling: make intercession
  For the treason of all clerks.

Because the darkness is never so distant,
And there is never much time for the arrogant
  Spirit to flutter its wings,
Or the broken bone to rejoice, or the cruel to cry
For Him whose property is always to have mercy, the
  author
  And giver of all good things.

THE UNKNOWN CITIZEN

(To JS/07/M/378
This Marble Monument
Is Erected by the State)

HE was found by the Bureau of Statistics to be
One against whom there was no official complaint,
And all the reports on his conduct agree
That, in the modern sense of an old-fashioned word, he
  was a saint,
For in everything he did he served the Greater Commu-
  nity.
Except for the War till the day he retired
He worked in a factory and never got fired,
But satisfied his employers, Fudge Motors Inc.
Yet he wasn't a scab or odd in his views,
For his Union reports that he paid his dues,
(Our report on his Union shows it was sound)
And our Social Psychology workers found
That he was popular with his mates and liked a drink.
The Press are convinced that he bought a paper every
  day
And that his reactions to advertisements were normal in
  every way.
Policies taken out in his name prove that he was fully
  insured,

And his Health-card shows he was once in hospital but
    left it cured.
Both Producers Research and High-Grade Living de-
    clare
He was fully sensible to the advantages of the Instal-
    ment Plan
And had everything necessary to the Modern Man,
A phonograph, a radio, a car and a frigidaire.
Our researchers into Public Opinion are content
That he held the proper opinions for the time of year;
When there was peace, he was for peace; when there
    was war, he went.
He was married and added five children to the popula-
    tion,
Which our Eugenist says was the right number for a
    parent of his generation,
And our teachers report that he never interfered with
    their education.
Was he free? Was he happy? The question is absurd:
Had anything been wrong, we should certainly have
    heard.

REFUGEE BLUES

SAY this city has ten million souls,
Some are living in mansions, some are living in holes:
Yet there's no place for us, my dear, yet there's no
    place for us.

Once we had a country and we thought it fair,
Look in the atlas and you'll find it there:
We cannot go there now, my dear, we cannot go there
    now.

In the village churchyard there grows an old yew,
Every spring it blossoms anew:
Old passports can't do that, my dear, old passports
    can't do that.

The consul banged the table and said;
"If you've got no passport you're officially dead":
But we are still alive, my dear, but we are still alive.

Went to a committee; they offered me a chair;
Asked me politely to return next year:
But where shall we go today, my dear, but where shall
  we go today?

Came to a public meeting; the speaker got up and said:
"If we let them in, they will steal our daily bread";
He was talking of you and me, my dear, he was talking
  of you and me.

Thought I heard the thunder rumbling in the sky;
It was Hitler over Europe, saying: "They must die";
O we were in his mind, my dear, O we were in his
  mind.

Saw a poodle in a jacket fastened with a pin,
Saw a door opened and a cat let in:
But they weren't German Jews, my dear, but they
  weren't German Jews.

Went down the harbour and stood upon the quay,
Saw the fish swimming as if they were free:
Only ten feet away, my dear, only ten feet away.

Walked through a wood, saw the birds in the trees;
They had no politicians and sang at their ease:
They weren't the human race, my dear, they weren't
  the human race.

Dreamed I saw a building with a thousand floors,
A thousand windows and a thousand doors;
Not one of them was ours, my dear, not one of them
  was ours.

Stood on a great plain in the falling snow;
Ten thousand soldiers marched to and fro:
Looking for you and me, my dear, looking for you and
me.

THE LABYRINTH

Anthropos apteros for days
Walked whistling round and round the Maze,
Relying happily upon
His temperament for getting on.

The hundredth time he sighted, though,
A bush he left an hour ago,
He halted where four alleys crossed,
And recognised that he was lost.

"Where am I? Metaphysics says
No question can be asked unless
It has an answer, so I can
Assume this maze has got a plan.

If theologians are correct,
A Plan implies an Architect:
A God-built maze would be, I'm sure,
The Universe in miniature.

Are data from the world of Sense,
In that case, valid evidence?
What in the universe I know
Can give directions how to go?

All Mathematics would suggest
A steady straight line as the best,
But left and right alternately
Is consonant with History.

W. H. Auden

Aesthetics, though, believes all Art
Intends to gratify the Heart:
Rejecting disciplines like these,
Must I, then, go which way I please?

Such reasoning is only true
If we accept the classic view,
Which we have no right to assert,
According to the Introvert.

His absolute pre-supposition
Is—Man creates his own condition:
This maze was not divinely built,
But is secreted by my guilt.

The centre that I cannot find
Is known to my Unconscious Mind;
I have no reason to despair
Because I am already there.

My problem is how *not* to will;
They move most quickly who stand still;
I'm only lost until I see
I'm lost because I want to be.

If this should fail, perhaps I should,
As certain educators would,
Content myself with the conclusion;
In theory there is no solution.

All statements about what I feel,
Like I-am-lost, are quite unreal:
My knowledge ends where it began;
A hedge is taller than a man."

Anthropos apteros, perplexed
To know which turning to take next,
Looked up and wished he were the bird
To whom such doubts must seem absurd.

TIME WILL SAY NOTHING
BUT I TOLD YOU SO

TIME will say nothing but I told you so,
Time only knows the price we have to pay;
If I could tell you I would let you know.

If we should weep when clowns put on their show,
If we should stumble when musicians play,
Time will say nothing but I told you so.

There are no fortunes to be told, although,
Because I love you more than I can say,
If I could tell you I would let you know.

The winds must come from somewhere when they blow,
There must be reasons why the leaves decay;
Time will say nothing but I told you so.

Perhaps the roses really want to grow,
The vision seriously intends to stay;
If I could tell you I would let you know.

Suppose the lions all get up and go,
And all the brooks and soldiers run away;
Will Time say nothing but I told you so?
If I could tell you I would let you know.

IF, ON ACCOUNT OF THE
POLITICAL SITUATION

IF, on account of the political situation,
There are quite a number of homes without roofs, and
     men
Lying about in the countryside neither drunk nor
     asleep,

If all sailings have been cancelled till further notice,
If it's unwise now to say much in letters, and if,
Under the subnormal temperatures prevailing,
The two sexes are at present the weak and the strong,
That is not at all unusual for this time of year.
If that were all we should know how to manage. Flood,
    fire,
The desiccation of grasslands, restraint of princes,
Piracy on the high seas, physical pain and fiscal grief,
These after all are our familiar tribulations,
And we have been through them all before, many,
    many times.
As events which belong to the natural world where
The occupation of space is the real and final fact
And time turns round itself in an obedient circle,
They occur again and again but only to pass
Again and again into their formal opposites,
From sword to ploughshare, coffin to cradle, war to work,
So that, taking the bad with the good, the pattern
    composed
By the ten thousand odd things that can possibly happen
Is permanent in a general average way.

Till lately we knew of no other, and between us we
    seemed
To have what it took—the adrenal courage of the tiger,
The chameleon's discretion, the modesty of the doe,
Or the fern's devotion to spatial necessity:
To practise one's peculiar civic virtue was not
So impossible after all; to cut our losses
And bury our dead was really quite easy: That was why
We were always able to say: "We are children of God,
And our Father has never forsaken His people."

But then we were children: That was a moment ago,
Before an outrageous novelty had been introduced
Into our lives. Why were we never warned? Perhaps
    we were.

Perhaps that mysterious noise at the back of the brain
We noticed on certain occasions—sitting alone
In the waiting room of the country junction, looking
Up at the toilet window—was not indigestion
But this Horror starting already to scratch Its way in?
Just how, just when It succeeded we shall never know:
We can only say that now It is there and that nothing
We learnt before It was there is now of the slightest use,
For nothing like It has happened before. It's as if
We had left our house for five minutes to mail a letter,
And during that time the living room had changed
    places
With the room behind the mirror over the fireplace;
It's as if, waking up with a start, we discovered
Ourselves stretched out flat on the floor, watching our
    shadow
Sleepily stretching itself at the window. I mean
That the world of space where events re-occur is still
    there,
Only now it's no longer real; the real one is nowhere
Where time never moves and nothing can ever happen:
I mean that although there's a person we know all about
Still bearing our name and loving himself as before,
That person has become a fiction; our true existence
Is decided by no one and has no importance to love.

That is why we despair; that is why we would
    welcome
The nursery bogey or the winecellar ghost, why even
The violent howling of winter and war has become
Like a juke-box tune that we dare not stop. We are
    afraid
Of pain but more afraid of silence; for no nightmare
Of hostile objects could be as terrible as this Void.
This is the Abomination. This is the wrath of God.

from FOR THE TIME BEING

722

W. H. AUDEN

WELL, SO THAT IS THAT

WELL, so that is that. Now we must dismantle the tree,
Putting the decorations back into their cardboard
    boxes—
Some have got broken—and carrying them up to the
    attic.
The holly and the mistletoe must be taken down and
    burnt,
And the children got ready for school. There are
    enough
Left-overs to do, warmed-up, for the rest of the week—
Not that we have much appetite, having drunk such
    a lot,
Stayed up so late, attempted—quite unsuccessfully—
To love all of our relatives, and in general
Grossly overestimated our powers. Once again
As in previous years we have seen the actual Vision
    and failed
To do more than entertain it as an agreeable
Possibility, once again we have sent Him away,
Begging though to remain His disobedient servant,
The promising child who cannot keep His word for
    long.
The Christmas Feast is already a fading memory,
And already the mind begins to be vaguely aware
Of an unpleasant whiff of apprehension at the thought
Of Lent and Good Friday which cannot, after all, now
Be very far off. But, for the time being, here we all are,
Back in the moderate Aristotelian city
Of darning and the Eight-Fifteen, where Euclid's
    geometry
And Newton's mechanics would account for our ex-
    perience,
And the kitchen table exists because I scrub it.
It seems to have shrunk during the holidays. The streets
Are much narrower than we remembered; we had for-
    gotten

723

The office was as depressing as this. To those who have
   seen
The Child, however dimly, however incredulously,
The Time Being is, in a sense, the most trying time of
   all.
For the innocent children who whispered so excitedly
Outside the locked door where they knew the presents
   to be
Grew up when it opened. Now, recollecting that mo-
   ment
We can repress the joy, but the guilt remains conscious;
Remembering the stable where for once in our lives
Everything became a You and nothing was an It.
And craving the sensation but ignoring the cause,
We look round for something, no matter what, to in-
   hibit
Our self-reflection, and the obvious thing for that pur-
   pose
Would be some great suffering. So, once we have met
   the Son,
We are tempted ever after to pray to the Father;
"Lead us into temptation and evil for our sake."
They will come, all right, don't worry; probably in a
   form
That we do not expect, and certainly with a force
More dreadful than we can imagine. In the meantime
There are bills to be paid, machines to keep in repair,
Irregular verbs to learn, the Time Being to redeem
From insignificance. The happy morning is over,
The night of agony still to come; the time is noon:
When the Spirit must practise his scales of rejoicing
Without even a hostile audience, and the Soul endure
A silence that is neither for nor against her faith
That God's Will will be done, that, in spite of her
   prayers,
God will cheat no one, not even the world of its triumph.

from FOR THE TIME BEING

Delmore Schwartz

THE BEAUTIFUL
AMERICAN WORD, SURE

THE beautiful American word, Sure,
As I have come into a room, and touch
The lamp's button, and the light blooms with such
Certainty where the darkness loomed before,

As I care for what I do not know, and care
Knowing for little she might not have been,
And for how little she would be unseen,
The intercourse of lives miraculous and dear.

Where the light is, and each thing clear,
Separate from all others, standing in its place,
I drink the time and touch whatever's near,

And hope for day when the whole world has that face:
For what assures her present every year?
In dark accidents the mind's sufficient grace.

ALL CLOWNS ARE MASKED

ALL clowns are masked and all *personae*
Flow from choices; sad and gay, wise,
Moody and humorous are chosen faces,
And yet not so! For all are circumstances,
Given, like a tendency
To colds or like blond hair and wealth,
Or war and peace or gifts for mathematics,

Fall from the sky, rise from the ground, stick to us
In time, surround us: Socrates is mortal.

Gifts and choices! All men are masked,
And we are clowns who think to choose our faces
And we are taught in time of circumstances
And we have colds, blond hair and mathematics,
For we have gifts which interrupt our choices,
And all our choices grasp in Blind Man's Buff:
"My wife was very different, after marriage,"
"I practise law, but botany's my pleasure,"
Save postage stamps or photographs,
But save your soul! Only the past is immortal.

Decide to take a trip, read books of travel,
Go quickly! Even Socrates is mortal,
Mention the name of happiness: it is
Atlantis, Ultima Thule, or the limelight,
Cathay or Heaven. But go quickly
And remember: there are circumstances,
And he who chooses chooses what is given,
He who chooses is ignorant of Choice,
—Choose love, for love is full of children,
Full of choices, children choosing
Botany, mathematics, law and love,
So full of choices! So full of children!
And the past is immortal, the future is inexhaustible!

TIME IS THE FIRE

CALMLY we walk through this April's day,
Metropolitan poetry here and there,
In the park sit pauper and *rentier*,
The screaming children, the motor car
Fugitive about us, running away,
Between the worker and the millionaire
Number provides all distances,

It is Nineteen Thirty-Seven now,
Many great dears are taken away,
What will become of you and me
(This is the school in which we learn. . .)
Besides the photo and the memory?
(. . .that time is the fire in which we burn.)

(This is the school in which we learn. . .)
What is the self amid this blaze?
What am I now that I was then
Which I shall suffer and act again,
The theodicy I wrote in my high school days
Restored all life from infancy,
The children shouting are bright as they run
(This is the school in which they learn. . .)
Ravished entirely in their passing play!
(. . .that time is the fire in which they burn.)

Avid its rush, that reeling blaze!
Where is my father and Eleanor?
Not where are they now, dead seven years,
But what they were then?
                                        No more? No more?
From Nineteen-Fourteen to the present day,
Bert Spira and Rhoda consume, consume
Not where they are now (where are they now?)
But what they were then, both beautiful;
Each minute bursts in the burning room,
The great globe reels in the solar fire,
Spinning the trivial and unique away.
(How all things flash! How all things flare!)
What am I now that I was then?
May memory restore again and again
The smallest color of the smallest day:
Time is the school in which we learn,
Time is the fire in which we burn.

DO THEY WHISPER
BEHIND MY BACK?

Do they whisper behind my back? Do they speak
Of my clumsiness? Do they laugh at me,
Mimicking my gestures, retailing my shame?
I'll whirl about, denounce them, saying
That they are shameless, they are treacherous,
No more my friends, nor will I once again
Never, amid a thousand meetings in the street,
Recognize their faces, take their hands,
Not for our common love or old times' sake:
They whispered behind my back, they mimicked me.

I know the reason why, I too have done this,
Cruel for wit's sake, behind my dear friend's back,
And to amuse betrayed his private love,
His nervous shame, her habit, and their weaknesses;
I have mimicked them, I have been treacherous,
For wit's sake, to amuse, because their being weighed
Too grossly for a time, to be superior,
To flatter the listeners by this, the intimate,
Betraying the intimate, but for the intimate,
To free myself of friendship's necessity,
Fearing from time to time that they would hear,
Denounce me and reject me, say once for all
That they would never meet me, take my hands,
Speaking for old times' sake and our common love.

What an unheard-of thing it is, in fine,
To love another and equally be loved!
What sadness and what joy! How cruel it is
That pride and wit distort the heart of man,
How vain, how sad, what cruelty, what need,
For this is true and sad, that I need them
And they need me. What can we do? We need
Each other's clumsiness, each other's wit,
Each other's company and our own pride. I need

My face unshamed, I need my wit, I cannot
Denounce them once for all, they cannot
Turn away. We know our clumsiness,
Our weakness, our necessities, we cannot
Forget our pride, our faces, our common love.

A DOG NAMED EGO

A DOG named Ego, the snowflakes as kisses
Fluttered, ran, came with me in December,
Snuffing the chill air, changing, and halting,
There where I walked toward seven o'clock,
Sniffed at some interests hidden and open,
Whirled, descending, and stood still, attentive,
Seeking their peace, the stranger, unknown,
With me, near me, kissed me, touched my wound,
My simple face, obsessed and pleasure bound.

"Not free, no liberty, rock that you carry,"
So spoke Ego in his cracked and harsh voice,
While snowflakes kissed me and satisfied minutes,
Falling from some place half believed and unknown,
"You will not be free, nor ever alone,"
So spoke Ego, "Mine is the kingdom,
Dynasty's bone: you will not be free,
Go, choose, run, you will not be alone."

"Come, come, come," sang the whirling snowflakes,
Evading the dog who barked at their smallness,
"Come!" sang the snowflakes, "Come here! and here!"
How soon at the sidewalk, melted, and done,
One kissed me, two kissed me! So many died!
While Ego barked at them, swallowed their touch,
Ran this way! And that way! While they slipped to
    the ground,
Leading him further and farther away,
While night collapsed amid the falling,
And left me no recourse, far from my home,
And left me no recourse, far from my home.

THE HEAVY BEAR

"the witness of the body"—WHITEHEAD

THE heavy bear who goes with me,
A manifold honey to smear his face,
Clumsy and lumbering here and there,
The central ton of every place,
The hungry beating brutish one
In love with candy, anger, and sleep,
Crazy factotum, dishevelling all,
Climbs the building, kicks the football,
Boxes his brother in the hate-ridden city.

Breathing at my side, that heavy animal,
That heavy bear who sleeps with me,
Howls in his sleep for a world of sugar,
A sweetness intimate as the water's clasp,
Howls in his sleep because the tight-rope
Trembles and shows the darkness beneath.
—The strutting show-off is terrified,
Dressed in his dress-suit, bulging his pants,
Trembles to think that his quivering meat
Must finally wince to nothing at all.

That inescapable animal walks with me,
Has followed me since the black womb held,
Moves where I move, distorting my gesture,
A caricature, a swollen shadow,
A stupid clown of the spirit's motive,
Perplexes and affronts with his own darkness,
The secret life of belly and bone,
Opaque, too near, my private, yet unknown,
Stretches to embrace the very dear
With whom I would walk without him near,
Touches her grossly, although a word
Would bare my heart and make me clear,
Stumbles, flounders, and strives to be fed

Dragging me with him in his mouthing care,
Amid the hundred million of his kind,
The scrimmage of appetite everywhere.

IN THE NAKED BED,
IN PLATO'S CAVE

In the naked bed, in Plato's cave,
Reflected headlights slowly slid the wall,
Carpenters hammered under the shaded window,
Wind troubled the window curtains all night long,
A fleet of trucks strained uphill, grinding,
Their freights covered, as usual.
The ceiling lightened again, the slanting diagram
Slid slowly forth.
     Hearing the milkman's chop,
His striving up the stair, the bottle's chink,
I rose from bed, lit a cigarette,
And walked to the window. The stony street
Displayed the stillness in which buildings stand,
The street-lamp's vigil and the horse's patience.
The winter sky's pure capital
Turned me back to bed with exhausted eyes.

Strangeness grew in the motionless air. The loose
Film grayed. Shaking wagons, hooves' waterfalls,
Sounded far off, increasing, louder and nearer.
A car coughed, starting. Morning, softly
Melting the air, lifted the half-covered chair
From underseas, kindled the looking-glass,
Distinguished the dresses and the white wall.
The bird called tentatively, whistled, called,
Bubbled and whistled, so! Perplexed, still wet
With sleep, affectionate, hungry and cold. So, so,
O son of man, the ignorant night, the travail
Of early morning, the mystery of beginning
Again and again,
     while History is unforgiven.

FOR THE ONE WHO WOULD TAKE MAN'S LIFE IN HIS HANDS

Tiger Christ unsheathed his sword,
Threw it down, became a lamb.
Swift spat upon the species, but
Took two women to his heart.
Samson who was strong as death
Paid his strength to kiss a slut.
Othello that stiff warrior
Was broken by a woman's heart.
Troy burned for a sea-tax, also for
Possession of a charming whore.
What do all examples show?
What must the finished murderer know?

You cannot sit on bayonets,
Nor can you eat among the dead.
When all are killed, you are alone,
A vacuum comes where hate has fed.
Murder's fruit is silent stone,
The gun increases poverty.
With what do these examples shine?
The soldier turned to girls and wine.
Love is the tact of every good,
The only warmth, the only peace.

"What have I said?" asked Socrates,
"Affirmed extremes, cried yes and no,
Taken all parts, denied myself,
Praised the caress, extolled the blow,
Soldier and lover quite deranged
Until their motions are exchanged.
—What do all examples show?
What can any actor know?
The contradiction in every act,
The infinite task of the human heart."

732

FATHER AND SON

"From a certain point onward there is no longer any turning back. That is the point that must be reached."
—FRANZ KAFKA

Father:
On these occasions, the feelings surprise,
Spontaneous as rain, and they compel
Explicitness, embarrassed eyes—

Son:
Father, you're not Polonius, you're reticent,
But sure. I can already tell
The unction and falsetto of the sentiment
Which gratifies the facile mouth, but springs
From no felt, had, and wholly known things.

Father:
You must let me tell you what you fear
When you wake up from sleep, still drunk with sleep:
You are afraid of time and its slow drip,
Like melting ice, like smoke upon the air
In February's glittering sunny day.
Your guilt is nameless, because its name is time,
Because its name is death. But you can stop
Time as it dribbles from you, drop by drop.

Son:
But I thought time was full of promises,
Even as now, the emotion of going away—

Father:
That is the first of all its menaces,
The lure of a future different from today;
All of us always are turning away
To the cinema and Asia. All of us go
To one indeterminate nothing.

Son:

Must it be so?
I question the sentiment you give to me,
As premature, not to be given, learned alone
When experience shrinks upon the chilling bone.
I would be sudden now and rash in joy,
As if I lived forever, the future my toy.
Time is a dancing fire at twenty-one,
Singing and shouting and drinking to the sun,
Powerful at the wheel of a motor-car,
Not thinking of death which is foreign and far.

Father:

If time flowed from your will and were a feast
I would be wrong to question your zest.
But each age betrays the same weak shape.
Each moment is dying. You will try to escape
From melting time and your dissipating soul
By hiding your head in a warm and dark hole.
See the evasions which so many don,
To flee the guilt of time they become one,
That is, the one number among masses,
The one anonymous in the audience,
The one expressionless in the subway,
In the subway evening among so many faces,
The one who reads the daily newspaper,
Separate from actor and act, a member
Of public opinion, never involved.
Integrated in the revery of a fine cigar,
Fleeing to childhood at the symphony concert,
Buying sleep at the drugstore, grandeur
At the band concert, Hawaii
On the screen, and everywhere a specious splendor:
One, when he is sad, has something to eat,
An ice cream soda, a toasted sandwich,
Or has his teeth fixed, but can always retreat
From the actual pain, and dream of the rich.
This is what one does, what one becomes

Because one is afraid to be alone,
Each with his own death in the lonely room.
But there is a stay. You can stop
Time as it dribbles from you, drop by drop.

Son:

Now I am afraid. What is there to be known?

Father:

Guilt, guilt of time, nameless guilt.
Grasp firmly your fear, thus grasping your self,
Your actual will. Stand in mastery,
Keeping time in you, its terrifying mystery.
Face yourself, constantly go back
To what you were, your own history.
You are always in debt. Do not forget
The dream postponed which would not quickly get
Pleasure immediate as drink, but takes
The travail of building, patience with means.
See the wart on your face and on your friend's face,
On your friend's face and indeed on your own face.
The loveliest woman sweats, the animal stains
The ideal which is with us like the sky. . . .

Son:

Because of that, some laugh, and others cry.

Father:

Do not look past and turn away your face.
You cannot depart and take another name,
Nor go to sleep with lies. Always the same,
Always the same self from the ashes of sleep
Returns with its memories, always, always,
The phoenix with eight hundred thousand memories!

Son:

What must I do that is most difficult?

Father:
You must meet your death face to face,
You must, like one in an old play,
Decide, once for all, your heart's place.
Love, power, and fame stand on an absolute
Under the formless night and the brilliant day,
The searching violin, the piercing flute.
Absolute! Venus and Caesar fade at that edge,
Hanging from the fiftieth story ledge,
Or diminished in bed when the nurse presses
Her sickening unguents and her cold compresses.
When the news is certain, surpassing fear,
You touch the wound, the priceless, the most dear.
There in death's shadow, you comprehend
The irreducible wish, world without end.

Son:
I begin to understand the reason for evasion,
I cannot partake of your difficult vision.

Father:
Begin to understand the first decision.
Hamlet is the example; only dying
Did he take up his manhood, the dead's burden,
Done with evasion, done with sighing,
Done with revery.
                    Decide that you are dying
Because time is in you, ineluctable
As shadow, named by no syllable.
Act in that shadow, as if death were now:
Your own self acts then, then you know.

Son:
My father has taught me to be serious.

Father:
Be guilty of yourself in the full looking-glass.

III

Poetry

of

The Forties

Editorial Note

This section, although called "The Forties", is to be taken, not as the complete story of the decade, but as a collection supplementary to the work of the well-established poets who also produced vital poetry during the forties but whose poems are included in Part II, the main section. Most of the work represented in the next hundred pages is that of younger or less well known poets and must be considered as interlocking with other important new poems and discoveries of the period. E.g., Wallace Stevens, Robert Frost, Robinson Jeffers, Marianne Moore, John Peale Bishop, E. E. Cummings, Allen Tate, Richard Eberhart and W. H. Auden (now a U. S. citizen, all of whose work used here was first published in America after 1939) published important work in the forties or at the turn of the decade. Then, too, poets of past periods have been discovered, and their books issued, only recently: Edward Taylor, a fine Colonial poet, and Samuel Greenberg, who wrote during the days of the first World War and was, perhaps, the most important of Hart Crane's influences. Hundreds of new poems written by Emily Dickinson before 1886 were also published for the first time in 1945.

It must be remembered that the war years belong in this decade and that poems arising against the emotional background of the war were written by poets of all ages, in and out of uniform.

In order to help the student or lover of poetry to understand the ferment, the extent and achievement of this remarkable decade, I have brought together the work of the younger poets in this supplement and, in the *Index of Authors and Titles* (pages 861 to 876), I have marked with an asterisk (*) each of the titles of those poems from the main section which should be considered, for one reason or another, part of the panorama of the forties.

O. W.

Joseph Bennett

COMPLAINT

Loss falls from the air as the tables turn
And the stage swings; and shepherds fasting their flocks
Set forth in the hills with the sun
Crossing the meadows and flowers.

Loss falls from the air, and as the tables turn,
The stage swings, and shepherds fast their flocks.
Flocks flowering the valleys
Abstain in gracious mourning.

Loss falls from the air, but the purity of flocks
Does not change with the tables; the sheep are white.
The stage swings the shepherds
Abounding in gracious morning.

Love, flocks fall from the air, in purity and white,
And tables turn with the stages; but shepherds die.
The sheep survive as chastened
In their flowery depths.

But shepherds die and love falls with loss,
So long was the day we led our fasting sheep.
Alas for flowers crushed
And taken in our path.

Loss falls from the air as shepherds fall,
And sheep all graciously gaze by.
Love, let us search the flowers
As the earth turns and swings.

739

The valleys turn and the sun diffuses; the meadows
And the hills revolve; so love declines
While the musing sheep proceed
Fasting and mourning in sleep.

TO ELIZA, DUCHESS OF DORSET

IN THE negro gardens negro birds
Plummet in the shadows, falling thirds.
Dorset in sable plumage comes.
A hawk! A raven in his tediums.

Daughter to that good Earl, once President
Of England's Council, and her Parliament,
Duchess, if that falling shadow strikes
And strikes no more, as Dorset softly likes,

And in your heart the spike its purple draws,
And on your coral neck the marble claws—
O Duchess feel the negro soil beneath
Your crushed mouth and your splintered teeth.

Eliza strangling on the lawn at Knole,
The flowers sinking toward the twilit Pole,
And walking, calling, Dorset now distends;
Dorset cock and cockatoo; and raven ends.

QUATRINA

THE mountaineer is working with his Bible
And all Kentucky echoes to his shotgun.
O mountains where our rivers rise and glisten,
Consider you the primitive with buckshot.
740

Forthwith the mountaineer he made him buckshot
And clambered where his liquors boil and glisten.
He struck at all Kentucky with his Bible
And clamorous he prophesied with shotgun.

Above the timberline, unquestioned shotgun
Could rule the mountaintops, the bald, with Bible.
Explicitly he cast the tiny buckshot
And poured his metal where the pinetops glisten.

The copperheads that on the mountain glisten
Lanced their tongues and coiled about his buckshot.
His sermon rumbled like the final shotgun
Gabriel fired to close the windy Bible.

Both wrathful Bible and the fuming shotgun
Saw the serpent glisten in their buckshot.

 John Berryman

PARTING AS DESCENT

THE sun rushed up the sky; the taxi flew.
There was a kind of fever on the clock
That morning. We arrived at Waterloo
With time to spare and couldn't find my track.

The bitter coffee in a small café
Gave us our conversation. When the train
Began to move I saw you turn away
And vanish, and the vessels in my brain

Burst, the train roared, the other travellers
In flames leapt, burning on the tilted air
Che si cruccia, I heard the devils curse
And shriek with joy in that place beyond prayer.

741

CONVERSATION

WHETHER the moorings are invisible
Or gone, we said we could not tell.
But argument held one thing sure
Which none of us that night could well endure:
The ship is locked with fog, no man aboard
Can see what he is moving toward,
There's little food, less love, no sleep,
The sea is dark and we are told it's deep.

Where is an officer who knows this coast?
If all such men long since have faced
Downward, one summon. Who knows how,
With what fidelity his voice heard now
Could shout directions from the ocean's floor?
Traditional characters no more
Their learnéd simple parts rehearse
But bed them down at last from the time's curse.

A broken log fell out upon the hearth,
The flaming harbinger come forth
Of holocausts that night and day
Shrivel from the mind its sovereignty.
We watched the embers cool; those embers brought
To one man there the failing thought
Of cities stripped of knowledge, men,
Our continent a wilderness again.

These are conclusions of the night, we said;
And drank, and were not satisfied.
The fire died down, smoke in the air
Took the alarming postures of our fear:
The overhead horror, in the padded room
The man who cannot tell his name,
The guns and enemies that face
Into this delicate and dangerous place.

WINTER LANDSCAPE

THE three men coming down the winter hill
In brown, with tall poles and a pack of hounds
At heel, through the arrangement of the trees,
Past the five figures at the burning straw,
Returning cold and silent to their town,

Returning to the drifted snow, the rink
Lively with children, to the older men,
The long companions they can never reach,
The blue light, men with ladders, by the church
The sledge and shadow in the twilit street,

Are not aware that in the sandy time
To come, the evil waste of history
Outstretched, they will be seen upon the brow
Of that same hill: when all their company
Will have been irrecoverably lost,

These men, this particular three in brown
Witnessed by birds will keep the scene and say
By their configuration with the trees,
The small bridge, the red houses and the fire,
What place, what time, what morning occasion

Sent them into the wood, a pack of hounds
At heel and the tall poles upon their shoulders,
Thence to return as now we see them and
Ankle-deep in snow down the winter hill
Descend while three birds watch and the fourth flies.

Elizabeth Bishop

A MIRACLE FOR BREAKFAST

AT six o'clock we were waiting for coffee,
waiting for coffee and the charitable crumb
that was going to be served from a certain balcony,
—like kings of old, or like a miracle.
It was still dark. One foot of the sun
steadied itself on a long ripple in the river.

The first ferry of the day had just crossed the river.
It was so cold we hoped that the coffee
would be very hot, seeing that the sun
was not going to warm us; and that the crumb
would be a loaf each, buttered, by a miracle.
At seven a man stepped out on the balcony.

He stood for a minute alone on the balcony
looking over our heads toward the river.
A servant handed him the makings of a miracle,
consisting of one lone cup of coffee
and one roll, which he proceeded to crumb,
his head, so to speak, in the clouds—along with the sun.

Was the man crazy? What under the sun
was he trying to do, up there on his balcony!
Each man received one rather hard crumb,
which some flicked scornfully into the river,
and, in a cup, one drop of the coffee.
Some of us stood around, waiting for the miracle.

I can tell what I saw next; it was not a miracle.
A beautiful villa stood in the sun
and from its doors came the smell of hot coffee.

744

In front, a baroque white plaster balcony
added by birds, who nest along the river,
—I saw it with one eye close to the crumb—

and galleries and marble chambers. My crumb
my mansion, made for me a miracle,
through ages, by insects, birds, and the river
working the stone. Every day, in the sun,
at breakfast time I sit on my balcony
with my feet up, and drink gallons of coffee.

We licked up the crumb and swallowed the coffee.
A window across the river caught the sun
as if the miracle were working, on the wrong balcony.

THE UNBELIEVER

He sleeps on the top of a mast.—BUNYAN

HE sleeps on the top of a mast
with his eyes fast closed.
The sails fall away below him
like the sheets of his bed,
leaving out in the air of the night the sleeper's head.

Asleep he was transported there,
asleep he curled
in a gilded ball on the mast's top,
or climbed inside
a gilded bird, or blindly seated himself astride.

"I am founded on marble pillars,"
said a cloud. "I never move.
See the pillars there in the sea?"
Secure in introspection
he peers at the watery pillars of his reflection.

A gull had wings under his
and remarked that the air

745

was "like marble." He said: "Up here
I tower through the sky
for the marble wings on my tower-top fly."

But he sleeps on the top of his mast
with his eyes closed tight.
The gull inquired into his dream,
which was, "I must not fall.
The spangled sea below wants me to fall.
It is hard as diamonds; it wants to destroy us all."

THE MAN-MOTH *

HERE, above,
cracks in the buildings are filled with battered moonlight.
The whole shadow of Man is only as big as his hat.
It lies at his feet like a circle for a doll to stand on,
and he makes an inverted pin, the point magnetized to
    the moon.
He does not see the moon; he observes only her vast
    properties,
feeling the queer light on his hands, neither warm nor
    cold,
of a temperature impossible to record in thermometers.

But when the Man-Moth
pays his rare, although occasional, visits to the surface,
the moon looks rather different to him. He emerges
from an opening under the edge of one of the sidewalks
and nervously begins to scale the faces of buildings.
He thinks the moon is a small hole at the top of the sky,
proving the sky quite useless for protection.
He trembles, but must investigate as high as he can climb.

Up the façades,
his shadow dragging like a photographer's cloth behind
    him,

* Newspaper misprint for "mammoth."

746

he climbs fearfully, thinking that this time he will manage
to push his small head through that round clean opening
and be forced through, as from a tube, in black scrolls on
the light.
(Man, standing below him, has no such illusions.)
But what the Man-Moth fears most he must do, although
he fails, of course, and falls back scared but quite unhurt.

Then he returns
to the pale subways of cement he calls his home. He flits,
he flutters, and cannot get aboard the silent trains
fast enough to suit him. The doors close swiftly.
The Man-Moth always seats himself facing the wrong
way
and the train starts at once at its full, terrible speed,
without a shift in gears or a gradation of any sort.
He cannot tell the rate at which he travels backwards.

Each night he must
be carried through artificial tunnels and dream recurrent
dreams.
Just as the ties recur beneath his train, these underlie
his rushing brain. He does not dare look out the window,
for the third rail, the unbroken draught of poison,
runs there beside him. He regards it as disease
he has inherited susceptibility to. He has to keep
his hands in pockets, as others must wear mufflers.

If you catch him,
hold up a flashlight to his eye. It's all dark pupil,
an entire night itself, whose haired horizon tightens
as he stares back, and closes up the eye. Then from the
lids
one tear, his only possession, like the bee's sting, slips.
Slyly he palms it, and if you're not paying attention
he'll swallow it. However, if you watch, he'll hand it over,
cool as from underground springs and pure enough to
drink.

747

CIRQUE D'HIVER

ACROSS the floor flits the mechanical toy,
fit for a king of several centuries back.
A little circus horse with real white hair.
His eyes are glossy black.
He bears a little dancer on his back.

She stands upon her toes and turns and turns.
A slanting spray of artificial roses
is stitched across her skirt and tinsel bodice.
Above her head she poses
another spray of artificial roses.

His mane and tail are straight from Chirico.
He has a formal, melancholy soul.
He feels her pink toes dangle toward his back
along the little pole
that pierces both her body and her soul

and goes through his, and reappears below,
under his belly, as a big tin key.
He canters three steps, then he makes a bow,
canters again, bows on one knee,
canters, then clicks and stops, and looks at me.

The dancer, by this time, has turned her back.
He is the more intelligent by far.
Facing each other rather desperately—
his eye is like a star—
we stare and say, 'Well, we have come this far.'

THE MONUMENT

Now can you see the monument? It is of wood
built somewhat like a box. No. Built
like several boxes in descending sizes
one above the other.

748

Each is turned half-way round so that
its corners point toward the sides
of the one below and the angles alternate.
Then on the topmost cube is set
a sort of fleur-de-lys of weathered wood,
long petals of board, pierced with odd holes,
four-sided, stiff, ecclesiastical.
From it four thin, warped poles spring out,
(slanted like fishing-poles or flag-poles)
and from them jig-saw work hangs down,
four lines of vaguely whittled ornament
over the edges of the boxes
to the ground.
The monument is one-third set against
a sea; two-thirds against a sky.
The view is geared
(that is, the view's perspective)
so low there is no 'far away,'
and we are far away within the view.
A sea of narrow, horizontal boards
lies out behind our lonely monument,
its long grains alternating right and left
like floor-boards—spotted, swarming-still,
and motionless. A sky runs parallel,
and it is palings, coarser than the sea's:
splintery sunlight and long-fibred clouds.
'Why does that strange sea make no sound?
Is it because we're far away?
Where are we? Are we in Asia Minor,
or in Mongolia?'
　　　　　　　　An ancient promontory,
an ancient principality whose artist-prince
might have wanted to build a monument
to mark a tomb or boundary, or make
a melancholy or romantic scene of it . . .
'But that queer sea looks made of wood,
half-shining, like a driftwood sea.
And the sky looks wooden, grained with cloud.

It's like a stage-set; it is all so flat!
Those clouds are full of glistening splinters!
What is that?'
                    It is the monument.
'It's piled-up boxes,
outlined with shoddy fret-work, half-fallen off,
cracked and unpainted. It looks old.'
—The strong sunlight, the wind from the sea,
all the conditions of its existence,
may have flaked off the paint, if ever it was painted,
and made it homelier than it was.
'Why did you bring me here to see it?
A temple of crates in cramped and crated scenery,
what can it prove?
I am tired of breathing this eroded air,
this dryness in which the monument is cracking.'

It is an artifact
of wood. Wood holds together better
than sea or cloud or sand could by itself,
much better than real sea or sand or cloud.
It chose that way to grow and not to move.
The monument's an object, yet those decorations,
carelessly nailed, looking like nothing at all,
give it away as having life, and wishing;
wanting to be a monument, to cherish something.
The crudest scroll-work says 'commemorate,'
while once each day the light goes around it
like a prowling animal,
or the rain falls on it, or the wind blows into it.
It may be solid, may be hollow.
The bones of the artist-prince may be inside
or far away on even dryer soil.
But roughly but adequately it can shelter
what is within (which after all
cannot have been intended to be seen).
It is the beginning of a painting,
a piece of sculpture, or poem, or monument,
and all of wood. Watch it closely.

R. P. Blackmur

BEFORE SENTENCE IS PASSED

I

I HAVE this to say, if I can say it.
Things are undone, your Honour. We are the same.
You also, Gentlemen: bench, box, and bar—
the same, with different vantages. This is mine.
—Here are my hands upon the rail, my voice
fretting your ears. The wood is sticky, my words
the tight quality of the air you breathe,
the air a cauling skin upon us. All this
that is dismay in you, in me disorder,
develops, envelops, this browning twilight air,
this room of screams and patience and rejoicing,
and hides without day the uncreated face.

(But look, Gentlemen, so good, so true:
These two fat bailiffs will catch me if I fall;
the Court keeps order; and you yourselves
observe decorum past your understanding.
Consider, the will you keep, in me
is voluntary, habit a conscious act.)

You will agree, and well within your time,
that nothing I can say here is digression,
and if you do not think so now, Wait;
you have not felt the focus closing, firming
on your vantage, not quite heard safety stop.
You don't even know, right now, if your watch has
    stopped.
The time will not be wasted if you look,

751

even if you look also at the big clock over your heads.
—My digressions are like that: inward occupations.

To be in a new place and tell the old story,
to fumble in the voice and say, "It is not so,
this rubbish of insurrection, treason, thought,
I stand here charged with," that would perjure me;
—oh, not in this Court nor in your Honour's Law!
My innocence, like my guilt, is radical,
and strikes a taproot down you cannot sever.
There is a face within me that coheres.

It is not easy to portray that face,
to prefigure what is long past, to show
the normal as a monster, to arrest God
visibly in his invisible escape;
to exhibit love as uncreated fear.

But what is hidden without looking may yet
transpire without being noticed. You shall see:
as you saw, just now, your watches were not right.

II

Asserted righteousness is avowed guilt,
Gentlemen; the mercy within your bowels
attests it, and the cold in the whites of your eyes.
Verdict-cold. This is an interdicted time.
Conviction—yours as well as mine—and yours,
your Honour, too, becomes the formal cry
we order up to cover the blank moment
saying, It is the Law. And if you ask—
and may it please your Honour, *you* should ask,
(for goodness and truth look not askance but boredom)--
Who interdicted what? I answer so:

It is my people, all my race and time,
the stuff I harbour, salvage that I am,
752

that gradually have lost in tension, lost,
that is, the keeping sod on the hill farms
(for we are hills at heart, whence cometh help),
and with the loss found various perfidy
of white hope and party-coloured withdrawals.
We have the forced, exhausting, unreplenishing crop.
No more. Ripeness is lost: which is tension itself.
Even the apple has lost its tartness, and
the potato cooks flat with no taste of death:
good chiefly for alcohol, intoxication.
But I do not wish to exaggerate the thunderclap
who did not feel the lightning strike. It is simple:
Erosion of good and evil, that's the phrase;
no tension to hold them together, no tragic need,
only the raging and indifferent perfidies
of opinionated unconvicted men.
Thus we clutch for untenable positions.

Your Honour knows just what I mean, and you,
my Gentlemen, are no more puzzled than I.
I am as dizzy with plain facts as you are:
the internecine battle of the frantic dead.
I too am distracted from this lower buzz.
Bats raid in the vault, I know, and gnats fly.
It is the evening; and in the actual world
which has neither faith nor perfidy nor hope,
it is the hour when eyes and ears take count
of vestiges and intimations, and
the gyrations in which these are merged and grow.
It is the sound through the open windows, high up.
—I need not remind you that we do not live
much in the actual world;
                              and hence, Gentlemen,
the sensation of irreducible distress, never death.
Take care, take care, you do not fly out the window.
The bats do, gnats do not—they settle,
sludge next morning in the residue of oil
(if you remember one generation back),

their distress always unequal in distribution.
It makes little difference that what is irrelevant
to gnats may be the next actuality for us:
the mass in darkness, the falling, the wiping up:
the deceit of fire seen only as light
or the worse fraud of light put up as fire.
You choose the phrase; I am the prisoner who sees.

But let us avoid that perspective. (I see a fly
rummaging the discoloured crease of that policeman's
    collar!)
This has become a very quiet place.
One feels a dislocation. One tries at last
to say what only the heart says, do only
what the buds do: flower by conviction:
the inward mastery of the outward act.

Is it a gulf, Gentlemen, this place
of falling off? Look, it is cloaca.
In either case the end-all and inter-regnum
where every issue joins and none cry out.

But all this is confusing, flies buzzing.
(Confusion: have you seen confusion when safety stops—
the miring of draft horses in the salt marsh
below the turnips?) One lets go only
what one has not held, the roughage of the mind.
One holds
only that which was already reserved,
the vestige brought out of turbulence, order
surviving only by digesting disorder:
the gravel in each mouthful that we eat.

Such fustian! unless imagination supervene
with items, like your face looking at mine,
your minds employing the words I employ,
your situation seen as the under half of mine:
my situation the guilty reward of yours.
754

III

It is like houses burning, here in this room,
right now, or soon, with all these people, my people,
swaying as I sway, and each thinking slowly
of his own house, not far off, afire by instinct.
The flues are dirty or the wiring faulty.
We think of little things,—of drafts and fuses,
of faces in the cut-off windows,—as large:
the unfinished work, the unattended wife—
as large as that! That is our history:
a holocaust of inattention, just
put out. It is in this sense that I burn.
It is your inattention set the fire
—oh not your present glare, your aching look
beyond, behind, the look to get away
of minds made up, and lost, while unawares—
I mean your inattention to yourselves,
until you saw me looking at you with both
your eyes and mine.
I doubt not you saw red—the beginning
sin of safety, the lower rim of blindness:
not only not to look, which may be forgiven,
but to act without looking, which is perfidy:
the final ignominy of giving in.

So you have come here, Gentlemen. So I.
And so your Honour. And all these people came,
a crowd sprung out of the cobbles, because of us:
the ever-springing hope of new guilt.
By this time, I think there is not one of you
feels quite at home. The first strangeness gone,
the new not wholly come. Even my bailiffs
grow tired with waiting: their eyes begin to creep.
There is disorder, like heavy breathing in the next room,
like people making way when no one comes.
The rest is not silence, except for me.
You will see shortly, all of you will see:
It is my right: I stand here in your stead.

John Malcolm Brinnin

VIEWS OF THE
FAVORITE COLLEGES

APPROACHING by the gate, (Class of '79,
All dead) the unimpressed new scholars find
Halls of archaic brick and, if it is April,
Three dazzling magnolias behind bars, like lions.

Unsettling winds among the pillars of wisdom
Assure them of harmonious extremes,
However academic. The bells, in key,
Covered with singing birds, ring on the hour.

Towering, but without aspiration, the campanile
Is known to sway an inch in a high wind;
But that, like the statue's changeable complexion,
Is natural. To find the unnatural,

Gradually absorb the industry
Of ten o'clock: the embryo pig slit through
With the proper instruments by embryos;
And Sophocles cut, for speed, with a blue pencil.

Prehensile sophomores in the tree of learning
Stare at the exiled blossoming trees, vaguely puzzled;
The lecturer, especially if bearded,
Enhances those druidical undertones.

What is the terminus of books? sing the birds.
Tell us about Sophocles! cry the trees.
And a crazy child on roller-skates skates through
The campus like a one-man thunderstorm.

John Malcolm Brinnin

EVERY EARTHLY CREATURE

The shifty limpet on his rocky shore
Contrives a conch to make life possible,
And the unbelievable giraffe achieves
A dainty salad from the lissom tree;
Pretending he is flora in the pond,
A silly fish will emulate a frond
To trick the appetite that savors him;
A rabbit in the snow will do the same.

Like tinted views from a dismantled fair,
These illustrations fail, being outworn;
Who would erect a summerhouse or myth
To shade him from the elements of love
Is naked of resource; since love like fate,
Omnipotent and unregenerate,
Keeps calendars that are a joke of time,
The newest grief retells the oldest theme.

Since war, the matter of a generation,
Blunts as it must the savior and the fool,
Fathers and sons in terror worlds apart
Communicate with pity and bare signs;
The accurate bombs that scatter sanity,
The child of Guernica who cannot see
That innocence is death, acquaints me now;
I have learned armor I would disavow.

What grace survives the city's glass and stone,
What facet points the cosmopolitan?
To eke a diamond from its mineral floor
Earth rakes its faculty for quake and tide;
Yet in the city's blaze the millions go
From crib to crypt, nor any gem to show.
Ah, there the heart of man knows less itself
Than the least pink shell upon a watery shelf.

Like feathers on a swan, indifference coats
The reptile remnant of our primacy;
Debauched of tongue in time's slow sabotage,
Both tragedy and outrage come to ash;
Then is the heart adaptable to death.
And creatures who employ the earth, and breathe
The vivid air, ascend, superior;
Who comes to his instruction, stays to fear.

The sun of Genesis is shining still,
Though God is shifted to his place in time;
May evil, here, pace like the captured leopard
Where the good contends dynastically with good;
May earth in its success provide for all
Who lack the logic of the sorry snail,
Who die without a candle, or remain
To citizen the natural state of man.

THE WIND IS ILL

ALL's ill and will be so
Until what will not wed is brought to bed
Charged with a savior's brief
Of coupling conscience with black flesh and blood;
Until the arch supports its crushing roof
And eggs in nests of snow
Tame the long undertow
With clattering allelulias from the shell
All's well so charily
The tongues of iron bells will fail to tell
A wiser homily than verily,
Say lack, say touch and go.

All hail wind-cocks that shift
The livelong architecture of hot sand

From leaf-pocked flesh to stone;
Where star-shaped seeds and seed-shaped stars are
    wound
Around the pillars strangled by a vine,
East comes soft, west comes swift
Until of all that's left
The lights of time patrol, yet cannot tell
All ails so bitterly
The marathon bird is buried where it fell,
And banished utterly
The little dog that laughed.

All hell pursues the pair
Who first touched fruits of flesh to find them sweet
And sadly separate;
The hunt is hot and what is chaste is caught,
Stripped of its leaf and tangled in a sheet
While the bored Glories sit
Before and after it,
Clocking the chores of ecstasy untouched.
Ah, well, the wind is ill
And if such sails as loom are seldom beached,
Farewell's the most of hail,
Here, there, and everywhere.

FÊTES, FATES

THEY come with, ah, fell footfall,
The merry wrist, thigh, lip and all their creatures,
Guests of my board and bed,
Companions of intolerable pleasure,
Self-sainted tongue, taut ankle, swiveled head
Who by blood's stream and vessel
Make picnic of my will,
Eating its music with an insect measure,
Unravelling its laws

759

Piecemeal until, in the disgrace of nature,
Whim is my wantonness
And wit's my jack-of-all.

Their host and cage long since,
I am death's head about them where they take
The welcome of my house,
Yet cannot be blindstruck, nor turn my back
When all my flying fragments kiss and toss
Sense to its blunted sense,
Love on its dear love's clowns.
To mend me, mind me, bind me where I break—
Heart's blood, mind's apse of light—
Is all my will; all, all, my lack:
Those meshings make my fate,
Those hungers call my dance.

Goodnight, when the door swings
And the great lock's shuttle tooth comes down
On darkness and hail fellow,
Goodnight, my smile, insatiate eye, bald frown.
Goodnight. In colder carnivals we'll follow
Our one pleasaunce among
A quietude, ere long,
That will our disparateness so bundle down
In earthen intimacy,
My ways and will and yours will move as one
When guest by host shall lie
Lengthwise, and right by wrong.

Gene Derwood

IN THE PROSCENIUM

THE night, too long illumined, comes a stranger
Driving to roof this audience hard-weathered
Through the play of rage and bitter luck of danger.
Born to these uniform seats, they claim
No hunter's pleasure, the historic name.

Long foundered is our prow that feathered
The warm archaic wave.

The limelight warns, the need to worship waits
A serious humour, the laud-lifted clown.
The lights are fluorescent,
Pale, pale and cold, ice flickering incessant
As at Asgärd's fall, were north gods' twilight
Ceaselessly from no star.
The nerveless curtain, like dead water, parts.
Increasing thousands raise their long slow stare
To the pacified shroud, our silver screen of fêtes.

No choral song arises, no drama starts.
This pantomime, like beauty, only lies
In the entrancèd eyes.
Our mask of shadow comes, there pantaloon
How massive stands, anabasis of stone
Toward the prickling cells: the final form of Gilles.
Quick with electric chill
All profiles right and left unending freeze
Not as at death's pole or Gorgon's locks,
But tight to one grounded wire, in paralysis.

761

Nothing will happen but fear's thrill on the nerve
Which makes the heart a nave.

If this were but enchantment or a dream
Even of solstice sacrifice, a rite
Of Druids moving with dark seasonal pace
Barefoot beneath Stonehenge's antique weight,
Endurance might enoble the tranced face
Or quell emotion with a natural light.

But here projection worse than mirror's spell
Our clown's oiled paradox
Drips from his skull and sockets' peacock pride.
The last cry for justice dies.
The sterile form of megalomaniac woe
Is malice; violence at recurrent speed
Is death's boredom motionless, thus is hell
Gone vacant, and so mocks.
The fawn has horned the doe.

The old, below their naked eyeballs' trance,
Recall Pierrot, the dance,
The silken lips, the fluttering love whose lease
Was years, fountains of smiles, the tears' duet
Before the risk was hate, the vines' empurpled lace.
The young lack memory. They fiercely throw
From the blank iris gun-glances for Gilles,
At Gilles, whose mask has the strength they make grow.

Innocent are their eyes, as pure as cruel,
Innocent of compassion, innocent as rue.
For the tuberose scent of love
Takes time and time to breathe;
This is amusement, to see the skull heave
Hard on the plastic ruff of hardened milk.

Even the young remember Punch. They're tough.

Punch had these heavy hands, but not this bat-winged
    hulk.
They have two hands for sticks, and hands enough.
Tyros of flowers and veterans of flight,
Born without firmament
In the planetary prison with a ceiling for skies,
One hour for love, short days,
They may not wing like bees through hearts of flowers
But wing like ants in regiments
Capturing aphides.

The undecipherable fate of Cain,
His mark, may saturate us with clown's pain.

Gilles sates our hunger and bloats hypnotized
In the proscenium. But he'll burst
In the easy rain of bombs, our aluminum sin.
The ascending dust will sift the son of Cain,
This generation dust, or lost, or dazed.

O animals were equal at the first.
We studied hunch of bison claw of cat
For duels. In the deep caves of the bat
Our risk was beautiful.
Now, at the slaughter pen, moans the young bull.

Christ's love! Who dreed our weird? Nobility
Troubles the heart in unexpected moments,
Heart's ease.
            New Human creatures tranquilly
New seasons will inhabit, safe as the wren,
Like the lion the chicken the hyena,
Natural as the veronica and the verbena,
In agricultural health.

ELEGY

On Gordon Barber, Lamentably Drowned
in his Eighteenth Year

WHEN in the mirror of a permanent tear
Over the iris of your mother's eye
I beheld the dark tremor of your face, austere
With space of death, spun too benign for youth,
Icicle of the past to pierce her living sigh—
I saw you wish the last kiss of mother's mouth,
Who took the salted waters rather in the suck
Of seas, sighing yourself to fill and drench
With water the plum-rich glory of your breast
Where beat the heart escaping from war's luck.

Gordon, I mourn your wrist, your running foot,
Your curious brows, your thigh, your unborn daughters,
Yet mourn more deep the drought-caught war dry boy
Who goes, a killer, to join you in your sleep
And envy you what made you blench
Taking your purple back to drought-less waters.
What choke of terror filled you in the wet
What fierce surprise caught you when play turned fate
And all the rains you loved became your net,
Formlessly yielding, yet stronger than your breath?
Then did you dream of mother or hopes hatched
When the cold cramp held you from nape to foot
And time dissolved, promise dissolved, in Death?
Did you cry 'cruel' to all the hands that stretched
Not near, but played afar, when you sank down
Your sponge of lungs hurt to the quick
Till you had left the quick to join the dead,
Whom, now, your mother mourns grief-sick.
You were too young to drown.

Never will you take bride to happy bed,
Who lay awash in water yet no laving
764

Needed, so pure so young for sudden leaving.

Gone, gone is Gordon, tall and brilliant lad
Whose mind was science. Now hollow his skull
A noble sculpture, is but sunken bone,
His cells from water come by water laid
Grave-deep, to water gone.
Lost, lost the hope he had
Washed to a cipher his splendour and his skill.

But Gordon's gone, it's other boys who live afraid.

Two years, and lads have grown to hold a gun.
In dust must splendid lads go down and choke,
Red dry their hands and dry their one day's sun
From which they earthward fall to fiery tomb
Bomb-weighted, from bloodying children's hair.

Never a boy but takes as cross Cain's crime
And goes to death by making death, to pass
Death's gate distorted with the dried brown grime—
Better the watery death than death by air
Or death by sand
Where fall hard fish of fear
Loud in unwetted dust.

Spun on a lucky wave, O early boy!
Now ocean's fish you are
As heretofore.
Perhaps you had sweet mercy's tenderness
To win so soon largesse of choice
That you, by grace, went gayly to the wave
And all our mourning should be to rejoice.

1942

765

N. B., SYMMETRIANS

WE, the symmetrians, seek justice here,
And asymmetric nature makes a drought.
We wrap up handouts for the martyred poor,
Making sure to put in books and tin-can beer.
Each man relieved goes home and gives a clout
To mrs man, or pal-man, and slams the door.

The speechful day in knowing languors goes,
We seek again for salt and summer sky.
The pure-blue meteor flares and falls unburnt;
We take to our heels standing on staunch tiptoes.
We read half-works of science for the why
And scheme to balance marxly with what's learnt.

Fastened and fasting in the bed-rock man
The assainted, snuffed-down halo strives to rise;
The unstabilized land still slips up out of ocean,—
Bears odd, imperilled flora built to plan.
A natural start is now no one's surmise,
To take things as presented, no one's notion.

They used to start a-fresh, but we try burdened,
Trimming the present's future with the past.
It's all the fault of inter-communication,
Mountains of dove-tailed pebbles and words wordened.
The newest prism is moulded from the last.
The simplest thing is: to laud the massive nation.

The moon still shines beside the daytime star,
The waters weave, rain cools, dunes move, grain grows,
Soft words bring soft replies, muscles expand.
Whether we say the stars are near or far,
The polar lights still paint the glacier floes,
The temperate zones are yet more fully manned.

GENE DERWOOD

BIRD, BIRD

AGE after age our bird through incense flies,
Angel or daw, dove, phoenix, falcon or roc,
Till this last net of wings dark charged to wreck
The hoops of heaven, dove's arc, and all that cries.
The clotted frets of Daedalus unlock
An egg of paradox the gods disguise;
Men as the organs of the bird demise
Heaven's breath under the bombers' moon, flac-flac.

Plunge, boy, to paradise that in heart's choir
Is home, rocked on the cords of birth, low
Again home, bringing to earth your found fire
Be hound or vine, not entrail to the crow
Of metal death,—explode the skies of fear—
Come down, O Icarus, come down, down, O.

WITH GOD CONVERSING

RED paths that wander through the gray, and cells
Of strangeness, rutted mouldings in the brain,
Untempered fevers heated by old kills,
By the pampered word, by the pat printed rune,
Unbalanced coil under glaucous blooms of thought,
A turning mind, unmitigated thinking that
Feeds human hunger and eats us alive
While cringing to the death, expecting love,—
Such make the self we are. And do you make it?
And practice on us? For we cannot take it.

Listen, Grow mild before the flicking lash
Seems welded to your hand, self-wounder.
What are we, cry we, while our pain leaps lush,
Too jungle thick: the jungle where we wander,
No seeded faith before, nor after, miracle,
Of bidden faith in things unseen, no particle.

For we think only through our troubled selves,
We note the worm that in the apple delves,
See gibbous moons and spots upon the sun,
Speak gibberish, and keep the poor in sin.

Plus birth and death must war-lash winnow
While every pod-burst leaf of May sucks life?
Because we think shall we be less than minnow,
Cat, carrot, rat, bat and such from sense aloof?
What doorless maze is this we wander through
With fuming souls parched of our morning dew?
Reason confounds as it presents to NAUGHT:
Earth worn, man moving into self-made night.
Reason-begotten science sets war's pace
And, civil-mouthed, makes civilization pass.

Created in your image, made up of words,
Till words reduce you to a zero-o,
We, then, reflecting you, are less than birds,
Bugs, or empty dugs, still less than minus no.
There must be something wrong with being wise—
Talking we go, wondering and wandering with woes,
Big thoughts have got us, hence we organize,
Govern our heroes with unmeant yeas and nays,
And breathe in dungeons of our nervous mesh
An air too blank to snare meandering flesh.

Night melting dawn shall turn the renewed sky,
Aurora Borealis and Australis
Fanfaring leap the poles, the moon fall by;
But if our science does not quickly fail us
How long for us will space blue light the dun
Of populaces, while wonderers eye the sun?
The gloomy silhouettes of wings we forged
With reason reasonless, are now enlarged,
The falsified subconscious, beast a-woken?
We-you? Post-suicides, shall we awaken?

Kenneth Fearing

CONFESSION OVERHEARD
IN A SUBWAY

ʋou will ask how I came to be eavesdropping, in the
    first place.
ʃhe answer is, I was not.
The man who confessed to these several crimes (call
    him John Doe) spoke into my right ear on a
    crowded subway train, while the man whom he
    addressed (call him Richard Roe) stood at my left.
Thus, I stood between them, and they talked, or some-
    times shouted, quite literally straight through me.
How could I help but overhear?
Perhaps I might have moved away to some other strap.
    But the aisles were full.
Besides, I felt, for some reason, curious.

"I do not deny my guilt," said John Doe. "My own, first,
    and after that my guilty knowledge of still further
    guilt.
I have counterfeited often, and successfully.
I have been guilty of ignorance, and talking with con-
    viction. Of intolerable wisdom, and keeping silent.
Through carelessness, or cowardice, I have shortened the
    lives of better men. And the name for that is
    murder.
All my life I have been a receiver of stolen goods."
"Personally, I always mind my own business," said
    Richard Roe. "Sensible people don't get into
    those scrapes."

I was not the only one who overheard this confession.
Several businessmen, bound for home, and housewives
    and mechanics, were within easy earshot.

769

A policeman sitting in front of us did not lift his eyes, at
the mention of murder, from his paper.

Why should I be the one to report these crimes?

You will understand why this letter to your paper is
anonymous. I will sign it: Public Spirited Citizen,
and hope that it cannot be traced.

But all the evidence, if there is any clamor for it, can
be substantiated.

I have heard the same confession many times since, in
different places.

And now that I think of it, I had heard it many times
before.

"Guilt," said John, "is always and everywhere nothing
less than guilt.

I have always, at all times, been a willing accomplice of
the crass and the crude.

I have overheard, daily, the smallest details of con-
spiracies against the human race, vast in their ultimate scope, and conspired, daily, to launch my own.

You have heard of innocent men who died in the chair.
It was my greed that threw the switch.

I helped, and I do not deny it, to nail that guy to the
cross, and shall continue to help.

Look into my eyes, you can see the guilt.

Look at my face, my hair, my very clothing, you will
see guilt written plainly everywhere.

Guilt of the flesh. Of the soul. Of laughing, when others
do not. Of breathing and eating and sleeping.

I am guilty of what? Of guilt. Guilty of guilt, that is all,
and enough."

Richard Roe looked at his wristwatch and said: "We'll
be twenty minutes late.

After dinner we might take in a show."

Now, who will bring John Doe to justice for his measureless crimes?

I do not, personally, wish to be involved.
Such nakedness of the soul belongs in some other prov-
ince, probably the executioner's.
And who will bring the blunt and upright Richard Roe
to the accuser's stand, where he belongs?
Or will he deny and deny his partnership?

I have done my duty, as a public spirited citizen, in any
case.

END OF THE SEERS' CONVENTION

WE were walking and talking on the roof of the world,
In an age that seemed, at that time, an extremely modern age
Considering a merger, last on the agenda, of the Seven
Great Leagues that held the Seven True Keys to
the Seven Ultimate Spheres of all moral, financial,
and occult life.

"I foresee a day," said one of the delegates, an astro-
analyst from Idaho, "when men will fly through the
air, and talk across space;
They will sail in ships that float beneath the water;
They will emanate shadows of themselves upon a screen,
and the shadows will move, and talk, and seem as
though real."

"Very interesting, indeed," declared a Gypsy delegate.
"But I should like to ask, as a simple reader of tea-
leaves and palms:
How does this combat the widespread and growing evil
of the police?"

The astrologer shrugged, and an accidental meteor fell
from his robes and smoldered on the floor.
"In addition," he said, "I foresee a war,
And a victory after that one, and after the victory, a war
again."

"Trite," was the comment of a crystal-gazer from Miami Beach.
"Any damn fool, at any damn time, can visualize wars, and more wars, and famines and plagues.
The real question is: How to seize power from entrenched and organized men of Common Sense?"

"I foresee a day," said the Idaho astrologer, "when human beings will live on top of flag-poles,
And dance, at some profit, for weeks and months without any rest,
And some will die very happily of eating watermelons, and nails, and cherry pies."

"Why," said a bored numerologist, reaching for his hat, "can't these star-gazers keep their feet on the ground?"
"Even if it's true," said a Bombay illusionist, "it is not, like the rope-trick, altogether practical."

"And furthermore, and finally," shouted the astrologer, with comets and halfmoons dropping from his pockets, and his agitated sleeves,
"I prophesy an age of triumph for laziness and sleep, and dreams and utter peace.
I can see couples walking through the public parks in love, and those who do not are wanted by the sheriff.
I see men fishing beside quiet streams, and those who do not are pursued by collectors, and plastered with liens."

"This does not tell us how to fight against skepticism," muttered a puzzled mesmerist, groping for the door.
"I think," agreed a lady who interpreted the cards, "we are all inclined to accept too much on faith."

A sprinkling of rain, or dragon's blood,
Or a handful of cinders fell on the small, black umbrellas they raised against the sky.

Lloyd Frankenberg

HIDE IN THE HEART

I

HERE is no shadow but cloudshadow and nightshadow
Moving across and rolling away and leaving
Only the purple avenues the ant
Drags his weight across from here to there
Between the leaning towers of his town.

Here are no voices but the gull's hard lot
Easing his discontent with all the beach,
Abusive tongues of terns, rheumatic crows'
Dry commentaries concerning tomorrow's weather
And pipers fleeing the sound of their own lament.

And the wind's singing is before all music
Picking the strings of grass and thumping the roof
And all the stops of the ocean to be pulled out
When anger is the howling of the wind
And all armies the marches of the sea.

And mornings bringing the white lies of peace,
The rags of truce upon the sea and sky,
Ambassadorial breeze from cloud to wave,
All solved and settled under a smiling sun
Blandly agreeing his hands to everything.

Until the fog with sidelong stratagem
Confers in huddled whispers with the earth—
And ships and birds are asking their way about
Of the whistling buoy that keeps its courage up
Through the long dark and vistas of the mist—

Then lifts again, its mission otherwhere
And leaves us this again our isle of quiet:
Surrounded with seas of grass and the glassy sea
Here in the sweet unreasonable weather
We think us safe, we think us housed in peace.

II

All day the storm stood off from about our door.
The tongues of sand lay panting in the sun,
We listening to the sounds of listless water
With wisps of ragtime over the dunes from town
And scraps of headline: BOMBING ALMERIA.

Who brought this newspaper in like contraband
To poison the horizons of our minds?
All day the sun was stored serenity
Before the cloud fulfilled its promised rain.
Now seeing the fire-edged cloud our thought is of war.

Our sea was water where we drowned our thoughts.
We plunged and lay like time—not like this time.
Our sea was not an endless belt of bullets
Round after round transmitted to the breech
To riddle time to tatters and red teeth.

Now more than ever we do not know how long
This little space of peace will be our own.
The nations run like nightmare toward the repeated
Dream's end and beyond the end and beyond,
Toward the waking up screaming and it's true! it's true!

III

Nations perpetuate the fatal motion
Letting their anger go from them with no
774

Power to retract, to make amends and an end.
The people standing under the balconies
Look up and become part of what they see.

The cannon standing at stiff-armed salute
Discharge their duties in the innocent air.
The bleak and bankrupt bones are all there is
To pay revenge its dividend and hate
Its pebble dropped, its circle widening.

IV

There is no hiding in these island seas.
The air is full of forebodings of disaster.
The gulls come up dead on the tide. It is one to them
Whether the world hold fish. The sandfleas dance
Burning alive on the phosphorescent beach.

The stars are a regiment of fixed bayonets;
The steelgrey seas a rank upon rank of helmets.
Clouds march and countermarch. Winds marshal them;
Roll on their spokes guncarriages of thunder.
The army of grass is led in all directions.

A large drop falls and that is all. The storm
Wheels to the skyline; leaves a sunspace; waits.
These little silly bombardments are but a device
To larger ends; rally the peace-protectors
About false standards, his eye upon another.

V

All day the storm stood off in a rift of cloud.
We thought us safe, we thought us housed in peace,
Ringed in by sun, chalked off by grass, passed by
In a lull of the storm, in a quiet isle. Till night
Darkened our door and the storm broke and the sea

Moving in fury upon the enduring beach
We put our windows against the rain, we drew
Bolts on the wind and shuttered out the storm.
All night the four walls shook like a heart in the gale
Shedding a light like blood on the troubled darkness.

Four walls in the wind are the wind's mouse and we
The heart in the mouse. The lightning lifts a paw,
Purrs in its throat and lets the paw fall slack.
The tail of the wind stirs lazily, shakes the floor
And we are alone with the taste of mouth on mouth.

VI

Hide in the heart. There is no help without.
The strong winds ramp about the world tonight.
The heart is wide enough to move about.
The heart is tall. In a world too small for flight
This is the only border out of doubt.

The light comes in as through the hand's devotion.
The world is held in the hollow of this hand.
Its own sea with its own moon-made motion
Rolls upon the shores of its own land.
Before all singing is the music of this ocean.

Find out this music pounding through the wrists.
Stop out the sounds of the feet tramping the roof.
Let the rain beat with all its mailed fists.
The heart is the only timber to be proof
Against all thunderclaps and lightningtwists.

Hide in this roof until the storm has been;
Till fear leaves us under the eaves of the blood
And one by one arising let them in
Disarming at the door the roaring flood,
The infantry of rain and the strong wind.

776

Jean Garrigue

THE STRANGER

Now upon this piteous year
I sit in Denmark beside the quai
And nothing that the fishers say
Or the children carrying boats
Can recall me from that place
Where sense and wish departed me
Whose very shores take on
The whiteness of anon.
For I beheld a stranger there
Who moved ahead of me,
So tensile and so dancer made
That like a thief I followed her
Though my heart was so alive
I felt myself the equal beauty.
But when at last a turning came
Like the branching of a river
And I saw if she walked on
She would be gone forever,
Fear then so wounded me
As fell upon my ear
The voice a blind man dreams
And broke on me the smile
I dreamed as deaf men hear,
I stood there like a spy,
My tongue and eyelids taken
In such necessity.
Now upon this piteous year
The rains of Autumn fall.
Where may she be?
I suffered her to disappear
Who hunger in the prison of my fear.

That lean and brown, that stride,
That cold and melting pride,
For whom the river like a clear,
Melodic line and the distant carrousel
Where lovers on their beasts of play
Rose and fell,
That wayfare where the swan adorned
With every wave and eddy
The honor of his sexual beauty,
Create her out of sorrow
That, never perishing,
Is a stately thing.

THE CIRCLE

THE wood, swollen with mushrooms,
Those rotting like excrement,
Those blooming in monkey scarlet,
Branch-brown and butter yellow,
The wood, swollen with voices,
Those high-blood, tortured sexual cries,
The penitential voice singing,
The wood, branch-brown, branched with weeping:

Who am I, am I,
Where the mirror has splashed its bloodless blood,
Who am I in the bloodless wood?
I said: eternity is this:
The formless past within the glass,
The flesh deprived of its true lust,
The inward virtue of the flesh
Corroded by the formless past,
I said: damnation is this eternity,
The mind divorced at last from act,
Distracted senses caged now judged,
Those thumping ranters damned who drag
The battered actor through such mire,

The act full-judged but not altered
(The crooked blood cannot run straight)
Perversity steals the old color
And red runs white in secret ill.

I said: eternity is this travel
Around and round the center of the wood,
Beset by cries, the sullied pool,
The light of mushrooms, moths running
As large as mice on the forest floor,
The flesh, that battered animal,
Asserting its ample sty has dignity.
I said: eternity devours the mind,
Devours and cannot change by its devouring.
The outward terror remains the same,
And the wood, swollen with mushrooms,
      the dark wood.

FROM VENICE WAS THAT AFTERNOON

FROM Venice was that afternoon
Though our own land's canal we viewed.
There willows clove the bluish heat
By dropping leaf or two, gold green,
And every tuft of hill beyond
Stood bright, distinct, as if preserved
By glass that sealed out light but not
Its gold or influence.
And floated on the speckled stream
A child of brilliant innocence
Where on the docks of green we stood
Naming it Love for its perfection.
This seemed to be . . . .
But the current carried the leaves swiftly,
So flowed that child away from us,
So stared we sternly at the water's empty face.

Ah, in the greenhouse of that hour
Waited in the tare and sorrel
The mouth of fleshliness that stopped;
The leaves that dappled on that breast
The five-sensed image of our pleasance
Have now destroyed its lineaments.
For the waters of that afternoon
Flowed through Negation's glassy land,
Where in this civil, gate-closed hour
The verges of those waters now
Drown that joy that was our power.
What tyranny imposed this pride
That caused love's gift to be denied
And our destroying features to
Cast perpetually on its brow
The glass accepting no leaves now?
In rages of the intellect
We gave to heaven abstinence,
Who said our love must issue from
No cisterns of the ruddy sun
But like the artifice of fountains
Leap from cold, infertile sources.
And our destroying features thus
Cast from that land its beingness
And strewed upon the green fleshed hills
Sands of our darkening great ills.

APOLOGIA

Agog, in rain house-deep,
Mud from the cars luxuriously
Splashed on feet, and lily leg
(In braces down from the knee),
The cripple lurched toward me.
She said: (O would you think
A beggar spoke so quick?)
Would you help me across the curb?

JEAN GARRIGUE

O she was pride-cheerful,
She cried: now don't you pity me.
Yes I will help you, I will
I will help you, I will, I will.

In quandary rain fell black
Muddy-eyed from the eye of night
And wind bent umbrellas back
(How many a skeleton lay on the walk!)
O you, I'd have said to her,
Disgust the callous deed I do.
Let watchers think I'm good, I'm not,
I'm caught in a deed I do not do
And false attendant thoughts about
The lots we're given, good or not,
And chance's power or God's pity,
Banalities that black the heart!

I want to know, I'd have said,
What—is it faith?—makes you abide
This groveling step from side to side,
This stagger, wrench, galvanic bend.
Your effort's joke on all of us
Who walk from pride to shame in ease,
From fear to failure comfortably.

For the hurdle achieved, she smiled.
Her thanks like flowers bumped my nose.
O not the causal thought which ran
In anguish imitative after her,
Poor toady to infirmity!
Nor thoughts on justice, God's pity,
Nor that necessity to face
Reality with physical honesty,
Consoled the need I had to meet
Those penalties I was not guilty of
That criticized the universe.

Addressed by her it was to fear—
As at an accident's loud burst—
Some test of supplication there
Though why her passionate effort tasked
My abstract and appalling help
I could not understand.
I felt no love but dread.

O fear and pity sport
(Despair for the gay oppressed)
Like flies in summer light
(Is cruelest test)
Kill the sorry content, the guile,
The ethic splurge with which they go
Athwart the sun of honesty.

Deliver us to our despair
When looking glasses accost
The looking glass we are
And who mends which for who?
In ignorance infamous we beg
That veteran pain, and will.

 Brewster Ghiselin

TO THE SOUTH

The umber slant lands under the Apennines
Clouded their sunward dust with pluffs and plumes,
Rust of peaches, pale of almonds and plums,
And lower yet a still green mist of vines;
These passed the slow train sliding down from the pines
And the winter rocks and the smoke-gray ravines.

782

Over the tiles of noon I saw upstart
The domes and pistil tower, as in a kiln:
Not like those shut steel buds of sleep at Köln
That close eternal winter on the heart
Nor like the April-folded stone of Chartres
Whose waiting is the unsummered spirit's hurt.

I came as from the ignominy of dream
Into the precincts of the sun's renown,
To feel the cycle of the night and noon,
To see on the shadowy river noonfire teem
And on the terra-cotta hills the gleam
Of fruit boughs whitening, a foam of time.

 Paul Goodman

MARCH 1941

RELYING on the disasters o' the war
to minimize my misery; and counting
those penalties that none can doubt as such
as the proof and price of private vices I
otherwise do not believe in—
           No!
I'll rather say it was our public crimes
that caused the world-wide calamity,
and that my private lapses get their wages
(small sins small death) in the very defect
of feeling that needs such a grandiose
analogy to burn me!
           Yet my *pleasures*
are moderated almost to the death
by the embarrassing imagination of
the agony of Europe. How is this?

A LITTLE PRAYER

HALLOWED be the Ordainer of
the world! through Whom this season of
delivery, let no accident
fall my beloved wife and friend,
but may the son or daughter, long
awaited, soon and safe be born;
I ask it who have sometime prayed
that other things would be destroyed.

 Alfred Hayes

THE SLAUGHTER-HOUSE

UNDER the big 500-watted lamps, in the huge sawdusted
government inspected slaughter-house,
head down from hooks and clamps, run on trolleys over
troughs,
the animals die.
Whatever terror their dull intelligences feel
or what agony distorts their most protruding eyes
the incommunicable narrow skulls conceal.
Across the sawdusted floor,
ignorant as children, they see the butcher's slow
methodical approach
in the bloodied apron, leather cap above, thick square
shoes below,
struggling to comprehend this unique vision upside down,
and then approximate a human scream
as from the throat slit like a letter
the blood empties, and the windpipe, like a blown valve,
spurts steam.

But I, sickened equally with the ox and lamb,
    misread my fate,
mistake the butcher's love
    who kills me for the meat I am
to feed a hungry multitude beyond the sliding doors.
    I, too, misjudge the real
purpose of this huge shed I'm herded in: not for my love
    or lovely wool am I here,
but to make some world a meal.
    See, how on the unsubstantial air
I kick, bleating my private woe,
    as upside down my rolling sight
somersaults, and frantically I try to set my world upright;
    too late learning why I'm hung here,
whose nostrils bleed, whose life runs out from eye and ear.

THE DEATH OF THE CRANEMAN

Happened like this: it was hot as hell
That afternoon, sand, stone dust, the sun,
We were in the mountains.
Drinking-water was by the gasoline drum,
We were all drinking like fish that day.
He must have come down from the crane
For a drink I guess, a cigarette
Might have done it, blew it bang up, that drum.
Like dynamite been dropped in it.
We came running down from the mountains.

The blacksmith got to him first: gasoline
Had made a bonfire of him, and we shouted
Craneman! Craneman! with the wops talking
Their language, and nobody knowing his name.
Standing there you could see him, a flame
Lighter and yellower than the sunlight,
And burning, hands and feet, his hair on fire,
Getting up from the ground, standing there,
Yelling out of the fire, flame shooting white

In the sunlight: Lemme alone! Lemme alone!
I'm all right!

Well, we get him here and here he dies.
And that's where we buried him out there,
In the goldenrod beyond them pines.
It's a Potter's Field and nobody'd care.
We dug the grave with our drills and hands.
You got to bury a guy somewhere.
Funny I thought as I looked at him
Blackened, with a pair of holes for eyes,
You bury a stiff and there he lies,
And Christ only knows where he come from
And whether there's kids somewhere or a dame,
We buried him like he came in this world,
A stiff, naked, without a name.

Ruth Herschberger

IN PANELLED ROOMS

THE love-grip, first excited by the eye,
Fastens its pleasing mortar; then the thigh
Moves like a tractor rocketing to fate.
The head reclines, the mind will gladly wait;
But pearly blood and sockets made of gum,
Less than immobile, seek the pleasing hum
Of fall and exaltation. Eyebrows made
Of ships and shaped like islands cannot shade
The walnut hull of eyes, the husk of brown
Under whose cover lies the kernel-down,
The certainty of love. Each jointed knee
Strolls in the wake of new fraternity,
And wishes elbows well; itself does grace
To flesh and bone, extracting from its place

All that made Solomon declare of myrrh,
Frankincense, flowers, upon touching her.

THE LUMBERYARD

WE watched our love burn with the lumberyard,
Bats in their wheeling showed our crazéd sense,
We stood in fields where weeds with chiggers scrambled,
And stood the heat flush in our face, immense.

Softly the crowd acclaimed the devastation,
And we, we smiled to see the embers twist,
Tottering towers and poles with flashing wires.
We shifted feet when shifting structures kissed.

Up in the sky the stars were red sparks shuttling,
Planes with a scouter's appetite hung by.
And at our backs the Negro huts were lit
With yellow mist, a ghostly gayety.

Sound above all: the cracking and the crocked,
As bones that, whetted by the warmer flames,
Edged into death, until the crimson glow
Vanquished the knotted amber boards, the names.

All banished, all decided, all cast in;
Far back beyond, the trees made silver white
By steaming flames, rose as cold piles of cloud
To cool this mirror of the blazing night.

And we beheld, we watched, as drunk as all,
And gladdened when the bursting peaked and sprung,
Rejoiced to see the threat of fire win,
And sang to see the worthy timbers wrung.

We watched our love burn with the lumberyard,
Magnificent the sight, the sin, the shame,
The vice profusely lavished; wheeled the bats
Silent as we, but crazed, crazed as the flame.

COUP D'ETAT

A tremor, like magnitude, shook the world,
It was an end-day, a beginning-hour.
The front lawns of the suburbs were not glad of it,
But the birds carolled endlessly, as ever.

The world imbibed this tremor with its coffee,
It ate of this magnitude with its bread;
Cake-eaters and bar-flies were caught up in it;
It was a day of imminent rejoicing.

But wailing too! What wailing! America
Had never descried the portents of the human throat.
What utterances were possible! What weeping!
Finally tears became as acceptable as laughter.

In small parks scattered amid cities,
The poor discussed the magnitude with longing:
"Have you ever in your day seen the like?"
Here was something the rich were sharing!

It was as terrible and hypnotic as the weather;
Some were wholly charmed, and some terrified.
Such effects are expected:
We have always with us, the unadventurous.

O let us be jubilant, my darlings;
We can cling together like brothers drowning,
And if, occasionally, someone feel the sharp teeth
Of another sinking into the flesh: quiet him.

Remembering that, tired of jubilation, we can weep;
Once weary of merriment, we can cry.
When we are dulled by sunlight, there is sleep;
And, gorged with terror, we have leave to die.

James Laughlin

A LETTER TO HITLER

LAST winter we were
short of firewood and

it was good and cold
so we used a lot of

old books that were
in the attic just old

novels nobody would
ever want to read but

we found they made
plenty of heat and

twice they set the
chimney afire when

a burning page went
up with the draft and

we found they would
smoulder a long time

after you thought the
fire was all out and

then suddenly burst
into flame & another

thing they made ashes
that wouldn't stay in

the grate but floated
out all over the room!

THE SUMMONS

HE went out to their glorious
war & went down in it and his
          last belief was

her love as he breathed flame
in the waves and sank burning
          now I lie under

his picture in the dark room
in the wife's bed and partake
          of his unknown

life does he see does he stand
in the room does he feel does
   he burn again

later I wake in the night while
she sleeps and call out to him
   wanderer come

return to this bed & embody the
love that was yours and is hers
   and is mine
   and endures.

 ## Coman Leavenworth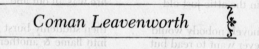

NORFOLK MEMORIALS

I

NORTH PICKENHAM

THE army was ours that spring. Landing in England
Captured an island much reduced by rain.
Deep in the humpbacked huts we cursed and cowered,
Waiting for mid-July, for now it seemed
Spring was the traitor, continually it seemed
The summit of the summer was the sun.

The planes got up and barked all over England,
And here rode such a ruddy Alexander
As England greened to look upon. His voice
Was Akron and Atlanta, but his eyes
Covered the skyline with a natural grace,
And when he took the air the air took fire.
This was the springboard, lifting him so high
He thought at first all diving was to fly.

His government provided scant instruction
As to the downward journey; then his life
Turned in the hand of God, he was on his own,
For where was the manual on how to die?
If he sometimes had to fall, his flaming hair
No more concerned the medical department
Than symptoms of an unprescribed surprise,
An unmilitary terror in his face.

Some only fell in love. For them the land
Hovered under the sky. They lay in meadows
Trimmed like movie sets, where bursts of green
Startled the flying bombs, and where the sun
Managed its cocktail parties all day long.
Much that they did was vital, but the stamp
Set on their records marked them as autre temps;
They loved love, when they should have laughed it off.
How could the brow describe so brave an arc
As that improvident parabola
Carved by the bomber on a screaming sky?

Incessantly the planes proclaimed disaster.
The lovers of the nightride in the lorry
Lingered as long as any could afford,
But when the runs of liberty were canceled
Even the least passionate embrace
Seemed overdone, so widely was it done.

And all the planes leapt overhead and soared.

II

RACKHEATH

We learned to laugh. Although the flying bombs
The V-2 rockets, the evidence of mortality,
Briefly forced our attention from the radio,
And some were absent at the dinner table

(Many went down to London on three-day passes),
Faces in the morning filled the places,
The movie reels revolved us into sleep,
And, notably, to some the weekend dance
Brought the intensity of true romance,
Which after all we longed for long ago.

Those who in the fields obscured by sunlight
Or under hedgerows darkened by the moon
Wound their lovers with the foreign flowers,
Turned their backs on what they could not love.
Laughing among the engines, these forgot
Tabus and special orders, could not tell
What they had come for when they had to come,
Sent from home by the elders. So they dance
Somewhat too lightly in a world of chance;
At dusk their shadows fall across the tomb.

A time for waiting. So we passed the time.
The time did not pass us; it seemed to rest,
To wait for our direction. Or it seemed,
In moments of fantastic acrobatics,
To follow on, sedately at the elbow,
Guiding the movement in a circling dream.
Here was a modest, but a true ringmaster;
Needless the whip to supervise the dance,
Since all the steps were settled in advance,
And soldiers wait to move at breakneck speed.

There were a few who sensed the time was wrong—
The unreal light, and evening falling so fast,
The tears so quickly urged, the ready laughter
Ringing too long in the darkened town (it seemed
Somewhere an echo listened, afraid to answer).
And yet how many had to be caught alone
Hanging heads together in the field red-handed,
How many had to be made to join the dance
When the season really got under way in France,
And all the rumbling planes got up and roared!

III
WENDLING

Here were planes. But everything else was gone.
Somewhere in the southern part of France
Peasants gathered like vultures, and the life
Seized from the grounded airman oddly bent
Under the platane, this life was flesh,
Love of our life caught in the upturned eyes.
Defying all the mockeries of maneuvers,
And violating all the secret commandments
It justified the war, and in its hand
Turned the neck of a flower like the stem
Of a wineglass, while the grateful peasants,
Raising their arms in prayer, proposed a toast.

Some read the numbers on the casualty list,
Counting the odds. Others, the erstwhile friends,
Showed shocked faces, thought as long as they dared
On the impossible event. Others shed tears
In private. Beyond these there were those
Who sleepwalked in the daytime, groping the air
For something that never seemed to be wholly there.
Their hands went out and faltered, and their eyes,
Dry and blind as mirrors, walked along
Like tourists who only have time to cover ground.

All this concerned the younger generation
(The oldest pilot would now be twenty-six).
Some who escaped wept on the ravished field,
Hiding their faces from their thoughts of home.
The lovelorn found it a time for awkwardness
In public places. The resigned pose came later.

Who could have said which look of love was real?
And how many knew what loves were gone forever,
In those days when the war wound up the war?

Now watch the planes move over the horizon,
Much like the elephants of Leconte de Lisle.

Robert Lowell

THE DRUNKEN FISHERMAN

WALLOWING in this bloody sty,
I cast for fish that pleased my eye
(Truly Jehovah's bow suspends
No pots of gold to weight its ends);
Only the blood-mouthed rainbow trout
Rose to my bait. They flopped about
My canvas creel until the moth
Corrupted its unstable cloth.

A calendar to tell the day;
A handkerchief to wave away
The gnats; a couch unstuffed with storm
Pouching a bottle in one arm;
A whiskey bottle full of worms;
And bedroom slacks: are these fit terms
To mete the worm whose molten rage
Boils in the belly of old age?

Once fishing was a rabbit's foot—
O wind blow cold, O wind blow hot,
Let suns stay in or suns step out:
Life danced a jig on the sperm-whale's spout—
The fisher's fluent and obscene
Catches kept his conscience clean.
Children, the raging memory drools
Over the glory of past pools.

Now the hot river, ebbing, hauls
Its bloody waters into holes;
A grain of sand inside my shoe

Mimics the moon that might undo
Man and Creation too; remorse
Stinking, has puddled up its source;
Here tantrums thrash to a whale's rage.
This is the pot-hole of old age.

Is there no way to cast my hook
Out of this dynamited brook?
The Fisher's sons must cast about
When shallow waters peter out.
I will catch Christ with a greased worm,
And when the Prince of Darkness stalks
My bloodstream to its Stygian term . . .
On water the Man-Fisher walks.

W. R. Moses

ANGINA PECTORIS

THE steady heart, which in its steadiness
Allows formation of the somewhat, life,
Unsteadies, stops, and so a thick debris
Drops to the sidewalk, where the poor limbs sprawl
Like things a child had made of mud, and all
The color leaves the face, pale as a knife.

When the man walked down the street in his mackinaw,
Or sat in a bar-room gurgling at his beer,
It was only a small usurper of oxygen
I noticed; I'd have seen him ship for Spain,
Or go to Dakota and die working with grain,
And never thought, or been glad he was not here.

But now that I see him neutral earth, to bury
In earth, for damp, or a pale, poetic swarm
Of worms to end, I'm sorry; I wish him what
I'd not wish other mud: that he ate tonight
With children he loved, that the meal was heavy and
        right,
That he slept with plenty of quilts to keep him warm.

AMERICAN HISTORY

Though the rough, bitter-sweet haw of pioneering
Seems now as remote as wheat in Egyptian tomb,
Grandparents actually ate it. In the big weather,
Under a strange heaven's gigantic bloom,
Between huge lakes, on huge prairies they dwelled.

And testified later: though dying children could tell you
That frontier doctors were dangerous as disease;
Though hail, tornado, or the cow in the kitchen garden
Could so disappoint as to make the heart freeze,
Those were their finest years, the first on the prairie.

Yes. The blue-green devils of nature are only wild,
And stubborn; and seldom dangerous in the end.
To valiant aggressors they give the flushing gift
Of victory softly, almost as to a friend.
It is hidden that they were the easy enemy.

Until those other devils, that should be red
From long enough pickling in the juice of the human
        heart,
By pressure and raid make conquerors realize
That an older, harder war is still at its start.
They long for the easy diversion, but that is gone.

Frederic Prokosch

THE FESTIVAL

The cello sobs, the symphony begins,
The fever flutters in the violins,
A hundred earrings tremble in the dark,
Sleek in their velvet squat the seven sins.

And sauntering down the river you and I
Discern the baffling planets in the sky,
Through the tall branches watch the tell-tale feet
And hear the voices of the summer sigh.

The castle fades, the distant mountains fade,
The silence falters on the misty glade,
The ducal lanterns hover on the hill,
The cathedral moves into the evening shade.

Softly upon you falls the casual light.
Your hair grows golden and your eyes are bright
And through the warm and lucid Austrian air
In love our arms go wandering to-night.

Far to the east extend the ancient seas,
The dear Danubian banks, the archaic trees
Among whose pillars still the restless dead
Dispel their homesick odours on the breeze;

Crete blows the night across her wicked floors
And Sicily now locks her little doors,
And up the Adriatic leap the clouds
And hurl a shadow on her sucking shores.

And northward through the benches of the park
Stealthily moves the thin conspiring dark:

797

The thieves and fairies huddle by the bridge
And hear the sickly hounds of Brussels bark.

In Norway demons dwell among the caves
Whose walls are bitten by the haggard waves
And on the emerald Carpathian slopes
The rancid wolves explore the village graves;

Each hungry orphan climbs into his bed
Afraid to face the usual midnight dread;
Across the cobbles past the pock-marked church
The hags go hustling with their crusts of bread,

The cripples stumble slowly up the stairs
And toss their curses on the stuffy airs,
The cellar-eyed, the sleepers in the ditches
Mutter their simple paranoiac prayers.

Listen, the rhythms of the night begin:
The little lamps are flickering in the inn:
Out through the door into the garden glides
The fretful elegance of the mandolin:

The night flies on, the coming tempest flies,
And all our lovely neighbours close their eyes.
Silent the paths of longing and regret
Which all our learning taught us to despise.

And you and I look out upon the stream
And by the lantern's mild and mirrored gleam
The inverted figures on the shore perform
The silly baroque postures of a dream.

O who is there to answer you and me?
The sky, the summer, the prolific sea?
The ground is shaking and we must not wait
Who one more moment feel alone and free

And hear the angels with their wingèd fears
Like serpents hiss their carols in our ears
And rediscover on this festive night
The hatreds of a hundred thousand years.

 Theodore Roethke

THE SHAPE OF THE FIRE

I

What's this? A dish for fat lips.
Who says? A nameless stranger.
Is he a bird or a tree? Not everyone can tell.
Water recedes to the crying of spiders.
An old scow bumps over black rocks.
A cracked pod calls.
    Mother me out of here. What more will the bones
        allow?
    Will the sea give the wind suck? A toad folds into
        a stone.
    These flowers are all fangs. Comfort me, fury.
    Wake me, witch, we'll do the dance of rotten sticks.
Shale loosens. Marl reaches into the field. Small birds pass
        over water.
Spirit, come near. This is only the edge of whiteness.
I can't laugh at a procession of dogs.
    In the hour of ripeness the tree is barren.
    The she-bear mopes under the hill.
    Mother, mother, stir from your cave of sorrow.
A low mouth laps water. Weeds, weeds, how I love you.
The arbor is cooler. Farewell, farewell, fond worm.
The warm comes without sound.

II

Where's the eye?
The eye's in the sty.
The ear's not here
Beneath the hair;
When I took off my clothes
To find a nose,
There was only one shoe
For the waltz of To,
The pinch of Where.

Time for the flat-headed man. I recognize that listener,
Him with the platitudes and rubbery doughnuts,
Melting at the knees, a varicose horror.
Hello, hello. My nerves knew you, dear boy.
Have you come to unhinge my shadow?
Last night I slept in the pits of a tongue.
The silver fish ran in and out of my special bindings;
I grew tired of the ritual of names and the assistant
    keeper of the molluscs:
Up over a viaduct I came, to the snakes and sticks of
    another winter,
A two-legged dog hunting a new horizon of howls.
The wind sharpened itself on a rock;
A voice sang:

        Pleasure on ground
        Has no sound,
        Easily maddens
        The uneasy man.

        Who, careless, slips
        In coiling ooze
        Is trapped to the lips,
        Leaves more than shoes;

Must pull off clothes
To jerk like a frog
On belly and nose
From the sucking bog.

My meat eats me. Who waits at the gate?
Mother of quartz, your words writhe into my ear.
Renew the light, lewd whisper.

III

The wasp waits.
        The edge cannot eat the centre.
The grape glistens.
        The path tells little to the serpent.
An eye comes out of the wave.
        The journey from flesh is longest.
A rose sways least.
        The redeemer comes a dark way.

IV

Morning-fair, follow me further back
Into that minnowy world of weeds and ditches,
When the herons floated high over the white houses,
And the little crabs slipped into silvery craters,
When the sun for me glinted the sides of a sand-grain,
And my intent stretched over the buds at their first
    trembling.

That air and shine: and the flicker's loud summer call;
The bearded boards in the stream and the all of apples;
The glad hen on the hill; and the trellis humming.
Death was not. I lived in a simple drowse:
Hands and hair moved through a dream of wakening
    blossoms.

801

Rain sweetened the cave and the dove still called;
The flowers leaned on themselves, the flowers in hollows;
And love, love sang toward.

v

To have the whole air!—
The light, the full sun
Coming down on the flowerheads,
The tendrils turning slowly,
A slow snail-lifting, liquescent;
To be by the rose
Rising slowly out of its bed,
Still as a child in its first loneliness;
To see cyclamen veins become clearer in early sunlight,
And mist lifting, drifting out of the brown cat-tails;
To stare into the after-light, the glitter left on the lake's
    surface
When the sun has fallen behind a wooden island;
To follow the drops sliding from a lifted oar,
Held up, while the rower breathes, and the small boat
    drifts quietly shoreward;
To know that light falls and fills, often without our know-
    ing,
As an opaque vase fills to the brim from a quick pouring,
Fills and trembles at the edge yet does not flow over,
Still holding and feeding the stem of the contained
    flower.

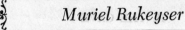

Muriel Rukeyser

AJANTA

NOTE: *In India, between the second century B. C. and the sixth century A. D., a school of Buddhist painter-monks worked on the walls of the Ajanta caves, keeping a tradition in painting that was lost in the East after them and never known in the West. Based on the religious analogy between the space of the body and the space of the universe, the treatment of bodies in these scenes of the life of the gods is such that the deepest background is the wall on which the paintings are done—the figures in the round but shadowless, start forward, seeming to fill the cave. Reality is fully accepted, then, the function of such an art is to fill with creation an accepted real world.*

CAME in my full youth to the midnight cave
nerves ringing; and this thing I did alone.
Wanting my fulness and not a field of war,
for the world considered annihilation, a star
called Wormwood rose and flickered, shattering
bent light over the dead boiling up in the ground,
the biting yellow of their corrupted lives
streaming to war, denying all our words.
Nothing was left among the tainted weather
but world-walking and shadowless Ajanta.
Hallucination and the metal laugh
in clouds, and the mountain-spectre riding storm.
Nothing was certain but a moment of peace,
a hollow behind the unbreakable waterfall.
All the way to the cave, the teeming forms of death,
and death, the price of the body, cheap as air.
I blessed my heart on the expiation journey
for it had never been unable to suffer:
when I met the man whose face looked like the future,
when I met the whore with the dying red hair,
the child myself who is my murderer.
So came I between heaven and my grave
past the serene smile of the *voyeur*, to
this cave where the myth enters the heart again.

803

II. THE CAVE

Space to the mind, the painted cave of dream.
This is not a womb, nothing but good emerges:
this is a stage, neither unreal nor real
where the walls are the world, the rocks and palaces
stand on a borderland of blossoming ground.
If you stretch your hand, you touch the slope of the world
reaching in interlaced gods, animals, and men.
There is no background. The figures hold their peace
in a web of movement. There is no frustration,
every gesture is taken, everything yields connections.
The heavy sensual shoulders, the thighs, the blood-born
     flesh
and earth turning into color, rocks into their crystals,
water to sound, fire to form; life flickers
uncounted into the supple arms of love.
The space of these walls is the body's living space;
tear open your ribs and breathe the color of time
where nothing leads away, the world comes forward
in flaming sequences. Pillars and prisms. Riders
and horses and the figures of consciousness,
red cow grows long, goes running through the world.
Flung into movement in carnal purity,
these bodies are sealed—warm lip and crystal hand
in a jungle of light. Color-sheeted, seductive
foreboding eyelid lowered on the long eye,
fluid and vulnerable. The spaces of the body
are suddenly limitless, and riding flesh
shapes constellations over the golden breast,
confusion of scents and illuminated touch—
monster touch, the throat printed with brightness,
wide outlined gesture where the bodies ride.
Bells, and the spirit flashing. The religious bells,
bronze under the sunlight like breasts ringing,
bronze in the closed air, the memory of walls,
great sensual shoulders in the web of time.
804

III. LES TENDRESSES BESTIALES

A procession of caresses alters the ancient sky
until new constellations are the body shining:
There's the Hand to steer by, there the horizon Breast.
and the Great Stars kindling the fluid hill.
All the rooms open into magical boxes,
nothing is tilted, everything flickers
sexual and exquisite.
The panther with its throat along my arm
turns black and flows away.
Deep in all streets passes a faceless whore
and the checkered men are whispering one word.
The face I know becomes the night-black rose.
The sharp face is now an electric fan
and says one word to me.
The dice and the alcohol and the destruction
have drunk themselves and cast.
Broken bottle of loss, and the glass
turned bloody into the face.
Now the scene comes forward, very clear.
Dream-singing, airborne, surrenders the recalled,
the gesture arrives riding over the breast,
singing, singing, tender atrocity,
the silver derelict wearing fur and claws.
Oh love, I stood under the apple branch,
I saw the whipped bay and the small dark islands,
and night sailing the river and the foghorn's word.
My life said to you: I want to love you well.
The wheel goes back and I shall live again,
but the wave turns, my birth arrives and spills
over my breast the world bearing my grave,
and your eyes open in earth. You touched my life.
My life reaches the skin, moves under your smile,
and your shoulders and your throat and your face and
          your thighs
flash.
      I am haunted by interrupted acts,

introspective as a leper, enchanted
by a repulsive clew,
a gross and fugitive movement of the limbs.
Is this the love that shook the lights to flame?
Sheeted avenues thrash in the wind,
torn streets, the savage parks.
I am plunged deep. Must find the midnight cave.

IV. BLACK BLOOD

A habit leading to murder, smoky laughter
hated at first, but necessary later.
Alteration of motives. To stamp in terror
around the deserted harbor, down the hill
until the woman laced into a harp
screams and screams and the great clock strikes,
swinging its giant figures past the face.
The Floating Man rides on the ragged sunset
asking and asking. Do not say, Which loved?
Which was beloved? Only, Who most enjoyed?
Armored ghost of rage, screaming and powerless.
Only find me and touch my blood again.
Find me. A girl runs down the street
singing Take me, yelling Take me Take
Hang me from the clapper of a bell
and you as hangman ring it sweet tonight,
for nothing clean in me is more than cloud
unless you call it.—As I ran I heard
a black voice beating among all that blood:
"Try to live as if there were a God."

V. THE BROKEN WORLD

Came to Ajanta cave, the painted space of the breast,
the real world where everything is complete,
there are no shadows, the forms of incompleteness.

The great cloak blows in the light, rider and horse arrive,
the shoulders turn and every gift is made.
No shadows fall. There is no source of distortion.
In our world, a tree casts the shadow of a woman,
a man the shadow of a phallus, a hand raised
the shadow of the whip.
Here everything is itself,
here all may stand
on summer earth.
Brightness has overtaken every light,
and every myth netted itself in flesh.
New origins, and peace given entire
and the spirit alive.
In the shadowless cave
the naked arm is raised.
Animals arrive,
interlaced, and gods
interlaced, and men
flame-woven.
I stand and am complete.

Crawls from the door,
black at my two feet
the shadow of the world.
World, not yet one,
enters the heart again.
The naked world, and the old noise of tears,
the fear, the expiation and the love,
a world of the shadowed and alone.
The journey, and the struggles of the moon.

Winfield Townley Scott

ANNUAL LEGEND

A MILLION butterflies rose up from South America,
All together, and flew in a gold storm toward Spain:
Eastward, the annual legend, a shining amber cloud
Driven homeward as it had been and would be again
Since the conquerors searching the harder shining
Brought for the bargain a handful of wings of flame.

Balboa lies dead somewhere and Pizarro's helmet
Is a spider's kingdom; yet here was the arrogant breath
And the dangerous plume burning across the foreign air
That danced like an ancient Andalusian noon:
A blaze, it rose leaving the jungle dark and the leaves
Heavy with silence, and the wheeltracks folding to doom
Where majesty wandered:

                      A million butterflies,
Wheeling eastward from the soil where the nugget lies
    lost,
Turned homeward in vast diurnal fire that marched one
    day
Burning toward Spain; and after that, for a while,
Spread like a field of death, gold on the sea.

Karl Shapiro

SCYROS

snuffle and sniff and handkerchief

THE doctor punched my vein
    The captain called me Cain
Upon my belly sat the sow of fear
    With coins on either eye
    The President came by
And whispered to the lords what none could hear

    High over where the storm
    Stood steadfast cruciform
The golden eagle sank in wounded wheels
    White negroes laughing still
    Crept fiercely on Brazil
Turning the navies upward on their keels

    Now one by one the trees
    Stripped to their naked knees
To dance upon the heaps of shrunken dead
    The roof of England fell
    Great Paris tolled her bell
And China staunched her milk and wept for bread

    No island singly lay
    But lost its name that day
The Ainu dived across the plunging sands
    From dawn to dawn to dawn
    King George's birds came on
Strafing the tulips from his children's hands

Thus in the classic sea
Southeast from Thessaly
The dynamited mermen washed ashore
And tritons dressed in steel
Trolled heads with rod and reel
And dredged potatoes from the Aegean floor

Hot is the sky and green
Where Germans have been seen
The moon leaks metal on the Atlantic fields
Pink boys in birthday shrouds
Look lightly through the clouds
Or coast the peaks of Finland on their shields

That prophet year by year
Lay still but could not hear
Where scholars tapped to find his new remains
Gog and Magog ate pork
In vertical New York
And war began next Monday on the Danes.

ELEGY FOR TWO BANJOS

HAUL up the flag, you mourners,
    Not half-mast but all the way;
The funeral is done and disbanded;
    The devil's had the final say.

O mistress and wife too pensive,
    Pallbearers and priestly men,
Put your black clothes in the attic,
    And get up on your feet again.

Death did his job like a scholar,
    A most unusual case,
Death did his job like a gentleman;
    He barely disturbed the face.

You packed him a handsome carton,
    Set the lid with silver screws;
You dug a dark pit in the graveyard
    To tell the white worms the news.

Now you've nothing left to remember,
    Nothing but the words he wrote,
But they'll never let you remember,
    Only stick like a bone in your throat.

O if I'd been his wife or mistress,
    His pallbearer or his parish priest,
I'd have kept him at home forever—
    Or as long as bric-a-brac at least.

I would have burned his body
    And salvaged a sizeable bone
For a paper-weight or a door-stop
    Or a garden flagstone.

I would have heaped the fire
    And boiled his beautiful skull.
It was laden like a ship for travels
    And now is but an empty hull.

I would have dried it off in linens,
    Polished it with a chamois cloth
Till it shone like a brand-new quarter
    And felt smooth as the nose of a moth.

Or I'd have hung it out in the garden
    Where everything else is alive,
Put a queen-bee in the brain case
    So the bees could build a hive.

Maybe I'd have wired the jawbone
    With a silver spring beneath,

Set it in the cradle with baby
    So baby could rattle the teeth.

O you didn't do right by William
    To shove him down that filthy hole,
Throw him a lot of tears and Latin
    And a cheap "God bless your soul."

You might as well leave off mourning,
    His photograph is getting dim,
So you'd better take a long look at it
    For it's all you'll ever see of him.

Haul up the flag you mourners,
    Not half-mast but all the way,
The funeral is done and disbanded,
    The devil's had the final say.

UNIVERSITY

To hurt the Negro and avoid the Jew
Is the curriculum. In mid-September
The entering boys, identified by hats,
Wander in a maze of mannered brick
    Where boxwood and magnolia brood
    And columns with imperious stance
Like rows of ante-bellum girls
    Eye them, outlanders.

In whited cells, on lawns equipped for peace,
Under the arch, and lofty banister,
Equals shake hands, unequals blankly pass;
The exemplary weather whispers, "Quiet, quiet"
    And visitors on tiptoe leave
    For the raw North, the unfinished West

As the young, detecting an advantage,
   Practice a face.

Where, on their separate hill, the colleges,
Like manor houses of an older law,
Gaze down embankments on a land in fee,
The Deans, dry spinsters over family plate,
   Ring out the English name like coin,
   Humor the snob and lure the lout.
   Within the precincts of this world
      Poise is a club.

But on the neighboring range, misty and high,
The past is absolute; some luckless race
Dull with inbreeding and conformity
Wears out its heart, and comes barefoot and bad
   For charity or jail. The scholar
   Sanctions their obsolete disease;
   The gentleman revolts with shame
      At his ancestor.

And the true nobleman, once a democrat,
Sleeps on his private mountain. He was one
Whose thought was shapely and whose dream was broad;
This school he held his art and epitaph.
   But now it takes from him his name,
   Falls open like a dishonest look,
   And shows us, rotted and endowed,
      Its senile pleasure.

KARL SHAPIRO

Theodore Spencer

THE INFLATABLE GLOBE

*"No. 43. A balloon in the shape of a globe, showing the main countries
of the earth and their possessions. Easily inflatable, it is instructive for
children learning geography. . . 50 cents."*

WHEN the allegorical man came calling,
 He told us all he would show us a trick,
 And he showed us a flat but inflatable ball.
"Look at this ball," he told us all,
 "Look at the lines marked out on this ball."
 We looked at the ball and the lines on the ball.
 England was red and France was brown,
 Germany orange and Russia green;
"Look at this ball," he told us all,
 "With a blow of my breath I inflate this ball."
 He blew, and it bounced, and bouncing, falling,
 He bounced it against the wall with a kick.
"But without my breath it will flatten and fall,"
 Said the allegorical man, and down
 Flat came his hand and squashed the ball,
 And it fell to the floor with no life at all,
 Once his breath had gone out of the ball. . .
 It seemed to us all a stupid trick.

CONTEMPORARY SONG

WHEN the weather is rough, said the anxious child,
 Is the wise man out or in?
 Which does the wise man love, said the child,
 His own, or another's skin?

814

What does the wise man do, said the child,
Does he watch the thread, or spin?
The heavens sagged; there was nothing to say.

When the guns are out, said the anxious child,
Does the wise man grasp a gun?
Which does the wise man hate, said the child,
Himself or everyone?
What does the wise man do, said the child,
When the battle's never won?
The heavens sagged; there was nothing to say.

EPITAPH

SHE was a high-class bitch and a dandy
Prancing man was he and a dandy
Man he was with that tall lady.

I should have known that a bitch and a dandy
Dancing man—and Oh, what a dandy!—
Would with a prance of a dapper dandy
Dance into grass; and to grass that lady.

Bitch as she was—and he was a dandy
Prancing man—it makes me angry
That those dance people should stagger and bend.
I think of that dandy and bitch and am angry
That over that bitch and over that dandy
Dancing man—and Oh, what a dandy
Man he was with that tall lady!—
Only crass grass should dance in the end.

Dunstan Thompson

THE LAY OF THE BATTLE
OF TOMBLAND

"WHATEVER you want is yours,"
  Said the Man with the Lopside Head;
"Girls, diamonds, and motor cars,
  If you'll love me, love me in bed."

So he prayed, and the sirens sang
  Their wrongs, O sang to me
Lost in the blackout, "You're young
  But wait till you're old as we."

I stayed where I was, afraid
  To leave the Club Foot Man;
"Behind the mirror," he said, "we'll hide.
  The dead have a death-ray plan."

"Welcome! Welcome!" the searchlights wrote.
  "The End of the World is here."
They spelt their names and then went out,
  And the poor lay everywhere.

What could I cry but "Bombs Away,"
  When the Man who was Hunchback spoke.
"O live through this, and be my boy,"
  He laughed, and his true voice broke.

"God, be nimble," the dicers begged,
  "Christ, be quick;" but they rolled too short,
Their fears embraced, and the whirlers bragged
  "In our heartbreak arms is sport."

316

The Harelip Man knelt down to drink
  Blood from the sewers, swore
"You'll kiss me yet, and you'll thank
  Me later, later, after the war."

Through air of flares the statues ran
  Shrouded in silk. "Be warned,"
They wirelessed, "for marble men
  Are the friends you never mourned."

O bathed in fire my mobster stood,
  The Man with the Artificial Eyes,
"Falling in love with love," he said,
  "Is falling in love with lies."

This piteous city gave up the ghost
  In the toll of all her towers;
Parachute princes held me fast,
  "Rest," they ordered, "the rest is ours."

THE MOMENT OF THE ROSE

A GOD of love among the silent flowers,
Your looks play rival to this sunlight view.
Late afternoon, the fragile, delicate time
Of sadness almost sorrow, overpowers
The languid air, as though these roses drew
Their perfume down long avenues of lime.
I see forget-me-nots are less than blue
When to their color your deep eyes are true.

Dear visionary, gloss the awkward guest
Abashed by plants and trees and foliage things;
Reflect this moment when the rainbow gives
Images of triumph to the sky—the least
Lasting enchantment; for past, perfect springs
Regaled those youths who lost their loving lives,

817

Some among gardens, some by seaside swings,
Or in a mean street, or where the nettle stings.

The dazzling slain companion you in arms.
Guardians, the watchers by the water clock,
They gaze like mica from a wall of moss.
These champions muster at the clanged alarms,
The one-toned coffin bells that muted mock
The rose, the willow, and the golden grass.
Against dead friends you need not ever lock
Your door, or wish them good or evil luck.

Now marble broken, now the gilt gone off
The princely monuments, one nobler tongue
Recites historic love, this land of blood,
The murderous kings, the ladies cruel enough
In lace and luxuries to bear a wrong
Made madrigal, and lords who understood
Their sentence by a sonnet—these belong
To terraces where flags suggest a song.

The end of love is that the heart is still
As the rose no wind distresses, still as light
On the unmoved grass, or as the humming bird
Poised the pure moment by an act of will.
Death may be like this, but here before night
Sends us to sleep murmuring a drowsy word
Of prayer, affection, or the idle flight
Of fancy, let us praise the rose and light.

Of gardens there is much to say, but now
I write as witness to an English one.
Between black clouds and white, between the hours
This island rides the misted ocean, how
Debonair appears the gallant shining sun.
Here I have found, as after thunder showers,
The friend my childhood promised me, when on
A desperate feast I met myself alone.

In summer when these blowsy roses break
The heart, and turn from pink to purple, deaths
Like butterflies exhaust their heavy scent,
And fluttering through vermilion mazes take
The time of day away, and take our breaths
Away as well. Then tragedies are spent
By gardeners on their ravelled funeral wreaths,
And wraithlike weather brings the almond moths.

But now the stars of heaven sail like ships
Above the trees, and round about your house
Ancestral ghosts are wandering, long come home
From wars and voyages. Now this garden sleeps
In shadow. Only the rustling field mice
And owls on vigil keep the hours. We dream
Of the rose and happiness, we dream until
The end of love is that the heart is still.

LARGO

For William Abrahams

Of those whom I have known, the few and fatal friends,
All were ambiguous, deceitful, not to trust:
But like attracts its like, no doubt; and mirrors must
Be faithful to the image that they see. Light bends
  Only the spectrum in the glass:
  Prime colors are the ones which pass
  The less distorted. Friendship ends
In hatred or in love, ambivalence of lust:
Either, like Hamlet, haunted, doting on the least
Reflection of remorse; or else, like Richard, lost
  In vanity. The frozen hands
  That hold the mirror make demands;
And flexing fingers clutch the vision in a vise.
Each one betrays himself: the ghostly glazer understands
  Why he must work in ice.

819

All friends are false but you are true: the paradox
Is perfect tense in present time, whose parallel
Extends to meeting point; where, more than friends, we
    fell
Together on the other side of love; where clocks
    And mirrors were reversed to show
    Ourselves as only we could know;
    Where all the doors had secret locks
With double keys; and where the sliding panel, well
Concealed, gave us our exit through the palace wall.
There we have come and gone: twin kings, who roam at
    will
    Behind the court, behind the backs
    Of consort queens, behind the racks
On which their favorites lie who told them what to do.
For every cupid with a garland round the throne still
    lacks
    The look I give to you.

The goddess who presided at our birth was first
Of those in fancy clothes fate made us hate to fight:
The Greeks with gifts, good looks, so clever, so polite,
Like lovers quick to charm, disarming, too well versed
    In violence to wear weapons while
    They take a city for a smile.
    By doomed ancestral voices cursed
To wander from the womb, their claws plucked out our
    sight,
Who nighttime thinking we are followed down the street
By blind men like ourselves, turn round again, and wait,
    Only to hear the steps go past
    Us standing lonely there, at last
Aware how we have failed; are now the Trojan fool
For all the arty Hellenistic tarts in plaster cast:
    The ones who always rule.

We are alone with every sailor lost at sea
Whose drowning is repeated day by day. The sound

Of bells from buoys mourning sunken ships rings round
Us, warning away the launch that journeys you and me
 On last Cytherean trips in spring.
  There the rocks are where sirens sing
  Like nightingales of death. But we,
Hearing excitements, music for the ear, have bound
Our voyage to find its ending where the sterile sand
Spends pearls and coral on a skull. The sailing wind
 Is with us now and then: blows high
  As halcyon clouds across the sky:
Falls fast to doldrums while the moon is also young,
Untided, half to harvest whole. See how your sirens die
   Before their song is sung.

What we have always wanted, never had, the ease,
The fame of athletes, such happy heroes at a game,
Beloved by every likely lad, is not the same
As what we have: these measured methods how to please
 An indolent and doubtful boy,
  Who plays at darts, breaks for a toy
  The sometime valued heart. Why seize
The moment in the garden, on the stair, to blame
Our nameless Eros for his daring? Too little time
Is left for love. When we come back, what welcome home
 Will he award our wounded eyes?
  What uniform be his disguise
In dreams, when sleeping sentries always march away
Once more to war? Now is our novelty: we may surprise
   The faun at end of day.

Make no mistake, my soldier. Listen: bugle calls
Revoke your leisure like a leave, invade your peace
With orders on the run, and, loud as bombs, police
Your life for death. The poet's blood-brick tower falls:
 Even his vanity is gone,
  Which leaves the loser all alone.
  Not private poems, but public brawls

Demand his drumbeat history, the pulse that must in-
crease
Until his heart is ransomed from its jewel. Revise
Your verse. Consider what king's killer did to those
    Who wrote their way between the shells
    That last delusive time. Farewells
Are folly to our serpent queen. She will not sign
Discharge of conscience for a masterpiece, but, hissing,
tells
    Failure in every line.

We are the mountaineers who perish on the slopes
Of heaven high and perfect Himalayan peak:
Exhausted by the cold, we can no longer speak
To one another—only signal by the ropes.
    Those best before us have, alas,
    Plunged through a gentian-blue crevasse:
    The snow-blind flaw. Their glacial hopes
Shine as a stream of desperate stars, icebound, and
bleak,
That mock their nimbused glory from a frigid lake.
Where we stand now, they stood much farther: climbing
like
    Legendary guides. But traps
Were waiting for their last collapse:
Inviting visions from the moon world air—misplace
A step to follow, dance to death. They fell, so we, per-
haps,
    May do as well with grace.

Now noble guests depart for good, wearing our loss
Like flowers.   O Damon, decked with asphodel, who
moves
Among the shadow dwellers. But he shall hear the hooves
Of unicorns at gallop, see them, coursing, toss
    Their fluted horns above the cool
    Unpoisoned waters in love's pool,
    And, kneeling, lay their heads across

A beatific virgin's breast. The day approves
His passage: sunlight on the secret river gives
Bright benediction to his boat. Elysian waves
   Bear him, the hero, far from us
   To join the gods. Illustrious!
No words may worship him. The laurel is not all
That withers at the roots, since we, lamenting him, are
      thus
   Autumnal for his fall.

Armed, say you? Armed, my lord. So, likewise, you and
   I,
Who with the butchered ghost must stalk the battle-
   ments,
Shall watch—cold-comfort guards—how lonely lie the
   tents
Where strangers sleep together just before they die.
   Look where their banners in the air
   Are half-staff hung. The cockcrow dare
   Of dawn is mourning in the sky.
Our thoughts like bayonets blood time. What precedents
Of passion shall we use to brave the coward? Once
Bombs are as roses, will he kiss the black-heart prince?
   Honor, more heavy than the sea,
   May overwhelm both you and me
To give no quarter choice at all: gay boys, whom war
Won janizary; youths, who flung away their shields. So
   we
   Are *mort à Singapore.*

Narcissus, doubled in the melting mirror, smiles
To see himself outfaced by tears, and, sorrowing, hands
His ace of love to harlequin of hearts, who stands
The distant edge of laughter. Time's joker still compiles
   Trick score of triumph, trumps the queen
   To play his knave of emeralds. Green
   Gamester reflects the water guiles

Of palming, reads the gambled cards, and then demands
Another pack to shuffle. But the glass partner bends
The fate five fingers round a saint's stigmata, wounds
    By dealing diamonds from his nails.
    No marveled metaphor avails
To vantage this beloved impersonator twin,
Whose coronet, crown crystal, qualifies a peer. My voice
    fails
    In your name poems begin.

 John Thompson, Jr.

A LOVE FOR PATSY

SEE the little maunderer
Stretch out on the grass!
His heart is burst asunder
The pieces cry Alas.

Upright, fat pink pieces
Of fluffy cloud float overhead.
The little facets of his eyes
Split by salty tears, so tired

Of seeing pieces of the world.
Close, and rustling grass,
Caws of an old unpleasant bird
Are sounds that say Alas;

They float like notes in the funny paper,
Round notes with sharp little tails.
Oh I'm blue, the supine moper
Says, I'm trapped in the toils

824

Of Patsy's black black hair.
Her hair is like the cool dry night
That waves through the window-bar
Where a moody jailbird sits apart

Shuffling his broken heart. I'm sad
As I can be. Her black
Black hair can never be compared
To dull dichotomic

Trees or prickly grass, inflated
Clouds, even a great
One draped on the sun. Over-rated
Senseless things to stare at,

One here one there they're strewn,
Impinging pieces left out of
The world. Her eyes are green!
Oh oh, he says, I die of love.

See the weeping little wretch
He rolls in a frenzy!
In all the world no two things match
But the green eyes of Patsy.

825

Peter Viereck

FROM ANCIENT FANGS

*(The time of this poem is in the far future, shortly after
peace and love return to earth.)*

I

LIKE lamp of intricate stained glass which hangs
    From curved blue ceiling,
A fat bright-bellied insect hangs up there.
    At night, on traveler,
It drops like rich and heavy poison welling
    From ancient fangs.

II

That insect's not the only thing which falls.
So many things must fall in their short day.
Careers and wine-cups; bombs and tennis-balls.
Even the sun. But sky? The sky must stay.

But now the sky itself is caving in.
O good old sky, O lid that keeps us snug,
Dear blue in which we always used to trust
As in the nurse our childhood bullied so,
When comfort was to see her loyal grin,
Ugly and safe, beam down on us below:
Dear sky, we pray to you, hold on, you must!
Hold tighter, sky. Be roof to us, not rug.

III

"It seems I'm being prayed to: I
    Am sky,

Older than hours and than miles more far,
    Your spectator.
When worlds grow honest, noble, clean, or clever,
    I fall and smother them forever.
To keep your high roof high, stop being good.
    All sights bore Me now but blood.
The main thing is to kill. And kill. And kill.
    First with your Springfield. Then with steel.

"And when steel breaks, with hands and stumps of
    hands.
And when you've killed all strangers, kill your friends.
And if you've used up humans, stone a rat.
Call it a whim—I like My world like that.
It's your world, too. The only world you'll get."

IV

"At school they never used to talk like You."
    "No, not like Me."
"People back home don't want such things to do."
    "Perhaps. We'll see."
"Men won't splash harmless blood just for Your thirst."
    "No, not at first."

DON'T LOOK NOW BUT MARY
IS EVERYBODY

MARY, long by Boss's kisses bored,
Quit desk and stole His yacht and jumped aboard.
Her lamb took she, for purer were his kisses.
Compass and pistol took she in her purse.
Free sailed she north to eat new freedom up.
And her helped ocean and grew calm and snored.
But when with bleating chum she cuddled up,
Unleashed His typhoons Boss; therein no bliss is.
Then knew she—by four signs—whose jig was up:

827

Her buoyed the life-preserver down, not up;
True was the pistol's aim, but in reverse;
The compass steered, but only toward abysses;
The little lamb nipped Mary's thighs and roared.

YOU ALL ARE STATIC; I ALONE AM MOVING

You all are static; I alone am moving.
Racing beyond each planted Pullman wheel,
   I pity you and long to reel
You through my thousand outstretched ways of loving.
Are you alive at all? Can non-trees *feel*?

Run while I may, for at my pith gnaws Night.
The winds—these are great stacks of anchored air;
   I thresh them with my hard-pronged hair;
I jump right through them, roaring my delight.
Live while I may—run, run, no matter where.

How marvelous—if you but knew—is speed!
You all must wait; I am your overtaker.
   Striding to green from yellow acre,
I toss you Spring. Each dawn, my tendrils knead
Stars into pancake-suns like a tall baker.

Trudging towards snowtime, I could weep for hours
To think of birds, the birds I leave behind.
   Why did the God who keeps you blind,
Instead give sight and sentience to my flowers?
Black questions in my sap outwear my rind.

Humans (I almost envy you your peace)
Are free of this gnarled urge for Absolutes
   Which sweetens and saddens all my fruits,
Dragging my twigs down when I'd fly towards bliss—
While bugs and diamonds agonize my roots.
828

NOW KINDNESS

This was the summer when the tired girls
Breathed in the parks another planet's air
And stretched like hyphens between Here and There,
Stretched and lounged and yawned on every lawn.
Then did the planet of the tired girls
Whirl from the constellation named The Fawn
(Goodbye mild starlight of the Sign of Fawn)
And ride into the galaxy named Fangs,
Where every dew-drop like a tear-drop hangs.
This was the summer-sob of wounded girls.

This was the tiredness when summer's girls
Grew soft and hidden griefs like downy curls.
Then was the drowsy melody of Languish
(Goodbye archaic waltzing-world of Languish)
Jazzed to the bad bad bad blues of Wild Anguish.
Serene old Mozart world—peace ethics laws—
Fades like girl-sighs. Or begs like kitten paws.
Or soars, unheeded like too pale a star,
Into the limbo where the tired are.
This was the faded June of fainting girls.

Then came the gnats who feed on sad young girls,
Winging and stinging through the gauze of dusk,
Buzzing and burning all that summer night.
Then did all perfumes bitterly take flight
Out of the stylish cloying of Sweet Musk
(Goodbye warm pensive world of sensuous musk)
Into that dark dark dream-flower named Take Fright.
Then girls discovered that their dolls were dead,
Hollow yet lovely like those gold skins shed
When locusts molt, found on old trees by girls.

Now kindness (wide-eyed as the dolls of girls),
Killed and redeeming, shines from all pale girls.

Robert Penn Warren

ORIGINAL SIN: A SHORT STORY

NODDING, its great head rattling like a gourd,
And locks like seaweed strung on the stinking stone,
The nightmare stumbles past, and you have heard
It fumble your door before it whimpers and is gone:
It acts like the old hound that used to snuffle your door and moan.

You thought you had lost it when you left Omaha,
For it seemed connected then with your grandpa, who
Had a wen on his forehead and sat on the veranda
To finger the precious protuberance, as was his habit to do,
Which glinted in sun like rough garnet or the rich old brain bulging through.

But you met it in Harvard Yard as the historic steeple
Was confirming the midnight with its hideous racket,
And you wondered how it had come, for it stood so imbecile,
With empty hands, humble, and surely nothing in pocket:
Riding the rods, perhaps—or grandpa's will paid the ticket.

You were almost kindly then, in your first homesickness,
As it tortured its stiff face to speak, but scarcely mewed;
Since then you have outlived all your homesickness,
But have met it in many another distempered latitude:
Oh, nothing is lost, ever lost! at last you understood.
830

But it never came in the quantum glare of sun
To shame you before your friends, and had nothing to do
With your public experience or private reformation:
But it thought no bed too narrow—it stood with lips
    askew
And shook its great head sadly like the abstract Jew.

Never met you in the lyric arsenical meadow
When children call and your heart goes stone in the
    bosom;
At the orchard anguish never, nor ovoid horror,
Which is furred like a peach or avid like the delicious
    plum.
It takes no part in your classic prudence or fondled axiom.

Not there when you exclaimed: "Hope is betrayed by
Disastrous glory of sea-capes, sun-torment of whitecaps
—There must be a new innocence for us to be stayed by."
But there it stood, after all the timetables, all the maps,
In the crepuscular clutter of *always, always,* or *perhaps.*

You have moved often and rarely left an address,
And hear of the deaths of friends with a sly pleasure,
A sense of cleansing and hope, which blooms from
    distress;
But it has not died, it comes, its hand childish, unsure,
Clutching the bribe of chocolate or a toy you used to
    treasure.

It tries the lock; you hear, but simply drowse:
There is nothing remarkable in that sound at the door.
Later you hear it wander the dark house
Like a mother who rises at night to seek a childhood
    picture;
Or it goes to the backyard and stands like an old horse
    cold in the pasture.

REVELATION

BECAUSE he had spoken harshly to his mother,
The day became astonishingly bright,
The enormity of distance crept to him like a dog now,
And earth's own luminescence seemed to repel the night.

Roof was rent like the loud paper tearing to admit
Sun-sulphurous splendor where had been before
But the submarine glimmer by kindly countenances lit,
As slow, phosphorescent dignities light the ocean floor.

By walls, by walks, chrysanthemum and aster,
All hairy, fat-petalled species, lean, confer,
And his ears, and heart, should burn at that insidious
    whisper
Which concerns him so, he knows; but he cannot make
    out the words.

The peacock screamed, and his feather fury made
Legend shake, all day, while the sky ran pale as milk;
That night, all night, the buck rabbit stamped in the
    moonlit glade,
And the owl's brain glowed like a coal in the grove's
    combustible dark.

When Sulla smote and Rome was rent, Augustine
Recalled how Nature, shuddering, tore her gown,
And kind changed kind, and the blunt herbivorous tooth
    dripped blood;
At Duncan's death, at Dunsinane, chimneys blew down.

But, oh! his mother was kinder than ever Rome,
Dearer than Duncan—no wonder, then, Nature's frame
Thrilled in voluptuous hemispheres far off from his home;
But not in terror: only as the bride, as the bride.

832

In separateness only does love learn definition,
Though Brahma smiles beneath the dappled shade,
Though tears, that night, wet the pillow where the boy's
head was laid
Dreamless of splendid antipodal agitation;

And though across what tide and tooth Time is,
He was to lean back toward that recalcitrant face,
He would think, than Sulla more fortunate, how once he
had learned
Something important about love, and about love's grace.

PURSUIT

The hunchback on the corner, with gum and shoelaces,
Has his own wisdom and pleasures, and may not be lured
To divulge them to you, for he has merely endured
Your appeal for his sympathy and your kind purchases;
And wears infirmity but as the general who turns
Apart in his famous old greatcoat there on the hill,
At dusk when the rapture and cannonade are still,
To muse withdrawn from the dead, from his gorgeous
subalterns;
Or stares from the thicket of his familiar pain, like a fawn
That meets you a moment, wheels, in imperious inno-
cence is gone.

Go to the clinic. Sit in the outer room,
Where like an old possum the snag-nailed hand will hump
On its knee in murderous patience, and the pomp
Of pain swells like the Indies, or a plum.
And there you will stand, as on the Roman hill,
Stunned by each withdrawn gaze and severe shape,
The first barbarian victors stood to gape
At the sacrificial fathers, white-robed, still;

And even the feverish old Jew regards you with authority
Till you feel like one who has come too late, or improp-
	erly clothed, to a party.

The doctor will take you now. He is burly and clean;
Listening, like lover or worshiper, bends at your heart;
But cannot make out just what it tries to impart;
So smiles; says you simply need a change of scene.
Of scene, of solace: therefore Florida,
Where Ponce de Leon clanked among the lilies,
Where white sails skit on blue and cavort like fillies,
And the shoulder gleams in the moonlit corridor.
A change of love: if love is a groping Godward, though
	blind,
No matter what crevice, cranny, chink, bright in dark,
	the pale tentacle find.

In Florida consider the flamingo,
Its color passion but its neck a question;
Consider even that girl the other guests shun
On beach, at bar, in bed, for she may know
The secret you are seeking, after all;
Or the child you humbly sit by, excited and curly,
That screams on the shore at the sea's sunlit hurlyburly,
Till the mother calls its name, toward nightfall.
Till you sit alone: in the dire meridians, off Ireland, in
	fury
Of spume-tooth and dawnless sea-heave, salt rimes the
	lookout's devout eye.

Till you sit alone—which is the beginning of error—
Behind you the music and lights of the great hotel:
Solution, perhaps, is public, despair personal,
But history held to your breath clouds like a mirror.
There are many states, and towns in them, and faces,
But meanwhile, the little old lady in black, by the wall,
Who admires all the dancers, and tells you how just last
	fall

ROBERT PENN WARREN

Her husband died in Ohio, and damp mists her glasses;
She blinks and croaks, like a toad or a Norn, in the hor-
    rible light,
And rattles her crutch, which may put forth a small
    bloom, perhaps white.

 Edward Weismiller

TO THE WOMAN IN
BOND STREET STATION

MADAM, you are right; the fight was a greaty pity.
Two soldiers against a third, an ally—perhaps
No worse could befall, as you feel, in this tense city.

Violence broke out so sharply: sudden fear
Fell on the watchers, who recoiled, and gasped,
And did not recall the girl who had disappeared.

Certainly the boy alone was very young.
It was brutal to smash at him with the torch.
    But, madam,
Though what I mean, and would say, is not on my tongue,

It was late; all three are gone now, home to their places,
Their hatreds dimmed. And those who today are damned
Are not such furious boys with blood on their faces.

835

John Wheelwright

FISH FOOD

An Obituary to Hart Crane

As you drank deep as Thor, did you think of mi'k or wine?
Did you drink blood, while you drank the salt deep?
Or see through the film of light, that sharpened your rage
    with its stare,
a shark, dolphin, turtle? Did you not see the Cat
who, when Thor lifted her, unbased the cubic ground?
You would drain fathomless flagons to be slaked with
    vacuum—
The sea's teats have suckled you, and you are sunk far
in bubble-dreams, under swaying translucent vines
of thundering interior wonder. Eagles can never now
carry parts of your body, over cupped mountains
as emblems of their anger, embers to fire self-hate
to other wonders, unfolding white flaming vistas.
Fishes now look upon you, with eyes which do not gossip.
Fishes are never shocked. Fishes will kiss you, each
fish tweak you; every kiss takes bits of you away,
till your bones alone will roll, with the Gulf Stream's
    swell.
So has it been already, so have the carpers and puffers
nibbled your carcass of fame, each to his liking. Now
in tides of noon, the bones of your thought-suspended
    structures
gleam as you intended. Noon pulled your eyes with small
magnetic headaches; the will seeped from your blood.
    Seeds
of meaning popped from the pods of thought. And you
    fall. And the unseen

churn of Time changes the pearl-hued ocean;
like a pearl-shaped drop, in a huge water-clock
falling; from *came* to *go*, from *come* to *went*. And you fell.
Waters received you. Waters of our Birth in Death dissolve you.
Now you have willed it, may the Great Wash take you.
As the Mother-Lover takes your woe away, and cleansing
grief and you away, you sleep, you do not snore.
Lie still. Your rage is gone on a bright flood
away; as, when a bad friend held out his hand
you said, "Do not talk any more. I know you meant no
harm."
What was the soil whence your anger sprang, who are deaf
as the stones to the whispering flight of the Mississippi's
rivers?
What did you see as you fell? What did you hear as you
sank?
Did it make you drunken with hearing?
I will not ask any more. You saw or heard no evil.

Richard Wilbur

POTATO

for André du Bouchet

AN underground grower, blind and a common brown;
Got a misshapen look, it's nudged where it could;
Simple as soil yet crowded as earth with all.

Cut open raw, it looses a cool clean stench,
Mineral acid seeping from pores of prest meal;
It is like breaching a strangely refreshing tomb:

Therein the taste of first stones, the hands of dead slaves,
Waters men drank in the earliest frightful woods,
Flint-chips, and peat, and the cinders of buried camps.

Scrubbed under faucet water the planet skin
Polishes yellow, but tears to the plain insides;
Parching, the white's blue-hearted like hungry hands.

All of the cold dark kitchens, and war-frozen gray
Evening at window; I remember so many
Peeling potatoes quietly into chipt pails.

"It was potatoes saved us, they kept us alive."
Then they had something to say akin to praise
For the mean earth-apples, too common to cherish or
    steal.

Times being hard, the Sikh and the Senegalese,
Hobo and Okie, the body of Jesus the Jew,
Vestigial virtues, are eaten; we shall survive.

What has not lost its savor shall hold us up,
And we are praising what saves us, what fills the need.
(Soon there'll be packets again, with Algerian fruits.)

Oh, it will not bear polish, the ancient potato,
Needn't be nourished by Caesars, will blow anywhere,
Hidden by nature, counted-on, stubborn and blind.

You may have noticed the bush that it pushes to air,
Comical-delicate, sometimes with second-rate flowers
Awkward and milky and beautiful only to hunger.

TYWATER

Death of Sir Nihil, book the *nth*,
Upon the charred and clotted sward,
Lacking the lily of our Lord,
Alases of the hyacinth.

Could flicker from behind his ear
A whistling silver throwing knife
And with a holler punch the life
Out of a swallow in the air.

Behind the lariat's butterfly
Shuttled his white and gritted **grin**,
And cuts of sky would roll within
The noose-hole, when he spun it high.

The violent, neat and practiced skill
Was all he loved and all he learned;
When he was hit, his body turned
To clumsy dirt before it fell.

And what to say of him, God knows.
Such violence. And such repose.

O

The idle dayseye, the laborious wheel,
The osprey's tours, the pointblank matin sun
Sanctified first the circle; thence for fun
Doctors deduced a shape, which some called real
(So all games spoil), a shape of spare appeal,
Cryptic and clean, and endlessly spinning unspun.
Now I go backward, filling by one and one
Circles with hickory spokes and rich soft shields
Of petalled dayseyes, with herehastening steel
Volleys of daylight, writhing white looks of sun;

And I toss circles skyward to be undone
By actual wings, for wanting this repeal
I should go whirling a thin Euclidean reel,
No hawk or hickory to true my run.

GRACE

" 'The young lambs bound as to the tabor's sound.' They toss and toss;
it is as if it were the earth that flung them, not themselves. It is the
pitch of graceful agility when we think that."—G. M. HOPKINS, Notebooks

So active they seem passive, little sheep
Please, and Nijinsky's out-the-window leap
And marvelous midair pause please too
A taste for blithe brute reflex; flesh made word
Is grace's revenue.

One is tickled, again, by the dining-car waiter's absurd
Acrobacy—tipfingered tray like a wind-besting bird
Plumblines his swinging shoes, the sole things sure
In the shaken train; but this is all done for food,
Is habitude, if not pure

Hebetude. It is a graph of a theme that flings
The dancer kneeling on nothing into the wings,
And Nijinsky hadn't the words to make the laws
For learning to loiter in air; he "merely" said,
"I merely leap and pause."

Lambs are constrained to bound. Consider instead
The intricate neural grace in Hamlet's head;
A grace not barbarous implies a choice
Of courses, not in a lingo of leaps-in-air
But in such a waiting voice

As one would expect to hear in the talk of Flaubert.
Piety makes for awkwardness, and where

Balance is not urgent, what one utters
May be puzzled and perfect, and we respect
Some scholars' stutters.

Even fraction-of-a-second action is not wrecked
By a graceful still reserve. To be unchecked
Is needful then: choose, challenge, jump, poise, run. . . .
Nevertheless, the praiseful, graceful soldier
Shouldn't be fired by his gun.

 Marguerite Young

DEATH BY RARITY

I fear, I fear the rarity
Of nighthawk, swift, ruby throat; I fear extinct
The roseate spoonbill and snowy egret slain
By no known enemy,

Slain by no known war of devastation
To all and one, the flamingo, the heath hen, and
     wild
Trumpeter swan, however covert they are
Slain where ever they are,

For rarity precedes extinction as sickness
Comes before death, there is weariness within
The perfection of the shell, and the perfect bird
Never will be born.

I fear that rarity overwhelming all marvelous
Names of birds whose names are poems
And the rarity of this so personal blood
Sleet in the golden vein.

SPECULATIVE EVENING

If there were no past, but specious present only, if
    twinkle ago,
By the edict of a heavenly geometer
Had been created this earth of pointed fir trees, De-
    cember snow,
Jewel eye, yet who would realize the colossal joke?

For with our equipment of memory,
Yet would this present seem entire fragment and whole
To sailor, soul, spectator of storms, and all would be
Exactly clouded, and the snow goose put on white at its
    maturity

And the albino crow who gets no partner in mortal
    marriage
Would tap at the window in surf among red berries,
And I myself would feel my crucial age
And cry for ambassadors like dolls among the wrinkled
    stars,

And I, poor pensioner in nature's house
In smoky beams of evening's blowing light
Would behold fallacious futures, impermanence of fact,
    brightest of all stars, Sirius,
And harpers harping on a sea of glass.

Appendix

Index of Authors and Titles

Index
of
Authors and Titles

Index of Authors and Titles

Poems preceded by an asterisk can be considered part of The
Forties.—*See Editorial Note, page 738.*

847

INDEX OF AUTHORS AND TITLES

849

Index of Authors and Titles

851

Index of Authors and Titles

INDEX OF AUTHORS AND TITLES

Marianne Moore, con-
tinued on next page

855

INDEX OF AUTHORS AND TITLES

Index of Authors and Titles

859